SOCIAL THE(

Social theory is the theoretical core of the social sciences, clearly distinguishable from political theory and cultural analysis. This book offers a unique overview of the development of social theory from the end of the Second World War in 1945 to the present day. Spanning the literature in English, French and German, it provides an excellent background to the most important social theorists and theories in contemporary sociological thought, with crisp summaries of the main books, arguments and controversies. It also deals with newly emerging schools from rational choice to symbolic interactionism, with new ambitious approaches (Habermas, Luhmann, Giddens, Bourdieu), structuralism and anti-structuralism, critical revisions of modernization theory, feminism and neo-pragmatism. Written by two of the world's leading sociologists and based on their extensive academic teaching, this unrivalled work is ideal both for students in the social sciences and humanities and for anyone interested in contemporary theoretical debates.

HANS JOAS is the Max Weber Professor and Director of the Max Weber Center for Advanced Cultural and Social Studies at the University of Erfurt. He is also Professor of Sociology and a member of the Committee on Social Thought at the University of Chicago.

WOLFGANG KNÖBL is Professor of Sociology at the University of Göttingen.

SOCIAL THEORY

TWENTY INTRODUCTORY LECTURES

HANS JOAS AND WOLFGANG KNÖBL

Translated by
ALEX SKINNER

CAMBRIDGE UNIVERSITY PRESS

CAMBRIDGE
UNIVERSITY PRESS

University Printing House, Cambridge CB2 8BS, United Kingdom

Cambridge University Press is part of the University of Cambridge.

It furthers the University's mission by disseminating knowledge in the pursuit of education, learning and research at the highest international levels of excellence.

www.cambridge.org
Information on this title: www.cambridge.org/9780521690881

Originally published in German as *Sozialtheorie. Zwanzig einführende Vorlesungen* by Suhrkamp 2004, © Suhrkamp 2004

First published in English by Cambridge University Press 2009 as
Social Theory: Twenty Introductory Lectures
© Hans Joas and Wolfgang Knöbl 2009

English translation © Cambridge University Press 2009

This publication is in copyright. Subject to statutory exception and to the provisions of relevant collective licensing agreements, no reproduction of any part may take place without the written permission of Cambridge University Press.

First published 2009
8th printing 2014

A catalogue record for this publication is available from the British Library

Library of Congress Cataloguing in Publication data
Joas, Hans, 1948–
[Sozialtheorie. English]
Social theory : twenty introductory lectures / Hans Joas, Wolfgang Knöbl, Alex Skinner.
p. cm.
Includes bibliographical references and index.
ISBN 978-0-521-87063-4 (hardback) 1. Social sciences–Philosophy–History–20th century. 2. Sociology–Philosophy–History–20th century.
I. Knöbl, Wolfgang, 1963– II. Skinner, Alex. III. Title.
H61.15.J6313 2009
300.1–dc22
2009015141

ISBN 978-0-521-87063-4 Hardback
ISBN 978-0-521-69088-1 Paperback

Cambridge University Press has no responsibility for the persistence or accuracy of URLs for external or third-party internet websites referred to in this publication, and does not guarantee that any content on such websites is, or will remain, accurate or appropriate.

For Björn Wittrock

CONTENTS

	Introduction *page* viii	
I	What is theory? 1	
II	The classical attempt at synthesis: Talcott Parsons 20	
III	Parsons on the road to normativist functionalism 43	
IV	Parsons and the elaboration of normativist functionalism 68	
V	Neo-utilitarianism 94	
VI	Interpretive approaches (1): symbolic interactionism 123	
VII	Interpretive approaches (2): ethnomethodology 150	
VIII	Conflict sociology and conflict theory 174	
IX	Habermas and critical theory 199	
X	Habermas' 'theory of communicative action' 222	
XI	Niklas Luhmann's radicalization of functionalism 249	
XII	Anthony Giddens' theory of structuration and the new British sociology of power 281	
XIII	The renewal of Parsonianism and modernization theory 308	
XIV	Structuralism and poststructuralism 339	
XV	Between structuralism and theory of practice: The cultural sociology of Pierre Bourdieu 371	
XVI	French anti-structuralists (Cornelius Castoriadis, Alain Touraine and Paul Ricoeur) 401	
XVII	Feminist social theories 432	
XVIII	A crisis of modernity? New diagnoses (Ulrich Beck, Zygmunt Bauman, Robert Bellah, and the debate between liberals and communitarians) 463	
XIX	Neo-pragmatism 500	
XX	How things stand 529	
	Bibliography 561	
	Author index 592	
	Subject index 599	

INTRODUCTION

This book is based on lectures originally conceived by one of the authors (Hans Joas) for a visiting professorship at the University of Chicago in 1985 and which he has held regularly since then. The first attendees, towards the end of the 1980s, were students at the University of Erlangen-Nuremberg, followed, for more than a decade, by students at the Free University of Berlin, along with their counterparts at various American and European universities during certain semesters. The younger of the two authors (Wolfgang Knöbl) contributed to the planning and constant improvement of these lectures at various stages of his academic career: as a student in Erlangen, as junior and assistant lecturer in Berlin and New York, and subsequently as a colleague at the University of Göttingen.

It goes without saying that the precise character of this lecture series has changed considerably over the course of time – not only because of the obvious necessity of keeping them constantly up to date, but also in response to students' needs and the imperative of clearing up points they struggled to understand; the authors' own ongoing theoretical projects have also had an important impact. We have now reached a point at which we feel confident enough in our basic approach and in the validity of our overview to sally forth from the lecture theatre and present our ideas to the reading public. We hope our survey will satisfy the needs of both students in the social sciences and those of non-specialist readers keen to understand international developments in the field of social theory since around the end of the Second World War.

To aid intelligibility we have largely retained the characteristic style of the oral lecture. Outstanding works of philosophy such as Ernst Tugendhat's *Traditional and Analytical Philosophy: Lectures on the Philosophy of Language* and Manfred Frank's lectures, published as *What is Neostructuralism?*, served as templates. A comparable work also exists in a subject area closer to our own: Jeffrey Alexander's *Twenty Lectures: Sociological Theory since World War II*. We follow Alexander's example not only as regards the number of lectures, but also in the inclusion of an initial chapter on the philosophy of science. We also agree with Alexander that the development of theory after 1945 may be divided into three major phases: first, a period in which the dominant forces were the work of Talcott Parsons and a modernization theory now considered overly conventional; one which saw this dominance come to an end and sociology disintegrate into rival, sometimes feuding 'approaches' whose political and moral arguments also clashed, mainly in the late 1960s and early 1970s; and the subsequent rise – as Alexander puts it – of a 'new theoretical movement', that is, the burgeoning of ambitious theoretical syntheses, partly anchored in the rival approaches, partly inspired by novel motifs.

But this is where our agreement with Alexander ends. *Thematically*, only our first eight lectures overlap with his book. Alexander's work is thoroughly America-centric and seeks to justify in quasi-historical fashion his own attempt to produce a neo-Parsonian synthesis (for a critique, see Joas, *Pragmatism and Social Theory*, pp. 188–213, esp. pp. 209–12). But given that the focus has shifted dramatically towards Europe since 1970, particularly in the field of theory, with the most ambitious and productive projects coming from Germany (Habermas, Luhmann), France (Touraine, Bourdieu) and Britain (Giddens, Mann), Alexander's account was already inadequate when it appeared (in 1987); it is even more so now. We have done our best to avoid reproducing such partiality in inverse form. We examine how proponents of modernization theory and Parsonianism have attempted to revise and develop these traditions and we scrutinize the renaissance of pragmatism and the rise of communitarianism – all largely intellectual products of North America.

The claim to completeness, proportionality and fairness expressed in these remarks points to the fact that we have one eye on the book's potential use as a tool of academic teaching. Yet it is not strictly speaking a textbook. This is not a neutral presentation of secure knowledge. As in philosophy, there is no certainty in social scientific theory, particularly when it goes beyond the empirical and explanatory, levels at which claims to certainty also frequently come to grief. As far as neutrality is concerned, in this field all one can aspire to do is to argue one's case fairly and comprehensively; it is impossible to forgo one's own theoretical perspective. By no means do we shrink from criticism and judgement. On the contrary, we very much see this book as part of our attempt to produce a comprehensive social theory capable of meeting contemporary needs; this it does by getting to grips with the achievements, problems and tasks germane to the field.

Unlike most of the lectures on which it is based, we have chosen not to call this book 'modern sociological theory'. While this title was well suited to university sociology curricula, it has always failed to capture the inclusion of ideas and stocks of knowledge (such as structuralism and pragmatism) whose intellectual home essentially lies outside of sociology. Rather than disciplinary affiliation, we have always been guided by how an author or movement has contributed to theories of the social. But what exactly do we mean when we speak of 'social theory'?

We lack a history of the use of the term 'social theory'. It seems to have been deployed, without further justification, in the late nineteenth century at the latest. On the one hand, much like the term 'social thought', it was used, in the absence of a more precise definition, for a field of thought to which sociology later laid claim: it referred to generalized statements about social realities or the regularities of social life. On the other hand, however, scholars applied it to a way of thinking, whether their own or that of others, which assailed 'individualism' or which aspired to transcend it. 'Social theory' thus ran counter to key premises of economic, political and psychological thought in the Anglo-Saxon world; implied here was a specific theoretical perspective on cultural and social processes. This was a work in progress marked by persistent theoretical clashes. A similar tendency to criticize individualism and the specific approach to social facts to which this critical stance gave rise influenced the discipline of sociology as it became institutionalized. As a result, the tension between the different meanings of 'social theory', one referring to specific empirical realities and one to a specific perspective on these phenomena, seems at first to have gone largely unnoticed.

However, as the subject became established and above all as it was increasingly professionalized, this tension inevitably became ever more apparent. From the point of view of professional sociology, with its orientation towards the empirical, theory largely meant 'empirical theory', that is, explanatory statements at a high level of generality (see Lecture I for further clarification). This *narrow* conception of theory tended to discourage the production of normative statements and interpretive templates. Even when such views held sway, however, scholars continued to engage in theoretical work *more broadly conceived*. Theory understood in this way was always regarded as useful, at least as a source of hypotheses and as a means of shoring up the discipline's historical identity. It is to this conception of theory that our lectures are dedicated. There are good reasons for this.

Not only has the understanding of the role of theory in the sciences in general changed substantially over the last decades (more on this too in Lecture I). New rivals have also emerged in neighbouring fields. The field of 'political theory', for example, which has become well established, discusses normative issues relating to communal life in good, just and well-organized polities; work in this field often achieves substantial public attention. And the humanities have generated a 'cultural theory', albeit a very nebulous one, at least as a field of discourse, which also tackles issues of significant normative interest, relating to gender relations or intercultural relations, for example. Were sociological theory to become fixated on its purely empirical, explanatory dimension it would inevitably fall behind these competitors.

If this were allowed to happen, two negative consequences would result. First, within the discipline of sociology itself, an overly narrow conception of theory would isolate theoretical from empirical work, which can only be to the detriment of both and puts disciplinary cohesion at risk. Second, the enormous potential inherent in the sociological tradition since Max Weber, Emile Durkheim and George Herbert Mead, both within a broader public context and within interdisciplinary dialogue, would likely remain untapped, squandering the prospect of being taken seriously as an overarching conception incorporating political and cultural dimensions. The term 'social theory' certainly aspires to such overarching status – which is not to say that our book realizes this ideal entirely. Our concern here is with where we direct our intellectual gaze rather than with making definitive statements.

Given its precarious position within the lattice of academic disciplines, some scholars have recently called for 'social theory' to be institutionalized as a discipline in its own right; it already has, they suggest, the requisite intellectual maturity in nascent form (see Stephen Turner's appeal in 'The Maturity of Social Theory'). We do not share this view; quite the contrary. Such a separation would do nothing but cement the state of mutual ignorance that risks emerging between social theory and empirical social science. In any case, in the absence of empirical substantiation and scrutiny, social theory would lose the very aspect which distinguishes it from philosophy and the mere exchange of ideas.

A word on the distinction between the term *social theory* and the German term *Gesellschaftstheorie* ('theory of society') which carries problematic connotations. *Gesellschaftstheorie* has often implied a more normative stance, of a left-wing, 'critical' hue, than is characteristic of sociological theory. Yet, as we argue in greater detail in Lecture XII, the concept of *Gesellschaft* or society is so implicitly bound up with that of an order based on the nation-state, with a clearly defined territory, that it has always been laden with conceptual baggage. Contemporary scholars are now so aware of this baggage that the concept of *Gesellschaft* has finally become problematic. Our understanding of societies constituted as nation-states, like that of all societies, must first be anchored in a theory of the social.

The present work is essentially concerned with the development of social theory since the end of the Second World War. Our point of departure is a book published a few years before this great historical turning point, Talcott Parsons' *The Structure of Social Action* (1937). We refrain from in-depth treatment of the classical figures of sociology, whose tremendous potential we have just underlined. Those wishing to learn about them will have to turn to other books. As will soon become apparent, however, this certainly does not mean that their thinking is ignored in this book. Its presence is constantly felt both in Parsons' work, which of course aspired to synthesize the classical figures' ideas, and in the writings of all subsequent authors who have incorporated more specific aspects in their work. The classical figures have attained this status precisely because their oeuvres have proved unceasingly productive – inexhaustible in fact. But those who believe that elements of their work remain untapped ought not merely to draw upon the classical figures; they must reflect on how much time has elapsed since their heyday and strive to tap their potential for present-day theoretical work. It is the work being done on contemporary problems and scholars' unceasing and productive recourse to older theories that generates the dynamism of 'social theory'; it is this dynamism for which we aspire to rouse interest in the present work.

We are tremendously grateful to all the friends and colleagues who read and provided critical comments on an initial draft of the manuscript. We have done our best to carry out the suggested improvements. Thanks are owed to Frank Adloff, Jens Beckert, Sibylle Kalupner, Christoph Liell, Nora Lindner, Katja Mertin, Gabriele Mordt, Florian von Oertzen, Hans-Joachim Schubert, Peter Wagner, Harald Wenzel, Patrick Wöhrle and Heinrich Yberg. The most outstanding services were rendered by Bettina Hollstein (Erfurt), who unearthed internal inconsistencies with extraordinary precision and whose suggestions helped resolve them. We are also immensely grateful to the University of Chicago (Albion Small Fund) and the University of Göttingen for funding the translation of our book into English.

I

What is theory?

Our decision to begin this lecture series on modern social theory with the question 'What is theory?' may raise some eyebrows. After all, a fair number of you have attended courses on the great figures of sociological theory – such as Emile Durkheim, George Herbert Mead and Max Weber – which featured no discussion of the 'nature' of theory. The course organizers rightly assumed that you already have an intuitive understanding of 'theory' or soon will have. At any rate, you should by now be in a position to characterize the quite different approaches to social reality taken by Weber, Mead or Durkheim. As is well known, Weber described the state or political phenomena from a completely different point of view from Durkheim; the former thus had a quite different *theoretical* conception of the nature of the political from the latter, though both referred to the same empirical facts in their sociological accounts. Mead's conception of social action clearly differed markedly from that of Weber, though some of the terms they used were similar, and so on. All these authors thus underpinned their sociological accounts with differing *theories* (plural!). But has this insight not brought us a decisive step closer to resolving the issue of the 'nature' of theory? If we were to compare all these theories and pin down what they have in common, thus finding the lowest common denominator, would we not, we might wonder, already have achieved an adequate understanding of theory (singular!)? A comparison of this kind would surely provide us with, as it were, the formal elements that make up a (sociological) theory; we could grasp what social theory in fact is.

Unfortunately, though, this proposed solution fails to take us very far. Since sociology was established in the nineteenth century, its academic practitioners have never succeeded in reaching a truly stable consensus with regard to its object and mission. They have never really agreed even about core concepts. It should therefore come as no surprise that the 'correct' understanding of theory has also been fiercely debated. The *relationship between theory and empirical research* was one subject of controversy, because certain social scientists assumed that we first need to carry out intensive empirical work to prepare the ground for a decent social scientific theory, while others asserted that empirical research without prior, comprehensive theoretical reflection would at best yield meaningless and at worst erroneous results. Social thinkers have also had very different ideas on the *relationship between theories and world views*. While some emphasized that sociological theory or social theory is a purely scientific affair remote from political or religious world views, others underlined that the humanities and social sciences can never entirely break away from such beliefs, and that the idea of a 'pure' science, of sociology for example, is therefore chimerical. The dispute over the *relationship between theory and normative or moral questions* was closely tied up with this. While some sociologists were of the opinion that science should in principle refrain from making any statements of a normative, political or moral nature, others called for a socio-politically engaged science which would not shrink from tackling 'oughts' (How ought people to act? How should a good or just society be structured?). On this view, science and particularly the social sciences should not act as though they merely make available research results with no responsibility for how these are used. Social scientific research certainly has consequences. Because of this, the discipline cannot be indifferent to what is done with its findings. Finally, the *relationship between theory and everyday knowledge* has also been subject to fierce debate. While some have postulated that science, including the social sciences, is generally superior to everyday knowledge, others have asserted that the humanities and social sciences are far too rooted in that everyday world, and dependent on it, to make such presumptuous claims. Thus, as you can see, the concept of theory itself is highly contentious. Any attempt, of the kind intimated above, to work out the lowest common denominator of the theories produced by the leading figures of sociology would come to nothing; it would remain impossible to answer the question 'What is theory?'. Even an endeavour of this kind would not help you reach a decision with regard to the debates which we have briefly outlined.

But do we need to thrash out and clarify so precisely what 'theory' is in the first place? At the end of the day, you have 'understood' the classical sociological authors, and have perhaps attended seminars on them, without having to explicitly question the concept of theory. Why then do we propose a debate on basic principles tackling the 'nature' of theory only at this stage – when considering *modern* sociological theory or social theory? There are two answers to this question. The *first* is informed by history or the history of the discipline. When, among others, Weber, Durkheim and Simmel, the so-called founding fathers, brought the discipline of 'sociology' into being, this often involved individuals struggling to assert the subject's scientific reputation and clashes with other disciplines that wished to deny the legitimacy of sociology. Of course, sociologists also disagreed with one another, quite often in fact, yet this was as nothing compared to the situation that pertained when sociology was finally established in the universities from the middle of the twentieth century on. Modern sociology, like the modern social sciences as a whole, now features a plethora of competing theoretical schools – not without good reason do we require another nineteen lectures to help you appreciate this diversity. And within this context of tremendous theoretical competition epistemological questions play a significant role, questions relating to the prerequisites for and characteristics of science and scientific theory construction. The dispute between the various social scientific theoretical schools was and is often about the correct understanding of theory. In this respect, you require at least a certain degree of insight into these issues in order to grasp how and why modern social scientific theories have developed as they have.

The *second* answer relates both to the history of the discipline and to pedagogical matters. The modern social sciences are characterized not only by a large number of competing theories, but also by an extremely damaging division between theoretical and empirical knowledge. Something of a division of labour, as it were, has arisen between those who see themselves as theoreticians and those who view themselves as empiricists or empirical social researchers. As a result of this strict division of labour, these two groupings scarcely register each other's findings any more. But theoretical and empirical knowledge cannot truly be separated. This lecture on the 'nature' of theory is thus intended to provide us with an opportunity to think about what theory is, its importance to empirical research and the way in which empirical knowledge always informs its theoretical counterpart. Through this lecture we wish to convey to the enthusiastic theoreticians among you – if there are any – that social theories are never free of empirical observations or assumptions. It is thus a mistake to look askance at 'number-crunching' empiricists. In this lecture, we also wish to help the current or future enthusiastic empiricists and (possible) despisers of theory among you to appreciate that empirical observations – however banal they may be – are never free of theoretical statements; there is, therefore, no harm in engaging with theory on an ongoing basis. This is true in part because, despite all the chatter about the declining influence of the social sciences, we should bear in mind that social scientific theories continue to have an enormous impact; we need only think of Marxian theory in the past or the highly consequential debates on globalization and individualization in the cultural and political sections of present-day newspapers. Theories not only imbue the instruments of empirical social research, they also inform the social world we wish to study; for this reason alone, even empirically inclined social scientists cannot simply pass over these theories by arguing that they wish to steer clear of all theoretical speculations and prefer to devote themselves to (empirical) reality. Once again: theoretical and empirical knowledge are too closely linked for such an attitude to be justified.

But if it is the case that, as described above, no uncontested understanding of theory has ever emerged within the social sciences, if it has proved impossible to definitively clarify the relationship between theoretical and empirical knowledge, between theory and world views, between theory and normative questions and between theory and everyday knowledge, does this mean that questions about the 'nature' of theory are meaningless? No, it does not. There are no grounds for resignation and cynicism, for two different reasons. *First,* you will rapidly come to appreciate, if you study sociology for example, that it is not the only discipline in which the question of the status of theory is discussed. The other social sciences, from political science through history to economics, face similar problems, even if arguments over basic issues tend to play a less central role there. And as you will see, even the seemingly unimpeachable natural sciences are not immune to such disputes. *Second*, it is certainly possible to achieve an understanding capable of attaining consensus, albeit one consisting of several steps, by drawing on the controversies over the status of theories, some of which have a very long history. This, however, requires us to examine precisely where and to what degree consensus has existed on the 'nature' of theory, at what point and why this consensus broke down and when, throughout the history of these controversies, attempts were made, again and again, to re-establish the previous consensus. This is precisely what we wish to elucidate.

At a very basic level, the different theoretical schools and disciplines are at least in agreement that theories should be understood as generalizations. To put it the other way around, which may be easier to grasp, we might say: every generalization is already a theory. We use theories of this kind all the time, particularly in everyday life. Whenever we use the plural, without actually having checked first whether our generalization truly applies to all cases, we are simultaneously deploying a theory: 'all Germans are Nazis', 'all men are macho', 'most sociologists say incomprehensible things', etc. are theories of this kind. On the basis of our observation that some Germans are in fact fascistic in their thinking, that many men do in fact behave in a misogynist manner, and that some sociologists struggle to speak generally intelligible English, we have concluded that *all* Germans are like that, that *all* men behave in this way, that *most* sociologists speak in that way. Of course, we have not really verified this. We neither know each and every German or male nor have we met most sociologists. When we make abstract statements such as these, we are therefore doing nothing other than utilizing a theory. You might also say that we are putting forward a hypothesis. The American logician, semiotician and philosopher Charles Sanders Peirce (1839–1914) has in fact shown to impressive effect that our entire perception of everyday life and our actions rest upon nothing but a wickerwork of hypotheses (or abductions as he calls them), without which we would be quite unable to live a meaningful life:

> Looking out of my window this lovely spring morning I see an azalea in full bloom. No, no! I do not see that; though that is the only way I can describe what I see.
>
> *That* is a proposition, a sentence, a fact; but what I perceive is not a proposition, sentence, fact, but only an image, which I make intelligible in part by means of a statement of fact. This statement is abstract; but what I see is concrete. I perform an abduction when I so much as express in a sentence anything I see. The truth is that the whole fabric of our knowledge is one matted felt of pure hypothesis … Not the smallest

advance can be made in knowledge beyond the stage of vacant staring, without making an abduction at every step.

(Peirce, Ms. 692, quoted in Thomas A. Sebeok and Jean Umiker-Sebeok, 'You Know My Method'. A Juxtaposition of Charles S. Peirce and Sherlock Holmes, p. 23)

Theory is as necessary as it is unavoidable. Without it, it would be impossible to learn or to act in consistent fashion; without generalizations and abstractions, the world would exist for us only as a chaotic patchwork of discrete, disconnected experiences and sensory impressions. Of course, in everyday life we do not speak of 'theories'; we use them with no awareness that we are doing so. In principle, working and thinking *scientifically* functions no differently, except for the fact that here of course the formation and deployment of theories occurs *quite deliberately*. Specific hypotheses or theories are proposed to deal with specific problems; one then tries to combine several such specific theories to make a more general theory that links together the various generalizations in consistent fashion. But all in all, the construction of theories, of generalizing statements, is a significant component of both everyday life and science. It is our only means of approaching 'reality'. The Anglo-Austrian philosopher Karl Raimund Popper (1902–94) expressed this elegantly, though not much differently from Charles Sanders Peirce:

> Theories are nets cast to catch what we call 'the world': to rationalize, to explain, and to master it. We endeavour to make the mesh ever finer and finer.
>
> (Popper, *The Logic of Scientific Discovery*, p. 59)

This understanding of theory, that is, its function with respect to generalization, is now almost universally accepted.

Historically, the first controversies began on the next level; but they too have been overcome because, as we shall see in a moment, one perspective emerged victorious, its superiority widely acknowledged.

The goal of scientific endeavour is not to produce generalizations of just any kind. Prejudices are also theories. They are also generalizations, albeit highly problematic or erroneous ones, as the above examples about the behaviour of Germans, men and sociologists clearly attest. But prejudices are the very thing that scientists claim not to produce; their concern is to formulate *accurate* generalizations on the basis of individual cases (inference from an individual case or individual cases to a universal statement is also termed 'induction' in the philosophy of science) or to explain individual cases *accurately* on the basis of theories ('deduction' – inferring individual cases from a generalization). But in order to speak of 'accurate' or 'inaccurate' theories, we require a yardstick. This must stipulate that theories are scientific (rather than prejudiced) only if they bear close scrutiny in light of reality, or can at least be checked against reality.

It was over this issue that consensus began to break down. People had different ideas about *what* exactly this process of checking against reality should involve. It seems obvious, for example, that *verification* should be the ideal of science. For a long time, until the early twentieth century, this was in fact the view commonly held by scientists and philosophers of science. If theoretical assumptions have to prove themselves against reality, then the best approach – it was presumed at the time – must be to first remove from science the entire stock of prejudiced everyday knowledge, in order to rebuild the edifice of scientific knowledge on absolutely solid ground. On this view, meticulous observation would lead to generalized statements which – repeatedly confirmed by individual observations and experiments – would become ever more certain. These principles and statements, verified in this way, that is, with their claim to truth confirmed, would then be combined, such that slowly but steadily more and more building blocks of *verified* knowledge could be accumulated and integrated. This would then lead to certainty, to 'positive' knowledge as it was called, which is one of the reasons why advocates of this conception of science are known as 'positivists'.

The problem with this positivist position, first clearly identified by the same Karl Raimund Popper mentioned above, is that verification cannot be a good yardstick of the scientific validity of statements for the simple reason that it is in fact impossible to verify most theoretical statements. As Popper lays out in his now very famous book *The Logic of Scientific Discovery*, which first appeared in 1934, in the case of most scientific problems we cannot be certain whether a generalization, that is, a theory or hypothesis, *truly applies in all cases*. In all probability, we will never be able to verify once and for all the astrophysical statement that 'All planets move around their suns along an elliptical trajectory', because we are unlikely ever to get to know all the solar systems in the universe and therefore we will presumably never be able to confirm with absolute certainty that every single planet does in fact follow an elliptical trajectory around its sun, as opposed to some other route. Much the same applies to the statement 'All swans are white'. Even if you have seen thousands of swans and all of them were in fact white, you can ultimately never be certain that a black, green, blue, etc. swan will not show up at some point. As a rule, universal statements cannot therefore be confirmed or verified. To put it another way: inductive arguments (that is, inference from individual instances to a totality) are neither logically valid nor truly compelling arguments; induction cannot be justified purely in terms of logic, because we are unable to rule out the possibility that *one* observation may eventually be made that refutes the general statement *thought to be* corroborated. Positivists' attempts to trace laws back to elementary observations or to derive them from elementary observations and verify them are thus doomed to failure.

This was precisely Popper's criticism. He then proposed a different criterion, for which he became famous, in order to mark off the empirical sciences from other forms of knowledge – from everyday knowledge and metaphysics. He championed *falsification*, underlining that '*it must be possible for an empirical scientific system to be refuted by experience*' (Popper, *Logic*, p. 41; original emphasis). Popper's position was thus that while generalizations or scientific theories are not ultimately provable or verifiable, they may be checked against reality intersubjectively, that is, within the research community; they may be repudiated or *falsified*. This may sound trivial, but is in fact an ingenious argument that lays the foundations for 'empirical science' and demarcates it from other forms of knowledge. With his reference to the fundamental testability and falsifiability of scientific propositions, Popper excludes *first* so-called universal 'existential statements' from the realm of science. Statements such as 'UFOs exist', 'God exists', 'There are ants the size of elephants' cannot be falsified: I can provide no evidence to refute the claim that God or UFOs or elephant-sized ants exist, as it is conceivable, at least theoretically, that if you searched long enough, you would eventually find a UFO, God or elephantine ants somewhere. Popper does not deny that such statements can be meaningful. The statement 'God exists' is manifestly highly significant and thus meaningful for many people. Popper is simply of the opinion that there is little point in entering into a *scientific* dispute about the existence of God, precisely because a statement to this effect cannot ultimately be disproved.

Second, the criterion of falsification now allows us to test and in fact verify so-called universal statements ('All Germans are Nazis'), because a single observation – of a German who is not a Nazi – can cause the assertion or theory to collapse. For Popper, the criterion of falsification is thus the only productive as well as the most efficient yardstick enabling us to distinguish scientific from other kinds of statements.

This brings a quite different dynamic to scientific work than pertained when the old 'positivist' conception of science and its principle of verification held sway. Popper's approach, which has triumphed over positivism, eschews a view of science as a slow accumulation of knowledge; for him, science means the *constant testing and questioning* of our theoretical assumptions by deliberately exposing them to the risk of falsification. Only the best theories survive in this (Darwinian) struggle. Science, Popper claims, is not set in stone: it is incapable of achieving absolute knowledge, truth or even probability; science is rather a steady forward march, a process of 'guessing' with respect to theoretical statements which are constantly put to the test. Theories can therefore only ever be described as 'provisionally warranted':

> it is not so much the number of corroborating instances which determines the degree of corroboration as *the severity of the various tests* to which the hypothesis in question can be, and has been, subjected.
>
> (Popper, *Logic*, p. 267; original emphasis)

Popper is thus less concerned to demand that scientists maintain distance from quotidian knowledge and its prejudices than with encouraging a willingness to repeatedly examine their own theory (or theories) for potentially falsifying evidence in order to get rid of all those theories with no chance of survival. Scientists should not be searching for evidence to confirm their own theories, but actively divesting themselves of all false certainties through consistent use of the principle of falsification! Popper puts it in typically pithy fashion: 'Those among us who are unwilling to expose their ideas to the hazard of refutation do not take part in the scientific game' (*Logic*, p. 280).

The superiority of the Popperian conception of science over its positivist predecessor is now widely recognized; falsification is generally thought to be a better criterion for defining what science is than verification. In this respect, there is once again consensus about what theory is and what it can do. Admittedly, scientists disagree over whether Popper's emphasis on scientific theories as generalizations that may be tested against reality and are thus falsifiable is really all that can be said about the concept of theory. Advocates of the 'rational choice' approach, which we examine in the fifth lecture, are in fact of this opinion insofar as they wish to reserve the concept of 'theory' only for those systems of statements in which social facts are *explained* quite explicitly *with the aid of a universal statement*, a general law. Here, 'theory' is understood *solely* as an explanatory system: 'Every explanation begins with the question of why the phenomenon under examination exists (or existed) in this way, functions (or functioned) as it does (or did) or changes (changed) in the manner it has been claimed to do' (Esser, *Soziologie. Allgemeine Grundlagen* ['Sociology: General Foundations'], p. 39). To explain things, you need, among other things, a universal statement – and it is only explanatory systems based on such universal statements that may be called 'theories' from the perspective of this approach. The rational choice approach refuses to honour other reflections, those not immediately concerned with producing law-like propositions, with the title of 'theory'.

At first sight this approach, which tallies with the Popperian conception of theory, appears reasonable and scarcely open to criticism. Furthermore, this definition of 'theory' has the advantage of being fairly narrow and precise: you know exactly what you mean then when you use the term 'theory'. However, this is not quite as unproblematic and self-evident as it might seem, because the relationship between theoretical and empirical knowledge throws up rather serious problems for the Popperian approach. The applicability of the criterion of falsification that Popper has brought into play (as well as that of the criterion of verification vanquished by him) rests on the assumption that the level of empirical observation and that of theoretical interpretation or explanation may be clearly distinguished, and thus that purely theoretical statements may be tested against separate, purely empirical observations. One can falsify and refute a theoretical statement with complete certainty only if one's observations, through which one is attempting to falsify it, are correct and beyond dispute. Observations cannot themselves entail yet more theories, because otherwise of course it is possible that, because one's observations may already contain a false theory, one is wrongly falsifying (or verifying) a statement. In other words, for falsification (or verification) to proceed smoothly we would require direct access to an unmediated, theory-free form of observation.

But we know, as the lengthy quotation from Peirce already brought home to us so powerfully, that this is not the case. Every observation made in everyday life, and every statement about it, is already permeated by theory. The same also applies to scientific observations and statements. Within a community of scientists, empirical observations must be formulated in an observer's language that either draws directly upon everyday language or, if explicitly specialist terminology is used in the process of observation, whose terms can be explicated and defined with the aid of everyday language. And this everyday language is of course always 'infected' with theory already. Peirce showed that *every* observation is a generalization and thus an elementary theory: observational languages *inevitably* entail theories already, which direct our attention towards certain phenomena and which help determine how we perceive phenomena. But this also means that we can never describe individual instances without implicit generalizations. It is thus impossible to maintain a strict division between empirical and theoretical knowledge. And the idea, which goes back to Popper, that it is possible to falsify theories in straightforward fashion, is untenable.

If there is no polarity, no strict division between empirical and theoretical knowledge, how are we to define their relationship? The American sociologist Jeffrey Alexander, whose work we will come across again in the course of this lecture series (see Lecture XIII) has made a very helpful suggestion in this regard. He speaks not of a 'polarity' but of a 'continuum':

> Science can be viewed as an intellectual process that occurs within the context of two distinctive environments, the empirical observational world and the non-empirical metaphysical one. Although scientific statements may be oriented more toward one of these environments than the other, they can never be determined exclusively by either alone. The differences between what are perceived as sharply contrasting kinds of scientific arguments should be understood rather as representing different positions on the same epistemological continuum.

(Alexander, *Theoretical Logic in Sociology*, vol. I, p. 2)

Thus, according to Alexander, scientific thought is constantly moving between the extremes, at which we never finally arrive, of what he calls the 'metaphysical environment' and the 'empirical environment' – which chimes with the Peircean argument that we are unable to access the world directly, without theory. Alexander has attempted to outline this in Figure 1.1 below (ibid., p. 3). The core message here is that observations are indeed relatively close to reality, that is, to the 'empirical environment', but that it is impossible to reproduce reality directly because observations are bound up with methodological assumptions, laws, definitions, models and even 'general presuppositions', which are relatively close to the pole of the 'metaphysical environment'. But this means – and we will return to this point later on – that it is quite misguided to try to limit scientific work to the construction of theories in the sense of explanatory systems and attempts to falsify them. If scientific argumentation does in fact take place along the continuum outlined by Alexander, then the task of scientific theorizing undoubtedly amounts to more than advocates of the 'rational choice' approach mentioned above, for example, assert. If 'general presuppositions', 'classifications', 'concepts', etc. play just as significant a role in the research process as 'laws' and observations – or at least a not unimportant role – there is no reason for us to accept that we can advance our understanding only by concentrating on these laws and observations. It would also be difficult to maintain the notion that the term 'theory' must be reserved exclusively for systems of statements consisting of laws and observations. And many social scientists have in fact adopted a more broadly conceived conception of theory.

But let us return immediately to the fact, problematic for Popperian falsificationism, that it is impossible to draw a strict dividing line between the levels

Metaphysical Environment

General presuppositions
Models
Concepts
Definitions
Classifications
Laws
Complex and simple propositions
Correlations
Methodological assumptions
Observations

Empirical Environment

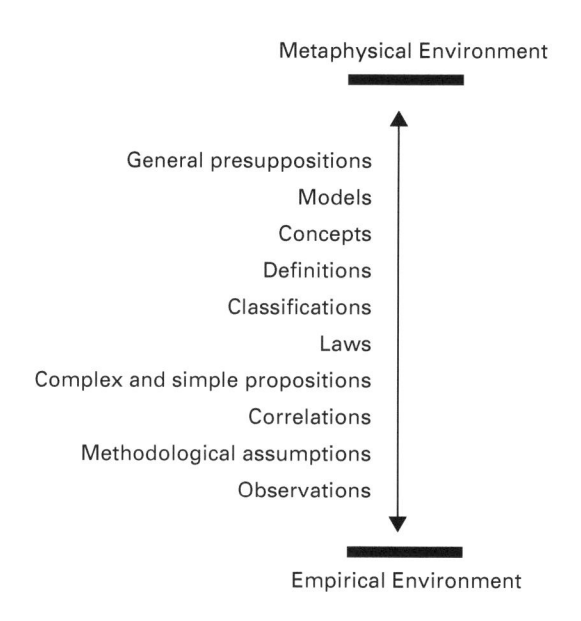

Figure 1.1

of theoretical and empirical knowledge. Popper himself – in his defence – certainly recognized this difficulty: '*There are no pure observations*: they are pervaded by theories and guided by both problems and theories' (Popper, *Logik der Forschung*, p. 76; original emphasis).[1] He too emphasized that every account of an observation, every statement about an event, every 'basic statement', uses concepts that cannot be corroborated by unmediated sensory data. He was thus also of the opinion that every attempt to test a theory must conclude or begin with some sort of basic statements upon whose correctness researchers must agree on the basis of *convention* or by making a *decision*. Science, for Popper, is thus not built upon a rock, but in a certain sense on (provisional) dogmas, on conventions or scientists' (more or less) arbitrary decisions to recognize as correct basic statements about observations. But this was no great problem for Popper since he was of the opinion that we may in turn – *if* any doubt arises as to their correctness – subject these basic statements to scrutiny, that is, *test* them.

As it turned out, philosophers of science and scientists carrying out research on how scientists actually work were dissatisfied with this Popperian defence of the method of falsification. One book, which was to become almost as famous as Popper's *Logic*, came to play a particularly important role in this debate: Thomas S. Kuhn's *The Structure of Scientific Revolutions* from 1962. Kuhn (1922–96), an American originally trained as a physicist, investigated the process of research in his home discipline in quasi-sociological fashion, focusing primarily on the historical development of physics (and chemistry) and more generally the way in which new theories come into being in the natural sciences. Kuhn made an astonishing discovery quite out of synch with the principle of falsification championed by Popper. The history of science certainly features countless cases in which specific scientific statements were falsified. However, what Kuhn observed in his historical-sociological analyses was that as a rule this did *not* then lead to the rejection of entire theories, from which these statements were derived, or to their replacement by others. Kuhn showed that the history of the natural sciences was replete with new discoveries, inventions, etc. which fundamentally contradicted the major theories of the day: Lavoisier's discovery of oxygen, for example, fundamentally contradicted the reigning theory of phlogiston, according to which this 'substance' is given off by all burning bodies. Yet Lavoisier's discovery did not lead to the immediate rejection of the 'old' and – as we now know – incorrect theory of phlogiston. On the contrary, it was made more specific, modified and reconstructed in order to render comprehensible Lavoisier's discovery; this discovery was not regarded as a falsification, but merely as a problematic observation,

---

[1] The quotation from Popper's *Logik der Forschung*, the German version of *The Logic of Scientific Discovery*, appears in an addendum inserted by the author in 1968; this was not included in the English translation.

a temporary puzzle, an 'anomaly' within a proven theory. Kuhn documented a multitude of such or similar cases in the history of science, drawing our attention to the fact – and this is the key point – that this adherence to the old theories was by no means an expression of dogmatism or irrationality. Again and again, there have been good reasons for this conservatism: the old theories have proved their worth in the past; it may be possible to integrate the new discoveries by further developing the old theories, by means of auxiliary hypotheses for example; the new theory has not yet been fully worked out and is often deficient or incomplete; it is possible that we are dealing merely with faulty measurements rather than genuine falsification, and so on. In brief, in the context of scientific practice, there has often been a complete lack of clear criteria by which to ascertain *when* a theory should be considered falsified.

Kuhn's book deals exclusively with the history of the natural sciences. But very similar accounts of the research process can of course also be found in the humanities and social sciences, where it seems to be even more difficult to destroy a theory, that is, to falsify it as a whole, by means of an empirical observation. We need only think of the history of Marxism. As a social scientific theory, Marxism can of course – and it itself demands no less – be tested against social reality. Now, many of the theoretical statements formulated or defended by Marx or Marxists, to put it carefully, conflict with empirical reality. Much of what Marx predicted never happened: the polarization of the population into a rich capitalist class on the one hand and a numerically huge proletariat on the other failed to occur; the socialist revolutions forecast by Marx and Engels did not take place or at least not where they were supposed to, namely in the industrially advanced countries under the leadership of the working class; successful revolutions took place at best on the global peripheries and with a significant role being played by the peasantry, that is, the 'wrong' group of people; the dissolution of all particularistic ties, predicted by Marx and Engels in the *Communist Manifesto*, supposedly propelled by the economy – among other things, they predicted that nation-states would disappear – did not happen either. In fact, the late nineteenth and twentieth centuries turned the assumptions of Marx and Engels upside down: this was the great age of nationalism and nation-states. If one adhered to the Popperian principle of falsification, all these observations would have inevitably led to conclusive refutation of Marxism and thus its definitive rejection. But this did not occur. Those convinced of the validity of Marxism as an approach to research always managed to persuade themselves, and clearly others too, of the productivity of the Marxist paradigm by means of a series of auxiliary hypotheses. The proletarianization of the majority of the population in the highly industrialized countries, so the argument goes, failed to occur because capitalism managed to relieve poverty 'at home' by intensifying exploitation of the 'Third World'; this was also the reason why revolutions failed to take place in the Western countries, in which the workers were 'bought' by 'capital', through welfare benefits for example, but took place instead in the countries of the impoverished and exploited Third World; and Marx and Engels may indeed have been too quick to forecast the end of the nation-state, but today – in the age of globalization – things were happening precisely as they had always predicted, and so on. In brief, Marxian theory is said not to be wrong, but merely to require adaptation to changed historical conditions.

You can decide for yourselves what you make of this defence of Marxism. For our purposes, all that matters is the insight that the natural and social sciences in general, and by no means only Marxism, appear to entail a fairly large number of defensive lines from which the proponents of a theory can shield it against empirical falsification. In fact, theories in the social sciences have in some ways proved even more resistant to unambiguous falsification than in the natural sciences. The former not only feature disagreements over precisely what falsification entails, but even about what exactly a theory is saying. While natural scientific theories are for the most part relatively clearly formulated, the social sciences and humanities are more often confronted with the problem that there is no real agreement over precisely what the content of a theory is. You may be familiar with this phenomenon from your seminars on the classical sociological authors or from reading the secondary literature on them. What did Marx, Durkheim, Weber, etc. *really* say? What is the correct, once-and-for-all *interpretation* of the theories of Marx, Durkheim, Weber, and others? But a theory whose very content is contested is, logically, scarcely amenable to unambiguous empirical falsification.

But let us return to Kuhn and his book *The Structure of Scientific Revolutions*. According to him, in the natural sciences at any rate, there are no compelling logical arguments against a theory; there can be no unambiguous falsification. And, Kuhn suggests, we should not be surprised if the daily routine of research passes off without much sign of criticism. Existing theories are used for long periods without being scrutinized, precisely because scholars are convinced of their fundamental fruitfulness. This routinized type of research Kuhn calls 'normal science'. Puzzling or contradictory occurrences, problematic experiments, etc. are not regarded as falsification in the course of 'normal science', but rather, to repeat, as anomalies, which one hopes to be able to remove or resolve *at some point* with existing theoretical means. 'Normal science' is research

> firmly based upon one or more past scientific achievements, achievements that some particular scientific community acknowledges for a time as supplying the foundation for its further practice.
>
> (Kuhn, *Structure*, p. 10)

Further, the history of science, according to Kuhn, only very rarely features instances of *individual* scientists suddenly embracing a new theoretical edifice in response to a persuasive argument or impressive experiment. The real breakthrough of genuinely new theories occurs in a manner that often has little to do with purely scientific criteria. The old theories often become overly complex because of the steady accretion of new auxiliary hypotheses to explain 'anomalies', intensifying the need for more simple theories. And this need is often articulated by a *younger* generation of scientists who suddenly ditch the old theory and *large numbers of whom* are willing to look afresh at the new discoveries and 'anomalies' and are therefore receptive to theoretical innovations. This is the moment which Kuhn terms a 'scientific revolution'. As Kuhn also states, a paradigm shift occurs. An old 'paradigm' – an old way of looking at phenomena, an old grand theory and associated research methods – is replaced fairly rapidly by a new 'paradigm', just as in the past 'Ptolemaic astronomy' and 'Aristotelian dynamics' were respectively replaced by their 'Copernican' and 'Newtonian' counterparts and 'corpuscular optics' gave way to 'wave optics'.

The crucial point in these revolutions in scientific work described by Kuhn is that there was never a clear *empirical* criterion that would have made it possible to justify cogently and persuasively to every scientist the necessary departure from the old paradigm and the change of direction towards a new one. In the history of science, it was not empirical knowledge as such that led to the final rejection of a theory formerly considered correct. Rather, decisions on such matters were often moulded by quite banal, 'everyday' circumstances. It was often 'biological' factors that helped a new theory break through, when, for example, one generation of scientists became too old and a new one open to theoretical innovations followed in its footsteps. But this also means that periods of 'normal science' as well as 'scientific revolutions' are accompanied by power struggles and clashes of opposing interests (between outsiders and established researchers, between older and younger scientists). Science is a venture that cannot be fully detached from the social phenomena which play a role in everyday life as well as other contexts.

The old and new theories are, Kuhn asserts, 'incommensurable'; they cannot in fact be compared and contrasted. Scientific revolutions do not, therefore, feature alternation between similar theories, but between theories so different that they may be described as differing 'world views', a term also used by Kuhn.

> Let us, therefore, now take it for granted that the differences between successive paradigms are both necessary and irreconcilable ... the reception of a new paradigm often necessitates a redefinition of the corresponding science. Some old problems may be relegated to another science or declared entirely 'unscientific'. Others that were previously non-existent or trivial may, with a new paradigm, become the very archetypes of significant scientific achievement. And as the problems change, so, often, does the standard that distinguishes a real scientific solution from a mere metaphysical speculation, word game, or mathematical play. The normal-

scientific tradition that emerges from a scientific revolution is not only incompatible but often actually incommensurable with that which has gone before.

(Kuhn, *Structure*, p. 102)

When the revolution has been successfully completed, science enters a 'normal' phase once again, and the research carried out by the scientific community is based on certain unquestioned rules and norms of research practice as it was formerly, until the occurrence of a new scientific revolution.

Kuhn's analyses in the history and sociology of science, as he pointed out, entailed profound consequences for the philosophy of science. To repeat, the process of science does not function remotely in line with Popper's attempt at standardization via his 'principle of falsification'. And on the basis of Kuhn's accounts, we can certainly conclude that it is 'good' if scientists refrain from proceeding in strict accordance with the principle of falsification. Normal science, that is, science which proceeds uncritically and in routinized fashion with respect to certain theoretical assumptions, may be highly productive. It may well make sense not to reject the theory every time a contrary observation crops up. This would sabotage or undermine the practice of research. It may make sense to initially interpret observations that contradict the theory as mere anomalies, in the hope that the problems internal to the theory may nonetheless be resolved at some point. This was in fact frequently the case in the history of the sciences. Furthermore, Kuhn showed that a fair number of *new and eventually successful* theories were initially falsified on the basis of experiences and observations accepted at the time and, had scientists adhered to Popper's criterion of falsification, they should have disappeared immediately. Popper's criterion, Kuhn asserts, is neither a helpful guide to the history of science nor is it of much help in the practical process of research.

Finally, we can draw one further conclusion from Kuhn's sociological analyses of the history of science. Kuhn's very choice of terms, his talk of 'paradigm shifts' and 'scientific revolution', shows us that scientific progress does not proceed without interruption, but is replete with tranquil periods as well as sudden upheavals. Here, Kuhn takes a stand against both positivism, whose advocates of course believed in the slow, continuous development of scientific knowledge, backed up by precise empirical observations, as well as against Popper, who underestimated the significance of the phase of 'normal' and routinized science. Science, Kuhn shows, is a process that disobeys the rational guidelines thought up by philosophers of science at their desks. In science, random factors play a role just as significant as the conflicts over status and power between generations of scientists mentioned above. (Should you be interested in a relatively short, well-written book on the debates within the philosophy of science, admirably geared towards the needs of the student, we would recommend A. F. Chalmers' *What is this Thing Called Science?*)

In any case, Kuhn's works were the point of departure for a vehement debate within the philosophy of science on the status of science, particularly in the 1960s and 1970s. While some criticized Kuhn for giving free rein to relativism (his talk of the 'incommensurability' of theories, whose quality could not be established *empirically*, was said to place science on the same level as any old world view, making rational discussion impossible), others welcomed the relativistic conclusions which – so they believed – could be drawn from Kuhn's analyses. The 'anarchistic' and for a time highly fashionable philosopher of science Paul Feyerabend stated, for example, that neither their methods nor results legitimate the ambitions of scientists: 'Science is one [i]deology among many' (*Science in a Free Society*, p. 106), that is, merely one form of knowledge among others (such as magic).

But both the orthodox defenders of science and their anarchistic critics interpreted Kuhn wrongly or at least in a very individual fashion. Kuhn did *not* assert that competing paradigms constitute totalities or world views hermetically sealed off from one another, between which, and with respect to their empirical fruitfulness, it is impossible to rationally choose, but in which one could at best profess one's faith – as with different religions. He merely argued that in many cases no truly clear *empirical* criterion exists enabling us to decide why we have to choose one paradigm rather than another. This is, however, not the same as saying that no arguments at all may be put forward for accepting or rejecting a theory (on this line of reasoning, see Bernstein, *The Restructuring of Social and Political Theory*, pp. 152–67). By no means did Kuhn launch a frontal attack on the rationality of 'science' in his account of the history of science. In his view, the transition from one theory to another is neither an unfounded choice between vocabularies nor a mysterious shift from one theoretical discourse to another. There certainly are *reasons* why it is necessary to adopt a new paradigm. It is possible to *discuss rationally* the paradigm shift to which one aspires or which one rejects; the pros and cons of the particular theory can be *weighed up*, even if we must give up the hope that there is one 'crucial experiment' that will make the decision for us.

What is more, Kuhn's analyses of the history of science – though his radical and problematical notion of the 'incommensurability' of paradigms appears to exclude this – almost always show that paradigms overlap substantially. The various theoretical edifices are connected by many corridors. In reality, not just the history of the natural sciences, but also that of the social sciences, shows that certain *empirical* findings are unanimously endorsed by the representatives of differing paradigms, and that even a fair number of *theoretical* statements meet with general approval beyond the boundaries of paradigms.

What does all this mean for the social sciences or for social theory? We can draw two conclusions from our discussion of the philosophy of science so far, particularly from the Kuhnian analyses, which are of great significance to the following lectures. *First*: the fact that the current theoretical landscape of the social sciences appears confusing, the fact that many different social theories or paradigms exist, some of which are at extreme variance with one another, does not mean that these theories or their theorists are incapable of engaging in a rational debate. In the nineteen lectures to come we will be introducing you to an array of theories. You will see – and this is one of the central theses of this lecture series – that the various theorists communicate with one another, that they make critical reference to one another, such that their theories overlap, resemble and complement one another to some degree. The fact that sociology, for example, is not based on *one single* paradigm arrived at through abstraction (as applies, for example, to economics, in which a specific theoretical school is clearly dominant or hegemonic), the fact that a much lamented, confusing theoretical diversity prevails within sociology, does *not* mean that the subject is fragmenting, or is bound to fragment, into a collection of disconnected approaches.

For you, who are now being introduced to the world of modern social theory, this leads to one inescapable conclusion. You will not, presumably, become experts on all the theoretical schools presented here during the course of your studies; no one could expect you to, especially since you would be hard pushed to find a professor of the social sciences who is truly up to speed with all these theoretical currents. But do not escape from this confusion by taking refuge in the first theory that takes your fancy. There are already too many students who know only one single theory really well and who are so enthusiastic about it that they disdainfully ignore all other approaches. Unfortunately, a fair number of your professors, who have not infrequently specialized in one and only one theory and consider all other theories in principle 'bad' or useless, are also a living example of such behaviour. As we have said, the various approaches that exist within sociology have much potential for mutual exchange. For this reason we advise you to engage in dialogue with *different* theoretical schools as you proceed with your studies. This will help you avoid one-sidedness and blindness to other perspectives. Given that, as we have shown, empirical and theoretical knowledge are very much connected, these are pitfalls that would surely rub off on your empirical work.

The *second* conclusion to be drawn from the 'debate' between Popper and Kuhn is directly relevant to the following lectures. If it is true that theoretical issues cannot be settled solely with empirical means, that the levels of empirical and theoretical knowledge cannot be clearly separated, that – as Figure 1.1 on page 10 produced by Jeffrey Alexander elucidates – we must work on the assumption that empirical and metaphysical environments are ranged along a continuum, then it is also clear that theoretical work within the social sciences must be more than the mere creation and falsification of laws or universal statements, as should be the case according to Popper and the rational choice theorists. Social theory must also concern itself with what are called 'general presuppositions' in Alexander's diagram. Theoretical issues thus range from empirical generalizations to comprehensive interpretive systems which link basic philosophical, metaphysical, political and moral attitudes to the world. Anyone wishing to be part of the social scientific world cannot, therefore, avoid engaging in critical debate on all these levels. Those hoping to stick with purely empirical theories will be disappointed. (It is surely unnecessary for us to repeat again that our conception of theory is not uncontested. As we have said, advocates of rational choice theories would not describe many of the theories presented in what follows as 'theories' in the first place. Should you wish to take a look at the controversy surrounding the question 'What is (social) theory?', you are advised to compare the first chapter of Jeffrey Alexander's book *Twenty Lectures: Sociological Theory since World War II* with the comments made by Hartmut Esser, one of Germany's leading rational choice theorists, in his book *Soziologie. Allgemeine Grundlagen*, chs. 3 and 4.)

If we take as our basis this broad concept of theory, does this not mean that the debate must necessarily run out of control, with every scholar his own theoretician and nothing standing in the way of an arbitrary increase in the number of theories? Quite simply, the answer is 'no'. It has in fact become apparent within the social scientific disciplines – and this brings us back to our first conclusion – that despite the great theoretical diversity, scholars are largely in agreement about what the fundamental or core research topics are. And it is possible to identify these. We believe that the theoretical development of the social sciences can be understood as revolving around three very specific questions. These are 'What is action?'; 'What is social order?'; and 'What determines social change?' All theorists – and this applies to both the *classical* authors of sociological theory as well as *modern* social theorists – have taken up these three questions. We should add that these are of course always closely linked: the *actions* of human beings are never entirely random. *Social orders* always develop, and these are subject to historical *change*. Though the writings of the theorists discussed in what follows approach these questions in markedly different ways – some were more interested in action than order, many were occupied more with social stability than social change – these mutually entwined questions have always been present. What makes these questions so particularly interesting is the fact that the process of answering them almost inevitably leads theorists to make certain diagnoses of their time. The various theorists' often highly abstract ideas about social action, social order and social change find expression – however directly or indirectly – in very concrete appraisals of the state of contemporary societies, their future 'developmental paths' and even of their pasts. Getting to grips with these three questions is thus not a purely formalistic exercise or an end in itself, but leads us straight to the heart of the field of activity which makes the social sciences so intellectually stimulating and attractive to a broad public: their striving to comprehend contemporary societies and detect future trends.

This very fact furnishes us with a basis on which to structure the following lectures. Our thesis is that the development of modern social theory may be understood as an unceasing search for answers to the three questions mentioned above and that the consequent debate was moved to a new level in the 1930s by a great American sociologist, to whom succeeding theorists repeatedly refer – implicitly or explicitly, approvingly or critically – to this day. We are referring to Talcott Parsons; in light of the significance of his work for modern social theory the next three lectures are devoted to him. The history of the reception of Talcott Parsons' work shows with the utmost clarity the very point which we have already touched upon and underlined above: by no means has sociology simply disintegrated into various theoretical schools, nor has this ever been its fate. Rather, it is a discipline in which the development of theory was propelled forward through communication, rational disagreement and controversial debates. Among other things, scholars' tendency to constantly refer back to the system of thought produced by Talcott Parsons created the unity which we now wish to depict in the subsequent nineteen lectures.

We shall convey to you in as much detail as the present context allows how Parsons understood social action, how he conceived of social order, what he had to say about social change, how he interpreted 'his era' – and how and why the other theoretical schools contrasted with his views. We also aim to briefly introduce you to the most important authors, the founders of the various theoretical schools. We intend to give you an overall view of the fields of empirical research in which the various theoretical schools were best able to develop their particular strengths, but also those that exposed their weaknesses. This last should be of particular interest to those of you whose interests tend or will ultimately tend towards the empirical. It will bring home to you once again a point we have addressed on several occasions: the ultimate impossibility of drawing a clear dividing line between empirical and theoretical knowledge.

II

The classical attempt at synthesis
Talcott Parsons

You will no doubt have already come across the founding fathers of sociology, the *classical* figures of the discipline, over the course of your studies or through your own reading. Indisputably, these include the German Max Weber (1864–1920) and the Frenchman Emile Durkheim (1858–1917). Their German contemporaries Georg Simmel (1858–1919) and Ferdinand Tönnies (1855–1936), and the Americans George Herbert Mead (1863–1931), William Isaac Thomas (1863–1947) and Charles Horton Cooley (1864–1929) are often mentioned in the same breath as the two disciplinary giants. Now we can argue till the cows come home about who else ought, or ought not, to be included in such a list of key authors, in the 'canon' of classical sociological theorists. The names of Adam Smith (1723–90) and above all Karl Marx (1818–83) crop up particularly often in this context and inspire intense controversy. Though not sociologists in a narrow sense, they have nonetheless had an enormous influence on sociological thought and, above all, on theory building in the social sciences as a whole.

As interesting as the debate on the classical status of certain authors may be, it is striking that the debaters tend to forget *who* was responsible for the formation of this canon, for drawing up this list of classical authors, *who* originally established the basic structure of the canon as pertains to this day. Should we examine this frequently neglected question, we will find that there is no getting away from the name of the American Talcott Parsons (1902–79). It was Parsons who, in the 1930s, during a very difficult period for sociology worldwide, managed to fuse together the pieces of a theoretical discussion increasingly fragmented after the discipline's foundation and, among other things, declared the substance of Durkheim's and Weber's writings the core of sociological thought. Parsons' first major work, *The Structure of Social Action* (often abbreviated as *Structure* or SSA), from 1937, was an attempt to create a canon, which determined the future development of sociology to an extent almost impossible to grasp today, especially given how long it took to have an impact. For the classical status of Durkheim or Weber now seems so taken for granted, even among neophyte students of sociology, and certainly among 'old hands', that one tends to feel no need to spend much time considering *how* they gained this status in the first place. We have none other than Parsons to thank for this, and this alone would justify a thorough investigation of *The Structure of Social*

Action. But this book of almost 800 pages, which is highly demanding and far from easy to read, and which, incomprehensibly, has yet to be translated into German, was more than a milestone in the process of canon formation. Parsons strove quite explicitly to glean the basic framework of a comprehensive sociological theory from the often fragmentary writings of the classical authors, which were shaped profoundly by national or even personal contexts, and to place the subject within the overall spectrum of the social sciences. We thus have good reasons for devoting this second lecture and even parts of the third to describing and analysing this in many respects pioneering work, which was hardly read when it first appeared, even in America, and was only 'discovered' by the academic community much later.

Parsons' life story is not particularly interesting, but rather embodies a typical, albeit highly successful, academic career. We can thus limit ourselves to a few biographical remarks (for more detail see Charles Camic, 'Introduction: Talcott Parsons before *The Structure of Social Action*'). Parsons was born on 13 December 1902 in Colorado Springs, Colorado, and grew up there in an ascetic Protestant household. His father, originally a Congregationalist minister, was professor of English and dean at Colorado College, before the family moved to New York City in 1917, where the young Parsons now had to prepare for college. He chose Amherst, initially focusing on biology, which was to prove significant to the theoretical development of his middle and later works in particular, before finally, as it seemed, opting for economics. After graduating from Amherst in 1924, he left the USA for a time with the help of a scholarship, initially in order to pursue further studies at the London School of Economics, where, among other things, he came into close contact with leading representatives of social anthropology such as Bronislaw Malinowski. In 1925 he went to Heidelberg, where the atmosphere was still very much imbued with the spirit of Max Weber, who had died five years before; Weber had lived and taught there for many years, leaving a lasting impression on local intellectual life. Here, Parsons also studied the works of other major German social scientists more intensively than before. He successfully completed his Ph.D. thesis on the concept of capitalism in the work of Karl Marx, Werner Sombart and Max Weber in 1927. By then, though, he had already returned to Amherst to work as a part-time lecturer in economics during the 1926/27 academic year. Thus, when Parsons obtained a position at Harvard in the autumn of 1927, his disciplinary orientation was yet to be finally settled. He had been appointed primarily to teach the students his basic knowledge of the *economic* theories then holding sway in Germany – which he had tackled to some extent in his thesis. This went on until 1930, when his increasing interest in things sociological found professional expression: Parsons began to teach at the Harvard sociology department, which had just been established by Russian émigré Pitirim Sorokin. As a result of personal and academic differences with Sorokin, however, Parsons initially faced difficulties here. It was only in 1937 – after the publication of *Structure* – that he was made associate professor, with the prospect of a permanent position. But from this point on Parsons was at least established in the sociology department, a milieu in which he was to remain for the rest of his academic life. He became a highly influential teacher and nurtured brilliant students; from the early 1950s, he managed to combine this with the production of a huge number of publications. *The Social System*, a second major work, appeared in 1951, and numerous books and essays, generally of first-rate theoretical calibre, were published in rapid succession. Parsons thus became the most respected and without doubt most important sociologist of the 1950s and 1960s, and not only in the USA, but across the world, his influence extending even to the Soviet Union. Yet his star began to fade in the late 1960s. He was subject to severe critical attacks. The view had taken hold, particularly within the student movement and the influential academic left, that Parsons' theoretical system, and also his more empirically oriented writings, featured a conservative, America-centric basic structure; it was thus thought necessary to smash the 'orthodox' Parsonian consensus in sociology. Regardless of the fact that this political characterization of Parsons and his work was far from accurate – studies of his life have revealed that he had much sympathy for Roosevelt's New Deal in the 1930s and presumably considered himself a leftish liberal, which also explains why he was later kept under close observation by the FBI – it impacted negatively on the reception of his work in the 1970s. While Parsons continued to be productive even in his later years, he was generally treated as an author whose time was past and who no longer seemed to fit within the contemporary theoretical landscape.

Surprisingly, though, this changed almost immediately after his sudden death on 8 May 1979 in Munich, where Parsons was staying for a lecture tour. In the late 1970s, scholars in various countries tried to overcome the theoretical diversity that had come to prevail within sociology, which many of them found unsatisfactory, through ambitious attempts at synthesis. In doing so, a number of theorists found it helpful to build on the edifice of Parsonian thought. A theoretical movement of this kind, modelled on the work of Parsons and aimed at synthesis, developed in the USA, and also in Germany, under such labels as 'neo-functionalism' or even 'neo-Parsonianism'; we shall return to this movement later (Lecture XIII). In Germany as well, two of postwar sociology's leading figures began to weave together their own arguments with core ideas from Parsons' oeuvre: Jürgen Habermas developed the ideas in his major work, *The Theory of Communicative Action* (1981), with explicit reference to *Structure*; and Niklas Luhmann was crucially inspired by Parsons' later writings, though not his earlier work. We shall look at these two authors in depth later on (Lectures IX–XI). Here, therefore, let us say only this with respect to *The Structure of Social Action*: it was precisely because Parsons had succeeded so brilliantly in this first major book in combining interpretive chapters on key figures in sociology with systematic theory construction that it was able to serve as a model for new attempts at *synthesis*, that is, for linking the arguments of very different theorists, apparently at odds, in order to develop a more comprehensive grand theory.

This brings us at last to the analysis of *The Structure of Social Action*, which we have touched upon several times already and which has had such a tremendous impact on the history of sociology, a book which bears the somewhat boring subtitle: *A Study in Social Theory with Special Reference to a Group of Recent European Writers*. But this subtitle refers to where this book gets much of its suggestive power from: to back up his 'social theory', Parsons elects a brilliant mode of presentation, which he combines with a very specific claim, destined to become famous under the label 'convergence thesis'. Parsons argues that between 1890 and 1920, four major European thinkers, renowned social scientists of their day, unconsciously and, above all, without making reference to one another, moved towards the development of a similar theoretical framework; their work had thus 'converged' on significant and, crucially, theoretically interesting points. These four authors – the German Max Weber, the Frenchman Emile Durkheim, the Englishman Alfred Marshall (1842–1924) and the Italian Vilfredo Pareto (1848–1923) – despite coming from differing national theoretical milieus and clashing intellectual traditions, had, Parsons claimed, found a common denominator with regard to important theoretical issues as their oeuvres developed. While the economist Marshall and the economist and sociologist Pareto were originally exponents of the utilitarian tradition, and the sociologists Durkheim and Weber were beholden, respectively, to French positivism and German idealism when they started out, they had, according to Parsons, increasingly modified these theoretical roots, *quite independently of one another*; that is, without mutual influence, they had come up with a remarkably similar critique of utilitarianism (which we will explain in a moment) and had at the very least made a start on the formulation of a 'voluntaristic theory of action'. Their theories had thus 'converged'. This was Parsons' striking assertion, which serves as our point of departure in what follows. All that matters for the time being is *why* Parsons championed a 'convergence thesis' of this kind, rather than what exactly is meant by this admittedly intimidating term. We will clarify that later.

The first crucial point is thus Parsons' claim to have *himself* identified and elaborated this similarity or convergence, of which the authors were quite unaware. He wished to achieve two things here. First, of course, he claimed to have succeeded, by means of a particularly interesting interpretation, in opening up a new way of looking at thinkers formerly perceived as very different. This in itself would be a major accomplishment. But Parsons had greater ambitions for his convergence thesis. It was intended, secondly, to furnish the reader with evidence, of a sort, of the correctness of his own theoretical endeavour. Parsons agreed with the criticisms of utilitarianism (allegedly) made by the four thinkers mentioned above and he wished to use their objections constructively to develop his own theory. At the same time, he also claimed to be able to retain and even synthesize their positive insights within the framework of a new, more comprehensive approach. Precisely because all four social scientists – this is what Parsons intended to be the main thrust of his convergence thesis – arrived at the same result independently of each other (in the contemporary natural sciences one would say: precisely because a 'multiple discovery' had occurred), Parsons was able to assert the plausibility of his argument that the critique of utilitarianism was both necessary and unavoidable. Parsons claimed that there was no way this critique could have arisen solely as a result of purely personal sensitivities, given that such different minds in different places had expressed their discontent with utilitarianism and ventured to adopt a new theory:

> In fact, within the broad cultural unit, Western and Central Europe at the end of the nineteenth and beginning of the twentieth century, it would scarcely be possible to choose four men who had important ideas in common who were less likely to have been influenced in *developing this common body of ideas* by factors other than the immanent development of the logic of theoretical systems in relation to empirical facts.
>
> (SSA, p. 14; original emphasis)

Parsons' ambition was thus to distil the important ideas put forward by these four authors, though these had been articulated only nebulously, and formulate them with analytical clarity, in order to provide sociology, and perhaps even the social sciences as a whole, with a firm or firmer foundation. The way in which he set about this was to interleave lengthy interpretive chapters on the four authors with purely theoretical expositions, relating all this to his convergence thesis. This was both brilliant and seductive, to a significant extent because his reference to these famous early authors placed him, as it were, 'on their shoulders', the 'shoulders of giants'. He thus interpreted the history of the social sciences (or of sociology) quite explicitly as a history of scientific progress. Parsons presumably thought (see the conclusion he reached in the above quotation) something like this: 'The history of utilitarianism necessarily results in its own critique in the shape of an immanent theoretical shift; at the same time, the first, albeit as yet imperfect, attempts were made to break free of the now untenable theoretical system of utilitarianism (as we can see in the work of the four authors), before I, Parsons, managed to develop a far clearer, more positive theory which, however, is also likely to be changed and perfected to an ever greater degree in future.'

According to Parsons' interpretation, the history of the social sciences can thus be written in much the same way as the success story of the natural sciences. On this view, we can clearly discern progress within the social sciences as well, and especially in sociology, which is of course of tremendous importance to the legitimacy of the discipline (and the social scientific subjects in general). In *The Structure of Social Action*, among other things, Parsons was always concerned to raise the profile of the still relatively young discipline of sociology vis-à-vis the overwhelming model of, for example, the natural sciences, but also economics, which was already significantly more developed and mathematized. His mode of presentation, which underlines scientific progress, is thus anything but accidental. But we would be doing Parsons an injustice were we to accuse him of having interpreted the history of social scientific thought in the particular way he did solely for selfish disciplinary reasons or were we to suggest that this interpretation was intended merely to hail his own status as the one who perfected the edifice of theory erected by these four thinkers. Had these been his only goals, Parsons could have made things far more simple for himself.

We need to recall at this point that Parsons, the American, placed *European* thinkers at the centre of his interpretations. This is relevant because when Parsons' study was published the influence of the European social sciences in the USA had become fairly negligible, if we disregard the increasing number of émigrés from Germany arriving in the country from 1933 onwards. *Before* the First World War, almost all famous American scientists studied in Europe and particularly in Germany at one time or another over the course of their career. But this began to change because the war had diminished Germany's prestige substantially. For many Americans, all of Europe was sinking in the political mire; one need only think of the rise of Italian fascism in the early 1920s, Hitler's assumption of power in 1933, the Spanish Civil War beginning in 1936 or the turmoil of the popular front government in France. From an American perspective it may have seemed very hard to grasp why, as Parsons proposed, one should build on the work of *European* thinkers – indeed exclusively – in order to establish a discipline and consolidate its position within the academy. Yet this is exactly what Parsons did, though his proposal was by no means guaranteed to meet with a favourable response given the origins of these thinkers. Parsons thus made it anything but easy for himself. He took a considerable risk in putting these thinkers on a pedestal, particularly Durkheim and Weber, to whom he devoted the longest sections in his book. By doing so, he contributed decisively to the emergence of these two scholars as the key figures in the modern-day sociological canon. For we must bear one thing in mind. Not only is it largely due to Parsons that the work of Durkheim and Weber has found such enduring acceptance within *American* sociology; not only is his creative way of dealing with these authors' work and his approach to theory building responsible for the fact that *American* sociology saw major progress in the theoretical field and attained a new, far greater degree of sophistication from the late 1930s on. We should also be especially alert to the fact that *even in Europe* the status of Durkheim and Weber was by no means secure (any longer); following the death of a fair number of its founding fathers, European sociology entered a period of stagnation in the early 1920s. This crisis was no doubt in part a result of the political upheavals of the time, but intellectual factors were also involved.

It was Parsons who, by concentrating on a small number of classical European figures, refocused the attention of scholars worldwide on the foundations of the discipline. It was Parsons who so successfully developed a canon – with the enormous consequences for the future development of sociology addressed above. This in itself is a good reason why a book on modern sociological theory must begin with Parsons.

So much for the presentational approach adopted by Parsons in *The Structure of Social Action* and his so-called convergence thesis. Our comments thus far have done little more than trace the formal structure of Parsons' work, but have as yet said nothing concrete about his other theoretical arguments or interpretations. This we shall now do in three steps, as we explain the significance of the key terms mentioned above.

Parsons devotes a significant portion of his argument in *Structure* to criticizing utilitarianism. *Criticism* of existing systems of thought, in this case utilitarianism, is thus a major component of the book. Parsons correctly assumes that he must first refute this influential theoretical current before he can seriously think about developing his own theory. For him, the constructive work must be preceded by an act of destruction.

What exactly is this 'utilitarianism'? We are immediately faced with difficulties in attempting to answer this question, because the term is somewhat unclear and Parsons himself often used it in a rather imprecise way. Nevertheless, clarification is vital, and you are therefore cordially invited to join us on a brief excursion into the history of philosophy.

First of all, 'utilitarianism' (from the Latin *utilitas* = utility, benefit) denotes a theoretical movement in the English philosophy of the late eighteenth and early nineteenth centuries. This approach is closely associated with the name of Jeremy Bentham (1748–1832), who formulated the basic utilitarian principles with respect to a theory of human action and a theory of morality. Bentham assumed that human action was governed by the dictates of 'pain and pleasure', that is, that human beings take action because they always and in all circumstances avoid pain and seek pleasure, because they – to put it slightly differently – wish to increase their utility. From this he then derived the ethical principle that the moral quality of human action is to be calculated on the basis of the extent to which it contributes to the greatest happiness, the greatest utility, of the greatest number of those affected by the action or of society. Bentham's basic ideas, which we have here outlined in brief, had a very far-reaching impact on intellectual history, particularly the English and Anglo-American variety, insofar as he had brilliant successors or interpreters who introduced his ideas to a broad public. One of them was John Stuart Mill (1806–73); in 1863, in a treatise entitled 'Utilitarianism', he undertook to marshal Bentham's arguments while to some extent modifying them. To help you enter the conceptual world of the utilitarians, we shall let him have his say in the following brief quotation. We suggest you pay particular attention to the phrases we have italicized, which relate to a theory of action.

> The creed which accepts as the foundation of morals, Utility, or the Greatest Happiness Principle, holds that actions are right in proportion as they tend to promote happiness, wrong as they tend to produce the reverse of happiness. By happiness is intended pleasure, and the absence of pain; by unhappiness, pain, and the privation of pleasure. To give a clear view of the moral standard set up by the theory, much more requires to be said; in particular, what things it includes in the ideas of pain and pleasure; and to what extent this is left an open question. But these supplementary explanations do not affect *the theory of life on which this theory of morality is grounded – namely, that pleasure, and freedom from pain, are the only things desirable as ends.*
>
> (Mill, 'Utilitarianism', p. 118)

Thus, like Bentham, Mill also defines human action as utility-oriented, as a process of weighing up the avoidance of pain and attainment of pleasure. It is precisely this action theoretical aspect of utilitarianism which Parsons vehemently assails – for reasons we will explain shortly.

Before setting about his critique, however, he points out that such a conception of human action, which privileges an orientation towards utility, was not characteristic solely of thinkers such as Bentham and J. S. Mill, who might be described as utilitarians in the narrower sense and who in fact described themselves as such. According to Parsons, the utilitarian conception of human action also had a profoundly formative influence on an entire discipline, namely economics, in the late nineteenth and twentieth centuries. This seems plausible when we look at how famous economists such as David Ricardo (1772–1823) and William Stanley Jevons (1835–82) were in fact influenced to a significant degree by utilitarian thinkers (personally in some cases). But Parsons goes one step further. He goes so far as to claim that utilitarian arguments were central to much of English political philosophy *long before* Bentham and Mill; he sees Thomas Hobbes (1588–1679) as a particularly good example of this, a point we will take a closer look at in a moment.

Parsons' notion of utilitarianism is problematic. It is in a sense too broadly conceived, attaching a single label to a large number of different currents within the history of philosophy. Nonetheless, his approach is understandable: key passages in *Structure* must be understood as intellectual historical analyses of the *roots* of this thought. Parsons draws our attention, for example, to the early Christian precursors of this type of thinking, which he calls 'utility-oriented' (as well as 'individualistic' or 'atomistic'), early forms whose typical features were toned down by medieval Catholicism. According to Parsons, it was only with the Reformation, which emphasized not so much the freedom of the individual as his *freedom of ends*, that the focus on utility again took on a more radical form (see SSA, pp. 51ff.). This, according to Parsons, is where the real origins of utilitarian thought lie, a way of thinking that is ultimately very one-sided, and which, as far as the topic of action is concerned, is interested primarily in the means with which the given ends of action may be achieved most efficiently. The efficient attainment of utility is thus centre stage. This tradition of thought often becomes linked, in highly opaque fashion, with modern empirical science, which also arose at the beginning of the modern age: scientific, rational experimentation was practically equated with utility-oriented action. Conversely, action intended to enhance utility was understood as the only type of activity that is truly rational and thus as action per se:

> in so far as it pursues ends possible within the conditions of the situation, and by the means which, among those available to the actor, are intrinsically best adapted to the end for reasons understandable and verifiable by positive empirical science.
>
> (SSA, p. 58)

In this sense, Parsons is able to argue – and this brings us to another as yet unexplained specialist term – that utilitarianism is a kind of current running within or even alongside the stream of 'positivism'. This is a school of thought which, Parsons claims, is especially characteristic of the French Enlightenment and French philosophy as a whole, according to which 'positive' science, a way of thinking shaped by the methods of the natural sciences, is the actor's only rational means of accessing reality (see SSA, pp. 60ff. and Lecture I, p. 6).

So much for Parsons' concepts, his understanding of utilitarianism and that complex of theories with which he grappled. The linchpin of his examination is Thomas Hobbes, *the* early modern political philosopher, who, Parsons tells us, most clearly fleshed out the action theoretical premises of utilitarian thought and, above all, systematically discussed its consequences, without, however, noticing the weaknesses of this concept of action.

At a crucial point in the argument presented in Hobbes' major work *Leviathan* (1651) he conducts a thought experiment, which Parsons found profoundly interesting. Hobbes asked what happens if people act in a 'state of nature', that is, in the absence of external rules, constraints, laws, etc., and indeed in a way that chimes with the utilitarian conception, namely if they *privilege utility* by attempting to increase their pleasure as much as possible and avoid pain. What happens if they behave in exactly this way – and in circumstances in which goods are scarce? (We can more or less take such circumstances for granted. When all is said and done, a surplus of every desirable good exists nowhere outside of Shangri-La; people have to compete for such goods everywhere else.) Hobbes' entirely plausible answer was that under such circumstances human action was bound to lead to pervasive 'force and fraud', because as people compete for scarce goods in the absence of constraining rules each individual merely seeks her immediate advantage, her utility. Other people are either utilized as a means of satisfying one's own needs and desires and may even be violently enslaved or they are deceived about others' intentions, swindled when exchanging goods, etc. These violent or underhand strategies, Hobbes asserted, would be deployed simply because they are very often an efficient way of achieving one's goals, and because everyone must work on the assumption that their fellow human beings will also resort to such means and strategies in order to attain their best advantage. The result of this situation, of such a 'state of nature', is everyday violence and a permanent sense of insecurity, restlessness, even fear of death. Even the enjoyment of property is at risk because its owners may be overpowered by other people at any moment. In such a situation, in which every individual merely pursues his egotistical utility unhindered, there can be no trust; in a 'state of nature' the war of all against all (*bellum omnium contra omnes*) would be the necessary result of human action geared solely towards utility enhancement. And this state, Hobbes tells us, is incapable of truly satisfying anyone.

If people really geared their actions towards utility enhancement as portrayed by Hobbes in his thought experiment on the state of nature, there could be only one way of ending this anarchic, warlike and untenable situation. Hobbes at least believed that this involves the subjugation of every individual under a single will, specifically, under the authority of a ruler or state, which will ultimately bring the war of all against all to an end, establish a monopoly of violence and thus obtain peace by force. Hobbes assumed that in the terrible, untenable and warlike state of nature, people have no other choice than to surrender all their power to the state. Hobbes calls this state – and his book – *Leviathan*, a name originating in the Old Testament and referring to a mighty sea monster. This peculiar choice of title itself points to the fact that Hobbes is ambivalent about his own 'proposed solution', the hegemony of the 'Leviathan', because while this monster does indeed bring about peace, it does so only at the expense of immense (political) inequality between the ruler, at the apex of the state, and the rest of the population. But according to Hobbes, it is only the state that enables people to escape such anarchic conditions and achieve a social reality in which they can enjoy, for example, the fruits of their labour, in other words property, in peace.

We could now, from a history of ideas perspective, investigate why Hobbes conducted this thought experiment, described the 'state of nature' just as he did and introduced the concept of the Leviathan. The book was certainly written at a time of massive political and social upheavals; England was in the grip of a bloody (religious) civil war. Attempts have also been made to relate his work to the emergence of a new social structure as capitalism began to transform the agricultural economy. Hobbes may thus have been thinking quite specifically of the England of his day when he came up with his thought experiment. And in this sense it is understandable that he thought the everyday violence of the civil war or – this is the other interpretation – the profound consequences of early capitalism could be tamed only by a 'monster', that the all-powerful, absolutist state appeared to him *the* solution to contemporary problems. Hobbes' 'solution', however, was to be joined by others. Another strategy which must be mentioned in this context has its origins in economic thought. The work of John

Locke (1632–1704) and Adam Smith, thinkers who, among other things, laid the ground for economics or facilitated its breakthrough in Great Britain, features the argument that human action aimed at utility enhancement can be rendered harmless if it is, as it were, 'diverted' into the realm of commodity exchange, of trade. According to Locke and Smith, the market, in which after all participants merely seek to achieve the greatest possible degree of utility, is distinguished by the fact that acts of exchange occur to everyone's mutual advantage. 'Truck and barter' are good-natured utility-oriented activities, through which *all* participants profit; they are the very condition for an enduring social order, that is, the order of the market. Comprehensively enforcing the market society, indeed, marketizing social relations to the greatest possible extent, is thus supposed to guarantee that calculations of utility which otherwise collide head-on, which are based on passions or unbridled desires and ultimately have a negative impact, are 'diverted' into the pursuit of rational market interests, coordinated in harmonious fashion. To put this notion of order in somewhat stereotypical form: the more market you have, the less people will succumb to passions and war, and the more peaceful, universally beneficial exchange will cause people to pursue their interests rationally, increasing the degree of harmony (see Albert Hirschman's excellent book *The Passions and the Interests: Political Arguments for Capitalism Before its Triumph*).

But an intellectual historical interpretation was not Parsons' intention at all. He was in fact interested in the *internal logic* of these arguments. He criticized the Lockean and Smithian idea that order is established via market transactions for being based on the 'metaphysical' assumption, which receives no further justification, of a natural identity of interests among market participants. Classical political economy, Parsons tells us, clearly assumed that market participants had objectives that could be unproblematically harmonized and that they interact to their mutual advantage. Regardless of whether such an assumption was correct or not (Parsons disputed this), it is an evasion – Parsons asserted – of the problem that Hobbes placed centre stage and in rather drastic terms: how order is established given the existence of *interests which are not in fact compatible* (see SSA, pp. 97ff.). By making this metaphysical assumption, the model put forward by classical political economy as a solution thus throws away, as it were, the opportunity to think through the question raised by Hobbes in truly *radical* fashion. It comes as no surprise that Parsons focuses primarily on the thought experiment originally conducted by Hobbes. His question, and this Parsons calls the 'Hobbesian problem' or the 'problem of order', was: How can order be established in the first place under conditions of pervasive utility-oriented action?

Now, Parsons does not dispute that state and market create order. But he is of the opinion that social order is an unquestionable fact, that there *is* order and that order is *not* therefore a truly mysterious phenomenon. In our everyday lives, we experience a huge number of social regularities, which have come about without the influence of the state or the market. One need only think of how uniformly – some would even say monotonously – interactions within the family or circle of friends pass off day in, day out, such that we can be fairly sure that they will proceed in the same or much the same way tomorrow as well. For Parsons it was therefore pointless to dispute that social order exists. He should not be understood, as is frequently suggested in the secondary literature, as having treated the problem of social order as an empirical problem to which he wished to propose a solution superior to that of Hobbes ('absolutism') or Locke ('liberalism'). This misunderstanding has arisen because of a misinterpretation of the exact nature of Parsons' argument. What Parsons doubted was the assertion that there can be stable order (whatever form this might take) *if people act purely to enhance their utility*. Here, Parsons deploys a 'transcendental' argument reminiscent of those put forward by the great German philosopher Immanuel Kant. Just as Kant thought about the conditions that must pertain in the first place for the science of physics, for example, to function as well as it does in fact function (Kant carried out no experiments and added to the theoretical edifice of physics no new propositions; he merely tried – and this he then calls 'transcendental' – to illuminate the conditions that must pertain on the part of the cognizing subject, for something, in this case natural scientific research, to be possible in the first place), *Parsons asked which qualities of human agents might render social order possible*. And within the framework of these transcendental considerations, Parsons tries to show that every author who premises his work on utility-oriented human action cannot hope to explain the existence of 'normal' social order, an order, that is, which has not come about as a result of subjugation (as in Hobbes) or market mechanisms (as in Locke and Smith). Not only that, but even order through violence or the market is based on elements which the model of utility-oriented action is quite incapable of conceiving.

Parsons demonstrates this very concretely with reference to Hobbes' proposed solution for overcoming the anarchy of the 'state of nature'. This fails to clarify how and why people suddenly grasp that they must give up the powers they have enjoyed hitherto to their own advantage and transfer them to a Leviathan. They might ask themselves: who exactly is going to guarantee that others will do as I do, that it is not just me that gives up my weapons (and power), but everyone else as well? Why should those currently doing well in the state of nature, that is, the rich and powerful, agree to take this step in the first place, when they can always hope to retain their power over the long term? After all, they possess the means to do so. Indeed, given that the creation of the Leviathan means that all but one will lose power and only he will gain massive power, why should one play this high-risk game, especially in light of the fact that while the dreaded civil war would indeed come to an end after the establishment of this all-powerful state, for the first time the perfect conditions would now be in place for the no less terrible war *between* states?

How that collective insight into the necessity of the Leviathan, how an agreement to this effect could come into being so suddenly among human beings always acting solely to enhance their utility, remained a mystery in Hobbes' theory. Parsons thus took the view that Hobbes' suggested solution was clearly undergirded by a conception of human action not based solely on utility maximization, otherwise it would be quite impossible for everyone to consent to the establishment of the Leviathan. Hobbes' solution to the problem of order, according to Parsons' thesis,

> involves stretching, at a critical point, the conception of rationality beyond its scope in the rest of the theory, to a point where the actors come to realize the situation as a whole instead of pursuing their own ends in terms of their immediate situation, and then take the action necessary to eliminate force and fraud, and, purchasing security at the sacrifice of the advantages to be gained by their future employment.
>
> (SSA, p. 93)

However, if a theory that conceives of action as *exclusively* utility-oriented is incapable of satisfactorily explaining social order or its origins, then – Parsons concludes – the utilitarian model of action must be wrong or at least inadequate from the outset. But before following Parsons' line of argument any further, let us pause for a moment to briefly summarize Parsons' ideas so far rather more abstractly.

Every sociologically interesting theory of action – and utilitarianism is or entails such a theory – must be able to explain how social order can come about. Because social order exists. The events which take place in our society, and also those which took place in Hobbes' England, do and did so in line with certain rules, because the goals of the members of a society are often identical. But this means that we *cannot* assume straightforward 'randomness of ends' (a term frequently used by Parsons) among the members of a society; it is wrong to assume that people have only very specific, individual goals and conceptions of utility, not all of which or which only randomly tally with those of others, if indeed there is any overlap at all. In any event, it is not enough – as tends to happen in economics and related disciplines, so profoundly influenced by utilitarianism – merely to postulate an identity of interests among subjects. It took economists a very long time even to consider the origins of actors' goals and notions of utility. They simply took it for granted that people act to enhance their utility without examining more closely what specifically actors adopt as their goals or declare to be their utility, and above all why or under what circumstances they do so. Parsons could not go along with such an approach, which simply ignores certain problems he felt to be of crucial importance. Rather, he asked: if order does in fact exist, the theory of action must be capable of *explaining* it; it must explain how it can be that the 'randomness of ends' that utilitarianism fails to problematize does not pertain in reality and how, instead, the quotidian coordination of ends is generally achieved without further ado. At this point, Parsons argues, utilitarianism lets us down, because it is unable to provide an answer to the question 'Where do the goals of action, actors' notions of utility, their "ends", in fact come from?'. Theorists or disciplines working with the utilitarian model thus merely establish that wishes, needs, ideas of utility, 'ends', etc. exist. They leave the question of *how* they arise to psychologists or biologists, saying nothing on the subject themselves. But this is to let slip the opportunity to explain why it is that the ends of human action do in fact match so often; understanding the origins of these 'ends' could provide us with an important, if not the decisive pointer in this regard.

Utilitarianism is thus indubitably beset by a grave theoretical problem. This was in fact acknowledged, at least by those in the know. Positivism, of which utilitarianism is only one form for Parsons, certainly attempted to answer these questions, but all its answers, asserted Parsons, who distinguishes two non-utilitarian variants, are unsatisfactory. In fact, they lead us to a point where all notion of human action as an active process evaporates, rendering the utilitarian model useless as a model of *action*. Why?

(a) 'Radical rationalist positivism' tackles the original problem that actors' goals, desires, conceptions of utility, their 'ends' could, on the premises of utilitarianism, agree only randomly and that we cannot therefore expect the long-term coordination of actions, that is, social order, by arguing that each actor pursues his ends through quasi-scientific methods. According to this conceptual model, highly rational actors coordinate the ends of their actions, and the very rationality with which they pursue these ends supposedly ensures the balancing of interests. Regardless of whether such all-round rationality really does cause things to balance out in this way, the consequence of this model is as follows. Human beings constantly find themselves in situations that leave them no real room for manoeuvre at all. They merely adapt to these situations, in which the rational choice of means is always already fixed. They are in fact, Parsons insists, quite incapable of formulating their own ends; they may at best make mistakes in the form of scientific errors.

> But this tenet had the inevitable logical consequence of assimilating ends to the situation of action and destroying their analytical independence, so essential to the utilitarian position. For the only possible basis of empirical knowledge of a future state of affairs is prediction on the basis of knowledge of present and past states. Then action becomes determined entirely by its conditions, for without the independence of ends the distinction between conditions and means becomes meaningless. Action becomes a process of rational adaptation to these conditions.
>
> (SSA, pp. 63–4)

(b) 'Radical anti-intellectualist positivism', meanwhile, attempted to do away with the bothersome 'randomness of ends' held by various actors by emphasizing the determining influence of circumstances in the environmentalist sense or the influence of one's genetic endowment as understood in theories of heredity. Exponents of this approach thus believed that it is environmental factors, such as the urban or rural social structure with its constraints and restrictions, or people's genetic endowment, which more or less unavoidably forces them to act in certain ways or within a particular order. This conceptual model is the polar opposite of 'radical rationalist positivism': it does not assume that actors' rationality guarantees that they coordinate their actions in an ordered way. Rather, order arises because forces *beyond* the rational control of the actors steer their actions, ensuring that certain patterns of action and thus social order itself are continuously reproduced. The problem, however, is that here again the element of *action* in the originally utilitarian theory of *action* vanishes, because the actors, as occurs at times in the naturalistic novels of Emile Zola, are portrayed as merely driven by their milieux or even as victims of a 'poor' genetic endowment, who no longer seem remotely capable of selecting their own ends.

In both these attempts at explanation, the goals, notions of utility, 'ends', etc. characteristic of human action coincide with the situation in which action takes place or with the conditions for action. *Utilitarianism's inherent inability to explain social order causes action itself to disappear from the proposed positivist solutions.*

Parsons is thus able to conclude that the utilitarian model of action as a whole is too narrow in scope, because it is incapable of shedding any real light on key issues, namely the origin of goals or 'ends' and thus how the goals and 'ends' of different actors are coordinated. According to Parsons, utilitarianism must therefore be overcome; our discussion of the positivist variants clearly shows that any superior theory of action must include an activist component. In explaining how people coordinate the ends of their action, the truly subjective aspect of human action, the freedom of choice that it entails, must play a role.

The observant among you may already have an inkling as to why we referred earlier to attempts to construct a 'voluntaristic theory of action' with respect to Parsons' interpretation of the four classical figures; the adjective 'voluntaristic' (Latin: *voluntas* = free will, decision) conveys the idea of freedom of choice, which is exactly what Parsons wishes to emphasize as he builds his own theory. But let's not get ahead of ourselves. It is clear that despite his sharp criticism of utilitarianism Parsons wishes to hold on to the correct insights it entails. Parsons sees positivism's contribution as lying in its entirely valid emphasis on the circumstantial factors that are the conditions of human action. This is an important point for Parsons. It is on this basis that he rejects 'idealistic' theoretical approaches which, while underlining the element of will in action and stressing human freedom, almost always – this at least is Parsons' interpretation – forget the (material) conditions to which action is subject. Parsons thus interprets idealism as a kind of 'emanationism', a way of thinking according to which human action emanates, as it were, from a collective spirit, as the mere expression of a *Volksseele* or national soul, certain world views, ideals, ideational complexes, etc. This one-sidedness must also be avoided, and Parsons, once again with a view to synthesis, makes a great effort to link the best insights of idealism and utilitarianism, in order – and this brings us to the second part of our account of *The Structure of Social Action* – to advance positively towards that 'voluntaristic theory of action'.

To come straight to the point: Parsons links his voluntaristic theory of action with a theory of social order which he describes as 'normative'; both theories are interrelated, precisely because, as we have already established, action theories, if they are to be sociologically persuasive, must also be able to explain social order. 'Normative' thus refers to both action *and* order, because for Parsons norms play a decisive role in both.

Let us turn first to the 'normativist theory of order'. What exactly does this mean? What Parsons means by this is that every social order always rests, in one way or another, on common values and norms, though of course these vary in strength depending on the circumstances. Thus, he asserts that utilitarians are wrong to assume the 'randomness of ends', which are in fact constrained by the presence of shared norms and values in many cases. In this sense, norms and values pre-structure the goals of action pursued by individual actors, thus ensuring that their goals are in synch. Parsons demonstrates exactly what he has in mind by distinguishing between 'normative order' and 'factual order'. Let us begin with the latter. By this Parsons means an order which has ultimately come about *unintentionally*. A prime example of such a 'factual order' are the congested roads in Germany during the holiday period. Vast numbers of people want to head south as quickly as possible, but as an unintended consequence of their setting off at the same time because their holidays coincide, they eventually find themselves stuck motionless on gridlocked roads. The result is a specific order, the traffic jam. This is a factual order which no one agreed to establish: people do not generally set off from home to sit in a traffic jam. No regulation stipulates that a massive traffic jam must be formed just outside Munich at least once a year and that every German in desperate need of a holiday must make his way there, every year, for precisely that reason. Another example that we have already touched on is the factual order to which the market gives rise. No one really intends the price of certain goods or of labour to form in conformity with the market; rather, this order develops, as it were, as a side-effect of the economic actions of numerous individuals. There was no agreement among all the actors involved, no rule that half a pound of butter must cost less than €1, though butter does in fact cost less than this in most shops.

This must be distinguished from the 'normative order', in which Parsons is clearly most interested and which he considers one of the central objects of sociology. This order is based on the fact that actors – consciously or perhaps more often pre-consciously – orientate themselves towards a common norm, towards shared rules of behaviour. It is thus always possible to discern a more or less tacit agreement or understanding of one kind or another, with respect to the establishment of order, among the actors involved. Parsons, starting with the normative order, describes how these two different types of order can link up:

> Order in this sense means that process takes place in conformity with the paths laid down in the normative system. Two further points should, however, be noted in this connection. One is that the breakdown of any given normative order, that is a state of chaos from a normative point of view, may well result in an order in the factual sense, that is a state of affairs susceptible of scientific analysis. Thus the 'struggle for existence' is chaotic from the point of view of Christian ethics, but that does not in the least mean that it is not subject to law in the scientific sense, that is to uniformities of process in the phenomena. Secondly, in spite of the logically inherent possibility that any normative order may break down into a 'chaos' under certain conditions, it may still be true that the normative elements are essential to the maintenance of the *particular* factual order which exists when processes are to a degree in conformity with them. Thus a social order is always a factual order in so far as it is susceptible of scientific analysis but ... it is one which cannot have stability without the effective functioning of certain normative elements.
>
> (SSA, pp. 91–2; original emphasis)

Parsons claims that while there is certainly a fundamental difference between a factual and a normative order, even the *long-term* persistence of a factual order can be explained only by the effects of norms. The examples mentioned above may serve as illustration here: the traffic jam is a social order, as revealed by statistical analysis (if a certain number of holidaymakers head south at the same time, then there is a specific degree of probability, depending on the condition of the transportation network, that the roads around Munich will be congested). But this congestion constitutes an order of very limited duration and is not, therefore, dependent on norms. Tyranny is different. The violent subjugation of human beings is an act not based on norms common to both rulers and ruled. But tyranny can endure only if at least some of the ruled develop an at least rudimentary acceptance of this domination, if they consent to it to some degree. The same goes for the market. We have already pointed out that the functioning of markets is something best understood as a result of the seemingly unintended interconnection of market participants' utility-oriented behaviour. Market participants do not carry out their transactions in order to ensure that the market functions. Nevertheless, and this was discovered by Durkheim (who tellingly refers to the non-contractual elements of the contract) and demonstrated by

Parsons on numerous occasions in various writings, the market participants undoubtedly do share certain norms without which the market as a whole would be unable to function. As Parsons underlined in a publication that appeared not much later, what appears to be the sheer self-interested behaviour of the market participants does not represent the most fundamental layer of motivation, but rather other motives exist 'underneath', as apparent in the fact that markets function quite differently in different cultures:

> It will be the principal thesis ... that 'economic motivation' is not a category of motivation on the deeper level at all, but is rather a point at which many different motives may be brought to bear on a certain type of situation. Its remarkable constancy and generality is not a result of a corresponding uniformity in 'human nature' such as egoism or hedonism, but of certain features of the structure of social systems of action which, however, are not entirely constant but subject to institutional variation.
>
> (Parsons, 'The Motivation of Economic Activities', p. 53)

If this is correct, if norms are crucial to generating *every single* stable social order and enabling it to function, then, Parsons concludes, we clearly need a theory of action in which norms and values play a key role. Parsons thus asserts that in analysing action, alongside the goals, utility calculations, 'ends', etc. that the utilitarians emphasize, we must pay at least as much attention to values and norms. These have been overlooked or erroneously explained away by the utilitarians. It is by no means the case that norms and values can be traced back to or regarded as identical to utility calculations, as some utilitarians appear to believe. This is apparent, among other things, in the fact that it is quite simply impossible to make our own values the subject of utility calculations. I cannot be seriously convinced of the value of absolute loyalty to my partner if I call this value into question every time the opportunity for an affair arises, because this ultimately provides me with momentary gratification in terms of sex or prestige, that is, utility. I cannot simply manipulate and overrule my *own* values. If I was to attempt to do so or even succeed in doing so, then these would not be real values, but at best half-baked ideas which I had somehow latched on to at some point. It is of course possible to manipulate values: advertising professionals and torturers, specialists in brainwashing, constantly do so or attempt to do so. But it is not their own values, of which they are convinced, which they manipulate, but those of *others*. And that is a very different matter. Parsons thus defines the normative, that is, norms and values, as 'a sentiment attributable to one or more actors that something *is an end in itself*' (SSA, p. 75; emphasis added). With respect to values, which are in a sense more general and involve a greater degree of personal commitment than norms, Parsons speaks of 'ultimate ends', because there are no circumstances under which one would turn these into means. They are in fact *ends in themselves*, ultimate values, which I cannot call into question without wrecking my self-image: 'Here I stand; I can do no other', as Luther so impressively proclaimed. If this is the case, then it also follows that notions of utility arise from these ultimate values in the first place, that is, that utility calculations rest upon individual, but sometimes also shared convictions ('a sentiment attributable *to one or more actors*'), because I can determine my utility, my 'ends', only on the basis of values. Values and norms themselves cannot therefore be subject to utility calculations, because they are constitutive of every criterion underpinning such calculations. Parsons believed that he had solved the 'puzzle' that fatally undermined utilitarianism. The social world is almost always an ordered one because human action is fundamentally moulded by common norms and values.

Parsons has now thrashed out what he believes to be the essential aspects of human action, in order to design a model of action which utilizes utilitarian insights, but also goes far beyond them. This model, this schema, he calls the 'action frame of reference' – a kind of basic conceptual apparatus for understanding human action. Here, what Parsons calls the 'unit act' consists of the following elements:

1. the actor
2. what Parsons refers to as the 'end', 'goal', or 'purpose' of action
3. the action situation, which is subdivided into the conditions of action, that is, those elements of the situation beyond the control of the actor, and the means of action, that is, those elements at the disposal of the actor
4. the norms and values of action (see SSA, p. 44).

Casting our minds back to Parsons' discussion of utilitarianism, it is apparent that the first three elements were certainly already present within the utilitarian theory of action, but that the crucial fourth dimension, that of norms and values, was missing. And this, we would add, is so important precisely because the 'normative', in contrast to the positivist explanatory elements discussed above (environment, genetic endowment), does not cause the individual's free will, her capacity to *act*, to vanish. Quite the opposite: I may also oppose norms and values, I may feel drawn to some and repelled by others; some exercise an almost irresistible power over me, others do not. The normative is for Parsons the specifically human aspect of action and thus the core of the voluntaristic theory of action. The complete 'action frame of reference' may therefore be depicted in graphic form in Figure 2.1.

Norms and values influence the course of the action in two ways. They have a selective effect on the means of action, some means being permissible and some being prohibited on normative grounds. If I adhere to certain values and norms, then I am expressly not allowed to deploy *any* means to achieve my goals. If I am convinced of the value of honesty, I cannot and will not use dishonest means in order to realize my goals. But as we have already established, norms and values also decisively structure the *ends* of action; they thus determine that which we consider good. We do not automatically consider

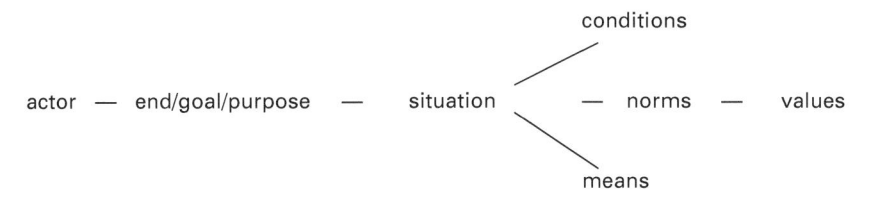

```
                                    conditions
                                       /
actor — end/goal/purpose — situation     — norms — values
                                       \
                                    means
```

Figure 2.1

everything we want or desire good. I may, for example, have certain sexual desires, but it is by no means the case that I consider all these desires desirable. I frequently resist them because they are morally unacceptable to me.

In every case, this influence of norms and values on both the means of action as well as the ends of action makes that coordination of action possible upon which social order depends, because norms and values are not primarily idiosyncratic, highly specific 'constructs' valid only for a small number of individuals, but rather are shared, held in common, by a specific group of people.

This account of Parsons' action frame of reference brings us to the end of the second step intended to help you appreciate *The Structure of Social Action*. But before taking the third and final step, we would like to make another point. You are urged to retain as clear an impression as possible of the form of the 'action frame of reference', to grasp how and why Parsons understood human action in this particular way. This is helpful because the lectures still to come are organized with this Parsonian model of action in mind. We utilize this model to help you understand the work of other theorists. It is our thesis that one can understand much of the development of modern sociological theory only if one sees it as a sometimes veiled, sometimes quite open argument with the Parsonian theoretical model.

This brings us to the third strand of our account. We claimed earlier that Parsons' convergence thesis is a specific interpretation of the work of classical figures in the social sciences and that, in a sense, it serves to 'prove' the correctness of Parsons' own theoretical endeavour. After Parsons set out his critique of utilitarianism and presented his voluntaristic theory of action in the first 125 pages or so of his book, the discussion of the classical figures that makes up the rest of it enabled him to demonstrate that these authors were already moving towards his position. Though their work was at times still rather vague and nebulous in this regard, Parsons suggested, they too had become aware of the importance of the normative elements of action. We now briefly summarize these extensive interpretations.

The English economist Alfred Marshall undoubtedly played a substantial role in formulating important elements of modern economic theory, which draw heavily on utilitarian thought. Yet at the same time, Marshall was one of the very few economists of his time to inquire quite consciously into the genesis or origins of needs, notions of utility, desires, etc. (SSA, p. 134), while refraining from declaring this a non-economic issue. Marshall saw clearly that economic action is tied to certain values in a range of ways. This is most apparent in the figure of the businessman, who is certainly keen to make a profit and augment his utility, but whose actions often rest in part on certain ingrained values, which we might express through terms such as virtuousness and 'honesty' and which thus clearly place limits on his 'wants' and the means he will deploy to satisfy them. Economic action cannot, therefore, be traced back to mere maximization of utility. Consequently, the existence of utility-oriented action does not in itself prove that certain values play no significant role in this milieu of action. Marshall thus saw very clearly – this at least is Parsons' interpretation – that economics fails to pay sufficient attention to values as a dimension of action and thus goes so far as to equate egotism and utility-oriented action with rational behaviour in a highly problematic way, which leads to empirically false accounts. According to Marshall, this is particularly apparent in the figure of the businessman, whose actions cannot be squeezed into a simple schema of utility maximization. On this view, the businessman is not rational purely because it is the smart thing to do or out of pure self-interest. Often, in fact, he evinces an ethical obligation to be rational; his rationality and striving for efficiency is based on a moral foundation (SSA, p. 164). This is what enables him to take certain investment risks and work tenaciously to ensure the success of his investments in the first place. In this sense, Parsons tells us, Marshall has already clearly shown us the way out of classical utilitarianism; the thrust of his work points to the 'voluntaristic theory of action' that Parsons favoured and which, among other things, recognizes and accepts the significance of values to action.

The ideas put forward by the Italian economist and sociologist Vilfredo Pareto differed from those of Marshall in a number of ways. In the work of Marshall, the rational businessman represents the crowning achievement of the process of civilization. In contrast, Pareto's view of history was *not* evolutionist; he did not believe in a straightforward unilinear historical process, in 'progress'. Because Pareto put far greater emphasis on the role of conflicts, of 'force and fraud', than, for example, Marshall, he had a markedly more pessimistic view of history than Marshall. What is more, their epistemological ideas also differed profoundly, in that Pareto's arguments were more polished; in fact, he advocated a position much of which Parsons was later able to develop. Yet despite all the differences between Marshall and Pareto, both arrived at similar theoretical conclusions with respect to a theory of action. In Pareto's case, this occurred because he became aware of the non-logical component of (economic) action, which he went on to investigate. His analyses not only brought home to him the importance of instincts, but also of rituals and certain subjective (non-logical) goals within human action. Pareto thus took his leave of the edifice of utilitarian and positivist thought which had been his initial frame of reference. And like Marshall he ultimately arrived at a conception very close to that of 'ultimate ends'.

> The settlement of conflicting economic claims between individuals involves more than economic considerations because here economic considerations are subsidiary to political, those of coercive power, so that every economic distribution is possible only within a general framework of distributive justice. But all these distributive questions concern only the settlement of potential conflicts of individual claims to wealth and power without indicating the basis of unity on which the structure as a whole rests. This basis of unity Pareto finds in the last analysis to lie in the necessary existence of an 'end the society pursues'. That is, the ultimate ends of individual action systems are integrated to form a single common system of ultimate ends.
>
> (SSA, pp. 249f.)

Emile Durkheim, meanwhile, unlike Pareto und Marshall, did not come from a milieu imbued with the theoretical debates of economics. According to Parsons, the roots of Durkheim's work lie in the French tradition of positivism, to which he was still beholden in his early work, before finally breaking with it (almost entirely) in his later writings. In his first studies, Durkheim described social structures as something solid, external, with which the individual finds herself confronted and which act as a force constraining her. In this connection he talked, above all in his book *The Rules of Sociological Method*, of 'social facts' which supposedly restrict and mould action in much the same way as do material factors, perhaps even – remember how Parsons grappled with radical anti-intellectualist positivism – as does one's genetic endowment. Only gradually, through his critical analysis of the concept of the collective consciousness, did Durkheim separate the social from the physical and elaborate the different forms of coercion affecting individuals. Durkheim ultimately placed the constraining power of conscience in a quite different category from that exercised by natural laws or social inhibitions enforced by the violence and power of others. It constrains the actions of individuals precisely because they feel an obligation to uphold their own norms and values and thus those of their society; they can act in no other way. The notion of the collective consciousness, with which Durkheim had long tussled, along with empirical observations, ultimately enabled him – Parsons asserts – to grasp how social, that is, shared norms and values, can be internalized.

> Now he makes the far-reaching empirical observation that since individual wants are in principle unlimited, it is an essential condition of both social stability and individual happiness that they should be regulated in terms of norms. But here the norms thought of do not, as do the rules of contract, merely regulate 'externally,' e.g., as the conditions of entering into relations of contract – they enter directly into the constitutions of

> the actors' ends themselves ... The individual elements in action are no longer identified with the concrete subjective individual, but the latter is recognized to be a compound of different elements. The element of ends as it appears in the means-end schema is no longer by definition 'individual' but contains a 'social' element. This is so important a step for Durkheim that in fact it constitutes a radical break with positivistic social theory.
>
> (SSA, p. 382)

While Durkheim, the roots of whose work lay in positivism, moved closer to a 'voluntaristic theory of action' through his examination of values, Max Weber, Parsons argues, did exactly the opposite. According to Parsons, Weber's work was anchored in the intellectual tradition of idealism, which was particularly strong in Germany; he was thus never in serious danger of downplaying the role of norms and values. In sharp contrast, the risk here was making the equally fatal mistake of forgetting the conditions and means which are of course just as important to action. Weber avoids this risk by going out of his way, from the outset, to emphasize the (utilitarian) form of 'instrumentally rational action' in his typology of action, which fully recognizes and includes value-oriented (normative) action, thus steeling himself against the temptations of idealism.

> Thus at this early critical stage of Weber's methodological work has appeared the concept with which this whole study started, that of the type of rational action which involves the means-end relationship as verifiable in terms of scientific generalization. For him, also, rationality in this sense plays a central role, methodologically as well as substantively. And it is especially interesting that its methodological role comes out in critical opposition to an idealistic theory.
>
> (SSA, pp. 584–5)

Parsons thus brings his examination of the writings of famous social scientists to a close. He thought he had managed to show that the path towards a voluntaristic theory of action was clearly traced out in the work of all four of these very different authors, and thus that their various studies converged. And at the same time, as we hope to have laid bare, with his critique of utilitarianism and reference to the criticisms which the economists Pareto and Marshall made of their own discipline, Parsons claimed that he and thus sociology had a superior understanding of human action, one which connects positivism and idealism and which also incorporates economic action. In a momentous move, he thus defined sociology as a science of *action*.

This brings to a close our account of *The Structure of Social Action*. The next lecture is devoted to the criticisms made of this hugely important work; we investigate the theoretical path trodden by Parsons *after* this book was published in 1937 as he strove to elaborate on the comprehensive sociological theory which it had laid out.

III

Parsons on the road to normativist functionalism

The Structure of Social Action, which appeared in 1937, attracted a great deal of criticism precisely because Parsons had such great ambitions for it (see Charles Camic, '*Structure* after 50 Years: The Anatomy of a Charter' and Hans Joas, *The Creativity of Action*, pp. 18ff. for comprehensive overviews). Some of the criticisms were made immediately after the book appeared, but many only after it had become very well known. As we pointed out in the previous lecture, *Structure* was received rather slowly at first. Over the course of time, however, coming to terms with Parsons became increasingly central to others' attempts to explain and contextualize their own equally ambitious theories, and inevitably criticisms became ever more systematic and comprehensive. In what follows, we shall present to you *those criticisms that were of the greatest significance to the development of theory*; in the second part of the lecture, we examine whether and to what extent Parsons answered or perhaps even anticipated these criticisms, as he attempted to refine his theoretical edifice.

If we look first at the debate on the so-called convergence thesis, it is apparent that it addressed a number of key problems; we examine these here. We can understand the sometimes passionate way in which scholars have grappled with this thesis only if we grasp that we are not dealing with a purely historiographical problem summed up by the question 'Whose interpretation of the classical figures is (at least somewhat) better?' Parsons claimed to have produced a *synthesis* of the work of these leading figures. Now if it should prove that Parsons' attempt to reconstruct the history of sociology was blighted by major omissions or straightforward misinterpretations, this would cast serious doubt on the plausibility of the main arguments in *Structure*. Above all, his assertion that his work constituted a (legitimate) continuation of that of the classical figures would be untenable. We must therefore allow the criticisms of the convergence thesis some space here.

1. As well as claiming that Parsons had at times failed to appropriately interpret the four 'classical figures', critics specifically attacked his convergence thesis for taking only Europeans *and no Americans* into account. Indeed, this is peculiar in that sociology as a discipline found broad institutional expression earlier in the USA than in Germany, France, the United Kingdom or Italy. As far as the establishment of chairs of sociology and the publication of sociological journals is concerned, the USA was indubitably

the pioneer. Yet American sociology was obviously quite insignificant for Parsons and the thrust of his theoretical work. How are we to understand this? In the last lecture we sang Parsons' praises for putting *European* social scientists 'on a pedestal' with such vigour during the difficult years of the 1930s. And this we stand by unequivocally. Yet at the same time, this had the unfortunate consequence that he neglected other contexts in which sociology arose or included these in his arguments only in highly abbreviated and thus somewhat distorted form. With regard to the intellectual history of the USA, he appeared to suggest that utilitarian, individualist and/or evolutionist thinkers à la Herbert Spencer (1820–1902) had dominated the landscape and that there was therefore no point looking for an instructive *critique* of utilitarian or similar theoretical constructs in America in the first place. Now the Englishman Herbert Spencer, whom Parsons discusses in the first three pages of the first chapter of *Structure*, undoubtedly had a significant influence and many admirers in the USA. But it is unfair to describe pre-1937 American intellectual history in its entirety as being under the sway of Spencer. It would be not merely unfair but quite simply wrong to apply such a description to American *sociology, social psychology* and *social philosophy* in particular, because many outstanding representatives of these disciplines such as George Herbert Mead, John Dewey, Charles Horton Cooley, William Isaac Thomas and Robert Park (1864–1944) never came close to embracing utilitarianism or the work of Spencer. Yet Parsons fails to make a single mention of any of these authors, let alone discuss their highly innovative theory of action, which was indebted to the philosophy of American pragmatism (see Lecture VI) and which might have furnished him with important inspiration. Spencer's thought was thus by no means representative of American sociology, as Parsons appears to suggest. Rather, to quote R. Jackson Wilson's pithy formulation (*In Quest of Community*, p. 155), Spencer was 'more whipping boy than master' in this discipline and its neighbouring subjects. Parsons clearly took a different view and was only too ready to deny that American intellectual history had any relevance whatsoever to his own theoretical project.

Later, Parsons was to fully own up to the deficiencies of his interpretation in *Structure* in this regard; but even then he conceded only that the internalization of values, addressed in the previous lecture, could have been dealt with more effectively by drawing on American social psychology and sociology. But this was all he was willing to concede. Why, then, did Parsons stubbornly refuse to acknowledge significant aspects of American intellectual history? Was this a matter of genuine ignorance? Or was the context in which Parsons acted perhaps characterized by veiled competition between Harvard University, where Parsons taught, and the University of Chicago, at which many of the pragmatist thinkers and sociologists we have mentioned had taught and where the influence of pragmatism could still be felt in 1937? We shall have something to say about this later on, when we deal with the theoretical school of 'symbolic interactionism', which was indebted to American pragmatism, in one of the following lectures. This will further clarify the exact significance of this deficit in Parsons' convergence thesis. His failure to take such important issues into account may point to difficulties in his theory building.

2. Even his selection of *European* thinkers inspired some protest. It was, for example, striking that Parsons says almost nothing about Georg Simmel in *Structure*, although he later admitted, in the foreword to a new edition of the book, for example, that he had originally intended to include a fairly lengthy chapter on Simmel and had in fact produced such a chapter in 1937. In this connection, he also acknowledges in self-critical fashion his neglect of American social psychology and sociology intimated above:

> Along with the American social psychologists, notably Cooley, Mead and W. I. Thomas, the most important single figure neglected in the *Structure of Social Action*, and to an important degree in my subsequent writings, is probably Simmel. It may be of interest that I actually drafted a chapter on Simmel for the *Structure of Social Action*, but partly for reasons of space finally decided not to include it. Simmel was more a micro- than a macrosociologist; moreover, he was not, in my opinion, a *theorist* on the same level as the others.
>
> (SSA, p. xiv)

Parsons attributes his neglect of Simmel, that is, his decision not to examine his work in detail in *Structure*, to lack of space or the lack of a clear theoretical orientation in Simmel's oeuvre. Some will accept this. Yet we might hesitate to do so, particularly as concerns the latter assertion. In fact, Simmel produced a highly sophisticated theory. However, this was based not on the idea of action undertaken by discrete individuals, but on the idea of the *relationship and interaction between individuals*. Simmel did not take individual (utility-oriented) action as his self-evident point of departure and then, like Marshall or Pareto for example, find himself confronted with the importance of norms and 'ultimate ends'. Rather, Simmel always worked on the basis that human beings start out as social beings, that the young person is entwined in social contexts from birth onwards. In this sense, Simmel certainly acknowledged the significance of norms and values, but it would have been difficult to describe him as a 'normal' action theorist and the development of his work as converging on a voluntaristic theory of action. Including Simmel in *Structure* would surely have disturbed the 'plot' of Parsons' 'story' quite substantially. Parsons himself conceded as much in 1979 in a letter to one of his admirers, the American sociologist Jeffrey Alexander, who we will discuss late in this lecture series. His failure to take Simmel into account may thus also point to a hidden theoretical problem.

3. Parsons' way of dealing with the work of Karl Marx is also problematic; while he chose not to devote a chapter specifically to him as he did to the other four classical European figures, he did at least discuss him at two different points in his book. But this discussion is far too short, above all because, interestingly enough, Parsons interprets Marx in a way which, in light of his own attempt to develop a voluntaristic theory of action, makes him appear a key figure. Parsons correctly interprets Marx as an author who, on the one hand, particularly while in exile in England, had placed himself clearly within the tradition of utilitarianism through his increasing concern with issues of political economy. Yet on the other hand, as a result of his German background, Marx had also, at least partially, internalized the edifice of idealistic thought characteristic of Hegel. If Parsons understood his own theory of action as a bridge between idealism and positivism or utilitarianism (SSA, p. 486), it would have made a lot of sense to examine in depth an author who fused the spirit of each.

> Marx may be considered to be understandable in terms of the logical framework of English utilitarian thought, though ... in a somewhat different way from most other utilitarians. Here, however, he tied his analysis into a theory of 'dialectic' evolution largely of Hegelian origin. Marx thus forms an important bridge between the positivistic and idealistic traditions of thought.
>
> (ibid.)

Even if Parsons correctly assumed that Marx's work failed to successfully integrate these theoretical elements, it would have been interesting, if not vital, particularly with respect to the thrust of his own theoretical work, to determine why this author, who had such an impact on the history of the world, proved incapable of producing a true synthesis. Why did Marx fail in this regard? Parsons leaves us in the dark.

4. Furthermore, there are good reasons to doubt the correctness of Parsons' assumption that French intellectual life was dominated by positivism. The French intellectual landscape was probably significantly more varied than Parsons acknowledged. It would otherwise be very difficult to explain why currents such as the philosophy of life (*Lebensphilosophie*) were able to spread so rapidly in France towards the end of the nineteenth century and why German theoretical traditions were then willingly embraced in the second half of the twentieth century (see Lecture XIV). Parsons might at least have drawn on the tradition of 'moralism' (see Johan Heilbron, *The Rise of Social Theory*) so strong in the seventeenth and eighteenth centuries and on Alexis de Tocqueville, in order to find arguments much like those that crop up in Durkheim and which could have backed up the thrust of his own theoretical work, namely his emphasis on values and norms.

5. In the same way, Parsons' assertion that German intellectual history was moulded largely by 'idealism' is open to criticism; not so much because this statement is entirely wrong, but because by applying this label we all too easily run the risk of thoughtlessly overlooking strands of this history of much relevance to a theory of action. It is certainly true that certain phases of German intellectual history featured much talk of the *Volksgeist* ('national spirit'), the 'German soul', etc. Particularly during the First World War, German intellectuals fell over themselves to deploy such martial terms, directed against the enemy, arguing as if every cultural phenomenon to be found in Germany directly embodied a 'heroic spirit'. In this sense, Parsons' characterization of the theoretical tradition prevailing in Germany as a kind of 'emanationism' was not entirely unfounded; this was a way of thinking that suggested that cultural and social phenomena are nothing other than the expression of supra-personal totalities such as the 'spirit' of a people or 'age'. But the philosophy of German idealism also rested to a very significant degree on a conception of human action which would have made it possible to cast doubt, with good reason, on a key aspect of the Parsonian 'action frame of reference'. Johann Gottfried Herder (1744–1803), for example, placed specific forms of action centre stage in his reflections, forms which Parsons' conceptual apparatus fails to capture: *expressive* action, in which the individual expresses himself, involves neither the pursuit of predetermined goals in rationalistic fashion (as utilitarianism imagines) nor the gearing of oneself (of which Parsons made so much) towards the common norms of a community or group. In a brilliant interpretation of this German 'expressivist anthropology', the great Canadian social philosopher Charles Taylor (b. 1931) has described this type of action as follows:

> If we think of our life as realizing an essence or form, this means not just the embodying of this form in reality, it also means defining in a determinate way what this form is. ... the idea which a man realizes is not wholly determinate beforehand; it is only made fully determinate in being fulfilled. Hence the Herderian idea that my humanity is something unique, not equivalent to yours, and this unique quality can only be revealed in my life itself. 'Each man has his own measure, as it were an accord peculiar to him of all his feelings to each other.' [Herder] The idea is not just that men are different; this was hardly new; it was rather that the differences define the unique form that each of us is called on to realize. The differences take on moral import; so that the question could arise for the first time whether a given form of life was an authentic expression of certain individuals or people.
>
> (Taylor, *Hegel*, pp. 16f.)

Two important points must be made about this quote from Charles Taylor (on what follows, you are referred in particular to Joas, *The Creativity of Action*, pp. 75ff.). First, Herder and the other thinkers within this tradition of expressivist anthropology understand action not as rationally planned, guided by given goals, conceptions of utility, etc., but as a phenomenon in which the meaning of the action for the actor emerges only in the act itself. Second, this action is not guided by a social norm. It comes, as it were, from within; it is more than mere compliance with norms. If you are wondering what everyday examples of such expressive action might be, we would initially suggest that you think of drawing a picture, singing a tune, the aesthetic production of the self through decoration of the body, types of movement such as dance, etc. You will surely concede that when you dance you do not, as a rule, wish (or at least not only) to pursue a predetermined goal; nor are you merely submitting to a norm. But Herder by no means wished to restrict this conception of action as actors' self-expression to aesthetic forms. Repelled by the high-handedness of self-proclaimed 'geniuses', he emphasized ever more vigorously that self-realization by means of action can also occur through acts of helping, the establishment of peace, etc.

Herder's non-rationalist and non-normativist conception of action may sound strange at first. But in fact you will be quite familiar with situations, particularly from everyday life, in which you have begun to take action not because you were driven by irrational urges, but because you had the feeling that the action itself was more important to you than all the goals or 'ends' which it might accomplish: expression of the ego, and not so much the goal of the action or compliance with norms, was the top priority. We shall elaborate on phenomena and problems of this kind in the lecture on neo-pragmatism, but first we want to make it clear that this model of expressive action can hardly be captured by Parsons' 'action frame of reference', which is thus indubitably deficient. The fact that Parsons failed to notice this is connected, among other things, with the specific form of his convergence thesis and its rash dismissal of entire national intellectual traditions. He failed to appreciate that the notion of the 'expression' of a 'national spirit' was ultimately anchored in an expressive model of action. While his criticism of 'emanationism' was quite correct, he was wrong to ignore this model.

To sum up, we can criticize Parsons' convergence thesis for implying a relatively unilinear notion of historical progress. At least, Parsons sees no contradiction between his preference for Pareto rather than Marshall, so clearly expressed in *Structure* (Parsons holds Pareto in such high regard in part because the latter did *not* share the optimism about progress typical of the Victorian era), or between his critique of evolutionist constructions of history à la Spencer and his own interpretation of intellectual history with its implicit belief in progress. And his interpretation certainly does entail such a belief, implying as it does that a clearly discernible, ascending path leads from the classical figures of sociology all the way to Parsons himself (the term 'convergence', of course, incorporates this notion). Now it may well be that Parsons' theoretical framework is superior to that of the classical figures. But this is not what matters to us here. Rather, we wish to warn against writing intellectual history *very generally* from the perspective of the 'victors', that is, the victorious theoretical constructions. For as we have just seen in the example of German expressivist anthropology around Herder, there were, are and always will be theoretical approaches which have something to tell future generations, even if 'progress' initially ignores these approaches by and large. We can often learn much of significance from them. The notion that 'progress' in the humanities would enable us to 'capture' the *entire* experiential content of human life and action valid in the past and then grasp it theoretically seems very strange to us, or at the very least over-confident. Sociologists, and not just historians, are thus well advised to take a look back through intellectual history. There is always something new to be discovered there. Contemporary German sociologists may spend a little too much of their time interpreting the classical figures and exploring the history of their own discipline. But such activities are in themselves entirely legitimate and indeed imperative, insofar as they involve drawing on old, forgotten, intellectual resources, which are always 'new', in order to enhance current theories and resolve theoretical problems.

So much for what we believe to be the really weighty objections to the form and content of Parsons' convergence thesis. Other criticisms seem to us less significant, if not quite misplaced. But since some of these crop up again and again, we need to take at least a brief look at them.

We addressed Parsons' extremely broad and sweeping use of the term utilitarianism in the previous lecture. But the claim that Parsons misrepresented utilitarianism and ignored some or even the most important of its moral philosophical and social theoretical arguments seems to be missing the point. For those who advocate an 'appropriate' interpretation of utilitarianism are often faced with the difficulty of delimiting this theoretical school with any precision, and in some cases one is entitled to ask whether all the moral philosophical arguments which they mention are really *utilitarian* in nature or whether the authors who supposedly document the breadth and diversity of utilitarian thought were truly *utilitarians*. Parsons merely asserted that much of modern Anglo-Saxon philosophy and classical political economy is imbued with utilitarian arguments. But this does not mean that every author working in this tradition was a true-blue utilitarian or that every author described as a utilitarian formulated nothing but unambiguously utilitarian arguments. Thus, it is not completely convincing to criticize Parsons' thesis (see for example the criticisms put forward by Charles Camic in 'The Utilitarians Revisited') by quoting, for example, from the work of Adam Smith or others and showing that it features highly sophisticated moral philosophical arguments that go far beyond Bentham's 'greatest happiness principle'. Parsons would have accepted this without hesitation. His line of argument centred on the logic and fateful theoretical consequences of a model of action narrowly focused on utility (that is, utilitarian), and not primarily on achieving a historically adequate definition or classification of authors. His aim was not to portray the history of British thought in all its complexities; he was concerned first and foremost with economics, which consistently took its lead from the utility-oriented model of action only from the mid-nineteenth century on.

Further, Parsons is criticized for seeing convergence where there was in fact divergence. Some critics (see Pope, Cohen and Hazelrigg, 'On the Divergence of Weber and Durkheim: A Critique of Parsons' Convergence Thesis') have claimed that the arguments and topics found in the work of Durkheim and Weber in particular drifted ever further apart and that for this reason alone Parsons' claim of convergence is absurd. For them, the real thesis to be defended is one of divergence. But this too is a misunderstanding. Parsons was not concerned to show that the work of the four authors he considered converged in all respects, but that they converged on a particular point, namely with respect to the development and elaboration of a voluntaristic theory of action, that is, with respect to the synchronous treatment of the basic sociological problems of action and social order.

We can now leave the debate on the convergence thesis behind us. We turn to the dispute over Parsons' 'action frame of reference', that is, the criticisms made of his conception of action. Here again, a number of significant objections must be mentioned.

1. You have already encountered the first criticism in our discussion of Herder's 'expressive action'. We shall therefore do no more than briefly ask again whether every instance of action can truly be crammed into the means–ends schema, whether there is not a type of action beyond the attainment of goals and fulfilment of norms. As our brief discussion of Herder showed, religious rituals, art, etc. resist such categorization (see Hans Joas, *The Creativity of Action*). But even on the 'opposite' side of the spectrum of action, if you will, there are activities which the means–ends schema fails to capture. Think of entirely routinized actions, actions which you carry out preconsciously, without really thinking. You will notice that a large number of everyday actions proceed in exactly this way: preparing breakfast for example, assuming that you do this often and not just once a year, does not involve a chain of clear goals in light of the given means, and reference to norms and values gets us no further here either. The actions you carry out in the kitchen (fetching the butter from the fridge, making the coffee, setting the table, etc.) certainly do not occur as an uninterrupted series of calculated acts. This may have been the case when you prepared

breakfast for your parents for the first time as a child and had to have a good think about whether breakfast really involves butter, coffee and a set table. You then had to make all these things happen by thinking them through and carrying out a series of individual actions. Nowadays when you make your usual breakfast the earlier process of goal-setting has long since been 'absorbed'; you no longer think about it. This is routinized action, in which these earlier goals are directly incorporated in the carrying out of the action; you do not reflect on what exactly you are doing or which goals you wish to attain. We shall return to all of this again in Lecture XII on the English social theorist Anthony Giddens, who recognizes that the Parsonian frame of action features certain deficiencies in this regard.

2. Parsons' 'action frame of reference' was also criticized for its 'objectivist' leanings. On this view, Parsons did not really take the cognitive capacities and weaknesses of actors into account with respect to how they deal with the action situation. Parsons' work creates the impression that it is quite clear that the actors see the means and conditions of action as they are – that is, objectively. But what actors know about the circumstances of their actions may vary a great deal; this cannot simply be determined externally – objectively – but rather the social scientist must first examine how the actors subjectively see things before making reliable statements about how they will act under given circumstances (see Warner, 'Toward a Redefinition of Action Theory'). A similar argument can be made about the norms and values of a society: these are not simply present or given, but must always be *interpreted* by the actors. We must get to the bottom of this feat of interpretation if we wish to understand the action undertaken; merely referring to 'objectively' existing norms and values fails to take us any further. All these points, however, only came to play a central role in the debate on theory within sociology later on, as you will find out in the lectures on symbolic interactionism, ethnomethodology and on the work of Anthony Giddens.

3. Closely bound up with the last point is the critical question of why Parsons, in his account of the 'unit act', scrutinizes the prerequisites for all action by referring to the situation of action, but ignored its *consequences*. Parsons writes as though this action is over and done with once its goal has been achieved. But this is a mode of analysis that regards the individual act in near-total isolation. This ignores the fact that the consequences of the action often have an immediate effect upon the actor. Ordered configurations are formed not only through the individual action *of various* actors; *my own* actions also form an interlocking chain, because the action I take has consequences to which I then have to respond. It would thus have been a very good idea to examine these consequences in more depth, especially as Parsons described and discussed Pareto's attempts to come to terms with the problem of side-effects in detail in *Structure*. Yet strangely enough, he

failed to draw on Pareto's insights in formulating his own action frame of reference. Among other things, the key distinction between the 'intended' and 'unintended consequences' of action, those I wished to produce and those I triggered without meaning to, was introduced only later by those close to Parsons, such as the American sociologist Robert Merton (1910–2003). But even this step is probably insufficient, because within the category of unintended consequences we still have to distinguish between those which are anticipated and those to which this does not apply. My actions may have consequences that are unintended, which I do not in fact wish to bring about – and I am quite aware of this. I will nonetheless act as planned, because achieving the intended consequences of my action seems more important to me than the unpleasant side-effects. Thus, in such cases I include these side-effects in my calculations, as I have foreseen them. But of course not all unintended consequences can be anticipated; those which can may in fact be a rarity. Social life is so complex that a single action often has tremendous consequences, which were literally impossible to predict when the action was taken. We need only think of the assassination in Sarajevo in 1914, when the murder of the heir to the Austrian throne involved consequences of which the assassins were surely unaware, because no one – not even they themselves – could have imagined that this would trigger the carnage of the First World War (see the illuminating remarks in Anthony Giddens, *The Constitution of Society*, pp. 10–14).

4. With respect to the consequences of action, the question arises as to what extent it makes any sense at all to take the action of the individual, an isolated action, as our point of departure. Does not Parsons' account of the 'unit act' warp our perspective by assuming that the actor generates his action more or less autonomously, off his own bat? Is it not in fact necessary to come at this problem from a quite different angle, one which we touched on briefly in relation to the neglect of the tradition of American theory and Simmel in *Structure* so often subject to criticism? Simmel's point of departure was not the individual actor, but rather the *social relation*, as he took the plausible view that it is the original sociality of the human being which makes action possible in the first place. The human being does not come into the world as an actor, but as a helpless baby or child, embedded in a social structure, who *gains the capacity for action from this structure*. On this view, sociality precedes the capacity for action, problematizing every attempt to make the isolated actor the central focus of theory building. The American pragmatists, particularly George Herbert Mead, have argued in much the same way, though bringing out the social psychological and action theoretical aspects with far greater sophistication and precision. But Parsons, as we have seen, leaves Mead out of the equation in his reconstruction of sociological thought as well. You will learn a good deal more about this in the lecture on symbolic interactionism.

5. Parsons' action frame of reference was also criticized for the obscurity of what we might call the 'normative'. In *Structure*, Parsons spoke of norms and values, and with respect to the latter also of 'ultimate ends', without truly making clear whether and how norms and values differ and how exactly they are connected. When he spoke of 'ultimate ends', he did indeed differentiate between personal 'ultimate ends' and those which may be characteristic of an entire society, but he failed to ask whether and how the two relate to one another. Ironically, one may criticize Parsons in much the same way as he himself did the utilitarians. Parsons asserted that the utilitarians had failed to inquire into the origins of notions of utility, desires, 'ends', etc. In a similar way, we must criticize Parsons for failing to make any effort to inquire into the genesis of values, where they come from, despite the fact that they are so central to his voluntaristic theory of action and that no term seems to be more important to his theory than 'values'. When one reads *Structure* (as well as Parsons' subsequent writings), one gains the impression that values are simply given. But how are we to conceive of the process by which something becomes a value as such for an individual? And how do values come to be *shared* in the first place? Parsons is silent on this, and we are forced to look for answers elsewhere (for an examination of the core features of this issue, see Joas, *The Genesis of Values*). You will hear about this in greater depth in the lectures on French sociology, particularly on Alain Touraine and those on neo-pragmatism.
6. The final criticism is on a rather different level than those above in that *Parsons himself* noticed a deficit in his theory, which he was quick to acknowledge. *The Structure of Social Action* fails to explore what drives human action. One may have certain goals and values, and even the means necessary to realize them, without in fact bringing oneself to accomplish them. Where, then, does the will, the exertion, the energy necessary to act come from? Noticing this lacuna, Parsons himself speaks of 'effort', of the dynamic force that takes aims and ends beyond their initial state as mere cognitions and enables them to *become realities*. He himself saw that more work was needed here.

It is vital that you keep in mind these six criticisms of the Parsonian *action frame of reference* for two reasons. First, *Structure* was of course not Parsons' final work, but his first. The question thus arises as to whether Parsons himself recognized these criticisms and worked out a response to them. This is of considerable significance to how we assess his later work. Second, as we hinted in our identification of numerous theoretical schools and theorists as we moved through the six points above, and as will soon be apparent in the way we have structured this lecture, many subsequent sociologists worked assiduously on Parsons' action frame of reference. The development of modern sociological theory can essentially be presented as an argument with the edifice of Parsonian thought.

We have now arrived at the second part of the lecture, where we leave *Structure* behind us at last and concentrate on Parsons' subsequent works. In terms of the evolution of his work, it is apparent that Parsons did in fact further refine his action frame of reference in *one* respect. As mentioned already, he fully recognized that he had neglected the true motive for action, that is, he had failed to sufficiently analyse which energies propel human beings to realize goals and values. It is at this point that Parsons began to take an in-depth look at psychoanalysis. He even submitted to a training analysis and drew on other, related psychological theories of the time in order to explain which motivating factors are anchored in the personality of the very young child, influencing her for the rest of her life. This intensive engagement with psychoanalysis finds clear expression in his writings, as he took up the criticisms of the original action frame of reference set out in point 6 above, putting them to productive use. In the immediate post-1937 period, however, he was initially focused on other topics and tasks, which, at first sight at least, are fundamentally empirical rather than theoretical.

First of all, Parsons began to develop an interest in the medical profession, studying the behaviour of medical students at Harvard Medical School for more than a year. Doctors, along with lawyers, etc. are among the representatives of the 'professions', which, while their tradition dates back to pre-capitalist relations, have lost none of their significance in modern (capitalist) society. On the contrary, the number of doctors and lawyers has grown steadily, and other professions structured in a similar way have also gained in importance. This is remarkable because while professionals such as doctors are paid according to market principles in a capitalist society, the egotistical market principle is at the same time subject to clear restrictions by the ethics firmly anchored in this professional group. In line with these, the doctor must see himself as the servant and helper of his patients, as one who certainly may not do or demand anything he likes in order to advance his immediate market or financial self-interest. The doctor must, for example, help patients even if desperate circumstances mean they are unable to pay; he may not undertake nonsensical medical interventions, even if a patient has requested them and is willing to pay for them, etc. For Parsons, the nature of the professions is so significant because it demonstrates that capitalism does not in fact follow an inexorable logic of its own, in which the principles of personal utility are *all* that count and all other elements are gradually eradicated. Rather, according to Parsons, the existence of the professions reveals that ethical systems can assert themselves while surrounded by the logic of the market; thus, not every non-market phenomenon – as Marx and Engels predicted in their *Communist Manifesto* and contemporary opponents and supporters of globalization continue to assert – 'melts into air'. As you can see, Parsons' empirical studies also have a theoretical tenor. If you would like to know more about this, you can do no better than to read Parsons' essay entitled 'The Professions and Social Structure' from 1939 (in Talcott Parsons, *Essays in Sociological Theory*).

The other key focus of Parsons' investigations in the late 1930s and early 1940s, which were of a more empirical nature, lay in the field of political analysis. Parsons, like many other American social scientists, was employed by the US government to help plan for the war and for the post-war period, simply because it needed to know about the society of the enemy, the problems affecting it, the prospects for democratic reconstruction, etc. Parsons therefore wrote essays and memoranda, some of them brilliant, on German society in the immediate pre-1933 period and under National Socialism. Here, he analysed the conditions in which Hitler rose to power and asked, among other things, whether there was a risk of an 'American Hitler' emerging in the USA. As classified documents, many of these essays were not published at the time. Today, you can of course read his work on National Socialism without problem. We recommend the anthology by Uta Gerhardt (*Talcott Parsons on National Socialism*, 1993) or – if you would prefer a brief review – the 1942 essay entitled 'Democracy and Social Structure in Pre-Nazi Germany' (in Talcott Parsons, *Essays in Sociological Theory*). While Parsons' assessments have been superseded by the findings of contemporary historians in many respects and require relativization, his analyses were for the most part streets ahead of those of other American sociologists of the day.

Given the nature of our account so far, one might suspect that the focus of Parsons' work increasingly shifted to empirical problems from 1937 on or – witness his engagement with Freud and psychoanalysis – that he carried out further work on his action frame of reference, trying to remedy its evident weaknesses as identified above. But this was not the case.

Rather, at almost the same time as he was engaged in the writing of *Structure*, Parsons began – as we know only on the basis of manuscripts published much later (see 'Actor, Situation and Normative Patterns', 1939) – to think about a comprehensive *theory of social order*. Parsons thus considered the action frame of reference that he had developed largely complete and adequate. His priority now was clearly to produce a theory capable of grasping and explaining different forms of empirical order. As you know from our exposition on *The Structure of Social Action*, Parsons' point of departure here was the observation that social order exists and that therefore the utilitarian concept of action is wrong or at least too narrow. He then developed his own 'voluntaristic' concept of action, which was intended to render comprehensible the unquestionable fact of social order. This order as such was not really his chief concern; he had not explicitly theorized it at all at that point. He now wished to make up for this. To get straight to the point: Parsons moved towards a theory of order, to which the literature on Parsons affixed the well-chosen label of 'normativist functionalism' and which can be seen in fully developed form in his second major work, *The Social System*, from 1951. Since this label will mean little to you, we shall begin by explaining the term 'functionalism' to help you understand the thrust of Parsons' theory of order.

'Functionalism' is a way of thinking that describes and explains social phenomena by pointing to the functions that they fulfil within a greater whole. One can show, for example, what (functional) contribution the family makes to society as a whole. One might spontaneously think of contributions such as the raising of young people, motivating them with respect to their future working lives, a task of tremendous societal importance, or the equally significant imparting of social norms by the parents, etc. One *might* then claim that the family emerged because it enabled functions important to the social whole to be fulfilled. This mode of argumentation, briefly outlined here through a first example, has a very long history and cropped up repeatedly in various systems of thought and disciplines over the course of the nineteenth and twentieth centuries. Who or what most influenced Parsons with respect to his adoption of functionalist concepts is hard to determine. Perhaps his contact with Bronislaw Malinowski at the London School of Economics in the mid-1920s was decisive; it was after all Malinowski (1884–1942) who did so much to advance functional analysis within anthropology. Perhaps it was his initial study of biology which made Parsons aware, for example, of the *functions* of organs within the body as a whole and their importance to its survival within a given environment. Perhaps, and this we intend as something of a provocation, his reading of Marx also played a key role, as there are functionalist arguments to be found here too. For our purposes, the question of what influenced Parsons is ultimately of no great importance. We wish instead to present a striking example of a functionalist argument from a Marxian theoretical context, in order to lay bare for you the specific logic of functionalist thought, its peculiarities and the difficulties it entails, and to help you understand that functionalism is relevant not only in those cases where authors explicitly mention it.

In his analyses of capitalism, among other things, Marx repeatedly drew attention to the existence of the so-called 'industrial reserve army' of the unemployed, which was in his opinion a typical feature of capitalism. This reserve army, he asserted, was extremely useful to the capitalists, because it reduces the prospects of workers with jobs achieving wage increases. The workers have no real means of applying pressure: in the case of a strike, for example, there exists a large number of people willing to work, and who would be happy to do so for a lower wage. Striking could thus never have much impact. One can claim, therefore, that the army of the unemployed fulfils a function vital to the structure and dynamics of capitalism, because it enables the capitalists to produce cheaply and exploit the workers. But Marx goes further still, claiming at certain points in his work that the unemployed exist *because* they ultimately serve the interests of capital or capitalism, because they are functional for the capitalist system. He thus argues that capitalism creates the unemployed in the first place.

All of this looks plausible at first sight, but once you begin to think about it you will soon notice that it may be problematic to make *both claims at the same time*. If one does so – as is typical of many functionalist arguments – the causes and the consequences of a phenomenon are conflated in peculiar fashion. In the first claim, unemployment is in principle the *prerequisite for* or *(one of the) causes* of the sound functioning of the capitalist system. In the second claim, meanwhile, unemployment is the *consequence* of the functioning of capitalism. Logically speaking, this is highly problematic, as the consequences or effects of a phenomenon can be seen only at a later point, while its prerequisites and causes must of course exist before it does. Functionalist arguments like the one above used by Marx must thus be taken with a large pinch of salt given their conflation of cause and effect, that is, their tendency to treat effects as causes. Above all, it is important to grasp that identifying the functions of a phenomenon is not generally sufficient to *explain* it. A simple example will suffice to show this. Animals may fulfil important functions for a family and especially for children within a family: one learns to behave responsibly by looking after them, one gains access to the natural world, etc. But by no means does this imply that all families necessarily keep pets, and it would be utterly absurd to claim that canaries or tortoises evolved *because* they must fulfil this function for the family. This example shows that while it is easy to 'identify' the functions performed by various phenomena, by no means does this necessarily tell us anything about what causes them. It is vital to be alert to the risk of simply equating functional claims with explanations.

As you will see, however, the social sciences and particularly sociology are brimming over with functionalist assertions or explanations. Such assertions appear in various contexts, among authors of both the left and right, among Marxists and non-Marxists. The use of the term 'function' has become nothing less than inflationary. Those using it generally fail either to clarify what exactly a phenomenon *contributes* to the greater whole, or to explain whether or how making a functionalist assertion equates or may equate with *explaining* something. It thus comes as no surprise that sociology all too often features what you might call a 'functionalist prejudice'. This refers to the assumption that whatever is happening at a given moment is always necessary to, that is, functional for, the survival of a greater whole. If the unemployment figures rise, then on this view this is undoubtedly functionally necessary to 'capital', especially because, as we have seen, it diminishes the workers' capacity to take industrial action and wages can be driven down; if the number of those unemployed falls meanwhile, adherents of this perspective state that this too merely shows how effectively capital can use and exploit the labour force and how functional the falling unemployment figures and the parallel increase in the number of jobs therefore is. The arbitrary nature of such arguments is thus given free rein; there is no way they can be said to provide genuine explanations. We shall return to this point in the lecture on Anthony Giddens, certainly one of the sharpest and cleverest critics of functionalism within the discipline of sociology, who has gone so far as to suggest that sociology would be better off doing without the concept of function for a few decades, rather than deploying it in this imprecise way.

Does this then mean that functionalist arguments as such are meaningless or wrong? No, not always. First, such arguments may in fact play a heuristic role in the research process, that is, they may help us gain purchase on reality. It is certainly true that references to functional relations in the social scientific literature are seldom linked with evidence that these relations do in fact exist. In this sense, a functionalist argument is initially no more than a plausible assumption. But assumptions can be subjected to empirical investigation. In other words, functionalist arguments may provide us with hypotheses open to falsification. Though a functionalist argument is not an explanation, it may *point the way* to one. Second, the conflation of cause and effect so typical of functionalism is permissible only if *actual processes of feedback* can be shown. That is, Marx's statement that the unemployed exist *because* they ultimately serve the interests of capital or capitalism and are thus functional is correct if he can show not only that an army of unemployed is useful for capitalists, but also that within capitalism specific actors – such as capitalists – pursue strategies which produce a certain reservoir of unemployed workers or which at least stabilize such a tendency. To put it in more abstract terms, one must show the consequences of a specific phenomenon and how these in turn have a specific effect – in the sense of a feedback mechanism – on the phenomenon, that is, that they also cause it.

These feedback effects may be simple or dynamic in nature. Body temperature is an example of the latter. The human body has a very specific temperature, which is maintained via energy supply, body hair, movement, etc. Should the body temperature rise through an excess of movement, this is counteracted by the formation of (cooling) sweat; once the period of movement is over, this may result in an excessive fall in body temperature; the body may begin to cool, causing the hairs to rise in order to warm it up again, and the body may need to be supplied with energy through food, etc. What we are dealing with here is a dynamic, constantly changing equilibrium; one can observe *concrete feedback processes* which allow us to use functionalist language in relatively unproblematic fashion. The question of course is whether functionalist arguments can be deployed in such a straightforward way in all contexts and disciplines.

In any event, our excursus on functionalism was intended to show that this theoretical construct *may* rapidly lead to questionable conclusions, particularly in the social sciences. Parsons makes use of such functionalism to construct a theory of social order, and we will be asking whether he managed to avoid its many pitfalls and problems. But before we do so, we need to make a final point directly connected with this issue. We have already established that *every* theory of action refers to a theory of order, that a theory of action requires a theory of order. From 1937 onwards, Parsons vigorously set about conceptualizing such a theory. But functionalism (especially Parsons' 'normativist functionalism') is just *one* example of such a theory of order; it is not *the* theory of order. What we are getting at here is that Parsons' theory of action *does not ineluctably* cause him to adopt functionalist ideas. Yet, while deploying the concept of system, Parsons makes straight for such a functionalism, drawing on ideas from biology, as is apparent in the 1939 paper 'Actor, Situation and Normative Patterns' mentioned above:

> In some sense a social system tends to 'stable equilibrium', to the maintenance of itself as a 'going concern', *as* a system, and the maintenance of a structural pattern either stably or through a course of development. In this respect it is analogous (*not* identical) to the organism and its tendency to maintain from a short-time point of view, a physiological equilibrium or 'homeostasis' and from a longer-run point of view, the maintenance of the curve of the life cycle.
>
> (p. 103; original emphasis)

We shall clarify what exactly Parsons means by a 'social system' in a moment, with respect to our analysis of *Toward a General Theory of Action* and *The Social System*, two books from 1951 in which his thoughts on functionalism appeared in their most mature form so far. But first we must shed light on what it means to call his functionalism *normativist*. This is in fact relatively straightforward, as you have already learned a good deal about Parsons' early work and about how tremendously important norms and values were to him. Parsons' functionalism differs from other functionalisms in that it attributes central importance to *values and norms* both as regards the actions undertaken by individuals and the stability of the social order. In fact, examining every social phenomenon in terms of how it functions to maintain and transmit *norms and values* became Parsons' core intellectual project. Norms and values thus constitute the point of departure for Parsons' functionalism, the ultimate point of analytical reference; this applies, of course, neither to biologists, for whom an organism's survival within a given environment represents this ultimate reference point, nor to other social scientific functionalists, nor even to Marx, who might be referred to as a 'materialist functionalist'. The term *normativist* functionalism is thus a fitting one, despite the fact that Parsons does not use the term in this way, speaking instead of a 'structural-functional' form of analysis (see *The Social System*, p. vii).

As you will have gathered from the above quotation, Parsons uses the concept of system to construct his theory of order. He refers to a 'social system', which in itself indicates that he is aware of *other* systems. But let us take one thing at a time. Our first priority is to clarify what Parsons means by 'system' in the first place. In order to do so, it is helpful to delineate precisely those of his ideas which he developed in greatest depth in *Toward a General Theory of Action*, a co-authored volume.

As the name *Toward a General Theory of Action* itself implies, in fleshing out his theory of order, Parsons' point of departure is action theory, that is, his 'action frame of reference', with which you are familiar from the previous lecture and which Parsons modified to a very minor degree. Though his terminology sounds different, Parsons has maintained his action theoretical stance: the actor always acts within a specific situation, that is, she relates to specific objects, to non-social (physical) as well as social objects, in the latter case therefore to other individuals (the actor may even thematize herself as an individual) or to collectivities or groups. In the process of taking action, the actor selects who or what she wishes to focus on, who or what she is *geared towards*. What an actor gears herself towards when taking action thus depends on a process of selection, and if these action orientations cluster, if regularities develop, Parsons talks of a 'system of action':

> The word *system* is used in the sense that determinate relations of interdependence exist within the complex of empirical phenomena. The antithesis of the concept of system is random variability. However, no implication of rigidity is intended.
>
> (*Toward a General Theory of Action*, p. 5, fn. 5)

Parsons' overriding concern in *Structure* was to investigate how the actions *of a number of actors* can link up, his aim being to resolve the utilitarian problem of the 'randomness of ends'. Parsons now goes one step further by asking how stable, regular action orientations can come about in the first place *within a single actor*. And this is also a 'response' to the criticism mentioned above that his action frame of reference lacks a motivational element, that he fails to clarify in *Structure* what actually drives the actor. Parsons makes use of his more intensive engagement with psychology and psychoanalysis, which began in the post-1937 period. He describes how stable *cognitive* and emotional or *cathectic* action orientations develop within the individual actor through past learning processes and particularly early childhood experiences, in which the sexual aspects of the parent–child relationship emphasized by Sigmund Freud (1856–1939) play a role. Parsons thus tried to capture the emotional forms of attachment to objects through the term 'cathexis' – the Freudian concept of libidinal attachment. Cognitive and cathectic orientations are then *integrated* by means of *evaluative*, that is, value-related orientations.

> The tendency of the organism toward integration requires the assessment and comparison of immediate cognized objects and cathectic interests in terms of their remoter consequences for the larger unit of evaluation. Evaluation rests on standards which may be either cognitive standards of truthfulness, appreciative standards of appropriateness, or moral standards of rightness.
>
> (*General Theory*, p. 5)

We can perhaps put it more simply and say that both cognitive and cathectic and ultimately – overarching both these – evaluative motivations enter into every action and that all of this explains the 'effort' and the will that stimulate the actor to take action.

This framework makes sense of the fact that Parsons understands the person as a 'system of action', for it is in the person himself that *stable* action orientations cluster in that mutual interlacing of cognition, cathexis and evaluation – on the basis of the experiences and learning processes that we have already addressed. The action undertaken by the individual is thus not random; his action orientations form a pattern. This is why Parsons refers here to a 'personality system': the actions carried out by the individual exhibit a certain consistency as a result of past experiences.

> This system will be called the personality, and we will define it as the organized system of the orientation and motivation of action of one individual actor.
>
> (ibid., p. 7)

But of course action orientations are *not only bundled within the individual*, but also *between individuals* – as we already know from the analysis provided in *Structure*. Because there are norms and values, stable action orientations and expectations develop, which also provide a basis for the orderly linkage of the actions taken by *a number of actors*. Parsons calls this the 'social system':

> The social system is ... made up of the relationships of individuals, but it is a system which is organized around the problems inherent in or arising from social interaction of a plurality of individual actors rather than around the problems which arise in connection with the integration of the actions of an individual actor.
>
> (ibid.)

But the 'personality system' and 'social system' are phenomena that cannot really be separated empirically; they are not spheres of reality in their own right. Rather, as the philosophy of science puts it, this mode of expression clearly involves an *analytical* distinction: in line with my interests as a researcher, I may pay more attention to the 'personality system' or to the 'social system'. For the actor is of course on the one hand an individual. But on the other hand he is embedded in contexts of interaction with other actors through one portion of his personality, and I am not, therefore, dealing with two truly separate 'objects' or 'phenomena' here.

Parsons now distinguishes still another system from these two systems, but one which he does *not* understand as an *action* system at this point in his development. This is the 'cultural system', by which he means the orderly linkage of cultural symbolizations. Here, he touches on the question of how ideas or belief systems are linked, how expressive symbols, styles or trends in art form a reasonably homogeneous unity or how the values of a society come to exhibit a degree of coherence:

> systems of culture have their own forms and problems of integration which are not reducible to those of either personality or social systems or both together. The cultural tradition in its significance both as an object of orientation and as an element in the orientation of action must be articulated both conceptually and empirically with personalities and social systems. Apart from embodiment in the orientation systems of concrete actors, culture, though existing as a body of artefacts and as systems of symbols, is not in itself organized as a system of action.
>
> (ibid.)

It will come as no surprise to you to learn that this system takes on much importance within Parsonian theory in as much as it touches on those values and norms which Parsons had already declared central to the coordination of actions in *Structure*. In fact, Parsons believes that the values from the cultural system must be anchored in the two action systems, through two processes: through *internalization* within the personality system and through *institutionalization* in the social system. As we shall be taking a more detailed look at institutionalization further below (p. 65), we shall restrict ourselves here to a few brief remarks on internalization, which we have touched on briefly already.

Parsons tried to make good at least *one* weakness in the original action frame of reference by paying greater attention to the *motives* of action, distinguishing between cognitive, cathectic and evaluative motives. The notion of cathexis referred to attachment to objects or the rejection of certain objects, and here, drawing on elements of Freudian theory, Parsons emphasized the role of sexuality and showed how biological urges are transformed into specific fantasies and then into motives of action. These human drive energies become interwoven with cultural values. It is the process of 'socialization' that facilitates the linkage or merging of cathectic and evaluative/value-laden motives, because the parents, for example, impart values, symbols and belief systems and the long-term absorption and adoption of these values, symbols, etc. occurs via diverted drive energies from the realm of infant sexuality. The drives are thus fused with values through socialization, rendering them socially tolerable. The child 'internalizes' the norms and values of the society.

So much for the key role played by the cultural system in processes of internalization. It can be realized only as part of an action system. 'Personality system', 'social system' and 'cultural system' are merely analytical distinctions.

Looking at the steps in Parsons' argument described so far, it is apparent that he has largely retained the action frame of reference, which has been expanded to some extent with reference to the cognitive, cathectic and evaluative *motivations* of action: what is really new is his bringing the concept of system into play at a crucial point, on the basis of which he develops his theory of social order. All of this, even the notion of different systems, was already present in embryonic form in the multi-authored *Toward a General Theory of Action*.

However, Parsons' ideas in this regard only took on the form of a genuine intellectual project with his second major work, which was published in the same year and which bore the revealing title of *The Social System*. Here, Parsons advocates the thesis that a general theory of action and order must pay attention to all three systems, but that different disciplines or subdisciplines would focus on different aspects. While the task of analysing the 'cultural system' would fall mainly to the sociology of knowledge (and perhaps to philosophy, theology, etc.), and it would be up to psychology to examine the personality system, sociology was to deal primarily with the 'social system'. The theoretical problems and empirical phenomena that emerge within this 'social system' were to be the main object of sociology.

But of course we can discover something about the object of sociology only if we inquire into what, in concrete terms, a 'social system' actually is; so far, Parsons has given us no more than a very abstract definition, merely telling us something about how this system differs from the two other systems. Parsons thus first underlines that society is the epitome of the 'social system':

> A social system ... which meets all the essential functional prerequisites of long term persistence from within its own resources, will be called a *society*. It is not essential to the concept of a society that it should not be in any way empirically interdependent with other societies, but only that it should contain all the structural and functional fundamentals of an independently subsisting system.
>
> (*The Social System*, p. 19)

On this view, society is thus the fundamentally independent, self-contained social system, which at the same time always contains within it a number, undetermined here, of other social systems as well, that is, less extensive but nonetheless ordered relations of action between individuals (such as institutions, groups, families, etc.). The idea is that groups, families, etc. are also social systems, though not as self-sufficient as 'society', which also means that these smaller systems are interwoven in one way or another with 'society' as the largest social system.

Parsons underlines that the first essential is to analyse the *statics* of social systems very generally, that is, to determine the elements of which a 'social system' consists, before we can move on to investigate *dynamics*, that is, how and by what means social systems change. This emphasis on the statics of social systems leads immediately to the idea of 'functional prerequisites', *the* conditions which must pertain for a system of action, in this case the 'social system', to exist over the long term:

> First, a social system cannot be so structured as to be radically incompatible with the conditions of functioning of its component individual actors as biological organisms and personalities, or of the relatively stable integration of a cultural system. Secondly, in turn the social system, on both fronts, depends on the requisite minimum of 'support' from each of the other systems. It must, that is, have a sufficient accordance with the requirements of its role system, positively in the fulfillment of expectations and negatively in abstention from too much disruptive, i.e., deviant, behavior. It must on the other hand avoid commitment to cultural patterns which either fail to define a minimum of order or which place impossible demands on people and thereby generate deviance and conflict to a degree which is incompatible with the minimum conditions of stability or orderly development.
>
> (ibid., pp. 27–8)

While you may not have understood every word of this, it should be clear that Parsons refers to a functioning 'social system' if a certain stability and relative absence of conflict pertains; but this is the case only if the personality systems of the parties to interaction within the social system have developed sufficient motivation to 'play along with' this 'social system', and if the cultural system is able to provide values and symbols in such a way as to ensure that the parties to interaction within the 'social system', get along together in an ordered way. The interpenetration of the social and personality system or of the social and cultural system is thus the minimal prerequisite for the existence of a 'social system'. Furthermore, Parsons adds that every social system must of course deal effectively with its allocation problems (allocation = the distribution of goods; the term refers to the fact that every system needs material resources in one way or another) and differentiate its internal tasks (*Toward a General Theory of Action*, p. 25). The family in a modern society thus requires both money and some way of organizing the division of labour between the family members if it is to survive over the long term without facing difficulties.

Turning to the question of what the *elements* of social systems might be, it comes as no surprise that Parsons identifies the individual action and the actor (the latter may also be a group or collectivity). But he also refers to another element, one which has cropped up already in the above quotation, namely the 'social role':

> We have, then, three different units of social systems referable to the individual actor ranging from the most elementary to the most composite. The first is the social act, performed by an actor and oriented to one or more actors as objects. The second is the status-role as the organized subsystems of acts of the actor or actors occupying given reciprocal statuses and acting toward each other in terms of given reciprocal orientations. The third is the actor himself as a social unit, the organized system of all

> the statuses and roles referable to him as a social object and as the 'author' of a system of role-activities.
>
> (*The Social System*, p. 26)

The reason why social roles or status-roles became so important to Parsons is linked with the problem of order with which you will now be more than familiar. This emerges whenever the actions carried out by a number of actors occur with reference to one another: how do actors manage to act in concert in the first place? This is in fact highly problematic and anything but self-evident from the analytic perspective of the social scientist, despite the fact that it is no real problem in everyday life. As is well known, Parsons' response was to refer to values and norms. But these must first be *specified, translated* into clear rules and anchored in institutions, if communication and cooperative action are not ultimately to come to grief. Values must be given concrete form by means of institutions, that is, *institutionalized* – and this is where the concept of roles enters the equation, one of *the* core concepts in the sociology of the 1950s and 1960s. Roles are behavioural patterns, clusters of regulations governing how to act, which I normally uphold on my own account, which I am required to uphold and which I also want to uphold. My fellow human beings also expect me to do so, so that if I disappoint their expectations by failing to act correctly, I run the risk of having sanctions imposed upon me in the shape of punishment, contempt, etc. In relation to interaction, roles – because they interpret values – ensure that people successfully coordinate their actions.

> It is only by virtue of internalization of institutionalized values that a genuine motivational integration of behavior in the social structure takes place, that the deeper 'layers' of motivation become harnessed to the fulfillment of role-expectation. It is only when this has taken place to a high degree that it is possible to say that a social system is highly integrated, and that the interests of the collectivity and the private interests of its constituent members can be said to approach coincidence.
>
> (ibid., p. 42)

The concept of role was crucial to Parsons' theory building during this period in two respects. First, placing this concept centre stage endowed sociology with a clear-cut identity. This allowed Parsons to continue what he had already tried to do, in *Structure* among other writings, that is, distinguish sociology clearly from other disciplines. It was because he considered the concept of role so important to the analysis of 'social systems' that he was able to argue that the social cannot be derived from nature; Parsons thus distances himself from biology. But this was not enough. Parsons' concept of role also allows him to point out that the social cannot be derived directly from culture either (this was his way of distancing sociology from the cultural sciences and to some extent from cultural anthropology), let alone from the mere aggregation of individual acts (this was intended to counter the claims of psychology). The concept of role was an excellent means of demonstrating the independence of the social and thus the necessity of the discipline of sociology.

Second, the concept of role embodies the ideas most fundamental to Parsonian 'normativist functionalism'. On the one hand, roles are norms and values made specific; on the other, they meet the functional needs of the system:

> Roles are, from the point of view of the functioning of the social system, the primary mechanisms through which the essential functional prerequisites of the system are met.
>
> (*The Social System*, p. 115)

The concept of role is an elegant means of illustrating how and by whom specific 'tasks' within a social system are performed, such as the contribution of the role of mother or father to the functioning of the social system of the family. What functions are performed by 'comedians' or 'outsiders' in a class of schoolchildren or small group? Have the roles of politicians in modern media-saturated societies changed and if so why? How exactly is the role of the chief executive of a major corporation defined, what is her function within it? It was a seemingly straightforward matter to broach all these issues through the concept of role, within a coherent theoretical framework.

Parsons himself surely did not understand his 'role theory' to mean that actors have no choice but to 'reel off' their roles more or less automatically without making any personal contribution. At certain points in his oeuvre he stated unequivocally that as well as behaving in conformity with norms, individuals may of course also feel a deep sense of alienation towards the system just as they may deal creatively with role expectations or change how they deal with them from one situation to the next (*Toward a General Theory of Action*, p. 24). And some of his colleagues, such as Robert Merton, to whom we referred earlier, highlighted the fact that there are inevitably conflicts and contradictions within and between the roles played by individuals, which may be of particular relevance to a theory of social change. But in Parsons' work the analytical spotlight was always on the prerequisites for the *maintenance* of systems – which also explains the distrust felt towards Parsonian thought within the social movements of the 1960s and 1970s; the critical questions which these raised, after all, related primarily to the potential for *overcoming* existing systems. The concept of role, meanwhile, is mainly suited to describing the functioning of *existing* structures. Parsons rarely mentioned system change. It is generally striking that at this stage Parsons had dealt almost exclusively with social action and social order in his theoretical work. The analysis, at least as important to sociology, of *social change* was for long marginal to his thinking. We will return to this issue in the next lecture.

In any event, with this structural-functionalist theory, Parsons managed to lay most of the foundations of empirical research practice within sociology as it then was. We would like to discuss this briefly at the end of the present lecture. For sociologists, and not only for Parsonians, Parsons' functionalism became the point of departure for an extensive programme of empirical research which focused on two key subject areas in particular – areas which Parsons had himself prefigured; *The Social System* included a chapter on learning roles or socialization and another on deviant behaviour. And Parsons' work did in fact provide socialization research with tremendous impetus. This in turn must be understood against the background of a sociology keen to assert itself; research on the *learning of social roles* was a good way of achieving that clear distinction between sociology and the disciplines of biology and psychology. Particularly with regard to the latter, it is evident that socialization research is concerned with a different set of themes than developmental psychology. The focus of attention here is not the development of the child's moral and cognitive capacities, which follows its own inherent logic, but rather how the individual comes to fit into a social order – a process, moreover, whose completion does not coincide with the end of childhood but which is and which must be gone through repeatedly and into one's later years.

The other thematic focus of attention was entirely at variance with the first: criminal sociology or the 'sociology of deviant behaviour' explores the circumstances which lead to the *failure* to internalize values among some individuals, or why the institutionalization of values in certain spheres of society fails to occur to a sufficient degree and deviant behaviour, i.e., behaviour that clashes with norms, occurs as a result. Parsons' theory exercised a major influence here as it was a first-class means of providing a theoretical structure for the field of research concerned with so-called deviant behaviour. However, it is important to avoid a potential misunderstanding here. Parsons and the sociologists working in his tradition merely claimed that social orders are held together by values and norms and that deviations from these are an issue in one way or another in every order – they may be punished severely, scoffed at or merely remarked upon with a shake of the head. Parsons and his colleagues did not mean that deviance *ought* to be punished. Though critics of the Parsonian research programme sometimes suggest otherwise, the functionalist theory of deviant behaviour was an attempt to describe and (perhaps) explain such behaviour. It was certainly not intended to imply a broader political or socio-political agenda.

But let us conclude this lecture with a return to pure theory. Parsons did not – and this reflects his tremendous productivity, particularly in the 1950s – cling to his theoretical position as outlined here. Rather, he worked on key aspects of the edifice of what he himself called his 'structural-functional' theory. Some earlier developments came to an end, some theoretical constructs proved to be dead-ends, but in many respects he also radicalized the positions already developed in *Toward a General Theory of Action* and *The Social System*. It is to this further elaboration of his theory that we now turn.

IV

Parsons and the elaboration of normativist functionalism

Having laid out the key foundations of his *theory of action* in *Structure* in 1937 and made vigorous efforts to develop a *theory of order* in *The Social System* and *Toward a General Theory of Action*, the multi-authored volume that appeared almost simultaneously at the very beginning of the 1950s, Parsons' subsequent work was also characterized by consistent attempts to resolve theoretical problems. However, it very quickly became apparent that a certain tension existed between his theory of action and his functionalist theory of order; it was unclear how these related to one another. While Parsons managed to further refine and enrich his theory of action, as well as adding new ideas to his functionalist concept of order, he ultimately failed to integrate the two theoretical models. In fact, the exact opposite seemed to occur: the more Parsons polished his subtheories, the more obvious it became that they were ultimately out of synch. Looking back on the development of Parsonian theory between the early 1950s and his death in 1979, we are left with the impression that while he made progress with many of the key points of his theory (or theories), he never again managed to achieve a true synthesis, a coherent grand theory. As we set out this stage in the development of Parsonian theory in the present lecture, you will probably have the sneaking suspicion, and for good reason, that Parsons' 'middle' or 'late' work is more a matter of disparate theoretical building blocks than a unified theory. We can in fact make out at least five theoretically significant but very different subject areas from the early 1950s on.

1. First, during the same period when *The Social System* appeared, in *Toward a General Theory of Action*, cited so often already, Parsons conceived the ambition of further developing his theory of action. On this basis he intended to take the *direct* route to a theory of order, that is, closely linking the theories of action and order. Parsons had at that point developed the 'action frame of reference' in purely abstract fashion, merely identifying the components of action without saying anything about what the thrust of this action is or may be, what its concrete goals are or may be, etc. One might say that in *Structure*, as in his subsequent works, which were influenced by psychoanalysis, Parsons dealt almost exclusively with the abstract 'form' of action, but not with its 'content'. This now began to change. In the early 1950s, Parsons took on the task of linking the action theory he had

developed so far with a comprehensive typology of action orientations or action alternatives, in order to be able to make statements about the content or *potential* content of human action or about what the feasible goals and orientations of action may in fact be. Parsons had a template here in Max Weber's famous typology of action (see Weber's 'Basic Sociological Terms', in *Economy and Society*), which distinguishes between instrumentally rational, value rational, traditional and affective action. Parsons has a similar system in mind, and to this end he draws up the so-called 'pattern variables'. What Parsons means by pattern variables or, more precisely, by the pattern variables scheme, is that all human action moves between five dichotomous and variable options, and thus that human beings must choose between five dichotomies, that is, mutually exclusive options, every time they take an action. According to Parsons, these options can be summed up as follows:

(i) Affectivity – Affective neutrality
(ii) Self-orientation – Collectivity-orientation
(iii) Universalism – Particularism
(iv) Ascription – Achievement
(v) Specificity – Diffuseness (*Toward a General Theory of Action*, p. 77).

As far as the first dichotomy is concerned, this means that I can and must gear my action towards emotions or refrain from doing so. In the case of some of my actions, emotions play a role, sometimes even determining the action I take in a decisive way. This is probably the case, for example, in my private life and love life. In other fields or situations, emotions should play a more subordinate role, in my professional life for instance, in which my role in the assessment of student performance is best kept free of excessive emotion ('affective neutrality'). I must, however, always decide what is appropriate with respect to my emotions in any given, concrete situation.

Every action, however, also entails a choice between 'self-orientation' and 'collectivity-orientation', that is, I have to choose whether to pursue merely my own interests or those of the community. The individual is not, after all, always able exclusively to pursue his own, possibly selfish aims; sometimes he has to bear the collectivity and its aims in mind.

With regard to all my decisions and actions – and this brings us to the third dichotomy – I also have to ask myself whether I am acting in line with criteria which relate to *all* human beings, or merely to a specific group of human beings. As a normative dimension is according to Parsons always inherent in human action, I need to be clear about who, concretely, the norms I consider valid are meant to apply to. Do I act in accordance with the same yardsticks vis-à-vis everyone or do I apply special criteria to my neighbours, friends or relatives? Does the precept 'Thou shalt not kill' protect everyone (making it a universal rule), or does it refer solely to those living in my community or even only to certain members of it, such that the killing of strangers or anyone 'different' would, for example, be entirely permissible, which would equate with a particularistic action orientation?

The fourth dichotomy refers to the fact that my action and judgements may differ with respect to whether I tend to assess others on the basis of their social origins, descent, beauty, etc., qualities, that is, for which they are not responsible ('ascription'), or whether I evaluate them on the basis of their own 'achievement'.

The final dichotomy is the choice between action which takes every possible aspect into account and which is thus rather diffuse, and that which is clearly dedicated to a narrowly delimited task and is therefore specific. The actions I take as head of the household are diffuse in that what I am expected to do encompasses both economic (I have to provide for the family), social (I may have responsibilities as a member of the parent–teacher association at the local school) and emotional aspects (as the loving father of my children). My job as a heating engineer meanwhile is defined in a more specific way: I must carry out my professional responsibilities precisely as defined.

It is crucial that we avoid two misunderstandings with respect to this now famous Parsonian pattern variables scheme.

First, the typology of action which Parsons sets out here is markedly more complex than that of Max Weber. This is not a matter of straightforward numerical difference. We cannot, for example, simply point to the fact that Weber's *four* types of action contrast with Parson's *five* pattern variables. It is true though that Weber identifies four types of action. For him, an action is, for example, either instrumentally rational or traditional, but not both at the same time; it is either affective or value rational, but not both at the same time. Parsons' five pattern variables are not, however, types of action but rather *dichotomies*, from which, at least theoretically, 32 types of action may be derived, because each dimension of these five dichotomies may in principle be combined. (This is also the origin of the term 'pattern *variables*'.) The combination of each dimension with the other dimensions produces 32 types of action, as you can easily work out for yourselves. That is, affective-neutral action may take an entirely different form in the four remaining dimensions; it may be simultaneously self-oriented, universalistic, achievement-oriented and diffuse or it may involve an entirely different combination of these variables and thus an entirely different orientation. Now the fact that Parsons has a significantly greater number of types of action at his disposal than Weber does not mean much in itself. Typologies, after all, must first prove their worth within the context of research practice, and Parsons himself was the first to admit that not all the action types derivable at least theoretically from the pattern variables can also be found in the empirical world. Yet this does nonetheless provide Parsons with a set of instruments enabling him to conceive of the highly variable range of orientations that may characterize human action with greater sensitivity than Weber, even if we may be sceptical about his claim that these pattern variables are so exhaustive and systematic that they cover *every* conceivable type of action. You may be able to come up with another dichotomy in addition to the five identified by Parsons.

Second, when Parsons states that every actor makes or must make a choice between the five dichotomies whenever she takes action, he does not mean that the action itself always proceeds in a highly rational way or that the actor, more or less like a calculator, always reflects upon the exact nature of the consequences of the complex choice between the five dichotomies every time she acts. Parsons merely says that a choice *is made* – explicitly or *implicitly*, consciously or preconsciously. The latter, the implicit or preconscious 'choice', however, already suggests that this choice is prestructured in line with these dichotomies, on the level of the personality system, social system and cultural system. All three systems always beat a path for our action, by relieving us of an entirely free and conscious choice of action orientation. In the case of the personality system: 'the person has a set of *habits* of choosing, ordinarily or relative to certain types of situations, one horn or the other of each of these dilemmas'. At the level of the social system, the prestructuring occurs because it involves definitions of roles, i.e. 'definitions of rights and duties of the members of a collectivity *which specify the actions of incumbents of roles, and which often specify that the performer shall exhibit a habit of choosing one side or the other of each of these dilemmas*'. And finally, with respect to the cultural system, one's choice is again not entirely free because most values, which are of course put into practice only when one takes action, are 'rules and recipes for concrete action' (*Toward a General Theory of Action*, p. 78; our emphasis). When it comes to our action orientations, our upbringing and the culture in which we live deny us total freedom. Our action orientations are always prestructured.

As these remarks lay bare, Parsons appears to succeed in smoothly linking his action theory, augmented by the notion of 'pattern variables', with the theory of order with which we are familiar from *The Social System* and its discussion of the three systems. As we have just seen in the quotation above, Parsons is seemingly able to 'incorporate' the pattern variables into his three systems. And these variables allow Parsons to do even more: they are – he quickly realized – important not only because they provide content for his *theory of action*, but also because they promise to solve central problems with respect to the description of concrete *social orders*, problems which had plagued classical sociology almost from the beginning.

In order to understand this we must have another brief look at *classical* sociological theory. A number of authors writing during the early days of sociology typically categorized types of social order in terms of dichotomies. Ferdinand Tönnies, for example, introduced the distinction between *Gemeinschaft* and *Gesellschaft* into the language of sociology, and, to differentiate specific forms of society, Emile Durkheim referred to the contrast between 'mechanical' and 'organic solidarity'. But simple dichotomies of this kind were found not only in the work of these authors. It must be added that they led to historical speculation – if not already in the work of Durkheim and Tönnies, then certainly in that of many of their successors. It seemed possible that the process of history would necessarily lead from societies featuring mechanical solidarity to ones featuring organic solidarity, from *Gemeinschaft* to *Gesellschaft*. Parsons now attended very consciously to these issues. He refers directly to Tönnies and sees his five pattern variables as a reconstruction of what he considered Tönnies' overly simplistic dichotomy between *Gemeinschaft* and *Gesellschaft*. Regrouping the elements found in the quotation on p. 69, he suggests that *one* aspect of the five dichotomies characterizes the spectrum of action typical of the *Gemeinschaft* ('affectivity', 'collectivity-orientation', 'particularism', 'ascription', 'diffuseness'), the other that of the *Gesellschaft* ('affective neutrality', 'self-orientation', 'universalism', 'achievement', 'specificity'). It is not just that Parsons' pattern variables scheme enables him to describe with significantly more precision what Tönnies may have meant by *Gemeinschaft* and *Gesellschaft*. In fact, working with the pattern variables enables us to resolve the fundamental polarity between these two social forms apparent, for instance, in the work of Tönnies and his successors, precisely because, to repeat, the dimensions of the five dichotomies can in principle be combined with one another in an absolutely variable manner. According to Parsons, social orders may be highly complex, far more complex than Tönnies' conceptual toolkit implies, because highly variable mixtures and combinations of action orientations and types of action may be institutionalized. At the very least, this enables Parsons to leave behind the latent philosophy of history that frequently became attached to the Durkheimian or Tönniesian concepts. For it is of course not the case – this is the point of the pattern variables scheme – that, for instance, ancient or traditional social forms are distinguished exclusively by affective, collectivity-oriented, particularistic, ascriptive and diffuse action orientations, while contemporary or modern social orders embody the exact opposite. However, as even some of his supporters failed to comprehend at times, Parsons is in fact making a quite different point here. He sees – as only the pattern variables scheme clearly shows – that modern society, for example, may be regarded as the institutionalization of a highly peculiar mixture of *very different* action orientations. Conversely, of course, this also applies to traditional forms of living together, which do not, as we might assume if we adopt Tönnies' categories, solely involve elements typical of the *Gemeinschaft*. This oddly composite reality can be well illustrated through the example of modern doctors, a profession which, as we discovered in the previous lecture, Parsons had investigated at an early stage. In practising his profession, the doctor frequently has to cope with almost contradictory action orientations. On the one hand, he has an obligation to regard patients' bodies as affectively neutral objects, which must be examined and treated scientifically, rather than, for example, as sexual or emotionally laden objects. At the same time, in his private life, the doctor himself is of course a human being with sexual desires. The doctor must simply put up with this tension, which is to some extent ratcheted up even further by the fact that he cannot exude scientific coolness and authority to the exclusion of all else in his professional life, but must also show empathy, understanding, emotionality, etc., if the doctor–patient relationship is to be a productive one. But even if one considers the doctor only in the context of his professional role, it does not follow that his options for action are restricted to the aspects of the pattern variables scheme relating to the *Gesellschaft*. Should the doctor's attitude towards the patient be scientific, coldly calculating, focused on specific tasks and affectively neutral, this by no means gives rise, as one might expect, to an action orientation that privileges the pursuit of his *own* goals and ends. The medical profession, as we learned in the previous lecture, has developed a set of professional ethics that entails certain obligations to the *collectivity*, such as the duty to provide medical assistance at all times, even if there is no prospect of financial compensation.

The 'pattern variables' open up the possibility of describing very different social forms *in all their complexity*, and Parsons immediately sees that this conceptual toolkit can also be used for comparative studies. How differently and to what varying degrees have societies institutionalized the dimensions of the 'pattern variables'? How, for instance, does German society differ from that of the United States with respect to the institutionalization of achievement orientations? How exactly do 'primitive societies' differ from modern Western societies in terms of the social anchoring and deployment of universalistic action orientations and norms? Parsons, and this is worth repeating, was very careful in his statements on these topics, in contrast to the supporters of modernization theory, which we shall look at later, who invoked Parsons' work to some extent. The various dimensions of the 'pattern variables' vary independently, which is why according to Parsons such simple dichotomies of social order as 'traditional versus modern societies', or '*Gemeinschaft* versus *Gesellschaft*' do more to distort reality than to elucidate it. As we have seen, Parsons assumed the existence of *complex* mixtures of institutionalized action orientations – and according to him this was true both of so-called 'simple' and of 'modern' Western societies.

So far, our remarks on Parsons' pattern variables sound extremely positive. They remain to this day an important means of analysing the orientation of action and the particular form taken by patterns of social order. Parsons himself, however – and we will be casting light on the reasons for this in what follows – was not entirely satisfied with this instrument, above all because of two interconnected and increasingly apparent problems. *First*, given the number of institutionalized action orientations possible in a society – you will recall the figure of 32 mentioned earlier – it was difficult to come up with a manageable classification system capable of dealing with different societies in a simple and persuasive manner, with which one might smoothly carry out empirical studies, particularly of a comparative nature. The pattern variables were to some extent overly complex. The dichotomy between traditional and modern society, so suggestive in later modernization theory, was anything but appropriate; but it was significantly easier to use, especially as this polarity facilitated a clear and at first sight convincing distinction between modern Western societies and the 'rest'. It seemed a near-hopeless task to replace this with the tremendously complex 'pattern variables'. *Second*, the pattern variables also proved rather more difficult to integrate into Parsons' own theory of order than was apparent initially. It was, it is true, easy enough to grasp the idea that only one particular expression of the 'pattern variables', specific to the individual, social fabric or culture, prestructures the actions taken within the personality and social system or the patterns identifiable within the cultural system. It was thus possible to suggest that the 'pattern variables' could be easily reconciled with functionalist role theory; after all, roles also prefigure the options for action open to individuals. But how the *content* of the pattern variables, those five dichotomous options for action, relate to functionalist thought as a whole, remained obscure. How do the 'pattern variables' or their concrete expression through action relate to the notion that the various systems feature abstract functional prerequisites? If action is, for example, affective-neutral, diffuse, particularistic, etc., does this have anything to do with the prerequisites for a system's survival? And if so, what exactly? Parsons was unable to answer these questions, as he concedes immediately in *Toward a General Theory of Action*:

> It should be clear that the classification of the value components of need-dispositions and of role-expectations in terms of the pattern variables is a *first step* toward the construction of a dynamic theory of systems of action. To advance toward empirical significance, these classifications will have to be related to the functional problems of on-going systems of action.
>
> (p. 93)

As Parsons' oeuvre developed further, he was to try again and again to incorporate the 'pattern variables' into his functionalist scheme of order. He attempted to explain how these are linked with the functional requirements of action systems or how the 'pattern variables', that is, these five action dichotomies *specifically*, can in fact be derived from these functional requirements; in this, he was far more loquacious than convincing. With tremendous doggedness he tried to show that the pattern variables, designed with action theory in mind, led smoothly to a functionalist theory of order. Yet perhaps Parsons himself secretly noticed that none of this sounded particularly plausible, which would explain why his subsequent theoretical efforts were increasingly focused on elaborating the theory of order, which involved further refining and even radicalizing his functionalist ideas; all of which he may have done as a result of a sense that, having failed to show that one could progress from action theory to a theory of order, he now had to take the opposite route, *progressing from a theory of order to action theory*. This brings us to the second focus of Parsons' theoretical work since the 1950s, one which clearly took hold only *after* the appearance of *The Social System* and *Toward a General Theory of Action*.

2. Parsons now began to put tremendous effort into developing the functionalist theory of order, attempting to systematize the functions which the various systems must perform. As we noted very generally in the previous lecture on the edifice of functionalist thought, it is always possible to identify a whole range of functions when observing social phenomena, which the latter perform with respect to a greater whole. Supposing that these functions can be shown to be plausible, it is of course unsatisfactory if differing numbers of perhaps quite disparate functional ascriptions are made depending on the specific case. Parsons, understandably, clearly felt the need to systematize in this regard, by asking whether the functions that systems must perform can be summed up in some way. Could one even claim that every social system has a certain number of clearly identifiable functions to perform? For the purposes of systematization, this would of course be ideal. Parsons had come to believe that it was possible to answer this question in the affirmative.

In *The Social System* and *Toward a General Theory of Action*, Parsons had already taken some initial steps in this direction. Among other things, he had established that at least two functions must be performed to maintain the equilibrium in systems: the allocation function, that is, the provision of resources for the particular system, and the integration function, in other words the coordination between the subunits within the system (see for example *Toward a General Theory of Action*, p. 108). His collaborative work with the social psychologist Robert Bales (1916–2004), who had already produced a series of studies on small group dynamics, enabled Parsons to develop this insight much further. Within the framework of his work with

Bales, Parsons came to the conclusion that it is possible to make generalizing statements about the functions which must be performed within small groups which far exceed his previous attempts to determine function. In a collaborative venture from 1953 (*Working Papers in the Theory of Action*) co-authored by the same Robert Bales and Edward A. Shils (1910–1995), Parsons, referring directly to Bales' studies, puts this as follows:

> basing himself on broad foundations of sociological theory, one of us has been at work for some years on an intensive analysis of the processes of interaction in small groups. This study has included the development both of methods of empirical observation and of theoretical analysis. ... Our present interest is not in the empirical methods, but in the theoretical scheme involved. The essential approach was to think of the small group as a functioning system. It was held that such a system would have four main 'functional problems' which were described, respectively, as those of *adaptation* to conditions of the external situation, of *instrumental* control over parts of the situation in the performance of goal oriented tasks, of the management and *expression* of sentiments and tensions of the members, and of preserving the social *integration* of members with each other as a solidary collectivity.
>
> (p. 64)

Parsons and his co-authors further generalize these already generalized hypotheses on the small group, asserting that *every* system, and not just the small group, has four fundamental functions to perform. These may be summed up, to modify the above quotation slightly, through the terms '*A*daptation', '*G*oal attainment', '*I*ntegration' (referring to the cohesion of the system's subunits) and '*P*attern maintenance' (that is, maintenance of the commitment to identity-forming values, or to put it more simply: preservation of structure via value commitment).

Parsons also uses the term '*L*atency' to refer to the latter function, because far from being apparent, these values are generally at work behind the scenes. We have now made you familiar with Parsons' famous AGIL scheme – an acronym made up of the four initial letters of the functions which each system must perform. Parsons' thesis is thus that each system has to adapt to the external environment or to other systems; formulate and attain certain goals; integrate its subunits and various parts; and be organized in such a way that certain values apply within it in binding fashion.

In this collaborative work Parsons again spends a lot of time trying to explain how the 'pattern variables' relate to the AGIL scheme, and one may perhaps, though only with a great deal of goodwill, accept his reasoning (see *Working Papers*, pp. 88ff.). In any case, it is evident that his argument here revolves not primarily around a given act, but around the prerequisites for the maintenance of systems. What we are trying to bring out here is that Parsons is increasingly concerned with the theoretical problems of *functionalist* thought and that this causes him to gradually lose sight of action, if indeed, as we shall see when we examine his later work, he does not in fact attempt to describe action itself in a functionalist manner or to *derive* it from the needs of the system.

Parsons now defines systems as 'boundary maintaining systems', which are delimited vis-à-vis their environment and other systems. If one argues from a macrosociological perspective, viewing, for example, whole societies as systems, and if one applies the AGIL model, also called the four-function paradigm, to them, this gives rise to the theory of functionally differentiated societal subsystems. One may then assert that within the system of society (as a whole) the subsystem of the economy performs the adaptive function (A), the subsystem of politics that of goal attainment (G), the subsystem of the 'societal community', Parsons' term for non-political and non-economic institutional structures very generally, that of integration (I) and the cultural subsystem or what Parsons terms the 'fiduciary system' that of maintaining commitment to identity-forming values (L) (see Figure 4.1).

The interesting point here is that according to Parsons this method of ascribing the four functions may be applied to every system. One may, as in the scheme below, regard the economy as a subsystem of society and ask which functions the economy must perform within the greater system of society. As a social scientist, however, one may also view the economy in its own right, as a more or less independent system, and again ask which

A		G
economy	politics	
societal community	culture (fiduciary system)	
I		L

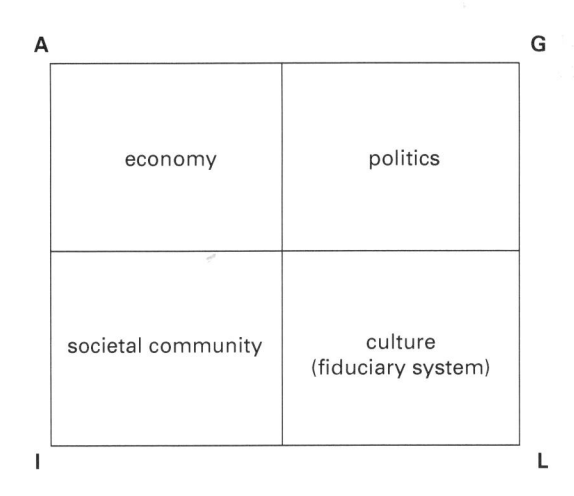

Figure 4.1

subsystems exist *within* the economic system, which perform the four functions necessary to the system of the economy. One could carry on asking questions like this for ever. One may 'descend' to the level of individual companies, or of branches of the same company, or even to the level of working teams within companies, etc., always asking which functions must be performed by which units. Thus, if one inquires into functions which must be performed, the issue of 'system references' inevitably arises, that is, the issue of which system one is in fact referring to. In relation to the system of society, the economy is a subsystem; if my reference system is the economy itself, however, I must ask which subsystems perform the four functions necessary to this particular system of the economy. Thus, depending on the interests of the observer, a system may or may not be a subsystem. In another publication that appeared a little later, Parsons expresses this very elegantly:

> *An economy* ... is a special type of social system. It is a functional sub-system of the more inclusive society, differentiated from other sub-systems by specialization in the society's adaptive function. It is one of four sub-systems differentiated on a cognate basis and must be distinguished from each of the others. It must also be distinguished from all concrete collectivities which, whatever their functional primacy, are *always* multifunctional. As a social system the economy has all the properties of such a system.
> (Parsons and Smelser, *Economy and Society*, pp. 306–7; original emphasis)

Parsons, however, hoped to be able to do more than merely systematize functional ascriptions with the AGIL scheme. He appeared to believe that this scheme, referring as it does to the different functional requirements of any given system, was capable of overcoming certain 'irritating' dichotomies that had long plagued sociological theory. According to Parsons, this four-function paradigm finally rids us of the Marxian dichotomy of base and superstructure and the problem of the relationship between interests and ideas analysed repeatedly by Max Weber, because it apparently allows us to show that social institutions and orders *always* involve a *complex fusion* of different functional requirements and corresponding processes and it is therefore *futile to ask* whether base trumps superstructure, or interests take precedence over ideas. In this respect, Parsons also thought it possible to evade a criticism directed at him ever since the writing of *Structure* – and which was in fact made of him for the rest of his life – namely that he was secretly indulging in cultural determinism and overemphasizing norms and values. The AGIL scheme seemed to allow him to show that his theory was in fact *multidimensional*, because it took *very different* factors and functions into account.

3. Parsons subsequently continued to work on and refine the theory of order associated with the AGIL scheme. In 1956, together with Neil Smelser (b. 1930), he produced the book *Economy and Society* mentioned above, in which he not only meticulously applies the four-function paradigm to a societal subsystem – the economy – but also points to the *processes* that occur between this subsystem and the other societal subsystems. Parsons and Smelser formulate a kind of theory of exchange relations with respect to the economy: what does the economy do for the other subsystems, which 'inputs' does the economy in turn receive from these other subsystems, etc.? All of this was intended, in part, to lend dynamism to the functionalist theory of order. Previously, Parsons had always referred only to functions; he now set out to reveal the processes through which these functions are performed. This was an attempt to deal with another criticism long made of functionalist thought, namely that it is fundamentally static, that it codifies inflexibility. For Parsons, his emphasis on *processes* is the first 'response' to this criticism, a response that he was to hone further as his work developed.

Parsons paid special attention to money as the means of payment in modern societies in *Economy and Society*; together with Smelser he investigated, among other things, how money can function as a means of payment in the first place. In this connection, both authors examined what precisely money is and what functions it performs within the processes of exchange which occur between the economy and the other subsystems of society.

But Parsons went further still, attempting to apply the findings he believed had emerged from his analysis of the subsystem of the economy to the other subsystems as well. Parsons quickly came up with the idea that rather than a single medium – money – there must be several, with each societal subsystem featuring a particular medium through which it communicates internally and creates links with the other subsystems. Money as the medium of the economy thus serves as his point of departure for reflections on subsystem-specific media in the fields of politics, societal community and culture. The end result of these reflections, which he outlined in several essays appearing during the 1960s (see 'On the Concept of Political Power', 'On the Concept of Influence' and 'On the Concept of Value-Commitments'), is, in his opinion, that we can interpret and define 'power', 'influence' and 'value-commitment' as, respectively, the media of politics, the societal community and culture. It is a genuine challenge to grasp this step in Parsons' thought process. It is of course quite possible, on the basis of everyday experience, to think of money as a medium. But it is far more difficult to think of the three other concepts identified by Parsons in similar terms. How exactly are we to understand his notions of 'power', 'influence' and 'value-commitment' *as media*?

Parsons himself quite consciously develops his ideas in this regard in close analogy with the medium of money, or to put it the other way around, precisely because money is *the* classic medium, Parsons tries to identify phenomena exhibiting similarly abstract qualities, in other words, which communicate or convey something much as money does (just as prices tell us something about the relationship between the supply and demand pertaining to a marketable good), phenomena which may be stored (one does not have to spend one's money immediately, one may hold on to it for use at a later date), which may be disposed of (just as I may hand over my money in exchange for a desirable good), etc. Do such phenomena comparable to the medium of money really exist? Parsons answers in the affirmative. To facilitate your understanding of his stance here, we shall attempt to help you appreciate Parsons' account of 'power' as a medium, especially in light of the fact that scholars who have commented upon and criticized Parsons' theory of media feel that his monetary analogy makes reasonable sense here, in contrast, perhaps, to the other media identified by Parsons of 'influence' and 'value-commitment'.

For Parsons, 'power' is the means or medium used to *gain control over the factors central to effectively achieving a society's goals*. Power is thus bound up with that societal subsystem which is defined in terms of its goal-attaining function – politics. According to Parsons, power is not identical to the factors which realize these goals. This follows directly from the monetary analogy, because money, the medium of the economy, is not a factor of production (such as labour or capital) but simply a medium. Comparable factors within the political subsystem would be, for example, tax law, the public sphere, etc., and these may be controlled through the medium of 'power'. Power thus allows us to influence certain factors within the political system such as tax law and the public political sphere. But at the same time, power also affects the other subsystems of society because, for example, it indicates to the other subsystems that 'leadership' is being made available to the society as a whole, that the politicians do in fact have leadership qualities with respect to society as a whole, enabling certain demands to be made of the other subsystems, such as an adequate inflow of resources from the economic system via taxes. But let us hear what Parsons himself has to say when he defines 'power':

> Power ... is generalized capacity to secure the performance of binding obligations by units in a system of collective organization when the obligations are legitimized with reference to their bearing on collective goals and where in case of recalcitrance there is a presumption of enforcement by negative situational sanctions – whatever the actual agency of that enforcement.
>
> (Parsons, 'On the Concept of Power', p. 308)

Much could be said about this definition, and in a quiet moment you might wish to draw comparisons with Max Weber's definition of power; as is well known, he understood power as the opportunity to have one's way despite any opposition that may exist. Here, we wish merely to affirm that Parsons understands power as a *'generalized* medium of communication', a symbolic medium which allows us to take actions of highly varying types, just as money enables us to signify and place many kinds of goods and achievements. Moreover, power – as apparent in the above definition – cannot be equated with violence. Parsons refers to the 'presumption of enforcement', the fact that the exercise of power entails an implicit threat, but that this threat must be carried out only in the rarest of cases; in the main, it is merely intimated symbolically. If power always had to fall back immediately on actual violence it would become blunted, or at the very least inefficient over the long term. No dictatorship, let alone democracy, is governed through violence alone. Were violence and power to coincide, power would no longer be a medium symbolizing something – namely the capacity to effectively realize goals and to oblige others to obey by threatening recourse to the means of violence. Power thus has a symbolic quality precisely because it does not always fall back immediately on violence or other devices; it *symbolizes* effectiveness and the capacity to oblige people to obey. In this sense, we may state that power may be maintained over time, especially given that there is no need to immediately make good on a threat that hangs in the air. Power may thus be stored, as it were.

If you understand Parsons' thinking here, you will also understand why his conception of power differs, sometimes markedly, from alternative versions; for Parsons, the way people deal with power is not a straightforward zero-sum game such that anyone whose power increases automatically takes the same 'amount' of power from others as a result. Parsons thought that it was entirely possible for legitimate power to increase in a society without certain groups within it necessarily losing some of their power. Parsons is thinking here in analogy to the economy and to the logic of money as a medium: just as one's credit facility is increased if one imparts to others faith in one's economic efficacy, power may also be enhanced within the political system if the key actors within it manage to symbolically communicate their ability to attain goals. Conversely, power may also undergo inflation, if this faith in the ability of political actors to influence certain factors in order to increase efficiency and attain goals disappears. So much for Parsons' monetary analogy and the conception of power to which it gives rise – which is interesting in many respects, but takes a great deal of getting used to.

In much the same way, Parsons now uses the analogy of money to determine the media involved in the other societal subsystems, that of the 'societal community' and the 'cultural system'. Because he understands money as a highly specialized language, as a generalized medium of communication, it is clear to Parsons that the medium characteristic of, for example, the 'societal community' must possess similar qualities. However, the monetary analogy comes up against greater problems here than in the subsystem of politics; the economy and politics constitute more or less narrowly defined, concrete fields, which function in line with specific, clearly identifiable rules. Within the tangible sphere of the economy, money plays a decisive role, and it may seem entirely plausible to the lay person that there must be something in the world of politics, which is also a rather narrow field, that has similar qualities to money. Parsons pointed to 'power', and we might be tempted to accept this despite a strange feeling that this 'power' is in fact far less 'concrete' than money. However, things become vastly more complicated – and Parsons himself recognizes that the monetary analogy is becoming increasingly problematic – if we look for a medium supposedly central to a subsystem as diffuse as that of the 'societal community'. This subsystem is not a clearly delineated field, it cannot be localized as can the economy or politics; rather, it contains everything outside of the economy and politics (and culture as well of course). It is entirely justifiable to ask whether there can really be a specific medium valid within this diffuse hotchpotch of institutions, groups and actors of many different kinds. Nonetheless, this is precisely what Parsons claims when he states that the medium of 'influence' performs much the same function here as do power and money in the other two systems discussed so far.

> Influence is a way of having an effect on the attitudes and opinions of others through intentional (though not necessarily rational) action – the effect may or may not be to change the opinion or to prevent a possible change.
>
> ('On the Concept of Influence', p. 406)

While money structures the consumption and production behaviour of the actors in the economic system, while power activates commitments among actors in the political system, within the subsystem of the 'societal community', according to Parsons, the medium 'influence' works by dint of the fact that here the actions of the parties to interaction are activated or coordinated by means of reasons and arguments. This is why Parsons then describes 'influence' as a 'symbolic medium of persuasion', while continuing to claim that the amount of influence also measures the degree of solidarity in the 'societal community'. However, commentators have expressed considerable doubts about how we are to conceive of the effect of 'influence' in concrete terms, whether talk of a medium of 'influence' is truly meaningful and above all whether it uncovers sociologically interesting facts. And much the same goes for the specific medium of the cultural system identified by Parsons – namely 'value-commitment', a medium that supposedly symbolizes the integrity of the cultural patterns within a society. 'Commitments as medium should be defined as generalized capacity and credible promises to effect the implementation of values' ('On the Concept of Value-Commitments', p. 456). Here, Parsons imagines these value-commitments circulating within societies just as money does in a market system (ibid., p. 457).

You will likely have trouble, in light of these definitions and statements, grasping how exactly these media work, especially as it is 'evident that influence and value commitment are less susceptible of being measured, alienated, and stored than money or even power' (Jürgen Habermas, *The Theory of Communicative Action*, vol. II, p. 275). Above all, it seems increasingly doubtful that it makes sense, for reasons of symmetry, to search desperately for media that do much the same as money does within the subsystem of the economy. It is hard to resist the sneaking suspicion that Parsons has merely logically derived rather than provided evidence of these media, at least those of 'influence' and 'value-commitment', according to the maxim: there are four different subsystems, therefore there must be four different types of media. Applying this theory of media *empirically* has in fact proved extremely difficult, and very few scholars have attempted to work seriously with Parsons' theoretical construct (for an exception to this, see for example Harald Wenzel, *Die Abenteuer der Kommunikation* ['The Adventures of Communication']).

Whatever your own assessment of Parsons' theory of media, whatever you think of his idea that all four of these media are mutually convertible, like currencies, you will undoubtedly come across similar ideas over the course of the present lecture series. German sociologists in particular have certainly taken up Parsons' ideas in this regard, albeit in a very different form at times. This will become clear when we introduce you to the work of Niklas Luhmann.

It is evident that the development in Parsons' argument described above is bound up with a profound radicalization of or even change in his thinking. First, by identifying various media and focusing on processes of exchange, Parsons has given up the notion of the special status of the cultural system, which he was still asserting as late as *The Social System*. Here, Parsons claimed that the cultural system was not a system of *action*. This has now been abandoned; Parsons subsequently conceived of the cultural system as a normal subsystem like any other. Further, the AGIL scheme and the notion of subsystem-specific media went hand in hand with an increasing tendency to formulate theoretical explanations of the functional requirements of systems in a language that drew consciously on biology (you will recall from Lecture II that Parsons originally enrolled to study biology) or cybernetics, the theoretical lodestar which became influential in biology as well as the other natural sciences in the 1950s in particular. For example, with respect to systems, Parsons referred to a cybernetic hierarchy in order to back up his *normativist* functionalism theoretically. Just as, for example, a thermostat regulates room temperature by gathering and processing information to control the heating system, in other words, this unprepossessing little instrument is de facto in control of a large energy system, Parsons now stated that the AGIL scheme is also pervaded by a cybernetic hierarchy. The control centre of every system is found in the L field, such that it is possible to claim that the values of a society, the cultural system, more or less control the other subsystems of the society. Thus, one ought in fact to refer to the LIGA rather than the AGIL scheme, because the function of 'pattern maintenance' or 'latency' takes priority over that of integration, as does integration over goal attainment, and as does this last in turn over adaptation. Thus, the idea of the cybernetic hierarchy elegantly sums up – at least, this is what Parsons thought – his thesis of the central importance of values, already present in *Structure*.

Critics, however – and Jürgen Habermas, who we discuss in later lectures, was one of the most prominent – claimed that Parsons problematically 'melts down basic action-theoretical concepts with the aid of systems theory' (Habermas, *The Theory of Communicative Action*, vol. II, p. 247) and that he had converted his theory 'from the conceptual primacy of action theory to that of systems theory' (ibid., p. 238): 'Once the scheme of the four basic functions has been torn from its roots in action theory ... the analytical components of action must now be conceived in turn as solutions to systemic problems' (ibid., p. 245). Parsons' attempt to expand his functionalist theory of order, characterized by ever greater theoretical refinement, ultimately led him to lose sight of action or merely to *derive* this action from the functional requirements of systems. But this did not constitute a genuine synthesis of a theory of action and theory of order, but rather the former was more or less sidelined by the latter. Parsons undoubtedly tried to derive the AGIL scheme from action theory at various points in his oeuvre, to show how the 'action frame of reference' could be reformulated in terms of systems theory; in this sense, he never truly broke the link with action theory, as Luhmann was to do at a later date (see Lecture XI). Yet these attempts at derivation were not particularly plausible. Habermas' critique of the primacy attained by systems theory within Parsons' work is entirely apt.

This tendency was further reinforced in the 1970s (see *Action Theory and the Human Condition*), when Parsons attempted to reconceptualize *action itself* at the highest level of abstraction with the aid of the four-functions scheme. The 'action system' was understood as a composite phenomenon consisting in turn of four subsystems, the 'cultural system' with the function of pattern maintenance or latency (L), the 'social system' with the function of integration (I), the 'personality system' whose function was goal attainment (G) and the 'behavioral system' with the function of adaptation (A). And this action system was in turn regarded merely as a subsystem of the system of the human condition. Within this system of human life in general, a system which of course again has four functions to perform, the action system, according to Parsons, performs the function of integration, the physical-chemical system the function of adaptation, the system of the human organism the function of goal attainment and what Parsons called the 'telic system' the function of binding people to values; this subsystem provides, as it were, the ultimate, transcendental or religious values characteristic of human life. However, with respect to these ideas, Parsons' following grew ever smaller; even many of his supporters failed to see why it was necessary to comprehend every sociologically relevant fact through the AGIL scheme or how this enhanced one's understanding. Parsons' ascription of specific functions to specific phenomena was perceived as rather arbitrary and basically implausible. (Why does the action system perform the function of integration within the system of the human condition? What exactly is being integrated here?) This does not, however, mean that Parsons' late work as a whole was uninteresting or unimportant. On the contrary, we can identify at least two thematic clusters that emerged during this period of creativity, of considerable relevance to this day and about which you should have heard at least something.

4. Since 1956 at the latest, the year of the appearance of *Economy and Society*, Parsons felt that he had solved a key problem of functionalist theory building. Having shown how media function and analysed the *processes* of exchange between the four societal subsystems, he felt able to counter the criticism that functionalism did no more than describe things in a static way. The focus on processes appeared to have initiated the analysis of social *dynamics*.

However, Parsons soon had to recognize that this had failed to satisfy his critics. Indeed, Parsons and Smelser had only ever described processes of change *within* social systems, and never changes *of* social systems. As to how societies change fundamentally, particularly how we are to grasp processes of social change from the first 'primitive' societies to 'modern' Western societies, Parsons' theoretical toolkit at that point could tell us very little.

When Parsons seriously set about developing a theory of social change in the 1960s, the problems he faced as well as his point of departure were relatively complicated. First, at the very beginning of his academic career – in the first few pages of his first major work *The Structure of Social Action* – Parsons took a very clear stand against grand evolutionist models and conceptions within the philosophy of history featuring a strong belief in progress à la Herbert Spencer. Sentences such as 'Who now reads Spencer? … Spencer is dead' (SSA, p. 1) were a clear expression of this stance, articulated again and again as the book proceeds, when, for example, Parsons – as you know already from Lecture II – gave preference to Vilfredo Pareto rather than Alfred Marshall with his faith in progress. With regard to the historical process, Parsons felt that the former had the more realistic, non-evolutionist perspective.

But developments in the late 1950s and 1960s provided an opportunity to reassess this strictly anti-evolutionist stance. First, it was no longer the case that neighbouring disciplines – above all social anthropology, with its strong empirical focus – dismissed reflections on the development of societies out of hand. On the contrary, within American social anthropology in particular, currents had emerged from the 1940s on which tried to take seriously Spencer and similar figures central to the history of science or to identify those elements of their theories worth holding on to (see Wolfgang Knöbl, *Spielräume der Modernisierung*, pp. 203–12). However, at the same time there was agreement among scholars that it was imperative to advance with caution across this theoretical 'minefield'. It was obviously out of the question to simply adopt wholesale Spencer's staunch evolutionism and his thesis that humanity had developed in a necessary and fairly linear manner from simple to complex social forms. Such a conception was all too palpably imbued with the spirit of the Victorian era with its faith in progress and extreme ethnocentrism, a time when the Anglo-Saxons saw themselves as the pinnacle of creation. Nonetheless, in the 1940s and 1950s numerous American social anthropologists as well as their counterparts abroad felt that it was at least possible to think about a *theory* of evolution, without becoming ensnared in evolutionist traps. That is, a 'theory of evolution', a theory of the development of humanity and human societies, does not necessarily have to be 'evolutionist'. Should you find the terms 'theory of evolution', 'evolutionary' and 'evolutionist' confusing, we suggest that you draw on your knowledge of Charles Darwin from biology class. Darwin and his successors had at their disposal a theory of evolution which identifies mechanisms – such as random genetic mutations and their differential selection – which enable us to explain why certain forms of life arise and why some of them become established, survive or even edge out others, etc. This construction entails no necessity, no – as academic language so often has it – teleology, according to which the natural world's developmental tendencies and goals are more or less predetermined. Quite the opposite: some mutations prove to be dead ends, developments may cease, etc. The Darwinian theory of evolution is not, therefore, evolutionist.

Harnessing this insight or distinction and applying it to anthropology and the neighbouring social sciences, we may ask: is it possible to identify stages in the history of humanity without simultaneously claiming that *every* people must pass through these stages in succession, and without assuming that the development from, for example, 'primitive' to 'modern' Western societies was a *necessary* occurrence, in line, as it were, with the laws of nature?

This is precisely what Parsons asked himself. Ironically, he did so in part because models of change had been cobbled together from hackneyed versions of his own theory, particularly within the American macrosociology of the 1950s and 1960s, which exhibited an unmistakable streak of evolutionism and which stood in need of correction. At the beginning of the present lecture we mentioned so-called modernization theory, an attempt to model processes of social change with the help of elements of Parsons' 'pattern variables'. The thesis put forward here was often that the macrosociological process of change proceeds from 'simple' social forms featuring particularistic and ascriptive action orientations or diffuse role expectations to complex forms featuring universalist and achievement-oriented types of action or specific rules governing roles, that is, in sum, from 'traditional' to 'modern' societies (see Lecture XIII).

As intimated above, Parsons thought this view of the process of social change one-dimensional; he, after all, worked on the assumption of a complex mixture of very different action orientations and role expectations in both 'traditional' and 'modern' societies. To assert a straightforward opposition between tradition and modernity was an out-and-out distortion as far as he was concerned. This meant, in light of developments in social anthropology and the predominance of a simplistic modernization theory, that he was now called upon to come up with his own theoretical take on the problem of *social change*, a topic which he had so far neglected because of his near-exclusive focus on social action and social order.

It comes as no surprise that Parsons approached this theoretical work once again with the aid of the four-functions scheme; neither will you be surprised to learn that a good number of readers and critics were to brand this approach highly dissatisfactory and arbitrary. Yet Parsons' basic ideas, laid down in two books, *Societies* (1966) and *The System of Modern Societies* (1971), proved so interesting that they form the point of departure for continuing reflections on social change to this day.

Parsons' basic idea was to describe social change as multidimensional or, to be more precise, four-dimensional, and to claim that the development of societies can take place in all four of the functional spheres which he distinguished between. His thesis – you will need to have another look at the AGIL scheme at this point – was thus that social change and development is possible, first of all, in the sphere of adaptation (A), which Parsons terms 'adaptive upgrading', meaning that societies may increasingly improve their capacity to adapt to the natural environment, to exploit resources more efficiently, etc. In the functional sphere of goal attainment (G), Parsons tells us, a process of change may occur which we might describe as 'differentiation'. He is alluding here to the fact that societies may become increasingly internally complex in order to deal with problems, that the division of labour advances and thus increasingly specific functions are performed by ever more specific institutions. Spencer, of course, advocated the same or much the same idea; in his notion of evolution from simple to complex social forms, he had already deployed this concept of differentiation, but in contrast to Parsons he emphasized differentiation *alone* and thus had a purely *one*-dimensional notion of change. Within the functional sphere of integration (I) – according to Parsons – a tendency towards change may make itself felt which he terms 'inclusion'. He is referring to a process in which societies may become increasingly efficient at integrating people as full citizens into the (political) community, by guaranteeing their civil, political and social rights. As you are probably aware, the granting of political rights, such as the right to vote, was a long and often contested process which came to a provisional end only recently in many countries. Even now, social rights are not guaranteed in many Third World countries, and we are thus unable to assert that everyone is truly a citizen of her society in the full sense of the word. In the USA, it took a long time for the rights of African-Americans to be recognized – a topic which Parsons examined on several occasions (see 'Full Citizenship for the Negro American?', 1967). Finally, within the functional sphere of 'pattern maintenance' or 'latency' (L), Parsons stated, we may observe a process he terms 'value generalization' because particularistic values are transformed into universalist ones, a lengthy process in which religious as well as political upheavals are involved.

Parsons combines these rather abstract remarks with more concrete propositions. With respect to world history, he refers to a specific sequence of revolutions which supposedly led all the way to 'modern' Western forms of society. While Parsons attempted to produce a fundamentally multidimensional theory of change, as shown above, it is in the main evidently the process of differentiation that guides his substantive statements. Parsons assumes that a relatively *undifferentiated* state pertained when human societies first developed, and that the functional spheres became increasingly *differentiated* over the course of several revolutionary stages, a process which then accelerated rapidly from the time of the Reformation in Europe. The Industrial Revolution, Parsons thought, thus finally separated the subsystem of the economy out from the 'societal community', or as he also puts it, the economy became differentiated through a process triggered by the Industrial Revolution. The democratic revolutions which occurred first in Britain, France and the United States in the seventeenth and eighteenth centuries meant the differentiation of the political sphere; the educational revolution which took place in the 1950s and 1960s, particularly in the highly developed societies of North America and Europe, had the same effect on the 'fiduciary system', that is, the cultural system.

A number of objections were made to Parsons' claims as presented here. These ranged from attacks on the arbitrary way in which the process of differentiation was attributed to the functional sphere of goal attainment to the question of whether the educational revolution was really so closely linked with the differentiation of the 'fiduciary system'. Indeed, critics frequently assailed Parsons' functionalist theory of order as a whole on grounds of arbitrariness. More important to us here, however, is another criticism, which we believe to be significantly more serious. The problem with the entire Parsonian theory of change was that its account of the four-dimensional process of change failed to make any causal statements; the identification of these four processes of 'adaptive upgrading', 'inclusion', 'value generalization' and 'differentiation' thus fails to explain anything. If you look, for example, at the concept of differentiation – one which was to play a hugely important role in sociological theories of change in the final third of the twentieth century among Parsons' successors – you will quickly notice that a process of change is only being *described* here. 'Something is being differentiated!' – but no statements are made as to the *causes* of this change or differentiation. The causes thus remain obscure, and many critics of Parsons' theory were quite justified in asking who, that is, which actors, which groups, etc., are in fact driving all these processes, who, so to speak, is responsible for differentiation or 'adaptive upgrading', 'inclusion' and 'value generalization'. Furthermore, and not without justification, it seemed to critics that Parsons' evolutionary approach had ultimately assumed a smoothly advancing historical process, which more or less airbrushed out the *conflicts* and *struggles* over the occurrences Parsons described.

At the same time, despite all the criticism, we should not overlook the fact that Parsons' fundamentally multidimensional theory of social change managed to temper substantially certain weaknesses characteristic of previous conceptions of change. His theory of evolution was first of all non-evolutionist. Parsons by no means believed that *every* society was bound to follow the path traced out by the Western countries. It is true that he referred to 'evolutionary universals', that is, institutions that have as yet been fully realized only in the West, such as rational bureaucracy, the market economy, a legal system based on rational principles and a democratic form of government; these are, in his opinion, better able to adapt to changing environments than institutional arrangements of any other kind. Ultimately, he was deeply convinced of the superiority of the Western model of society. Yet at the same time, he certainly believed that other forms of society survive within their niches and that societies may skip certain stages of evolution, clearly leaving behind the unilinear conception of history typical of Spencer and his Victorian contemporaries. What is more, and this we emphasize as it sets him apart, once again, from Spencer and other theorists of social change, Parsons had a multidimensional theory of change, even if he was to lay a good deal more emphasis on processes of differentiation than on the other three processes that he brought into play, at least in his concrete analyses. Still, his fundamentally multidimensional approach enabled him to draw a more multifaceted picture of historical development and modernity than his theoretical competitors and even his supposed supporters among the modernization theorists, who oversimplified social reality and its dynamics with their crude dichotomy between traditional and modern societies. That Parsons' conception was significantly more sophisticated and commensurate with reality is evident in his remarks on a topic which he was to take up in the last few years of his life, religion. Here, Parsons proved astonishingly perceptive and markedly more reliable in his prognoses than many of his contemporaries. We shall conclude our lecture with a brief examination of this subject.

5. In one of his last major works, a 1978 collection of various of his essays entitled *Action Theory and the Human Condition*, mentioned above, Parsons engaged intensively with religious matters. And it is striking, particularly from a contemporary perspective, how worth reading these texts, almost entirely neglected in the secondary literature on Parsons, still are.

First, Parsons provides us with an interpretation of modernity and modern society which baulks at the explanations put forward by most social scientists in the 1960s and 1970s and which can still be heard today. This common interpretation runs roughly as follows. The breakthrough of modernity, the emergence of modern society with its civil rights and freedoms, constitutional guarantees and democratic gains, is claimed to have been achieved largely *in opposition to* religion, to Catholicism for example; it was supposedly only the age of Enlightenment, often critical of religion or atheistic, which realized, and was able to realize, the democratic values that pertain today against religious irrationality. And the victory of the Enlightenment was supposedly a final one, which will cause religion to recede ever further, leading to what has been called the 'secularization' of the world, from which religious values will one day vanish entirely.

Parsons now turns fervently against this interpretation. While there is no time in this lecture to adduce the evidence that many of his opinions were quite correct, a few remarks are appropriate. In *Action Theory and the Human Condition*, Parsons shows in detail just how much the Judaeo-Christian tradition has shaped the Western world, a world on which the Enlightenment thinkers built. Much of the time, there was no question of a head-on battle between Enlightenment thinkers and religion. The idea of 'inclusion', for example, the brotherhood of all human beings, was nothing new to Christianity; this was no invention of the French Revolution. Individualism, which we have become accustomed to interpreting as a purely secular phenomenon, had its roots in certain Protestant sects, as

Max Weber himself of course acknowledged (see for example the essays 'Christianity' and 'Durkheim on Religion Revisited' in *Action Theory and the Human Condition*). If this Parsonian perspective is correct, if, for example, human rights have their origins in religion (see Joas, 'The Gift of Life'), then this would require us to think about whether there may be good reasons, in the largely secularized, perhaps continuously secularizing societies of modern Europe, for example, to provide institutional protection for that space *remaining to* religion, rather than further undermining it by means of legislation or legal rulings. At the very least, reading Parsons may *sensitize* us to such issues.

Parsons even manages to correct the common thesis of the inexorable secularization of the world. It ought by now to be clear that this thesis is unambiguously Eurocentric. The notion that religion is on the retreat in the modern world applies at most to Europe, but is quite wrong even with respect to the USA, and much the same can be said of other parts of the world, in which religious life continues to display tremendous vitality. Parsons' achievement was to show in various essays that rather than being on the wane, the religious impulse persists, and that the impression of advancing secularization often rests on no more than a false perspective. In many contexts, such as the USA, religion is not simply disappearing, but is at most being transformed: religious values such as brotherliness and individualism are being recast in secular form. Problematically, according to Parsons, secularization is generally interpreted as the unilinear decline of religion or as the replacement of religious by secular values. Meanwhile, another at least as plausible interpretation is only rarely taken into consideration, 'namely that the secular order may change in the direction of closer approximation of the normative models provided by a religion, or by religion more generally' (*Action Theory and the Human Condition*, p. 240).

Even now, this shift in how we see the process of secularization, described so often by social scientists, a shift for which Parsons called in the 1970s, can dislodge ingrained perspectives within sociological research on religion that all too often give rise to highly problematical interpretations of the contemporary era. Because there is one thing which practically everyone agrees on: traditional secularization theory as formulated by many social scientists from the 1960s on has failed dramatically outside of the European context. Recourse to Parsons' near-forgotten later works would surely help rectify much of this problem.

We are nearing the end of our three lectures on Parsons, whose work, as you are probably beginning to realize, was of impressive and perhaps unmatched theoretical complexity. If you would like to take another brief look at his oeuvre as a whole, we advise you to read the precise account 'Talcott Parsons' by Victor Lidz; for a more in-depth engagement with Parsons, we particularly recommend the fourth volume of Jeffrey Alexander's *Theoretical Logic in Sociology*.

Both accounts are in sympathy with Parsons' theoretical endeavours and manage to comprehend and convey the internal logic of his system of thought. But as you already know, Parsons' work was also received with a great deal of scepticism, and in the late 1960s there were far more critics than advocates. While, as we have mentioned, we will be showing in the following lectures how succeeding sociologists have slaved away to develop Parsons' insights, we shall sum up here with an overview of the key criticisms made of Parsons' oeuvre, some of them politically motivated:

(A) We have already touched on the first point several times. As it will continue to crop up again and again there is no need to discuss it further here: all in all, Parsons clearly failed to match his theory of action with a satisfactory theory of order. Functionalism was ill-suited to the task. Or to put it the other way round: his attempt to synthesize action theory and functionalism was unsuccessful.

(B) Parsons – critics assert – ultimately presented social order as a value in itself, particularly as his theoretical toolkit seemed unsuited to the study of conflict. This criticism is based in part on a misunderstanding, as Parsons' concepts were of course meant to be analytical rather than normative. When Parsons spoke of deviant behaviour, by no means did he see his role as that of a social therapist determined to save society from social conflicts. There is nonetheless a grain of truth in this criticism. This is apparent, for instance, in the fact that Parsons' image of modernization very much conveys the impression of a smooth process passing off without a hitch; very little attention is paid to internal tensions, as even American and German Parsonians such as Jeffrey Alexander and Richard Münch were to concede. And in this sense it is not too difficult to grasp why the leftist student movement of the 1960s assailed Parsons as a representative of the dominant political and social system, especially in light of the fact that he singled out Western societies, particularly the USA, in which he believed those institutions he termed 'evolutionary universals' had been realized in especially pure form. Today, of course, following the collapse of socialism, we would be far less harsh in our assessment of Parsons' views. For many people, the thesis of the superiority of the rule of law, a rational bureaucracy, democracy and the market over other forms of order no longer seems quite so outlandish.

(C) Finally, Parsons was fiercely criticized because his influence and the nature of his contribution supposedly led to a dangerous divorce of theoretical from empirical knowledge. C. Wright Mills (1916–62), the American sociologist and firm critic of Parsons, had the latter and his 'grand theory' in mind when he wrote:

> the systematic theory of the nature of man and of society all too readily becomes an elaborate and arid formalism in which the splitting of concepts and their endless rearrangement become the central endeavor.
>
> (Mills, *The Sociological Imagination*, p. 23)

But even authors very well-disposed towards Parsons endorsed this critique, fearing that tinkering around with grand theories of this kind would lead ultimately to the neglect of empirical work, as many of the concepts put forward by Parsons were not amenable to empirical verification. It was Robert Merton who, against Parsons, propagated the development of so-called 'middle range theories', understood as clearly testable hypotheses on concrete sociological phenomena and problems, in order to link empirical and theoretical knowledge more closely. Again, the underlying critique of Parsons was surely justified. It led social scientists astray nonetheless. Parsons was of course aware that his work on basic concepts did not always hold out the promise of instant empirical applicability or usability, but this work is necessary if we are to meaningfully access reality in the first place. Whether Parsons himself really achieved such access with his concepts is another question. Yet it is indisputable that work on basic concepts is imperative. In this sense, the propagation of 'middle range theories' may be interpreted as a flight from theory rather than a compromise between theory-construction and empirical research, particularly given that the work of sociologists 'close to the ground' frequently led to a 'mindless empiricism' no less sterile than Parsons' abstract flights of speculation.

In any case, Parsons' theory set the standard for all subsequent theoretical work. This makes his dramatically declining influence from the 1970s all the more astonishing. Many insights already present in his work had, as it were, to be rediscovered by others, and became associated with their names. Before turning to later attempts at theoretical synthesis, it is vital to examine the theoretical schools that were to combat so successfully the Parsonian hegemony that pertained from the 1950s on.

V

Neo-utilitarianism

In light of the increasing dominance of the Parsonian school in the 1940s and 1950s, first in the United States and then internationally, one might have presumed that the age of utilitarian intellectual movements was finally past. Parsons' incisive arguments had demonstrated the inadequacy of utility-oriented models of action; in his first major work, *The Structure of Social Action*, he had already shown how the edifice of utilitarian ideas had disintegrated from within and how leading theoreticians from various disciplines had turned away from this theoretical model as a result. According to Parsons, this was because utilitarianism had never managed to conceptualize the existence of a stable social order in consistent and non-contradictory fashion. After this great feat of criticizing utilitarianism comprehensively yet precisely, there was some justification for Parsons' view that it was no longer possible to take models of utility-oriented action seriously as theoretical approaches within sociology. He did not dispute the applicability of these models to the discipline of economics. But he considered them unacceptable as an integrative theory of the social sciences.

Despite all that, utilitarianism underwent something of a renaissance in the late 1950s; its supporters even launched massive counter-attacks on the edifice of Parsonian thought. One of the reasons for the revival of an intellectual movement that had been presumed dead was that the concept of 'utility', which was constitutive of utilitarianism and gave it its name, was multifaceted and thus open to interpretation. Some believed that Parsons' objections could be got round if one understood 'utility' somewhat differently.

In the preceding lectures we have presented utilitarianism as a theoretical school in which the actor is understood as one who always pursues his own immediate and egotistical utility. In demonstrating the inherent contradictions and problems of utilitarianism, Parsons too imputed to it a conception of this kind. This was and is justified insofar as the early utilitarian philosophers, such as Jeremy Bentham who we heard from above, did in fact declare the increasing of pleasure and the avoidance of pain the decisive maxims governing action for all human beings. And Adam Smith, the founder of modern economics, also stated with admirable clarity, if ironically: 'We are not ready to suspect any person of being defective in selfishness' (quoted in G. Becker, *A Treatise on the Family*, p. 172).

Now, we are of course not bound to define the concept of 'utility' so narrowly. It is certainly possible to extend its scope. In fact, some utilitarian thinkers of the nineteenth century had already recognized this, placing the notion of the greatest utility for the greatest number of people centre stage. A similar emphasis characterized the renaissance of utilitarianism within the sociology of the late 1950s. Ultimately, 'utility-oriented action' can also be understood to mean increasing the utility of a collectivity or of others. In this sense, utility would of course not be defined in terms of *egotism*. We could take it to refer to *altruistic* behaviour as well. Admittedly, extending the concept of utility in this way involves hidden dangers. To describe altruistic acts as utility-oriented is to declare the enhancement of others' utility (that of those who benefit from one's actions) as the well-spring of one's own actions, or to put it differently, in the language of economics: it is to declare that the altruistic giver/donor, etc. enjoys the consumption of the recipient/beneficiary. This sounds unproblematic at first. We all know how good it feels to make other people happy. We give a friend a birthday present and take pleasure in her joyful reaction. In this specific case, we can in fact state that we enhance our own utility by increasing that of others. Nevertheless, and this is the crux of all such arguments, the word 'altruism' loses all meaning if this behaviour is based *solely* on the utility increase experienced by the giver/donor, however it may be obtained. At the end of the day, the altruist would be no more than a closet, highly sophisticated egotist. Amitai Etzioni, one of the acutest contemporary critics of the old and new forms of utilitarianism, lays bare the absurdity of such an argument:

> If one assumes that only the quest for pleasure (and avoidance of pain) *can* motivate people, one must conclude that saints enjoy their sacrifices; they 'must be' masochistic.
>
> (Etzioni, *The Moral Dimension*, p. 26; original emphasis)

This is clearly a real problem, and this insight into the difficulties of the concept of utility was to lead many economists and some advocates of the utilitarian approach within sociology either to strip the concept of its original meaning or to ditch it entirely:

> indeed during the early history of economic analysis, it was assumed that goods provided utility or usefulness in some measurable, psychological sense. Although that misleading psychological conception has been abandoned, the name 'utility' has stuck. So it is now simply a name for the ranking of options in accord with any individual's preferences.
>
> (Alchian and Allen 1977, quoted in Etzioni, *The Moral Dimension*, p. 29)

Much of the time, therefore, sociology of a utilitarian persuasion, which some authors also call 'individualist social theory', no longer speaks of 'utility' at all, but merely of ends or preferences. What was originally a clearly delimited and psychologically defined concept of utility is now nothing more than a formal category. The assumption now is merely that an actor pursues ends (selfish, altruistic, etc.) of one kind or another in a goal-directed way, all of which are fairly unwavering and which the actor can consistently rank in order of priority. This does in fact allow us to leave behind the problems of a concept of utility that can only ever be defined in psychological terms; however, we will immediately have landed ourselves with a new problem. This highly insubstantial talk of 'preferences' inevitably causes us to ask what in fact compels us to categorize such tangible and very different phenomena as egotistical utility maximization on the one hand and altruistic devotion on the other under a single, generic term, and a vague one at that. What is more, such terms tell us nothing about how these preferences arise or how they may change. The old concept of utility was at least anchored in a psychology, however primitive, based on the weighing up of 'pleasure and pain'; the term 'preferences' meanwhile is a mere shell which first requires filling, psychologically (which psychological approach do we adopt?), biologically (which variety of biology?), sociologically (which theory of socialization?), and so forth. As even advocates of the neo-utilitarian approach concede: 'Until we have a robust theory of preference-formation, or a rich body of data, the persuasiveness of explanations based upon preferences will hinge on readers' perceptions of their intuitive appeal' (Friedman and Hechter, 'The Contribution of Rational Choice Theory to Macrosociological Research', p. 203).

Thus, as we have seen, a sociology rooted in utilitarian arguments faces a number of problems as it tries to set itself apart from or modify the old utilitarianism of the nineteenth century. Nonetheless, it has managed to attract new supporters because, in terms of its fundamental conceptual toolkit, it has abandoned the bizarre assumption of individuals acting in a purely egotistical way and has thus succeeded, or so it seems at first sight, in immunizing itself against objections, especially Parsonian ones.

However, before getting to this utilitarian renaissance, to those approaches emerging in the second half of the twentieth century which we call *neo*-utilitarianism, we must address a question related to the logical status of utilitarian theories already subject to fierce debate during the nineteenth century. It may be put as follows: what precisely does it mean, within the framework of this approach, to state that actors always seek to maximize their utility, pursue their goals or assert their preferences? Does this entail an anthropological claim to the effect, for example, that people *always*, and indeed independent of historical period or culture, act in line with these maxims? Or are we aiming at a more limited proposition, for example, that people *often* behave in this way or do so *in certain circumstances*? Or does it mean that people *ought to* pursue their goals, preferences or utility, though we know that this is not always, or is in fact rarely, the case?

If we look at the debates and discussions on this subject since the nineteenth century, it is evident that participants adopted at least three different stances. While Bentham – this is the first stance – produced a kind of anthropology with his references to 'pleasure and pain', that is, he asserted that, empirically speaking, human beings' basic psychological apparatus causes them to seek always to avoid pain and achieve as much pleasure as possible, other social scientists took a quite different view. Max Weber, for example – this is the second stance – did not care greatly for bastardized Benthamite psychology, which seemed to him to unduly simplify the complexity of human decisions and actions. At the same time, however, Weber did not attack the prevailing (utilitarian) model of action characteristic of some strands of economics at the time, insofar as this enabled one to trace the functioning of markets back to the utility-maximizing and thus rational decisions of market participants. He was of the opinion that this model of economic behaviour aptly described an ever greater number of realms of social reality. Just as this model of action, Weber believed, captures the actual behaviour of participants in modern (capitalist) markets with reasonable accuracy (but not the behaviour typical of *pre*modern markets), contexts other than economic ones would also be determined by actors oriented towards utility within the framework of an advancing 'process of rationalization'. For him, the model of the actor used in economics was an increasingly apt means of describing reality. Thus, Weber did not attribute an anthropological status to utility-oriented behaviour, but rather placed it, as it were, in a historical context: he believed that it was only with the advent of capitalism that the idea of the utility maximizing actor was reflected in reality (see for example Weber, 'Marginal Utility Theory and the So-called Law of Psychophysics', esp. pp. 33f.). Others meanwhile – this is the third stance – argued that the notion that human beings are oriented towards utility or ends does not, and should not seek to, describe empirical reality. Analyses of utility-oriented behaviour ought merely to inform us about the actual attainability of goals and ends, enlighten the actor as to which obstacles may lie between him and his goal, and show him how best to achieve his goal. In line with this, the idea of utility-oriented behaviour is thought not to imply a theory to be confirmed or falsified empirically, but rather to present a *normative analytical* model which, because it examines the conditions, settings and prospects characteristic of the rational pursuit of goals, opens up options for action and alternative actions. It is only when actual human behaviour and actions approach the norm of rationality that this model, initially conceived solely in normative and analytical terms, becomes empirically productive. The discipline of economics, for example, has taken this idea to heart in that it assumes that actors in firms and markets do in fact largely behave in the *most rational* fashion.

These three very different stances on the logical status of the theory (or theories) of utility-oriented action still have their supporters, though the influence of the approach described above as 'anthropological' has greatly diminished. Of course, it is at times unclear in the case of a fair number of authors which stance they are in fact adopting, and thus on which level they are arguing: the empirical or the normative and analytical. If we look at the development of neo-utilitarian theories within sociology it is apparent that two key theoretical currents have arisen from the 1950s on, which partly – though one needs to avoid inflated claims here – reflect the differing views on the logical status of the utility-oriented model of action outlined above (see Wiesenthal, 'Rational Choice', p. 436). Firstly, the advocates of the so-called 'exchange theories' quite determinedly picked up the thread of the early political economists and wished to understand social realities as an accumulation or aggregation of individual actions. Just as Adam Smith, for instance, had presented the market as the result of acts of economic exchange carried out by individuals, the so-called exchange theorists now wanted to derive social order in general from the interrelated, utility-oriented actions of individuals. Secondly, the proponents of the 'rational choice approach' also lean on a utility-oriented model of action, used above all in economics, but their view of the logical status of the theory is in the main normative and analytical rather than empirical. Rather than the constitution of social order on the basis of individual actions, the primary focus of their investigations – and here they pick up where the contract theorists of political philosophy à la Hobbes and Locke left off – is on how such a thing as cooperation can arise out of the rational and utility-oriented actions of individuals in the first place, how we should view the relationship between individual and collective rationality and what the constraints and limitations on individual 'rational choice' might be, but also what opportunities it might entail.

It was the so-called exchange theorists who first attacked Parsons' theory in the late 1950s. We shall therefore begin with them.

One of the first sociologists in the neo-utilitarian camp that existed within post-war American sociology to attain a fair degree of prominence, largely thanks to his brilliant critique of Parsonian functionalism, is George Caspar Homans (1910–89). Homans was himself originally a student of Parsons, eventually becoming his colleague at Harvard University. He became known among the wider academic community in 1951 with the appearance of one of his major works, *The Human Group*, a more descriptive than theoretical investigation of human behaviour in small groups. In terms of its proximity to or distance from Parsons, this work was not, therefore, particularly revealing or spectacular. Homans' attitude towards Parsons' oeuvre was, however, soon to change. From the mid-1950s at the latest, a number of well-placed publications marked him out as a staunch critic of his old teacher.

This critique of Parsons' work and that of his functionalist supporters was focused primarily on three points:

1. Homans asserted that the edifice of Parsonian thought could not really be described as a theory, at least not one that could seriously claim to *explain* facts. Homans was willing to concede only that functionalism was a method by means of which one could *describe* certain social objects and phenomena. Functionalism, he thought, merely provides us with categories but, however skilfully these might be linked and interleaved, they do not yet constitute a theory (see Homans, 'Bringing Men Back In', pp. 810f.). This criticism is of course based on a specific and – as the first of our lectures lays bare – far from undisputed conception of theory. For Homans, theories are solely systems of propositions that make certain claims about the connections between qualities and objects in the social or natural world:

   > To constitute a theory, the propositions must take the form of a deductive system. One of them, usually called the lowest-order proposition, is the proposition to be explained, for example, the proposition that the more thoroughly a society is industrialized, the more fully its kinship organization tends towards the nuclear family. The other propositions are either general propositions or statements of particular given conditions. The general propositions are so called because they enter into other, perhaps many other, deductive systems besides the one in question. Indeed, what we often call a theory is a cluster of deductive systems, sharing the same general propositions but having different explicanda. The crucial requirement is that each system shall be deductive. That is, the lowest-order proposition follows as a logical conclusion from the general propositions under the specified given conditions.
   > (Homans, 'Bringing Men Back In', pp. 811–12)

   As Homans was to state at a later point, a theory is nothing unless it can explain something. And in line with the above quotation, an explanation must be structured in such a way that the more complex and specific connections (such as those between industrialization and the trend towards the nuclear family) can be derived directly from more simple law-like propositions relating to individual behaviour (such as that of individuals within families in a given set of circumstances). This lays bare Homans' epistemological programme. For him, the social sciences must facilitate the explanation of complex social facts by means of deduction from simpler causal relationships. As functionalism fails to do this, it is unable to truly advance our understanding. Ultimately, functionalism for Homans was a dead-end street in which sociology risked getting stuck.

2. Homans also criticized Parsons for making his 'theoretical construct' – if we can call it theoretical in the first place, which Homans of course disputes – overly normative. The analysis of norms was Parsons' point of departure. Social behaviour reined in by institutions, that is, constrained

by norms, was always centre stage. It was no accident that the concept of roles had become a core concept of functionalist sociology. The question of how and why norms and institutions emerge in the first place was meanwhile neglected, precisely because it was simply assumed that people always act within an institutional context. If we accept this description of the 'achievements' of functionalism and the critique of Parsons that underlies it, that is, if we want to explain how institutions and norms arise in the first place, then according to Homans we need to turn our attention to 'elementary' forms of behaviour of which the superordinate and normatively regulated units are initially composed:

> Since sociologists often call things like roles and their attendant sanctions *institutions*, and behavior so far as it conforms to roles *institutionalized* behavior, elementary social behavior might be called *subinstitutional*. But remember always that the institutional framework of elementary social behavior is never rigid, and that some elementary social behavior, pursued long enough by enough people, breaks through the existing institutions and replaces them. Probably there is no institution that was not in its germ elementary social behavior.
>
> (Homans, *Social Behavior*, p. 5; original emphasis)

While functionalists have always placed emphasis on the (normative) 'constraints' on the actor or the inhibitions he faces, with this proposition Homans points to the possibility and fact of normatively unrestricted acts of choice, which are for their part capable of explaining the *genesis* of institutions.

3. Finally, and this is of course closely bound up with the above criticism, Homans finds fault with Parsons' sociology as a whole, which he claims is anti-individualist or collectivist, because it understands the behaviour of individuals more or less as a consequence or effect of institutional arrangements. Homans, meanwhile, wishes to turn this on its head and show how macro-phenomena can be understood *and can in fact only be understood* as an aggregation, as a cluster of individual choices and decisions.

All these criticisms are reflected in the striking phrase 'Bringing Men Back In', the title of Homans' presidential address to the American Sociological Association (ASA) at its 1964 conference, which was published the same year: functionalism, he asserted, had thematized institutions, roles and values, that is, *the circumstances* in which human action takes place, but had done no more than describe these things. Homans, meanwhile, called for sociologists to give pride of place to the *actual behaviour of human beings* ('men') in their analyses and to *explain* it as well. But what exactly is this actual human behaviour? How are we to conceptualize it?

In an important programmatic essay entitled 'Social Behavior as Exchange', published in 1958, and then in his key work *Social Behavior: Its Elementary*

Forms (1961), which appeared soon after it, Homans had already left readers in no doubt that he sees the answers to these questions as lying chiefly in behavioural psychology and economics. Homans wishes to understand interactions between people as 'an exchange of goods, material and non-material' ('Social Behavior as Exchange', p. 597). In typical utilitarian fashion, he is of the opinion that all action – and he believes this to be empirically verifiable – revolves around avoiding costs, pain, punishment, etc. and maximizing pleasure or rewards. In other words, the bargaining which takes place between people is an exchange of material or non-material goods, which act as reward or punishment depending on the nature of the good and which actors either want more of, as in the case of rewards, or less of, as in the case of punishment. He borrows these findings on human nature – Homans assumes a fundamentally unchanging human nature that is everywhere the same (*Social Behavior*, p. 6) – from so-called behaviourist psychology, whose chief American proponent was his friend B. F. Skinner (1904–90). Skinner based his theoretical propositions on laboratory experiments with animals, whose behaviour he attempted to condition and thus influence by means of incentives: in the form of rewards or punishments, these stimuli can reinforce or weaken animal behaviours, generating explanatory propositions such as the statement that the more frequently an animal is rewarded for a certain activity, the more often it will engage in it. The greater the frequency with which, for example, one rewards a pigeon with a grain for pecking in a certain place, the greater the frequency with which it will exhibit this particular behaviour and peck at this particular spot. Homans does not assert that human and animal behaviour is completely identical, but does claim that there are similarities in the reactions to certain stimuli and the learning which results from this.

> Taking our departure, then, from what we know about animal behavior, we shall state a set of propositions that seem to us fundamental in describing and explaining human social behavior, or human exchange.
>
> (*Social Behavior*, p. 31)

Homans then goes on to present a whole series of principles of the type '*x* varies as *y*', that is, quasi-natural scientific statements which, for example, entail propositions about the relationship between the similarity of incentives and the probability of respondent behaviour, or that between the value of a reward and the likelihood of a particular behaviour, about the theorem of decreasing marginal utility, used by economists among others ('The more often a man has in the recent past received a rewarding activity from another, the less valuable any further unit of that activity becomes to him', *Social Behavior*, p. 55), or the relationship between frustration and aggression ('The more to a man's disadvantage the rule of distributive justice fails of realization, the more likely he is to display the emotional behavior we call anger', *Social Behavior*, p. 75).

In formulating these principles, Homans is a *neo*-utilitarian: he accepts the premises of political economy, with its utilitarian roots, almost without exception, though he does correct or modify the notion of *homo economicus* in one respect:

> The trouble with him ['economic man'] was not that he was economic, that he used his resources to some advantage, but that he was antisocial and materialistic, interested only in money and material goods and ready to sacrifice even his old mother to get them. What was wrong with him were his values: he was only allowed a limited range of values; but the new economic man is not so limited. He may have any values whatever, from altruism to hedonism, but so long as he does not utterly squander his resources in achieving these values, his behavior is still economic.
>
> (*Social Behavior*, p. 79)

Homans thus takes a step which we addressed at the beginning of this lecture. He takes the early narrow utilitarian concept of utility and makes it more differentiated, or extends it. This, he believes, allows him to grasp altruistic behaviour as well and thus to avoid, for example, the Parsonian objections. At the same time, we again need to be clear about what exactly Homans means when he talks of altruism or values. For Homans, values are merely the result of an earlier situation in which one received a reward. Because novel forms of reward or punishment may arise, they are in no way '*ultimate* ends', as Parsons puts it, but depend entirely on the situation, which is subject to the actor's calculations. This is something quite different from what Parsons understood by values and from that which we have tried to illustrate with our example of Martin Luther ('Here I stand; I can do no other').

Homans' conception of values, like similar neo-utilitarian interpretations, is thus undergirded by a tendency to deny their importance or to trace them back to something else. The crucial factor that led Homans to do this was certainly his belief that the surest and best way for people to live together in a sensible, functional manner is for them to admit with complete frankness that interests, including differing interests, are a fact of life. He was convinced that human beings living together in a society get on best if people, who inevitably behave selfishly, admit this to one another, and refrain from concealing it behind a veil of morality: after all, hypocrisy and moral criticism, he thought, only lead to more and more irrational conflicts. For a fair number of other authors, neo-utilitarian approaches appeal because they wish to 'unmask' social reality. Just as the appeal of Marxism was often anchored in its apparent ability to show how ideas and ideologies do no more than conceal certain interests, uncompromising neo-utilitarians could often boast that they had unmasked the noblest of moral stances, tracing them back to mere calculations of utility. A 'cultivated hard-nosed crassness', in James Buchanan's apt phrase (Etzioni, *The Moral Dimension*, p. 249), really no more than a pretentious display, could suggest to the naive interlocutor that one possessed superior knowledge and, of course, enable one to consider oneself better than other actors, whose base motives, as a neo-utilitarian, one had already seen through.

So much for Homans' analyses of the elementary forms of behaviour, his explanations of human action derived from behaviourist psychology and the background to his particular form of theory building. Should you be wondering how this type of sociology differs, for example, from the *behaviourist psychology* championed by B. F. Skinner, Homans' answer would have been: solely with respect to the broader range of topics which sociologists work on. And Homans did in fact consciously strive to *reduce* sociology to propositions emanating from behaviourist psychology. He described himself, in uncompromising fashion, as the 'ultimate psychological reductionist' ('Social Behavior as Exchange', p. 597). On this view, the task of sociology can only be to study the behaviour of individuals, explained psychologically as outlined above, with a view to determining how it combines to bring about higher forms as several actors bargain with each other, or, to turn it around, to investigate how meso-phenomena (such as behaviour in groups) or macro-phenomena (the structures of large organizations) arise out of the 'elementary behaviour' of individuals. However, we should note here that Homans failed to produce much in the way of such macrosociological research, as the focus of his work was chiefly at the micro-level. What is more, and despite having criticized the Parsonians for merely describing norms rather than explaining them, he himself failed to make progress here. But this is merely a peripheral criticism. The main critique of Homans must privilege other matters, as indeed it did, and these we deal with in what follows.

Homans had couched his critique of Parsons' theoretical programme in spectacular terms, and he certainly touched a number of 'sore points' with some of his above-mentioned objections. Indeed, in our own critique of Parsons presented in the last few lectures, we too have repeatedly asserted that Parsons' attribution of function was at times highly arbitrary and that functionalism all too often blurred the boundaries between description and explanation. We may therefore well concur with the first of Homans' criticisms quoted above, even if we do not share his limited understanding of theory (which sees theoretical work as consisting merely in the formulation of 'x varies as y' statements). Homans also has a point when he criticizes the excessive normativism in Parsons' work: as we touched on earlier, Parsons went so far as to *derive* human action from the functional requirements of normatively integrated systems, especially during the middle and later years of his career.

A justified or partially justified critique is one thing. But whether Homans truly succeeded in offering a theoretical alternative that meets his own scientific demands or which is at least better than the theory of his 'opponents' is something else again. In fact, it seems quite doubtful that Homans' endeavour can be described as a success. The weaknesses of his entire theoretical set-up are all too apparent.

One need look no further than Homans' assertion that his approach satisfies the criteria of natural scientific research, that it is truly 'explanatory', etc. This seems highly questionable, as his approach is immediately beset with the problem of tautology, that is, it explains phenomena by reference to the very things that need explaining. If we claim – as does Homans – that people always seek rewards or their utility, we clearly have to establish what exactly actors perceive their utility to be, what precisely they interpret as a reward. How, though, are we to do this? There are in principle two possibilities. First, one could assert that everyone everywhere and in every historical period has certain goals in common. The problem with that, of course, is that there are no such specific goals to which everyone aspires. The statement 'everyone strives to increase his wealth', is clearly false empirically. There are certainly people, quite a lot of people in fact, who do not strive to augment their wealth. We thus have to rule out this possibility, and in fact no contemporary social scientist seriously claims that this is a convincing route to determining utility. The differences between people and cultures are too great.

We therefore have to look for another option. The second possibility is to ascribe to human beings a subjective standard: what exactly does an actor regard as utility or reward? We have to ask questions about this; she must tell us about her motives, and perhaps relate what prompts her to act. Only then can we establish whether the person involved was thinking in terms of utility, and that this did in fact cause her to act accordingly, or whether the underlying motives were actually quite different. What we need, therefore, is a standard *independent of* behaviour in order to gauge whether the thesis that human beings always pursue their utility, always seek to obtain rewards, etc., is correct. That is, we need to know *before* an action is carried out what the actor regards as utility. It is only when we observe the ensuing action that we can really discover whether the individual we are studying acted with utility in mind. In any case, what we must *not* do is *infer* the utility or reward structure from the action itself, for to do so inevitably traps us in a process of circular reasoning and we forgo all prospect of coming up with truly causal propositions. The problem here is that an individual's action increases her utility by definition. The theory has become tautological, and thus worthless: it explains nothing. The following example brings this out. If I, as a social scientist, omit to shed light on what a given individual is thinking with regard to utility *before* the action to be investigated is carried out, and if I assert at the same time, as Homans does, that people always pursue their utility, then if an armed robber steals from a charitable organization, we can in fact describe this by stating that the perpetrator was trying to increase his utility by lining his pockets with other people's money. The problem with this is that, according to Homans' premises, I could also describe and 'explain' the 'opposite' act in precisely the same way. By giving generously to the local workers' welfare association, the donor again simply wished to augment his utility: he acted as he did because giving generously makes him feel like a good person and this gives him pleasure and thus utility. This means that whatever someone does, he does it with a view to enhancing his utility. Such a theory explains literally nothing; it is quite impossible to falsify. But this means that Homans' own theory fails to meet his demand for a natural scientific approach. Against this backdrop, his vehement criticisms of Parsonian theory for failing to truly explain anything ring rather hollow.

What is more, the prestige and influence of *behaviourist* psychology, the foundation of Homans' theory, declined markedly within its own discipline, because its capacity to produce meaningful findings proved limited: at the end of the day, the assumption of incessant utility maximization, whether among animals or human beings, failed to capture persuasively the reality of behaviour or action. Other approaches have risen to prominence within psychology, and superior alternatives exist even for the analysis of animal behaviour (within the *Verstehen*-oriented ethological research of Konrad Lorenz for example). Admittedly, the key assumption of utilitarianism has not vanished entirely; it appears to some extent to have 'migrated' to the disciplines or sub-disciplines of sociobiology and genetics. Here, based on the Darwinist idea of selection, the assumption is that the organisms which will ultimately prevail are those that *maximize* their 'reproductive fitness', that hold their ground against other organisms or species, that is, those which, relatively speaking, manage to produce the greatest number of surviving progeny. This is the context in which the notion of 'selfish genes' emerged. But in an astonishing parallel to the debate on the concept of utility in neo-utilitarianism described above, scholars within these disciplines also soon began to ask why 'altruistic' behaviour, in the shape of brood care or caring for 'relatives' for instance, exists at all. Again the parallels to the social scientific debate are amazing. The answer that these scholars came up with was structured in an almost identical way, in that they believed it possible to affirm that such altruistic behaviour always arises in cases where it increases the 'reproductive fitness' of the species, at least in the long term. Once again, altruism was 'elegantly' traced back to genetic egotism. None of this is terribly persuasive. However, as the influence of sociobiology and population genetics on sociology remains generally negligible, these issues need concern us no further here. What really matters is not whether the notion of '*selfish* genes' is meaningful or not. More important to sociological theory in this context is the question of the extent to which genes do in fact influence human action. In any case, the findings produced thus far by sociobiologists do not suggest that 'traditional' sociology urgently requires a firmer anchoring in biology and genetics. It does, however, need always to engage with biology and its explanatory pretensions.

Finally, and this is the last of our comments on the problems thrown up by Homans' theory, we may also ask whether his radical attempts to anchor sociology in the micro-level, the way he puts complex sociological facts down to the actions of individuals (which he interprets in purely psychological terms) is really as feasible as he implies. It is in fact all too obvious that seemingly 'elementary behaviour' in micro-situations is always predetermined by institutional frameworks, subliminal norms and expectations, socially imbued orientation patterns, etc., which cannot simply be traced back yet again to the actions of individuals. Franz Fühmann's story 'Drei nackte Männer' ('Three Naked Men') – practically the polar opposite of Gottfried Keller's novella *Kleider machen Leute* ('Clothes Maketh the Man') in terms of its sociological message – brings this out very well. Fühmann's depiction of a scene in a sauna shows how even in a state of nakedness, in which there are no external indications of power and domination – after all, everyone in the sauna is naked and thus equal, a case of pure 'elementary behaviour' – the structures that prevail beyond the sauna are immediately reproduced by means of subtle rituals of domination and subordination. Those present are quicker to laugh at the jokes of their superiors – even under these conditions. It is thus impossible to radically reduce action to the micro-level, that is, we cannot understand micro-situations without referring back to macro-structures. Homans' project thus comes to grief as a result of this theoretical demand as well, which he himself imposed. When all is said and done, the 'elementary forms' of social behaviour which he described are not so elementary after all – too great is the 'suspicion that exchange relations are also guided by norms and that exchange-like orders lacking an institutional and normative framework (such as the norm that "contracts must be adhered to") cannot endure' (Wiesenthal, 'Rational Choice', p. 436). However, if we always have to assume the pre-existence of institutions if acts of exchange are to pass off smoothly, then it becomes highly doubtful that, as Homans persisted in believing, we can solve the problem of the *genesis* of institutions with the same means as that of the *functioning* of these institutions (ibid.).

In view of all these intellectual and theoretical difficulties, it is no wonder that exchange theory, as originally developed by Homans, could not be developed much further. This was apparent, for example, in the theoretical work of Peter M. Blau (1918–2002), who was a tremendously productive researcher from an empirical point of view, primarily in the field of organizational sociology and the sociology of social inequality, but who also had more far-reaching theoretical ambitions. Blau published a theoretical work entitled *Exchange and Power in Social Life* in 1964, whose very title explicitly evoked the term 'exchange theory' coined by Homans, though this approach was often referred to by sociologists as 'behavioural sociology' as well. Blau, who alluded to Homans among others, did develop some of his premises further: he too referred to processes of exchange between individuals and even went a step beyond Homans, bringing out how relations of power and domination are reproduced out of processes of exchange – an issue neglected by Homans: 'While reciprocal services create an interdependence that balances power, unilateral dependence on services maintains an imbalance of power' (Blau, *Exchange and Power*, p. 29; for a similar perspective, developed at about the same time, see Richard M. Emerson, 'Power-Dependence Relations'). Yet at the same time, Blau distanced himself from key Homansian premises: he did not strive to anchor human action in, or reduce it to, the micro-level in the radical way Homans tried to do, because he recognized that not all social structures can be traced back to individual behaviour; he thus consistently refused to embrace psychological reductionism. He was even prepared to acknowledge the positive significance of certain values to social processes, without immediately putting consensus on values down to utility calculations, as did Homans. This in itself points to the fact that he conceived of the theorem of utility or rewards in a significantly less radical way than Homans. Blau referred to both 'extrinsic' and 'intrinsic' goods, that is, those for which no immediate material *quid pro quo* is demanded. He thus left Homans' narrow utility-oriented model of action far behind: 'In intrinsic love attachments ... each individual furnishes rewards to the other not to receive proportionate extrinsic benefits in return but to express and confirm his own commitment and to promote the other's growing commitment to the association' (Blau, *Exchange and Power*, p. 77).

But all these corrections to Homans' original theoretical framework, as necessary and useful as they were, ultimately blurred the distinction between this approach and other theoretical currents, including Parsonianism. The approach was almost forcibly 'watered down'. One could certainly glean interesting insights into the peculiarities and various forms of social interaction by reading Blau's analyses. At the same time, however, since *Exchange and Power in Social Life* frequently alluded to Georg Simmel as a classical authority, readers often questioned whether such analyses could not be undertaken at least as successfully with the help of a theoretical language other than that of exchange. Blau's fusion (see Müller, *Sozialstruktur und Lebensstile* ['Social Structure and Lifestyles'], pp. 71ff.), yet to be fully clarified, of the aspiration to quasi-natural scientific theory building, which rested upon Homans' legacy, and very different theoretical dimensions and categories (his constant references to Simmel being an example) was ultimately responsible for the failure of his theoretical programme to evolve further, despite its many useful corrections to Homans' approach. It is difficult today to name a single contemporary exchange theorist who seriously claims to pursue an independent theoretical programme, especially one clearly delimited from other approaches. Homans' legacy thus proved a dead end. This, however, by no means applies to the project of neo-utilitarianism as a whole.

From the mid-1960s, another variant of neo-utilitarianism began to emerge within sociology, a theoretical school labelled 'rational choice' or 'rational action'. Its point of departure differed from that of Homans' project. The key question here was how it is possible for utility-oriented individuals to join forces in pursuit of a *common* goal in the first place. This is a point of contact with the seventeenth- and eighteenth-century exponents of political philosophy and the social contract who asked: under what conditions might such individuals agree to act collectively, to conclude a contract for example? Parsons of course had already discussed this issue with reference to the Hobbesian problem and pointed to the existence of norms and values as the 'solution'. The exponents of neo-utilitarianism take a different approach. They tackle the problem of order from a very different perspective; initially it was not central to their work. The clever thing about their argument, which takes the assumption that all actors pursue their utility *as a theoretical model rather than an empirical finding*, is that it demonstrates the often paradoxical or counter-intuitive macro-processes or consequences for society as a whole that may result. All of this may seem very abstract to you, but fortunately we are able to refer you to an extremely well-written book which is relatively simple to read and which was responsible for the fact that the abstract issues outlined above gained traction once again within sociology. The book in question is Mancur Olson's *The Logic of Collective Action*.

This book by the American economist (1932–98), which appeared in 1965, was so impressive because it broke with a widely held assumption regarding the origins of collective action, that is, the origins of groups, organizations, rebellions, revolutions, etc. This may be stated roughly as follows: on the basis of similar interests, ends and goals among individuals, collective actions or organizational forms arise almost automatically to realize these interests. This assumption, which seems plausible at first glance, can be found in various social scientific theories, and plays a particularly prominent role in the work of Marx or within Marxism, when it assumes for example that organized class struggle, in which the proletarians unite to overthrow the capitalist order on the basis of a common interest and the capitalists seek to defend it, results from the differing interests of proletarians and capitalists, each class consisting of those with similar interests.

Anyone arguing in this way (in Marx's defence, it must be said that he distinguished clearly between the 'class in itself' and 'class for itself'), that is, anyone who wishes to derive collective action from individual actors' utility-oriented pursuit of their interests, has, according to Olson, a problem. In fact, it is possible to demonstrate that, in the impressive formulation of French sociologist Raymond Boudon,

> an unstructured group of persons with a common interest, aware of this interest and having the means to realise it, will in fact under a very wide range of different conditions do nothing to promote it. Community of interest, even when quite conscious, is not in itself enough to bring about the shared action that would advance the general interest. The logic of collective action and the logic of individual action are two very different things.
>
> (Boudon, *The Unintended Consequences of Social Action*, p. 30)

But why is this the case? Why is collective action on the basis of individual utility calculation so unlikely, if not impossible, despite what appear to be highly favourable conditions? The reason is simply that collective goods or so-called 'public goods' always throw up the 'free rider' problem. Public or collective goods are those which no one or practically no one can be excluded from using. 'Clean air' is an example of such a good because everyone can enjoy it; 'military security' is another case in point as not just a few people but in principle everyone within the nation-state benefits from it. We could list a whole series of additional public goods of this kind, such as scientific findings, a country's cultural heritage, its transport infrastructure, etc. With regard to the proletariat, from a Marxist perspective a collective good of this kind would, for example, be a successful revolution, from which *all* proletarians (not just some or the majority) benefit significantly. The provision of all these public goods, however, entails a special feature: they are made available more or less *independently of the individual's contribution*. Everyone appreciates 'clean air'. As a German citizen I certainly do. At the same time, however, I also know that my contribution to maintaining air quality or air pollution is relatively tiny. Whether or not I behave in an ecologically sound fashion affects the overall quality of air in my country very little or not at all. But because I know this, very simple utility considerations now come into play: because I benefit from the public good of 'clean air' regardless of my own contribution to it, I no longer make the effort to act with the environment in mind. I drive a car that uses 20 litres of petrol per 100 km, because it would cost me far too much money, effort, etc. to switch over to a more environmentally friendly model. At the same time, I assume that everyone else will behave in environmentally compatible fashion, refraining from polluting the air. I thus become a 'free rider', and enjoy the benefits of the 'public good' without myself contributing anything, just as 'fare dodgers' on the underground enjoy the benefits of public transport, happy to leave the paying to others, but are unwilling to cough up themselves. The actions carried out by trade unions present us with a similar situation. As a worker I obviously wish to benefit from the improved working conditions or higher wages or salaries achieved by the trade unions. Yet at the same time, I know that my own contribution to the success of union strategies is negligible; it does not depend on me personally. This then gives rise to the realization that it is more expedient and rational for me to eschew participation in the work of the unions and pay no fees. Even as a non-union member, the fruits of the unions' work simply fall into my lap, because improved working conditions and higher wages apply to all workers. I can thus hope that I will nonetheless benefit from what *others* have achieved through their hard work and the risks they have taken.

The crucial point in all these examples is that it is *not just me* who will think in this way, *everyone else will probably do so as well*. The peculiar result is that although everyone has an interest in 'clean air', every underground passenger has an interest in an adequately funded public transport system and all workers have an interest in a strong union, insofar as everyone merely acts with utility in mind and no other factors come into play, these collective goods will never be made available. This insight is of course of singular importance, as the problems which Olson describes arise in principle in *all* organizations; it is very generally the function of organizations to supply their members with public or collective goods. Let us allow Olson, who examines unions and their organizational difficulties in depth in his book, to help elucidate the 'free rider problem':

> The individual member of the typical large organization is in a position analogous to that of a firm in a perfectly competitive market, or the taxpayer in the state: his own efforts will not have a noticeable effect on the situation of his organization, and he can enjoy any improvements brought about by others whether or not he has worked in support of his organization.
>
> (Olson, *The Logic of Collective Action*, p. 16)

If we accept Olson's insight, this generates novel research perspectives. The research focus is no longer exclusively on social problems and the resulting, seemingly objective interests – Olson has shown that collective actions do not automatically arise from the shared experience of social problems and identical interests. Instead, researchers are paying more attention to why certain individuals take action to achieve a collective good in the first place and which social structures make it probable that people will work together towards a common goal; Olson himself attempted to tackle this in his book and it has been pursued further by one strand of neo-utilitarianism.

Olson himself came up with several answers to these questions as he tried to establish which factors in an organization counteract the 'free rider problem', such that common interests give rise to common action. Olson is of course aware that revolutions have occurred, that organizations, especially in the modern world, play a massive role, in short, that collective action does in fact happen fairly often in reality.

1. According to Olson, there is a fundamental difference between groups with many members and those containing just a few. In small groups, the contribution that each individual can make to achieving the collective good, that is, the aim of the group, is comparatively large – indeed, the smaller the group the larger the contribution. In this sense, it may be entirely rational for the individual to make an effort to achieve a valuable collective good at relatively great cost, even if he has to assume that some others will 'shirk' their responsibilities. In small groups, even one's own contribution offers good prospects of ensuring the provision of a highly valued collective good:

> Thus, in a very small group, where each member gets a substantial proportion of the total gain simply because there are few others in the group, a collective good can often be provided by the voluntary, self-interested action of the members of the group.
>
> (*The Logic of Collective Action*, p. 34)

The larger the group becomes, however, the less probable it is that action taken by an individual contributes significantly to provision of the collective good. The prospect of collective action diminishes. What is more, it is significantly easier to 'keep an eye on' the individual members of small groups than large ones. That is, in small groups the actions of individuals tend to be visible; one is always aware of what the other is doing. But this also means that a kind of social control exists which makes things fairly difficult for 'free riders', with the result that group members are more willing or are compelled to contribute to the provision of the collective good. In larger groups too, of course, the more noticeable the potential 'free riders' are, the greater the prospects of pursuing the common goal. Large organizations can encourage this by, for example, creating decentralized units or subunits, quasi-federal structures in which the members are better able to monitor or supervise one another than in a huge unstructured institution.

2. Groups, organizations, etc. are for the most part capable of *forcing* their members to contribute. This applies, for example, to taxation. Every citizen, of course, enjoys the collective goods financed by means of tax revenues, from water supply to motorways. Here again, a great temptation exists to 'free ride' and refrain from paying tax, because the modest amount of tax paid by the individual, to construct an entire motorway for example, contributes only to a very marginal degree and everyone else will surely pay their taxes. The danger, however, is that everyone might think like this and thus evade taxes. In this case, the state cannot rely on voluntary compliance by citizens, but must supervise the paying of taxes and collect them by force if necessary, and punish tax evasion with fines or imprisonment, etc. In much the same way, non-state organizations also have certain means of enforcement at their disposal, such as expulsion or the threat of expulsion from the organization, denying the former member access to the collective good in question. Or – this is the alternative approach – organizations attempt to ensure that compulsory membership is prescribed in their particular field of activity. This is the case, for example, when trade unions succeed in establishing a so-called 'closed shop' system, which means that *only trade union members* are allowed to work in a firm. This too enables one to tackle the 'free rider problem', because membership in a union and thus the payment of union dues are directly linked with a particular place of work. Olson is expounding a view here that clearly contradicts the prejudice held by a fair number of social scientists, that 'rational choice' theorists

are dyed-in-the-wool market-oriented liberals in all respects. Olson thus affirms that unions have a right to use coercive measures, viewing them as a legitimate means of ensuring that they are in fact able to effectively provide 'their' collective good. For Olson,

> the conventional creed which says that unions should not have the power of coercion because they are private associations, and that the expansion of the public sector inevitably entails the loss of economic freedom, is based on an inadequate understanding.
> (*The Logic of Collective Action*, p. 97)

3. A fairly large number of organizations also offer so-called 'secondary benefits' or 'selective incentives' to motivate members to remain in the organization and pay their fees. Trade unions, for example, offer their members legal protection, outings, cut-price books through union-owned book clubs, etc., to get the free rider problem under control in a different way. After all, the wage increases negotiated by the trade unions benefit all employees, not only those in the union. The trade unions attempt to counteract this quasi-invitation to consume a collective good free of charge, to 'free ride', by offering additional, *non-public* goods, reserved *exclusively for union members*, such as legal protection, cheap books, etc. This increases the incentive to remain in or join the union.

Olson's theory has given rise to a whole series of research topics and a number of conclusions of theoretical interest. Olson himself had already remarked that the so-called pluralist theory of democracy, according to which all groups within a democratic polity have a more or less equal chance to make their concerns known, is wrong if for no other reason than because the level of difficulty faced by different groups in forming enduring organizations varies tremendously. According to Olson, the size of the group itself means that relatively small groups are better able to organize on a voluntary basis, that it is easier for small groups to articulate their views effectively in the public sphere (Olson, *The Logic of Collective Action*, p. 126). Other scholars developed these themes further by investigating, for example, the differing organizational requirements of employers and employees. In an essay that built on but went far beyond the ideas of Olson, and which by no means restricts itself to rational choice theorems, for example, the German sociologists and political scientists Claus Offe (b. 1940) and Helmut Wiesenthal (b. 1938) have pointed to the fact that the organizational behaviour of employees is *necessarily* based on very different principles than that of employers, because the size of these groups differs and because the potential for member mobilization does so also ('Two Logics of Collective Action'). Olson's theoretical toolkit also made it easier to grasp the 'iron law of oligarchy' formulated by the German sociologist Robert Michels (1876–1936), according to which all organizations, including democratic ones, tend to erect structures of domination that enable the leaders of the organization to shirk the 'normal' members' demands and supervisory efforts. They thus impose their ideas upon them despite the fact that the constitution or articles of association entitle the members to determine the organization's policies. As a prominent French exponent of the rational choice approach put it, as a consequence of the ratio of members (numerous and thus hard to organize) to functionaries (few) itself,

> when the organization representing the constituents pursues a politics that clearly diverges from their interests, they are in most circumstances incapable of expressing their opposition to what is happening.
> (Boudon, *Unintended Consequences*, p. 35)

Finally, in the analysis of social movements and revolutions, elements of Olson's arguments were deployed to draw attention to certain accelerating effects in the field of collective action. The German rational choice theorist Karl-Dieter Opp (b. 1937), for example ('Repression and Revolutionary Action'), pointed out that the structure of costs facing individuals within revolutionary movements may change dramatically once the movement has attained a certain size. Its success no longer depends on whether I as an individual take part in demonstrations or fighting, etc., as my contribution is negligible. I might therefore rationally decide to 'stay at home'. Yet at the same time, of course, the cost to the individual of taking part in the revolutionary movement also decreases, because it is easier to evade the watchful eyes of the state as part of a huge crowd or because it has become quite impossible for the state to punish an enormous number of protesters and demonstrators. The Monday demonstrations in Leipzig prior to the fall of the GDR regime, for example, can be analysed from this perspective, as the growing number of protesters very rapidly attracted ever more discontented East Germans, who at the same time faced an ever diminishing risk of individual punishment by the state. A kind of momentum was thus able to develop because the cost structure of dissenting action changed dramatically as a result of the growing number of demonstrators; the costs sank while the 'chances of winning' – of a change in the political situation – increased markedly.

Thus, as we can see, the fruitfulness of the research approach based on the work of Olson is beyond doubt. At the same time, however, there is equally little doubt that this approach itself entails significant theoretical problems. This is in fact recognized by rational choice theorists. In identifying the three supposed prerequisites for collective action, Olson fails to elucidate how the state manages to coerce its citizens, to pay tax for example, and why and how they submitted to this domination at some point in the past and continue to do so. Olson thus always assumes the existence of the state or some kind of coercive power. His reference to 'selective incentives' is also rather unconvincing, first because it is empirically false to state that, for example, the material value of the incentives determines or explains the durability or transience of organizations in some way. Second, these incentives themselves also have to be produced collectively and the question therefore immediately arises of who exactly is willing to volunteer to make these incentives available: 'If selective incentives have to be produced in order to assure production of the joint good, then they are merely another kind of joint good, one whose production must also be regarded as costly, and, therefore, problematic' (Hechter, *Principles of Group Solidarity*, pp. 35–6). Reference to selective incentives, according to Michael Hechter, thus merely defers the original problem of how it is possible for collective action to arise in the first place. One may, of course, attempt to remedy these deficits using the tools of rational choice theory, which is precisely what Hechter does, but all this in itself points to the fact that Olson's theory, so elegant at first glance, is ultimately rather difficult to apply.

A more serious objection, however, concerns the field of application of Olsonian theory. Olson had clearly understood his model of the utility-oriented individual as an analytical one; he was the first to concede that it was quite incapable of dealing with certain empirical facts such as philanthropic or religious phenomena (Olson, *The Logic of Collective Action*, p. 6, fn. 6). At the same time, however, he claimed that his model could certainly be applied to some, even many, realms of reality, above all the milieu of economic organizations, precisely because we must assume that the individuals within them act to enhance their utility and that these organizations do in fact primarily serve the interests of their members. Admittedly, which spheres can be counted part of that 'milieu' of economic organizations is a matter of controversy. We are certainly entitled to ask whether, for instance, we can meaningfully investigate the *origins* of revolutions with this theoretical toolkit, as do the rational choice theorists who have extended Olson's approach. Olson, after all, merely criticized Marx's theory of revolution and class struggle, rather than attempting himself to analyse revolutions, rebellions or social movements. This is striking in that Olson's book came out at the very peak of the social protests of the 1960s (see Oliver and Marwell, 'Whatever Happened to Critical Mass Theory?', p. 294). And it is in fact very difficult, if not entirely implausible, to examine these phenomena solely on the premise that individuals act in line with their ends or utility. Indeed, everything seems to suggest that revolutions, for example, will not break out – yet they do. To repeat, why should I take part in activities in which every act may cost not only money, and of course time, but even my life, but to which my own contribution is quite insignificant? Even participation in elections is something of a mystery for rational choice theorists. They struggle to explain why people (still) vote in such large numbers, though they must be well aware that their vote can scarcely have much impact on the result. Why do they expend energy and time going to the polling station? Rational choice theorists always have to turn to norms (or unconditional beliefs) for help in such cases, which, however, they then tend to subsume under the concept of individual preferences or utility maximization. But this point of departure is in itself highly implausible, as implausible as every *radically* individualist approach to social phenomena, which was of course the approach favoured by Olson. Like consistent rational choice theorists in general, he always assumed that each individual makes decisions *in isolation* and *independent of* other actors on whether or not to contribute to a collective good. Yet empirical studies of revolutions have repeatedly shown that in fact *groups* took action, and social *networks* existed in which individual decisions were taken and which decisively moulded these decisions. Olson's successors, meanwhile, equated dissidents, revolutionaries, etc. with the customers of mail order companies, who sit alone on the sofa studying the best deals, weighing things up precisely and maximizing their utility from this cosy vantage point. This is also the criticism of rational choice theory made by the so-called 'resource mobilization' approach to research on revolutions and movements, a criticism which we can to some extent categorize as a 'family argument'. While this approach does break with 'rational choice' over a fairly important issue, it undoubtedly develops it further in other respects. We might also say that it merely counters the rational choicers' *individualist* rationalist approach with a *collectivist* rationalist perspective, according to which the pivotal issue is how the organizers of social movements manage to mobilize scarce resources such as time and money to further their aims. The exponents of this perspective (such as the American authors Anthony Oberschall, Doug McAdam, John D. McCarthy and Mayer N. Zald) acknowledge that movements and revolts/revolutions always started out as groups. Such large-scale collective events are unimaginable without the social and normative cohesion of groups, because otherwise the free rider problem emerges and the political dissatisfaction felt by individuals is not converted into collective action. In this sense, the resource mobilization theorists break with the *individualist* rationalism of 'rational choice'. But they then proceed on the basis of rationalist premises and assert that these relatively stable *groups* or *collectivities* certainly act in accordance with considerations of cost and utility, when, for example, they attempt to prevail over other groups, overthrow the old state machinery, etc. If the state is weak, according to resource mobilization theorists at least, revolutions occur

> in those societies and at those times when large numbers of groups, with strong allegiance from their individual members, have *rational expectations of positive net benefit* from revolutionary or protest actions.
>
> (Goldstone, 'Is Revolution Individually Rational?', p. 161; our emphasis)

Of course, we may also question this thesis of an unambiguous group rationality – and we will be saying something about that in the next lecture on 'symbolic interactionism'. For the moment though, we still want to find out what became of Olson's research programme.

At the same time as rational choice theories were growing in strength, so-called *game theory* also took off. This theory of strategic games, the foundations for which were laid at the end of the Second World War, is concerned with situations in which the result of action taken by each participant is directly dependent on expectations of how the others will behave. We will look at precisely what this means in a moment. First, though, it is important to underline that we are dealing here with the analytical, abstract formulation of a rationalist theory of action, that is, a theory of action which espouses the premises of neo-utilitarianism. More or less artificial action situations are simulated and analysed by means of at times highly elaborate mathematical procedures, in order to model the logic of action characteristic of rational actors and the results of their aggregated action. Game theory continues Olson's work in that it is again faced with the problem of collective goods, but in a much more extreme form. Game theorists deal with situations in which rational action leads the isolated individual – as Olson has of course already shown – to suboptimal collective and individual results. And conversely, in the same way as Olson's book, game theory contradicts the prejudice that we can make inferences about the actions of individuals on the basis of the potential for enhancing collective utility. Even if the collective utility seems clearly evident, rational actors will not act in such a way as to ensure that it is in fact realized. Thus, game theory also breaks with the assumptions of classical economic theory, which always assumed that the actions of individuals (in the market) more or less automatically end up producing optimal outcomes (by means of the Smithian 'invisible hand').

The various situations simulated or constructed within game theory generally have their own, sometimes very peculiar or amusing, names – such as the 'assurance game', 'chicken game' or 'prisoner's dilemma'. The last of these is certainly the most famous, which is why it is so often discussed by non-game theorists or even by critics of 'rational choice'. We describe it briefly here.

Let us assume that the following situation has arisen (see Boudon's remarks, easily comprehensible even for non-mathematicians, in *Unintended Consequences*, pp. 79f.): two people are arrested, accused of jointly carrying out the same crime, but each is *interrogated separately*, such that they have no opportunity to exchange information. In court, the judge offers them the following options in order to obtain a confession: each will receive five years in prison if both confess, or two years if neither confesses. But if only one of them confesses, he will be acquitted, while the one who fails to confess will be stuck with a ten-year prison sentence.

For the prisoners, let us call them Smith and Brown, this is a tricky and peculiar predicament. Because whatever Smith does, for him alone it is *always* better to confess: Smith receives five years (rather than a possible ten) if Brown confesses, and an acquittal if Brown fails to confess. Brown, of course, will

		Smith	
		confesses	fails to confess
Brown	confesses	5/5	0/10
	fails to confess	10/0	2/2

Figure 5.1

be thinking along the same lines. If he fails to confess, he risks ten years in prison (namely if Smith were to confess), but if he confesses, he receives either five years (if Smith confesses as well) or an acquittal (if Smith fails to confess). Although, or in fact because, both Smith and Brown act rationally and confess, the outcome for them is comparatively poor or suboptimal. Both are sentenced to five years in prison, whereas it would have been possible for them to get away with two years each through consistently denying their crime. In graphic form this looks as shown in figure 5.1; the number before or after the slash refers to the number of years in prison to which Smith and Brown would be sentenced depending on which strategy they choose.

All of this may seem rather artificial to you. This is in fact a fair description; these are after all simulated situations. But such simulations can serve not only to analyse the problem of cooperation described by Olson far more exactly and in far greater detail, but also to disentangle very real conflictual situations and highlight options for action which would otherwise simply remain hidden or at least opaque. Other ways in which such analyses may be utilized, to elucidate the mutual imbrication of collective actors for example – such as that characteristic of unions, employers' associations and the state – and the sometimes irrational net results produced by their actions, can be seen in exemplary form in the work of Fritz Scharpf (b. 1935) (*Games Real Actors Play: Actor-Centred Institutionalism in Policy Research*). Scharpf cannot be considered a devotee of rational choice, but rather uses game theoretical arguments merely as ancillary tools of analysis. The arms race between major powers can be studied in much the same way, because in deciding whether to increase or reduce their stock of arms, the actors find themselves in a situation similar to that of the prisoners Smith and Brown in the courtroom; their entirely rational decisions may lead to a result which, from an external point of view, is suboptimal, that is, in need of improvement.

We would like to introduce you to some other prominent and especially brilliant exponents of this approach. Thomas C. Schelling (b. 1921), a professor of political economy at Harvard, caused a stir in the early 1960s when he deployed game theoretical ideas in a book on military strategy. *The Strategy of Conflict* (1960) is a brilliant analysis of the options for action open to opposing states which, in widely varying circumstances or with widely varying resources, have threatened and continue to threaten each other with war. More important for our purposes, however, is his 1978 book *Micromotives and Macrobehavior*. Here, in nothing less than exemplary form, he shows through consideration of various phenomena how 'innocent' individual behaviour may lead to highly questionable collective consequences at the macro-level. Schelling brings this out with regard to the phenomenon of ethnic or 'racial' segregation in cities through a simple model or game, which you yourselves will be able to relate to. You have a chessboard with 64 squares and a total of 44 coins, of which 22 are one-cent and 22 are two-cent coins. First distribute the coins randomly across the squares of the board. Your task is now to move or position the coins in such a way that if possible no coin of one type is in a 'minority', spatially speaking, in other words, outnumbered by coins of the other type. That is, coins of one kind cannot be placed in such a way that they are surrounded by coins of the other type; no real 'minority' must arise in any area of the board. Keeping this rule in mind, you may move these coins around the board as often as you like: patterns featuring a high concentration of one type of coin are always produced. Applied to the phenomenon of ethnic or 'racial' segregation in cities, this means that people, even if they are not racist and thus have no desire to be spatially divided from other ethnic groups, that is, when they wish merely to avoid being in a (numerical) minority in their immediate neighbourhood, produce a highly segregated pattern through their ensuing behaviour when moving home or migrating. That is, through aggregation effects, the 'innocent' actions of individuals may give rise to so-called 'perverse effects', those which no one actually meant to produce. In light of the omnipresence of such effects or the unintended consequences of action, Raymond Boudon (b. 1934) drew interesting conclusions with respect to a theory of social change. For the pervasiveness of these unintended consequences contradicts the assumption, found all too often among sociologists, of a unilinear historical process, just as it makes one sceptical of all attempts to 'engineer' society (Boudon, *Unintended Consequences*, pp. 7ff.).

The Norwegian philosopher and political scientist Jon Elster (b. 1940) is concerned less with the aggregate consequences of individual action than with this individual action itself. Elster spelled out in detail the different forms that rational action may take and what can in fact be achieved with rational means. In an essay tellingly entitled 'Imperfect Rationality: Ulysses and the Sirens' (in his book *Ulysses and the Sirens*), Elster shows the disciplining mechanisms that actors may use to guard against the possible irrationality of their own future behaviour. Just as Ulysses had his crew tether him to the mast of his ship so that he was able to listen to the sirens' song without succumbing to their fatal seduction, individual as well as collective actors develop disciplining practices:

societies adopt constitutions, for example, to regulate certain procedures and bind themselves with regard to the future such that certain options for action are no longer open to them. But Elster also showed that various goals cannot be achieved or manufactured rationally: it is impossible to manufacture spontaneity, for example. The exhortation 'Be spontaneous!' has no prospect of success because spontaneity is at most a by-product of other activities, but cannot itself be the result of intention, because this would destroy the spontaneity. Falling asleep involves similar issues; it rarely happens when you most want it to. In addition, Elster made a name for himself as a trenchant critic of functionalism, his extremely good nose enabling him to detect in the writings of various very prominent sociologists so-called functionalist explanations, which are in fact nothing of the kind, but in the main mere suppositions, vague assumptions, etc. (see also Lecture III). Mounting scepticism about the fruitfulness of the rational choice approach itself is also evident in Elster's work. As his work has developed, Elster has gradually discerned the significance of the normative; it is fair to say that he is retracing the steps of some of the classical sociological thinkers, from economists to sociologists proper. Elster's major book (*Alchemies of the Mind: Rationality and the Emotions*), in which he tries to anchor the social sciences in a social psychological foundation by drawing on the sociology and psychology of the emotions, seems to complete this process. Little remains of the model of utility-oriented action originally provided by economics.

The work of the great Chicago sociologist James S. Coleman (1926–95) was devoid of such 'defeatist' characteristics. Coleman was *the* champion of 'rational choice' in the USA; he combined his reflections on social action, moreover, with a compelling theory of society. Coleman vividly brought out how corporative actors (organizations) determine the dynamics of action in contemporary societies and argued that the action undertaken by individuals requires reassessment in light of this, because these individuals are always already either integrated into organizations or are confronted with such organizations as they take action (see Coleman, *The Asymmetric Society*). Theoretically, Coleman was particularly innovative in that he was one of the first members of the neo-utilitarian camp to attempt to illuminate the *origins* of norms. Neo-utilitarians of every shade and colour have always struggled to clarify the nature of norms, phenomena which, unless their very existence was denied, had to be taken into account, but which could not really be elucidated using the means permissible or available within this theory. Coleman at least managed to show how norms, which he defined as legitimized and thus accepted rights of control over certain goods or actions, may emerge under quite specific circumstances:

> The condition under which interests in a norm, and thus demands for a norm, arise is that an action has similar externalities for a set of others,

yet markets in rights of control of the action cannot easily be established, and no single actor can profitably engage in an exchange to gain rights of control. Such interests do not themselves constitute a norm, nor do they ensure that one will come into being. They create a basis for a norm, a *demand* for a norm on the part of those experiencing certain externalities.

(Coleman, *Foundations of Social Theory*, pp. 250f.; original emphasis)

However, Coleman was unable to show that this type of norm formation is the most common one. The conditions which he identified for the development of norms, to which still others must be added (see Coleman, *Foundations*, p. 257), were certainly too restrictive, too rarely found in the empirical world, for this. But regardless of this, Coleman's influence was and is so great primarily because he managed, towards the end of his career, in the work *Foundations of Social Theory* mentioned above, to present a kind of synthesis that attempts to resolve consistently all the theoretical problems of sociology worth mentioning from the perspective of the rational choice approach. A similarly ambitious project is currently being undertaken in Germany by Hartmut Esser (b. 1943). In his introductory volume *Soziologie* (1993) (which is followed by another six volumes of the same title, each of which tackles a specific theoretical field within the discipline), he attempts to achieve a codification of sociology similar to that to which Coleman aspired in his day.

Finally, we must mention the Chicago-based Nobel Prize winner in economics, Gary S. Becker (b. 1930), who contributed much to the development of the theory of human capital, which acted as a decisive spur to the economics of education. It was also Becker who tried to consistently apply the utility-oriented model of economic action to sociological facts. This he did in studies on criminality and deviant behaviour as well as on the family, which he described from the perspective of the actors, the family members, all of whom, he asserted, parents and children, find themselves in a process of 'bargaining for sex, subsistence, and security' (Alan Ryan, 'When It's Rational to be Irrational', p. 20). But as this pithy and provocative way of putting it intimates, Becker is frequently tempted to abandon the normative and analytical understanding of this model of action at which many rational choice theorists have arrived and to conceive of it, like Bentham, as a quasi-anthropological thesis comprehensive in scope. And this is highly problematic.

Let us draw this lecture to a close with some concluding remarks on the importance of neo-utilitarianism. We have discussed how the strand of neo-utilitarianism that may be labelled 'rational choice' or 'rational action' differs from 'exchange theory' in that the model of the utility-oriented actor is understood here as a normative and analytical one. The problem of tautology is thus less troubling than in the work of Homans. Nonetheless, the theorists to whom we have referred are of course interested in applying this model to reality, in order to produce explanations: all are interested in coming up with *empirically* accurate theories of choice and decision-making. The question then is in which fields we can in fact refer, with a reasonable degree of plausibility, to rational actors. And here the limits of this model very rapidly become evident. It is almost always possible, in every conceivable context, to demonstrate empirically that actors are constrained in ways which make it impossible for them to act even remotely as the rational model of action requires them to. Actors always lack certain information; it is moreover often far too costly and awkward to obtain all the information necessary to making the decisions and choices with which they are confronted. Sometimes there is far too much information available to them, such that the actors are no longer able to grasp all these data, and come up against the limits of their cognitive capacity to process it, and so on. Even those scholars working with 'rational choice' and decision theory have increasingly acknowledged these problems. One of the consequences was that a number of authors gave up the idea of utility maximization and worked instead with that of 'satisficing', which refers to the adequate satisfaction of needs (Herbert Simon, 'Theories of Decision-Making in Economics and Behavioral Science', p. 262). The actor whose aim is 'adequate satisfaction' is no longer truly 'rational', but rather breaks off his search for the aptest means of carrying out an action or the best information for making a decision when he has found a solution that fits his level of aspiration; he often acts in a rather arbitrary fashion as well in order to successfully take action at all, given all the difficulties that arise in real life. The actor is then characterized as 'more or less rational' ('bounded rationality'). But as soon as one concedes this, we immediately have to ask what exactly 'more or less' means here. How far away is this less rational actor from the ideal typical utility maximizing actor? Just a little or a great deal? Should the latter be the case, then it is clear that the model of the utility maximizing actor is generally a quite inappropriate means of grasping social phenomena empirically (for a critique see Etzioni, *The Moral Dimension*, pp. 144ff.).

If this is the case, the fascinating question arises as to who in fact really does behave like the utility maximizing actors in this model. Empirical studies of these problems (such as Marwell and Ames, 'Economists Free Ride, Does Anyone Else?') have been produced. Interestingly enough, the everyday behaviour of most groups of people differs greatly from the rational model of action. According to these studies, the rational model represents a good empirical approximation of the behaviour of just one group of people, and this group consisted of students of economics! Whether we are dealing here with a consequence of selection or socialization, whether all such students chose this subject on the basis of affinity or whether this particular intellectual approach moulds their behaviour, remains unresolved. What is certain is that the 'neo-utilitarian' model of action features far too many limitations and restrictions. In the following two lectures we will therefore devote ourselves to theoretical approaches which, far from contenting themselves with calls for a return to the more comprehensive Parsonian model of action, go so far as to criticize Parsons' model for its *lack* of sophistication and comprehensiveness.

VI

Interpretive approaches (1)
Symbolic interactionism

In this and the following lecture we shall be getting to grips with two different sociological theories, symbolic interactionism and ethnomethodology, which are often referred to in the literature by the generic term 'interpretive approaches' and are even confused from time to time as a result. The term is quite problematic, but at least captures the important point that there were undoubtedly other significant approaches than the neo-utilitarian paradigm of exchange theory or 'rational choice' and the normativist-functionalist theory of Talcott Parsons within the sociology of the 1950s and 1960s – approaches, moreover, of enduring vitality. Those authors to whose work we may apply the term 'interpretive approaches' advocated a fundamentally different model of action than the representatives of *rational* choice theory, but also one which differed from that developed by Parsons, with his emphasis on *normative* aspects of action. This also explains the literal meaning of the label 'interpretive approaches'. First, it gives expression to the existence of a camp hostile to Parsons and his model of action; the representatives of the 'interpretive paradigm' complained that Parsons' notion of norms and values, to which action always relates, was insufficiently complex. They were not disputing the importance of norms and values in human action. Quite the reverse. But what Parsons had overlooked, they asserted, is the fact that norms and values do not simply exist abstractly for the actor and cannot be unproblematically converted into action. Rather, on this view, norms and values must first be specified and thus *interpreted* in the concrete action situation. Parsons had thus overlooked the *dependence* of values and norms on *interpretation* – and this was thought to be his theory's key deficiency, giving rise to a whole host of problematic empirical consequences.

Second, the term 'interpretive approaches' refers to the fact that the theoretical schools involved are often – though not necessarily – closely associated with *ethnographic* traditions of research and the methods of *qualitative* social research. As it may be assumed that the application of norms and values, but also of entirely non-normative goals and intentions in concrete situations is always a complex and never entirely consistent process, it seems a good idea to examine in detail the milieu in which individuals take action and thus to *interpret* their options for action, rather than working with voluminous quantities of data in a very raw state, which inevitably throw up major problems. For the exponents of the 'interpretive paradigm' it is inappropriate to collect the large quantities of data common, for example, in survey research on attitudes, convictions, etc., because the material gained in this way and its statistical processing tell us little about how people actually behave in specific action situations. Of course, those with a preference for qualitative methods did not differ significantly from Parsons, who never really committed himself as far as methodological issues are concerned, but did set themselves apart from those sociologists (and there are a fair number of them within the neo-utilitarian camp in particular) who try to back up their theoretical statements chiefly with quantitative methods.

Thus, the label 'interpretive approaches' was and still is applied to the theoretical schools both of symbolic interactionism and of ethnomethodology. They have certain points in common, but it must be emphasized that we are dealing here with two clearly distinguishable approaches, whose roots lie in competing strands of modern philosophy. While ethnomethodology, which we shall be dealing with in the next lecture, is in the tradition of Husserlian phenomenology, we are now going to look at symbolic interactionism, which derives from American pragmatist thought. This philosophical current, which we shall describe in more detail shortly, was closely associated with early American sociology. The work of authors such as George Herbert Mead, William Isaac Thomas, Charles Horton Cooley and Robert Park was a direct continuation of this tradition of thought; in fact, these thinkers helped to create and elaborated on this tradition. In as much as symbolic interactionism leaned heavily on pragmatist thought, it was not a *new* theory at all. Rather, it was a *continuation* of the 'Chicago School' of sociology, a strand of research taught and practised with much success under the direction of William I. Thomas and Robert Park between 1910 and 1930 at the University of Chicago. This school of research, which dominated American sociology at the time, was later marginalized by the hegemony of the Parsons school, whose status was becoming apparent in the 1940s and was an established fact by the 1950s.

As we learned in the third lecture, when Parsons reconstructed the history of sociology in *The Structure of Social Action* he (consciously?) neglected to subject the representatives of this school to serious examination. But when symbolic interactionism, as an approach explicitly in competition with functionalism, rose to prominence within the discipline of sociology in the 1950s and especially the 1960s, it was sociologists who had studied directly under the representatives of the original 'Chicago School' of sociology who formed the front line of criticism of Parsons' work. We shall have more to say on this later. The first essential is to explain just what American pragmatism and the adjoining 'Chicago School' of sociology are all about. Four points, it seems to us, are particularly worth mentioning.

1. What is particularly interesting about the philosophical tradition of American pragmatism is that it sees itself as a philosophy of action. In this sense, significant points of contact could have been explored by Parsons, with his early action-theoretical ambitions. The fact is, however – and this is surely also why Parsons disregards this tradition in *Structure* – that the pragmatists developed their model of action against a completely different background. While Parsons came up against the problem of social order and attempted to 'solve' it by making much of the normative aspects of action, within American pragmatism, whose principal exponents were the logician Charles Sanders Peirce, the philosopher John Dewey (1859–1952), the psychologist and philosopher William James (1842–1910) and the social psychologist and sociologist George Herbert Mead, who we mentioned in the first lecture, the central problem was a quite different one. For the pragmatists, it was the *connection between action and consciousness*, rather than that between action and order, that stood centre stage; among other things, this led to new philosophical insights (on what follows, see Joas, 'Pragmatism in American Sociology'). What was revolutionary about American pragmatism was that it broke with a basic premise of modern Western philosophy in tackling this issue. Since the time of the French philosopher René Descartes (also known as Cartesius, 1596–1650), this philosophy had made the individual and his cognition the starting point for philosophy and scientific analysis of any kind. Descartes' argument was that one might doubt everything in principle, but not one's own existence, because the very act of doubting points ultimately to a doubting consciousness, to an ego. That is, even if I was determined to doubt everything, I could not contest that it is *me* who is thinking, that it is *me* that exists: *Cogito, ergo sum*, as Descartes famously put it. Because one's own self-consciousness is the only thing that is certain, it must – Descartes concluded – be made the point of departure for philosophy. To put it the other way round: philosophy requires a firm foundation, and self-consciousness, the ego, the ego's certainty of its own existence, provides this. On this basis, this absolutely secure foundation, philosophy, as well as science, must begin its work; both must be constructed on this bedrock.

Descartes' radical 'Cartesian doubt', as it is known in the philosophical literature, and his attempt to provide a foundation for philosophy and the sciences had a tremendous impact on Euro-American culture as a whole; as intimated above, it shaped much of modern philosophy, at least for those who, like Descartes, make the individual consciousness the focal point of philosophy, and who are thus engaging in the 'philosophy of consciousness'. But this philosophy of consciousness also faced substantial theoretical difficulties, centred on the issue of whether the theoretical move performed in such exemplary fashion by Descartes – falling back on the individual consciousness and the indubitable fact of its existence – itself entails problems.

Cartesian doubt led to a situation in which the ego was the only thing that could be regarded as certain, and one could not take for granted that the rest of the world, including objects and one's fellow human beings, existed. But how does this abstract ego, imagined in isolation, reconnect with the world, to objects, to other subjects? This was a serious problem, a problem caused by the radical dualism between the ego (the soul, the spirit, consciousness – or whichever similar terms one might wish to mention) on the one hand and the objective, animate or inanimate world on the other, a dualism between the immaterial substance of the spirit and the material world of visible action. From the outset, the philosophy of consciousness sought repeatedly, but always in vain, to overcome this theoretically unsatisfactory dualism so fraught with problems.

The reason why it was incapable of doing so, according to the revolutionary thesis of American pragmatism, formulated towards the end of the nineteenth century, was that Cartesian doubt itself involved a highly artificial cognitive move, which led philosophy along the wrong path, to the dualisms mentioned above. The pragmatists' argument was that Descartes' doubt was entirely abstract, thought up in the philosopher's study as it were; but it never really takes and never could take this form in everyday life, including the quotidian world of philosophy and the sciences. It is impossible to doubt *deliberately*. Anyone who tries to do so is quite well aware, at a certain level of her consciousness, that something is the case. Furthermore, it is impossible to doubt *everything at the same time*, as this would lead to complete paralysis and an inability to act. If I seriously wished to doubt that the university is an institution with the object of research and teaching rather than, for example, entertainment and generally passing the time, that taking a course in sociology is a meaningful thing to do, that there is such a thing as lectures in the first place, that the students in the lecture hall do in fact exist, etc., I would be overwhelmed by the severity of the problems; I would no longer be able to take action in light of all the questions simultaneously assailing me. Thus, the pragmatists were not calling for an uncritical attitude to imparted knowledge, but for the adoption of a stance within philosophy that corresponds with a 'real and living doubt' (Peirce, 'The Fixation of Belief', p. 232; on Cartesian doubt as a whole see his essay 'Some Consequences of Four Incapacities'), a doubt which really does arise *in concrete situations*, indeed *in action situations*. If one argues in this way, casting doubt on the meaningfulness of Cartesian doubt itself, the assumption of a single isolated consciousness as the fixed point of thought becomes superfluous. There is no longer any need to assume a purely abstract ego, producing nothing but rational thoughts and separate from the rest of the world. Rather, one may think of the ego as a *sensory* ego, an ego *within* the world and within its social setting. Among other things, it is then possible to see the cognitive process as a cooperative one, one in which several individuals might be involved. All in all, this gives rise to entirely different philosophical problems, but also to new solutions different to those proposed by Descartes' 'successors'.

The pragmatists spoke of doubt *in concrete action situations* and denied the legitimacy and relevance of Cartesian doubt, but they did not stop there. They now had the opportunity to overcome the dualism that had plagued almost every theory of action rooted in Cartesian premises – the dualism between the immaterial substance of the spirit, however conceived, on the one hand and visible action on the other. The pragmatists argued that without action it would be impossible to conceive of mind, consciousness, thought, etc. in the first place. Or to put it differently: thoughts arise in problematic action situations. Thinking and acting are intimately related. This undermines or dissolves Cartesian dualism, without merely countering the idealistic stance of the philosophy of consciousness (based on the principle that action somehow springs from the mind) with a radically materialist stance (along the lines, for instance, that consciousness can be derived solely from biological or physiological processes). For the pragmatists, mind, thought and consciousness are not material or immaterial substances at all. Rather, consciousness, thought and mind are understood *in terms of their functional significance with respect to action*: in the view of the pragmatists, the work of consciousness is done whenever we find ourselves facing a problem within a given situation. This is precisely the point at which *thinking* occurs. It is problem situations which irritate the actor, necessarily making him aware of new objects and aspects of reality. These he then attempts to order and understand. In short, he begins to think. Only when the quasi-natural flow of everyday action is interrupted by a problem are the components of the situation, formerly taken for granted, reanalysed. If a solution is found, it can be stored by the actor and retrieved in similar situations in future.

So much for the *philosophical* consequences of pragmatist thought. Its *sociological* relevance is probably not yet apparent, excepting perhaps the fact that this theoretical tradition conceives of the actor as an *active* being, as seeking and problem solving, rather than a passive one spurred to action only if certain stimuli appear. Thus, stimuli as such do not exist, but are defined as such within the particular action situation. It was only with the writings of John Dewey and above all George Herbert Mead that the relevance of pragmatist thought to the disciplines of *sociology* and *social psychology* became completely clear.

2. The crucial thing about Mead's thought is that, rather than focusing his analyses on situations of action vis-à-vis the material environment, he emphasized situations of interpersonal action (on what follows, see Joas, *G. H. Mead: A Contemporary Re-examination of his Thought*). Particularly in everyday life, there are many situations in which I myself affect other

individuals, in which my action triggers something off in the other. I myself am, as it were, a source of stimuli for others. Should a problem of communication arise as these interpersonal events take place, I notice *how* I affect others, in as much as these others react to me in turn. We might say that my ego is reflected back to me in the reaction of the other or others. With this idea, Mead laid the foundation stone for a theory of the process of identity formation, which became the core of a theory of socialization as well. With the conceptual tools of pragmatism, he shed light on the genesis of 'self-consciousness' in situations of interaction. Our attention here cannot be focused on the individual actor alone, but on the actor *among other actors*. Mead thus broke fundamentally with the notion that social psychology or sociology could be based on the individual subject. Instead, he underlined that the social sciences and humanities must resolutely embrace an *inter*subjective perspective. But in order to be able to do so, in order to grasp intersubjectivity, it was necessary to put together an anthropological theory of *communication*, for which Mead also laid the foundations.

3. For Mead, human beings are unique in that they use symbols. Symbols are objects, gestures or speech sounds which people use to signal something to others, to represent something. Crucially, the meaning of these symbols arises within the interaction. Symbols are thus defined *socially* and thus differ greatly from one culture to another. Animals use gestures as well, but these are not symbols. When dogs bare their teeth, for example, their aggressiveness is certainly clearly apparent. But one would hardly state that the dog had decided to express its rage in this particular way. These gestures are instinctual and thus, apart from certain modifications formed during early stages of development, always the same. Human gestures used as symbols function quite differently. Extending the middle finger of the right hand is a common aggressive and obscene gesture in Central Europe, but its meaning is not immediately understood on the margins of this cultural area because this meaning is assigned to a different physical gesture. Human beings may also think about symbols, consciously attempt to deploy or avoid them, modify them, use them ironically, etc., all of which is impossible in the animal kingdom. It was one of Mead's great achievements that he managed to tease this out, with the faculty of speech the fulcrum of his reflections. For Mead, language too can be understood only in light of the 'vocal gesture', of sounds and gestures.

4. Building on this theory of communication, merely hinted at here, and the underlying ideas about the potential for self-consciousness to arise, Mead also devised a highly innovative and enormously influential developmental psychology centred on the question of how children learn to put themselves in others' shoes, and how they develop over time an independent self through this very process. Mead explained that the self develops in several stages. At first, the baby or infant does not truly understand the

consequences of his actions. Initially, the child cannot even distinguish between himself and the world of objects. Parts of his own body – such as the toe at the other end of the blanket – may be regarded as extraneous objects in the environment. Even when they refer to themselves, toddlers talk as if of an exterior object, their stories often deploying their name rather than 'I'. Little Johnny may say 'Johnny doesn't like that' rather than 'I don't like that'. This is not because he is unaware of the relatively simple word 'I', but because he still sees himself entirely from the perspective of others. He has yet to claim a perspective of his own. Little Johnny understands that it is *he himself* who triggers others' reactions to him, and in this sense he perceives how his mother, father or sister see *him*. He thus gains an image of himself, but one divided into discrete external perceptions ('me-s'). When we succeed in synthesizing these various external perceptions into a coherent self-image, we become social objects in our own eyes. We begin to look at ourselves and to develop a self or an '(ego) identity'. Little Johnny now sees himself in his name. By carrying out various actions, he has learned not only to identify with his immediate reference persons, but also to recognize his own role with respect to them. Through 'play' (as in 'mummies and daddies' or 'doctors and nurses'), he has learned to put himself in the place of others; he has learned from others' reactions what his actions have triggered in them. He is able to adopt the perspective of his father, his mother, his closest friends, and to playfully take on their roles. And at a later stage – with the help, for example, of games such as football in which one must adhere to abstract rules – he is soon capable of understanding not only the roles of the individuals in his immediate environment and their expectations of him, but also the rather more general expectations of a larger community (the team) or even of society ('the generalized other'). A clearly recognizable identity thus takes shape, because as one deals with all kinds of different people one's own ego is reflected back through their reactions. At the same time, the individual is able to adopt the perspective of large numbers of other people, such as that of one's own mother as well as that of the relatively unknown right-back, policeman or salesman.

By this point in his development, the actor is thus able to see himself; he can quite consciously objectify himself, because he is able to adopt the role or perspective of the other ('role-taking'). But this also means that for Mead and all the other authors who endorsed his views, the self is not a truly solid and immutable entity, but one which is constantly defined and, as the case may be, redefined, through and as a result of interaction with others. The self is thus more a process than a stable structure, a constant feat of structuring with no concealed substance.

So much for the core ideas of American pragmatism, which went on to exercise a strong influence on the more narrowly *sociological* studies of the 'Chicago

School' of sociology, though the connection between these basically philosophical and social psychological theoretical building blocks and research practice in the Chicago of the day is not always immediately apparent.

Both pragmatism and the Chicago School suffered a decline in popularity in the 1940s and 1950s, their formerly great influence diminishing markedly. It was one of George Herbert Mead's students who did more than anyone else to counter this trend, eventually managing to gather around him a number of comrades-in-arms. We are referring to Herbert Blumer (1900–87), who had been a member of the sociology department at the University of Chicago between 1927 and 1952, before moving to Berkeley in California. Consciously drawing on the Meadian legacy, Blumer had established himself in the department at Chicago, becoming a kind of intellectual role model for those committed to this legacy. At the same time, at the *national* level, he emerged as the driving force behind efforts to organize those sociologists who wished to draw on the pragmatist tradition. He was so successful in this that he served as editor of the *American Journal of Sociology*, the most influential American sociological journal, between 1941 and 1952, and was elected president of the American Sociological Association in 1956.

It was Blumer who coined the term 'symbolic interactionism' in an article on social psychology in 1938. This composite concept requires explication. 'Interaction' refers to the *reciprocity* of *action*, the way in which the actions performed by several individuals are mutually intertwined; 'interaction' was in fact the original translation of Simmel's term *Wechselwirkung*. This refers to the insight, found above all in the work of Mead, that the task of sociology is not to view the human being in isolation, but as a being which always acts in *inter*subjective contexts, which is enmeshed in a whole panoply of actions carried out by two or more individuals. So much for 'interaction'. The adjectival component of the term, 'symbolic', should not be misunderstood. It does not mean, of course, that interactions are purely symbolic or imparted in character, that they are not, as it were, 'real'; neither does it mean that symbolic interactionism concerns itself only with actions with a high symbolic charge, as we may know them from religious rituals. Rather, the term suggests that this theory understands action as 'symbolically mediated' interaction (this is the more fitting expression introduced by Jürgen Habermas), as action dependent on symbol systems such as language or gestures. And this symbolically mediated character of human action receives special emphasis because it allows us to draw conclusions unavailable to other theoretical schools.

The term 'symbolic interactionism', however, took hold only very slowly. It gained little currency over the next two decades, and it was only in the 1960s and 1970s that a series of volumes and anthologies featuring this label in their titles were published, helping to ensure that the theoretical movement dating back to Mead did in fact receive an enduring name. One may certainly question how uniform this tendency really was (Plummer, 'Introduction: The

Foundations of Interactionist Sociologies', p. xii), but since schools or traditions often depend on retrospective constructions, this is of no further interest to us here. We should now look at how Blumer took up Mead's legacy, what kind of sociology he propagated and which topics he and his fellow combatants managed to install within the sociological debate.

In a now famous collection of essays from 1969 (*Symbolic Interactionism: Perspective and Method*), Blumer defined 'symbolic interactionism' with reference to three simple premises:

> The first premise is that human beings act toward things on the basis of the meanings that the things have for them. ... The second premise is that the meaning of such things is derived from, or arises out of, the social interaction that one has with one's fellows. The third premise is that these meanings are handled in, and modified through, an interpretative process used by the person in dealing with the things he encounters.
>
> (Blumer, 'The Methodological Position of Symbolic Interactionism', p. 2)

These three premises, which might be described as social psychological or even anthropological assumptions about the nature of the human capacity to act and the nature of human communication, are indeed very simple. And you will probably be wondering whether it is possible to construct a theory on the basis of such simple, perhaps even trivial statements, one capable, for example, of seriously competing with the complex edifice of Parsonian theory. Do not allow yourselves to be deceived. What Blumer is identifying here are no more than premises and assumptions, not complete theories. If you were to look for such premises in Parsons' theoretical construct, or other complicated-sounding theories, you would certainly come across similarly simple statements, though not, perhaps, the same ones. Parsons might even have accepted these three premises without protest. We cannot exclude that possibility. On the occasion of a debate carried out indirectly between him and Blumer on an essay by Jonathan H. Turner revealingly entitled 'Parsons as a Symbolic Interactionist' (see also Blumer's and Parsons' replies of 1974 and 1975), Parsons was irritated by the interactionists' attacks while asserting that he had in fact always integrated interactionist thought and its premises into his theory. 'Where' – as we might paraphrase Parsons' line of thought here – 'are the theoretical differences? What is the basis of the interactionists' attacks? I am after all well aware that people confer meanings and have the capacity for language.' Blumer's response might be summed up as follows: 'It may well be that you, Professor Parsons, agree with these premises at a superficial level. But in reality you fail to take them sufficiently seriously. If you really accepted and consistently adhered to these premises, you would never have been able to produce the kind of theory that you have in fact produced!'

The three Blumerian premises, which appear so simple, give rise to a large number of far-reaching theoretical consequences, which produce a completely different type of theory than that with which you are now familiar from our lectures on Parsons, as well as that on neo-utilitarianism.

Let us begin with the first premise, the proposition that people act vis-à-vis objects on the basis of the meanings which these possess for them. This entails, first of all, the simple observation that human behaviour is not determined by the influence of quasi-objectively existing forces or factors. These seemingly objective factors and forces are in fact always already interpreted by actors; *meaning* is attributed to them by actors. A tree is not simply a tree in the sense of a material object, and nothing more. Rather, for the actor, the tree is located within a specific context of action. For the biologist, for example, it may be a practical object of research that can and must be analysed in an emotionally neutral way; for another person, however, it has a romantic meaning, perhaps because the tree – that lovely oak at the edge of the woods – reminds him of his first rendezvous. Thus, objects do not determine or 'spark off' human action. Quite the reverse: they obtain their meanings from human beings because they are located within a specific context of action. This does not, of course, apply only to material objects, but also to social rules, norms and values. These do not determine human behaviour either, because people have first to interpret them. In other words, a norm may 'impact on' the actor quite differently from one situation to another, because how the actor interprets this norm becomes clear only in the situation itself. But this must lead us to conclude that any conception according to which societies feature norms that act as fixed determinants of action misses the crucial fact that actors confer meaning and have room for manoeuvre in making their interpretations. We addressed this particular point in the third lecture when we listed the criticisms of Parsons' action frame of reference. The claim that Parsons' work featured an 'objectivist bias' centred on Parsons' failure to consider seriously how actors impart meaning and their cognitive achievement in general.

Now, the second and third premises, which tell us that 'the meaning of social objects arises through interaction' and that 'meanings are constantly reproduced and changed in an interpretive process' are not really very surprising or spectacular either. In the case of the second premise, Blumer merely wishes to convey the idea that the meanings which objects have for us are not to be found in the objects themselves, as if the meaning of the tree could somehow be derived from its physical reality, or the physical object that is the tree contains the idea or meaning 'tree' – as if, that is, the tree embodied this idea. But neither, according to Blumer, are meanings constituted in a purely internal psychological, more or less individual manner. Rather, meanings develop from the interactions between people, partly because of the fact that we are socialized into a particular culture. As you may know, Germans are said to have a special relationship to woods and trees – perhaps as a result of the Romantic movement. Germans are therefore particularly likely to associate trees with romantic experiences, which might be met with little understanding in another culture. In brief, the process by which actors impart meaning as they act is far from being purely psychological and carried out in isolation. In fact, *intersubjective contexts* play a major role here. Yet at the same time – this is the real significance of the third premise – Blumer also tells us that existing meanings, thought to be secure, may be subject to repeated change. Consider, for example, the personal computer, which you are able to operate skilfully – until you are suddenly faced with a problem. Until that moment, the computer may have been no more than a new kind of typewriter for you, whose smooth functioning you could take for granted. But this 'typewriter' is now malfunctioning and you are suddenly required to *deal with* it, read manuals, etc. You enter into a process of communication with yourself, asking yourself which faults may be involved, what you ought to do next, which key you should hit, which cable you should insert into which socket. And as you go about this potentially long-drawn-out and nerve-racking task, this object takes on a new meaning for you, because you learn how it works; you begin to see it 'with new eyes'.

All these premises seem perfectly innocuous – and Blumer does in fact regard them as self-evident. Nonetheless, he draws conclusions on their basis which remain inaccessible to Parsonian functionalism and neo-utilitarianism.

First, the foundation on which the symbolic interactionist theory of action is built is fundamentally different. Its point of departure is always *inter*action – and not, as in Parsons' *The Structure of Social Action* or in neo-utilitarianism, the individual act or actor. As Blumer states, social interaction is 'a process that *forms* human conduct instead of being merely a means or a setting for the expression or release of human conduct' (Blumer, 'Methodological Position', p. 8; original emphasis). The actions of others are thus always already a component of individual action and not merely of the milieu in which it occurs. Blumer therefore frequently refers to 'joint action' rather than the 'social act' (Blumer, *Symbolic Interactionism*, p. 70), to make it clear how inseparably others' actions are always already enmeshed with my own:

> a joint action cannot be resolved into a common or same type of behavior on the part of the participants. Each participant necessarily occupies a different position, acts from that position, and engages in a separate and distinctive act. It is the fitting together of these acts and not their commonality that constitutes joint action.
>
> (ibid.)

The concomitant of this is that Blumer and the symbolic interactionists have a markedly different notion of the form of the self than is the case in other theoretical traditions – with consequences for the theory of action. Directly taking up Mead's ideas on the origins of self-consciousness (see above), interactionists emphasize that the human being is also the object of his *own* action: I can relate to myself because I am always entangled in interactions and my actions are reflected back to me through the corresponding reactions of my fellow human beings. I can thus think about or reflect upon myself. I may feel annoyed with myself because I behaved rather stupidly in a given situation. I may sink into self-pity because my partner has left me. I may stride along, my chest swelled up with pride, having just carried out yet another heroic deed, etc. Sociality thus means something quite different here than in the Parsonian theory of action. Of course, Parsons also worked on the assumption that human beings are social beings. Were this not the case, it would be impossible for norms and values, which Parsons tells us are institutionalized in societies and internalized in the individual, to function as they do. But for Parsons, this process of internalization is a rather unilinear one, which proceeds from the society to the individual.

The interactionists' point of departure is itself quite differently conceived. For them, the self's communication with itself is pivotal – there is no question of internalization being a smooth and continuous process. Rather, as we have suggested already, for them the self is more a process than a fixed structure. But this also means that as we seek to grasp this processual self and its actions we cannot simply deploy the concepts otherwise common in sociology or social psychology. The inner world

> cannot be caught, consequently, by reducing it to fixed elements of organization, such as attitudes, motives, feelings and ideas; instead, it must be seen as a process in which such elements are brought into play and are subject to what happens in such play. The inner world must be seen as inner process and not as fixed inner psychical composition.
>
> (Blumer, 'George Herbert Mead', p. 149)

For a theory of action this means that it is inappropriate to assume the existence of given goals, desires, intentions and utility calculations (as is the case in neo-utilitarianism), and of fixed and unchanging norms and values (as Parsonian theory imagines), which are then converted into action. In this sense, Blumer also considers the concept of roles, as utilized in Parsonian theory (see Lecture IV), highly problematic, suggesting as it does – disregarding the processual nature of the self – that there exist fixed role expectations fulfilled straightforwardly by the individual in everyday life. This perspective turns the self into nothing more than a medium that merely executes societal expectations in order to produce actions; it is denied any active component (Blumer, *Symbolic Interactionism*, p. 73).

This leads directly to the next qualification which must be made to the action theoretical ideas typical of sociology. And this brings us once again to a point to which we have already drawn your attention in our critical appraisal of Parsons' action frame of reference (see Lecture III). Of course, when Blumer and the interactionists underline the processual character of the self and the non-determinist nature of human action, part of what they wish to convey is that the human being is not a passive being that merely responds to stimuli. Rather, the human (and animal) organism is described as one that acts in active fashion, which exhibits, as it were, seeking behaviour, and whose goals may therefore change rapidly as new predicaments crop up, requiring the actor to pay attention to new factors. One's original goals and intentions may change very quickly, because objects constantly produce new meanings within the ceaseless process of interpretation so typical of human beings.

This puts the idea found in the work of Parsons – that fixed means and ends are a vital component of the 'action frame of reference' – into a quite different perspective. Human action, according to Blumer, is not always embedded in means–ends relationships. Not only is this apparent in certain distinct forms of action such as ritual, play, dance, etc., that is, expressive acts which we brought to your attention in our remarks on Herder and German expressivist anthropology in Lecture III. In general, actors often lack any truly clear goals or intentions as they go about their everyday lives, just as there are only rarely clear-cut norms, regulations, etc., which have only to be converted into deeds. What we have to do, like what we wish to do, is often very poorly defined. Ultimately, action is highly indeterminate. Action unfolds only within a complex process which it is impossible to determine in advance. In the main, action is contingent rather than determined.

This perspective on human action differs markedly from the view typical of other sociologists who, like many neo-utilitarian theorists, assume that utility calculations and preferences are unambiguously predetermined and therefore that the means of action are also selected on a rational basis, or those who, like Parsons, assume that normative guidelines are clear. Interactionists, in contrast, conceive of action *very generally* as fairly undetermined and fluid. The American sociologist Anselm Strauss (1916–96), himself a famous interactionist, captured this as follows:

> But the future is uncertain, is to some extent judged, labelled and known after it happens. This means that human action necessarily must be rather tentative and exploratory. Unless a path of action has been well traversed, its terminal point is largely indeterminate. Both ends and means may be reformulated in transit because unexpected results occur. Commitment, even to a major way of life or destiny, is subject to revision in process.
>
> (Strauss, *Mirrors and Masks*, p. 36)

Action is a process of interpretation, an interactive process involving direct communication with others and oneself. This is why the notion of given and unchanging goals is misleading (we shall have more to say on this in the lecture on neo-pragmatism).

This brings us directly to another point. Because individual action never proceeds in truly unilinear fashion and because the self must be understood as active and processual, the notion of *fixed* social relations between persons and of course that of larger *fixed* and *stable* webs of action, as with institutions or organizations, is also highly problematic for interactionists. The relations between people are only rarely pregiven or defined in advance. When we encounter other people, there is a tussle over the definition of the situation, which is sometimes carried out openly and at other times discreetly. Every interaction involves a relational aspect which is not simply present but which must be *negotiated*. You yourselves will have had this experience on countless occasions, and it will often have been a painful one. Think of your relationship with your parents. During your childhood, you will certainly have tried on occasion to speak or negotiate with them as equals, at 'eye level' as it were. No doubt you were sometimes successful in this, and they accepted you as an equal, rational, almost grown-up individual. But your mother or father will also have acted the big boss at times, failing to acknowledge you as an equal partner in certain discussions. You tried to act as an equal member of the family, but were rejected as such. And such situations occur constantly in everyday life. You may be happy for close friends to take many liberties, but not everyone is allowed to do so; you would refuse to tolerate the same things from some of your acquaintances. In other words, you would reject their attempts to propose a certain definition of the situation.

We can therefore conclude that social relations are always tied in one way or another to *mutual* recognition by the parties to interaction and that, because the outcome of this shared definition of a given situation cannot be predicted or the parties to interaction may fail to produce a shared definition, social relations are open in terms of their development and form. And of course the same goes for more complex webs of relations consisting of large numbers of people such as organizations or societies. Interactionists therefore also conceive of 'society' as a process of action, rather than a structure or system, because this problematically implies that social relations are fixed. Symbolic interactionism

> sees society not as a system, whether in the form of a static, moving, or whatever kind of equilibrium, but as a vast number of occurring joint actions, many closely linked, many not linked at all, many prefigured and repetitious, others being carved out in new directions, and all being pursued to serve the purposes of the participants and not the requirements of a system.
>
> (Blumer, *Symbolic Interactionism*, p. 75)

Symbolic interactionists thus aspire to proceed *consistently* in line with action theory when explaining and describing group phenomena. You may also find exponents of neo-utilitarianism who try to do this. However, the model of action used here is quite different, in that it conceives of action as constituted intersubjectively.

A social scientist of course must assume that actions are interwoven – we do this constantly in everyday life when we talk about marriage, groups, organizations, war, etc., that is, phenomena in which by definition more than one actor is involved. But it is important to realize that these are not terribly stable entities, but are in fact composed of actions carried out by individuals and are therefore fluid. Even seemingly stable forms of shared action – as found in organizations – are often more changeable than one might assume. Even action taken in supposedly fixed contexts depends to a significant extent on processes of interpretation.

> Rather than viewing organizations in rigid, static terms, the interactionist sees organizations as living, changing forms which may outlive the lives of their respective members and, as such, take on histories that transcend individuals, conditions and specific situations. Rather than focusing on formal structural attributes, the interactionist focuses on organizations as *negotiated* productions that differentially constrain their members; they are seen as moving patterns of accommodative adjustment among organized parties. Although organizations create formal structures, every organization in its day-to-day activities is produced and created by individuals, individuals who are subject to and constrained by the vagaries and inconsistencies of the human form.
>
> (Denzin, 'Notes on the Criminogenic Hypothesis: A Case Study of the American Liquor Industry', p. 905; original emphasis)

Interactionists are thus suspicious of talk of the 'internal dynamics' of institutions and even of the notion of 'system requirements' so typical of functionalism. This is because it is always action, itself an act of interpretation, which produces, reproduces and changes structures; it is not the logic of an abstract system, however conceived, which changes an institution or adapts it more effectively to its environment. (On Blumer's critique of Parsons, see the remarks by Colomy and Brown, 'Elaboration, Revision, Polemic, and Progress in the Second Chicago School', pp. 23ff.)

This immediately has another consequence with respect to the conceptualization of societies. Blumer and the interactionists are also sceptical of the normative element in Parsons' functionalism. Because the interactions of members of a society are described as fluid and dependent on their own acts of interpretation, the idea that societies are held together by a consensus about certain values seems problematic. To argue this is to overlook the fact that societies emerge out of interactions, that different people are networked, linked or isolated in different ways, and that 'societies' are thus better described as webs comprising of disparate worlds of meaning or experience – the 'worlds' of art, crime, sport, television, etc. (see Strauss, *Mirrors and Masks*, p. 177; Blumer,

Symbolic Interactionism, p. 76) – than as entities fully integrated by fixed values. This integration via values should at least be investigated empirically, rather than merely postulated – as in the premises of Parsonian theory.

Finally, Blumer's three premises, which seem so straightforward, lead to at least one further conclusion of great sociological importance – one related to the problem of how to conceptualize *social change*. Because Blumer makes so much of the element of interpretation when describing action and underlining the process of mutual definition in situations, it is evident to him that unanticipated factors crop up again and again in these processes of action and definition. Action – because it is carried out searchingly and tentatively in everyday contexts – is always hedged in by uncertainty. We never know precisely where our action is taking us, whether we might be distracted, or come up with new goals, etc. Action therefore entails an element of the *creative* and thus of the *contingent*. But if this is the case and if at the same time society is regarded as many people acting together, this means that every social process, and indeed history as a whole, proceeds in contingent fashion: 'uncertainty, contingency, and transformation are part and parcel of the process of joint action. To assume that the diversified joint actions which comprise a human society are set to follow fixed and established channels is a sheer gratuitous assumption' (Blumer, *Symbolic Interactionism*, p. 72).

Blumer made this clear in a major, though posthumously published study of the phenomenon of industrialization (*Industrialization as an Agent of Social Change*). Industrialization, that is, the rise of modern industries, an urban infrastructure, electricity supply, etc., by no means determines the path which a society must ultimately follow. The idea that every society will respond in the same way to the 'impact' of industrialization is completely wrong according to Blumer. It is wrong because there exist very different and, moreover, quite differently *perceived* points of contact between social groups and economic-technological 'structures'. Depending on what kind of labour market is created by industrialization, what degree of group solidarity pertained in the preindustrial society, to what extent rural and urban areas are incorporated into the new industrial structures, how much political agencies intervene, etc., industrialization will follow a unique trajectory in each country – with quite different consequences. The view which long dominated both the sociology of development and the functionalist theory of change – that Western societies showed the countries of the Third World how their future would be because they would inevitably follow exactly the same path and simply had to catch up with the West – is for Blumer crudely simplistic and distorted for theoretical reasons. Economic structures do not simply come up, objectively as it were, against very different societal structures; interpretation again plays a decisive role here, because it is down to the members of the society to interpret the process of social upheaval and to act accordingly (see also Maines, *The Faultline of Consciousness: A View of Interactionism in Sociology*, pp. 55ff.).

So much for the far-reaching sociological consequences of Blumer's three premises. On this basis, Blumer also formulates a *thematic* programme intended to be clearly distinct from its Parsonian counterpart. For Blumer it is clear that Parsonian functionalism, dominant for so long, left out various topics or failed to deal with them in sufficient depth. Blumer counters functionalism's inherent preference for the description of stable system conditions with the sociological study of social change. He counters functionalism's typical focus on ordered processes which endlessly reconfirm systems with the need to study processes of social disorganization. He finds these so interesting because they demonstrate, again and again, the potential for the emergence of *new* ways of action and new structures. He counters the functionalist tendency to see uninterrupted processes of socialization (internalization being the key word here) with the imperative of viewing such processes as entailing elements of self-control and social control that coexist, sometimes antagonistically, in complex fashion (Blumer, *Symbolic Interactionism*, p. 77).

In its heyday between the late 1950s and early 1970s, symbolic interactionism did indeed focus on some, though not all, of these topics. A kind of division of labour with functionalism arose, in that symbolic interactionists focused mostly on topics found in social psychology, the sociology of deviant behaviour, of the family, medicine and professions and the field of collective behaviour, largely and very willingly leaving the other fields of inquiry – particularly macrosociology – to functionalism. With reference to this historical phase of sociology, observers of the sociological scene spoke of symbolic interactionism as a 'loyal opposition' (Mullins and Mullins, 'Symbolic Interactionism', p. 98), because while the interactionists criticized functionalism, they came to terms with it by means of a kind of topical division of labour. Symbolic interactionism managed to become firmly established, at least in those fields which it seriously tackled. It succeeded in founding genuine research traditions. Here, in many respects, the symbolic interactionists carried on the empirical studies of the Chicago School.

1. In the *sociology of the family*, authors such as Ralph Turner (*Family Interaction*) demonstrated in concrete terms that family members are not, as assumed by utilitarians, utility-focused and thus calculating individuals, but neither, as Parsons assumes, do they merely carry out set roles. Rather, they constantly try out new forms of interaction, are always engaging in fresh forms of action, are involved in complicated processes of negotiation, etc. What Turner (b. 1919) found was not fixed structures but fluid processes of interaction.

2. Another field of research in which symbolic interactionism is also very strongly represented is the still young *sociology of emotions*. This field, which has existed only since the mid-1970s, is of much interest insofar as emotions were generally regarded as biologically determined and thus

as asocial. Interactionists managed to show that emotions are very much shaped by one's social milieu and – perhaps even more importantly – that people *work* on these emotions. Emotions are best understood as a process of self-interaction. Feelings such as anger, fear or rage are certainly very real and are expressed physically in one's facial expressions and gestures. But of course this does not happen entirely automatically; we have a certain degree of control over it. And because we do, we also anticipate how others will react to our emotions, which in turn makes us want to control them more effectively or to express them in a different way (see Denzin, *On Understanding Emotion*, pp. 49ff.). If this is the case, if we work at our feelings, then it is worthwhile investigating, for example, where within society and by which groups of people a particular instance of emotional work is carried out. One groundbreaking study in this field is that by Arlie Hochschild (*The Managed Heart*) on the commodification of emotions among specific occupational groups. Taking stewardesses as her example, Hochschild (b. 1940) shows how they are trained to control their emotions, enabling them to greet passengers' most outrageous behaviour with a friendly smile and to view this as 'normal' – a particularly imperative type of emotional work, as unfortunately stewardesses are unable to escape from lunatics, the inebriated, sexists, etc. within the narrow confines of the aircraft.

3. In the social psychological field concerned with the *formation and development of the self*, Anselm Strauss is one of the leading as well as best-known authors. His *Mirrors and Masks*, to which we referred earlier, is a brilliant little essayistic book which elaborates on and develops further the thought of Mead and Blumer. With tremendous sensitivity, Strauss describes the never-ending process of human self-formation and self-discovery, because we are forever interpreting the past in new ways; the past is never truly over and done with. For Strauss, socialization is a life-long process. It does not end during adolescence, with only marginal changes in one's identity still to come. Rather, Strauss brings out how new and surprising elements constantly break into people's lives. Again and again, this forces them to reinterpret themselves and their past. Strauss paid particular attention to phases in people's lives in which such acts of redefinition are particularly striking; life, after all, is itself a series of so-called 'status passages' which everyone has to master – the transition from a 'genderless' child to an adolescent with sexual desires, from an adolescent mainly interested in having fun to a gainfully employed adult, from sexually promiscuous bachelor to faithful husband, from husband to father, wife to mother, and even from living to dead. Among other texts, Strauss analysed this last transition in collaboration with Barney G. Glaser in a now famous book entitled *Awareness of Dying*, a study of the interaction between nursing staff, dying patients and their relatives in a hospital.

This brings to light the various smokescreens put up by those involved, as well as the painful process of articulating and accepting the fact of imminent death. Here, the loss of options for action itself becomes the object of action theoretical analysis.

In the neighbouring field of the analysis of the presentation of the self, one author in particular stands out. While his books were hugely successful, he is an at best marginal figure within symbolic interactionism. We are referring to Erving Goffman (1922–82). Though he was a student of Everett Hughes, a famous interactionist at the University of Chicago, and took up a post at the University of California at Berkeley on the invitation of Herbert Blumer in 1958, he was basically a theoretical one-man-band – his thought being highly independent and, perhaps, eccentric. Goffman was a brilliant observer of everyday life, as manifest in his first book, *The Presentation of Self in Everyday Life*, in which he described in detail the techniques of stage-management and presentation deployed by individuals as they deal with their fellow human beings. He used theatrical metaphors to underline that people often direct their everyday lives as artistically, and perform them with as much sophistication, as do actors on a real stage. The social scientific literature has often referred to a 'dramaturgical' model of action with respect to Goffman's work, because in both the above-mentioned book and subsequent studies, rather than describing action, as do utilitarians, as guided by preferences and utility-maximizing, or, like Parsons, as geared towards norms, or even, like the pragmatists and 'normal' interactionists, as exploratory and searching, Goffman described it as entirely a matter of self-presentation. Our goal is to maintain our self-image, to *appear* as a certain type of person vis-à-vis others; this is why we stage-manage ourselves and frequently subordinate everything else to this end.

In subsequent empirical studies, Goffman examined life in so-called 'total institutions' such as psychiatric hospitals (*Asylums: Essays on the Social Situation of Mental Patients and other Inmates*) and analysed the action strategies of people whose identity is damaged, by disability or racial discrimination for example, and who have to deal with and live with this deficiency (*Stigma: Notes on the Management of Spoiled Identity*). It was not until his later books (especially *Frame Analysis: An Essay on the Organization of Experience*) that Goffman began to systematize his empirical observations and place them within a theoretical framework. Goffman's books sold and continue to sell very well not only in the USA but also in Germany. Among other things, this has something to do with the fact that he wrote in a very straightforward, easy-to-understand fashion, without much in the way of sociological jargon, as well as opening up exotic and thus interesting worlds, with his studies on psychiatry for example. The way he presents his insights also suggests a cynical understanding of how we behave in everyday life, which many readers obviously find appealing.

Competing interpretations of Goffman's work exist with regard to this last point. While some critics complained that his model of action was aimed merely at the cynical manipulation of the other party and that his description of total institutions takes no account of patients' bargaining power and thus neglects the processual nature and variability of action that exists in every institution and organization (see for example the critique in Meltzer, Petras and Reynolds, *Symbolic Interactionism: Genesis, Varieties and Criticism*, pp. 107ff.), others have pointed out that, particularly in his later work, Goffman was in fact close to Durkheim, secretly taking up and further developing the latter's emphasis on the significance of rituals to societies in an innovative way. Goffman 'is explicitly following Durkheim's point that in differentiated modern society, the gods of isolated groups have given way to worship of the one "sacred object" we all have in common: the individual self' (Collins, *Three Sociological Traditions*, pp. 156–7). On this view, the practices he analyses must be understood more as mutual face-saving rather than one-sided strategic 'impression management'. In his microstudies on techniques of individual self-presentation, Goffman is thus claimed to have pointed, as it were, to the sacrality of the individual in modern society, as manifest also in the belief in human rights.

4. Symbolic interactionism became especially popular in the field of *deviant behaviour*, which again worked with concepts known to you already. The most famous and in many ways groundbreaking book in this field was Howard S. Becker's *Outsiders: Studies in the Sociology of Deviance*, a highly readable and theoretically substantial study on deviant subcultures and their 'members', such as dance musicians and marijuana users (the empirical studies of these exemplary cases were undertaken in the 1950s; we might still refer to the subculture of drug users today, though consumers of marijuana would hardly be the first to spring to mind). What was innovative about Becker's 1963 book was, first of all, the fact that he described deviant behaviour as a behaviour sequence rather than a one-off act, a process through which one slowly but surely grows into a deviant subculture. Here, Becker (b. 1928) deployed the term 'career' to suggest that deviance is in fact a fluid process of slipping into a behaviour which eventually becomes firmly established. At the same time – and this was Becker's truly spectacular second point, which caused quite a stir – it is a process which unfolds not only between the novice drawing closer to a particular subculture and those already entrenched in it, but especially between the members of the subculture and the agencies of social control, such as the justice system or police. This last aspect unleashed both tremendous theoretical momentum as well as inspiring fierce controversy because Becker saw deviance not primarily as a genuine problem of the subculture, but as one which *becomes a problem only because society construes it as such*:

> social groups create deviance by making the rules whose infraction constitutes deviance, and by applying those rules to particular people and *labelling* them as outsiders. From this point of view, deviance is not a quality of the act the person commits, but rather a consequence of the application by others of rules and sanctions to an 'offender'. The deviant is one to whom that *label* has successfully been applied; deviant behavior is behavior that people so *label*.
>
> (Becker, *Outsiders*, p. 9; our emphasis)

Becker, so to speak, turns the conventional perspective familiar from everyday life (and sociology up to that point) on its head. Deviant behaviour is not in itself repugnant, 'anormal', unusual, etc.; rather, a particular type of behaviour is rendered deviant by certain groups or authorities within society. Labelling a particular behaviour as deviant is thus bound up with interests and power relations. It is the powerful groups within a society that criminalize shoplifting while regarding tax evasion as a trivial offence and toning down its legal implications; it is the powerful who drive heroin addicts out of parks while themselves snorting cocaine at high society parties. 'Who can, in fact, force others to accept their rules and what are the causes of their success? This is, of course, a question of political and economic power' (*Outsiders*, p. 17).

Becker's work on deviant cultures marked the birth of so-called labelling theory, which emphasized this aspect of deviance and which was associated with scholars such as John Kitsuse (1923–2003), Kai Erikson (b. 1931) and Edwin Lemert (1912–96) (see the bibliography for some of their writings). As you can no doubt imagine, particularly in the turbulent 1960s, the theory attracted a great number of students who saw themselves as critical of power; the 'underdog perspective' typical of the labelling approach (Becker's question 'Whose side are you on?', for example, became quite famous) suited them down to the ground. By now, it must be said, this approach within the sociology of crime has lost much of its sheen; it has become only too apparent that, with its almost exclusive emphasis on the role of agencies of social control, it cannot satisfactorily explain deviant behaviour. However, the other aspects of Becker's theory, his reference to the learning of certain patterns of behaviour as a process, and his notion of 'career', have lost none of their influence in fields such as subculture research; their relevance to the present is undiminished (for a brief overview of symbolic interactionism within the sociology of deviant behaviour, see Paul Rock, 'Symbolic Interaction and Labelling Theory').

5. Another important field in which symbolic interactionism became well established was that of *collective behaviour*. Blumer himself saw collective behaviour, which he had studied as early as the 1930s, as a phenomenon of central importance to every society. He believed he could discern here the

potential for new social patterns and forms of social action to emerge. In fact, the older members of the Chicago School saw the analysis of collective behaviour as *the* key task of sociology. Structural functionalism, meanwhile, had long ignored this phenomenon entirely, and in the 1950s and 1960s Blumer's students were in fact more or less the only ones to tackle these themes (see Shibutani, 'Herbert Blumer's Contribution to Twentieth Century Sociology', p. 26).

A very wide variety of phenomena were included under the label of 'collective behaviour', ranging from fashion through rumours and panics to violent mass movements. Blumer's students had a particular nose for all these aspects of social reality; their studies of what we would now term 'social movements' have emerged as their most important contribution in this area. Interactionists were in the 'front line' of empirical studies of the American civil rights movement, the international student movement, the women's movement, the environmental movement, etc., developing their own unique theoretical perspective.

What is interesting about the interactionist approach to these phenomena is that it contrasted sharply with traditional social scientific styles of research and thus shed light on dimensions which remained outside of their remit. In the 1960s, two theoretical schools dominated sociological research on social movements. The first was structural functionalism, which had only recently discovered this field and traced social movements back to 'social strain'. The problem with this approach was that a clear distinction was always made between social movements and the institutional structures of society. The impression arose that only insufficiently adapted groups tended to engage in protest; irrationality was thus always thought to be at play in one way or another in social protests and movements. You have already met the other approach of central importance at the time, resource mobilization, in Lecture V; it states its case in such out-and-out rationalistic fashion that it creates the impression that social movements are solely a matter of social groups battling to augment their power while weighing up risks and (political) opportunities. But both schools, asserted the interactionists, disregard the fact that collective action is not simply unilinear – whether conceived as rational or irrational. Furthermore, collective behaviour cannot be understood as a mere aggregation of individual forms of behaviour. The interactionists showed, by means of empirical studies, how, for example, participants' goals change in and through the concrete situation of the mass gathering, and thus that mass behaviour is subject to development of a processual nature, a specific dynamic that completely contradicts the notion of the rational pursuit of goals.

Depending on the context and the nature of the situation, new meanings quite different from any that existed before are particularly likely to arise within social movements, just as the interactionist model of action might lead us to expect. In analysing the race riots in Watts, Los Angeles, in 1965, it was possible to show that a new definition of the situation developed very quickly out of a banal incident: a confrontation with police ensued after a motorcyclist was pulled over and an initially very small crowd of people gathered. The actions of the policeman were suddenly reinterpreted as typical of the repression of the white police force as a whole; a commotion relating to a local event was suddenly interpreted as an uprising against the 'white system'. None of those originally present in this small crowd of people started out with these ideas. They took shape only as the various actions of those present unfolded, and in this process cognitive and affective outlooks, and beliefs, were then transformed.

This is the moment of the 'emergence' of new norms, in as much as new meanings and patterns of behaviour arise in a given situation; these redefine the situation and reinterpret the reality, producing a break with everyday routines. The new symbols which arise rapidly attract people's interest – they become the focus of action beyond all considerations of utility. The storming of the Bastille in the French Revolution did not take place because it was strategically the most important place in the French capital or the central prison in which the largest number of political prisoners were incarcerated, but because this fortress had become a symbol of royal rule. But this focus of collective action on symbols cannot simply be interpreted as a sign of irrationality, because the action does in fact follow a certain logic – quite apart from the fact that it is not irrational to attack symbols! All in all, the interactionist approach within social movements research facilitated a quite different perspective on mass phenomena, often one more commensurate with reality than 'traditional' sociological theories could manage (on the specific features of this interactionist approach within research on social movements, see Snow and Davis, 'The Chicago Approach to Collective Behavior').

6. Finally, one of the important thematic fields of symbolic interactionism is the *sociology of occupations and work*, particularly the sociology of professions. Here, of course, competition with functionalism inevitably arose. Parsons himself, as you know from Lecture III, had already developed his interest in this subject at a very early stage. Sociologists of professions soon talked of competition between the Harvard approach (Parsons) and the Chicago approach, the last being closely associated with Everett Hughes (1897–1983). Hughes criticized Parsons for taking too seriously and failing to question sociologically the ethics upheld by the professions with respect to the attitude of service towards clients, the objective adequacy of academic or university knowledge, emphasized so frequently by Parsons, and the necessity for professional self-management, which Parsons evoked with equal vigour. In contrast, Hughes interpreted these phenomena, from the standpoint of a critique of ideology, as attempts to maintain power

and exclude other groups which encroach on this occupational field and threaten the sinecure of the established professions, and as a means of increasing autonomy vis-à-vis clients. In the same vein, he interpreted efforts by occupational groups to develop into 'real' professions, to 'professionalize', as a quest for more

> independence, more recognition, a higher place, a cleaner distinction between those in the profession and those outside, and a larger measure of autonomy in choosing colleagues and successors. One necessary validation of such changes of status in our society is introduction of study for the profession in question into the university.
> (Hughes, 'Professions', in *On Work, Race, and the Sociological Imagination*, p. 43)

In Eliot Freidson (1923–2005) and Andrew Abbott (b. 1948), whose key writings on this subject you can find in the bibliography, Hughes found worthy successors in the sociology of professions. They further developed analyses featuring this Parsons-critical thrust, with a clear overlap emerging with the conflict theoretical approach discussed in the lecture after next.

So much for the traditional concerns of symbolic interactionism. There is, however, another field on which this school has also exercised a marked influence – and this is the realm of sociological research methods. Because of their particular perspective on social phenomena, the interactionists saw how imperative it was to capture this reality with social scientific methods in keeping with the character of these phenomena. Blumer himself had already referred to the fact that in light of the fluidity of social processes recognized by the pragmatists, empirical social research also requires special concepts. Blumer spoke of 'sensitizing concepts' (Blumer, *Symbolic Interactionism*, p. 149), ones which help us grasp the meaning of whatever we are studying, in contrast to those which merely allow the phenomena to be subsumed under them without elaborating on what precisely they mean and how one has generated them. In their book *The Discovery of Grounded Theory*, Barney G. Glaser and Anselm L. Strauss put this right in sensational fashion. Glaser and Strauss produced a manifesto of qualitative social research, setting out with the help of numerous examples the 'best strategy' for generating theory in empirically grounded, step-by-step fashion. We should not – as Parsons was criticized for doing – deduce theory logically from an abstract action frame of reference or the like. Rather, they suggested, the ideal way to achieve an empirically grounded theory consists in approaching the object of investigation carefully and without bias, subjecting it to intensive study and *comparing* it with other objects for similarities and features in common (many descriptions of 'grounded theory' forget all about comparison), before creating categories and formulating hypotheses. We must, however, refrain from delving further into the methodological aspect of symbolic interactionism in these lectures on theory.

We conclude with a look at current trends in symbolic interactionism. Three points at least are worthy of mention. First, some exponents of interactionism have since the late 1980s become increasingly involved in the debate on postmodernism, a particular focus being the intensive analysis of the media and their role in modern society. Norman Denzin (b. 1941), whom we have met already, belongs in this category in that he has made film the key focus of several studies – in part because he believes that postmodern identities are inconceivable without it (and other media); for him, film and television furnish people with images with which they then identify (Denzin, *Images of Postmodern Society: Social Theory and Contemporary Cinema*). Denzin undoubtedly touches on important empirical questions about changes in the formation of identity here. This also applies to his work on 'epiphanies', shattering events such as divorce, rape, loss of status, conversion, and so on. However, the profound radicalization of Mead's insight into the fundamentally processual and never-ending nature of identity formation, characteristic of some postmodern writings, has generated untenable exaggerations. Here, interactionism runs the risk of being absorbed into so-called 'Cultural Studies' and losing its professional identity as social science.

The second recent trend within symbolic interactionism, the further development of action theory, looks more promising. Once again, Anselm Strauss made a key contribution, formulating with tremendous clarity a large number of hypotheses on social action in his 1993 book *Continual Permutations of Action*. But many of the developments in this field of action theory are taking place within *philosophy* and *social philosophy*, because pragmatism has taken hold there as a bona fide movement on the back of a wholesale pragmatist renaissance. We shall have more to say on this in Lecture XIX.

Many were surprised that one particular field was affected by the third and final recent trend which we must mention here. We are referring to macrosociology. The development of symbolic interactionism from the 1950s was after all shaped by a division of labour with functionalism, adherents of the former focusing mainly on *micro*sociological topics. It is true that Blumer had identified social change as one of the subjects that symbolic interactionism ought to tackle as he sought to expand its scope. Yet his comrades-in-arms generally did very little to advance his agenda, particularly with respect to social change. Blumer himself had certainly written a fair amount on industrialization, but this was a critique of existing approaches rather than an attempt to produce an autonomous and constructive macrosociology.

The interactionists' macrosociological abstinence was peculiar in that the 'Chicago School' of sociology originally had far broader sociological interests. Authors such as Park and Thomas were very strongly focused on urban sociology and had written important studies on immigration and migration, ethnicity and collective behaviour. In fact, in the symbolic interactionism of the 1950s and 1960s, all that was left of these macrosociological topics was a concern with 'collective behaviour'; 'bigger' issues were left out of account. Initially, then, symbolic interactionism merely carried on the *micro*sociological aspect of the old Chicago School. Some scholars then complained, not entirely without justification, that by concentrating on the micro-level of actors interacting directly with one another, this approach was ahistorical and ignored economic aspects and social power relations entirely, that it had an inherent 'astructural bias' (Meltzer, Petras and Reynolds, *Symbolic Interactionism*, p. 113).

Symbolic interactionism was in fact very slow to tackle this problem; its path towards macrosociology was to prove a particularly stony one. The point of departure was the sociology of professions, as it investigated organizations such as hospitals in which the members of professional groups work. Once again, it was Anselm Strauss who spoke of 'negotiated orders' in relation to these organizations, in other words, of structures as the result of processes of negotiation which take place in every organization – however stable and unshakeable it may appear. Hospitals are by no means structured on the basis of an unambiguous organizational goal; many structures can be understood only if one understands them as official or unofficial arrangements between various groups (doctors, nurses, health insurance schemes, patients, etc.). The concept of 'negotiation' provided an opportunity to consider more deeply the relationship between action and structure: 'Structure is not "out there"; it should not be reified. When we talk about *structure* we are, or should be, referring to the structural *conditions* that pertain to the phenomena under study' (Strauss, *Negotiations*, p. 257; original emphasis). These studies in organizational sociology increasingly threw up the question of whether one might also deploy the figure of 'negotiation' to describe configurations of actors on a larger scale, *between* institutions and organizations, and whether, in fact, one might even understand entire societies in this way:

> The model of a society that derives from the negotiated order is one characterized by a complex network of competing groups and individuals acting to control, maintain, or improve their social conditions as defined by their *self*-interests. The realization of these interests, material and ideal, are the outcomes of negotiated situations, encounters, and relationships.
> (Hall, 'A Symbolic Interactionist Analysis of Politics', p. 45; original emphasis)

The idea of 'negotiation' was first used to macrosociological ends in Norman Denzin's impressive essay 'Notes on the Criminogenic Hypothesis: A Case Study of the American Liquor Industry', in which he examined with equal dexterity the historical context and the relevant collective actors and structures involved: the distilleries, the distributors, the bars, the consumers and the legal system. The interactionist camp's first attempts to grasp political phenomena are equally worthy of note, though the focus here was generally on the techniques of image cultivation deployed by political representatives rather than the many and varied processes occurring *between* political actors (Hall, 'A Symbolic Interactionist Analysis of Politics').

Various authors of the symbolic interactionist school then began to make vigorous efforts to make their theory more relevant to macrosociological concerns. The key names here are, once again, Anselm Strauss, David R. Maines (b. 1940) and Peter M. Hall (see the relevant entries in the bibliography), who thought long and hard about how the gulf between the micro-level of actors and the macro-level of organizations and society might best be bridged via the theoretical construal of networks of relations, practices, conventions, etc. Maines' concept of the meso-structure ('In Search of Mesostructure: Studies in the Negotiated Order') was and is an interesting starting point here. However, all three authors – Strauss, Hall and Maines – were to discover that they were anything but alone in this field, because the traditional (non-interactionist) sociological theories continued to regard the so-called micro–macro problem as difficult to solve and existing macro-theoretical arguments as unsatisfactory. And this is why, suddenly, certain authors were surprised to find themselves interested in each other's work, because they had until then moved within seemingly very different subject areas and theoretical traditions (see Adler and Adler, 'Everyday Life in Sociology', pp. 227ff.). You will be hearing more on this in lectures still to come, such as those on the works of Pierre Bourdieu and Anthony Giddens for example, in as much as they drew in part on a body of thought present in the same or similar form in American pragmatism and symbolic interactionism. One symbolic interactionist (David Maines, *The Faultline of Consciousness*) has even claimed that much of contemporary sociology leans towards interactionist ideas without entirely realizing it. Again, this confirms our hypothesis, put forward in Lecture I, that the various sociological theories, supposedly sealed off from one another so tightly, are linked by numerous corridors.

VII

Interpretive approaches (2)

Ethnomethodology

As we learned in the previous lecture, symbolic interactionism is not the only theoretical school to which the label 'interpretive approach' has been attached. The other is what is known as ethnomethodology, whose frighteningly complex name alone might be enough to scare one off. In fact, the name is less complicated than it looks: it consists of two components, each of which is perfectly understandable in itself. The first element, 'ethnos', alludes to sociology's neighbouring discipline of ethnology (also known as anthropology), while the second is the term 'methodology'. This in itself helps us begin to grasp the agenda of this theoretical approach. Here, the methods of ethnology, a subject which investigates other ethnic groups, are deployed to examine one's own culture, in order to reveal its taken-for-granted and characteristic features, of which we are often entirely unaware – precisely because they are taken for granted.

Defamiliarizing one's own culture is intended to unveil its hidden structure. But ethnomethodologists had even more ambitious aims in mind. They not only sought to identify the unnoticed structural characteristics *of their own* culture; their aim was ultimately to uncover the fundamental *universal, quasi-anthropological* structures of everyday knowledge and action. How must this knowledge, the knowledge held by each member of each society, be structured to enable action to take place? This was the central issue which the ethnomethodologists wished to address – one which they believed had been utterly neglected by traditional sociology.

This interest in action theoretical matters was no coincidence. The founder of ethnomethodology, Harold Garfinkel (b. 1917), was a student of Talcott Parsons, who had supervised the PhD he obtained from Harvard in 1952. He was thus very familiar with the latter's work. In fact, in keeping with the thesis advocated in the present work that modern sociological theory began with Parsons, Garfinkel made it abundantly clear that his theoretical point of departure, and that of his comrades-in-arms, was *The Structure of Social Action*:

> Inspired by *The Structure of Social Action* ethnomethodology undertook the task of respecifying the production and accountability of immortal,

ordinary society. It has done so by searching for, and specifying, radical phenomena. In the pursuit of that programme, a certain agenda of themes, announced and elaborated in *The Structure of Social Action*, has over the years offered a contrasting standing point of departure to ethnomethodology's interest in respecification.

(Garfinkel, 'Respecification', p. 11)

As hinted at in this quotation, however, Garfinkel's theoretical work developed in a markedly different direction than did Parsons'. We might put it more bluntly: ethnomethodology, which became so hugely fashionable in the 1960s, reflected a shift away from Parsonianism. But unlike symbolic interactionism, this was no 'loyal opposition' within a sociology still dominated by Parsonian functionalism. Rather, a significant number of ethnomethodologists – including Garfinkel on occasion – took on the role of critics of fundamental aspects of sociology as a whole. They assailed the discipline for having failed to sufficiently elucidate the everyday knowledge held by members of a society and thus having contributed practically nothing of any substance to the investigation of social reality.

But let us begin at the beginning, with Garfinkel's early work. The points of divergence from Parsons' oeuvre were already apparent in his unpublished dissertation. Here, he criticized Parsons for having failed to shed light on exactly how and through which procedures actors define their action situation, which considerations enter into the carrying out of action and what the conditions for completing an action are in the first place. The Parsonian 'action frame of reference', he claimed, was insufficiently complex in that Parsons refers to goals and values as a matter of course without going on to examine how actors relate to these in concrete terms (Heritage, *Garfinkel and Ethnomethodology*, pp. 9f.).

As his career progressed, Garfinkel was to sharpen his critique of Parsons further still; this was due, among other things, to the new findings that emerged from his empirical research. After completing his dissertation at Harvard and following a sojourn in Ohio, Garfinkel took up a post at UCLA (University of California, Los Angeles), where he studied, among other things, the decision-making behaviour of jury members in court cases through relatively small studies carried out in the 1950s. He established that the behaviour of jurors was not clearly predictable, even when the legal norms involved and the facts of the case were unambiguous. One might have assumed that a certain verdict was more or less certain in such cases. After all, there appears to be little for the jurors to think about. But as Garfinkel showed, they *always* found it difficult to apply a legal norm to the facts of the case. The complexity of real life had always first to be 'aligned' with a legal norm, and reality interpreted accordingly, especially given that the opposing sides in the trial generally gave very different accounts of the alleged offence and its particulars.

Further, Garfinkel demonstrated that a multitude of heterogeneous considerations entered into the decision-making process and that the jurors 'cobbled together' their view of the case only gradually in order to render comprehensible the parties' contradictory statements. According to Garfinkel, this process cropped up constantly in various forms. The assumption that jurors – though of course this applies not only to the particular group of people studied by Garfinkel, but to every human being making decisions in everyday contexts – have *from the outset* a clear notion of which conditions must pertain if they are to reach a verdict is problematic, if not in fact wrong. It is only *after the event*, looking back, that it often seems *as if* a clear decision-making strategy had always existed.

> In the material reported here, jurors did not actually have an understanding of the conditions that defined a correct decision until after the decision had been made. Only in retrospect did they decide what they did that made their decisions correct ones. When the outcome was in hand they went back to find the 'why', the things that led up to the outcome, and then in order to give their decisions some order, which namely, is the 'officialness' of the decision.
>
> (Garfinkel, *Studies in Ethnomethodology*, p. 114)

The results of these studies demonstrate to Garfinkel that sociology is poorly served by identifying norms in order to explain why people behave one way rather than another. The mere reference to norms and rules leaves out of account the complex processes of deliberation in which actors must engage if they are to adhere to a norm in the first place. It also conceals the fact that the aptness of a norm is established through these processes of deliberation. According to Garfinkel, the research results suggest, among other things, that the action theoretical model which Parsons takes as his basis is excessively unilinear (and of course the neo-utilitarian conception of action even more so). There can be no question of fixed goals and values in the context of everyday action: the values and goals underpinning a decision are often determined only *after the event*.

One might have thought that Garfinkel would turn to American pragmatism and symbolic interactionism to flesh out his critique of certain theoretical conceptualizations of action. Ultimately, as we learned in the previous lecture, these schools of thought also placed a question mark over excessively linear notions of action, underlining the fluidity of social processes; scholars such as Herbert Blumer had heavily criticized the rigid normativism inherent in Parsonian role theory. It was not that the interactionists rejected any notion of roles – the concept, after all, is drawn from Mead's analysis of interaction – but they loosened up the Parsonian concept significantly. Ralph Turner, for example, who exercised a major influence on interactionist role theory, always described interaction in the context of roles as a 'tentative' and searching process; he tended to refer to 'role-*making*' rather than the mere carrying out of certain normative expectations:

> Roles 'exist' in varying degrees of concreteness and consistency, while the individual confidently frames his behavior as if they had unequivocal existence and clarity. The result is that in attempting from time to time to make aspects of the roles explicit he is creating and modifying roles as well as merely bringing them to light; the process is not only role-taking but *role-making*.
>
> (Turner, 'Role-Taking: Process versus Conformity', p. 22; original emphasis)

It very soon became apparent, however, that *this* critique of Parsonian role theory was not enough for Garfinkel and the ethnomethodologists, and that they wished to reconstruct action theory at a 'deeper' level than symbolic interactionism had managed. According to Aaron Cicourel (b. 1928), another leading ethnomethodologist, even Turner's flexible theory of roles neglects, for example, the issue of

> how the actor recognizes relevant stimuli and manages to orient himself (locate the stimuli in a socially meaningful context) to the behavioral displays so that an organized response can be generated that will be recognized as relevant to alter. The actor must be endowed with mechanisms or basic rules that permit him to identify settings that would lead to 'appropriate' invocation of norms, where *the norms would be surface rules and not basic to how the actor makes inferences about taking or making roles.*
>
> (Cicourel, 'Basic and Normative Rules in the Negotiation of Status and Role', p. 244; original emphasis)

To put it slightly differently, this means that reference to creative 'role-making' still tells us nothing about how and according to which (fundamental) rules the role is organized or what, concretely, the actor gears himself towards, etc.

This leads us to the key differences between Garfinkel's theoretical agenda on the one hand and that of Parsons and the rest of sociology on the other. These we shall list here, although they will only become truly clear as we move through this lecture.

1. Particularly in relation to Parsonian theory, Garfinkel argued *that the relationship between the motive of an action and the carrying out of that action had been conceived far too narrowly and smoothly*. Parsons, Garfinkel asserted, acted as if the presence of a motive – when, for example, a norm or value that necessitates a certain activity has been internalized – directly triggers the carrying out of an action. But this is certainly not the case, as Garfinkel of course demonstrated with the help of the complex processes of deliberation characteristic of jurors faced with the need to reach a verdict.

Because Parsons neglects these processes, Garfinkel polemically calls the actors in the former's theory 'cultural dopes' or 'judgmental dopes':

> By 'cultural dope' I refer to the man-in-the-sociologist's-society who produces the stable features of the society by acting in compliance with preestablished and legitimate alternatives of action that the common culture provides.
>
> (Garfinkel, *Studies in Ethnomethodology*, p. 68)

The term 'cultural dopes' is meant to suggest that Parsonian theory allows actors practically no initiative of their own; they appear incapable of dealing with norms and values in autonomous fashion. Rather, they merely follow predetermined norms blindly, as if controlled by outside forces. Parsons denied his actors the ability to reflect on the norms and values they had internalized. Values and norms – Garfinkel tells us – are de facto described as fixed causal entities in Parsonian theory, which actors must and ultimately do obey.

Should this criticism be correct, then Parsons comes dangerously close to advocating a stance that he had roundly criticized in *Structure*, when, for example, he attacked positivism for lacking a theory of action. For Parsons, positivism robbed actors of all freedom, presenting them as driven either by their environment or by their genetic endowment – thus failing to capture the initiative involved in human action. According to Garfinkel, Parsons' model of action is not so very different from that of the positivists. The part played by the environment or genetic endowment for the positivists is taken on by norms and values for Parsons. *In both cases,* Garfinkel asserted, actors' capacity for reflection and deliberation is disregarded. Garfinkel is doubtful as to whether the Parsonian model of action is capable of capturing the reality of everyday action.

For the same reason, he claimed that, rather than a genuine theory of action, Parsons had at best a theory of dispositions towards certain actions, because he had failed to fill in the 'gap' between the motive for and the carrying out of action. Garfinkel, meanwhile, became profoundly interested in how actions do in fact occur. To illuminate this, empirical studies must first reveal *what actors know*, what stock of knowledge they are able to draw upon, and how they deploy this knowledge in such a way that collaborative social action can come about in the first place (see the quotation on p. 153 from Aaron Cicourel). Here, Garfinkel's concern was to understand actors as 'knowledgeable actors' and action itself as an 'endless, ongoing, contingent accomplishment' (Garfinkel, *Studies in Ethnomethodology*, p. 1). It will be clear by this point that this not only represented a shift away from Parsons, but also from neo-utilitarianism, with its talk of (fixed) utility calculations and preferences. Because it is doubtful, as Garfinkel's study of the decision-making process among jurors shows, that actions are guided by norms in such linear fashion as Parsons assumes, ethnomethodologists replaced Parsonian normative determinism with the concept of actors' 'normative accountability'. In as much as they act with reference to norms, actors' 'account' of why they behaved in a particular way is at best delivered *retrospectively*. This cannot simply be equated with what *actually* happened. Because both Parsonianism and neo-utilitarianism fail to take into account or entirely disregard the processes of deliberation in which actors engage and their frequently retrospective attempts to endow what has occurred with meaning, ethnomethodologists have always suspected that these theories are capable of explaining very little (Heritage, *Garfinkel and Ethnomethodology*, p. 112).

2. Parsons' emphasis on norms was always inadequate in that he *failed to specify how exactly actors understand norms*. Parsons simply took the comprehensibility of language and other symbol systems, in which norms are embedded, as givens. He left open the question of how norms come to share the same meaning and particularly how multiple parties to interaction come to understand norms in identical fashion in concrete action situations. Parsons – though this of course applies to others as well – lacked a sophisticated theory of language capable of remedying this. He may even have lacked the feel for the fact that norms are never specified with any real clarity while rules are, for the most part, extremely vague. Whatever the truth of this, we cannot, Garfinkel tells us, assume that the coordination of action simply ensues from the internalization of norms. We can bring this out by looking at norms of greeting. In our society there exists the norm or rule that one ought to greet one's acquaintances or respond to their greetings. But knowing about this norm helps us very little in everyday life, however firmly we may have internalized it. For in order to apply this norm in everyday contexts, we must distinguish clearly between *groups of people to be greeted in a particular way*. Whose hand do we shake or refrain from shaking? Who do we merely nod or wave to? Who do we not wish to greet and who ought we, perhaps, not greet (outsiders of one kind or another)? How, in the context of a sizeable gathering, for example, do we greet close friends differently, without being too conspicuous about it, from mere acquaintances and people we do not know at all (we do not, after all, want to offend our friends), etc.? Adhering to the simple norm of greeting thus necessitates a wealth of knowledge about 'parameters', knowledge which everyone must possess in order to truly 'live' the norm. Parsons says very little about this. He failed to analyse convincingly the problem of specifying norms, and his concept of roles is of equally little help.

3. Finally, Garfinkel and the ethnomethodologists criticized Parsons for tackling the problem of order in the wrong way or in relatively superficial fashion. Their argument was that *the problem of order does not arise*

only when conflicts of interest crop up between actors. In discussing the Hobbesian problem, Parsons had argued that social order was inconceivable on the basis of strictly utilitarian premises, that in this case unregulated conflicts of interest would lead to an endless war of all against all; only norms can explain the stability of social life. Garfinkel, on the other hand, emphasized that everyday order is always being established *independently of diverging interests*, because without referring explicitly to norms, actors themselves always mutually confirm the meaningfulness of their actions and their world as they interact. They find immediate confirmation that their linguistic statements are comprehensible and thus that their actions dovetail with those of others, yet there is no sign at all of the norms to which Parsons so frequently alluded. Before norms even become an issue, a species of trust is actively produced between the actors – and this is the foundation of social order. To put it a bit differently: because norms do not truly determine and structure how actions develop (see the first point in Garfinkel's critique of Parsons), the internalization of norms and values, which Parsons underlined so often, is *not* the main pillar on which social order rests. Rather, we need to look at a much *deeper* level for the mechanisms through which human beings find assurance of their reality in everyday life, because (again, see the quote from Aaron Cicourel on p. 153) it is on the basis of *these mechanisms* that people can relate explicitly to norms in the first place. The real foundations of social order are thus to be found somewhere other than Parsons assumed.

These three criticisms of Parsonian theory – though they apply not only to it but also to most other sociological approaches – may sound rather abstract. As we move through the lecture, you can expect further clarification on this point, as we will be presenting the *empirical* research programme put forward by Garfinkel and the ethnomethodologists. But first we shall turn again briefly to theoretical matters, asking on what philosophical basis the edifice of ethnomethodological theory was constructed.

In the previous lecture, we referred to the fact that both approaches within so-called 'interpretive sociology' – ethnomethodology and symbolic interactionism – can be traced back to currents within modern philosophy. While the theoretical foundations of interactionism lie in American pragmatism, Garfinkel and the ethnomethodologists drew on phenomenology, which originated largely in Germany, particularly in the work of Edmund Husserl. This school of thought appealed to the ethnomethodologists primarily because it had developed ideas aimed at bringing to light the generally unacknowledged, taken-for-granted features of human action and human perception; this of course fit neatly with the ethnomethodologists' objective of rendering one's own culture unfamiliar in order to reveal its hidden structures.

The philosophical programme developed by Edmund Husserl, who was born in Moravia in 1859, taught in Halle and Göttingen and from 1916 in Freiburg, and who died in 1938, was in essence an attempt to elucidate the structures of our consciousness, to investigate *how* objects appear to our consciousness. This may not seem terribly stimulating at first sight, but is in fact an exciting endeavour with far-reaching consequences. Among other things, Husserl's justification for phenomenology as a 'rigorous' science was based on a critique of certain axioms of the then dominant naturalistic or positivist psychology, which took for granted the existence of a kind of passive consciousness which does little more than process sensory data. According to Husserl, this overlooks the fact that sensory data are endowed with meaning only on the basis of the achievements of consciousness itself. This insight, as it happens, is not so very different from the one we discussed in Lecture I, when we quoted from C. S. Peirce to point to the fact that all perception is necessarily or inevitably derived from theory. Whatever the precise relationship between these philosophical currents, the simplest way to grasp the constitutive achievements of consciousness to which Husserl referred may be the ambiguous figure which the observer, depending on where she focuses her attention, may see as two quite different images, whose meaning may thus 'flip' dramatically (Figure 7.1).

Depending on where you direct your attention, you may see this figure as a stylized goblet or as two faces looking at each other. Crucial achievements of

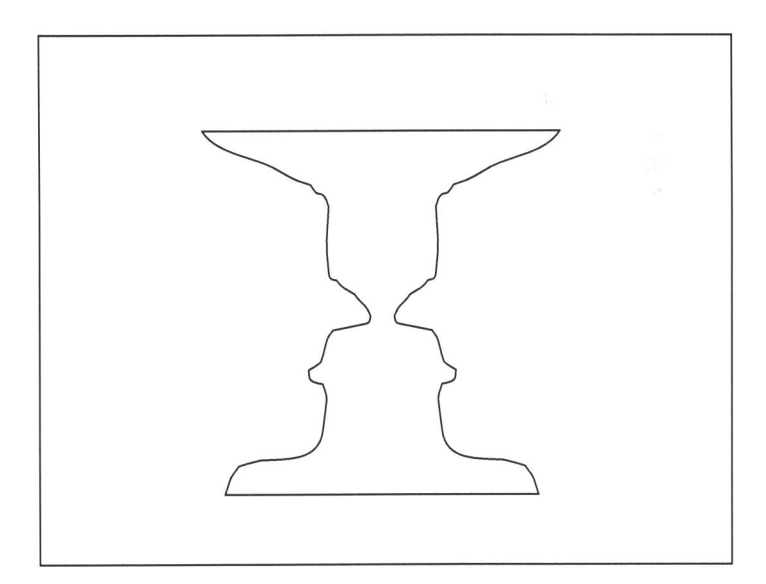

Figure 7.1

consciousness, in other words, are part and parcel of perception; you do not simply see things free of all assumptions. But this does not of course apply only to such experimental or exotic phenomena as these ambiguous figures. Rather, as Husserl brought out, our everyday perception is based fundamentally and is dependent on such achievements of consciousness. Think, for instance, of the lecturer who holds up an important book during a lecture or seminar, which he urges you to read. You perceive a book, although in reality – and this is what makes Husserl's method of inquiry so fascinating – you do not of course 'see' a book at all. What you may see in the distance is at most the book's front cover. You see no back cover, and probably not even its edges. What you see is at most a surface of one colour or another with words printed on it which you may be able to read. You see no more than this. Therefore, you do not really 'see' a 'book'. Rather, it is down to the achievements which your consciousness goes on to perform that the image of a book crystallizes in your perception, a sensory object which of course has a reverse side, edges and thus pages, which you can touch, which you can handle, and indeed read, etc. That which appears to you as a book is the end result of a series of unconscious and automatic operations and achievements performed by your psyche; you are helped by the fact that you have held a book in your hands before, that you know what it looks like, how it feels, etc.

What Husserl wished to do was to shed light on these achievements of consciousness, which are always at work in everyday life – in our 'natural attitude' as Husserl puts it – when we perceive our world and take action. His phenomenology took up the task of analysing how objects are experienced in this natural attitude. But in order to be able to do this, phenomenology must distance itself from this natural attitude; it must, as Husserl states, undertake a 'phenomenological reduction'. While we simply perceive the book as such in everyday life, phenomenology must analyse precisely *how* we see the book as a book, *how* it appears in my consciousness 'as a book'. This is why Garfinkel was so interested in Husserl's phenomenology. Just as Husserl wished to unravel and thus cast light on our quotidian perceptual models, Garfinkel too was determined to render the world unfamiliar in order to illuminate its innermost structures and thereby to demonstrate the meaning of the 'natural attitude' to the world.

Husserl's phenomenological programme had far-reaching consequences for the history of philosophy. It exercised a major influence on twentieth-century German philosophy, the philosophy of Martin Heidegger (1889–1976) being perhaps the best example. Conveyed via various complicated routes, it became hugely influential in France from the 1930s, in as much as authors such as Jean-Paul Sartre (1905–80) and Maurice Merleau-Ponty (1908–61) took up certain phenomenological ideas, linking them with motifs found within existential philosophy. Particularly in the late 1940s and 1950s, French existentialism was a tremendously influential movement that captivated numerous intellectuals, particularly in Western Europe. But it was not these authors who ultimately influenced Garfinkel, but the Austrian economist and social theorist Alfred

Schütz (1899–1959), who fled Europe with the rise of Hitler and arrived in the USA in 1939, where he took up a post at the New School for Social Research in New York City. Schütz himself was from the outset greatly interested in fundamental issues characteristic of action theory. In his first major work, *The Phenomenology of the Social World*, which appeared in 1932, he grappled intensively with Max Weber's conception of action, which he wished to free from what he felt was an overly narrow, rationalistic straitjacket. By means of Husserl's ideas, Schütz set about breaking down more precisely than had Weber how meaning is constituted for the actor, how it is possible to understand others in the first place, etc. Schütz was to continue to work on these problems for the rest of his life. He became aware of a theme and concept already present in Husserl's later work which – as we shall discuss again later in the lectures on Jürgen Habermas – was to exercise an enormous influence on theoretical debates within German sociology in the 1970s at the latest. We are referring to the concept of the *Lebenswelt* or life-world.

In his last major work, *The Crisis of European Sciences and Transcendental Phenomenology*, the published form of a lecture series which began in 1935, Edmund Husserl launched a sharp attack on the ceaseless advance of the natural sciences and their emerging hegemony within Western thought as a whole. In his critical reconstruction of natural scientific arguments since Galileo and Descartes, Husserl pointed out that the origin of these natural sciences had lain in the sensory, actually perceptible world, *but that this origin had been suppressed by the natural scientists and 'their' philosophers in favour of the increasing mathematization, mathematical idealization, abstractification, etc. of the world*, which led, among other things, to a situation in which even psychology tended to naturalize the psychological (Husserl, *The Crisis of European Sciences*, p. 67). In contrast, Husserl believed that the priority must be to deploy phenomenology to shed light on and to some extent rehabilitate the everyday 'life-world as the forgotten meaning-fundament of natural science' (*Crisis*, p. 48) as well as doing the same for all other contexts of action. What Husserl means by the 'everyday life-world' or the 'life-world based attitude', is largely identical to that which we characterized above as a natural attitude. To some extent, the 'life-world' refers to the opposite of the universe of the (natural) sciences; it refers to the very *naive givenness of the world* which we encounter unquestioningly and without reflection, upon which we construct all our everyday actions and which we can question only with much effort. Husserl, in contrast to the natural scientific way of thinking, puts it as follows:

> the ontic meaning [*Seinssinn*] of the pregiven life-world is a *subjective structure* [*Gebilde*], it is the achievement of experiencing, pre-scientific life. In this life the meaning and the ontic validity [*Seinsgeltung*] of the world are built up – of that particular world, that is, which is actually valid for the individual experiencer. As for the 'objectively true' world, the world of science, it is a structure at a higher level, built on

prescientific experiencing and thinking, or rather on its accomplishments of validity [*Geltungsleistungen*].

(*Crisis*, p. 69; original emphasis and insertions)

This 'life-world', in which we are always entangled as actors, is the outcome of the actions and experiences of past generations, our grandparents and parents, who have created a world that we have come to take for granted, which we do not question in everyday life, at least as regards its basic structures, because it is constitutive of the carrying out of action. The 'life-world' is, so to speak, the foundation of all our action and knowledge.

It was Alfred Schütz's great accomplishment that he further developed Husserl's concept of the life-world and, above all, rendered it sociologically useful. (On his oeuvre and on the man himself, see Helmut R. Wagner, *Alfred Schütz: An Intellectual Biography* and Ilja Srubar, *Kosmion. Die Genese der pragmatischen Lebenswelttheorie von Alfred Schütz und ihr anthropologischer Hintergrund* ['Cosmion: The Genesis of Alfred Schütz's Pragmatic Theory of the Life-World and its Anthropological Background'].) This he did in a number of essays and then in a fragmentary work completed and posthumously published by his student, the leading phenomenological sociologist Thomas Luckmann (b. 1927) (Alfred Schütz and Thomas Luckmann, *The Structures of the Life-World*). Here, Schütz strove to shed light on the structures of *everyday knowledge* as the core component of the life-world, which he also described as the 'province of reality', 'which the wide-awake and normal adult simply takes for granted in the attitude of common sense. By this taken-for-grantedness, we designate everything which we experience as unquestionable; every state of affairs which is for us unproblematic until further notice' (Schütz and Luckmann, *The Structures of the Life-World*, pp. 3f.). Schütz elaborated in detail how the understanding of the other, the understanding of his actions, proceeds. People use *typification*, ascribe *typical* motives and *typical* identities, identify *typical* actions – drawing on taken-for-granted social interpretive patterns to make sense of the actions of others. Understanding thus depends on a number of social conditions, in as much as we must draw on the interpretive patterns with which our life-world provides us. In everyday life, we attempt to capture through typifying categories, to understand, to *normalize* as it were, even those things which we are unable to interpret immediately. The entire process of carrying out everyday action is geared towards preventing doubt about the world, as it appears to us, from arising in the first place – an insight which, as we shall see, was to have a nothing less than electrifying effect on Garfinkel.

Because this is the case, because we are always dependent on typifications in our everyday lives, we may state that our actions take place within a certain 'horizon' of the familiar and taken-for-granted; we simply have certain perceptual patterns and recipes for action at our disposal, which we may deploy in highly variable and specific contexts and which we therefore do not question. But at the same time, there are also phenomena – day-dreams, ecstatic experiences, crises such as death, and the theoretical stance characteristic of the sciences – in which the matter-of-factness of the life-world is, as it were, undone, in which another reality suddenly appears or the potential for another reality becomes conceivable (Schütz and Luckmann, *The Structures of the Life-World*, vol. II, pp. 117ff.).

Where Schütz led, the ethnomethodologists were to follow. Garfinkel and his comrade-in-arms Harvey Sacks (1935–75) put it this way: 'Schütz's writings furnished us with endless directives in our studies of the circumstances and practices of practical sociological inquiry' (Garfinkel and Sacks, 'On Formal Structures of Practical Actions', p. 342).

First, the typical patterns of perception and recipes for action rather vaguely referred to by Husserl and more specifically by Schütz may also be demonstrated *empirically*, in fact far more effectively and more plausibly demonstrated than the philosopher Husserl and the philosophizing social theorist Schütz managed to do. In this regard, Garfinkel proposed an ingenious methodological tactic in order empirically to 'get at' the facts which the phenomenologists had in mind. His empirical method was based on the idea that taken-for-granted perceptual patterns and recipes for action are most and above all most immediately apparent when one wilfully destroys them. For the destruction of the taken-for-granted distresses the affected actors. This state of 'being distressed' may at the same time serve as an indication that a taken-for-granted rule of quotidian existence is being broken. Garfinkel puts this as follows:

> In accounting for the persistence and continuity of the features of concerted actions, sociologists commonly select some set of stable features of an organization of activities and ask for the variables that contribute to their stability. An alternative procedure would appear to be more economical: to start with a system with stable features and ask what can be done to make for trouble. The operations that one would have to perform in order to produce and sustain anomic features of perceived environments and disorganized interaction should tell us something about how social structures are ordinarily and routinely being maintained.
>
> (Garfinkel, 'A Conception of, and Experiments with, "Trust" as a Condition of Stable Concerted Actions', p. 187)

The 'breaching experiments' which we shall discuss in a moment are intended to shed light on the 'formal structures of practical actions' (Garfinkel and Sacks, 'On Formal Structures of Practical Actions', p. 345), those 'grammatical structures' (Weingarten and Sack, 'Ethnomethodologie' ('Ethnomethodology'), p. 15), which, as it were, exist beneath the level of reference to norms, disputes over norms, etc. on which Parsons always had his sights set.

Second, some of Garfinkel's comrades-in-arms developed a keen interest in the 'other worlds' which also fascinated Alfred Schütz, especially non-Western cultures and the other rationalities to be found there, because comparison cast light on the taken-for-granted features of Western culture and its life-world. An interest in other ways of living and forms of rationality became highly fashionable, soon culminating in a deeply problematic debate on relativism, which was centred on the question of whether scientific knowledge can and ought to lay claim at all to an elevated status vis-à-vis other types of knowledge.

But let us turn first to Garfinkel's breaching experiments. Garfinkel set himself and his students the task of laying bare the implicit structures of everyday action by causing controlled deviations from that which one would expect, from 'normal' behaviour, in an experimental situation. What exactly did this involve? Garfinkel organized games of chess, for example, in which an unsuspecting test person faced the experimenter, who systematically broke the rules of the game, made wrong moves, suddenly switched the position of his own pieces, rearranged his opponent's pieces, etc. The result was almost always confusion on the part of the test persons. But at the same time, it was also immediately apparent, and this is the sociologically interesting thing, that the test subjects tried to *normalize* the situation, to offer 'normal' explanations, in order to render the experimenter's behaviour comprehensible *to themselves and at the same time to suggest to the experimenter the existence of a normal situation*. The test subjects attempted to interpret the whole situation as a joke or prank, or wondered whether the experimenter was playing some kind of clever, subtle game with them, not 'chess' but perhaps something quite different, or whether the experimenter was indeed playing chess, but was – rather ineptly – cheating, or perhaps the whole thing was really an experiment and thus not 'real', etc.

For Garfinkel, the theoretical insight thus obtained was that not only in the quasi-artificial situation of the game, but also in the context of normal everyday action, people constantly and almost desperately attempt to categorize the unusual, distressing, impermissible behaviour of the other as normal, 'to treat the observed behavior as an instance of a legally possible event' (Garfinkel, 'Conception', p. 22). The other is always immediately offered, in fact has forced upon him, acceptable and plausible explanations for his deviant conduct. We feel nothing less than compelled to refer to the *meaningfulness* and *comprehensibility* of our action. As we carry out actions in everyday life, we actively produce normality, thus assuring ourselves of the normality of our world, in as much as we categorize deviant and distressing events within our familiar interpretive framework, thus explaining them or explaining them away. In light of this active production of everyday normality, Garfinkel and the ethnomethodologists describe the reality with which we are confronted not as something automatically given, but as 'reflexive activity' (Mehan and Wood, 'Five Features of Reality', p. 354).

Another breaching experiment frequently described in the literature, one which you can easily carry out yourself, tells us something about the corporeality of our action. Action is not only a mental process, but also one in which gestures, facial expressions, etc. and thus bodily aspects play a decisive role, as we have learned from Mead and the symbolic interactionists in particular. When interacting with others, for example, maintenance of an *appropriate* physical distance between the parties is vitally important, and this distance varies from culture to culture. When we talk to another person, we intuitively position ourselves at a certain physical distance away from her, very much in line with the nature of the situation. And this distance can be determined quite precisely through breaching experiments. It is quite simply irritating for the salesman if you, as the customer, get so close to him that your noses are practically touching. He will inevitably move back in order to re-establish the 'normal' distance. On the other hand, it would be considered impolite and extremely unusual were you always to insist upon a 3.5 metre space between you and every quotidian interlocutor, in the absence of any pressing need for such a great distance.

At the same time, people immediately try to normalize the situation whenever the typical distance is not maintained. City-dwellers, for example, experience this almost every day when they use over-crowded buses or underground trains. The culturally specific normal distance between bodies is automatically infringed, especially when the faces of complete strangers are mere centimetres away or when one's arms and hands come close, perhaps 'dangerously' close, to the genitals or breasts of others amid the tumult. Such negligible distance is only really permissible in unambiguously sexually defined situations. But travelling by underground train is not a situation of this kind, which is why all those who find themselves in these difficult situations and do not in fact have any sexual intentions try to *normalize* them in such a way as to exclude all sexual content. If you find yourself on an underground train just two centimetres away from the tip of a complete stranger's nose, you do not make things even worse by looking her in the eye; rather, you stare off into space, look at the ceiling or close your eyes, etc.!

Finally, we wish to present one more breaching experiment, one which shows yet again how greatly Garfinkel's methods were influenced and inspired by the thought of Schütz. From Schütz and his analyses, Garfinkel knew that when dealing with one another in everyday life, people take it for granted that others generally agree on the aspects of the action and of the situation relevant to them; when one meets another, talks to him, etc., one typically assumes that one leaves behind the specific, individual aspects of one's biography and that as one interacts one is operating on a level on which *both* parties can somehow relate to the same situation in the same way. This statement sounds more complicated than it is, so let us turn straight away to the experiment carried out by Garfinkel and his colleagues which elucidates it.

One of Garfinkel's students (experimenter = E) brought about the following situation involving her husband (subject = S):

> On Friday night my husband and I were watching television. My husband remarked that he was tired. I asked, 'How are you tired? Physically, mentally, or just bored?'
>
> (S) 'I don't know, I guess physically, mainly.'
> (E) 'You mean that your muscles ache, or your bones?'
> (S) 'I guess so. Don't be so technical.'
> (S) (After more watching) 'All these old movies have the same kind of old iron bedstead in them.'
> (E) 'What do you mean? Do you mean all old movies, or some of them, or just the ones you have seen?'
> (S) 'What's the matter with you? You know what I mean.'
> (E) 'I wish you would be more specific.'
> (S) 'You know what I mean! Drop dead!'
>
> (Garfinkel, *Studies in Ethnomethodology*, p. 221)

This experiment illustrates at least three theoretically interesting facts.

1. In the course of everyday communication, we always assume the kind of agreement mentioned above on what is of relevance to the actors involved. In remarking on his own tiredness, the husband merely states that he feels tired (*somehow*), that he feels a *vague* sense of tiredness; he has no clear goal in mind in making this statement. He is merely relating his mood. In fact, much of our everyday communication is like this, with both parties to the interaction talking for the sake of communication, neither of them pursuing a particular, clearly formulated goal. In her role as experimenter, the wife consciously eschews this assumption and adopts the technical approach of a doctor by asking for a description of what exactly the poor husband means by 'tired'. But this attitude is entirely inappropriate while watching television on an evening in one's own home, which is why the husband reacts with understandable irritation.
2. The example of communication outlined above shows everyday language to be inexact and vague. This is particularly apparent in the second half of the conversation. The statement 'All these old movies' is in fact ambiguous and probably wrong, at least if one were to examine it in scientific-theoretical mode. This is exactly what the wife does, profoundly unsettling her husband. This lays bare how we always reciprocally ascribe clarity to the statements we make when engaging in everyday communication. We assume that our statements are meaningful and that others grasp this meaning without trouble. Our quotidian world is thus structured in such a way that we can live with the unavoidable obscurity of our communication without further ado. Garfinkel (*Studies in Ethnomethodology*, pp. 38f.)

Table 7.1

Husband: Dana succeeded in putting a penny in a parking meter today without being picked up.	*This afternoon as I was bringing Dana, our four-year-old son, home from the nursery school, he succeeded in reaching high enough to put a penny in a parking meter when we parked in a meter parking zone, whereas before he has always had to be picked up to reach that high.*
Wife: Did you take him to the record store?	*Since he put a penny in a meter that means that you stopped while he was with you. I know that you stopped at the record store either on the way to get him or on the way back. Was it on the way back, so that he was with you or did you stop there on the way to get him and somewhere else on the way back?*
Husband: No, to the shoe repair shop.	*No, I stopped at the record store on the way to get him and stopped at the shoe repair shop on the way home when he was with me.*
Wife: What for?	*I know of one reason why you might have stopped at the shoe repair shop. Why did you in fact?*
Husband: I got some new shoe laces for my shoes.	*As you will remember I broke a shoe lace on one of my brown Oxfords the other day so I stopped to get some new laces.*
Wife: Your loafers need new heels badly.	*Something else you could have gotten that I was thinking of. You could have taken in your black loafers which need heels badly. You'd better get them taken care of pretty soon.*

demonstrated this by recording everyday conversations and attempting to restate them in precise and unambiguous language in which – as far as possible – all tacit assumptions and suppositions find explicit expression (see the right-hand column in italics in Table 7.1).

In this connection, following Husserl, Garfinkel refers to the notion that everyday language is saturated by 'occasional expressions', by words 'whose sense cannot be decided by an auditor without his necessarily knowing or assuming something about the biography and the purposes of the user of the expression, the circumstances of the utterance, the previous course of the conversation, or the particular relationship of actual or potential interaction that exists between the expressor and the auditor' (Garfinkel, 'Aspects of the Problem of Common-Sense Knowledge of Social Structures', p. 60).

The reference to the 'occasional' or 'indexical' character of language is also implicitly of key importance to Garfinkel's critique of the Parsonian model of the actor, according to which actors relate without a hitch to norms or objects. For Garfinkel, meanwhile, every statement and act is merely the starting point of a complicated process of interpretation (Heritage, *Garfinkel and Ethnomethodology*, p. 140) which actors must perform and sociologists cast light on. This also has consequences for empirical social research, as the ethnomethodologists are suspicious of all methods that fail to pay attention to this unavoidable *indexicality* of everyday language or which tend to exclude it – through standardized questionnaires, for example. They are doubtful that these methods are capable of capturing the complex everyday processes of interpretation in any meaningful sense. At the same time, the ethnomethodologists see that the scientific process itself, every instance of communication between scientists and every perusal of collected data, is also dependent on everyday language and thus the apparent objectivity of science is inevitably 'contaminated' by it. We need to think about this rather than airbrushing it out if we are to avoid coming to flawed conclusions. 'We must assume that the normal attitude found in everyday life holds sway not only within the practical sociological investigations carried out *on a daily basis* by members of society, but also in those carried out by professional sociologists. The normal attitude of everyday life is no more restricted to the "man in the street" than are sociological investigations to professional sociologists' (ibid., p. 195; original emphasis). When Garfinkel talks about the 'sociological investigations' carried out by normal members of society, he is referring to the fact that certain ethnomethodologists attempted to deny science its special, elevated status vis-à-vis other 'worlds' and to make the social sciences themselves the subject of research (Psathas, 'Die Untersuchung von Alltagsstrukturen und das ethnomethodologische Paradigma' ['The Study of Everyday Structures and the Ethnomethodological Paradigm'], pp. 186ff.). We shall return to this topic later, when we discuss ethnomethodology's preferred research fields.

3. The communication experiment involving the husband and wife watching television – particularly the husband's concluding remarks – ultimately gives rise to the theoretically highly interesting insight that we place genuine trust in others' achievements of interpretation as we go about our daily lives. 'Trust', a pivotal concept for Garfinkel, is a phenomenon directly connected with the third element in his critique of Parsons and lends plausibility to his assertion that Parsons discussed the problem of order at the wrong level.

The husband responds angrily and gruffly to his wife's questions and answers. But, as Garfinkel demonstrated by means of a whole series of other breaching experiments, this is not a characteristic specific to this particular test person. In fact, *almost all* test persons respond in this way, if over the course of the experiment it turns out that their faith in the normality of the everyday world is being subverted. Sanctions ensue – the test person becomes furious, angry, shouts, etc. – if the rules of everyday living and everyday knowledge are broken, if the taken-for-granted aspects of the everyday world are threatened. This is something very different from what happens when, for example, certain deeds are punished or people are made into (deviant) offenders, as explored in the sociology of deviant behaviour. The wife is not offending against a written or unwritten instantly identifiable norm. What she is infringing and causing to collapse is rather her husband's *faith in the normality of the world*, and *this* is what he reacts to so angrily. What guarantees social order is the self-evident validity of our everyday world, which is protected and buttressed by a high degree of trust. This explains why the ethnomethodologists argue that the moral rules emphasized by Parsons are merely secondary phenomena, as social order is constituted on a quite different, far deeper level than Parsons assumed. Garfinkel himself provided a powerful account of this. With reference to the relationship between the (Parsonian) normative regulation of action and the taken-for-granted, trust-based stability of everyday action (elucidated by ethnomethodology), he claimed that

> the critical phenomenon is not the 'intensity of affect' with which the 'rule' is 'invested', or the respected or sacred or moral status of the rule, but the perceived normality of environmental events as this normality is a function of the presuppositions that define the possible events.
>
> (Garfinkel, 'Conception', p. 198)

The decisive or substantiating dimension with regard to social order – Garfinkel tells us – is not the 'strength' or the binding nature of moral rules emphasized so often by the likes of Durkheim and Parsons, but the normality of everyday life, on the basis of which people relate to norms in the first place. Or, to recall once again the quote from Cicourel: as the structures of everyday knowledge and action, the fundamental rules determine the applicability of norms.

From the outset, ethnomethodology as a whole was concerned to analyse the hidden grammar of everyday knowledge and action. A whole number of important and fundamental rules were undoubtedly 'discovered' here, which were of course of tremendous importance to the theory of action and the critique of existing sociological theories. But it was not solely due to its theoretical insights that ethnomethodology became so hugely fashionable and attracted the younger generation of sociologists in particular, especially in the 1960s. It also appealed because it enabled one to adopt – as in the breaching experiments – a clownish attitude, to consciously behave 'foolishly', because the experiments were aimed 'at problems which, from the point of view of those who wish to *do* something in the world, are not problems at all' (Wieder and Zimmermann, 'Regeln im Erklärungsprozeß' ['Rules Within the Process of Explanation'], p. 124). One could have fun destroying trust in the structures of the everyday world, knowing all the while that one was producing relevant knowledge. The proximity to the theatre of the absurd, which was quite popular in the 1960s, was unmistakable; in both cases, rules and norms were deliberately offended against. In the case of ethnomethodology, there was always a risk that these experiments might degenerate into 'happenings', undermining its claim to the status of serious theoretical player.

This danger was further amplified by ethnomethodology's great interest in different and unfamiliar cultures and rationalities. In the days of the hippie movement and so-called counter-culture, in which the world of drug-taking exercised as much fascination as the unfamiliar world of India and the literature of Carlos Castaneda, which was wrongly considered to constitute ethnography, this interest was unsurprising and in keeping with the times. But what captivated many ethnomethodologists were different world views which, if one accepts their premises, certainly function in line with a consistent logic insofar as the 'unfamiliar' actors involved also ceaselessly produce *their version* of everyday normality. By making comparisons with sometimes radically different cultural grammars, one could obtain certain insights into the functioning of our own 'world' while encouraging understanding of unfamiliar cultures and their assumptions about the nature of rationality. For example, ethnomethodologists – again drawing heavily on Schützian ideas – pointed out that one of the essential premises of our culture is that of the constancy of objects, the conviction that objects remain the same objects, that they do not suddenly change and become something quite different and that they do not, in as much as we are dealing with inanimate objects, move independently, disappear, etc. (see also Mehan and Wood, 'Five Features'). This may be a rather trite insight, but in certain circumstances it can become quite interesting.

Imagine that you have mislaid an object, such as your sunglasses. When you entered the relatively dark front hall of your flat, having just been outside, you took them off and placed them on the shelf by the front door. Twenty minutes later, on this beautiful sunny day, you again want to leave the house. You go to the shelf – and the glasses are no longer there, although there was and is no one else in the flat. You could have sworn that you put the glasses right there on the shelf. But they are not there. You begin to scour the flat in search of these glasses, until at length you discover them on the TV. As a rule, you will react by explaining the whole thing to yourself: 'Although I was absolutely sure I had put the glasses on the shelf, I obviously didn't. I was probably off in another world; that happens a lot actually. I really am scatterbrained sometimes. I must have somehow subconsciously put the glasses on the TV.' These are no doubt the kind of thoughts that would pass through your mind in such cases. Despite being absolutely sure, when you began searching, that you had put the glasses on the shelf, there is one thing you do not do: you do not seriously consider the possibility that glasses move independently, that they can fly, perhaps as the result of some kind of magic, or that they sometimes prefer to sit on the shelf and sometimes on the TV. But if you were really so sure about the location of the glasses, this would have been a plausible and entirely rational attempt at explanation – at least as plausible and rational as your retrospective and thus rather unconvincing admission of your own muddle-headedness. Precisely because we are convinced of the constancy of objects in our culture – the object in this case being an inanimate one – we exclude the possibility that glasses can fly. This is why we look for another rationalization to explain what has happened.

But there are cultures in which the assumption of object constancy is not self-evident and in which the basic situation described above might be explained as follows: the disappearance of an object is due to the influence of the gods, or the magical powers of the sorcerer, etc. Such explanatory strategies can indeed be found in certain cultures. Ethnomethodologists have pointed out that this is anything but irrational. In light of the premises characteristic of these cultures, these explanatory achievements are entirely understandable. In other cultures too, the actors ceaselessly produce normality and act in an entirely rational fashion. And just as we in our Western culture always assume that our actions are rational, individuals in other cultural settings do so as well – in a way, in fact, that is extremely plausible *given the particular premises* that pertain.

This line of thought rapidly led on to the question of whether our Western culture can lay claim to higher standards of rationality than non-Western cultures and whether science in particular boasts a higher form of rationality than other forms of knowledge, such as magic. A rather controversial and at times obscure debate on relativism kicked off (see for example Kippenberg and Luchesi, *Magie. Die sozialwissenschaftliche Kontroverse über das*

Verstehen fremden Denkens ['Magic: The Social Scientific Dispute over How to Understand Other Ways of Thinking']). The value of this debate was questionable at times, particularly as, in light of the undeniable fact that knowledge is temporally and spatially bound and thus context-dependent, many of the debaters rushed to the conclusion that all forms of knowledge are *equally* valid or cannot be compared in the first place and are not therefore amenable to assessment. But this is certainly not the case. It is absolutely possible to compare forms and stocks of knowledge and then to produce a balanced assessment of them. This is often difficult, and at times it may prove impossible to come to a clear conclusion. But this predicament is not all that different from that in which scientists find themselves when, as described in Lecture I, they have to choose between two competing paradigms. Even in the absence of a 'crucial experiment' to clear things up, it is certainly possible to *discuss and compare reasonably*. In much the same way, it is possible to contrast the stock of quotidian knowledge found in different cultures.

The fact that a fair number of ethnomethodologists rejected this notion, often drawing relativistic conclusions from their investigations, and the fact that at least some enjoyed their role as critics of science and of sociology in particular far too much, had a generally deleterious effect on this school of thought. From the mid-1970s, ethnomethodology rapidly lost influence in the USA and elsewhere; it does not appear capable of providing sociology with innovative new ideas at present. The fact that this long-ignored theoretical current is currently undergoing something of a revival in France, where it has suddenly taken on a new importance, does nothing to change this (see Dosse, *Empire of Meaning*, pp. 67ff.).

Turning to the thematic foci of this theory, it is striking that *macro*sociology was little affected by it and that its key authors rarely make even general statements on social change. The strength of ethnomethodology lay and lies still in the highly detailed description of *micro*situations, which can provide us with important insights germane to a *theory of action*. It was the empirical research spurred by breaching experiments that enabled Garfinkel and those of like mind to formulate statements of great action theoretical import. The field of empirical research known as conversation analysis (Harvey Sacks, Emanuel A. Schegloff, b. 1937), which developed out of these stimuli, attempts to thoroughly illuminate the mechanisms of conversation as well as non-verbal communication such as eye contact (see for example Schegloff, 'Accounts of Conduct in Interaction: Interruption, Overlap, and Turn-Taking'). As far as the *theory of order* is concerned, we have already addressed the ethnomethodological critique of Parsons and the concurrent emphasis on the taken-for-granted nature of everyday knowledge; again, key insights have penetrated the 'other' theoretical approaches within sociology, as we shall see once again, for example, in Lecture XII (on Anthony Giddens).

In addition, ethnomethodology continues to exercise a significant influence in five key areas or empirical fields:

1. Ethnomethodology's powerful critique of traditional action theory and the recognition of the indexicality of everyday language has inspired a new caution and circumspection within the general sociological debate on methods. Sociologists reflect a good deal more on how data are generated and obtained than they did before ethnomethodology appeared on the sociological stage. This is due in no small part to a book which continues to be of central importance, Aaron Cicourel's *Method and Measurement in Sociology*, an in-depth investigation of the research process, particularly the adequacy of certain tools of data collection. For anyone wanting to get to grips with the problems of quantitative social research, for example, Cicourel's 1964 book remains indispensable. Jack Douglas' book *The Social Meanings of Suicide* (1967) is a particularly graphic and spectacular exposition of the significance of the ethnomethodological critique of methodology. In contrast to Durkheim's project in his book on suicide, Douglas was interested mainly in *how data on suicide are collected* by national or local authorities. By showing exactly which underlying assumptions, prejudices, etc. are involved in the construction of an 'official' suicide, Douglas made it clear that official statistics cannot be taken at 'face value'. This of course has ramifications for some of Durkheim's findings, in as much as he had avoided serious consideration of how his data were produced and had reached his theoretical conclusions, without a hitch, on the basis of the available official information – rendering them highly questionable according to Douglas. Similar reservations apply to crime statistics. Ethnomethodological research has demonstrated how the relevant data are produced. Investigation of these statistics reveals, for example, the curious fact that an increased police presence leads to a dramatic increase in crime figures. This is not because more crimes are committed when the number of police in a given neighbourhood increases, a highly implausible outcome, but because these police officers record more crime: always on the go in one way or another, they log offences more or less in passing.
2. This last point leads us to the next field in which ethnomethodology has a strong presence: the sociology of deviant behaviour. Here, the conduct and 'offence-producing' activities of supervisory authorities such as the police were investigated in great detail. Authors such as Egon Bittner (b. 1921; 'Police Discretion in Emergency Apprehension of Mentally Ill Persons') and Harvey Sacks ('Notes on Police Assessment of Moral Character') brought out the tremendous room for manoeuvre enjoyed by the police as they go about their daily duties, the highly contingent criteria, which have nothing to do with the letter of the law, that spur them to action in certain

situations, and how differently their perception of everyday incidents is structured from that of 'lay people'.
3. In light of our previous remarks, it will come as no surprise that the authors influenced by Alfred Schütz also exercised a significant influence on the field of the sociology of knowledge. Here, rather than in ethnomethodology, founded by Garfinkel, it was certain aspects of Schütz's work, which could be linked with the critique of ideology characteristic of some of the classical figures of sociology, that took centre stage. One work in particular broke new ground in this regard, *The Social Construction of Reality* by Peter L. Berger and Thomas Luckmann. This commanding book deployed Schütz's ideas to undergird or amend the work of classical authors who had dealt with topics in the sociology of knowledge, such as Karl Marx, Max Scheler (1874–1928) and Karl Mannheim (1893–1947). Particularly in the 1960s, which saw renewed interest in the work of Marx, this book, which appeared in 1966, provided important food for thought with respect to the associated debate on the 'nature' and content of ideologies. Despite the fact that the ideological-political disputes characteristic of Western societies in the 1960s have since become less significant, and the same fate has befallen the sociology of knowledge as a result, the classical status of this work by Berger and Luckmann which, to repeat, has little in common with the Garfinkelian research tradition, remains undiminished.
4. The themes covered in point 3 bear closely on the sociology of science. Given that ethnomethodologists set out to examine how reality is produced by comparing different 'worlds', it is unsurprising that the analytical spotlight soon fell on science itself. Garfinkel himself was involved in research of this kind, his interest lying, for instance, in the reality of the laboratory, the ways in which facts are produced and interpreted in such settings (Lynch, Livingston and Garfinkel, 'Temporal Order in Laboratory Work'). By drawing on ethnomethodological ideas, a sociology of science taking an ethnographic approach showed, for example, how greatly even this supposedly highly rational research process is moulded by the structures of everyday action, how arbitrary decisions determine this process, how chance occurrences influence how the research develops, how researchers must first acquire the ability to see 'facts' through constant practice, how seemingly clear rules of research are often thrown overboard or bent, how even here – as with the jurors – research reports retrospectively stylize the actual course of events and how greatly 'dependent' even highly technical experiments are on the interaction of scientists, who decisively shape how the data are analysed (see for example Karin Knorr-Cetina, *The Manufacture of Knowledge: An Essay on the Constructivist and Contextual Nature of Science*).

5. Ethnomethodology has also exercised a significant influence on feminist research and theory building. We shall be going into this in more detail in Lecture XVII.

This brings us to the end of our lectures on the 'interpretive approaches'. Along with neo-utilitarianism, symbolic interactionism and ethnomethodology rebelled against the Parsonian hegemony in the 1950s and 1960s. Another school of thought existed, however, which we have not yet mentioned and which also competed with Parsonian theory. We are referring to conflict theory, which demands discussion before we can consider subsequent developments, and to which we turn in the next lecture. The late 1970s were to see a turning point: taking all these critiques into account and trying once again to productively continue where Parsons had left off in his attempts at theoretical synthesis, sociologists produced new large-scale syntheses. This was the only way to ward off the danger of the subject fragmenting into a disconnected juxtaposition of 'schools' or 'approaches'.

VIII

Conflict sociology and conflict theory

Both neo-utilitarianism and the interpretive approaches of symbolic interactionism and ethnomethodology were reactions to the dominance of the Parsons school in the 1950s and 1960s. In both cases, the concept of action was the key subject of debate. While the neo-utilitarians found the Parsonian model of action overly normative and generally too complicated, believing that it had tended to weaken the explanatory power of sociology, the interactionists and ethnomethodologists thought Parsons' normative conception of action inadequate and insufficiently complex. The neo-utilitarians thus tried to revive the tradition of utilitarianism to which Parsons had bid farewell, while the symbolic interactionists stood in continuity with the American pragmatists whom Parsons had ignored, especially in his early work; by taking up phenomenological ideas, the ethnomethodologists set off along new, one might say dissident, paths. But all three schools wrestled primarily with the Parsonian conception of action, while the problem of social order, let alone that of social change, was paid far less attention.

The rise of so-called conflict sociology in the mid-1950s must be seen against this background; in every sense, it represents an antithesis of Parsons or of a certain understanding of Parsons. Many sociologists felt that Parsons' theoretical conception of order and change made too much of the normative elements of social reality. As a result, according to them, it merely assumed the existence of a stable social order, proceeding without reflection on the premise that societies are static and well-ordered. The conflict sociologists countered this with an alternative theory that emphasized the role of power relations and naked conflicts of interests in social life, thus highlighting the dynamism and often rapid change characteristic of social orders. In short, social 'conflict' was placed firmly centre stage in the process of sociological theory building in an effort to evade Parsons' normative model of order at a basic conceptual level. Unsurprisingly, this conflict sociology exercised a particular appeal in the 1960s, a time when various social movements, especially the student movement, were becoming increasingly critical of the Western, particularly American, model of society, singling out Parsonian theory as a reactionary defence of the state of American society. But we wish to underline that the conflict sociological critique of Parsons was by no means restricted to the *left* of the political spectrum.

Whatever the critics' political motivation may have been, Parsons himself felt that they had misunderstood him, badly in some cases. He had after all been arguing at a higher level of abstraction in his early action- and order-theoretical analyses in *Structure* as well as in his middle period of structural-functionalist writings. By no means did he intend to defend a particular social and political order such as that of the USA. He had just as little interest in denying the existence of social conflicts. The main thrust of his argument – this at least is how he saw things – was in fact 'transcendental' in the Kantian sense: he had asked what the basic prerequisites for social order are. And the answer to this question has nothing to do with whether one tends to see empirical evidence of order-creating or conflictual factors at work within a particular social reality. Parsons worked on the assumption of the empirical existence of order, but did not of course deny the existence of conflicts. The conflict sociologists' attacks thus inevitably seemed misplaced to him, particularly given that he had explicitly attempted to come up with a theory of social change from the 1960s on (see Lecture IV). Was the rise of conflict sociology due to a misunderstanding, the consequence of a distorted or merely very one-sided perception of Parsonian theory? Yes and no. Parsons was certainly correct in his insistence that his action- and order-theoretical analyses were beyond direct empirical criticism. For the most part, he did in fact argue at a higher theoretical level than many of his conflict sociological critics. On the other hand, and even Parsons' followers were eventually to concede this, the entire Parsonian theoretical framework lacked a set of sensitive conceptual tools with which to grasp the nature of conflicts. The critics were thus by no means entirely wrong to criticize Parsons' writings – particularly his empirical analyses – for their strong tendency to emphasize harmony, generally disregarding the existence of massive conflicts and clashes of interest and thus presenting social change as continuous and linear in a quite inadequate way. Parsons' late work in the field of evolutionary theory, which saw him grapple with the problem of macrosocial change, failed, as we have seen, to truly refute this criticism. There were thus good reasons why some suspected that a 'harmonious bias' was built into the very foundations of Parsons' theoretical edifice or that this edifice was constructed in such a way that it is difficult to focus primarily on social conflicts.

But let us turn now to conflict sociology itself, which immediately confronts us with a certain conceptual difficulty or ambiguity. One may use the term conflict sociology to refer to a sociological subdiscipline: just as the sociology of the family deals with families, and the sociology of religion concerns itself with religion, conflict sociology, understood in this way, deals with conflicts. This is one way of understanding the term. But – and this is of rather more interest to us within the framework of our lectures on modern social theory – conflict sociology may also refer to a *theoretical approach in its own right*. We shall therefore use the term 'conflict *theory*' to refer to this latter meaning. This choice of terminology makes sense to us as it helps avoid confusion: historically, the origins of conflict *theory* are in fact found within conflict *sociology*.

There are good reasons why we suggested above that Parsonian theory failed to afford a central place to the topic of conflict. For conflicts were in fact never *central* for Parsons and his followers, despite the fact that they studied them as empirical phenomena. Those sociologists close to Parsons began to modify or expand on Parsonian role theory at an early stage by pointing – like Robert Merton (see for example 'Continuities in the Theory of Reference Groups and Social Structure') – to intra- and inter-role conflicts, to the fact that different, conflicting behavioural expectations must often be met within one and the same role (a child's mother and father have different expectations of him, for example) or the fact that individuals almost always have a variety of roles to perform (women often perform the role of mother and worker at the same time), which cannot be seen as straightforwardly compatible, and which thus give rise to conflicts. But these further developments were not meant as a far-reaching critique of Parsons, especially given that Merton immediately referred to the techniques with which actors generally defuse or master these problems; neither did they constitute a shift of emphasis within structural-functionalist theory towards the analysis of social conflicts. The edifice of Parsonian normative theory remained intact; space was merely made, as it were, for the study of quite specific conflicts, that is, *role* conflicts.

A notable advance occurred through the work of Lewis Coser, who was born in Berlin in 1913 and emigrated to the USA in 1941 (d. 2003). While Coser's work was closely aligned with that of Parsons and his theoretical approach, in 1956 he formulated a detailed critique in *The Functions of Social Conflict*. Among other things, he criticized the fact that functionalists such as Parsons had for the most part interpreted conflicts as psychologically determined phenomena, as individual lapses, sometimes even as 'illness'. This, he claimed, was because this theoretical tradition interprets the social status quo as normal, and any deviations from it can only be interpreted as disturbances, as cases of *individual* maladaptation. In his view, Parsons in particular had shown almost no serious interest in conflictual social processes, in part because he had been too much of a Durkheimian and not enough of a Weberian. What Coser meant was that Parsons had been too quick to embrace Durkheim's emphasis on values with respect to social integration while generally ignoring Max Weber's correct insight into the significance of struggle to the social system (*The Functions of Social Conflict*, pp. 21ff.).

Coser was certainly to the left of Parsons politically and frequently championed his democratic socialist ideals openly and vigorously. But his critique of Parsons' generally static model of the social world is not due solely to this particular difference. Rather, a cultural factor appears to have played a role here. Coser was Jewish and was himself influenced by a Jewish author, one of the founding fathers of German sociology, who had already made a substantial contribution to the analysis of conflicts by the threshold of the twentieth century. We are referring to Georg Simmel, whose book *Soziologie* (1908) contains a brilliant essay entitled 'Conflict'. Here, among other things, Simmel presented a typology of conflict, analysed the consequences of this form of social relationship and provided revealing insights into those situations in which a third party may exploit a dispute between two others, true to the saying: 'When two fight, the third wins'. But it was not the specific observations made by Simmel that were crucial to Coser. Far more important was the fact that Simmel clearly diverged from the cultural tradition then (and perhaps still) dominant in Germany, which immediately attaches a negative label to arguments, conflicts, disputes, etc. Simmel in contrast had a very positive view of this type of social relationship, which was certainly due in part to the rabbinical culture of argument that had developed over the centuries, in which conflicts were by no means interpreted as a threat to the community. And it is precisely this positive or at least neutral attitude towards argument and conflicts which Coser adopted by carrying it over into functionalist arguments. As the title of Coser's book (*The Functions of Social Conflict*) suggests, and as he states explicitly in the preface, his central concern is the function fulfilled by social conflicts. Coser understands conflict as a type of sociation:

> This means essentially that ... no group can be entirely harmonious, for it would then be devoid of process and structure. Groups require disharmony as well as harmony, dissociation as well as association; and conflicts within them are by no means altogether disruptive factors. Group formation is the result of both types of processes.
>
> (Coser, *The Functions of Social Conflict*, p. 31)

Drawing, sometimes heavily, on Simmel, Coser pointed to the potential of conflicts to 'clear the air' and thus to act as a kind of safety valve. He underlined that by no means every conflict is inevitably accompanied by aggressive acts and, above all, and this was directly aimed at the narrow focus of Parsonian theory, that the absence of conflicts in itself tells us nothing about the stability of a social system: the lack of conflicts may point to subliminal tensions, which may erupt at a later point in uncontrolled fashion. In other words, if conflicts are settled in an open way, this may well be a sign of stability (Coser, *The Functions of Social Conflict*, p. 94). Coser takes a step further. Particularly in a subsequent work entitled *Continuities in the Study of Social Conflict* from 1967, he claims that conflicts often have a highly positive effect on entire societies, in that they may trigger learning processes and provide an opportunity for the establishment of new rules and institutions. If societies permit no conflicts, they are, he asserts, incapable of learning and in the long term incapable of surviving.

> What is important for us is the idea that conflict ... prevents the ossification of the social system by exerting pressure for innovation and creativity.
>
> (Coser, *Continuities*, p. 19)

The plausibility of this thesis is evident in the case of environmental movements, which encountered a significant degree of resistance in the 1970s and 1980s in West Germany. Conflicts were by no means unusual, and violent clashes occurred at times. But these conflicts were permitted within the framework of democratic politics, giving rise to learning processes that have ultimately induced all political parties to champion environmental protection. Even if one considers the steps actually taken to protect the environment rather unimpressive, and feels that the political parties enjoy varying degrees of ecological credibility, it is surely impossible to deny that the violent suppression of ecological movements in East Germany and the withholding of relevant information in that state hampered the learning process, such that environmental destruction continued unabated into the 1980s.

Despite all these criticisms of Parsons, Coser's arguments essentially remained a development *within* functionalism. However, at the time of the publication of *The Functions of Social Conflict*, other developments were already beginning to emerge within sociology which were to lead to a radical break with that creed. The phenomenon of conflict was now turned *against* functionalism. Attempts were made, step by step, to establish conflict sociology as an independent *theoretical approach* in competition with it.

In the USA, this emerging movement was particularly associated with the name of Reinhard Bendix. Bendix (1916–91), like Coser of German-Jewish origin, had emigrated to the USA in 1938 and begun a highly successful academic career at the University of Chicago, later moving to Berkeley. While Coser had found his theoretical lodestar fairly rapidly in Simmel, whom he attempted to link with the Parsonian theoretical tradition in highly complex fashion, the development of Bendix's work is best described as a tentative search for 'suitable authors' and a suitable theory of change. Bendix was undoubtedly influenced by Marx, but was from the outset keenly aware of his great theoretical weaknesses; these he strove to overcome with the conceptual tools provided by Alexis de Tocqueville (1805–59) and above all Max Weber. His essay 'Social Stratification and Political Power' from 1952 is characteristic of this groping towards an adequate theory of social change. In it he vehemently criticizes the empirical failure of Marxian theory, due to its hopeless attempts to trace *every* conflict back to class conflicts. For Bendix, the *diversity* of conflicts in the social world is far too great for such reductionism to lay claim to any explanatory power. Yet he is unwilling to break completely with Marx; he describes Marxism as a basically 'interesting' theory of social change. What was crucial, he believed, was to defend Marx's sociological insights, rescuing them from Marx himself and his supporters.

> we should not ... abandon the genuine insight which makes the Marxian theory attractive: that the many antagonisms created in a society, and especially the conflicts inherent in its economic structure, may, but need not, give rise to collective action and that it is the task of the analyst to discover the circumstances under which collective action does or does not arise. I believe that Marx forfeited his genuine insight into the indeterminacy of the relationship between class situation and class action by his prophetic fervor, which prompted him to forecast the capitalist development with a certainty often belied by his own historical sense.
>
> ('Social Stratification', p. 600)

This motif of rescuing Marxian insights from Marx crops up again and again in conflict theory, including *European* conflict theory, which we shall discuss in a moment. The first thing we should note are the conclusions Bendix drew with respect to this emerging, massive reformulation of Marxian theory. Bendix, as we saw in the above quotation, called into doubt the close link between class situation and class action and saw that the collective action performed by groups and the political action carried out by individual actors is fairly independent of the abstract class situation. He therefore rejected the notion that the process of social change could be predicted, which is an integral feature of Marxian theory. Rather, he advocated the view that the historical process is subject to contingent circumstances, that parties to conflict and social movements are continuously shaped by 'local conditions, historical antecedents, the acuteness of the crisis' ('Social Stratification', p. 602); ahistorical generalizations about these phenomena are thus of highly dubious value. Bendix's propositions were clearly intended as an attack on the Marxian conception of history. But given that he adopts Marx's insight into the importance of conflicts to historical processes, it is no surprise that an increasingly critical stance towards Parsonian figures of thought emerged as his work developed, though this largely remained implicit.

Bendix's book *Work and Authority in Industry: Ideologies of Management in the Course of Industrialization* from 1956 was a decisive step in this direction. His historical-comparative study of the process of early industrialization in England and tsarist Russia and 'mature' industrialization in the USA and GDR was utterly out of synch with Parsons' accounts of organizations and the studies in differentiation theory and evolutionary theory produced by Parsons and his students a few years later. Bendix begins his book with the provocative conflict theoretical statement: 'Wherever enterprises are set up, a few command and many obey' (*Work and Authority*, p. 1); even at the level of description, he adopts a very different perspective from Parsons, who had always viewed organizations as based primarily on a division of labour, supported by certain values, with the object of enhancing efficiency. And while the literature on social change influenced by Parsons interpreted history as a more or less linear process in which modern social structures had, as it were, established *themselves* because of their superior rationality, Bendix described these processes as highly conflictual. For him, industrialization was not a self-propelled process, but one in which groups (aristocracy and bourgeoisie, industrialists and workers, state bureaucrats and managers) struggled one against the other and in which this struggle was dressed up in ideological garb or legitimized with the aid of ideologies. 'The few, however, have seldom been satisfied to command without a higher justification ... and the many have seldom been docile enough not to provoke such justifications' (ibid.). In a preface to a new edition of the book, Bendix underlined that while he had drawn on de Tocqueville and Marx in his analyses, he was in fact most indebted to Weber's sociology of domination (*Work and Authority*, p. xxv).

Indeed, of the classical figures of sociology, Max Weber was to become *the* reference author for a fair number of conflict theorists. While Durkheim, for example, was on the receiving end of severe criticism and was even regarded with contempt within this tradition (see Coser's trenchant critique in *Continuities*, pp. 153–80), Weber's work seemed a suitable point of departure for attacking both Marxism and structural functionalism. This, however, was a very different Weber from the one that Parsons had presented to the American public in works such as *Structure*. Here, Parsons had interpreted Weber chiefly with reference to his convergence thesis, that is, to the effect that his thought, together with that of Marshall, Pareto and Durkheim, whose background lay in the traditions of utilitarianism or positivism, had led him ever closer to a 'voluntaristic theory of action' that acknowledged the special importance of norms and values. In his *Max Weber: An Intellectual Portrait*, Bendix explicitly took aim at this normativist interpretation of Weber. In this book, which appeared in 1960, Bendix places struggle, and thus the sociology of domination, centre stage in his interpretation of Weber, rather than his analyses of world views within the sociology of religion as Parsons had done. And with this interpretation, Bendix disputes that Parsons and the structural functionalists were justified in identifying Weber as their intellectual progenitor in the first place. Bendix thus makes use of Weber in order to profoundly, if implicitly, critique Parsons:

> The view of society as a balance between opposing forces is the reason why Weber quite explicitly rejected the attempt to interpret social structures as wholes, at least in the context of sociological investigations. For him, sociology was a study of the understandable behavior of individuals in society, and collectivities like a state or a nation or a family do not 'act' or 'maintain themselves' or 'function'. ... Weber's approach conceived of society as an arena of competing status groups, each with its own

economic interests, status honor, and orientation toward the world and man.

(Bendix, *Max Weber: An Intellectual Portrait*, pp. 261–2)

Probably because of the overwhelming dominance of the Parsonian paradigm, the critique generated within American sociology concerning the topic of 'social conflict' was initially either compatible with functionalism (see Coser) or was indeed fundamental but remained implicit and lacked clearly formulated theoretical ambitions. This was the case in the work of Bendix, but also, for example, in that of an influential academic outsider, the left-wing social critic C. Wright Mills, who produced an important study on American society, *The Power Elite* (1956). Some European sociologists, meanwhile, particularly in Great Britain and Germany, were far more open-minded about Parsons' work in the 1950s. Following the fundamental critique of Parsons, attempts were made to develop a theoretical alternative – namely conflict *theory*.

In Britain, two authors in particular shaped the conflict theory of the 1950s and 1960s, David Lockwood and John Rex. Lockwood (b. 1929) made a name for himself during this period chiefly through large-scale empirical studies on class theory, drawing particularly on Weberian categories to analyse the consciousness of white- and blue-collar workers. What is more significant within the context of the present work is that he was also one of the first British authors to launch a vehement attack on Parsons' *The Social System* and whose goal was to develop his own theoretical perspective independent of that of Parsons. His now famous 1956 essay 'Some Remarks on *The Social System*' rails against the excessive emphasis on the normative and concurrent theoretical marginalization of material 'life chances' and non-normative interests in Parsons' work. Lockwood called for scholars to take an at least balanced approach to norms and material interests and to pay as much heed to the Marxian topic of exploitation (of specific groups) and the resulting social conflicts as to the Parsonian topic of socialization. Yet Lockwood certainly did not assume that Marxian categories could be applied without further ado. Quite the reverse: as Bendix had done, he expressed the non-Marxian view that social conflicts do not result solely from economic structures. With reference to the historical studies of Otto Hintze (1861–1940) and above all Max Weber's sociology of domination, he underlined that one must also take into account military and political power conflicts which cannot be traced back to economic circumstances. But quite apart from this, he asserted that while Marx's insights require modification, they are important enough to act as a crucial corrective to the Parsonian analytical strategy. In short, Lockwood stresses that Parsons' approach and the conflict theoretical approach with its roots in Marxism are 'complementary in their emphases'. He thus calls for a fusion of both approaches, because social reality is characterized both by normative patterns of order and power-based 'factual orders' – a demand he intended to comply with in a work that appeared much later (see *Solidarity and Schism: 'The Problem of Disorder' in Durkheimian and Marxist Sociology*). But as early as 1956, he stated:

> Every social situation consists of a normative order with which Parsons is principally concerned, and also of a factual order, or substratum. Both are 'given' for individuals; both are part of the exterior and constraining social world. Sociological theory is concerned, or should be, with the social and psychological processes whereby social structure in this dual sense conditions human motives and actions. The existence of a normative order in no way entails that individuals will act in accordance with it; in the same way the existence of a given factual order in no way means that certain kinds of behaviour result.
>
> (Lockwood, 'Some Remarks', pp. 139–40)

John Rex (b. 1925) is the other prominent British representative of conflict theory. Originally from South Africa, he arrived in England in the late 1940s, making a name for himself chiefly through the analysis of ethnic conflicts. In *Key Problems of Sociological Theory*, Rex criticized Parsons primarily for his one-sided theoretical development. While *The Structure of Social Action* deserved praise as a work 'without parallel as an analytical history of sociological thought' (*Key Problems of Sociological Theory*, p. 96) and whose action theoretical perspective at least allows us to think about the existence of conflicts, Parsons had, he claimed, since his structural functionalist phase at the latest, adopted a stance that merely permits exceptions (such as the deviant behaviour of individuals) to otherwise smooth and uninterrupted processes of institutionalization.

> For although we may argue with Parsons that normative elements enter into the sort of unit act which occurs in social systems, this by no means implies that social systems are completely integrated by such elements. And this is the point to which Parsons' thought continually seems to be moving, even in *The Structure of Social Action*, but much more obviously in *The Social System*.
>
> (*Key Problems*, p. 98)

Parsons' theoretical construct, Rex claimed, was ultimately idealistic, because – and Rex's argument here is very close to that of Lockwood – he no longer questions whether stable orders and normative patterns may themselves be the expression of power structures, whether, for example, the belief in the legitimacy of a particular order of ownership is the result of the institutionalization of power conflicts, perhaps stretching back over a lengthy period of time. In this connection, Rex refers to the fact that the concept of legitimacy had been introduced by Max Weber 'as one of the possible bases of *imperative co-ordination*' and 'not ... as arising from any sort of consensus of norms' (ibid., p. 181; original emphasis). He thus asks rhetorically and with a view to criticizing Parsons, 'whether it would not be better to start one's analysis with the balance of power or the conflict of interests which this balance of power is supposed to settle, rather than beginning by assuming the existence of norms' (ibid., p. 116). But Rex does not entirely reject the Parsonian perspective. Rather, like Lockwood, he regards the Parsonian 'theory of integration' and Weberian–Marxian conflict theory as complementary: the key, but very different problems of the social, he believed, can be resolved only through a combination of both theoretical approaches: 'There would be a property problem, a power problem, an ultimate value problem and a religious problem in any society' (ibid., p. 179).

But the most radical critique of Parsonianism and the most emphatic defence of the conflict theoretical approach came from a German: Ralf Dahrendorf. Dahrendorf, who was born in the same year as David Lockwood and is the son of the leading social democrat and anti-fascist resistance fighter Gustav Dahrendorf, enjoyed a meteoric rise to success within German sociology as a result of his brilliant insights; among other things, he held professorships at the universities of Hamburg, Tübingen and Constance. As he was also hugely successful as a journalist, opportunities soon opened up in the political sphere. From 1969, he was briefly parliamentary secretary for the FDP at the foreign ministry, before becoming a member of the Commission of the European Communities in 1970. His path led him to England, where he was director of the London School of Economics from 1974 to 1984 and where he was ultimately ennobled, making him Lord Dahrendorf (see Ralf Dahrendorf, *Über Grenzen. Lebenserinnerungen* ['Across Boundaries: A Memoir']).

Dahrendorf, who had completed a substantial portion of his academic education at British universities, produced a conflict theoretical critique of Parsons' structural functionalism *before* Lockwood and Rex. It is thus quite fair to say that British conflict theory derives to a significant extent from his contributions; but at the same time, Dahrendorf was himself deeply influenced by British traditions of thought within sociology, which also explains the fact that his work generally made a greater impact in the English-speaking world than in Germany. Dahrendorf's important essay 'Struktur und Funktion. Talcott Parsons und die Entwicklung der soziologischen Theorie' ('Structure and Function: Talcott Parsons and the Development of Sociological Theory') from 1955 crucially influenced Lockwood's argument with Parsons. It thus comes as no surprise that the criticisms later made in the British context already feature in his work. With respect to the development of Parsons' work, Dahrendorf concluded that there was in fact no need for Parsons to move from the theory of action to a *functionalist* theory of order (as you will no doubt recall, we dealt with this criticism in Lecture III), especially given that this inevitably led him to evade causal analysis; what is more, dysfunctions received no systematic treatment, lending Parsonian theory its static character. But at this point in time, Dahrendorf still spoke of the desirable extension of Parsonian theory rather than its refutation ('Struktur und Funktion', p. 237). In his book *Class and Class Conflict in Industrial Society* from 1957, he continues to adhere to this line: while structural functionalism – Dahrendorf tells us – is certainly capable of analysing the integrative forces within a society, it lacks a similar analytical tool for explaining or describing *structure-changing* forces (*Class*, pp. 122f.). Like Lockwood and Rex, Dahrendorf sees the potential for supplementing the Parsonian approach with a heavily modified Marxian theory of class, one, however, which must be cleansed of all 'metaphysical' ballast, that is, of any trace of philosophy of history and anthropology, but also political economy; it must be reduced down to its sociologically valuable core – the explanation of social conflicts. On this basis, it could advance to the status of a theory of change capable of explaining structure-changing forces. Dahrendorf believes that we can get past Marxian class theory only if 'we replace the possession or nonpossession, of effective private property by the exercise of, or exclusion from, authority as the criterion of class formation' (ibid., p. 136). As for Bendix, Rex and Lockwood, for Dahrendorf the control of the means of production is merely a special case of domination; relations of domination also exist in other contexts and these cannot necessarily be reduced to economic structures.

> But Marx believed that authority and power are factors which can be traced back to a man's share in effective private property. In reality, the opposite is the case. Power and authority are irreducible factors from which the social relations associated with legal private property as well as those associated with communal property can be derived. ... Property is by no means the only form of authority; it is but one of its numerous types.
>
> (ibid., p. 137)

This, then, is Dahrendorf's intellectual programme: power and domination are the basic concepts of sociology; other phenomena can, as it were, be derived from them, and on this basis we can analyse societal dynamics. For wherever there is domination, there are people subject to it, who attempt to fight the status quo in one way or another. Wherever there is domination, there is conflict, though Dahrendorf believed that most societies are characterized by a wide variety of different associations and thus by different kinds of conflict: 'In theory there can be as many competing, conflicting, or coexisting dominating conflict groups in a society as there are associations' (ibid., p. 198).

With this kind of class theory, Dahrendorf now appears to have at his disposal the key to a *theory of social change*. But his theoretical ambition found full expression only in a later essay entitled 'Out of Utopia: Toward a Reorientation of Sociological Analysis'. Though Dahrendorf has no desire to claim for his model of conflict 'comprehensive and exclusive applicability' (ibid., p. 127), he does in fact come up with a clear alternative to Parsons' theoretical programme in this work from 1957, and indeed with a conciseness which distinguishes him from Rex and Lockwood, and particularly from Coser and Bendix. His conciliatory reference to the possibility or even necessity of cross-fertilization between the Parsonian approach and conflict theory cannot obscure the fact that for Dahrendorf conflict theory is the more convincing approach and that the future belongs to it:

> As far as I can see, we need for the explanation of sociological problems both the equilibrium and the conflict models of society; and it may well be that, in a philosophical sense, society has two faces of equal reality: one of stability, harmony and consensus and one of change, conflict and constraint. Strictly speaking, it does not matter whether we select for investigation problems that can be understood only in terms of the equilibrium model or problems for the explanation of which the conflict model is required. There is no intrinsic criterion for preferring one to the other. My own feeling is, however, that, in the face of recent developments in our discipline and the critical considerations offered earlier in this paper, we may be well advised to concentrate in the future not only on concrete problems but on such problems as involve explanations in terms of constraint, conflict and change.
>
> ('Out of Utopia', p. 127)

We have now introduced you to the key authors who developed the conflict theoretical approach in the 1950s and 1960s. What is striking in comparison with the other approaches we have looked at is the fact that there was no *one* definitive author who 'led' the development of conflict theory; neither were there authoritative texts which might have demonstrated conclusively the fruitfulness of the new 'paradigm': there was no Talcott Parsons (as in the case of functionalism), Harold Garfinkel (as there was for ethnomethodology) or Herbert Blumer (as in the case of symbolic interactionism), nor was there a book such as Mancur Olson's *The Logic of Collective Action*, which was so vital to neo-utilitarianism. Furthermore, there existed no uniform tradition to nourish the conflict theoretical approach. It is true, as mentioned above, that among the classical figures of sociology Max Weber was the key reference author for conflict theorists. Georg Simmel also played an important role. They also grappled with Marx, though with sometimes markedly different political objectives. All of them tried to combine Marxian insights with those of Weber or to exorcize Marx's errors with Weberian means. Just how much distance one must put between oneself and Marx was, however, a subject of considerable disagreement. So-called Weberian Marxism or Left Weberianism, which remained fairly close to Marxism, attracted many on the political left, especially in Great Britain; authors such as Lockwood and Rex can be placed within this rather diffuse context. But while it leaned heavily on Marxist ideas, as was clearly apparent for the most part, conflict theory was by no means a left-wing project. Raymond Aron (1905–83), for example, whom we shall mention only briefly here, was a major French sociologist of the post-Second World War era, whose primary inspiration was Weber. He was the first to adopt conflict theoretical standpoints within a French discursive landscape strongly shaped by Durkheim. As a journalist, he was a trenchant critic of all politics with Marxist leanings and was the great antagonist of the French left-wing intellectuals around Jean-Paul Sartre. In the case of Ralf Dahrendorf, as we have seen, explicit reference to Marx certainly played an important role, but he too was certainly no Weberian Marxist. Dahrendorf, the social liberal, *massively corrected* Marx with the help of Weber, but also with reference to thinkers such as Gaetano Mosca and Vilfredo Pareto, some of whom were close to Italian fascism, and who were well aware of the power of political elites.

Taking all these differences between the individual theorists into account, can we really speak of a coherent theory? Was there such a thing as *conflict theory* in the first place? The answer is 'yes', at least in the 1950s and 1960s, before this theory was transformed or found a new home in various sociological sub-disciplines. We shall have more to say on this later. First, we shall flesh out in greater detail what all the authors and theorists mentioned above have in common. This we shall do by making four points:

1. The point of departure for conflict theory is not the problem of social order, but the question of how to explain *social inequality* between individuals or groups. The problem of social inequality is of course by no means new and has preoccupied many thinkers, including some leading ones. Other than social philosophical writings such as those of Jean-Jacques Rousseau (1712–78), the prehistory of sociology saw the well-known, basically journalistic research of Friedrich Engels, *The Condition of the Working Class in England*, published in 1845, and cartographic studies on the varying living conditions in American cities, such as the famous Pittsburgh Survey, which appeared in six volumes between 1909 and 1914. This was then continued during the period when sociology was constituted as a discipline; there was certainly no lack of analyses on inequality and poverty. But what distinguished conflict theory from mere descriptions, and of course what it had in common with Marxism, was the *theoretically* informed question as to the *causes* of this inequality. Gerhard Lenski (b. 1924), an author who had tried to integrate conflict theoretical and functionalist approaches in a large 1966 book on social stratification (*Power and Privilege: A Theory of Social Stratification*), though the conflict theoretical element clearly predominated, summed up this theoretical interest in the pithy formula 'Who gets what and why?' As Lenski and the conflict theorists underline, there are reasons why goods are distributed so unevenly in societies. But

these are different reasons than those mentioned in structural functionalism. Parsons too had certainly studied stratification or social inequality. His thesis was always that, for example, the differing pay structure in modern industrial societies was by and large an expression of core social values, such that doctors, with crucial responsibility for the cherished value of health, are also located high up within the stratification system. This is exactly what the conflict theorists contested with their thesis that social inequality, the unequal distribution of goods in a society, *cannot* be explained as a result of the society's normative structure.

2. This brings us to the second point. The conflict theorists' answer to the question posed by Lenski was that social inequality is ultimately a question of *domination*. Lenski argues roughly as follows: because goods have a status value as well as a use value and, moreover, are always scarce, people struggle over these goods in every society. Because for various reasons some have emerged and continue to emerge from this struggle as winners and others as losers, structures of domination are established in order to secure the unequal distribution of goods over the long term. Certain groups in a society thus have an active interest in maintaining and defending privileges, while others rebel against this. This is an answer to Lenski's question 'Who gets what and why?', though it fails to adequately define or delimit the conflict theoretical stance. The following two points enable us to do just that.

3. When conflict theorists speak of *goods* or *resources*, which can be secured with the aid of relations of domination and which can themselves be used in turn to capture positions of domination, they mean this in a very comprehensive sense. Conflict theorists criticized Parsons, for example, for saying practically nothing about material resources because of the overriding emphasis on norms and values evident in his theory. But Marxists too, they asserted, were guilty of severe one-sidedness here, in that they only ever referred to *one* type of resource, namely *economic* resources, specifically ownership of the means of production. But according to conflict theorists, there are significantly more 'interesting' resources, over which and with which people fight and whose distribution is determined through relations of domination. Conflict theorists pointed in particular to the significance of, for example, *political* resources (such as positions of authority), as these exercise a great influence on the form of social inequality. They also treated means of violence, weapons, as resources in their own right, in that they facilitate domination and thus the enjoyment of privileges, without necessarily being explicable in terms of economic or political resources: as is well known, the role of the means of violence in human history should not be underestimated, and it was not always the most economically or politically 'advanced' societies that were most successful at waging war. Randall Collins, one of the leading later conflict theorists, ultimately pointed also to *immaterial* resources, such as 'sexual gratification' (see below) and to

what he called 'emotional energy', which certain individuals or groups may acquire in order to further bolster their dominion. Think, for example, of the 'morale of the troops' described so often in military history, which may be strengthened, among other things, by 'suitable' images of the enemy, and you may begin to get a sense of just how significant a resource this 'emotional energy' can be. In all, the conflict theorists thus highlighted a whole range of resources which are fought over within relations of domination and which are therefore distributed unequally.

4. Finally, for conflict theorists disputes are *constant* features of human history. They work on the assumption of the all-pervasiveness of social struggles and thus distance themselves markedly from Parsons' highly integrated notion of society, but also from Marxism, in as much as it assumes that we will arrive at the 'end of history' and of class struggle as soon as the socialist or communist system has been established. Conflict theorists consider this an utterly unfounded superstition, which stems from the fact that Marxists pay heed solely to economic resources, neglecting all other kinds. Even if the private ownership of the means of production was to be abolished and economic resources distributed equally, so the conflict theorists tell us, other types of conflict (between the sexes, between administrators and the administrated, etc.) will by no means disappear. Of course, conflicts are sometimes brought to an end; there have been and will continue to be historical periods in which conflicts are few and far between. But conflict theorists always interpret this 'peace' as no more than a *passing* compromise, a *temporary* ceasefire, because ultimately the underprivileged party will not accept the unequal distribution of resources and goods over the long term and conflict will eventually break out again.

As a result of these assumptions, key themes of Parsonian sociology are re-evaluated or reinterpreted in conflict theory; most social phenomena are viewed 'realistically' or 'soberly', which is brought out very clearly by contrasting these two standpoints. While for Parsons social orders are based on values, for conflict theorists they are merely temporary compromises between the parties to conflict which may be abandoned at any time; while for Parsons values were 'ultimate ends' which, insofar as they really believe in them, actors cannot manipulate or question, the conflict theoretical perspective takes a rather cynical view of these values, generally interpreting them as justifications for social inequality, as ideology, as a façade; while for Parsons political power is an expression of the value commitments of citizens, who entrust to certain representatives the task of governing because of these very values, from the perspective of conflict theory it appears to be no more than one means of maintaining social inequality, and the state is considered a means of cementing the class structure; while rebellions, revolutions and violent uprisings were ultimately dangerous exceptions for Parsons, in the view of the conflict theorists they are taken-for-granted events; rather than irrational flare-ups, they are rational interventions aimed at changing the structure of social inequality.

This 'realistic' theoretical perspective, markedly different from Parsonian theory, has stimulated a whole series of research fields and left traces in a fair number of sociological subdisciplines.

(A) The *sociology of education* must be mentioned first. Here, sensitivity to power did in fact manage to produce new findings and insights into the mode of operation of educational institutions. Randall Collins' investigations stand out here. Born in 1940, and thus younger than Coser, Bendix, Rex, Lockwood and Dahrendorf, it was he who most clearly and distinctly continued the conflict theoretical programme. Collins, a student of Reinhard Bendix, demonstrated the fruitfulness and, he thought, superiority of a conflict theoretical approach to the analysis of educational institutions in a brilliant 1971 essay entitled 'Functional and Conflict Theories of Educational Stratification'. Collins showed that functionalist interpretations and explanations of the trend, observable in all modern industrial societies, towards ever longer periods of school and university education and thus ever higher levels of education among employees are quite unconvincing. This is because such explanations are based on the highly questionable assumption of increasing (technologically determined) *demand* for a well-educated workforce. Empirically, though, so Collins tells us, it can neither be shown that job requirements are becoming increasingly complex nor that better qualified workers are in fact more productive than less qualified ones. What is more, most occupational skills are learned 'on the job' and *not* at school or university, further undermining the demand thesis. Thus, according to Collins neither economic nor technological pressures can be straightforwardly held responsible for the ever increasing number and ever higher level of educational certificates. In other words, from the point of view of society as a whole, the *content* of the knowledge necessary to acquire certain school or university qualifications cannot be of crucial importance. For Collins it is therefore vital to come up with an alternative interpretation, especially in light of the fact that even in the seemingly so egalitarian twentieth century, professional success is still closely linked with social background. Collins asserts that the trend towards ever greater levels of education can be explained far more simply with reference to *status groups' struggle* to gain social and economic advantages or to maintain the status quo. How are we to understand this? For Collins, schools' primary educational task is the teaching of 'vocabulary and inflection, styles of dress, aesthetic tastes, values and manners' ('Functional and Conflict Theories', p. 1010). Different kinds of school and schools enjoying varying degrees of prestige and with different financial means at their disposal, which are particularly characteristic of the American education system, thus teach different status groups, as not all parents are able to send their children to the top-ranking or prestigious educational establishments. This reproduces the already existing structure of social stratification, especially given that the employers also favour those higher up the ladder in their recruitment practices: '(a) schools provide either training for the elite culture, or respect for it; (b) employers use education as a means of selection for cultural attributes' (ibid., p. 1011). But this only explains why it has proved impossible to significantly reduce social inequalities through educational institutions. Why, though – and this was the key question for functionalist sociologists of education as well – does the general level of education keep growing? Collins' answer was as follows: the lower classes do indeed strive to enhance their status through acquisition of qualifications, to climb the social ladder by means of education, but the middle and upper classes counter this by enhancing their own educational qualifications in order to set themselves apart from the lower classes: 'Led by the biggest and most prestigious organizations employers have raised their educational requirements to maintain both the prestige of their own managerial ranks and the relative respectability of middle ranks' (ibid., p. 1015). The lower classes' efforts to increase their upward mobility by means of education thus merely leads to an overall rise in educational levels, but not to substantial change in the structure of stratification or to the uncoupling of social background and professional success. Collins then laid out his hypotheses in more detail and placed them on a firmer historical footing in a volume entitled *The Credential Society: An Historical Sociology of Education and Stratification*. In this 1979 work, as in his earlier essay mentioned above, it is striking how strongly Collins' findings resemble those of the French theorist Pierre Bourdieu, who we deal with in a later lecture, in as much as he too showed the great extent to which people may deploy cultural goods – including educational qualifications and the knowledge gained in school – to mark themselves off from those lower down the social ladder aspiring to enhance their status, for the purposes of 'distinction', in Bourdieu's terms.

(B) Conflict theoretical insights were also put to productive use in a neighbouring research field, the *sociology of professions*. The professions were something of a favourite subject for Talcott Parsons. Parsons studied professionals (see Lecture III), among other things, in order to demonstrate that the development of modern societies cannot be interpreted in terms of the increasing edging out of normative aspects. Even in markets, seemingly dominated by purely instrumentally rational considerations, even in a capitalism allegedly rationalized root and branch, there exist important niches and occupations in which professional conduct is subject to a high degree of normative regulation and opposed to the logic of the market. Thus, when describing and analysing professions, Parsons and those researchers associated with him within the sociology of professions had always drawn particular attention to the phenomenon of professional ethics, even declaring this ethics central to the definition of professions. The so-called Chicago School of the sociology of professions, which was influenced by conflict theory, responded by asserting that the so-called Harvard School had merely been taken in by the semi-official ideology of certain professional groups. Conflict theorists believed that this professional ethos underlined by Parsons and articulated by representatives of the professions themselves was by no means simply an honest expression of certain values, but for the most part merely an effective means of securing ideologically one's own professional position within the public sphere and maintaining privileges (see also our remarks in the lecture on symbolic interactionism). An important book in this regard was Magali Sarfatti Larson's *The Rise of Professionalism: A Sociological Analysis*. In her 1977 study, Larson showed just how much groups such as the medical profession use their supposedly secure knowledge and their authority to establish their status as the only 'real' professional group and create a monopoly in order to exclude competitors (such as naturopaths, wise women and midwives, etc.), how specialist language serves to deprive patients of the right of decision and thus enhance the power of medical experts and finally how and why only certain professions (doctors and lawyers) succeeded in establishing themselves as fully fledged professions with all the accompanying privileges, while engineers, for example, never really managed this 'breakthrough'.

(C) The *sociology of deviant behaviour* also benefited substantially from conflict theoretical insights; a certain proximity to approaches influenced by symbolic interactionism and ethnomethodology is apparent here to some extent. Labelling theory, which we discussed in Lecture VI, incorporated the insight that processes of definition backed by *power* and guided by interests crucially determine whether certain offences are branded crimes and certain offenders branded criminals while others are not. Conflict theorists emphasized power even more than exponents of the interpretive approaches.

(D) Conflict theoretical insights have also made an impression on a field which we have already encountered in connection with neo-utilitarianism. The resource mobilization approach, within the field of research concerned with *social movements*, is based on the rationalist assumption that social movements require or are dependent on favourable political opportunity structures in order to keep the costs for participants as low as possible and the chances of winning as high as possible. Here, it is not the individual, but groups or classes that are assumed to be performing cost–benefit calculations; this also entails the conflict theoretical idea of a permanent power struggle between rulers and ruled, power-holders and those excluded from power, such that it is no surprise that neo-utilitarianism and conflict theory are closely interwoven in the work of certain movement researchers. This is clearly apparent, for instance, in the work of authors to whom we have already referred such as John McCarthy (b. 1955) and Mayer N. Zald and also in that of the leading historical sociologist Charles Tilly (1929–2008) (see the bibliography for some of their writings).

(E) The *sociology of gender relations*, which we will be taking a closer look at in Lecture XVII, is another field enriched by conflict theoretical arguments. One of the first *male* sociologists to take this field seriously in the 1970s was Randall Collins, who we have mentioned several times already. In a systematic 1975 survey of the field (*Conflict Sociology*) he had attributed much importance to gender relations in processes of social change and attempted to theorize the inequality between men and women from perspectives which were novel at the time. In extremely cold, matter-of-fact language, Collins described the family as a typical structure of domination in which hierarchy was maintained by means of brutal relations of power and violence and which – however much the form may have changed – persists to this day. According to Collins, every human being was and is willing to coerce others, use violence, live out their sexuality, etc. But the capacity to do so is distributed in line with gender. According to Collins, the physical strength of men and the biologically determined vulnerability of women (during pregnancy for example) have historically made women the booty of men, their prize as they fight each other for power. Ultimately, the family is the product of these struggles, and the family as an organization is thus a stable form of sexual ownership, though there are of course major cultural and social differences. Thus we are not, according to Collins, dealing solely with sexual domination and violence. Structures of domination entail relations of ownership, while ideologies also play a role, which explains the historical variability of gender relations:

> Family organization, as stable forms of sexual possession, can be derived from conditions determining how violence is used. Political organization is the organization of violence, hence it is a major background variable here; when the political situation restricts personal violence and upholds a particular kind of economic situation, economic resources accruing to men and women can shift the balance of sexual power and, hence, the pattern of sexual behavior.
>
> (*Conflict Sociology*, p. 230)

But the sexual act itself – Collins tells us – often involves an element of coercion and violence, and this is one of the key reasons why the social division of labour between men and women is as it is, namely to the disadvantage of the physically weaker sex.

It is hardly surprising that Collins' basic ideas appealed to feminists, as this approach broke with the functionalist notion, often perceived as patriarchal, according to which the family primarily fulfils 'the human need for love' and the woman's subordinate role in family and society is merely due to functional requirements. Parsons' sociology, with its strict allocation of the instrumental aspects of action to the male gender role and of emotional-expressive aspects to the female role, mirrors the golden age of the nuclear family in the post-war United States. But Collins also broke with the 'prudery' (Collins) of the Marxist tradition, in as much as it always immediately reduced sexual relations to property relations, already marginalizing the sexual dimension and sexual violence at the theoretical level. Collins' ideas made it possible to modify traditional theories on the 'sexual division of labour' and supplement them with specifically conflict theoretical perspectives (see Collins' collaboration with feminist sociologist Janet Saltzman Chafetz in Collins *et al.*, 'Toward an Integrated Theory of Gender Stratification').

Despite the uncontested productiveness of the conflict theoretical perspective in a fair number of fields of empirical research, it ultimately failed to achieve the breakthrough which theorists such as Dahrendorf and Rex had hoped for in the mid-1960s. This was due in significant part to the internal difficulties of the theory, namely the fact that its roots were too diffuse to establish long-term stability, and ultimately to the fact that when analysing processes in modern societies, it became ever more difficult to clearly identify the *core* patterns of conflict.

Let us begin first with the theoretical difficulties, with the question of immediate relevance to this book, of whether conflict theory does in fact represent a theoretical advance on the Parsonian approach. We must take two factors into account here, which are linked to some extent. First, the conflict theoretical perspective seems at first sight particularly 'realistic' or capable of convincingly describing reality, in as much as, against Parsons, it asserts that conflicts are all-pervasive, underlining that periods of social calm are never more than temporary ceasefires in the ceaseless battle between groups and classes. However, one might ask sceptically whether this notion is not gravely overdrawn and whether it unjustly elbows out core insights produced by none other than the reference authors of conflict theory. Georg Simmel, for instance, also refers to how an argument or conflict may be transformed into a longer-term process and how it changes those involved in the conflict. Disputes do not simply end in temporary ceasefires 'unloved' by more or less all those involved. Rather, they often trigger learning processes as a result of which the conflict loses its original virulence and what had been a compromise is now experienced as valuable, meaningful, etc.

This thesis is not intended to revive Marxian hopes of an end of history or an end to conflicts in general; it merely points out that while conflicts may repeatedly recur, their structure may change. Simmel recognized this. Coser too, following Simmel, referred to the fact that conflicts 'clear the air'. Radical conflict theorists such as Dahrendorf in the 1960s seem all too rapidly to have forgotten this insight; they failed to follow up the potential for conflicts to be transformed, though Max Weber had some important things to say here as well. It was after all Weber who recognized that compromises reached in the context of conflicts may take on a life of their own, if, for example, these compromises are systematically 'processed' and give rise to tendencies towards bureaucratization and juridification. The history of the Western world in the nineteenth and twentieth centuries was saturated with intense labour conflicts, conflicts over civil rights and women's equality and equal rights in marriage and society. Many of these conflicts featured violent phases, but were eventually juridified and thus mollified to some extent. And those compromises reached through legal means are anything but fleeting or unstable. This is not only because the law in itself is sluggish and can for the most part be changed only with difficulty or very slowly, but also because the legal form of the compromise can often count on the assent of large sections of the population, on both sides of the original conflict, such that many people feel a value-laden attachment to this legally based compromise. Because of this, it is difficult to imagine that the conflicts will break out again in their old form. Social conflicts are thus transformed fundamentally; at the same time, social trends (such as 'juridification') develop, which would not have come about in this way without these conflicts.

Think, for example, of the long history of the women's movement and its struggles. You can of course still find numerous forms of sex discrimination in modern Western societies; it is not difficult to identify chauvinists for whom the equality of women is a thorn in the flesh. Nevertheless, one must also recognize that the idea of equality between the sexes has become taken-for-granted and value-laden among broad sections of the population, including large numbers of men, and that it is at present impossible to seriously imagine social or political changes leading to a shift away from this, such that women would revert, for example, to the legal status that pertained in the eighteenth century. One may therefore willingly accept that sexual violence played a role in the historic formation of the family as outlined by Collins; one may also accept that sexuality entails an element of power, without signing up to his conclusion that it is *these* factors which *crucially* or *ultimately* determine the form of the sexual division of labour in family and society, especially in light of the fact – as Collins himself concedes – that 'ideologies' shape the relationship between the sexes. If we use the term 'value-laden attachment' rather than the derogatory 'ideology', it becomes apparent that conflicts, including that between the sexes, are not a natural given merely covered up by ideologies for a brief period. Rather, it is clear that some aspects of this particular conflict may perhaps be cast in certain enduring forms in such a way that both parties to the conflict – men and women – can 'live' with the resulting compromise, as legal regulations capable of meeting with widespread consent are formulated.

This leads us directly to the second problematic feature of the conflict theoretical approach. Conflict theory always ran the risk of theoretically exaggerating actors' rationalism and thus approaching a neo-utilitarian or rational choice stance. When we identified some of the research fields in which the conflict perspective was particularly productive, we pointed out that attempts were occasionally made to achieve a certain symbiosis between these two approaches, as in the case of the resource mobilization approach within the sociology of social movements. And this was no accident: both theoretical schools tended to view norms and values sceptically, generally interpreting them as mere camouflage for interests. This then led them to interpret political structures and institutions, for example, merely as crude structures of domination, the state and law as no more than a means of securing power, while culture as a whole was seen as mere ideology, as manipulation in the style of Enlightenment theories of priestly deception. Just as religion was claimed to be a cunning invention of the 'clerics' designed to keep the people quiet and extort money from them into the bargain, the law, values and norms, debates on the legitimacy of rule, etc. could also be understood as sophisticated constructions generated by groups engaged in a perpetual power struggle. Empirically, though, all of this is quite implausible and incorrect; such a stance both *overestimates* the human capacity for instrumentally rational action (people rarely act in the strategic and utility-oriented fashion assumed by conflict theorists and neo-utilitarians) and *underestimates* the potential of ideas and cultural patterns to take on a life of their own: these can neither be easily manipulated nor can they be interpreted as the straightforward outcome of earlier attempts at manipulation.

These theoretical difficulties were responsible, among other things, for the fact that conflict theory failed to make the breakthrough its protagonists had originally hoped for. But a second aspect also played a role here, perhaps even a more important one. We have already intimated that conflict theory lacked both key foundational authors and authoritative texts, making the development of a coherent paradigm problematic. What is more, the conflict theoretical camp lacked *political* unity. It would be wrong to claim (as is done so often) that conflict theory was somehow to the 'left' of Parsonianism. Simplistic political ascriptions of this kind simply fail to appreciate the diversity of theoretical motives driving the conflict theorists' break with Parsons. The thesis of an eternal struggle over power can also be used as Machiavellian justification for one's own lack of principles, amorality and the survival of the fittest. Because of these political differences, it was more difficult for this approach to establish itself as a coherent and enduring school of thought and to retain its original form. Ultimately, it is no great surprise that Coser, Bendix, Rex, Lockwood and Dahrendorf had only a few successors 'of like mind'. Indeed, from the 1970s, hardly any younger sociologists championed conflict theory *as a theoretical approach in its own right*. Randall Collins was practically alone in seriously attempting this – in his 1975 book *Conflict Sociology*, mentioned above, for example. It is true that Collins' work was only beginning to appear during this period; he continues to produce impressively multilayered and thematically diverse studies to this day, in which conflict theoretical arguments frequently appear. He recently turned out a sociological interpretation of the world history of philosophy (*The Sociology of Philosophies: A Global Theory of Intellectual Change*) and a comprehensive microsociological theory of violence (*Violence: A Micro-Sociological Theory*). In this sense, one could certainly state that the 'torch' of conflict theory has been passed on to the next generation. But even Collins could not help but stray from the original, clear-cut conflict theoretical approach and incorporate elements from authors such as Goffman into his theoretical programme, elements that can scarcely be described as basic to *conflict* theory. The same applies to him as to the entire discipline: 'a clear and distinct conflict approach is no longer so evident in sociology' (Turner, *The Structure of Sociological Theory*, p. 162).

Ultimately, this 'blurring' of a clear and distinct conflict approach also had something to do with changes in society, which made it ever more difficult to explain social change in terms of clearly structured conflicts and to establish the superiority of conflict theory on this basis. This was Dahrendorf's original preoccupation and his intellectual project in the mid-1950s, when he was still able to confidently assert that class conflicts develop on the basis of structures of domination, and thus that classes and class conflicts always appear wherever there are associations. More than a decade later, in *Konflikt und Freiheit* ('Conflict and Freedom') from 1972, he was already becoming sceptical about the theory's scope of application: he concedes that his original formulation of the theory applied only to very specific conflicts, namely those *within* an association, and therefore failed to illuminate ethnic and international disputes, for example (*Konflikt und Freiheit*, pp. 15ff.). He also accepts that even with a massively modified conflict theoretical class theory it is almost impossible to grasp social change in contemporary societies; social reality has become too diffuse, and the actions of various kinds of collective and individual actors, with their highly variable interests, are proving too confusing for the originally dichotomous class theory, on which Dahrendorf built his conflict theoretical approach, to generate genuinely novel insights:

> Because many political parties in the modern world do not represent interest groups that have developed out of quasi-groups of common

interests and positions of power, the link between political events and their social basis has become more problematic. In other words, it would appear that the social structure of interests no longer leads us directly to parties and conceptions of political conflict; interests seem to be lost, or perhaps satisfied, before they even enter the arena of group antagonism. Replacing Marx' theory by a more general one based on structures of power rather than property, one which explains the rhythm and direction of change, rather than taking it for granted, may have been sufficient for an earlier period of political development. But it is no longer enough. The new theory of class conflict must itself be replaced in order to explain what we see going on around us in today's world.

(Dahrendorf, *Konflikt und Freiheit*, p. 85)

It is thus unsurprising that conflict theory in its 'pure form' – if this be a meaningful term – exists at most in a field of research which we have not yet addressed, but which we will take a closer look at in Lecture XIII, namely historical sociology. It would appear that the conflict theoretical toolkit is a particularly appropriate means of analysing macroprocesses in *premodern* societies or at least in societies in the *pre-twentieth-century* period. Because the number of actors and groups to be taken into account is limited and interests can be attributed to various sources of domination with relative ease for these historical periods, the concepts of power and conflict appear to have an inherent potential to dissect historical processes (Turner, *The Structure of Sociological Theories*, p. 211). Processes of state formation, spurred by disputes between kings and nobility or between states, processes of class formation, that is, the evolution of peasants or workers into collective actors capable of taking action, actors of real significance on the political stage, and processes of democratization, such as the struggle of certain groups to achieve participation in political power, have been analysed with much success from a conflict theory perspective; among other things, this has opened up new insights into the *violent* origins of European and North American modernity, an aspect to which the Parsonian theory of change and evolution had paid practically no attention. Thus, the conflict theory of the 1950s and 1960s found 'a new home' in historical sociology, which, particularly since the late 1970s, has experienced a massive upturn, mainly in the Anglo-American world.

All in all, though, conflict theory failed to endure as a theoretical school *in its own right* in the sense of a genuine *alternative* to the approaches we have discussed so far. Theoretical developments in the 1970s, a time when conflict theory's best days were already behind it, were inspired by a problem which conflict theory proved just as unable to resolve as had the Parsons school: the link between power and culture. The critique of conflict theory had laid bare the necessity of paying serious attention not only to power, but also to the role of culture when analysing conflictual processes. The question of how to adequately synthesize culture and power proved a significant motif, which pointed the theoretical debate within sociology beyond that between Parsons and the exponents of the interpretive paradigm on the one hand and the conflict theorists on the other, spurring on the development of theory. The golden age of these attempts at synthesis began in the late 1970s; certain outstanding sociologists endeavoured to retain all that was valuable in existing theoretical approaches and integrate them into a new theoretical synthesis. The work of Jürgen Habermas emerged very quickly at the centre of the debate, and it is to him that we devote the following two lectures.

IX

Habermas and critical theory

Any attempt to describe the development of sociology worldwide from the mid-1960s must inevitably make mention of the palpable shift in the locus of theoretical production that occurred during this period. If modern sociological theory was initially linked closely with the name of the American Talcott Parsons, and if the rival approaches of neo-utilitarianism, ethnomethodology, symbolic interactionism and – with major caveats – conflict theory were also ventures strongly influenced by their American context of origin, theoretical work in sociology was subsequently 'Europeanized' to a quite astonishing degree. The reason for this change is, paradoxically, to be found above all in the higher degree of professionalization characteristic of US sociology, which was established as an independent university discipline with a clear profile more rapidly than in Europe. As a result, scepticism towards the theoretical diversity that emerged following the end of the Parsonian hegemony set in very quickly and to a greater extent than in Europe. Many American sociologists interpreted this diversity as the fragmentation of the discipline or as an expression of damaging (political) ideologization that threatened to undermine the professional identity of sociology that had taken so much hard work to achieve. Thus they either stuck with *existing*, seemingly 'tried and tested' theoretical schools (primarily Parsonianism and the rational choice approach), attempting merely to refine or slightly modify them – or they turned away from grand theories entirely, concentrating exclusively on empirical research. In brief, theoretical work was increasingly marginalized. This was facilitated by the American context, where the high degree of professionalization and specialization characteristic of the discipline sealed it off tightly from other subjects in the humanities in which comparable processes were occurring, most notably philosophy.

The division between sociology and philosophy was far less marked in Europe during this period, which clearly helped keep alive the interest in theoretical questions within sociology. In any case, European sociologists took the opportunity to venture into the theoretical lacunae abandoned by their American colleagues. As emphasized at the close of the previous lecture, it soon emerged that the most pressing question was whether the diversity of the theoretical landscape might be overridden by new *theoretical syntheses*.

Jürgen Habermas was among those scholars for whom the close connection between philosophical and sociological arguments was a matter of course; it is perhaps because of this that he became aware of the need and potential for a new theoretical synthesis so quickly and with such sensitivity. His major work *The Theory of Communicative Action* from 1981 represents such an attempt at synthesis. With this book, Habermas achieved an *international* breakthrough; he is now recognized and respected across the world, both within and beyond academia, as one of the great intellectuals of the twentieth century. But Habermas' route to this status was anything but simple. Following a brief biographical outline, we shall thus be tackling his early writings in this lecture; his major work, referred to above, takes centre stage only in the following lecture. Our initial task is to get a sense of the basic ideas which informed the development of Habermas' theoretical conception.

Habermas – like Lockwood and Dahrendorf born in 1929 – grew up in a bourgeois Protestant family in the predominantly Catholic Rhineland. His childhood and adolescence occurred during the period of Nazi rule, and Habermas never denied that he had embraced to some extent the supposed ideals of the regime as a member of the Hitler Youth. He experienced the fall of the so-called Third Reich as a major biographical turning point. His shock at the extent of the atrocities committed, which he would never have thought possible, as well as his own youthful credulousness, had a decisive influence on the rest of his life. It is impossible to achieve an adequate understanding of Habermas' academic and journalistic activities without taking these factors into account: many of his central arguments can be read as a process of coming to terms (whatever form this may have taken) with this dark period in German history and as a defensive reaction to the various temptations of totalitarianism (of both left and right).

Habermas' most important academic teacher as well as doctoral supervisor was Erich Rothacker (1888–1965), a typical representative of philosophical anthropology and of the German tradition of the humanities generally. This, along with his dissertation on the romantic-idealist philosopher Friedrich Wilhelm Joseph Schelling (1775–1854), point to the fact that Habermas' original home was philosophy rather than sociology. But because he was also highly successful as a journalist in the early 1950s, tackling political and socio-political issues in intellectual journals as well as daily and weekly newspapers (see for example some of the essays reprinted in the volume *Philosophical-Political Profiles*, originally published in 1971), it soon became apparent that philosophy alone was not enough for him and that he was keen to open up points of contact with other disciplines. In line with this, he became a research fellow at the famous Institute for Social Research in Frankfurt in the mid-1950s. This institute, which was founded in 1923 with the help of an endowment and which undertook interdisciplinary research informed by Marxism (though it had no party affiliation), had to relocate outside Germany during the Nazi period. Following the Second World War, it was rebuilt largely due to the efforts of Max Horkheimer (1895–1973) and

Theodor W. Adorno (1903–69), who had returned to Germany after emigrating to the USA.

In 1961, though yet to qualify as a university lecturer, Habermas was elected to the chair of philosophy at Heidelberg, where he taught until 1964. He completed his habilitation soon after taking up his post in Heidelberg – not in Frankfurt, as one might have expected in light of his biography and academic interests, but in Marburg, under the supervision of none other than the political scientist Wolfgang Abendroth (1906–85), the only prominent self-confessed Marxist elected to a chair in West Germany. Habermas' decision to complete his habilitation in Marburg was not, however, entirely 'voluntary': Horkheimer's aversion to him made it more or less impossible for him to do so in Frankfurt. Horkheimer considered Habermas too left-wing and overly sympathetic to Marxism, which ran counter to his efforts to cut the Institute for Social Research off from its Marxist taproots. Nonetheless, Habermas succeeded Horkheimer at the Institute in 1964 following the latter's age-related departure, as well as becoming – again as Horkheimer's successor – professor of philosophy and sociology at the University of Frankfurt (for details of Habermas' early career, see Rolf Wiggershaus, *The Frankfurt School*, pp. 537ff.).

Habermas left the University of Frankfurt in 1971, not least because he opposed the ever more radical student movement, whose hatred he had earned by famously accusing it of 'leftist fascism'. Habermas took up a quieter post – at least in terms of its setting and public – as a director at the Max Planck Institute for the Study of the Living Conditions of the Scientific-Technological World in Starnberg, which he headed together with Carl Friedrich von Weizsäcker (1912–2007). During this period he worked on his magnum opus, *The Theory of Communicative Action*, before returning to his chair at Frankfurt (that of philosophy alone this time around) in 1983. Habermas retired in 1994, though this has as yet had little real effect on his still enormous yield of publications or the frequency of his visiting professorships at universities in America and elsewhere.

In parallel with his illustrious *academic* career, Habermas increasingly established himself in Germany as a key *figure in public life*, with great influence on important scientific and political debates. In the 1960s, he played a key role in the dispute over positivism that occurred within German sociology. In the early 1970s, his clash with Niklas Luhmann caused quite a stir among sociologists. Habermas also exercised a major influence on the heated so-called historians' dispute in the early 1980s, which saw him warn that some German historians risked retrospectively exculpating National Socialism; he has also influenced the contemporary debate on bioethics and genetic engineering.

We have now gained some insight into the biography of Jürgen Habermas. This has not, however, elucidated the intellectual traditions informing Habermas' work or the sources motivating him to attempt the synthesis of *The*

Theory of Communicative Action. We believe that three key intellectual traditions can be identified as forming the background to Habermas' thought.

1. Marxism was certainly one of its well-springs. This is worthy of note in that it was rather unusual for West German academics to have a positive relationship with Marxism in the 1950s and early 1960s, *before* the student uprisings. 'Positive' here means that Habermas approached Marx's work very differently from most conflict theorists, particularly Dahrendorf. While the theory of social change with its core thesis of class struggle was the only thing Dahrendorf found interesting in Marx, rejecting all other elements of Marxian thought as metaphysical, non-sociological speculation, which he considered of no value to sociologists (he declared the Marxian economic theory of surplus value to be wrong and the philosophical-anthropological content of Marx's early writings useless), Habermas viewed the work of Marx with a rather more open mind, as evident particularly in his great 'Literaturbericht zur philosophischen Diskussion um Marx und den Marxismus' ('Review of the Philosophical Discussion on Marx and Marxism') from 1957 and his essay 'Between Philosophy and Science: Marxism as Critique' from 1960. Here, with tremendous sensitivity and understanding, Habermas takes up the debate on central problems in Marx's oeuvre, in all its international permutations, taking these problems very seriously. In contrast to Dahrendorf, he had no interest in playing the supposedly sociological core of Marx's thought off against his philosophical speculations. Quite the reverse: Habermas sees Marxism's interleaving of scientific and philosophical-normative arguments, of (scientific) theory and a praxis capable of changing society and tapping human potential, as a particularly attractive feature, because a fusion of this kind is the only means of effectively criticizing existing social relations and going beyond them. With Dahrendorf in mind, Habermas put this in the following way, which is admittedly not easy to understand:

> In the recent sociological debate on Marxism, this division into scientific and non-scientific elements leads ... to the formal construction of models on the very level of reifying abstraction that inspired Marx's objection – that social relations are 'presented as governed by eternal natural laws which are independent of history, and at the same time bourgeois relations are clandestinely passed off as irrefutable natural laws of society in abstracto'.
> ('Literaturbericht', pp. 415–16; see also Marx, *A Contribution to the Critique of Political Economy*, p. 192)

In concrete terms, for Habermas this means that excising the philosophical elements from Marx's work ultimately leads one to raise the thesis of the all-pervasiveness of conflict to the status of a law of nature. One then lacks all conceptual means of moving beyond this state of affairs; the original critical potential of Marx's writings is lost. A (conflict) sociology relating to Marx in this fashion, Habermas thought, merely describes reality without ever succeeding in imagining *another* reality.

This motif of 'salvaging' what was often referred to at the time as the 'emancipatory' content of Marxian theory, against Dahrendorf and other conflict theorists, by no means caused Habermas to read Marx uncritically, let alone gullibly, or naively to join any of the existing factions which had been battling over the 'correct' interpretation of Marx for many decades. Rather, Habermas pursued his own course from the outset, attempting to distance himself from two interpretations of Marx in particular, highly influential at the time though very different in nature.

(a) Habermas made no bones about the fact that the doctrine of 'Marxism-Leninism', originally authorized by Stalin, or the Soviet political model of the Stalinist and post-Stalinist era, constituted both a bleak philosophical project and a failed political one:

> Finally, the Russian revolution and the establishment of the Soviet system are *the* historical facts by which the systematic discussion of Marxism, and with Marxism, has been paralyzed to the greatest extent. Initiated by a weak proletariat and supported by petty bourgeois and prebourgeois peasant masses, the anti-feudal movement which liquidated the dual power of Parliament and Soviets in October 1917 under the direction of Leninistically schooled professional revolutionaries had no immediate socialist aims. But it established a rule of functionaries and party cadres, on the basis of which, a decade later, Stalin was able to initiate the socialist revolution bureaucratically from above, by the collectivization of agriculture.
>
> ('Between Philosophy and Science', pp. 197f.; original emphasis)

Habermas' disdain for this way of reading Marx was all too obvious, as was his aversion to the political conclusions which the communist party cadres had reached on this basis.

(b) But this does not mean that he concurred with the interpretations of Marx advocated by certain Eastern European dissidents in the 1950s. For him, the work of these authors, who drew primarily on Marx's early philosophical writings with their strongly humanistic tenor (see p. 212 below), were and are deficient in a manner antipodally at variance with conflict theoretical interpretations of Marx. Just as Marxism cannot be understood as pure sociology, as pure science, neither can it be adequately conceived as *pure philosophy* ('Literaturbericht', pp. 396f.). According to Habermas, an exclusively philosophical approach without corresponding political and economic analyses is impotent; it is *mere* philosophy, incapable of acting as a guide to practical political action. It is therefore equally mistaken to discard the political-sociological aspects of Marx's writings.

However, and this lays bare Habermas' theoretical reservations about Marxisms of every interpretive stripe, this political-sociological content requires massive revision, the *general direction* of which is fairly clear but the *extent* of which cannot yet be determined. At this point, the only thing which Habermas seems entirely clear about is that Marx's own or the subsequent Marxist labour theory of value was scarcely tenable in as much as it had thus far ignored the 'scientific development of the technical forces of production as a possible source of value' ('Between Philosophy and Science', p. 226); the classical Marxist take on the relationship of base and superstructure too was no longer convincing because the interventionist welfare state had interfered massively in the market; the 'dependence' of the (state) superstructure could no longer be taken for granted (ibid., p. 195); and finally, thought Habermas, Marxism had failed to grasp the tremendous force of social progress in capitalism, in that the proletariat, in the sense in which Marx meant this word, as a materially *impoverished* class, no longer exists, at least in the Western countries. With this last point, Habermas proves especially allergic to all arguments, to be found in Marxism in particular, which assume the existence of great subjects – the notion of the proletariat as a mover of history is an example – without studying empirically whether and how collective actors capable of taking action develop in the first place. When all is said and done, Habermas tells us, the political-economic-sociological content of Marxism can be convincingly overhauled only through a greater emphasis on *empirical research*, which would reveal how many of the original Marxist elements a renewed 'materialist' theory of this kind can retain:

> A materialist dialectic must prove its power afresh with respect to historical realities by producing concrete analyses. It must not merely superimpose the dialectic schema on these realities.
>
> ('Literaturbericht', p. 454)

Habermas managed to find a productive route out of the difficulties of Marxism, *without throwing away or ignoring its normative-philosophical impulses*, and this had partly to do with the fact that he was able to draw on other major intellectual traditions, one of which he learned about from his doctoral supervisor Rothacker.

2. We are referring to the German tradition of hermeneutics within the humanities. Hermeneutics is the art of *Verstehen* or 'understanding'; it is above all texts, particularly authoritative texts, that are to be *understood*.

This may sound rather mysterious, yet the underlying issues are relatively straightforward. As you are no doubt aware, there are texts which the reader struggles to cope with or whose meaning is not always obvious. In such cases the reader faces a challenge, the ease of reading vanishes due to the effort to understand, and from time to time it is even necessary to think methodically about *how* and *why* a text must be understood in one particular way rather than another, *why* one interpretation may be better or more appropriate than another. This problem of *Verstehen* has cropped up with respect to a number of pivotal cultural phenomena over the course of Western intellectual history.

The first and perhaps most prominent example of this is the 'correct' interpretation of the Bible. As *the* authoritative text of Christianity, the Bible is by no means easily accessible. Many parables are hard to understand, and some stories make little sense to later generations, even seeming implausible or illogical. The problem arises of how such a text is to be understood and related to contemporary life. For it was and is neither satisfactory for pious Christians merely to interpret the text as the expression of a distant past, whose content has become insignificant to them, nor can the Bible be interpreted exclusively from the perspective of later centuries, as this would mean calling into question the meaningfulness of the faith of earlier generations; the current generation could always claim for itself the 'truer' faith, which would clearly be nonsense. How then do we reach an appropriate understanding of the Bible, how should it be interpreted? A similar problem also arose in relation to the interpretation of Classical poetry. In an age in which, in Europe for example, the literature of ancient Greece and Rome set the standard for all literary production, this poetical language, often hard to grasp because its origins lay in an unfamiliar world, had first to be decoded. This too presented the reader with substantial problems of much the same kind. Finally, similar considerations apply to the understanding of legal texts or legal norms. In the continental European legal tradition, for example, there has always been the difficulty of how to relate a norm, which may have been formulated long ago and is abstract in nature, to a specific case, to a concrete situation. Once again, if a lawyer has to decide what the legislature may have meant and whether the concrete case at hand can be subsumed under this abstractly formulated law in the first place, she must practise the art of *Verstehen*.

It is a peculiarity of the history of knowledge that for various reasons it was at the universities of Germany that the art of *Verstehen* flowered in the nineteenth and early twentieth centuries. We can go so far as to say that it was one of the strengths of the humanities in Germany at the time that scholars in a variety of disciplines – theology, jurisprudence, philosophy, history – dedicated themselves with much earnestness to this problem of understanding, raising the methodological level, that is, the level of reflection on the foundations of and prerequisites for scholarship in the humanities, to new heights. Here, the problem of *Verstehen* was broadened to encompass the understanding of images, great deeds, everyday actions, etc. rather than merely that of texts. Though the nationalistic exuberance characteristic of the era often endowed hermeneutics, within the discipline of history for example, with an elitist slant, with an overemphasis on the need to understand the deeds of *great men*, such as Martin Luther, Frederick the Great or Bismarck (which often included dubious justifications for these deeds), this did not alter the fact that sociology too had to grapple with hermeneutic insights. The arguments put forward by the German founding fathers of sociology such as Max Weber or Georg Simmel were also closely bound up with this problem of *Verstehen*.

Habermas' work certainly stands in continuity with these developments. He was educated in this hermeneutic tradition and is well aware of the importance of *Verstehen*, particularly to the formulation of a theory of action; should we wish, for example, to produce a typology of action, we must first understand actions. Habermas' style of argumentation as a whole, in his later works as well, is deeply imbued with this hermeneutic tradition of thought, a tradition characterized by attempts to construct arguments by grappling intensely with earlier authors and their texts. While Talcott Parsons attempted to come to terms systematically with other authors mostly in *The Structure of Social Action*, but then did his best to perfect his theory by drawing on elements from highly disparate fields, ranging from biology to cybernetics, while ethnomethodology and symbolic interactionism fell back on *highly specific* philosophical traditions while largely ignoring all the others, Habermas' work is characterized by the hermeneutic effort to understand the entire range of philosophical problems and subjects particular to Western history. Habermas develops his position by engaging closely with a large number of key philosophical and sociological authors. He strives to maintain constant 'dialogue' with their writings and tries to understand their theoretical problems and attempted solutions. Despite an often caustic style of argumentation, one can therefore always make out a certain humility common to all hermeneuticians in their respect for the (theoretical) accomplishments of their predecessors, whose insights ought to be preserved.

3. A third tradition undoubtedly upheld by Habermas is political in nature. From the outset, he was oriented towards Western liberal-democratic thought. The experience of being seduced by National Socialism as an adolescent, and his equally sharp condemnation of Soviet Marxism and all its political permutations, led him to place an extremely high value on democratic ideals as articulated and given institutional form in Great Britain, France and the USA. He always regarded democratic traditions in Germany, meanwhile, presumably for biographical reasons, with a fair

degree of mistrust; they had after all ultimately been too weak to protect the country from the temptations of totalitarianism. West Germany ought therefore – Habermas thought – to dedicate itself to Western democratic thought, in order at all costs to avoid any repetition of that terrible civilizational rupture. However, in the 1950s and 1960s, it was often rather unclear how precisely his high regard for the Western democratic constitutional state could be reconciled with his emphatic recourse to certain aspects of Marxism, his attempt to develop a practically relevant 'materialistic' theory and his continuation of the hermeneutic tradition, and above all what this meant for his political stance in concrete terms. But Habermas was undoubtedly always aware of the value of research freedom and was therefore a vigilant defender of the system of democratic institutions which made it possible.

We have now identified the three major traditions that decisively influenced Habermas' thought. The secondary literature on Habermas, however, tends to refer to another major tradition – generally discussed first – which we, so it might appear, have neglected entirely. It is usually claimed that Habermas is a representative of critical theory and, as it were, the legitimate successor of Max Horkheimer and Theodor W. Adorno. We are rather sceptical that this categorization of Habermas is correct, that he was really so greatly influenced by critical theory, and shall briefly explain why in what follows. To this end, we must first explain what is meant by 'critical theory'. The term was coined by Max Horkheimer in 1937 to refer to a particular form of Marxism, as developed theoretically at the above-mentioned Frankfurt Institute for Social Research and as championed by its members in exile. In the 1920s and 1930s, this institute was the setting for an interdisciplinary social science that incorporated psychoanalysis and whose political orientation was decidedly revolutionary but also rather vague. Its exponents had hoped to be able to overcome the political, economic and social crisis of the Western world by means of the theoretical tools of Marxism without, however, really being able to identify a revolutionary subject. For they viewed the German working classes, who had either made do with the reformism of the SPD or had embraced an ever stronger National Socialism, with suspicion. And they kept their distance from the Stalinist KPD, as Soviet Marxism too was surely quite incapable of realizing their predominantly humanistic ideals.

When Hitler seized power, the institute was relocated abroad, its members forced to emigrate. But this did not cause them to cease publishing or to publish less; it was in fact only in exile that the *Zeitschrift für Sozialforschung* ('Journal for Social Research'), the key organ of publication for the members of the institute and its sympathizers, which it published between 1932 and 1939, truly flourished. Another important publication from around the same time was the collectively produced research report 'Authority and the Family' from 1936. This work, based on data collected under the Weimar Republic and drawing heavily on psychoanalytic interpretive categories, tackled the spread of authoritarian attitudes and aspired to provide insights into the causes underlying the rise of National Socialism. The most famous work to emerge from the context of the institute, however, was the *Dialectic of Enlightenment*, a collaboration between Adorno and Horkheimer which appeared in the early 1940s. This philosophical book was marked by a deeply pessimistic if not tragic undertone that took to an extreme Max Weber's thesis of rationalization and asserted that the modern, technological-rational world of the Enlightenment would almost inevitably tip over into violent barbarism (of a National Socialist or communist stripe).

The claim that Habermas was particularly influenced by these writings in exile is in our opinion quite unconvincing. He certainly did not share the pessimistic view of history characteristic of *Dialectic of Enlightenment*. The most that can be said is that Habermas was very close to those writings produced in the early days of the Frankfurt Institute for Social Research and during the period of its foundation, and to those published by various authors in the *Zeitschrift für Sozialforschung*. Yet Habermas was not really familiar with these early writings. When Horkheimer re-established the institute in West Germany (which was still very conservative at the time), he was keen to conceal its Marxian roots. Issues of the *Zeitschrift* – as an institutional legend fittingly had it – lay behind lock and key in the cellar while Habermas was carrying out research there in the late 1950s. It is thus more accurate to say that Habermas, rather than being *influenced* by this early form of critical theory, was more or less unconsciously *moving gradually towards it*, though initially unaware of the fact. It was only during the 1960s that Habermas began to stylize himself as a representative of this critical theory and that others declared him a key figure in the so-called second generation of the 'Frankfurt School' (another term for the representatives of critical theory), especially when the student movement began to place great hopes in this critical theory. But with respect to the history of intellectual influences, this is probably a misinterpretation. We must in fact assume that Habermas was influenced predominantly by the first three major traditions we have mentioned, which also suggests that his thought was far more self-contained and independent than implied in the claim that he was decisively influenced by critical theory.

Though our focus is now on three (rather than four) major traditions as the basis for the development of Habermasian thought, it is immediately apparent that these traditions are rather out of synch and present problems of compatibility. At best, all we have outlined thus far is a *field of tension*. One might suspect that the major differences between these influences make Habermas' work highly eclectic, a mere juxtaposition of quite different ideas lacking a unifying thread. But this is not in fact the case, because all these influences were held together or channelled by an idea initially graspable only as pre-scientific intuition, but which Habermas was to explicate with increasing clarity and systematicity, namely that of the *special nature of human language*, the *special nature of human communication*. Habermas was enthralled by the wonder of language, so vastly different from forms of animal communication. And his enthusiasm for this topic had major consequences in that this insight into the central importance of language for human social life could be linked with a whole number of philosophical, historical and sociological research topics.

In terms of *philosophy*, it was possible to relate this insight to the idea, frequently articulated in the history of Western thought, that language features an inherent conciliatory or rationalizing potential. Habermas very much made this idea his own, though he primarily emphasized the *potential for rationality* which language entails. As his work developed, he was to explain in great detail why rational arguments exercise a characteristic pressure on the parties to discussion, how and why better arguments lead to consensus and thus to the coordination of action, which is superior to all other forms of coordination (such as violence or markets). From a *historical* point of view, one could ask when, how and by which routes this rationalizing potential of human communication developed, how, for example, over the course of history, certain forms of domination lost their legitimacy through the force of the better argument, when and where political power came to be accepted only as *argumentatively justified* rule (that is, ultimately legitimized by democratic forms of discussion) and no longer as beyond discussion – because of religious assumptions for example. Finally, this diverse range of emerging issues touched directly on a *sociological* problem which had been a central concern of 'traditional' critical theory, and indeed of Western Marxism as a whole, and even of a diffuse cultural criticism that often defies easy political categorization: will capitalism and the technical or instrumental rationality inherent in or at least related to it, which makes everything into a commodity and permits us to think only in terms of economic ends and means, come to dominate to such an extent that all other forms of life, all other forms of thinking and acting, will be destroyed? Will the supposedly destructive triumph of capitalism and its 'instrumental' rationality prove unstoppable? Habermas shared with critical theory, but also with cultural critics of a very different political stripe, the idea that we must resist the triumph of 'technical-instrumental' rationality; but he *did not* share the tragic undertone of their arguments, because he saw language, with its inherent comprehensive (rather than one-sided or limited) potential for rationality as an effective or at least potential counterbalance to 'technical-instrumental' rationality.

Later on, in the early 1980s, Habermas was to take advantage of this idea of the potential rationality of language to formulate his own theoretical synthesis, which promised a fusion of the strengths of all existing theoretical schools within sociology. The path to this synthesis was, however, a long one. First (and it is the 1960s to which we refer in the following part of the lecture), in a number of studies Habermas tested out the sociological viability and productiveness of the idea of communication. To put it another way, his books and essays written in the 1960s (this phase of Habermas' biography was marked by genius; he was hugely productive, publishing one important work after the other), despite their apparently highly disparate subject matter, are best analysed and understood in terms of this idea of the special nature of human communication, even if Habermas considers some of these texts ultimately unsatisfactory, and some of them were to prove dead ends.

1. *The Structural Transformation of the Public Sphere*, Habermas' postdoctoral thesis published in 1962, is perhaps his most appealing and most readable book, making it a particularly good point of entry to his work. It is a historical-sociological study of the (political-philosophical) *idea* of the public sphere and particularly of its *institutions* in the bourgeois age, in other words the eighteenth and nineteenth centuries. Here, Habermas describes how a public sphere developed, initially in non-political settings such as coffee houses, private reading and discussion circles, clubs and *Tischgesellschaften* (dining clubs), in which literary, artistic, and 'social' problems and social affairs in the broadest sense were openly discussed. With the spread of newspapers and magazines, this public sphere became rapidly politicized; people increasingly asserted their right to a say in the *political* sphere:

   > A public sphere that functioned in the political realm arose first in Great Britain at the turn of the eighteenth century. Forces endeavouring to influence the decisions of state authority appealed to the critical public in order to legitimate demands before this new forum. In connection with this practice, the assembly of estates became transformed into a modern parliament – a process that was, of course, drawn out over the entire century.
   >
   > (*The Structural Transformation of the Public Sphere*, p. 57)

   According to Habermas, at least in this initial phase (*before* the rise of parties with fixed structures and professional politicians) this parliament is a place of serious debate, in which participants struggle to show that their policies are best by means of the better argument; this is an assembly of reasoning representatives of the middle classes rather than a gathering (as was often the case later on) of those merely representing various interests, compelled to stubbornly defend their views to the bitter end.

   As people reflect on these political and non-political *institutions* of the public sphere, the philosophical-political *idea* of the public sphere arises, which is regarded as fundamental by philosophers and intellectuals because one can get to know other views of the world only in the liberal space that is the public sphere. Only in the public sphere is it possible to lay one's own interests open to rational discussion, opening up the possibility that these interests may be changed and that it may be possible to achieve consensus. And as Immanuel Kant (1724–1804) already suspected and as Habermas affirms in the following quotation, only in the public sphere can autonomous decisions be reached on matters of general interest.

> Before the public it had to be possible to trace all political actions back to the foundation of the laws, which in turn had been validated before public opinion as being universal and rational laws. In the framework of a comprehensively norm-governed state of affairs ... domination as a law of nature was replaced by the rule of legal norms – politics could in principle be transformed into morality.
>
> (ibid., p. 108)

While these regrettably brief remarks cannot bring out the richness of Habermas' historical-sociological reconstruction of the idea and institutions of the bourgeois public sphere, it should nonetheless be clear that his thoughts here are again informed by his enthusiasm for the astonishing capacity of human language and that the idea of the public sphere is closely linked with the phenomenon of language, with its potential for rationality with respect to the exchange of arguments. In this sense, this is Habermas' first major attempt to investigate the effectiveness and significance of language with respect to politics and society as a whole.

As brilliant and suggestive as the book is, it suffers from one significant weakness, which Habermas was later to concede openly (see his preface to the new 1990 edition of the book). Habermas wrote his account from a critical perspective that assumes cultural decline. He describes the institutional reality of the eighteenth and nineteenth centuries as if the philosophical-political idea of the public sphere had truly been *put into practice*, while at the same time, with reference to processes of commercialization and the advance of professional and party politics, he can see no more than a debased form of the public sphere in the contemporary era. To put it differently and more simply, influenced by cultural criticism, he presents an overly idealistic picture of the past, of that bourgeois age in which reason supposedly still held sway unchallenged and in which the full force of reason was unleashed within institutions. Inevitably, his portrayal of the present is all the darker in tone as a result. But as we shall see, Habermas was increasingly to restrain this highly problematic critical stance as his work developed, primarily because linguistic analysis furnished him with a means of avoiding the implications of this cultural criticism.

2. *Theory and Practice* is a collection of essays that originally appeared in 1963, including 'Literaturbericht zur philosophischen Diskussion um Marx und den Marxismus' ('Review of the Philosophical Discussion on

Marx and Marxism') and 'Between Philosophy and Science: Marxism as Critique', both mentioned earlier. The volume also contains pieces of a largely theoretical and socio-political nature from the early 1960s; it was to exercise a significant influence, particularly on the later student movement. In those essays that grapple directly with Marxism, Habermas conceived of it as an 'empirical philosophy of history with practical intent' ('Between Philosophy and Science', p. 212), the adjective 'empirical' being intended as a sideswipe at dogmatic Marxism-Leninism. Marxism should and must genuinely open itself to the empirical, it must be 'scientifically falsifiable', in line with one of Habermas' chief concerns: 'understanding Marx better than he understood himself' (ibid.) – a monstrous idea in the eyes of those who saw themselves as the guardians of orthodox Marxism.

It is evident – even in its title – that Habermas' arguments in this collection of essays are still crucially informed by the concept of 'praxis', which has a complex history within Marxist debates. It played an important role in the thought of the famous Italian Marxist theoretician Antonio Gramsci, but was also a key anti-Stalinist concept for dissident intellectuals in the Eastern bloc, thinkers – particularly in Hungary, Czechoslovakia and Yugoslavia – who opposed their regimes with the help of the conceptual tools of Marxism, and thus continued to adhere to Marxism despite the bitter reality of real existing socialism, a different Marxism, admittedly, than that which the various dogmatic party ideologues wished to codify. These dissidents clung to Marx's early philosophical-anthropological writings and the concept of praxis found in them, a concept – drawing, among other things, on the philosophy of Aristotle (384–322 BC) – which was also pervaded with romantic elements: 'praxis' here did not refer primarily to instrumentally rational activities, such as goal-directed work carried out to maintain one's existence, but the realization of the human potential for action, derived from the world of art, creative self-expression in other words, as well as the realization of a good and reasonable way of living, brought about collectively and consciously. All these motifs found in the early Marx served Eastern European intellectuals as a means of criticizing their own political system, in as much as these motifs found no institutional expression in the bleak reality of the Eastern bloc societies. Habermas too was still dependent on this concept in the early 1960s and deployed it accordingly, if only to discuss what constitutes a rational social order. This indicates that at this point in time his intuition with regard to the theoretical significance of linguistic analysis is as yet too weak and he lacks the means to derive from such analysis a critical foil capable of illuminating existing realities. He had not yet managed to produce a sufficiently sophisticated and sociologically usable theory of language, leaving him with no other choice, for the time being, than to use the conceptual tools of the early Marx and Eastern European dissidents in order to critique the advance of technological rationality as found in capitalism and, albeit in a quite different way, in Soviet socialism:

> the real difficulty in the relation of theory to praxis [arises] ... from the fact that we are no longer able to distinguish between practical and technical power. Yet even a civilization that has been rendered scientific is not granted dispensation from practical questions; therefore a peculiar danger arises when the process of scientification transgresses the limit of technical questions, without, however, departing from the level of reflection of a rationality confined to the technological horizon. For then no attempt at all is made to attain a rational consensus on the part of citizens concerning the practical control of their destiny.
> (*Theory and Practice*, p. 255)

In this quotation, Habermas criticizes the ceaseless advance of science and scientific-technical rationality, which 'debases' highly political issues relating to the rational regulation of the communal life of society – issues that ought to be thrashed out between citizens – and turns them into mere technical-rational problems; according to him, this may mean the replacement of political debate by the rule of experts. This critique of contemporary civilization is thus developed with the aid of the concept of praxis – and it was to be some time before he relinquished this, giving up the dichotomy between 'technical and practical power' in favour of the distinction between 'labour' and 'interaction' (see further below), interaction here meaning that type of action among human beings which is anchored in *language*.

3. The dispute over positivism in German sociology began at the 1961 conference of the German Sociological Association in Tübingen, its main protagonists being Theodor W. Adorno and Karl Raimund Popper. This was one of the more ill-starred developments in the social sciences in Germany, not least because the influence of the Frankfurt School caused the opposing camps to talk past each other; this hugely impactful debate sent whole generations of students off down the wrong track or at least down highly problematic ones (see Adorno, *The Positivist Dispute in German Sociology*). At the heart of this dispute, in which Habermas played a significant role, lay Adorno's vehemently expressed claim that the (increasing) use of quantitative methods in the social sciences represented a major problem insofar as these conceive of the social world from the perspective of its disposability and are geared towards the model of the – equally objectionable – technological domination of nature; this, Adorno asserted, would ultimately lead to human beings' self-enslavement. Underlying Adorno's view here was a normatively charged conception of science which adopted a clear-cut stance towards the problem of how to conceive of 'theory', a problem which, as mentioned in Lecture I,

had never really been resolved within sociology. For Adorno, theoretical work can never be separated from normative issues; science must never lose sight of the goal of emancipating human beings. For him, the use of quantitative methods entails precisely this risk. As far as the last point is concerned, Habermas did *not* adopt this extreme stance. Quite apart from the fact that he took for granted the use of analogous methods, intended to render disposable the natural world, within the natural sciences, and in any case did not share Adorno's perspective on these disciplines, which was informed by cultural criticism, Habermas certainly accepted the use of quantitative methods in the social sciences for certain purposes. In principle though, he defended Adorno's emancipatory scientific ideal, which Adorno's rival Karl Raimund Popper simply could not understand. He had always insisted that normative issues, 'oughts', must be kept out of the scientific debate; the notion of an 'emancipatory science' was inevitably an alien one to Popper.

What made things so confusing for many people and underlay the destructive influence of the debate as a whole was, first, the fact that the opponents of Adorno and Habermas – notably Popper – were successfully characterized or branded as positivists, though Popper was anything but a positivist; in fact, it was he who had given the edifice of positivist thought a good shaking, as addressed in Lecture I. Second, judging by the heatedness of the debate, one would think that one was dealing here with *immutable* views of fundamental issues touching on the self-understanding of the (social) sciences. What was overlooked was the fact that the disagreement was in reality fairly minor, in as much as Habermas clearly moved closer to Popper's scientific ideal a few years later, with respect to many if not all of its aspects.

4. The 1968 book *Knowledge and Human Interests*, despite its brilliant line of argument, was in a sense a continuation of the dispute over positivism and was to prove no more than a transitional work, despite – and this we mention only in passing, though it is important to Habermas' later work – its extensive discussion of American pragmatism, the philosophical tradition that gave rise to symbolic interactionism. Here, Habermas seeks to broadly analyse the epistemological self-conception of the most varied range of disciplines and expounds the thesis that no form of knowledge – including the scientific – can be understood as a reflection of the world arrived at in a vacuum or as an 'unadulterated' reproduction of the world. Rather, all knowledge relates to deep-seated, anthropological *interests* – hence the book's title. While the *technological interest* concerned with the mastery of nature is claimed to be apparent in the natural sciences, the hermeneutic traditions aim to *enhance understanding* between human beings. Psychoanalysis and materialist-revolutionary thought are alleged to be alone in being inspired by an *emancipatory-critical* interest, the

liberation of human agents from unnecessary domination and repression, *and in grasping how all science and knowledge is tied to certain interests.* Habermas puts this as follows:

> The process of inquiry in the natural sciences is organized in the transcendental framework of instrumental action, so that nature necessarily becomes the object of knowledge from the viewpoint of possible technical control. The process of inquiry in the cultural sciences moves at the transcendental level of communication, so that the explication of meaning structures is necessarily subject to the viewpoint of the possible maintenance of the intersubjectivity of mutual understanding. Because they mirror structures of work and interaction, in other words, structures of life, we have conceived of these two transcendental viewpoints as the cognitive expression of knowledge-constitutive interests. But it is only through the self-reflection of sciences falling within the category of critique that the connection of knowledge and interest emerges cogently.
>
> (*Knowledge and Human Interests*, p. 286)

Knowledge and Human Interests reflected an ongoing disagreement with Popper, in that Habermas accused him of producing a one-sided scientific ideal. Habermas believed that Popper's conception of science, geared towards the process of knowledge production within the natural sciences, airbrushed out the fact that the natural sciences represent just one of three fundamental human interests, while utterly neglecting the other two anthropologically rooted interests – that concerned with the 'explication of contexts of meaning' or with improving understanding and that which revolves around emancipation and liberation from violence. Habermas claims (for himself and presumably also for critical theory; by this point he has successfully placed himself within this tradition) to possess a broader conception of rationality, which includes technical-instrumental reason but which also goes way beyond it.

However, Habermas subsequently dissociated himself from this stance, at least as far as his thesis of the existence of a critical-emancipatory interest is concerned; he soon abandoned the hope that certain disciplines (psychoanalysis and a social science indebted to Marxism) would play a revolutionary or pro-revolutionary role. He was no longer to harbour such great expectations. *But he clung to the idea that we need another form of rationality to supplement technical-instrumental rationality.* The above quotation gives a hint of what exactly this might look like with its reference to the contrast between 'labour and interaction'; and it is this conceptual dichotomy which allows him to bid farewell to the concept of praxis which he was still using in the 1950s and 1960s.

5. This is first clearly evident in a 1967 essay entitled 'Labour and Interaction: Remarks on Hegel's "Jena Philosophy of Mind"'. In this text on the early Hegel (1770–1831) and on Marx, Habermas tries to explain *why the process of the formation of the human species may be understood as the interplay and conflict between two forms of action*, namely labour *and* interaction; this he does by drawing, among other things, on George Herbert Mead's theory of communication and, presumably, Hannah Arendt's (1906–75) *The Human Condition*, though Habermas makes no reference to it. As he explains, making positive reference to Hegel's insights: 'A reduction of interaction to labour or derivation of labour from interaction is not possible' ('Labour and Interaction', p. 159). Marx on the other hand, he asserts, had carelessly or pre-emptively fused both these forms of action – with highly problematic consequences for his theory building:

> precise analysis of the first part of the *German Ideology* reveals that Marx does not actually explicate the interrelationship of interaction and labour, but instead, under the unspecific title of social praxis, reduces the one to the other, namely: communicative action to instrumental action. ... Because of this, Marx's brilliant insight into the dialectical relationship between the forces of production and the relations of production could very quickly be misinterpreted in a mechanistic manner.
>
> (ibid., pp. 168–9)

Habermas' essay is clearly directed against Marx and above all against an interpretation of Marxism which hopes to advance the lot of the human race solely by developing the forces of production. Habermas, on the other hand, wishes to hold on to the idea that each form of action is irreducible to the other. For him, interaction or communicative action must not be mistaken for instrumental or instrumentally rational action; the logic of action in each case or, if you will, the anthropological interests underlying this action, are utterly different. This is also why Habermas – we refer you again to the quotation – wishes to take leave of the concept of praxis, as it entails the risk that the necessary conceptual differentiation between labour and interaction will be blurred or overlooked.

But if one insists on the irreducibility of labour and interaction, this immediately has significant consequences for the interpretation of the historical process, and these contradict entirely the basic assumptions of orthodox Marxism, that is, one interpreted in the sense of an economic determinism. The development of the forces of production in and of itself is no guarantee of social progress: 'Liberation from hunger and misery does not necessarily converge with liberation from servitude and degradation, for there is no automatic developmental relation between labour and interaction' (ibid., p. 169).

The Habermasian distinction between 'labour' and 'interaction' had a profound impact on the development of his oeuvre; he retains it to this day. This was a necessary critical step vis-à-vis orthodox Marxism, but also vis-à-vis the Marxism espoused by Eastern European dissidents, which emphasized the concept of praxis. But this step was also associated with certain theoretical costs: the related question arose of what – in light of Habermas' interpretation of the Marxian concept of labour as purely instrumentally rational action – had become of the insight into the potentially *expressive character of work*, retained in Marx's early writings and especially in the concept of praxis, that is, work as the self-expression of the working human being. The question was thus whether the typology of action, expressed here through the terms 'labour' and 'interaction', was not overly simplistic.

6. The essay 'Labour and Interaction' was republished in 1969 in a slim volume entitled *Technik und Wissenschaft als 'Ideologie'* ('Technology and Science as "Ideology"'). The opening essay of the same name is an initial systematic diagnosis of the times, and thus thoroughly sociological. Here, Habermas makes use of the distinction, introduced earlier, between 'labour' and 'interaction', in order to analyse macrosociological changes in modern societies. Habermas asks himself a straightforward question in this essay: how do we explain the fundamental structural change characteristic of the manner in which capitalism justifies itself? How do we explain the fact that, as never before, a technocratic ideology has become *the* legitimizing trope in contemporary capitalist societies? To answer this question, Habermas develops a Marxian theoretical framework, or at least one that borrows Marxian ideas, but which takes neither a technologically nor economically deterministic approach, and which thus refrains from asserting the primacy of either technology or the economy within the framework of societal development. Habermas breaks with the Marxian dialectic of forces and relations of production because, as he pointed out in 'Labour and Interaction', the Marxists had misunderstood this dialectic, conceiving of it mechanistically, because of their simplistic conceptual framework (again, see the quotation on p. 216). Habermas replaces this with another dialectic, namely that pertaining between the *systems* or *subsystems* of instrumentally rational action on the one hand and the institutional framework of a society or *life-world*, regulated by means of processes of communication on the other (we shall discuss this term, which you have already been introduced to in our analysis of ethnomethodology, in more detail in the following lecture); the dichotomy of concepts of action is thus repeated as a dichotomy between two spheres of society. Labour or purposive-rational action is the model of action that prevails within subsystems, while the life-world develops out of interactions or communicative acts.

> So I shall distinguish generally at the analytic level between (1) the institutional framework of a society or the socio-cultural lifeworld and (2) the subsystems of purposive-rational action that are 'embedded' in it. Insofar as actions are determined by the institutional framework they are both guided and enforced by norms. Insofar as they are determined by subsystems of purposive-rational action, they conform to patterns of instrumental or strategic action.
>
> ('Technology and Science as "Ideology"', pp. 93–4; chapter in *Toward a Rational Society*)

This set of conceptual tools, borrowed from both phenomenology and systems functionalism, facilitates Habermas' diagnosis of the contemporary era, which is as follows. Habermas refers to the restructuring of the state which has occurred in all Western countries, the shift from the classical night-watchman state, whose tasks were limited to the maintenance of order and security, to the modern interventionist welfare state. However, according to Habermas this means that the state can no longer be treated, as Marxists believe it can, as a purely superstructural phenomenon: the critique of society can no longer be merely a critique of political economy, because the state no longer intervenes solely in the process of distribution, but also directly in the process of production – via research and technology policy for example. But classical political economy itself has also become irrelevant: the thesis of fair exchange between market participants, which it had once been possible to believe in – at least during the era of laissez-faire liberalism, though it was rather implausible even then (see the remarks by Parsons in Lecture II, p. 30) – has now been fatally undermined. This is because both exchange and production are shaped by state policies. It has thus become quite absurd to speak of a naturally just market.

But what supersedes this basic ideology of fair exchange in capitalist societies? Habermas claims that it is the welfare state that ensures the loyalty of the masses. At the same time, though, he suggests, this imbues politics with a purely negative image; at the very least it loses its formative character. This is because welfarist policies are directed solely at tackling dysfunctions. The sole priority is to solve technical and monetary problems; the practical substance of politics, such as new ideas on how to rationally organize social relations, are airbrushed out completely. For Habermas, the question of what constitutes the 'good life', a question at the heart of classical political philosophy, and above all the public discussion of this subject, no longer plays any role in such a political landscape. Practical political issues have become technological ones – a view which Habermas had already adopted in *Theory and Practice* (see p. 213); political issues now revolve solely around objectives *within* existing social structures. The populace becomes depoliticized as a result, which is ultimately a constitutive feature of the functioning of welfare capitalism, based as it is on the assumption that the people are the *passive object* of well-meaning measures drawn up by experts.

Overall, this means that what Habermas believes to be the fundamental distinction between 'labour' and 'interaction' may drop out of the public consciousness, just as it was already blurred in the work of Marx, because the potential of the forces of production has been tapped on a massive scale and the majority of the population has achieved a fair degree of prosperity as a result of welfarist intervention. In contemporary public consciousness, societal development seems determined by technological progress *alone*. In other words, issues of justice, of what constitutes a rational society and above all one worth living in, are being pushed aside in favour of supposed practical necessities. Habermas sees a danger here, which he was to explicate more precisely in his later works, namely that the institutional framework of society, the life-world, might be marginalized entirely by the subsystems of purposive-rational action, and we are thus faced with a world in which

> the structure of one of the two types of action, namely the behavioural system of purposive-rational action, not only predominates over the institutional framework but gradually absorbs communicative action as such.
>
> (ibid., p. 106)

Habermas is in fact describing the 'technocratic spirit' of the 1960s and 1970s, common in politics and among broad sections of the population, quite well here; this was a time when the belief in the capacity to make and remake social relations within the framework of the existing social structure seemingly knew no bounds, when the solving of tangible problems was more or less equated with what politics is and such a politics still enjoyed much acclaim. John F. Kennedy's governing team, numerically dominated by brilliant experts ('the best and the brightest'), exuded this air, as did the West German cabinet under Chancellor Helmut Schmidt in the 1970s, in as much as resistance to measures drawn up by the government was all too quickly put down to ignorance or lack of expert knowledge.

These statements clearly entail a critique of Western capitalism, but Marx does not come away unscathed either. Habermas refers to the need to reformulate the 'category framework ... in the basic assumptions of historical materialism' (ibid., p. 113). For Habermas, it is clear that class struggle, that pivotal category of Marxian thought, can no longer claim pride of place in contemporary theoretical analyses of society, because the welfare state has brought this struggle to an end or pacified it; as a result, class antagonisms exist at most in latent form. What is more, Habermas believes, the fundamental distinction between 'labour' and 'interaction' produces more adequate analyses of the danger, with which Western societies are faced, of a blurring of technological and practical political issues than the Marxian dialectic between forces of production and relations of production. To counter the temptation to reduce 'labour' to 'interaction' and vice versa, Habermas again emphasizes that we must distinguish clearly between the rationalization characteristic of the subsystems of purposive-rational action and that typical of the level of interaction. The rationalization of the institutional structures dependent on communication is not measured by the increasing domination of nature, but according to whether and to what extent societies enable their members to freely reach agreement, thus reducing the repressiveness and rigidity of social relations. The rational potential inherent in language should, according to Habermas, therefore be used to expedite the institutional restructuring of societies with a view to organizing social structures more rationally. Again, his key idea with respect to the functions and tasks of language is expressed very nicely here.

Habermas' essay was certainly a compelling diagnosis of the late 1960s; yet with hindsight, it inevitably raises at least two critical questions.

(A) Why did the technocratic ideology rapidly become quite insignificant, or better, fall to pieces, in the mid-to-late 1970s? Habermas cannot, of course, be expected to predict the future; on the other hand, one must inevitably wonder how deep-seated this technocratic ideology really was, how important or necessary it was to Western capitalism in the 1960s, if it had so little influence a mere decade later. The technocratic consensus came to an end fairly quickly as a result of the environmental and anti-nuclear movements which burgeoned in the early 1970s, when the citizens of Western societies, particularly the younger and often academically educated ones, became increasingly sceptical of the mania for feasibility so typical of the political and scientific establishment, and indeed of economic growth as such. Moreover, this technocratic consensus was broken on a quite different front as well, when traditional patterns of the legitimation of capitalism declined dramatically, particularly in Great Britain under Margaret Thatcher and in the USA under Ronald Reagan. In the eyes of many British and American voters, the welfare state evidently seemed to be the problem, and no longer the solution; contrary to expectations, the idea of the market and of the fair exchange which allegedly prevails within it seemed to regain its power and persuasiveness. The retreat of the state from economic and social policy thus seemed no more than logical. This trend too was impossible to foresee, let alone predict, on the basis of Habermas' diagnosis of the times.

(B) The second criticism is directed more at abstract theoretical matters than political diagnoses. Habermas' notion of 'subsystems of purposive-rational action' may be suspected of being overly simplistic. The idea of the 'exclusivity' of purposive-rational forms of action, of a logic characteristic of certain spheres of society which is truly pervasive and rests *solely* on instrumental rationality, which the concept of system implies, is in reality quite inconceivable. As we know from Lecture III, Parsons himself pointed out that markets rest upon norms, and it therefore seems highly problematic when Habermas speaks as though, for example, the subsystem of the economy *as a whole* is moulded by purposive-rational forms of action. Every study in industrial sociology shows that a whole range of actions takes place in firms, that they feature processes of *negotiation*, that norms, habits, irrational privileges, etc. play a massive role. Habermas' conceptual strategy captures none of this. Habermas proves a very quick study in this regard, though. He was soon to distinguish clearly between *types of action* and *types of action system*, conceding that the subsystems of society cannot be characterized by a single type of action. In his later *Theory of Communicative Action* he was to conceive of this quite differently.

We have now traced the development of Habermas' work to the late 1960s, a period of brilliance characterized by tremendous productivity. Our question now is what direction his oeuvre took in the 1970s and 1980s and how he succeeded in making the first major attempt at synthesis after that of Talcott Parsons, an endeavour to which we have referred on several occasions. For Habermas' influence was ultimately limited to sociology until the late 1960s. It would be quite fair to classify Habermas during this period as a Western Marxist, albeit a *highly innovative* one, who differed from other neo-Marxist authors primarily in the emphasis he placed on the unique structure of human intersubjectivity in his arguments. But this was not enough to satisfy the theoretical needs of those who had good reason to distrust the Marxist traditions as a whole or who expected very little of them. The notion that the complexity and multidimensionality of Parsons' oeuvre, and the lively discussion between conflict theorists, symbolic interactionists, ethnomethodologists and the exponents of rational choice could be overridden with the aid of a Marxian approach, albeit a modified one, seemed rather implausible. Where did Habermas' theoretical journey take him next? What enabled him to achieve his influential theoretical synthesis?

X

Habermas' 'theory of communicative action'

The crucial turning point in Habermas' career came in the early 1970s, when he broke finally and unmistakably with key elements of the Hegelian and Marxian legacy; it was in this context that he wrestled with the utopias of the student movement. Habermas thus cut the cord connecting him to this tradition, which he previously seemed to be continuing with mere critical modifications. As a consequence of this break, he was to introduce a number of new theoretical elements into his thought, enabling him to advance towards his own theoretical synthesis.

First, Habermas abandons the idea that history can be understood as a process of the formation of *the human species* as a whole. In the work of Marx, humanity had been conceived in Hegelian fashion as, so to speak, a macro-subject. Following lengthy periods of alienation, this subject would regain consciousness in the post-capitalist era. This *single* subject of humanity as a whole – Habermas emphatically states – *does not exist*; the notion that later generations as a whole are always able to stand on the shoulders of those who came before and that we can thus expect humanity as such to develop further in seamless fashion is an utterly unjustified idealization. It is simply not the case that the knowledge held by the forebears is simply transferred to all their descendants, that the future generations need only to build on that which the forefathers knew and what they established in fixed and immutable fashion. Rather, we must assume that it is initially *individuals* who learn, and *individuals* who (in the context of the family for example) absorb or perhaps reject the experiences of their forebears. People always have to make a new start. They come into the world in a state of 'not knowing' and must first acquire their own individual stock of knowledge.

All of this may sound relatively unspectacular or even trivial, but the step taken by Habermas here is of great significance. It entails the rejection of the idea, not unusual in the work of Marxian thinkers, that the good of later generations justifies the suffering and sacrifices of the previous generations of humanity, such that the suffering of current generations can be accepted given that the living conditions of future generations are expected to be better – a very dangerous idea, particular as regards political practice, which has repeatedly led to criminal consequences throughout modern history. Humanity – according to Habermas – is *not a singular subject*; we cannot simply weigh up the sufferings and joys characteristic of specific developmental periods, societies or people in light of other periods in its supposed process of formation. Social change, he concludes, must be grasped without recourse to this notion so central to the Hegelian-Marxian philosophy of history. Rather than rushing to identify the supposed learning processes characteristic of *the species*, Habermas therefore begins to examine the real learning processes typical *of individuals*. He begins to study how and in which dimensions of action individuals learn; for learning processes begin within the concrete individual. Of course, this does not exclude the possibility that processes of collective learning may also occur, that groups or even whole societies can learn, but this learning can only be understood as the successful fusion of individual learning processes, determined by the specifics of the situation, and should not be assumed to be the automatic result of a developmental process characterizing humanity *as such*.

In line with this idea, authors who have studied these individual learning processes, authors in the field of developmental *psychology*, now took on great importance for Habermas. The Swiss psychologist Jean Piaget (1896–1980) and the American social psychologist Lawrence Kohlberg (1927–87), both of whom studied cognitive, but above all *moral* learning processes among children and adolescents in a highly innovative way in the 1950s, 1960s and 1970s, became the crucial reference authors for Habermas as he set about investigating how the findings of developmental psychology might be combined with a theory of evolution. Are there any parallels between the stages of cognitive and moral development in individuals and the developmental stages typical of humanity as a whole? How does 'ontogeny', the development of the individual being, relate to 'phylogeny', the history of one's tribe or species, and, should it exist, how exactly are we to conceive of this parallelism? This is the question *alluded to, but not answered* in the following quotation, which is Habermas' primary concern in the 1970s and which he will not – and this he realizes at a fairly early stage – manage to resolve in an entirely satisfactory way.

> The components of world-views that secure identity and are efficacious for social integration – that is, moral systems and their accompanying interpretations – follow with increasing complexity a pattern that has a parallel at the ontogenetic level in the logic of the development of moral consciousness.
>
> (*Legitimation Crisis*, p. 12)

For Habermas, like all theoretically informed and thus cautious theorists of evolution, will be able to state only that it is possible to discern a logic in the sequence of developmental stages characteristic of humanity – which parallels the cognitive and moral development of individuals in a certain sense, though exactly how is left unclarified. *But it is almost impossible to say anything about the mechanisms, the causal factors, which led to new stages.* Habermas thus distinguishes between the developmental *logic* of the historical process *and the historical process itself.* Evolutionary and social theorists can reconstruct the logic of developmental history only in retrospect; however, no precise statements can be made about the concrete historical processes involved. Evolutionary theory proceeds reconstructively, not by means of causal analysis.

> Historical materialism does not need to assume a species-subject that undergoes evolution. The bearers of evolution are rather societies and the acting subjects integrated into them; social evolution can be discerned in those structures that are replaced by more comprehensive structures in accord with a pattern that is to be rationally reconstructed. In the course of this structure-forming process, societies and individuals, together with their ego and group identities, undergo change. Even if social evolution should point in the direction of unified individuals consciously influencing the course of their own evolution, there would not arise any large-scale subjects, but at most self-established, higher-level, intersubjective commonalities. (The specification of the concept of development is another question: in what sense can one conceive the rise of new structures as a movement? Only the empirical substrates are in motion.)
>
> If we separate the logic from the dynamics of development – that is, the rationally reconstructible *pattern* of a hierarchy of more and more comprehensive structures from the *processes* through which the empirical substrates develop – then we need require of history neither unilinearity nor necessity, neither continuity nor irreversibility.
>
> ('Toward a Reconstruction of Historical Materialism', p. 140; original emphasis)

For historians and all those interested in detailed analyses of process, this is of course inadequate or unsatisfactory. Nonetheless, speculative Hegelian Marxism with its highly problematic theory of social change has been replaced with an evolutionary theory based on insights from developmental psychology which, moreover, as Habermas stresses in the quotation above, is also non-evolutionist (see our remarks on the distinction between 'theory of evolution' and 'evolutionist' in Lecture IV, p. 86). In any case, this theory of evolution takes on crucial strategic importance in Habermas' work. Regardless of the surely irresolvable issue, which we have just touched on, of which concrete *mechanisms* underpin the assumed parallels between phylogeny and ontogeny, the thrust of Habermas' arguments amounts to the thesis that in the sphere of production or in the realm of world views, cognitive or moral learning processes occurred which, in line with the fundamental distinction between 'labour' and 'interaction', were relatively independent of one another. In other words, Habermas again argues, against Marx, that bolstering the forces of production does not automatically lead to moral progress in the sense of a more rational way of organizing social relations. We must assume that moral action follows its own logic, which precludes the notion that the economy is the key factor in explaining social change. Habermas, using Marxian concepts, but against Marx, puts this as follows:

> The development of productive forces can then be understood as a problem-generating mechanism that *triggers but does not bring about* the overthrow of relations of production and an evolutionary renewal of the mode of production.
>
> (ibid., p. 146; original emphasis)

Second – taking another step away from the legacy of Hegel and Marx, though this is linked with the first step in some respects – Habermas eschews all reference to idealized superordinate subjects. Here, his arguments were clearly directed against the Hungarian Marxian theorist Georg Lukács (1885–1971) and his book *History and Class Consciousness* from 1923, a hugely influential work, particularly in the student movement. *History and Class Consciousness* was one of the major reference texts of left-wing cultural critics into the 1970s due to Lukács' impressive and suggestive account of the culturally destructive effects of capitalist commoditization in a chapter on 'The Phenomenon of Reification'. What was highly problematic was the fact that Lukács tied his hopes for an end to this reifying and reified state of affairs entirely to a Leninist party, which he saw as the embodiment of an objective proletarian class consciousness, which alone can point the way out of the 'antinomies of bourgeois thought' and bourgeois society:

> The *conscious* desire for the realm of freedom can only mean consciously taking the steps that will really lead to it ... It implies the conscious subordination of the self to that collective will that is destined to bring real freedom into being and that is today earnestly taking the first arduous, uncertain and groping steps towards it. This conscious collective will is the Communist Party.
>
> (Lukács, *History and Class Consciousness*, p. 315; original emphasis)

The alarming thing about Lukács' figure of thought was not just that he took it upon himself to declare empirical class consciousness null and void and – because *he* as a Marxist philosopher has obviously known how the process of history will turn out all along – to counter it with an 'objectively correct class consciousness'; also alarming was Lukács' unhesitating identification of this real class consciousness, and thus the progress of humanity, with a specific political party, and furthermore with one whose legitimacy was anything but democratic: the Leninist vanguard party.

Habermas now rejected out of hand all thinking even vaguely reminiscent of this, which, given the circumstances at the time, meant battling sections of the student movement of the late 1960s and early 1970s, when Leninism, surprisingly, was booming and a troupe of obscure figures frequently laid claim to knowledge of the laws of motion governing human history and thus the best (revolutionary) strategies to pursue in a way that seems laughable today, but which dominated at some universities at the time. As early as *Theory and Practice* and the chapter on Marxism which it contains, Habermas had stated that the analysis of historical processes must not be derived deductively from a 'dialectic schema', but determined through empirical analyses, and that this also applies to assumptions about groups' and classes' capacity to act (see Lecture IX, p. 204). The alarm felt at the excesses of the student movement now led Habermas to declare more vehemently than ever that the notion of idealized superordinate subjects was wrong and reprehensible. He also saw a similar tendency at work in the right-wing Hegelian notion of the realization of the *nation* as a 'historical mission'. His destruction of the idea of superordinate subjects is thus directed politically against the dangers of totalitarianism of the left or right.

From now on, Habermas was in fact to view every systematic attempt to conceive of collective actors theoretically with enormous scepticism – even in cases in which this is quite justifiable empirically. For him, the 'superordinate subject' idealized in the history of philosophy is hiding behind every 'collective actor'. Habermas goes further yet. On the level of theory, he adopts a construction which renders the very idea of such superordinate subjects more or less impossible. We are referring to the functionalist concept of system. Via the reception of Luhmann's work (see the following lecture), Habermas – as may have been evident in some of the quotations presented in the last lecture – had adopted the Parsonian concept of system as early as the late 1960s. In light of the analyses of Luhmann and Parsons, it seemed to him beyond doubt that all theories of action are of limited potential. The underlying idea here is as follows. As Luhmann tried to show in his 1968 book *Zweckbegriff und Systemrationalität* ('The Concept of Ends and System Rationality') for example (and as we shall explain in more detail in the next lecture), organizations, institutions, etc. are not guided simply by predetermined, rational aims. In other words, actors' objectives, including those of actors at the managerial level within an organization, are often near-impossible to bring into line with the concrete way in which the organization functions. The objectives of the many actors involved in an organization are too diffuse, too diverse and involve too great a degree of overlap to sift out a clear and unambiguous organizational goal. *Rather, organizations act according to their own functional logic* – regardless of the aims of action taken by individuals. For Habermas, this insight confirms that fairly large gatherings of people come about in this way, and that it is thus impossible to derive the functioning and operational logic of the collective entity from the concrete notions of action which people hold. According to Habermas, the concept of system is needed here. We should, he believes, accept the functionalists' argument that the concept of action alone is insufficient to analyse social processes.

But Habermas goes on to use this purely theoretical argument for political ends; he precludes the possibility that systems or collectives can behave *like* subjects. This is clearly apparent when Habermas writes: 'Systems are not presented as subjects' (*Legitimation Crisis*, p. 3). For Habermas, the notion of *the* proletariat or *the* nation and their missions is absurd because the interconnection of actions which these terms denote do not add up to a whole which can be meaningfully grasped through the concept of subject, whatever form this may take. In this sense, the introduction of the concept of system into Habermas' work may be interpreted in part as an attempt to deflect totalitarian temptations of every hue.

As commendable as this political motive may be, as right as Habermas may be to take a firm stand against all Leninist and nationalist temptations and to warn against the use of *idealized* collective subjects in this regard, one can at the same time hardly deny that collectives and collective actors do in fact exist. We may therefore wonder whether Habermas' clear shift towards the functionalist concept of system was rather hasty, because his theory no longer considers or is no longer able to consider the constitution of collective actors. The notion of collective actors does not automatically rest upon a kind of historical idealization. Rather, one must establish empirically whether and to what extent one can describe certain phenomena as collective forms of action. But because of his alarm at the often absurd consequences of the student rebellions, Habermas, rather like Parsons, is willing – and able – to imagine social order as a whole *solely in functionalist terms*, solely as constituted by systems. Conceiving of social order as the often fragile and only temporarily ordered 'interplay' of different collective and individual actors seems to him an unworkable approach, while it seems vastly preferable to embrace functionalism rather than the interactionist insight into the fluidity of social orders (see Lecture VI).

Politically and theoretically, this prefigures the fraught fusion of functionalism and hermeneutics, of systems and action theory; Habermas tries out this approach in the 1970s, which may be seen as a period of searching. Habermas first presents his interim findings, ranging from diagnoses of the contemporary world (*Legitimation Crisis*, 1973) to purely theoretical analyses ('Toward a Reconstruction of Historical Materialism' [1976] in which – as intimated earlier – he attempts to reformulate Marxism by means of evolutionary theory). Of far greater importance, however, is his magnum opus, *The Theory of Communicative Action* from 1981, eight years in the making, which is our key focus for most of the remainder of this lecture.

We can break down *The Theory of Communicative Action*, a two-volume work of more than 1,100 pages, into four topical clusters. It offers (1) a theory of rationality, (2) a theory of action, (3) a theory of social order and (4) a diagnosis of the contemporary era. According to Habermas, all four fields are inseparably and necessarily linked, a claim which can certainly be disputed.

You shall hear more about that later. We first wish to underscore Habermas' tremendous ambition in attempting to tackle such a broad and comprehensive set of topics. His aim is thus to achieve a synthesis, to unify a sociology disintegrating into various theoretical schools by taking up the claims and concerns of each of them. It is no coincidence that *The Theory of Communicative Action* is constructed on the model of Talcott Parsons' *The Structure of Social Action*, which tends to be overlooked entirely in the philosophical reception of Habermas' work. As in *Structure*, systematic theoretical sections alternate with interpretive chapters on specific authors in Habermas' major work and, like Parsons, Habermas deals in detail with Max Weber and Emile Durkheim. In contrast to Parsons, however, Habermas does not discuss the more economically oriented authors such as Alfred Marshall and Vilfredo Pareto; rather, he grapples with other key figures in the social sciences, including, tellingly, George Herbert Mead, neglected by Parsons, the leading lights of critical theory, Max Horkheimer and Theodor W. Adorno, and Parsons himself. Talcott Parsons, who had died shortly before and who – as we mentioned in Lecture II – did so much to establish the canon of classical sociological authors, is himself raised to the status of classical figure.

While the first volume of *The Theory of Communicative Action* tackles Weber and critical theory, the second examines the work of Mead, Durkheim and Parsons. There are specific reasons for this which have nothing to do with any chronology relating to the biography or work of these authors. Rather, this layout reflects a clear, though not undisputed thesis, namely that a paradigm shift is emerging within sociology, a notion Habermas argues vigorously in favour of in this work. On this view, the weakness of a theoretical construction which supposedly places *purposive-rational* action centre stage (Weber, critical theory) is increasingly being recognized by sociological theorists; they are coming to appreciate the need to adopt a very different model of action. Contemporary theoretical debate is converging on the idea of *symbolically mediated interaction*, found in the work of Mead, and to some extent in that of Durkheim as well. According to Habermas, we can overcome the difficulties of current theoretical approaches within sociology only by taking into account the ideas present in the work of these authors. Finally, Parsons is cited as an authoritative source to show that the theory of action, about whose scope, as we just mentioned, Habermas was extremely sceptical, requires a *functionalist* theory of order, although, according to Habermas, Parsonian functionalism is ultimately too radical.

So much for the book's layout and presentational approach. We turn now to the key themes in *The Theory of Communicative Action*, the first of which is Habermas' theory of rationality.

1. The simplest way to get at Habermas' conception of rationality is by appreciating how it developed *through a process of grappling* with two other highly

influential conceptions of rationality. Habermas' critique obviously aims at all those theories that see rationality merely as a balanced relationship between means and ends, thus equating rationality with the optimal choice of suitable means for realizing given ends. This mainly refers, of course, to the rational choice perspective which – as apparent in the name itself – advocates a conception of rationality of exactly this kind. But he is not referring solely to the rational choice approach *within* neo-utilitarianism, but rather to *all* utilitarian and neo-utilitarian theories, which, according to Habermas, advocate a far too narrow conception of rationality, in that they appear to render impossible any *rational* answer to the question of why people choose particular *ends* (as opposed to means). From the perspective of thinkers adopting this approach, ends are arbitrary, subjective, etc., which inevitably means that scientific, or indeed any form of rational investigation, can provide insights only into the *choice of means* for accomplishing given ends, which are not amenable to further analysis.

The other set of opponents Habermas has in mind in developing his concept of rationality, but to whom he refers only very indirectly, are those who subject rationality as such to fundamental critique. We have come across such thinkers already in the case of the anarchist theorist of science Paul Feyerabend (see Lecture I), who became one of the progenitors of the postmodern critique of science with his extreme radicalization of Kuhn's theses; we shall meet them again when we discuss poststructuralism (Lecture XIV). According to Habermas, they share the narrow conception of rationality typical of utilitarians and neo-utilitarians. But while the utilitarians grant rationality an important role, albeit in a highly circumscribed sphere – exclusively as regards the choice of means – postmodern thinkers had, Habermas tells us, taken leave of rationality entirely. For them, science as a whole and rational thought as such have no greater claim to legitimacy than other forms of knowledge (such as magic); science is no more than another type of ideology deployed to back up claims to power.

Habermas wishes to escape this dead end. He is unwilling to follow either the (neo-)utilitarians or the postmodernists, so he attempts to formulate a more comprehensive conception of reason and rationality, which he terms 'communicative rationality' or 'communicative reason'. It comes as little surprise that the intuition that lies behind this conceptual apparatus again has to do with language. It may be expressed as follows: there is no compelling reason for us to adopt the narrow conception of rationality which is the point of departure for utilitarianism. For when we talk to each other in everyday settings, we refer to very different issues and phenomena, yet at the same time, there is an expectation that agreement, that *a rational consensus can be achieved*. Everyday practice thus shows that most people clearly believe reason to be capable of substantially more than do the utilitarians. But Habermas is not content merely to allude to the intuitive suspicion that everyday practice and human language have great potential for rationality. Drawing heavily on the findings of analytical philosophy, he proceeds to analyse this potential for rationality more precisely. Analytical philosophy, particularly the speech act theory of the American philosopher John Searle (b. 1932), investigated language and human speakers in detail, analysing what exactly we do when we speak, what the achievements of language are, what exactly is expressed in a speech act and how this happens. What emerged from this was that speech acts may refer to quite different aspects of the world – and it is this idea that is taken up by Habermas. He expounds the thesis, fundamental to his broad or comprehensive concept of rationality, that every utterance, and in principle every action, entails precisely three 'validity claims', that every utterance we make and every action we take produces, as it were, three different forms of reference to the world, which we are prepared in principle to defend.

(a) In every utterance we refer to something in the world, we assert that things are like *this* rather than like *that*. In Habermas' terminology, we make a *validity claim to truth*. For utilitarians, this is the only point of departure for rational or scientific debate: we argue over whether or not a statement about the world is empirically correct. This aspect is certainly far from unimportant. When all is said and done, labour and the objectification of nature, natural sciences and technology are based on the fact that we can make statements about the world, but can also dispute, correct and revise them, etc. In this sense, every instrumental action also entails this claim to validity. But for Habermas, the notion that rationality should be anchored in *this validity claim alone*, that rational argument is possible only via 'constative speech acts', constitutes a profoundly inadequate conception of language and action. The reasons for this are as follows.

(b) Every utterance we make and every action we perform defines a social relationship and says something about whether or not an action is appropriate and normatively correct from a social point of view. In Habermas' diction: we make a *validity claim to normative correctness*. Here, of course, Habermas is addressing an issue with which you are already familiar from our lecture on symbolic interactionism, the fact that interactions between people do not follow a fixed and stable pattern, but that the level on which we speak and interact with one another must often be negotiated first. We sometimes find ourselves confronted with people who think that they can issue us with commands or order us around, throw their weight around as if they were our superiors, etc. This involves the assertion that a particular normative framework exists, within which they command and we obey. But we can of course reject this implicit or explicit definition of the situation; in brief, we can dispute the validity claim relating to the normative correctness of the other's actions, that is, we can assert the existence of a different norm. But in doing so, we have already entered into a debate over this validity claim, a debate which – as Habermas sees it – can in principle be carried on with rational arguments. But Habermas goes a step further. He asserts that

(c) we can also identify a *validity claim to truthfulness* in relation to our experiences and desires or the authenticity and consistency of our actions in every act or utterance. This insight, derived both from the work of Goffman and from theories of art, means that people act and speak not only with reference to the external world and to the form of normatively regulated social relations; rather, all their (speech) acts also express the *subjectivity* of the speaker or actor. The presentation of the self, as Goffman shows so impressively in his analyses, is a key component of every interaction; we are at pains to communicate our action to others as authentic, rather than artificial or false. We wish to present ourselves as truthful, as 'our true selves', and all our actions as an understandable and consistent expression of our identity. Here again, we may argue over the extent to which actions and utterances are authentic, and this we constantly do in our everyday lives, when we doubt, for example, whether another has told us what he really thinks, when we suspect that he is merely putting on an act, etc. In much the same way, Habermas tells us, artists claim to be expressing themselves through their work, a claim which art *critics* may in turn subject to scrutiny.

We have now outlined the framework within which, according to Habermas, it is possible to engage in argument, a framework far broader than that which typifies other conceptions of rationality. But let us hear from Habermas himself:

> *Normatively regulated actions* and *expressive self-presentations* have, like assertions or constative speech acts, the character of meaningful expressions, understandable in their context, which are connected with criticisable validity claims. Their reference is to norms and subjective experiences rather than to facts. The agent makes the claim that his behaviour is right in relation to a normative context recognized as legitimate, or that the first-person utterance of an experience to which he has privileged access is truthful or sincere. Like constative speech acts, these expressions can also go wrong. The possibility of intersubjective recognition of criticisable validity claims is constitutive for their rationality too. However, the knowledge embodied in normatively regulated actions or in expressive manifestations does not refer to the existence of states of affairs but to the validity of norms or to the manifestation of subjective experiences. With these expressions the speaker can refer not to

something in the objective world but only to something in a common social world or in his own subjective world.

(Habermas, *The Theory of Communicative Action*, vol. I, pp. 15–16; original emphasis)

This is not to say that each of the three validity claims is made *with equal force* in each utterance or action. In some actions, the aspect of cognitive truth is certainly more important than in others, in scientific laboratories, for example, compared with religious ceremonies. Yet the other two validity claims always play a role as well – at least as boundary conditions, because even natural science is embedded in a normative context and one must at the same time assume that the utterances made by the scientists involved are truthful. But if this is the case, a more comprehensive concept of rationality must be open to *all* three of these quite different validity claims. For all three validity claims may be disputed or refuted *through rational argument*. All three are thus amenable to discussion – Habermas refers to 'discourses' – at least if the discussions take place under the ideal or idealized condition of absolute freedom from external and internal constraints. And because we may argue over these three very different validity claims, learning processes are possible in all these spheres. According to Habermas, we now have a model of rationality which can claim to encompass, and in fact to synthesize, the assumptions about rationality found in other sociological theories (of action), which were always one-sided in their original context.

Habermas' conception of rationality proved to have far-reaching consequences. While his remarks on the third validity claim, that of truthfulness, remained rather unclear, patently fusing together a number of different dimensions (everyday truthfulness is surely quite different from authenticity in art), his sharp delineation of the validity claims of truth and normative correctness met with a very strong response. Habermas' discourse theory of truth and morality was and is the central point of departure for many contemporary debates within epistemology, philosophy of science and ethics. In Lecture XIX, which examines neo-pragmatism, we return to some of these issues, which are certainly more philosophical than sociological.

2. Habermas' theory of action is very closely, in fact inseparably, linked with the conception of rationality presented above. This comes as no surprise, given that Habermas developed this theory of action on the basis of his theory of rationality. This is undoubtedly an appealing approach, simple and highly elegant. It almost effortlessly assigns types of rationality, as we shall see in a moment, to types of action. Yet such a procedure is not free of problems. At least two critical questions arise: first, if the theory of action is constructed on the basis of the theory of rationality, does this not almost automatically result in action being understood in a highly rationalistic

way, with forms of action which fail to jibe neatly with the model of rationality being overlooked or even consciously neglected? Second, does the approach chosen by Habermas not contradict vital insights from the philosophical tradition of American pragmatism with respect to the relationship between thinking and acting? Here (see Lecture VI), thinking was conceived not as a substance, not as mind or consciousness, but as a process *which occurs in situations of action*. The American pragmatists interpreted thinking as functional with respect to problems of action. But because Habermas begins his theoretical construction with a theory of rationality and *only then* progresses to a theory of action, he appears to have ignored this insight.

We can of course only hope to answer these questions if we are familiar with Habermas' theory of action. What form does this take? Habermas essentially distinguishes between three types of action, though he attributes these to the three validity claims mentioned above, which are made in every utterance or action, in a highly idiosyncratic, or at least rather asymmetrical way. One might have expected that Habermas would construct the various types of action *in parallel with* the validity claims he has elaborated. And he does in fact do so when he distinguishes between *teleological* action, which is intended to manipulate the external world, *normatively regulated* action based on the appropriateness of social relations, and *dramaturgical* action, fundamentally concerned with the problem of self-representation (ibid., vol. I, pp. 85ff.). Yet Habermas did not go on to make *this* form of symmetrical or parallel classification the point of departure in his discussions of action theory. For his typology of action is ultimately based largely on the distinction between rational action in a narrow sense, which he subdivides into 'purposive-rational action' and 'strategic action' on the one hand, and 'communicative action' on the other, which is based on a comprehensive conception of rationality. Why did he choose this approach and what exactly does this mean?

According to Habermas, *purposive-rational action* relates to material objects; it is action which involves choosing suitable means in order to render nature disposable, manipulate objects, etc. As Habermas states:

> The actor attains an end or brings about the occurrence of a desired state by choosing means that have promise of being successful in the given situation and applying them in a suitable manner. The central concept is that of a decision among alternative courses of action, with a view to the realization of an end, guided by maxims, and based on an interpretation of the situation.
>
> (ibid., vol. I, p. 85)

Strategic action does *not* relate to material objects, but to other subjects, though once again the means–ends schema guides the action. Typical examples of such action situations can be found in game theory (see Lecture V); they involve mutually imbricated actors choosing their best options for action and thus rendering each other mere means for achieving certain ends. The teleological model of action

> is expanded to a strategic model when there can enter into the agent's calculation of success the anticipation of decisions on the part of at least one additional goal-directed actor. This model is often interpreted in utilitarian terms; the actor is supposed to choose and calculate means and ends from the standpoint of maximizing utility or expectations of utility. It is this model of action that lies behind decision-theoretic and game-theoretic approaches in economics, sociology, and social psychology.
>
> (ibid., vol. I, p. 85)

Communicative action, meanwhile, contrasts markedly with instrumental and strategic action, but also with the normatively regulated and dramaturgical action addressed above. Normatively regulated, dramaturgical and communicative action do have certain features in common in that, in contrast to instrumental and strategic action, they do not assume an *actor in isolation*, who merely manipulates material objects or other subjects as if they were objects. When our actions are guided by norms, we fulfil the behavioural expectations held by a *group*, taking our lead from norms *held in common*, just as we 'stylize the expression' of our experiences *'with a view to the audience'* in the case of dramaturgical action (ibid., vol. I, p. 86); and communicative action is of course underpinned by an identical framework, which does *not* assume the existence of an isolated actor. But communicative action differs from the normatively guided and dramaturgical types of action in that the individuals interacting here wish to achieve a genuine *understanding*. Normatively regulated action is based on the *taken-for-granted* validity of norms, while dramaturgical action is anchored in the conventions of self-representation, which are initially regarded as *unproblematic*. It is only communicative action that investigates the unquestioned prerequisites and taken-for-granted features characteristic of these action situations; the actors discuss the various validity claims made and attempt to produce consensus. 'The actors seek to reach an understanding about the action situation and their plans of action in order to coordinate their actions by way of agreement' (ibid.).

Communicative action – and this is its special feature, distinguishing it from normatively guided and dramaturgical action – is *not* teleological, that is, it is not aimed at achieving a specific goal. It is geared neither towards achieving *specific ends* with selected means, adherence to unquestionably *given* norms, nor *successful* self-stylization. Rather, communicative action is distinguished by the fact that it suspends the validity of predetermined goals, because it revolves around honest discussion with other people, which cannot and must not be aimed at achieving a fixed goal. If I engage in such discussion with others, I have to expect my goals and ends to be revised, refuted, *convincingly* rejected. In other words, this form of discussion requires all interlocutors to open up; they must have an open mind about the outcome of the conversation. *Under these circumstances of open discussion*, there are no predetermined ends which those involved wish to accomplish. And this means that communicative action, action geared towards understanding, is non-teleological action. Let us hear once again what Habermas himself has to say:

> Only the communicative model of action presupposes language as a medium of uncurtailed communication whereby speakers and hearers, out of the context of their preinterpreted lifeworld, refer simultaneously to things in the objective, social, and subjective worlds in order to negotiate common definitions of the situation.
>
> (ibid., vol. I, p. 95)

We can now understand why Habermas posits communicative action as a counter-concept to instrumental and strategic action: this is a type of action that always necessarily requires other actors capable of engaging in argument *and which is at the same time* non-teleological. This may be presented in graphic form (see Habermas, ibid., vol. I, p. 285) by a fourfold table, featuring the axes 'nonsocial action situation' versus 'social action situation' on the one hand and 'action orientation oriented to success' versus 'action orientation oriented to reaching understanding' on the other (Figure 10.1).

If we compare this scheme with Parsons' action frame of reference, we notice that Habermas does indeed break with the teleological model of action – by means of his notion of communicative action. While Parsons

Action situation / Action orientation	Oriented to success	Oriented to reaching understanding
Nonsocial	Instrumental action	–
Social	Strategic action	Communicative action

Figure 10.1

could only imagine action as geared towards goals and ends – although he took values and norms into account of course (see Lecture II and our critique in Lecture III) – in Habermas' work, communicative action is distinguished by the fact that actors do not have their sights set on *predetermined* ends or norms; rather, these ends are at the disposal of the actors engaged in discussion.

Finally, this scheme lays bare Habermas' *synthetic* intentions with respect to theory building. With his conception of action, Habermas claims to encompass the models of action developed within sociology (in the work of Parsons or Goffman for example), to incorporate the intentions of the various authors – to synthesize their theoretical insights. The idea of communicative action allows Habermas to stand, as it were, on the shoulders of earlier sociologists. Here again, the parallels with Parsons' ambitions in *The Structure of Social Action* are unmistakable: Parsons claimed to have brought together and conceptualized with greater clarity the intuitions already appearing in the work of Durkheim, Weber, Pareto and Marshall by means of his action frame of reference. Habermas argues in much the same way, legitimating his own approach by drawing on the interpretations of classical authors. Here, his thesis ('The Paradigm Shift in Mead and Durkheim: From Purposive Activity to Communicative Action') states that the shift towards communicative action, though it may not yet have been clear or complete, had already occurred during the early days of the establishment of sociology. For Habermas, it was above all George Herbert Mead (the progenitor of symbolic interactionism discussed in Lecture VI) and the late Emile Durkheim (primarily in his work in the sociology of religion), who truly recognized the significance of language or of symbolically mediated interaction, spurring on a conception of rationality as well as one of action broader and more comprehensive than those available to Max Weber and upon which critical theory, as in the case of Adorno and Horkheimer, had to build, and whose hypotheses on the rationalization of the world proved extremely one-sided.

It is certainly possible to raise certain questions about this view of the history of sociology, that is, Habermas' interpretation of the classical figures of the discipline. The hyper-rationalist interpretation of Durkheim's sociology of religion, which Habermas presents in the guise of the 'linguistification of the sacred', has been subject to particularly intense criticism (see Joas, 'The Unhappy Marriage of Hermeneutics and Functionalism'). But these aspects are not our concern here; rather, we will be *critiquing* Habermas' typology of action.

(a) You will notice that one field of the diagram, that of non-teleological relations with non-social objects, has been left empty. Habermas was convinced that no such relations exist. This had partly to do with a point made in the previous lecture – that he had already broken down the Marxian concept of praxis by means of the dichotomy of 'labour' and 'interaction', which meant that he could now conceive of 'labour' only as purposive-rational action. Here, we can already see in embryonic form the idea that relations with material objects can only be captured through the categories of ends and means. Yet one can certainly dispute the notion that such relations inevitably take this particular form. Habermas might have learned from American pragmatism that there exist forms of action vis-à-vis objects which elude the means–ends scheme. This is exactly what happens in the case of children's playing or playful interaction with objects, and artists' work with various forms of matter is surely not informed by a fixed objective. This playful or aesthetic interaction with objects is more than merely marginal for the pragmatists in that they see within it the creativity of human action (see Joas, *The Creativity of Action* and Lecture XIX). Habermas fails utterly to take account of this, such that one can certainly criticize his seemingly comprehensive typology of action for being too narrow or lacking certain elements. Habermas thus pays the price for basing his typology of action on his conception of rationality rather than an independent and extensive phenomenology of various forms of action.

(b) Furthermore, Habermas is so exclusively interested in the distinction outlined above between communicative action on the one hand and instrumental or strategic action on the other that he fails to discuss what is *common to all action*, what, for example, distinguishes all the types of action discussed by him from animal behaviour. He thus evades an anthropological discussion of human action, which is certainly possible and perhaps even necessary. This is problematic in that he thus forgoes the opportunity to correct or supplement his rationalistic typology of action. The insights garnered by philosophical anthropology in particular, but also many psychological and biological studies, into the specific *corporeality* of human action, thus have no impact on his theory. We have at least indicated how this aspect of every action can be taken fully into account in our discussion of symbolic interactionism and ethnomethodology. We shall have more to say on this in subsequent lectures (on Giddens, Bourdieu and neo-pragmatism).

3. Habermas' theory of order is also closely and directly linked with his conception of rationality and action. He refers to two types of social order, that of the *life-world* on the one hand and that of *systems* on the other. To some extent, Habermas derives these two types of order, which he distinguishes in dichotomous fashion, from his action theoretical distinction, elaborated above, between communicative action on the one hand and instrumental

or strategic forms of action on the other. As we know from the previous lecture, Habermas had used the terms 'life-world' and 'system' as early as the late 1960s. In his magnum opus, he reformulates these concepts and sets new trends, conceiving the two types of order in accordance with a distinction going back to Parsons with which you are already familiar.

In *The Structure of Social Action*, Parsons had drawn attention to the distinction between a 'normative order' and a 'factual order', and thus to the fact that we can distinguish forms of joint action in line with whether the ordered patterns of action between actors have come about on the basis of shared norms or merely constitute a random aggregation of actions thrown together – like the traffic jam, share prices or the market price of butter – to produce an unintended, normatively unregulated pattern. It is precisely this idea that Habermas now takes up in his definitions (admittedly inconsistent at times) of system and life-world. In line with Parsons' 'normative order', he views the *life-world* as an ordered context which individuals help generate in as much as they refer to common norms, a common understanding, common culture, etc. *Systems* meanwhile correspond structurally to what Parsons calls the 'factual order', in that the ordered patterns do not express the specific intentions of the individuals involved; rather, this order is merely the unintended result of the actions of a large number of individuals. Here, it is the *consequences* of action that give rise to patterns, as with market prices which are generated *only as a result* of the consumption and production behaviour of market participants. Habermas thus wishes to distinguish

> mechanisms of coordinating action that harmonize the *action orientations* of participants from mechanisms that stabilize nonintended interconnections of actions by way of functionally intermeshing *action consequences*. In one case, the integration of an action system is established by a normatively secured or communicatively achieved consensus, in the other case, by a nonnormative regulation of individual decisions that extends beyond the actors' consciousnesses. This distinction between a *social integration* of society, which takes effect in action orientations, and a *systemic integration*, which reaches through and beyond action orientations, calls for a corresponding differentiation in the concept of society itself.
>
> (ibid., vol. II, p. 117; original emphasis)

Habermas thus refers, first, to the *social integration* of a society, in which its members are integrated via shared action *orientations* – a state of affairs elucidated through the application of the phenomenological concept of life-world; second, he believes, societies also feature *mechanisms of system integration*, the actions being linked by means of the *consequences* of action, a form of linkage which, according to Habermas, we can get at only through functional analysis and which thus requires the concept of system.

So far, the distinction between these two fundamental types of order seems clear. Yet Habermas is obviously dissatisfied with this: he adds two further distinctions. We might wonder how these relate to the first two definitions emphasizing the *consequences* of action and action *orientations*. First, Habermas asserts that system and life-world can also be differentiated in line with whether or not the parties to interaction are co-present. While the systemic coordination of action, in capitalist markets for example, comes about through acts carried out by individuals – such as the consumer and producer – who generally do not know one another, and thus occurs in abstract fashion, integration within the life-world is distinguished, among other things, by the fact that the actors face each other directly or at least fairly directly *within a concrete action situation*; they are physically co-present, enabling them to coordinate their actions precisely.

> A *situation* is a segment of *lifeworld contexts of relevance* [*Verweisungszusammenhänge*] that is thrown into relief by themes and articulated through goals and plans of action; these contexts of relevance are concentrically ordered and become increasingly anonymous and diffused as the spatiotemporal and social distance grows.
> (ibid., vol. II, pp. 122–3; original emphasis and insertion)

Second, Habermas also differentiates between system and social integration on the basis of their differing degrees of cognitive accessibility. While at least the external observer, the scientist, can get at system integration by means of functional analysis, the life-world is characterized by a unique form of existence. As we know from Lecture VII, the term originated in phenomenological contexts, where, as Habermas makes clear by quoting from Schütz and Luckmann, it refers to the 'unquestioned ground of everything given in my experience, and the unquestionable frame in which all the problems I have to deal with are located' (quoted in Habermas, ibid., vol. II, p. 131). On this view, the life-world forms the partially inaccessible background to all our actions; it is the taken-for-granted context of our thought and activity and cannot, therefore, be grasped cognitively in the same way as the systemic mechanisms of action coordination, which are in principle objectifiable and which we can hope to understand intellectually.

All these *additional* definitions, through which Habermas attempts to capture the two dichotomous types of order, point to the fact that he has reached a crucial stage in terms of theoretical strategy; but it may also indicate that these manifold definitions conceal certain difficulties. For it is not always clear how action coordination on the basis of action orientations, or within the context of actors' co-presence, or on the basis of a (cultural) background regarded as taken for granted, relate to one another. All three definitions are intended to define the socially integrative mechanism of the life-world. But it is unclear whether, for example, action coordination is dependent on co-presence, and if so to what extent; what is more, it seems peculiar that it is only within systems that the *consequences* of action are claimed to be of great significance, but not in the life-world, which actually contradicts everyday experience, in as much as we are constantly confronted with the unexpected consequences of our actions. But if this is so, would one not have to deploy functional analysis to illuminate situations of co-presence, an approach Habermas wished to reserve for the study of systemic contexts? And why in fact does the existence of action consequences compel us to adopt a functionalist analytical framework, given that the analysis of the unintended consequences of action – as we saw in Lecture V – is one of the key concerns of neo-utilitarianism, particularly rational choice theory, which has regained traction precisely on the basis of a justified critique of Talcott Parsons' functionalist paradigm? These are all points in need of clarification, and ultimately raise the question of whether Habermas has succeeded in fusing two concepts of order drawn from very different traditions – that of the life-world, which can be attributed more or less to the interpretive approaches, and that of system, whose origins of course lie in functionalist thought – or whether he has engineered a mismatch leading to insurmountable theoretical problems (see Joas, 'The Unhappy Marriage of Hermeneutics and Functionalism').

However this may be, Habermas now ascribes the two basic types of action to the two concepts of order. While the concept of life-world is claimed to be a 'concept complementary to that of communicative action' (Habermas, *The Theory of Communicative Action*, vol. II, p. 119), action within systems *predominantly* (though not exclusively) takes the form of instrumental or strategic action. He adds to this set of ideas the thesis, which he backs up with reference to evolutionary theory, of the historical 'uncoupling of system and life-world'. By this, Habermas means that the earliest societies in terms of evolution, such as 'primitive' tribal societies, can be understood exclusively as socio-cultural life-worlds. Here, the social structure was substantially and immediately determined by normatively guided interaction, that is, the coordination of action between the members of the tribe occurred exclusively via action orientations in circumstances of co-presence; language was the key and in fact the only medium through which the actors came to an understanding, while the *consequences* of action had not yet taken on independent form. This, Habermas believes, happened only later, at a higher level of social evolution, when the emergence of political domination in the form of states and – in capitalism – the emergence of free markets, gave rise to orders that had finally severed the ties binding them to immediate linguistic communication. Habermas, closely following Parsons and other functionalist theorists, claims that a process of differentiation has set in, which has given rise to systems such as politics and the economy which are regulated via symbolically generalized media of communication such as power and money and which are no longer accessible to the intuitive understanding of all members of society:

> The uncoupling of system and lifeworld is experienced in modern society as a particular kind of objectification: the social system definitively bursts out of the horizon of the lifeworld, escapes from the intuitive knowledge of everyday communicative practice, and is henceforth accessible only to the counterintuitive knowledge of the social sciences developing since the eighteenth century.
>
> (ibid., vol. II, p. 173)

The terminology itself clearly lays bare the borrowings from Parsons (see for instance the concept of differentiation and the adoption of his theory of media). Habermas' historical thesis, outlined above, serves above all to justify the incorporation of functionalist arguments in his system of thought. Precisely because politics and the market have emerged as distinct spheres, according to Habermas, interpretive approaches to the analysis of modern societies are insufficient, as is their concept of order, the life-world, which is why one must introduce the concept of system. At the same time, deploying the concept of life-world and system in parallel can help produce a viable diagnosis of the contemporary era, thus facilitating a critical perspective on modern societies.

4. This brings us to the fourth major theme of *The Theory of Communicative Action*, the diagnosis of the modern world. This will come as little surprise in light of our discussion of Habermas' writings of the 1960s and 1970s, in which we set out – at least in rudimentary form – some of the basic features of this diagnosis.

Habermas' diagnosis of the contemporary world is directly linked with his evolutionary reflections. Habermas portrayed social evolution as a process of the decoupling of system and life-world that occurs in stages, describing how specialized systems, particularly the market and the state, became differentiated out from very simple societies which were lifeworlds in themselves; these discrete systems function in line with their own unique dynamic by means of their own specific media – money in one case, power in the other. With his theory of differentiation undergirded by a theory of evolution, it is already apparent here that Habermas is very close to the thought of Parsons. As is well known, Parsons too declared differentiation the dominant trend of historical development. And in his theory of media too, Habermas patently and openly borrows from Parsonian theory. Habermas, however, is by no means driven by the overwhelming need to systematize characteristic of Parsons. Unlike the latter, Habermas does not engage in an almost desperate search for media comparable to money. Quite the reverse: Habermas weighs up carefully in which spheres of society the concept of system contributes to describing social conditions and in which it does not. He comes to the conclusion that only the economy and – to some degree – politics became differentiated out from the sphere of direct interaction among members of society over the course of socio-cultural evolution and then began to function in a way which increasingly differed from everyday communication – through the use of the media of money and power. It is these media which more or less replace communicative understanding in these functional spheres. Even here, though, Habermas is rather hesitant and tentative, particularly with respect to the medium of power, and in any event more cautious than Parsons, who places power on a par with money as a matter of course because of what he asserts to be the former medium's degree of abstraction and efficiency. Habermas notes – and this is not only a criticism of Parsons, but far more of Luhmann (see the following lecture) – that power is far less partitioned off from everyday communication than is money, and above all is far less divorced from the issue of its own *legitimacy*. While the use of money now requires practically no normative justification, the use of power depends on legitimacy:

> *It is only the reference to legitimizable collective goals that establishes the balance in the power relation built into the ideal-typical exchange relation from the start.* Whereas no agreement among the parties to an exchange is required for them to make a judgment of interests, the question of what lies in the general interest calls for a consensus among the members of a collectivity, no matter whether this normative consensus is secured in advance by tradition or has first to be brought about by democratic processes of bargaining and reaching understanding. [In any case], the connection to consensus formation in language, backed only by potential reasons, is clear.
>
> (ibid., vol. II, pp. 271–2; original emphasis)

The ties that bind politics and its medium of 'power' to everyday communication stand in stark contrast to the consistent functionalism advocated to some extent by Parsons and later elaborated in far more radical form, particularly by Luhmann, a functionalism according to which the various systems and subsystems function *exclusively* in line with a logic of their own and are utterly disconnected from quotidian issues and problems. Habermas is unwilling and unable to adopt this radical approach: *from the outset* he had striven to produce a *synthesis* of action and systems theory; he is thus unwilling to allow action and, as he elaborated in his theory of action and rationality, the validity claims inherent in every action simply to be marginalized by the functional requirements of systems. For if language and action are closely bound up with certain features of rationality, if the development of humanity and human society is measured by the extent to which the rational potential of language is tapped, then this rationality must be allowed to blossom fully; we must not get to a point where this comprehensive rationality is superseded by the highly circumscribed rationality characteristic of 'systems of purposive-rational action', in which efficiency is the sole imperative.

This points directly to Habermas' diagnosis of the contemporary world. His concern is to determine what constitutes a reasonable relationship between life-world and systems, a relationship which lives up to the rational potential of human language as well as paying heed to the need for efficiency characteristic of modern societies. Habermas' thesis is that this 'healthy' equilibrium does not currently pertain, that systemic factors are making ever greater inroads and that the systems and processes regulated by political and economic mechanisms increasingly threaten to unilaterally influence the life-world. Habermas captures this through the powerful metaphor of the 'colonization of the life-world by the systems', the idea that systemic contexts are at the point of gaining the upper hand over those of the life-world. All of this no doubt sounds very abstract; it may become clearer if we very briefly outline what Habermas is aiming at politically with his thesis of the contemporary relationship between system and life-world.

(a) Habermas' original goal in incorporating systems theory was to hamper, at the theoretical level itself, any attempt to refer to collective subjects, particularly idealized superordinate subjects of Hegelian or Marxian provenance. This we have pointed out already. At the same time and not entirely unrelated to this goal, the use of systems theoretical arguments helps capture certain 'facts' about the way modern societies are constituted, against the ideas of the extreme left. For Habermas defends the need for uncoupled systems; he accepts that the economy and – in certain respects at least – politics became differentiated into discrete systems for good reason: over the course of socio-cultural evolution, this was the only means of ensuring a high degree of efficiency. Contrary to the utopian dreams of the left, he argues that money and rational (political) administration are indispensable functional mechanisms of modern societies and that if the producers were to hold power in unmediated fashion or money were to be abolished, both efficiency and rationality would be severely impaired. While the differentiation of these two subsystems has given rise to fields no longer directly accessible to everyday communication and *its* rationality, these subsystems have unleashed the potential for efficiency inherent in society and this cannot and should not be abandoned.

(b) On the other hand, Habermas warns against giving free rein to the systemic mechanisms and allowing them to penetrate too far into the life-world. According to Habermas, this occurs when everyday activities are monetarized, when, for example, the venerable tradition of neighbourly help, provided as a matter of course, is altered in such a way that people expect to be paid for their efforts, or when the only way to get family members to help out with household chores is by paying them, when the delightful daughter or much-loved son will take the dog for a walk, do the dishes, help their siblings or even tidy their own room only if they have a monetary reward to look forward to. Habermas describes such monetarization of certain spheres as a form of colonization of the life-world, because market transactions threaten to edge out other forms of human relationship. The taken-for-granted validity of norms or the processes of negotiation through which people determine what a just state of affairs in fact is, are simply replaced or bypassed by the medium of money, which is inserted between actions.

But according to Habermas, it is not just the market, but the state too, which threatens to colonize the life-world. The welfare state itself, with its tendency towards detailed bureaucratic and legal regulation of social relations, runs the risk of ousting interactions characteristic of the life-world, when, for example, every type of living situation is defined in precise legal terms in order to determine certain claims to state benefits, and legal disputes occur in which it is ultimately no longer 'normal' people that are arguing and communicating with one another, but lawyers in courts, whose rulings are then implemented by the state administration. Here again, the life-world risks being pushed to the margins as power-backed interventions increasingly replace everyday communication.

For Habermas, this diagnosis of risks to the life-world also entails significant prognostic potential, given his conviction that the potential for protest specific to modern societies is apparent in the conflict between systems and life-world – the environmental movement for example, which protests against the ceaseless advance of ecologically deleterious technologies, as well as a diffuse alternative movement that articulates a sense of unease about the hyper-rationality of modern societies in which there is no longer any space for expressive forms of action.

At the same time, and here again his claim to theoretical synthesis is apparent, Habermas' diagnosis of the modern era embodies the assertion that he is the heir to the diagnoses produced by earlier sociologists and social theorists. He believes that his conceptual apparatus is superior to that of Marx, Weber or older forms of critical theory associated with Adorno and Horkheimer. This theory, he alleges, enables him to reformulate the legitimate features of Marx's critique of capitalism, to relativize

Max Weber's anxiety about the tendency towards objectivization found in modern society and to take up and assimilate in productive fashion the critique of technology produced by the early Frankfurt School. To put it differently: according to Habermas, the necessary critique of the alienating aspects of modern society can be formulated and specified in a manner far more in keeping with the times, making it possible to take up the traditional left-wing as well as a politically non-specific cultural critique, without adopting their pervasive cultural pessimism. Habermas believes that his theory of rationality has allowed him to come up with a fitting criterion for assessing the reasonableness of the processes of differentiation in modern societies, a criterion which also underpins hopes of resistance, as people will take action to defend themselves if systemic mechanisms intervene too directly in their everyday lives.

As successful as Habermas' diagnosis of the age was as a result of his catchy and formulaic notion of the 'colonization of the life-world' and as much as his book defined the public debate on the present and future of modern societies in the 1980s, numerous critics raised many serious objections to his work, of which we shall briefly address just three here.

(a) In his diagnosis of the modern age, Habermas focuses almost exclusively on the interplay and problematic relationship *between* system and life-world, but says very little about possible internal malfunctions on the system level. He thus practically ignores the inherent problems of the economy, apparent, for instance, in recurrent economic cycles, the tendency towards monopolization, etc., as he does the problems that characterize the political system, which, as is particularly apparent today, is struggling to meet the demands of the rest of society. Habermas' diagnosis certainly failed to address developments in the early 1980s, when the state began to withdraw from the economy as political conservatism grew in strength in many Western democracies and Germany suffered economic crises and a high level of long-term unemployment.

(b) In his diagnosis, Habermas merely mentioned the possible source of social movements and collective actors, referring to the interface between systems and life-world. Quite apart from the fact that this reference is rather vague, enabling one to explain 'causally' practically any social movement, he fails to examine how the existence of collective actors can be reconciled with the dualistic conceptual framework of system and life-world. To put it the other way round: collective actors represent forms of joint action which seem to resist the concepts of life-world and system or which are at least difficult to capture with this conceptual toolkit; Habermas had of course introduced the concept of system quite intentionally in order to nip in the bud any talk of macro-subjects. But this leaves unclear what systematic importance collective actors might have within Habermas' theoretical framework. Empirically, they cannot be interpreted merely as *indicators* of a disturbed relationship between system and life-world. One would need to have a peculiar, hyper-stable understanding of societies were one to reduce social, religious, political and economic movements, which have characterized modernity – not to mention other historical eras – from the very beginning, to this indicative function.

(c) Furthermore, Habermas never managed to develop empirically useful criteria for the 'correct' relationship between system and life-world on the basis of his theory of rationality, or to indicate how and when exactly the life-world is threatened by the advance of systemic mechanisms. This lack of definition makes it easy for him to refer to pathologies, to disturbed social relations, etc. But in the absence of clear, intersubjectively understandable criteria for determining at precisely what point a systemic mechanism ought to be classified as legitimate in light of its efficiency or as expanding pathologically, Habermas often seems to be merely positing a hypothesis.

Of course, Jürgen Habermas' theoretical development was by no means over in 1981. As mentioned earlier, this impressive theoretician continues to be hugely productive to this day, long after his retirement. There is no space here to list all his subsequent works, so we shall restrict ourselves to two particularly influential books which appeared in 1985 and 1992 respectively. The first, *The Philosophical Discourse of Modernity*, is essentially a major attempt to come to terms with so-called postmodern and poststructuralist thinkers, and above all a critique of French philosophers and sociologists who, under the influence of Nietzsche (1844–1900), took the critique of reason so far that they ended up denouncing reason itself as a project of domination. Habermas accuses these thinkers of having abandoned rationality as a whole – partly on the basis of justified criticism of an overly narrow model of rationality. For him, this is a rash move which prevents one from recognizing and appreciating the rational potential of language. We shall return to these issues in Lecture XIV, where we provide our own account of the schools of thought under attack here. In a sense, Habermas' book 'protects the flanks' of his theory of communicative rationality and of communicative action against postmodern scepticism about reason.

Between Facts and Norms: Contributions to a Discourse Theory of Law and Democracy, the second book that we shall address briefly here, can also be considered a continuation of the subjects touched upon in *The Theory of Communicative Action*, and even more as an attempt to resolve some of the problems which that book failed to get to grips with. It is first and foremost a treatise in the philosophy of law that tackles the question of what role law plays in contemporary societies. With his dualistic conception of order, which works with the concepts of system and life-world, Habermas had never quite managed to clarify how the two orders *fit together*, or indeed how one is to conceive of the integration of societies. Habermas of course always insisted on the primacy of the life-world, which he believes can be justified historically by the fact that systems have become differentiated *out from* the life-world. But it remained quite unclear in *The Theory of Communicative Action* how unity can be established in ethnically and culturally fragmented societies, for consensus is neither pre-given, nor is it plausible to imagine a discussion taking in the whole of society through which a general consensus is eventually reached. By what means, then, are modern societies integrated? Habermas is deeply suspicious of the obvious answer – by means of certain values, by means, for example, of the *belief*, anchored in religion or other motivating factors, in the validity of the human rights enshrined in a constitution, the *belief* in the validity of revolutionary principles, the *conviction* of one's ethnic group's cultural or political superiority, etc. – because he regards *all* such values as particularistic, as not really amenable to rational discussion and thus ultimately incapable of achieving consensus. In the book under discussion here, he hits on the solution of ascribing this integrative role to the *law*, because it occupies a key strategic position between system and life-world and, in his opinion, has an integrative effect precisely because of this: 'Because law is just as intermeshed with money and administrative power as it is with solidarity, its own integrating achievements assimilate imperatives of diverse origin' (*Facts and Norms*, p. 40). For Habermas, the prodigious rational potential of communicative reason preserved in the law makes it an apt means of pulling together the differing interests found in modern, fragmented societies. Collective identity, Habermas tells us, is no longer guaranteed by common values – modern societies are too complex and it is implausible to expect people to reach agreement on specific values – but at best by people's commitment to the rationality of the constitution and the rational legal procedures based upon it. Nowadays, Habermas believes, we can be both patriotic and rational only with respect to a constitution, in as much as we are convinced of the rationality of legal provisions and procedures – constitutional patriotism rather than value-based patriotism is thus claimed to be the appropriate contemporary form of collective identity of Germans, Americans, Russians, etc.

Clearly, Habermas is saddling the law with a major responsibility, and one may well wonder whether he is grossly exaggerating its integrative capacity. Further, one might go on to ask whether Habermas was not too quick to abandon the idea that identity may be generated through values. We would therefore encourage you to re-read the last few pages of Lecture IV on the later work of Talcott Parsons. Parsons does *not* distinguish so sharply between values and (constitutional) norms as Habermas always quite rightly proposes we should do and as he himself indeed does. Extending Parsons' ideas, it is, however, possible to discuss whether universal human rights, as codified in the Western constitutional states, are not in fact historically beholden to a (highly specific) religious context of origin and to explore how, to this day, these human rights, which apply in principle to every individual, are surrounded by a somehow religious aura, however transformed.

From a critical perspective, we may thus wonder whether Habermas, as a result of his premise of the pervasive secularization of the world ('the linguistification of the sacred'), was too hasty in disregarding insights to which Parsons showed great sensitivity. Of course, not all values are universalizable, and those that are may in fact be thin on the ground, and this is even more true of the (nationalistic) belief in the superiority of a nation. But some values – including some of the most widely recognized – inspire commitment not because of their rational plausibility, but because they encapsulate collective experiences or individual experiences shared by millions of people. Thus, if one has doubts about the role of law in establishing identity or consensus, one ought at least to consider these questions, central to the philosophy of values, rather than rejecting them at the outset with the argument that values are not amenable to discursive justification (see Joas, *The Genesis of Values*).

Admittedly, Habermas himself recently seems to be moving very cautiously in this direction – his acceptance speech on receiving the peace prize of the German book trade being an example. For the time being, though, this process of opening lays bare even more starkly the almost complete lack of a systematic and empirically grounded examination of issues in the philosophy of values and theory of religion in his work so far. In the contemporary era, however, such issues (see our remarks on communitarianism in Lecture XVIII and on neo-pragmatism in Lecture XIX) are proving ever harder to avoid.

We close with some suggested reading. If you would like to find out more about Jürgen Habermas' magnum opus, you will find numerous essays tackling various aspects of the book in the anthology *Communicative Action: Essays on Jürgen Habermas' 'The Theory of Communicative Action'*, edited by Axel Honneth and Hans Joas. Should you wish to familiarize yourself with Habermas' theory as a whole, we recommend chapters 7 to 9 of Axel Honneth's *The Critique of Power: Reflective Stages in a Critical Social Theory* as a good introduction, and Thomas McCarthy's highly detailed book *The Critical Theory of Jürgen Habermas*.

XI

Niklas Luhmann's radicalization of functionalism

Niklas Luhmann was the other major figure within German sociology who, like Jürgen Habermas, was unwilling to accept the theoretical diversity apparent from the 1960s on, which we have described in the previous lectures, and strove instead to achieve a new synthesis of his own. Admittedly, we cannot take the word 'synthesis' too literally in Luhmann's case. Habermas, in an enormous hermeneutic effort, did in fact attempt to comprehend the various theoretical schools and preserve those insights he considered valid while developing his own theoretical construct in such a way that certain elements of these 'source theories' remained quite apparent in its architecture. Luhmann, meanwhile, took a far more direct approach. He lacked the grasp of hermeneutics that is such a major feature of Habermas' work. Rather, he endeavoured to evade or reformulate the key concerns of the competing theoretical schools within sociology – with the help of a functionalism markedly more radical than that of Parsons. *From the very beginning* Luhmann made use of the functionalist method of analysis, which he gradually turned into a kind of 'super theory' as his work developed over time and with which he attempted to assert his claim to synthesis or, we might better say, comprehensiveness. Thus, in comparison to that of Habermas, Luhmann's oeuvre developed in amazingly straightforward fashion. Though Luhmann himself and his supporters have been talking about a theoretical reconstruction (the 'autopoietic turn', which we shall look at later) since the early 1980s, the foundations of his theory have remained unchanged.

Niklas Luhmann was born in Lüneburg in 1927 and is thus of the same generation as Jürgen Habermas. His middle-class background is also rather similar: Luhmann's paternal grandfather was a senator in Lüneburg and therefore a member of the influential city patriciate; his father owned a small brewery and malthouse in Lüneburg, while his mother hailed from a family of Swiss hoteliers. Unlike most members of his generation, Luhmann had no liking for the National Socialists and thus his experience of that regime's collapse and the end of the war in 1945 was also quite different. While others experienced this historic upheaval as a profound turning point in their own biography, which shook all previous convictions to the core, Luhmann appears to have been merely 'taken aback' and 'bewildered'; this gave rise to his later, fundamentally 'distant' attitude to socio-political events. Conscripted as an auxiliary into the *Luftwaffe* at 15, he was captured by the Americans towards the end of the war. Treated by his captors in a way he experienced as very unfair, he remained captive until September 1945. For him, 'liberation' lacked the emphatically moral significance which Habermas always attached to it, because he found himself confronted with a situation that he was unable to interpret through the categories of 'guilt' or 'innocence'. For him, it was rather an experience whose origins may be conveyed by a theoretical concept which was to play a key role in his theory, that of 'contingency'. Up until 8 May 1945, one particular (National Socialist) order pertained, and subsequently a quite different one – somehow, everything might be different, and this is exactly what came to pass in 1945. Because of this very fact, because we must assume that social phenomena are contingent, we ought – Luhmann concludes – to be sparing with moral categories. We shall return to these insights and the associated theoretical concepts later.

First, though, let us track Luhmann's path through life a little further. After studying law in Freiburg, Luhmann became a high-level civil servant, initially as assistant to the presiding judge of the higher administrative court of Lüneburg and then as adviser in the Lower Saxony ministry of culture in Hanover. But this post quickly began to bore him; he clearly felt unchallenged and in 1960/61 he therefore seized the opportunity of a scholarship at Harvard University, where, among other things, he came into close contact with Talcott Parsons. Luhmann, who had studied law, had so far read sociology merely as a hobby during his stint at the Lower Saxon ministry – partly in order to understand why his administrative work bored and failed to challenge him – and it was thus in the USA that he first got to know academic sociology from the inside.

This resulted in a first, brilliant book in which Luhmann put his professional experiences to good use theoretically: *Funktionen und Folgen formaler Organisation* ('Functions and Consequences of Formal Organization') from 1964 was a large-scale study in the sociology of organizations, a highly critical take on previous work in this research field from a Parsonian-functionalist perspective. Despite this noteworthy publication, however, Luhmann had as yet by no means made a new home for himself in the academy. While he had left Lower Saxony in 1962 and taken up a post as consultant at the research institute attached to the university of administrative science in Speyer, it was only in the mid-1960s that Helmut Schelsky (1912–84), the great post-war conservative sociologist in Germany, went out of his way to support him, helping him enter the academic world of sociology. With Schelsky's backing, Luhmann gained his doctoral and post-doctoral qualifications in 1966 in a single year(!) and was immediately appointed to a post at the reform university of Bielefeld founded by Schelsky. As the university in general and the sociology department in particular were being built up, a famous incident occurred which tells us something about Luhmann's theoretical ambitions, which were already becoming apparent. When Luhmann was asked to name his research projects on a form, he tersely entered: ' "theory of society"; length: 30 years; costs: none' (on these biographical details, see Luhmann, 'Biographie im Interview' ['A Biographical Interview']).

But even in the late 1960s and within the discipline itself, Luhmann was seen primarily as an organizational or legal sociologist rather than a social theorist. This changed only in 1971 as a result of the so-called Habermas–Luhmann controversy briefly outlined in the previous lecture, which was documented in the book *Theorie der Gesellschaft oder Sozialtechnologie* ('Theory of Society or Social Technology'). With his functionalist-systems theoretical approach, Luhmann made his mark as the leading adversary of Jürgen Habermas and his 'critical social theory'; as a result, in the 1970s, when enthusiasm for theory was riding high, many German sociologists joined the Habermas or Luhmann camp, while other theoretical schools beyond this polarization risked being marginalized. Luhmann had thus achieved his breakthrough *at least in Germany*. Above all because of his unusual productivity, he has managed to extend his influence continuously since then, such that it is certainly greater at present than that of Habermas within German sociology – though not in philosophy. The founding of the journal *Soziale Systeme* ('Social Systems') in 1995, the main organ of Luhmann's followers, is an expression of this tremendous influence in as much as no other theoretical school in Germany has managed to establish a similar journal to promote its interests.

But it was not until the 1980s that Luhmann became well known *internationally*. In countries such as Japan and Italy, Luhmann now has a large number of followers or disciples; his reception is not limited to sociology, but extends to jurisprudence and political science in particular. Interestingly, however, his influence has always been negligible within American sociology, which is undoubtedly bound up with the fact, first of all, that he has lacked a highly gifted 'translator' such as Thomas McCarthy (b. 1945), who played this role for Jürgen Habermas, a figure capable of rendering the German discursive context accessible to the American readership. Second, generally speaking, Luhmann's extremely abstract theory building has been viewed with suspicion by a highly professionalized and often empirically oriented American sociology. Further, while Luhmann's work was seen in Germany as a continuation of that of Parsons and, as it were, as a more modern version of structural functionalism, the American Parsonians tended to regard it as deviating from Parsons and closed their minds to him.

Despite this 'American lacuna', however, in the 1980s and 1990s Luhmann became an ever more fashionable thinker, a kind of pop star among scholars no less, whose writings and ideas are often quoted even by those who do not really understand them. After retiring from the University of Bielefeld in 1993, Luhmann produced a constant stream of new writings in near-feverish fashion until his death in 1998, and since then finished or half-finished unpublished manuscripts have continued to appear as books. It will be some time before Luhmann's oeuvre reaches its final form.

As in our discussion of Jürgen Habermas, we must now investigate the intellectual traditions into which Luhmann's work fits or which influenced him. And as in the case of Habermas, we can identify at least three.

1. One of the decisive influences in Luhmann's intellectual career was undoubtedly his encounter with Talcott Parsons, to whom Luhmann owes many ideas. Yet Luhmann was never an 'orthodox' Parsonian; he was too much of an independent thinker for that. Rather, Luhmann made *certain* of Parsons' ideas his own, while disregarding entirely other arguments central to Parsons' thought.

    Luhmann was not interested in Parsons' theory of *action*; he seems to have been little impressed by Parsons' *early* work as a whole. What Luhmann took from Parsons were the structural functionalist or systems theoretical figures of thought from his middle or later creative period. But once again, Luhmann very much followed his own path, in as much as he increasingly radicalized the theoretical components borrowed from Parsons, ultimately reformulating them. Parsons had always asked which functions a social phenomenon fulfils for a greater collectivity or whole, what role, for example, the family plays within society. Thus, for Parsons, the point of departure was a (stable) structure whose existence was ensured by certain functional achievements which the theorist must identify. Luhmann was dissatisfied with this structural functionalist approach, with its characteristic tendency to analyse structures first and functions second. He accepted the criticisms so often made of the Parsonian structural functionalist approach, such as the objection that the social sciences are unable to determine exactly what structures or systems require to survive, because – in contrast to biological organisms – they do not feature the empirical phenomenon of death. This objection does indeed represent a problem for every theory which takes structures and systems as its point of departure in this fashion and *only then* examines functions, as it problematizes the unambiguous identification of the stability or existence of a social phenomenon.

    Luhmann therefore decided to reverse Parsons' analytical strategy and to place particular emphasis on the functionalist aspect of systems theory, which enabled him to advance to a position quite different from that of Parsons. This was also apparent in Luhmann's terminology, when he announced that he wished to replace Parsonian 'structural functional' systems theory with a 'functional structural' theory.

    > The underlying reason for the shortcomings of structural-functional systems theory lies in its guiding principle, namely its prioritizing of the concept of structure over the concept of function. In doing so, structural-functional theory forgoes the opportunity

to problematize structures per se and investigate the purpose of structure formation, and indeed to scrutinize the purpose of system formation itself. However, reversing the relationship between these two basic concepts, putting the concept of function before that of structure, allows us to do just that. A functional-structural theory can probe the function of system structures, without having to make a comprehensive system structure the point of reference for any investigation.

(Luhmann, 'Soziologie als Theorie sozialer Systeme' ['Sociology as a Theory of Social Systems'], p. 114)

As a consequence of this theoretical switch, Luhmann's thought contrasted with that of Parsons in at least three linked respects. First, because Luhmann does not take *existing* structures which must be maintained at all costs as his point of departure, the problem of order does *not* represent *the* key problem of sociology for him as it did for Parsons, whose earliest work centred on action theory. In line with this, Luhmann's conception is not dependent on values or norms, which (supposedly) hold the social system together. He thus automatically leaves behind the normativist character of Parsonian theory, which – as you will recall – led to the subsystems that fulfil the function of 'latent pattern maintenance' being identified as the top of the cybernetic hierarchy of control in his later systems functionalist phase. Luhmann is able to disregard Parsonian normativism entirely for theoretical reasons; what is more, from an empirical point of view, he believes that norms and values no longer play an integrative role in modern societies in any case.

Second, if systems are no longer defined in terms of concrete elements required for their survival and if one no longer needs or is no longer able, in contrast to Parsons, to point to the integrative role of values and norms, systems must be conceived more abstractly, much more abstractly in fact. Luhmann borrows his notion of how exactly this occurs primarily from biology, which observes and analyses how organisms maintain their stability, by constantly regulating their body temperature for example, in a changeable environment which in principle represents an ever-present threat to the organism. Luhmann applies this originally biological model to *social* wholes and defines social systems as interrelated actions *delimited from* other actions. Systems, *including social systems*, are separate from their environment, which refers not only to the natural or ecological setting as in everyday usage, but to everything which is not part of the system itself.

> Social systems can only be observed empirically if we conceive of them as *systems of action*. ... [For the] functional systems theory emerging in the social sciences, as well as contemporary biology, the technology of automatic control systems and the psychological

theory of personality ... stability is no longer considered the true essence of a system, which excludes other possibilities. Rather, the stabilization of a system is understood as a problem that must be resolved in light of a changeable, unheeding environment that changes independent of the system and which thus makes a continual orientation towards other possibilities indispensable. Thus, stability is no longer to be understood as an unchanging substance, but as a relation between system and environment, as the relative invariance of the system structure and of the system boundaries vis-à-vis a changeable environment.

(Luhmann, 'Funktionale Methode und Systemtheorie' ['Functional Methods and System Theory'], p. 39; original emphasis)

Luhmann thus conceives his functional-structural systems theory quite explicitly as a 'systems-environment theory' (ibid.), allowing him to extend his analysis of organizations beyond their internal mechanisms to include a broader context. This also enables him to drop one of the core hypotheses of traditional organization theory, which states that it is ultimately the organization's internal goals or certain internal values which regulate what happens within it. Luhmann was to show that everything is far more complicated and that the many ties binding systems and subsystems to the wider environment rule out such a simple assumption.

Third, Luhmann points out that the basic problems of social systems are not solved once and for all by existing structures; rather, they are always *only provisionally* tackled, more or less successfully, in a particular way. These problems may also be solved (again, provisionally) by very different forms and structures; here, Luhmann finally bids farewell to the survival-oriented functionalism expounded by Parsons, who believed that it is possible to identify and determine the concrete features of systems. Luhmann terms his functionalism, logically, equivalence functionalism, to constantly remind us that equivalent solutions can if necessary always be found or identified that (provisionally) solve the problems of systems. The only condition is that 'The system structure must be organized and institutionalized in such a way that it permits the requisite degree of self-variation with respect to the ongoing adaptation to the environment' (Luhmann, *Funktionen und Folgen formaler Organisation*, p. 153).

Luhmann's shift towards an equivalence functionalist theory of this kind also has the advantage of seemingly being able to evade another fundamental criticism of conventional functionalism. As we discussed in Lecture IV, functionalist arguments must not be confused with causal statements: the fact that a subunit performs a function for a greater whole tells us nothing about why this subunit came into being in the first place. Thus, critics assailed the fact that functionalist theories merely furnish us with descriptions or causal hypotheses rather than genuine explanations.

From the very beginning of his career, Luhmann confronts these accusations and criticisms head-on, taking the bull by the horns with his equivalence functionalist perspective. He immediately concedes that the function of an action does not explain its factual occurrence. As Luhmann notes, functionalists had therefore repeatedly attempted to produce causal statements hedged in by clauses or of an indirect nature through a variety of arguments rooted in survivalist functionalism, in order to be able to 'explain' the existence and stability of a system after all. But according to Luhmann, this was tenable neither empirically nor logically, so the functionalists ought finally to understand and accept that it simply cannot be their task to formulate causal statements (see Luhmann, 'Funktion und Kausalität' ['Function and Causality']). Rather, the apparently unavoidable survival functionalism, with its problematic or false claims to identify causality, must be replaced by an equivalence functionalism. The final abandonment of causal statements that this entails should not, Luhmann tells us, be seen as a deficiency. For Luhmann, it must in any case be conceded that in complex systems of action it is extremely difficult to identify clear-cut causes and effects, making predictions and prognoses almost impossible. Luhmann believes that this opens up an opportunity for equivalence functionalism, because, rather than the factual occurrence of *particular* functional accomplishments, it points to a huge number of possibilities, namely equivalent accomplishments, by means of which systems can stabilize their external borders vis-à-vis their environment. This thinking in categories of *possibility* which equivalence functionalism entails allows the social theorist to run through theoretically the effects of a multitude of very different causal relationships. Luhmann thus redefines the weakness of functionalism, namely its inability to produce clear-cut causal statements, as a strength. The functionalist sociologist is not concerned with uncovering concrete cause–effect relationships, but with *possible* causal relationships; the functionalist theory is thus a heuristic one, a guide to understanding, which allows us to tackle the widest range of issues in an expansive manner, issues related to the stabilization problems characteristic of systems within a particular environment, which are solved in a variety of ways.

> Functionalist thought will presumably require us to redefine human freedom. Functionalist analysis does not define the actor in terms of a once-and-for-all, absolute end of his action; it does not attempt to come up with an accurate conception of his goals. Nor does it attempt to explain action on the basis of causes and in line with laws. It interprets it in terms of select, abstract and thus

interchangeable aspects, in order to render action comprehensible as one possibility among others. ... The social sciences can solve the problem of stability in social life not by putting forward and verifying hypotheses about social laws; it can do so only by making it the central point of analytical reference and searching for the various functionally equivalent options for stabilizing behavioural expectations on this basis.

(Luhmann, 'Funktion und Kausalität', p. 27)

2. Another important influence on Luhmann's thought were theoretical and empirical developments within biological research, in which he took a great interest. We have already seen the great extent to which his functionalist systems-environmental theory took up the findings of biology, but in his later work too Luhmann was to borrow frequently from this field.

What was perhaps even more important, however, was the fact that in a number of respects Luhmann picked up the thread of a very German 'discipline' – though in highly selective fashion. We are referring to so-called 'philosophical anthropology'. This school of thought understands (understood) itself as an interdisciplinary 'empirical' philosophy, which strives to elaborate the specific features of human existence and human action with the help of the findings and tools of understanding of biology, anthropology and sociology. This type of research and thinking has always provoked a great deal of interest in the German-speaking world in particular – and one can identify famous forerunners in German intellectual history who carried out pioneering work in this regard (see Honneth and Joas, *Social Action and Human Nature*). We have already discussed Herderian expressive anthropology in the late eighteenth century in Lecture III, and for the nineteenth century one would have to mention the work of Ludwig Feuerbach (1804–72) and the early philosophical-anthropological writings of Karl Marx. In the twentieth century it was thinkers such as Max Scheler and Helmuth Plessner (1892–1985) who embodied this philosophical anthropology. It was through their efforts that these approaches developed into a vigorous philosophical school and a cultural critique with a wider public impact. Alongside these two thinkers, the name of Arnold Gehlen (1904–76) must be mentioned. A brilliant thinker, but one who is highly controversial because of his involvement in National Socialism, Gehlen's profoundly conservative stance on socio-political issues was hugely influential; he held chairs in sociology in Speyer and Aachen.

Gehlen's magnum opus, *Man: His Nature and Place in the World*, originally published in 1940, revised in the post-war period and reprinted many times, laid the foundations of a philosophical anthropology that understood the human being as a *Mängelwesen*, a creature that lacks. This term may sound peculiar at first, but the notion to which Gehlen was referring is relatively easy to explain. Gehlen was pointing to the fact that the human being, in contrast to the animal, is not really bound or constrained by instincts and drives. These cause animals to react more or less *directly* to a given situation, that is, to a stimulus, and the behaviour triggered by the stimulus then proceeds quasi-automatically. Human beings – so Gehlen tells us – are *Mängelwesen* precisely because they *lack* such drives or instincts. On the other hand, though, this dearth of instincts and humans' open-minded outlook open up certain opportunities for them. Human behaviour is disconnected from the function of serving instinctive drives, which makes it possible to learn in an active and above all comprehensive fashion. It is only in this way that 'action' becomes possible in the first place. As Gehlen states, the human being is not 'fixed'; rather than being controlled by his drives, he must 'determine' himself. He can and must shape his world by applying his intelligence and through contact with others.

The human being's lack of instinctual apparatus, however, also forces him to acquire behavioural security: habits and routines *relieve the burden* (German: *entlasten*) of motivation and control which every action ultimately requires, enabling one to draw on earlier successful learning easily or unproblematically and thus preventing one from feeling permanently overwhelmed (Gehlen, *Man: His Nature and Place in the World*, pp. 57ff.). We have now been introduced to the concept of *Entlastung*, relief or unburdening, which was to be of key importance to Gehlen's theory of institutions and was ultimately to exercise a great influence on Luhmann's theory building as well. For it is not only individual routines and habits that relieve the strain on human beings, but also institutions and traditions. Institutions

> are those entities which enable a being, a being at risk, unstable and affectively overburdened by nature, to put up with his fellows and with himself, something on the basis of which one can count on and rely on oneself and others. On the one hand, human objectives are jointly tackled and pursued within these institutions; on the other, people gear themselves towards definitive certainties of doing and not doing within them, with the extraordinary benefit that their inner life is stabilized, so that they do not have to deal with profound emotional issues or make fundamental decisions at every turn.
>
> (Gehlen, 'Mensch und Institutionen' ['Human Beings and Institutions'], p. 71)

It is easy to come to conservative conclusions on the basis of such arguments. Gehlen's argument that the human *Mängelwesen* requires relief from the strains of life and that institutions provide this led him to call for a strong state. This inspired his favourable view of the Third Reich. He saw every criticism of established social structures as a threat, as contributing to the 'downfall of the West'. His stance made him a key figure in the conservative critique of culture in the 1950s and 1960s in Germany.

Luhmann took up some of Gehlen's key ideas. Let us leave aside the question of whether he did so on the basis of similar political or culturally critical motives; it is a difficult one to answer, because Luhmann, a strikingly aloof scholar, only rarely expressed a clear political stance; rather, he allowed this to emerge in his work, often in veiled form only. In any case, Luhmann used Gehlen's concept of *Entlastung*, partly for theoretical reasons, translating it into the language of systems theory in the shape of the phrase 'reduction of complexity', which has become so popular and with which you are no doubt familiar. This process of translation, however, was bound up with Luhmann's own project – and this was very different from Gehlen's. While Gehlen, like all exponents of philosophical anthropology, placed the human being at the centre of his reflections, defined the human being as an acting being and was thus a theorist of action, Luhmann was rather uninterested in action as such.

It thus comes as no surprise that Luhmann used the idea of *Entlastung* primarily for *systems theoretical* purposes. Luhmann, as we have seen, strengthened the functionalist elements within the original edifice of Parsonian systems theory, and drawing on Gehlen's figure of thought offered him particular opportunities in this regard. For Luhmann answers his own questions – 'What is the function of systems or structures as such?' 'What is the function of the production of structure itself?' – to which Parsons paid no heed, by pointing to 'the reduction of complexity'. Institutions, stable structures or systems, prescribe certain forms of interaction, limit the options for action open to the parties to interaction, reducing their number, which is in principle unlimited, and thus not only ensure individual behavioural security, but also ordered interaction among human beings. Just as Gehlen argued that the human capacity for action is dependent on easing routines, habits and ultimately institutions, Luhmann argues that 'in light of the unalterably meagre extent of the human attention span, increased efficiency is possible only through the formation of systems, which ensure that information is processed within a meaningful framework' (Luhmann, 'Soziologische Aufklärung' ['Sociological Enlightenment'], p. 77). Social and other systems thus reduce the, in principle, infinitely complicated environment by laying down relatively limited options for action, thus making 'increased efficiency' possible. But at the same time, this sets them apart from the environment, from other systems for example, which in turn privilege highly specific options for action. Systems, to repeat, reduce the complexity of the environment, but construct in turn complex internal structures, as will be well known to anyone who has ever had anything to do with public authorities or a major industrial firm, whose organizational structures may be highly internally differentiated.

3. Finally, Luhmann was also influenced by the phenomenology of Edmund Husserl. We have come across this philosophical tradition already in Lecture VII on ethnomethodology, so you will be familiar with some of its basic ideas. But while the ethnomethodologists were interested first and foremost in the concept of life-world found in the late Husserl, Luhmann picked up the thread of his studies in the psychology of perception. Husserl, very much like the American pragmatists, had shown that, rather than a passive process, perception is necessarily dependent on active achievements of consciousness. In the context of these investigations in the psychology of perception, Husserl coined terms such as 'intentionality', 'horizon', 'world' and 'meaning', to demonstrate that our action and perception is not concerned with the whole world, but is focused and thus always refers only to a part of this world, such that meaning and sense arise in the context of a specific perceptual horizon. Luhmann applied these phenomenological insights and categories, obtained on the basis of studies of individual perception, to social systems, which he treats and understands as quasi-subjects: systems in general and social systems in particular – as we have seen – reduce the infinite complexity of the world; it is this complexity which becomes the pre-eminent point of reference for functional analysis, because it is only by means of such reduction that meaning can be produced. It is no longer the *existence* of systems – as in Parsons' work – which forms the point of departure for every functional analysis, but the complexity of the world, because it is only on this basis that we can grasp the function of systems. Without the reduction provided by systems, we would sink into an infinite and thus fundamentally incomprehensible sea of perceptions; it is only the construction of systems that makes it possible to confer meaning in the first place, because systems force us to concentrate on a comparatively small and thus in principle controllable part of the world. Psychological and social systems thus produce meaning, laying down what can and cannot be thought and said. In the social subsystem of the economy, for example, (monetary) payments and 'profit' constitute the key point of reference of all communication and action, rather than aesthetic pleasure, athletic elegance or an upright character. Systems register only part of the world. They function against the background of a *highly specific* horizon and thus quite differently from the systems found in their environment. Systems, according to Luhmann's more or less implicit thesis, are structured in much the same way as cognizing individuals in the work of Husserl: their perception is always limited, and one can understand their internal logic only if one grasps how they perceive the world and how they produce meaning.

We have now identified the three influences that decisively shaped Luhmann's thought. It is hard to say whether these three influences are more or less heterogeneous than those to which we referred in discussing the development of Habermas' oeuvre. But this need not concern us here, because, as with Habermas, these different influences were linked by certain crucial intuitions. Luhmann's synthesis of basic Parsonian, philosophical-anthropological and phenomenological ideas was powerful and persuasive because he made use of experiences gained over the course of his career in the legal profession and in a bureaucratic organization and because his theoretical analyses of various empirical fields were informed by the problems characteristic of administrative authorities or formal organizations. While Habermas was inspired by the achievements of language and therefore developed a special interest in the rational force of unconstrained discussion and the importance of the public political sphere, Luhmann was fascinated by the achievements performed by bureaucratic institutions and the procedures developed by formal organizations in order to assert themselves within an environment and set themselves apart from it, and in order to function in highly routinized fashion.

This lays bare yet another difference from Habermas' project. While Habermas' work, in line with his intuition regarding the achievements of language, featured a clear normative tendency, and while Habermas attempted to construct a well-founded critique of existing social structures by referring to the notion of the rational potential inherent in language, Luhmann's venture was decidedly non-normative; in fact, it was out-and-out anti-normative. Luhmann would not dream of engaging in social criticism. At most, he would permit one to ask which functions such critique, or far more generally, the invocation of values and norms, might have in a modern society. Luhmann's fundamentally non-normative stance is probably connected with his particular experience, to which we have already alluded, of the conditions that pertained in 1945. But it is not the exact biographical background as such that is crucial here. Rather, what is important is that the concept of 'contingency' has always played a pivotal role in Luhmann's theoretical framework. Luhmann was in fact always fascinated by the 'contingency' of social phenomena and orders, by the idea that everything might be different; Luhmann defines as 'contingent' that which is 'neither necessary nor impossible', emphasizing the fact that something is 'just what it is (or was or will be), though it could also be otherwise' (Luhmann, *Social Systems*, p. 106).

As it happens, Luhmann's definition comes from the pragmatist philosopher and psychologist William James. James uses it in his 1907 book *Pragmatism: A New Name for Some Old Ways of Thinking* (see esp. pp. 137ff.) to underline a particular political stance, namely a cautious, anti-utopian reformism (James refers to 'meliorism'), which is aware of the limitations of all political action, whose results are 'contingent' and which cannot therefore really be predicted, a reformism intended to prompt those in power to adopt a politics of small steps. Luhmann also refers to the radical contingency of every social order, which might always be quite different, but, typically, comes to very different conclusions from James in light of this.

This thesis not only serves to justify his abstention from clear-cut causal statements, outlined above, and his use of the equivalence functionalist method. The thesis of the fundamental contingency of social phenomena also crucially shapes Luhmann's argumentative *style*: because social orders are 'neither necessary nor impossible', one must refrain from making moral judgements, because morality always assumes that specific actions necessarily give rise to specific effects. It is as a result of this very attitude that Luhmann's work achieves its literary effects; his writings are notable, and this is surely something the 'normal' reader is quite unused to, for their *systematic* and *consistent* abstention from moral judgements. This has a significant defamiliarizing effect, further intensified by Luhmann's highly abstract language, with which he describes even the most trivial circumstances. Luhmann refers to this himself: in terms of theory, what is at issue

> is not an interest in recognizing and curing, nor an interest in preserving what has been in existence, but first and foremost an analytic interest: to break through the illusion of normality, to disregard experience and habit.
>
> (Luhmann, *Social Systems*, p. 114)

Effects of this kind have also played an important role in literature – in the work of Bertolt Brecht for example, who 'defamiliarized' everyday phenomena on the stage in order to lay bare their changeability. But while a deeply moral and political impetus was at work in the case of Brecht, this was absolutely not the case for Luhmann. The defamiliarizing effects which he achieved are more reminiscent of forms of irony, as deployed by Romantics such as E. T. A. Hoffmann or Ludwig Tieck, in order to give literary expression, for example, to the knowledge of the inevitable dichotomy between ideal and reality.

Like certain Romantic ironists, Luhmann too is to some extent 'aloof'. While the social theorist shows why people in society believe in norms, values, religion, etc., he eschews embracing such beliefs, and can therefore react to the facts which he observes only with more or less mild irony. It is impossible to pin down Luhmann's place within society; he is in a sense an analyst who resists definition. He speaks from 'off-camera' as it were. And it is this position which comprises much of the fascination of Luhmann's thinking; it is surely the reason why his theory has attracted so many followers, particularly from the 1980s on. Just as Marxism and neo-utilitarianism (see Lecture V) recruited their adherents on the basis of the motif of unmasking, Luhmann acquired his 'disciples' in much the same way. But while the factor of truth was decisive in the case of Marxists and neo-utilitarians (who tried to reveal the economic and utility-oriented/selfish realities behind the pleasing 'normative' façade),

Luhmann consciously refrains from locating himself in this way. While pointing out that everything might be quite different does have a de-masking effect, the search for truth is in vain from the outset *because of the problem of contingency*. What remains is the air of ironic, aloof observation, a point of view which implies superiority and which may therefore become particularly attractive at certain times. Luhmann himself referred to this Romantic irony, in his last major work for example, but, typically, without stating explicitly whether he sees himself as such an ironist:

> One ... can always choose whether to privilege forms of representation that express shock and sympathy, which almost inevitably means taking sides within respect to a given issue, or whether one presents one's reflections by means of (romantic) irony, which, despite everything, expresses one's involvement in the matter at hand in terms of distance.
> (Luhmann, *Die Gesellschaft der Gesellschaft* ['The Society of Society'], p. 1129)

In light of this (indirect) reference to Romantic irony, it is probably correct to interpret Luhmann as a highly individual representative of the 'sceptical' post-war generation, one described in an influential sociological study by Luhmann's patron, Helmut Schelsky, whom we mentioned earlier. This was a generation which – having been seduced all too often, particularly by National Socialism – had lost all its great ideals and was thus no longer willing to fight moral and political battles. Luhmann's hordes of followers, however, were and are younger; they cannot, in any case, be categorized as the *war* generation. Many are of the 1980s generation often described as cynical or hedonistic; after the apparent failure of their parents' struggles in the 1960s and 1970s, they too have lost faith in great ideals and have a 'sceptical' attitude as a result.

So much for Luhmann's intellectual background and key ideas. In light of his tremendous productivity and thus the large number of his published writings, the following discussion cannot hope to provide a comprehensive overview of how his work as a whole has developed over time. Instead, we shall attempt to briefly outline particularly important works or those which allow us to access Luhmann's thought with relative ease, as well as identifying the most important phases in his intellectual development. In what follows we shall attempt to do this in three stages.

(A) The vast majority of Luhmann's writings published in the 1960s grapple with topics in organizational, legal and political sociology and in this sense seem to be of interest to a small specialist audience only. However, to focus solely on Luhmann's empirical studies would be to overlook the fact that intimations of his broader theoretical perspective already appear in his early works, which in fact laid the ground for his later grand theory. It is thus imperative that we turn our theoretical gaze to this period, during which Luhmann was so productive.

Three monographs from this period have become particularly well known and influential: the study *Funktionen und Folgen formaler Organisation* ('The Functions and Consequences of Formal Organization') from 1964, mentioned above, the book *Zweckbegriff und Systemrationalität. Über die Funktion von Zwecken in sozialen Systemen* ('The Concept of Ends and System Rationality: On the Function of Ends in Social Systems') published in 1968, and finally *Legitimation durch Verfahren* ('Legitimation through Procedure') from 1969, whose key arguments we wish to bring out briefly in what follows. Our aim here is to bring to life for you Luhmann's way of thinking and the main ways in which he differed from other sociological theoreticians by drawing on key areas of empirical investigation.

Funktionen und Folgen formaler Organisation was basically a critical examination – replete with empirical evidence – of the core assumptions of traditional organizational sociology. The classical figures of this subdiscipline such as the German-Italian sociologist Robert Michels (1876–1936) and Max Weber tried to describe and explain organizations, particularly bureaucracies, through the concepts of domination and obedience, ends and means. Both Weber and Michels had assumed an elective affinity between the instrumentally rational model of action, as may be applied to individual actors under certain circumstances, and the ends pursued by organizations. To put it somewhat differently, both Michels and Weber understood bureaucracies as bodies promoting rational action on a large scale, as quasi-machines programmed to fulfil certain aims and which do in fact function in just this way. Max Weber's description in his *Political Writings*, among other texts, reflects this: the administrative bureaucracy is a compliant instrument in the hands of the various ministers and must be such; it has to carry out the politicians' intentions. Bureaucracies are thus comprehended as hierarchical organizations headed by individuals who formulate goals, while subordinates, advisers, ministry officials, administrative experts, etc. do the preparatory groundwork for them.

Luhmann doubts that organizations and bureaucracies can be adequately described in this way, and he can point here to a diverse range of empirical studies published since the time of Michels and Weber. Among other things, these showed what a huge role so-called informal relationships play in bureaucracies, how important, for example, a positive and trusting relationship between boss and secretary is, how significant friendships are within bureaucracies or how useful 'non-existent' information channels between different departments may be. Acting through semi-official channels, such as a short informal phone call, often solves problems far more quickly than the slow and arduous prescribed channels, involving large numbers of formally responsible officials. If one takes

Weber's ideal typical account of formal organizations and bureaucracies as one's basis, such informal processes would be no more than a 'spanner in the works'; one would have to describe them as disturbances or at least as of no real importance. Yet this would fail utterly to capture the realities of functioning organizations.

These research findings in the sociology of organizations, which demonstrate that members' motives for action by no means jibe at all times with the objectives held by the leadership, also point to the fact that key assumptions of classical organizational sociology must be taken with a large pinch of salt, while substantial modifications must be made to the ideal typical notion of the bureaucracy and organization. This insight is also present, for example, in symbolic interactionist studies, in as much as they underlined the fluidity of social processes even in highly regulated institutions by means of the concept of 'negotiated order' (see Lecture VI).

But Luhmann wishes to go further. He not only wants to supplement or in some cases revise existing research, but to shake these classical assumptions *to the core* and contest the notion that bureaucracies or organizations can be understood with reference to a set organizational goal in the first place. This – Luhmann asserts – is simply not the case; objectives play no or only a very minor role in the analysis of organizations:

> In most cases, people certainly band together for reasons of which they are consciously aware or indeed to achieve particular goals: to satisfy needs or solve problems. In this way, the foundation is laid for a formal ideology underpinning their association. These reasons are one thing, the problems which crop up when people live and work together over a span of time are quite another. Not all the needs which arise, not all meaningful impulses and opportunities can be subsumed under the aegis of the foundational structure, not even if this is modified and adjusted here and there. A social system develops which must satisfy complex requirements and which must be defended on several fronts.
>
> (Luhmann, *Funktionen und Folgen*, p. 27)

You will recall from Lecture IX that Jürgen Habermas considered this statement by Luhmann a very cogent and momentous argument; Habermas accepted that action theory is incapable of shedding sufficient light on macrosociological contexts, because the goals of individuals do not appear at this level of aggregation. This was the crucial theoretical factor prompting him to adopt the concept of system and incorporate it into his theory.

Thus, for Luhmann, maintaining an organization or system requires more than the achievement of an objective set at one point in time or another. If one accepts this, then the various parts and subdivisions of the organization or system must also do more than merely serve this alleged objective (ibid., p. 75). The differentiation of the system or organization into subunits and subdivisions cannot, in any event, be derived from the highest goal of the organization or system. This would limit profoundly the functioning of the system or organization, leading to maladaptation to its environment:

> First, not all the tasks necessary to the system can be related to a single system goal or to several smoothly interconnected system goals. This would require a perfectly ordered, stable environment which maintains the system for the sake of its goals. As this requirement can never be entirely fulfilled, every system must develop strategies of self-preservation alongside its objectives. Only if such mechanisms of self-preservation are present does it make any sense to speak of a system. Second, concrete actions can never be related exclusively to a goal. This would be to ignore their side-effects. Actions always have a wide range of consequences, which affect the various system problems in both advantageous and disadvantageous ways. Every effective action, every concrete substructure of a system is in this sense multifunctional.
>
> (ibid., pp. 75–6)

If one accepts this as well, one must conclude that systems cannot 'be rationalized in accordance with a single criterion, such as a goal'; they must in fact be 'organized multifunctionally' (ibid., pp. 134–5). The sociology of organizations must pay heed to this and must no longer assume that consistency and total stability are absolute system imperatives; rather, it must accept that systems *need* inconsistencies if they are to exist in an environment which can never be entirely controlled (ibid., p. 269).

Looking back across the years to Luhmann's first major book, it is striking that he was still very much interested in problems of action theory; at the very least, he discusses them. He points, for example, to the fact that it is not only at the level of organizations or bureaucracies that justified criticisms have been and continue to be made of the means–ends categories most often deployed, but also at the level of individual actors. Tellingly, he again cites Arnold Gehlen (ibid., p. 100, fn. 20), in this case his book *Urmensch und Spätkultur* ('Primitive Man and Late Culture') in which Gehlen, drawing on American pragmatism, explains that rather than interpreting action at all times merely as the realization of goals, it can also be seen as activity without a specific aim, in which the action becomes an end in itself (see our critique of Parsons in Lecture III; see also Lecture VI). This might have prompted Luhmann to take a look at action theory, to ask whether the problems of the Weberian or Michelsian model of bureaucracy are due to a theory of action which is in itself problematic, one which for various reasons has always privileged instrumental rationality, inevitably tending to regard other forms of action as deficient or incapable of theoretical elaboration. On this view, Weber (and Michels) had produced ideal typical notions of orders such as organizations and bureaucracies at the macro-level which once again placed instrumentally rational action centre stage, and which failed to capture the reality of the processes occurring within organizations and bureaucracies as a result. Symbolic interactionists argued in the same or much the same way when they attempted – in the 'negotiated order approach' – to get beyond the notion, so firmly entrenched within sociology, of hyper-stable organizations. Here, a pragmatist theory of action rather different from Weber's was used to produce a notion of how organizations function that was closer to the empirical reality (again, see Lecture VI).

Luhmann does *not* opt for this approach. He does not set about correcting the problematic notions of action fundamental to traditional organizational sociology, in order then to ascend to ever 'higher' levels of aggregation on the basis of an enhanced theory of action. Rather, his strategy was to 'convert' immediately to systems theory.

Even more clearly than in *Funktionen und Folgen formaler Organisation*, Luhmann ultimately took leave of action theory in another famous book from the 1960s informed primarily by the sociology of organizations, namely *Zweckbegriff und Systemrationalität. Über die Funktion von Zwecken in sozialen Systemen* ('The Concept of Ends and System Rationality: On the Function of Ends in Social Systems'). The book's title and subtitle embody its key concerns, literally.

In this work, Luhmann grapples even more directly and above all in a more detailed way than in the book discussed above with the *action* theoretical problem of the concept of ends. Luhmann thus cites, among other figures, John Dewey and the 'American pragmatists', picking up on their critique of the idea of action as a process always guided by particular goals and ends as well as their critique of the 'teleological model of action' (see *Zweckbegriff*, pp. 18ff.). Dewey, for example, to whom Gehlen also made reference, did not understand the flow of human action causalistically, assuming the existence of a specific cause that triggers the action, which automatically determines the act itself. For this – as the symbolic interactionists and ethnomethodologists were to underline so often – would fail entirely to bring out the actors' reflexivity, their achievements of deliberation, and their creativity as they deal with new situations (see Joas, *The Creativity of Action*, pp. 152ff. and Lectures VI and VII).

Luhmann agrees with this, but does not set about producing an improved, non-teleological theory of action; rather, he immediately goes over to *asking*, from a systems theory perspective, *what functions ends and values fulfil*, or what functions it serves when actors claim to be acting in line with certain values and ends. Luhmann knows or appears to know that it is near-impossible to identify clear chains of causality within the natural and social sciences. With respect to the applicability of the causal scheme, he asserts that 'there can be no precise predictions of the necessary effects of particular causal factors, only probabilities which depend on the distribution of possible causes within causal contexts necessary to effectively bring about a particular effect' (*Zweckbegriff*, p. 26, fn. 7). Much the same may be said of values, which in reality never provide clear instructions with regard to action; it is in fact inconceivable that they could furnish us with an unambiguous guide to action. But why then do people constantly refer to objectives, to supposedly guiding values, both in everyday contexts and in organizations and bureaucracies? Luhmann's answer is that objectives and values merely serve to reduce complexity for the actor. Objectives, or the idea underlying them that actors can in fact produce calculable and foreseeable causal effects, like values, structure actors' horizon of action for rational problem solving. Luhmann puts forward the thesis

> that the human potential for complexity, the ability to grasp and process complex facts, lies primarily in subconscious processes of perception, whereas all the higher, consciously selective achievements of cognition are capable of grasping only a very limited number of variables at the same time. While I have no trouble choosing between two baskets of fruit, if one contains four oranges and the other five, it is far more difficult to choose between baskets containing a variety of fruit, even if the difference in value is significantly greater. I either have to settle on a very strong, dominant preference – value bananas above all else for example – or compare prices; in any event, I must take an indirect route in order to first reduce complexity. For the same reason, one rapidly loses track of causal connections if one has to deal with a chain of causal factors as variables at the same time. In much the same way as the simplifying approach outlined in the example of the fruit baskets, distinguishing between causes and effects helps us escape this problem. For it makes it possible to vary one factor only in light of the constancy of the others, and then, having finished reflecting on this, to apply the same schema to entirely or somewhat different factors.
>
> (ibid., pp. 31–2)

Assumptions of cause and effect, like values, thus have the function of reducing complexity. This entails the assertion that an epistemologically informed *science* cannot meaningfully work with these categories. If it is impossible to make unquestionable causal statements, then the sciences must find another way of thinking; if diverse sets of arguments have caused us to take leave of the concept of action because neither the concept of ends nor that of values is particularly helpful in structuring action, then – so Luhmann suggests – it is only logical to adopt a new conceptual apparatus. And of course he proposes that systems theory provides us with one, *his* systems theory, which, it is true, merely sets out to identify functional equivalents, but which is nonetheless able to clarify the *function* of objectives and values, and of claims of causality, as well.

The title of the book should thus be taken to mean: instrumental rationality *versus* system rationality. The epistemological and other weaknesses of (teleological) action theory, with its reference to ends, compel us – so Luhmann believes – to turn to systems theory. And as we shall see, as his work progresses and he develops his systems theory, Luhmann ultimately comes to regard action itself as produced by systems: the point of references to action and actors is merely to structure communication and to attribute communication to a particular personal or social system. Within the ceaseless flow of communication, the notion of action helps structure the context and demarcate the present from the past. For Luhmann, we must deploy systems theory to understand 'action'.

The systems theory developed by Luhmann by this point, which we have just outlined, is markedly different from that of Talcott Parsons, despite all the influences from this great American sociologist. In the 1960s, this was expressed nowhere as clearly as in the third book which we discuss here, *Legitimation durch Verfahren* ('Legitimation through Procedure'). Even Parsons' late systems theory had assumed that societies are integrated by values; Parsons' term 'cybernetic hierarchy of control' (see Lecture IV) entailed the notion that social systems or societies are ultimately integrated through values and are held together via 'latent pattern maintenance'. Parsons' normativist theory thus took for granted that societies feature an identifiable control centre.

All of this changes completely in Luhmann's work. Luhmann follows through on the assertion that modern societies are functionally differentiated, that the functional spheres of science, the economy, politics, etc., all follow their own logic, without being ordered hierarchically by a superordinate system or by values. This does not mean that nothing now remains of 'stratificatory' or other forms of differentiation: classes continue to exist, differences between rich and poor, between the centres of a society and its margins, etc. But the division of modern societies into various *functional* spheres has become so dominant and pervasive that it is now impossible to identify any clear 'up' or 'down', any ordering principle.

Luhmann demonstrates this view very clearly in his analysis of democratic politics and the legal system. According to Luhmann, democratic elections and judicial proceedings are not tied to a supreme value, to truth or justice, such that we might state that the legitimacy of the political system or judiciary depends on achieving true or correct policies by means of elections or on passing just sentences through the code of procedure, that is, on complying with or enforcing certain values. This was what Parsons thought, and much the same assumption is present in the work of Jürgen Habermas, who ascribes to normatively based law – and to it alone – a tremendous integrative effect in his most recent writings in philosophy of law (see the previous lecture). Luhmann meanwhile breaks completely with this assumption so steeped in tradition; for him, truth and justice are terms which fail to refer to anything tangible:

> By now ... in a process linked with the development of the sciences, modern thought has defined the concept of truth more precisely, linking it with very strict methodological prerequisites; it has thus undermined the idea of natural law and positivized the law, that is, refounded it in terms of decision-making procedures. In light of all this, it is difficult to see how, other than through *prejudice*, one can adhere to the notion that true knowledge and true justice are the goal and thus the essence of legally regulated procedures, and if this is so, how one might achieve such a goal.
>
> (Luhmann, *Legitimation durch Verfahren*, p. 20; emphasis added)

Of course, we still hear a great deal about truth and justice to this day, but for Luhmann, this discourse too merely fulfils certain functions which ease the burden on human beings by reducing complexity. But legitimacy today is no longer attained because citizens truly believe in such noble values and expect correct or true decisions to be made. Legitimacy is now produced within the political or legal system itself, when people participate in free elections or legal proceedings and, solely by taking part in them, gain the feeling that they can somehow accept the verdict, whatever its specific content may be. Procedures such as elections or legal proceedings thus transform issues of truth and justice so that ultimately all that is at stake is the *psychological acceptance* of the various procedures by those affected. And this acceptance is achieved on the basis that people are integrated into the political or legal system by granting them different roles, that because they have their roles to play, there is pressure on them to accept the rules of procedure. As regards legal proceedings, Luhmann describes this as follows:

> By submitting to a certain code of conduct and adapting their behaviour to the developing procedural system in order to achieve their aims, the parties to conflict acknowledge one another's roles as parties. This is possible because the ruling itself is not determined in advance. Each party gives the other, as it were, carte blanche to oppose him, without influencing the outcome of the conflict. In this sense, the principle of equality of the parties is a key procedural principle.
>
> (ibid., pp. 103–4)

This has nothing – so Luhmann asserts – to do with issues of truth or justice. It is the participation in these procedures that determines the legitimacy of decisions and thus that of subsystems in general; it is both inconceivable and impossible for these decisions to be anchored in values or norms shared by society as a whole. But this means that Luhmann has thrown overboard all trace of normativism, including that characteristic of Parsonian systems theory, and has struck a blow against all socially critical analyses, which necessarily work with concepts such as truth and justice. It is solely the logic of the subsystems and of their specific procedures that ultimately determines their stability and dynamics. While these subsystems are in principle dependent on their environment, they feature a distinct dynamic of their own; they can neither be controlled from without by objectives or values, nor are they dependent on such external values. Luhmann was subsequently to radicalize ever further this idea of the dynamics and logic unique to the various societal subsystems as well as substantiating it theoretically in new ways.

(B) In the 1970s and early 1980s, Luhmann continued to demonstrate his tremendous productivity, publishing numerous books on very different theoretical and empirical topics. While the sociology of law, organizations and administration remained Luhmann's key concern, slim theoretical volumes on *trust* and *power* (each topic originally the subject of separate books in German, appearing in 1968 and 1975, though amalgamated in the English edition, *Trust and Power*) and a major 1981 study on *Political Theory in the Welfare State* also became influential. And it was around this time that Luhmann began his studies in the sociology of knowledge, which ultimately comprised several volumes (*Gesellschaftsstruktur und Semantik* ['Social Structure and Semantics']), in which he described how the meaning of certain crucial terms, that is, semantics, changed in modern society, which is no longer hierarchically structured but functionally differentiated. A prime example is his 1982 study on the rise of the Romantic 'semantics of love' (*Love as Passion: The Codification of Intimacy*).

As productive as he was, it is nonetheless fair to say that Luhmann's approach remained essentially the same. He worked with the same theory, merely applying it to new fields. In light of this unchanging theoretical framework, critics claimed that the findings of his studies, as interesting as some of the details might be, offered few surprises.

The first signs of theoretical innovation appeared only in the early 1980s, becoming particularly apparent in *Social Systems*, Luhmann's magnum opus from 1984, which was in part conceived as a response to Jürgen Habermas' *The Theory of Communicative Action,* published three years before. To be precise, Luhmann's 'turn' here is in fact nothing of the kind, but merely a further radicalization of systems theory. First,

Luhmann rids himself of the idea, present in Parsons and in his own earlier work, that reference to 'systems' was merely analytical, that sociologists used this theoretical toolkit merely in order to obtain improved or more adequate access to reality. His new understanding of systems is realistic, that is, he assumes that social phenomena really are systemic in character, as is unmistakable in the first few lines of the first chapter of *Social Systems*:

> The following considerations assume that there are systems. Thus they do not begin with epistemological doubt. They also do not advocate a 'purely analytical relevance' for systems theory. The most narrow interpretation of systems theory as a mere method of analyzing reality is deliberately avoided. Of course, one must never confuse statements with their objects; one must realize that statements are only statements and that scientific statements are only scientific statements. But, at least in systems theory, they refer to the real world. Thus the concept of system refers to something that is in reality a system and thereby incurs the responsibility of testing its statements against reality.
>
> (Luhmann, *Social Systems*, p. 12)

What exactly Luhmann means in this last sentence when he refers to testing systems theory against reality, and above all how we are supposed to figure out whether something is really a *system*, remains somewhat unclear and appears a rather dogmatic assertion. In any event, this is the step taken by Luhmann, who claims at the same time that his systems theory is capable of encompassing all the theoretical problems with which sociology has grappled hitherto. His aspiration to generate a theoretical synthesis thus finds expression at the heart of systems theory. Systems theory – the confident Luhmann tells us – has now become a 'supertheory ... with claims to universality (that is, to including both itself and its opponents)' (ibid., p. 4).

Second, Luhmann mounts his systems theory, as he himself states, on a new foundation. He notes that system theoretical thought, which has now been successfully established, particularly in the natural sciences, for several decades, has undergone constant development; in his opinion, it is about time the social sciences embraced this advance in our understanding. Luhmann distinguishes between three phases of systems theoretical thought (see *Social Systems*, pp. 5ff.): the first, still highly immature phase, was distinguished by an understanding of systems as a relationship between part and whole. But for various reasons, this version of the concept of system, the notion that the whole is somehow more than the sum of its parts, proved unproductive and imprecise; the next step in the development of systems theory thus involved placing the system–environment problem rather than the part–whole problem centre stage. Systems, on this view, are distinct from their environment but at the same time open enough to adapt to it. As you have probably noticed, this is a position to which Luhmann himself subscribed in the 1960s and 1970s, when he placed particular emphasis on the 'achievements of adaptation' performed by systems with respect to their environment. But now, according to Luhmann, recent developments have taken place within systems theory, particularly biology and neurophysiology, which cast doubt on the system–environment model that has held sway thus far and which instead point towards a theory of *self-referential systems*. What does this mean?

To put it in very simple terms, this perspective suggests that living organisms are better understood if, rather than their exchange with the environment, we place their *operational autonomy* centre stage. Such organisms may be *physically* open, in that they take in certain materials from the environment. But the way in which they process this material follows a logic entirely internal to the system, just as the information which flows into this organism adheres to the logic of the organism and is not dependent on the environment. This was conveyed in particularly cogent and vivid form in the neurophysiological studies produced by two Latin American scientists, Humberto R. Maturana (b. 1928) and Francisco J. Varela (1946–2001), which formed Luhmann's primary point of reference. While investigating the perception of colour, Maturana and Varela made the astonishing discovery that there are clearly no straightforward connections between the activities of certain nerve cells in the eye behind the retina and the physical qualities of light. Thus, there are no clear causal relationships between light source and nervous system (for more detail, see Kneer and Nassehi, *Niklas Luhmanns Theorie sozialer Systeme* ['Niklas Luhmann's Theory of Social Systems'], pp. 47ff. and Bernhard Irrgang, *Lehrbuch der evolutionären Erkenntnistheorie* ['Handbook of Evolutionary Epistemology'], pp. 147ff.). If this is in fact the case, one might conclude, like Maturana and Varela, that the nervous system is a *self-contained system*, that is, nervous systems or perceiving organisms do not produce a perfect copy of their environment, but construct *their own unique world* by means of *their own operational logic*.

Living organisms function as self-generating systems that refer only to themselves. Maturana and Varela speak of *autopoietic* (autos = self; poiein = to make) *systems*, systems which are organizationally closed and thus autonomous, at least in the sense that the components of a system are reproduced within the system itself. There is of course contact with the environment; there is, to use the specialist terminology, a 'structural linkage'. Yet no elements relevant to the system are provided by the environment: systems are merely irritated by the outside world, but they respond to this irritation in line with their own logic and with their own methods. Further, the qualities of living systems cannot be determined by reference to their components, but only by the organization of these components, that is, by the processes occurring between the components. The nervous system, for example, cannot be defined in terms of the neurons, but by analysing the manner in which information is conveyed between the neurons, which respond to the irritations conveyed to them, for instance, by the retina, in their own particular way.

Luhmann now applies these findings from biology and neurophysiology to social systems, paying no heed to the fact that Maturana and Varela expressed scepticism about the applicability of their theory to the social sciences. Luhmann conceives of psychological and, of particular interest to sociologists, social systems as autopoietic systems. He explains what he hopes to achieve with this 'autopoietic turn' as follows:

> In general systems theory, this second paradigm change [away from system/environment theory towards the theory of self-referential systems] provokes remarkable shifts – for example, from interest in design and control to an interest in autonomy and environmental sensitivity, from planning to evolution, from structural stability to dynamic stability.
>
> (Luhmann, *Social Systems*, p. 10; our insertions)

Here, Luhmann is expressing his intention to further radicalize his functionalism, to push the idea of functional differentiation as far as possible. And this new theoretical toolkit does in fact enable him to abandon entirely any notion of a social whole, as we discuss in more detail later on. As Luhmann sees it, the functionally differentiated subsystems, such as science, the economy, religion, art, the law, education and politics, now follow their own logic. They function according to their own code (here, there are of course clear parallels with Parsons' theory of symbolically generalized media of communication, see Lecture IV), are programmed in a specific way and cannot therefore be regulated or controlled from outside. These subsystems can only be irritated from outside. What they do with these irritations is down to the subsystem's specific programme. Any notion of planning as regards society as a whole ('from planning to evolution') is thus superfluous. Luhmann yields to no one in his pessimism about planning and makes fun of political attempts to intervene in the economy; for him, though, the same applies to state intervention in the science system, legal system, etc. more generally.

> As with the rain dance of the Hopi Indians, reference to stimulating the economy, ensuring Germany's status as a good place to do business and creating jobs seems to perform an important function, at the very least giving the impression that something is being

done and that [the government] is not simply waiting around for things to change by themselves.

(Luhmann, *Die Politik der Gesellschaft* ['The Politics of Society'], p. 113)

Luhmann harbours no doubts that no matter what politicians say or do, they will not impress or influence the economy. 'The place for economics is the economy' – Luhmann would not hesitate to sign up to this credo of a former German liberal minister for economic affairs, though he would add that the same applies to art, science, etc. Art is made in the art system, science in the science system. Modern societies are *functionally* differentiated; the various functional spheres are no longer structured hierarchically. According to Luhmann, the notion of planning or control is thus misguided from the outset. Systems and subsystems evolve. They cannot be planned. This is clearly a particular way of diagnosing the modern era as well, and we shall be looking at this more closely in the last part of this lecture.

Luhmann's approach in relation to the thesis of the primacy of functional differentiation in modern societies has certainly become more radical since the so-called 'autopoietic turn'; yet on the other hand, for Luhmann this theoretical innovation obviously did not entail the necessity of revising significantly or even rejecting his previous accounts of societies or social subdivisions. In this sense, the autopoietic turn may be seen as no more than a further turn of the functionalist screw.

In the present context, however, what is interesting is a theoretical consequence of the autopoietic turn, which Luhmann himself addresses, namely the 'radical temporalization of the concept of element':

> The theory of self-producing, autopoietic systems can be transferred to the domain of action systems only if one begins with the fact that the elements composing the system can have no duration, and thus must be constantly reproduced by the system these elements comprise.

(Luhmann, *Social Systems*, p. 11)

And in applying the autopoietic model to social contexts, Luhmann does indeed implement this temporalization of elements. Luhmann, who distinguishes between machines, organisms, psychological systems and social systems, his primary focus being on the latter as the object of sociology, underlines that systems theory breaks and must break with what he calls the 'traditional European' concept of subject, placing other elements at the centre of the theory building inspired by Maturana and Varela, elements which 'can have no duration, and thus must be constantly reproduced by the system these elements comprise' (see the quotation above).

For Luhmann, this means that social systems are not constructed on the basis of human beings and are not composed of actions, but of communication. Acts of communication are the elementary units of social systems; it is through such acts that meaning is produced and reference to meaning is constantly made. Luhmann, out to shock and defamiliarize as much as he is able, tells us that the human being is not part of the social system, and that it is not people who communicate but communication itself (Luhmann, *Die Gesellschaft der Gesellschaft*, pp. 29f., 103ff.). While communication is indeed dependent on psychological systems, on the consciousness of human beings, we cannot look inside others' minds, and communication can therefore only ever relate to that which is communicated.

As a consequence, social (and psychological) systems are defined not by fixed units, but by the constant reproduction of meaning; the theory of system differentiation refers to the form of the particular act of communication, not to the affiliation of people or acts. The science system, for example, forms a unified whole and is able to constantly reproduce itself because reference is made to truth, because it functions in line with the distinction between 'true' and 'false'. In science, constant reference is made to true or false statements, the correctness of hypotheses is tested, and this is then precisely what characterizes the system of science: a very special form of communication takes place here, a particular 'binary code' is deployed. Thus, the science system is not a unified whole because certain people belong to it – as is well known, scientists are more than just scientists; they are at the same time citizens who are political, make money, assert their rights, are artistically inclined, etc. It is therefore impossible, according to Luhmann, to determine the existence of a system with reference to specific individuals, or to specific actions, because one and the same action may appear in the most diverse range of contexts, in artistic or scientific contexts; but which meaning is produced depends on the particular code involved.

> We cannot assign people to functional systems in such a way that each individual is a member of just one system, that is, participates only in the law, but not the economy, or only in politics, but not the education system. The ultimate consequence of this is that we can no longer claim that society is composed of people; for people clearly cannot be placed within a subsystem of society, that is, they can no longer be placed anywhere in society.
>
> (Luhmann, *Die Gesellschaft der Gesellschaft*, p. 744)

Social systems, and the most extensive social systems are societies, are thus defined, so Luhmann tells us, through ceaseless flows of *communication*. Society ends wherever communication ends, which is why, in an age in which communication spans the world, we must speak of a global society. In the modern age, the nation-state seems to Luhmann an utterly outmoded point of departure for analysing social processes.

Communication and meaning, rather than 'actors' or 'action', are thus the core, elementary concepts in Luhmann's sociology. Reference to 'action' or 'subject' is for Luhmann merely an example of attribution or ascription: psychological systems refer to actions, that is, clearly delineated processes which are ascribed to an individual in order to reduce complexity. But of course Luhmann 'knows' that actions as such do not exist, at least not as a practicable description of real processes:

> Actions are constituted by processes of attribution. They come about only if, for whatever reasons, in whatever contexts, and with the help of whatever semantics ('intention', 'motive', 'interest'), selections can be attributed to systems. Obviously, this concept of action does not provide an adequate causal explanation of behavior because it ignores the psychic.
>
> (Luhmann, *Social Systems*, pp. 165–6)

The remnants of any possible action theoretical problem were thus eradicated, and – at least on the basis of his system theoretical premises – Luhmann can now assert that his functionalist super-theory encompasses the stock of knowledge and findings of sociological theory.

(C) We have already discussed the fact that Luhmann's radical thesis of the functional differentiation of modern societies and his equally radical pessimism about planning are an expression of a particular diagnosis of the contemporary era, of the detached stance of the observer who has long since abandoned any faith in the possibility of changing social conditions and can only cast an ironic glance at the futile efforts of socially engaged activists.

Luhmann only rarely expanded on this diagnostic element in his writings, and it is therefore useful here, as we conclude this lecture, to examine briefly a slimmer volume from 1986, in which he does so openly. We are referring to *Ecological Communication*. This book – as its title suggests – is a response to the environmental movement which has become increasingly important from the 1970s on and which has had a significant political or socio-political influence since the founding of the political party Die Grünen in Germany at the latest. Luhmann's response here is rather revealing.

Luhmann begins his book – and this makes it the most accessible of his works even for neophyte sociologists – with a fairly compact and easily understandable introduction to his theory. He explains once again that modern societies (in as much as one can talk of nations in isolation in the first place these days) consist of different subsystems – politics, the economy, the law, science, religion, education (as it happens, Luhmann was to devote a number of books, highly comprehensive for the most part, to each of these subsystems in the 1980s and 1990s). All of these, as it were, speak their own language, use a 'binary code', through which the information within the system is processed. The economy for example, which Luhmann understands as 'all those operations transacted through the payment of money' (*Ecological Communication*, p. 51), works with the code have/not have or pay/not pay; science with the code true/false; the modern-day political system with the code government/opposition, etc. None of these subsystems is capable of taking control of the other subsystems; no code somehow takes priority over the others.

It is of course possible to investigate the relationship between the economy and politics, art and religion, or science and law. But one must not assume that one subsystem can guide or control the others. The economy can respond to politics only by means of the code pay/not pay; it has no other language at its disposal. Art can respond to religious influences only with the help of the aesthetic code, while religion can respond to legal influences only through the code transcendence/immanence. The various codes cannot be smoothly translated one into the other.

Luhmann's perspective is certainly interesting. As with Parsons' systems theory, this is a research heuristic which helps bring out the specific logic according to which the various social subsystems function and the nature of the processes of exchange between the subsystems, should there be any. This probably furnishes us – and this is what Parsons claimed to have done with respect to his AGIL scheme – with a rather more realistic feeling for the analysis of social processes than that provided by, for example, the crude Marxian base–superstructure theorem.

But Luhmann's theoretical construct, namely the thesis that social (sub)systems are autopoietic systems which function exclusively in line with their own systemic logic and which can be irritated but not controlled from outside, rules out any prospect of planning or regulation. The subsystems can merely observe one another and can only ever translate external attempts to influence them into their own unique language – and they can do no more than this. These constraints also apply to the political system, which so often experiences the fundamental inaccessibility of other systems, in accordance with the motto we encountered earlier: the place for economics is the economy. The question inevitably arises as to whether such a radical supposition is realistic.

But let us turn first to the question posed by Luhmann in the book's subtitle: can modern societies adapt to ecological threats, to the dangers of nuclear power for example, as laid bare so strikingly by Chernobyl? Luhmann's answer – and this will surely come as no particular surprise – is 'no'. His argument is as simple as it is revealing. In modern, highly differentiated societies, there is simply no longer any vantage point from which individuals or groups might gain an overview of the whole entitling them to warn 'society' about various dangers, let alone enabling them to protect society against these dangers. For Luhmann, any attempt to construct an overall macro-intention supposedly representative of society as a whole – including attempts made with respect to the avoidance of alleged ecological threats – is simply ridiculous and bound to fail. He then goes on to interpret the environmental movement from this perspective, with a bluntness and harshness surprising in a representative of Romantic irony; he refers to the 'blasé moral self-righteousness observed in the "Green" movement' (Luhmann, *Ecological Communication*, p. 126).

Luhmann is certainly not blind to the dangers facing modern societies. In the last major work published before his death, he states:

> The actual consequences of the excessive exploitation of the environment are still within reasonable bounds; but it takes little imagination to realize that we cannot go on like this.
>
> (Luhmann, *Die Gesellschaft der Gesellschaft*, p. 805)

But Luhmann is radically pessimistic about our capacity to influence what happens. Various measures will of course be taken to protect the environment, emissions will be capped, nuclear power stations shut down, etc. But no one should believe that this political system can truly be influenced or controlled from outside, such that genuinely 'effective' measures might be taken; it may at most be irritated, and it will then react to these irritations with its own unique logic of communication. For Luhmann, this means that 'the new social movements have no theory' – what they lack is of course Luhmann's systems theory, and thus the insight into the primacy of functional differentiation. And this is why he feels such disdain for these movements:

> Thus, for the most part, goals and postulates are determined in very simple and highly specific fashion, and the distinction made between supporters and opponents and the typical moral evaluation put forward tend to be correspondingly simplistic.
>
> (Luhmann, *Ecological Communication*, p. 125)

It is the moral stance which he appears to find particularly insufferable; in functionally differentiated modern society, there is simply no longer any standpoint which might represent the whole, and moralizing is thus utterly out of place, particularly in light of the fact that chains of causality are impossible to identify in the environmental sphere and questions of guilt and innocence are therefore irresolvable. The moral high ground occupied by the environmentalists must be judged in exactly the same way as any public outcry against immigrants (see *Die Gesellschaft der Gesellschaft*,

p. 850, fn. 451): both stances are stupid and arrogant in Luhmann's eyes. Protests and movements of this kind can only be injurious to the functional differentiation so constitutive of modern society. Here, Luhmann appears to want to adopt the position of a personified modern society, which either bestows praise on actors, such as the established political parties, or, like the unbearably moralizing 'Greens', rebukes them. Why Luhmann, despite this no longer ironical but extremely cynical or even fatalistic position ('as if a net rational improvement could be attained from the closing of nuclear plants or from constitutional reforms effecting a change in the majority rules', *Ecological Communication*, p. 131), has become something of a fashionable author among sections of the German green movement and its intellectuals, is very hard to grasp, and can probably be understood only in light of this movement's complex historical genesis.

However this may be, Luhmann's critique of the environmentalists has something of the air of the traditional conservative attack on intellectuals, masterfully exemplified by Luhmann's patron Helmut Schelsky, who we encountered earlier, as in his famous, rather resentful and at times reactionary polemic entitled *Die Arbeit tun die anderen. Klassenkampf und Priesterherrschaft der Intellektuellen* ('Someone Else Does the Work. Class Struggle and the Intellectuals' Priestly Hegemony') from 1975, which, incidentally, Luhmann thought a 'remarkable critical observation' and was therefore perplexed as to why it was considered 'conservative' (Luhmann, *Die Gesellschaft der Gesellschaft*, p. 1108, fn. 382).

But Luhmann's critique of the ecological movement is problematic primarily for *theoretical* reasons (opinions will differ widely on his political evaluation), because he conflates an (ecological) warning about *specific forms* of functional differentiation with criticism of functional differentiation *as such*. Luhmann acts as though warnings about the ecological threats facing modern industrial society came primarily from those who would ideally like to go back to a *pre*modern, functionally non-differentiated society. But this is not only empirically false, because the protests have come and continue to come from very different groups, but also nips in the bud theoretically any possibility even of thinking about a society that is *differently* constituted, that is *differentiated in a new way*. Even in existing Western industrial societies, cross-national comparison reveals massive differences in how social differentiation is institutionalized: the economic, religious, political, legal, etc. institutional structure exhibits major differences from one country to another. But there are surely reasons for this, and this would seem to suggest that there have in the past been conflicts over *forms* of differentiation, conflicts which have differed from one society to another, and that there will always be such conflicts. Decisions about these forms of differentiation are made in the political or democratic process; they are not determined by (Luhmannian) social theorists. Hans Joas has summed this up in the phrase 'democratization of the differentiation question'. In this sense, Luhmann's radical pessimism about control seems exaggerated; the outcome of struggles over the form of institutions cannot in fact be predicted, but it is quite insufficient to speak of mere 'irritations', because it is certainly possible to make out battle lines within these conflicts as well as 'winners' and 'losers' as actors struggle over a specific institutional structure. We shall have more to say about the fact that another theoretical perspective is entirely possible, namely one which takes this factor into account, particularly with respect to the interpretation of ecological movements, over the course of this lecture series, when we discuss the works of Alain Touraine and Ulrich Beck.

Finally, there are three texts we would like to recommend to you. There are numerous introductions to Luhmann's work or systems theory, which, however, generally have one serious disadvantage: they are almost exclusively written from a systems theoretical perspective and thus often refrain completely from criticizing or at least relativizing the theoretical edifice they describe. Nonetheless, we would single out three slim volumes in particular: Detlef Horster's *Niklas Luhmann* is to be recommended not only because it provides a concise introduction, but also because it contains an interesting biographical interview carried out a few years before Luhmann's death; *Niklas Luhmanns Theorie sozialer Systeme* ('Niklas Luhmann's Theory of Social Systems') by Georg Kneer and Armin Nassehi is perhaps the most compact introduction to Luhmann's work; while Helmut Willke's *Systemtheorie. Eine Einführung in die Grundprobleme* ('Systems Theory. An Introduction to the Basic Issues') is, as the title suggests, a more comprehensive introduction to systems theory more generally.

This brings us to the end of our lecture on Luhmann. We have now examined the two major attempts at synthesis made in *Germany* in the 1970s and 1980s. But as we have intimated, it was not German sociology but *Western European sociology* as a whole which began to lead in the production of sociological theory during this period in a discipline in which 'America' had formerly set the tone. Attempts at synthesis were also made elsewhere, in Great Britain for instance, where one name in particular began to dominate the debate from the 1970s on, that of Anthony Giddens.

XII

Anthony Giddens' theory of structuration and the new British sociology of power

While it was essential to examine the biographies of the two German 'grand theorists' considered in the previous lectures in a fair degree of detail, in order to bring out the ideas central to their theories, this is not necessarily the case with respect to Anthony Giddens. It is quite possible to explain Giddens' attempt at synthesis in light of the trends emerging from the 1960s, particularly within British sociology, without digressing into his personal history. The key here is conflict theory, which we examined in Lecture VIII; two developments in particular were to play an important role for Giddens.

1. British conflict theory in the 1950s and early 1960s had been closely associated with the names of John Rex and David Lockwood, who – in contrast to the significantly more radical Ralf Dahrendorf – had never broken entirely with the theoretical approach of Parsons, but merely wished to see conflict theory established alongside Parsonian functionalism on an equal footing. Mere 'co-existence', however, could never entirely satisfy even the protagonists of conflict theory, and at least the theoretically ambitious Lockwood clearly attempted to break up the rigid opposition between power and conflict theoretical approaches on the one hand and functionalist (as well as interpretive) approaches on the other. In other words, he tried to produce a kind of synthesis. Groundwork had thus been completed that helped pave the way for the later attempts at 'grand' synthesis – those of Habermas, Luhmann and Giddens himself.

    David Lockwood's essay 'Social Integration and System Integration' from 1964 pointed the way forward in a number of respects. Lockwood, who, we again emphasize, comes from a Weberian Marxist tradition, analyses various functionalist and conflict theoretical approaches with regard to their tenable and productive theoretical statements, in order to produce, by developing his own conceptual apparatus, a reasonably coherent theoretical framework. Lockwood's position here, as in the 1950s, was that functionalism and conflict theory should not be seen as mutually negating alternatives: norm–consensus–order should not be considered incompatible with power–alienation–conflict; rather, in the social world, *both complexes* are always linked and interwoven in a quite specific way, though this varies greatly from one society to another. Any theory which, like that of Dahrendorf (and to some extent that of Rex) focuses in a one-sided way on power, conflict and alienation, would fail to capture key aspects of social reality, because it is impossible to adequately analyse conflicts separately from the form and development of value systems: 'For, given the power structure, the nature of the value system is of signal importance for the genesis, intensity, and direction of potential conflict' ('Social Integration', p. 248). As was to apply in the work of Habermas as well, the spotlight here is on the relationship between power and culture, between instrumental and other forms of rationality. This prefigures a crucial theoretical goal, which most later attempts at synthesis had in their sights.

But according to Lockwood, an overly radical conflict theory is not only deficient because it airbrushes out the relationship between culture and power. It is also problematic because its statements regarding social change are insufficiently systematic and because it fails to acknowledge that while social change is frequently associated with conflict, not all conflicts – not even those on a massive scale – necessarily lead to social change. 'Conflict may be both endemic and intense in a social system without causing any basic structural change' (ibid., p. 249). Some conflicts do in fact lead to social change in the sense of a change in the institutional structure of a society, while others do not. Evidently, then, we must distinguish clearly between two complexes of problems: it is one thing to ask whether actors or groups/classes within a society struggle with or fight one another, quite another to ask whether the structure of this society really changes as a result. This consideration inspires Lockwood to introduce a pair of terms with which you are already familiar: *social* and *system integration*, terms which Habermas was also to use later on, though in modified form. According to Lockwood, we have to distinguish *between the relationships among the actors* in a system (social integration) and the *relationship among the parts* of a system (system integration). It may well be that there exist numerous contradictions or system problems within a society that are not necessarily reflected or expressed at the level of action – in which case there are no visible protests, no open conflicts, no class struggles, etc. Conversely, there may well be protests and conflicts within a society without this leading to a change in the relationships between its subsystems, its overall structure. This Lockwoodian distinction between social and system integration clearly reflects the political experience of the Western European left that economic crises do not necessarily lead to intensification of class struggles, but that conversely such intensification may well occur during periods of economic prosperity.

Radical conflict theory – so Lockwood tells us – ultimately lacks this insight insofar as it is interested merely in manifest conflicts rather than the phenomenon of system integration: it discusses conflicts, as it were, only superficially, without asking whether and how these conflicts cause genuine system change or whether and how these conflicts spread to or affect the parts of a social system. For Lockwood, using the concept of system and adopting functionalist ideas seems not only possible but absolutely imperative if we are to analyse modern societies successfully. Only by tackling the problems of social *and* system integration *concurrently* can we construct a convincing social theory. This is also the point of departure for Lockwood's critique of Parsonian (normativist) functionalism, in as much as the latter, assuming the absolute primacy of normative (social) integration, sees no tensions between the parts of the system because *all* institutions and sub-systems are merely the embodiment of value complexes spread throughout society and thus – in Marxian terms – a contradiction between the institutional order and its 'material basis' is quite inconceivable. Lockwood thus accuses Parsons of having covered up the potential problems of system integration within societies through the all-pervasive notion of normative integration.

Lockwood's deservedly famous essay, which we have briefly outlined here, had thus already laid out a course that would lead ultimately to a theoretical synthesis. Yet Lockwood himself failed to achieve a real *breakthrough* in this respect; his ideas were probably too firmly anchored in Marxian thought, despite all his criticisms of Marx. Lockwood emphasizes repeatedly, for example, that the idea of a complex interplay between social and system integration is built into Marxian theory. But he lacks adequate theoretical and philosophical means to retain this insight *while at the same time* – like Habermas – ridding himself of key aspects of the Marxian approach, above all the utilitarian and economistic figures of thought found in the work of Marx, which suggest that there is very little prospect of achieving a synthetic conception of the relationship between power and culture on this basis. Nonetheless, it was possible to develop Lockwood's ideas further – and in the British context this occurred primarily through Anthony Giddens, who, however, interpreted the concept of 'social versus system integration' in a quite different fashion, such that very little remained of Lockwood's and later Habermas' original ideas.

2. The development of Giddens' work should not be seen solely against the background of Lockwood's first attempt at synthesis, which was incomplete but greatly inspiring, but also in light of a sociology of power which privileged historical arguments and that began to flourish in Great Britain in the 1970s, a sociology of conflict, as we discussed towards the end of Lecture VIII, that had 'migrated' to the field of historical sociology.

There are at least three reasons why this *historically oriented* sociology of power or conflict began to take off in Great Britain (in much the same way as it did in the USA, but in sharp contrast to West Germany). First, non-orthodox Marxian historians and intellectuals such as Edward P.

Thompson (1924–93), Eric Hobsbawm (b. 1917) and Perry Anderson (b. 1938), with their at times strongly sociologizing reflections, and historical studies that drew on a rich range of materials, stimulated sociologists, who felt spurred on to link their analyses of the present more strongly to history. The existing Weberian Marxist school within sociology, to which Rex and Lockwood belonged, opened itself up to historical subjects to a quite astonishing degree. Second, the influence of Norbert Elias was felt far earlier in Great Britain than in West Germany. Elias (1897–1990), who was expelled from Germany during the Nazi period and whose great historical-sociological book *The Civilizing Process* (1939) became truly well known in West Germany only in the second half of the 1970s, finally established himself in Great Britain as a lecturer at the University of Leicester in 1954 following a typical émigré's odyssey across several countries; here, he exercised a significant influence on British sociology, primarily through his teaching. His historical macrosociology, with its central thesis of the disciplining effect of processes of state formation, of macro-processes which decisively shape even people's most private feelings as they increasingly internalize the control of the self, was bound to stimulate a sociology concerned with power and social conflicts. Third, highly theoretical and historically oriented sociological research on the development of the (British) welfare state, associated with the names of Richard M. Titmuss (1907–73) and Thomas H. Marshall (1893–1982), flourished in Great Britain as early as the 1950s and 1960s. This formed another point of contact for those sociologists with historical-sociological interests.

Moulded by this intellectual climate, a number of younger sociologists established themselves in this historical-sociological field from the 1970s; Anthony Giddens was one of those who came into contact with these figures. The name of Michael Mann (b. 1942) must be mentioned here first. Mann caused a stir with his extremely ambitious project, set out in several volumes, for a sociologically informed universal history (*The Sources of Social Power*), and he was made a number of attractive offers from American universities following the appearance of the first volume in 1986; he now teaches at the University of California, Los Angeles. Mann, who characterizes himself as a left-wing Weberian and who was from the outset equally sceptical of Parsonianism *and* Marxism, believing neither in the integration of whole societies through values nor in the fundamentally revolutionary role of the labour movement, started out as a theorist of class in the 1970s, publishing a number of studies on workers' consciousness and the role of intellectuals in Western societies. But his interests rapidly shifted to history, and indeed as early as the late 1970s, as it seemed to him that historical-sociological analysis was the only means of getting to the bottom of certain seemingly self-evident yet highly problematic and harmful premises of sociological thought. Mann pushed for the revision of traditional sociological perspectives in at least three respects (on what follows, see Haferkamp and Knöbl, 'Die Logistik der Macht' ['The Logistics of Power']).

(a) Michael Mann was one of the authors who attempted to do away with the holistic concept of society in quite radical fashion. Since the era of its foundation, sociology had made this concept a key analytical category, without taking into account that the idea of 'society' as a discrete unity was closely bound up with the nation-state, which was becoming firmly established in the nineteenth century. That is, the concept of the nation-state was equated with society, despite the fact that such self-contained entities simply did not exist in premodern times or outside of North America and Europe, because there were no strictly policed borders or – as in the early modern Holy Roman Empire – a large number of territorially small states existed, a political order which is impossible to capture through the idea of a discrete, let alone 'national-cultural' unity. The concept of society is of no use in such contexts. As a consequence, Michael Mann defines the human being not in terms of 'society' as such, but as a 'social being', taking leave of the concept of society as a *basic* concept in the sociological armoury.

(b) In place of the holistic concept of society, Michael Mann now refers to only partially overlapping *networks of power*: human beings – according to Mann's key thesis – exist within various networks (he mentions four: the ideological, economic, military and political) or are 'forced' to cooperate in a more or less ordered way by these networks. With this thesis, he is pursuing at least three strategic theoretical goals. First, Mann turns against Marxism, which has always taken the fundamental primacy of the economy as its point of departure, however much it may hedge this in with qualifications. This is unacceptable to Mann. Very much in line with the traditions of conflict theory, he stresses the existence of several types of resource or sources of power, over which there may be conflict; which of the four sources of power dominates at a particular moment of history must be determined empirically. Second, Mann then opens up sociology directly to historical analysis, because the following questions immediately arise: By what means has it proved possible to organize human beings economically, politically, militarily and ideologically over the course of history? How did these power networks develop? Has there been an increase in the capacity for organization? Mann proves a master of historical-sociological analysis in this connection, when he shows, for example, which means of communication and transport made it possible to integrate people into stable networks, and at which historical junctures such attempts at integration repeatedly failed. Finally, Mann's reference to the only partially overlapping sources of power prevents any relapse into the holistic notion of society, because it provides an insight into the fact that some power networks may have a large radius of action, while others have only a small one. Thus, one cannot simply assume – as does reference to 'societies' (conceived on the basis of nation-states) – that political, economic, ideological and military power networks were and are always identical in scope. This simultaneously opens the door to current political-sociological debates, such as those concerned with the oft-cited 'globalization', as Mann's theory of power networks allows us to evaluate with much sophistication which networks are at present truly global and which are not.

(c) It was as a result of his preoccupation with history that Michael Mann had become alert to the significance of wars in the formation of 'societies', particularly modern Western 'societies'. The rulers or state administrations always played a key role in the creation of 'intra-societal' relations, primarily because states often went to war and the collection of taxes to this end involved massive intervention in the social structure. Mann thus rejects the 'endogenous' view of historical processes common within sociology, according to which societies develop predominantly or even exclusively on the basis of a particular internal logic (as the Parsonian theory of evolution assumes) or as a result of the progress of the forces of production (as Marxism claims). Instead, he demonstrates that it was frequently *exogenous* forces, such as the sudden effect of military force, that decisively moulded the nature of class formation and thus the overall structure of 'society'. This may seem excessive at first sight, but there are good reasons why the renowned German historian Thomas Nipperdey (1927–92) began his three-volume history of Germany (1800–1918) with the sentence 'In the beginning was Napoleon' (p. 1). Here, Nipperdey draws attention to the fact that one cannot understand early nineteenth-century German history without taking the role of the Napoleonic machinery of domination and its armies into account, because it was only *in response to this* that German 'society' began to mobilize and change – to 'modernize' – in unprecedented fashion. With his emphasis on the role of states and the wars triggered by them, Mann also laid the ground for the revision of an overly linear view of history common among sociologists and an overly harmonious interpretation of modernity, which had long predominated among those close to Parsons, and in many other quarters besides, but which was to be decisively rejected in some of the diagnoses of the contemporary era produced in the 1980s and 1990s (see Lecture XVIII).

At around the same time, John A. Hall (b. 1949), a friend of Michael Mann, made a name for himself within a historical-comparative field of research that privileged conflict theoretical arguments. Hall's 1985 book *Powers and Liberties: The Causes and Consequences of the Rise of the West* is a highly elegant comparison of civilizations; he went on to grapple with issues of international diplomacy, war and peace, from a sociological perspective (see for example *Coercion and Consent: Studies in the Modern State*). His aim in constructing many of his arguments is the same as that of Michael Mann, in as much as he too places the military role of the state in the genesis of the modern era centre stage.

Giddens follows the example of these authors, adopting many of their figures of thought. This was not, however, to be a smooth process, for Giddens quickly sees that the macrosociology propagated by Mann and Hall suffers from action theoretical deficiencies. Their work is incapable of achieving the *synthesis* of power and culture on which Lockwood had set his sights. To put it in highly simplified terms, Mann and Hall are almost exclusively theorists of conflict and power rather than culture. Michael Mann's work, for example, simply places economic power networks *alongside* ideological (cultural) ones, without going on to scrutinize the relationship *between* the two, to examine whether, for example, the economy as such can exist in the first place if it is not embedded ideologically and culturally. This was an ongoing concern not only of Max Weber but also of Talcott Parsons, as described in Lectures II and III; yet neither Mann's nor Hall's theoretical framework deals adequately with this topic. Giddens sees the need to correct these approaches, and this can only be done on the basis of thoroughgoing consideration of action theoretical issues. And he did not 'forget' the action theoretical roots of his arguments in his reflections on the theory of order; he was thus far more consistent than Habermas, who, he believed, and this tallies with our critique, influenced by Luhmann and Parsons, was too quick to embrace a functionalist and thus actor-less approach as he attempted to construct an adequate theory of order.

So much for the key influences on Giddens and the disciplinary context in which his writings originated. Before scrutinizing Giddens' theoretical position more closely, a few brief remarks on his career will provide you with a more vivid picture of this outstanding figure in contemporary British social science. Giddens, who spent key phases of his academic career at the elite English university of Cambridge and who was until recently director of the famous London School of Economics, was born in 1938, making him about ten years younger than his German 'competitors' Habermas and Luhmann. Like them, he displayed an astonishing degree of scholarly productivity while still relatively young. He started out as an innovative interpreter of the classical sociologists Durkheim and Weber; in this connection, he produced a textbook entitled *Capitalism and Modern Social Theory* in 1971 which was quite influential in the English-speaking world. From the very beginning, he also sought to come to terms with Talcott Parsons' theory and his interpretation of the history of sociology, with which Lecture II on *The Structure of Social Action* familiarized us. Giddens vehemently rejected Parsons' *normativist* theory of order and his assertion that classical sociological thought arose through a purely intra-theoretical process of grappling with utilitarianism. Giddens expounded a *political* interpretation and understood sociology in its early days – partly in light of its diagnoses of the modern era – as a response to the crisis of liberalism towards the end of the nineteenth century (see for example his essay 'Classical Social Theory and the Origins of Modern Sociology' from 1976).

As early as 1973, however, alongside these studies on the history of sociology, he produced a book on *The Class Structure of the Advanced Societies*, which has had a huge influence internationally. In this book, he gets to grips with the class theories of Marx and Weber, building on their work to analyse the class structure of both capitalist and state socialist societies. The developmental trends characteristic of the working and middle classes form a particular focus for him here. Giddens presents himself here as a left-wing social theorist, but one who, rather than 'clinging' to Marxian ideas in orthodox fashion, attempts to generate a productive fusion of Marxian *and* Weberian ideas – in line with the Weberian Marxism mentioned earlier. This book includes mention of a term which Giddens was later to make famous, that of 'structuration'. By this, Giddens wishes to underline the fact that, from a historical and empirical point of view, one can *only very rarely speak of fixed classes and class boundaries*; for the most part, what we find are *variable* 'stages' of class formation, influenced both by a society's mode of production as well as the degree of intergenerational mobility, which is potentially subject to change (see *Class Structure*, pp. 107ff.). Giddens initially used this concept of structuration solely in the context of class theory, but applied it to social processes very generally and provided it with an action theoretical foundation in the late 1970s and early 1980s, in order to shake up sociology's generally static conceptual apparatus. Giddens no longer refers to (fixed) structures, but to structur*ation*, pointing to the fact that dynamic processes are always at work in societies, that seemingly fixed structures come into existence and fade away and are continuously changed *by actors*. Here, he is taking up an idea popularized in the early 1960s by the English Marxist social historian E. P. Thompson which was to prove hugely influential, an idea expressed in the title of his most famous work, *The Making of the English Working Class*. Thompson referred quite consciously to the *making* rather than the *development* of the working class in order to indicate that class formation is a process actively driven by the actors rather than one which, as it were, unfolds automatically. The Marxist Thompson thus rejected the approach of those Marxist class theorists who place such great emphasis on structures (the relations of production) that they lose sight of acting subjects. Giddens adheres broadly to Thompson's approach in this respect, but generalizes his insights into the idea, consistent with action theory, that structures are both made *and* makeable in a general sense, an idea which Thompson related to processes of class formation; Giddens extends this to incorporate the idea of structur*ation*, which is constantly driven by actors, consciously *or* unconsciously. This is practically the exact opposite of the notion of systems and structures found in the work of Luhmann, with which you are already familiar, as well as that characteristic of structuralism, which we shall be looking at in Lecture XIV.

From the mid-1970s, Giddens begins to examine and critically analyse the various theoretical currents within sociology, ranging from ethnomethodology to symbolic interactionism (see for example *New Rules of Sociological Method* from 1976), from structuralism to German critical theory (see for example *Central Problems in Social Theory: Action, Structure and Contradiction in Social Analysis* from 1979). In the early 1980s, he published an analysis of historical materialism intended to run to several volumes but which has ultimately remained incomplete (*A Contemporary Critique of Historical Materialism. Vol. 1: Power, Property and the State*), which lays bare how strongly Giddens was influenced by the historical-sociological theory of power and conflict forming in Great Britain at the time.

His tremendous productivity in what appeared to be an excessive number of fields and his reception of highly disparate theoretical approaches, referred to above, gave him a reputation, from the late 1970s at the latest, as a mere commentator and highly eclectic theorist, whose work lacked internal cohesion and consistency. But Giddens managed to convincingly refute this criticism through the publication of a major systematic book, *The Constitution of Society: Outline of the Theory of Structuration,* which appeared in 1984, three years after Habermas' *The Theory of Communicative Action* and at the same time as Luhmann's *Social Systems*. In this book, Giddens undertook to weld together the various theories he had studied into a coherent framework; the following analysis of his theory thus draws largely upon this systematic magnum opus.

A year later, the second volume of his analysis of historical materialism appeared; *The Nation-State and Violence* is a weighty work of historical sociology that advances an interpretation of modernity in which political power plays a key role and which devotes particular attention to war.

In 1989, unusually for a high-ranking theorist, Giddens produced an 800-page textbook of sociology (*Sociology*). In the early 1990s, there then appeared a number of slimmer volumes on modernity (*The Consequences of Modernity*) and on identity in modern societies (*Modernity and Self-Identity: Self and Society in the Late Modern Age*; *Transformation of Intimacy*, 1992), which reached a broader public, but which are far less systematic and important for social theory than the work he produced in the mid-1980s: American sociologist Jeffrey Alexander coined the rather nasty term 'Giddens light'.

Giddens did in fact become more and more of a policy adviser. Close to Tony Blair, he was the key figure delineating the so-called 'Third Way', a renewed European social democracy, his various publications an attempt to reflect the political course of a moderate left that no longer believed in the state (see for example *Beyond Left and Right: The Future of Radical Politics* from 1994; and *The Third Way: The Renewal of Social Democracy* from 1998). It is fair to say that while Giddens' emergence as policy adviser made him even better known, especially on the international stage, it did little for his scholarly reputation. His most recent publications were too reminiscent of political pamphlets and too partial, while their sociological content left much to be desired. Nonetheless, his books, particularly those which appeared in the mid-1980s, remain milestones in the development of a synthetic social theory. (We return to his later writings and their diagnosis of the modern age in Lecture XVIII.)

We turn now to his systematic magnum opus, *The Constitution of Society*. In what follows, in order to avoid repeating points made in the previous lectures, we wish to present only those of Giddens' arguments which go beyond the theoretical positions discussed so far. In terms of *action theory*, at least six points are particularly worthy of note (on the following, see Joas, 'A Sociological Transformation of the Philosophy of Praxis: Anthony Giddens' Theory of Structuration').

1. Giddens' reception of ethnomethodology and symbolic interactionism in the 1970s influenced his work in that he adopted or modified many of the ideas developed by them. Crucial in this connection is the fact that he vehemently rejected the very first basic assumption of Parsons' action frame of reference. Parsons took the 'unit act' as his point of departure and tried to determine the elements of every action on this basis. Giddens sees this as the wrong place to start, though it was adopted by analytical philosophy and a whole number of other schools within the social sciences and humanities. As he sees it, action is not made up of atomistic individual acts, such that, for example, one discrete action is superseded by the next and these isolated acts could be analysed individually. Rather, Giddens asserts – and here he is able to draw on phenomenological and pragmatist-interactionist insights – that we must think of action holistically as an uninterrupted flow of action.

> Human action occurs as a *durée*, a continuous flow of conduct, as does cognition. Purposive action is not composed of an aggregate or series of separate intentions, reasons and motives. ... 'Action' is not a combination of 'acts': 'acts' are constituted only by a discursive moment of attention to the durée of lived-through experience.
>
> (*The Constitution of Society*, p. 3)

Only with hindsight, Giddens' thesis suggests, can we isolate individual acts through an intellectual effort and refer to (bounded) acts. But action, as it is being carried out, does not take this form. Rather, we must take the continuous flow of action as our starting point, the *durée*, a term borrowed from the French philosopher of life Henri Bergson (1859–1941).

With the aim of resisting a hyper-rationalist philosophy and psychology, Bergson had used this term in his doctoral thesis in 1889 to characterize the processes of our consciousness, to describe moments at which 'our ego lets itself live, when it refrains from separating its present state from its former states' (Bergson, *Time and Free Will*, p. 100). Bergson, certain aspects of whose work also influenced Edmund Husserl, the founder of phenomenology and philosophical progenitor of ethnomethodology, and William James, one of the founders of pragmatism, understood our consciousness not as the stringing together of isolated thoughts, but as a stream of experience in which cognitions blend into and fuse with one another rather 'as happens when we recall the notes of a tune, melting, so to speak, into one another. Might it not be said that, even if these notes succeed one another, yet we perceive them *in one another* …?' (ibid., p. 100; our emphasis). Bergson was particularly interested in the distortion which affects our subjective awareness of time when it is 'spatialized', that is, made subject to an objectivistic schema, namely that of physical time. Subsequently and as a result of his work, the topic of 'time', in the sense of subjectively experienced temporality, became a topos of post-1900 cultural criticism – in both literature (Marcel Proust) and philosophy (Martin Heidegger). Giddens was to adopt this idea – see the above quotation – but apply it to action as well. According to Giddens, precisely because Bergson was right to describe states of consciousness as *durée*, as a flow of pure duration which can be broken through and interrupted only by mental effort, it is insufficient to limit this idea to processes of *consciousness*. *Action* must also be understood in this way. Action is not acts strung together but a continuous flow halted only temporarily when obstacles crop up and which can be divided into discrete unit acts only in retrospect.

2. Giddens – much like ethnomethodology and symbolic interactionism – breaks with the idea that action is *preceded* by clear goals. This idea too is of course directed at Parsons' action frame of reference. But it is by no means only there that we find such a teleological conception of action. Parsons had described action in terms of goal realization: actors set themselves goals, which they set about achieving in light of situational factors, available means and above all prevailing norms and values. Giddens meanwhile emphasizes that the bulk of human action occurs *without* the preceding development of an intention. Intentionality is thus not something which is external to action, such that people first set themselves a goal and then act in order to achieve it. Rather, goals are often only formed *as people act*; it is

only as they act that actors become aware of the intentions welling up within them, intentions which are or may be revised again and again as the action occurs. Thus, for Giddens, intentionality means something different than in conventional action theory. He takes it to be the capacity for reflexive self-control within the process of action itself, the 'reflexive monitoring of action' as he puts it (*Constitution*, p. 3). The goals and intentions which individuals have settled upon are not simply realized through action. Rather, Giddens tells us, people are always looking over their shoulders, and thus observing themselves; in this process, they modify their goals and execute their actions differently. This is graphically expressed by the metaphor of 'monitoring'. In reality, action is thus a far more complex process than the typically evoked temporal sequence of 'goal-setting–action–achievement of goal' suggests.

This thesis that action *precedes* intention is probably one of the reasons why Giddens refrains from constructing a typology of action. It is no less than striking that he, who grappled so often and so explicitly with the early Parsons, and also with Habermas, quite consciously eschews such an endeavour: action clearly seems to him far too fluid a process for it to be meaningful to bring it to a standstill, as it were, by means of a typology. However, his decision to do without systematic consideration of the various 'paths' that action may take also entails certain dangers, evident, for instance, in his macrosociological analyses. For want of a sophisticated typology of action, he is occasionally led astray, his arguments expressing a one-dimensional theory of power which appears to leave very little room for the autonomy of culture (see p. 304 below).

3. Giddens departs from 'conventional' models of action in another, though closely related respect. He asserts not only that action often precedes the development of a clear-cut intention; he also calls into question an overly rationalistic conception of action that assumes that actors *consciously* control the action. Giddens takes the view that everyday life is governed largely by *routines*, by preconscious mechanisms. Action – Giddens' thesis suggests – always unfolds to a significant degree through routines and does so *inevitably*. It is his concern to liberate the concept of routine from its negative connotations and move away from the idea of an absolute opposition between autonomous, entirely transparent action on the one hand and opaque, lethargic action carried out in routinized fashion on the other. He wants to get away from the idea that 'autonomous action' and 'routine' form a mutually exclusive pair of opposites. This is most impressively apparent (see *Constitution*, pp. 60–4) in his remarks on situations of extreme crisis. Reports on concentration camp inmates describe how the total collapse of familiar everyday routines brought about by conditions in the camp rendered many prisoners utterly incapable of taking action, in a way that could not be explained solely as a result of the horrendous physical conditions.

The psychological shock of such disruption to one's routine made the already tremendous physical suffering far worse: death was sometimes due just as much to psychological as to physical suffering:

> The disruption and the deliberately sustained attack upon the ordinary routines of life produce a high degree of anxiety, a 'stripping away' of the socialized responses associated with the security of the management of the body and a predictable framework of social life. Such an upsurge of anxiety is expressed in regressive modes of behaviour, attacking the foundation of the basic security system grounded in trust manifested towards others. ... Ordinary day-to-day social life, by contrast ... involves an ontological security founded on an autonomy of bodily control within predictable routines and encounters.
>
> (ibid., pp. 63–4)

This means, then, that routines and the autonomy of action cannot be separated: it is only the maintenance of routines that ensures the potential for action. Thus, far from being solely or primarily constraining, routines in fact feature an enabling aspect. Though Giddens does not particularly emphasize or recognize this, he is very close here to American pragmatism, the philosophical school that informed symbolic interactionism, in as much as the pragmatists also referred constantly to the importance of 'habits' to people's capacity for action.

4. This emphasis on the routine character of human behaviour leads Giddens immediately on to another point passed over in most theories of action. When we speak of routines, of 'habits', we almost inevitably end up – see the above quote – talking about the *corporeality* of human beings and of human action as well. We know very well that much of the action we take in everyday life consists of quasi-automated physical movements. As children, we learn at some point to tie our shoelaces. When we perform this task as adults, we no longer think about how exactly one makes a bow. It is not us, but our hands that produce the bow – this task has become second nature or, as the German saying puts it so well, it has 'passed into our flesh and blood'. And everyday life features many such activities: it takes no more than a few moments of reflection to come up with a long list of them, from riding a bike to the coordinated movement of one's fingers at the computer keyboard. Giddens claims that it is wrong to draw a clear dividing line between mere movements of the body and 'real' action, as if one can talk of 'action' only if the bodily movements involved are controlled *consciously*. Rather, he emphasizes that the preconscious control of the body and action must be inseparably interwoven in the healthy and functioning human being. Studies of brain-damaged patients show that they are often incapable of using their own bodies in routinized fashion; they must, for

example, command their arm to stretch out and pick up an object. These patients have to consciously make their bodies carry out the most everyday movements, expending substantial amounts of energy in a way that the healthy person does not. People in good health do not generally have this kind of 'instrumental' relationship to their bodies. Rather, they *are* bodies; for them, action always takes place on the basis of routinized physical movements; action and such routinized movements are directly linked. Like American pragmatism (see Lecture VI), Giddens spurns the dualism of body and mind, of 'mere' movement and 'real' action; with much irony, he shows that this dualism is an apt description of the problems of the brain-damaged, but not of everyday human action. Another point follows on immediately from this.

5. Because Giddens' consideration of the concept of routine has brought him into contact with the topic of the human body, he is also significantly more willing than other theorists of action to recognize the *centrality of the body to human interaction*. Giddens underlines, for example, that the human body is no unity: anthropological and sociological studies have, he suggests, shown in many different ways the outstanding significance of the human face as a means of expression and communication as compared with other parts of the body. At the same time, expressions such as 'lose face' and 'keep face' demonstrate that facial expressions, gestures, expressive behaviour, etc., in as much as these depend on the facial features, have partly moral implications, and that it would thus be wrong in every respect to treat such bodily responses merely as insignificant components of communication. Giddens took a great deal from the American sociologist Erving Goffman (see Lecture VI), who displayed tremendous sensitivity to human expressive behaviour, always underlining the centrality of the physical presentation of the self in his studies. Giddens fully takes on board Goffman's insights, repudiating more or less explicitly theorists such as Habermas who reduce communication essentially to *linguistic* utterances. Processes of communication – according to Giddens – do not occur between intelligent machines who merely throw up certain validity claims. Rather, at least in the case of direct forms of communication, language is always closely intertwined with corporeality, with gestures and facial expressions; the meaningful content of the interaction is not seamlessly transformed into language. This is why the concept of 'copresence' is of key importance to Giddens' theory, because the actors – when they find themselves in conversation or in any kind of interaction with one another – are not merely disembodied intellects, but always bring their physicality with them. 'Copresence', the awareness of being seen and knowing that one's own seeing is also being observed by the other, is for Giddens *the* basic experience of human intersubjectivity, *the* elementary experience in comparison with which other forms of communication and interaction have a derived status.

6. Finally, Giddens, in contrast to Parsons, goes out of his way to underline the cognitive dimensions of action. Parsons' 'action frame' always had a peculiarly objectivizing slant in that it failed to investigate *how* the actors perceive the conditions of action. Parsons assumed that all actors see them just as they are. Giddens explicitly introduces the distinction between the acknowledged and unacknowledged conditions of action, thus characterizing actors, like Garfinkel and the ethnomethodologists, as 'knowledgeable actors' able to draw upon specific, though varying stocks of knowledge in everyday life. And Giddens also differentiates – see Lecture III – between different forms of unintended consequences of human action (*Constitution*, pp. 8ff.). But unlike certain functionalists (such as Robert Merton), he does not use the fact that unintended consequences of action exist as an argument for adopting a *functionalist* theory of order: they had opted for functionalism partly because – so they claimed – the existence of such unintended side-effects on a massive scale could be understood only as a process of subjectless reproduction adhering to the same unvarying pattern. For them, the market, for example, cannot be traced back solely to the intentional acts performed by the actors involved; rather, the impenetrable fusion of intended actions and their innumerable side-effects could be meaningfully captured only with the aid of the concept of system. But for Giddens – just as for rational choice theorists – this is not a convincing argument. He comes to radically different conclusions than the functionalists or system theorists. The very fact of inevitable unintended side-effects of every action – so Giddens tells us – blows a hole in the alleged functionality of so-called systems. Because new side-effects constantly crop up, the notion of *stable system conditions and thus every functionalist theory of order is highly problematic*. It is of course possible to identify structures, but these are in a permanent state of flux. They are never the same, but rather – very much in line with the idea of structuration – are constantly being reproduced in new forms by actors. Giddens thus refers to the 'duality of structure' to convey the notion that while structures have a constraining effect, they make action possible in the first place, and that while they appear to be solid constructions merely reproduced by actors, they are in fact constantly transformed by them.

So much for Giddens' theory of action and its characteristic features. The last of these mentioned above marks the point at which we pass from a theory of action to a theory of order, to asking which set of concepts allows us to capture the interconnection of the actions of several or many people. The specific features of Giddens' theory of order are as follows.

(A) Giddens, as we have suggested, is an anti-functionalist, and in a radical sense. He wrestled with functionalism as early as the 1970s and early 1980s, assimilating the epistemological arguments against this way of thinking (see Lecture III). He agrees with the criticism that functionalism features a peculiar conflation of causes and effects and implies causal relationships where none exist (Giddens, 'Commentary on the Debate'). But he does not rely solely on epistemology in making his criticism, but also brings empirical arguments into play. In his opinion, functionalism is wrong because it assumes that social relations are stable and that actors can do nothing about them. Giddens' notion of structuration is based on the contrary observation that the actors not only reproduce the structures, but also produce and change them. The functionalist notion of systems – his critique asserts – assumes that social structures are hyper-stable in a highly questionable way, an assumption that seems entirely unjustified and which also makes the analysis of historical *processes of change* unnecessarily difficult.

This does not mean that Giddens rejects entirely the concept of 'system' and its use in the social sciences. He fully recognizes that there are *also* highly stable patterns of action in the social world, that actors or even generations of actors perform the same actions time and again, thus producing highly stable structures which point to the need for the concept of system and justify its use. But this should not lead us to conclude that *all* social structures and processes exhibit such stability. In contrast to Parsons, who used an *analytical* concept of system, and Luhmann, who simply assumed in *essentialist* fashion that systems exist and thus works with his functionalist-systems theoretical toolkit without further justification, Giddens has an *empirical* understanding of systems: on this view, the concept of system is applicable only if the empirical conditions are such that one may assume a high 'degree of systemness' when observing a social phenomenon. In other words, only if one observes precisely and with absolute certainty that the interaction produces consequences which affect, via feedback loops, the initial conditions of the action carried out by the actors and which trigger the same forms of action again and again, can one truly speak of a 'system'. Such systems rarely occur in social reality. But even when they do:

> Social systems should be regarded as widely variable in terms of the degree of 'systemness' they display and rarely have the sort of internal unity which may be found in physical and biological systems.
>
> (*Constitution*, p. 377)

If it is impossible for Giddens to embrace a theory of order of a functionalist or systems theoretical persuasion, if at various points in his oeuvre he criticizes Habermas for incorporating into his theoretical architecture a functionalist theory of order in grossly uncritical fashion, merely juxtaposing it with his alternative conception of order based on the 'life-world', the question immediately arises as to what Giddens himself can offer in the way of an order theoretical 'replacement' for functionalism. It is a Giddens 'trademark' that he does in fact strive with great consistency to develop a theory of social order on the basis of action theory, that he does not attempt to supplement or even replace action theory with a subjectless systems theory. He is protected from such temptations by his concept of power, though this is a concept whose meaning jibes neither with everyday understanding nor with that of many other sociologists.

(B) We must begin by mentioning that Giddens ties the concept of power directly to that of action. This, as we are about to see, is not the obvious approach; but it is in line with Giddens' arguments, which are consistently anchored in action theory. For if one wishes to take individual actors and their actions as one's starting point, 'ascending' on this basis to ever more complex entities, one becomes almost automatically aware of the phenomenon of power, because several or many actors may be linked or integrated through power. This seems very abstract at first sight; we shall therefore proceed step by step in order to help you appreciate Giddens' thinking here.

The first thing to notice is that Giddens considers Max Weber's concept of power inadequate. Weber (*Economy and Society*, p. 53) defined power as follows: '"Power" [*Macht*] is the probability that one actor within a social relationship will be in a position to carry out his own will despite resistance, regardless of the basis on which this probability rests.' This means that Weber – to put it in terms of game theory – regards power as a zero-sum game: the sum of power remains ever the same; however much power one loses, another gains the same amount, and vice versa. Social scientists working with such a concept of power almost inevitably develop an intense and sometimes near-exclusive interest in the *distribution* of power. In the history of sociology, however, such a concept of power has encountered criticism, being regarded as inadequate. This unease was articulated most clearly by Talcott Parsons, who, as you know from Lecture IV, understood power as a kind of medium. Regardless of whether or not one considers this terminology felicitous, Parsons was surely right to claim that power can also be *accumulated or produced, without any of those involved in the power relationship necessarily losing*. Power, like capital, may increase when, for example, people in a group cooperate, achieving significantly more than any individual could have on her own. In this case, power is produced, power has been accumulated, despite the fact that no 'losers' can be singled out.

Giddens takes up this Parsonian idea, which can be found in much the same form in political philosophy – in the work of Hannah Arendt for instance (see, for example, *On Violence*) – and develops a particular interest in the *production* of power. He underlines, in a genuinely

Giddensian move, that *every* action is linked with power. This, he suggests, is apparent even at the level of etymology, in that there is an identity between the words for 'power' and 'to do' in certain languages. In French, 'pouvoir' means both 'power' and 'to be able (to do)'; in English, 'power' refers both to the capacity to influence the course of events as well as to physical 'strength' and to 'abilities'. 'To act' and 'to have power' – so Giddens tells us – thus both refer to the ability to 'intervene in the world' (*Constitution*, p. 14).

> Action depends on the capability of the individual to 'make a difference' to a pre-existing state of affairs or course of events. An agent ceases to be such if he or she loses the capability to 'make a difference', that is, to exercise some sort of power. ... Expressing these observations in another way, we can say that action logically involves power in the sense of transformative capacity. In this sense, the most all-embracing meaning of 'power', power is logically prior to subjectivity, to the constitution of the reflexive monitoring of conduct.
>
> (ibid., pp. 14–15)

This equation of acting and power also means that situations of absolute powerlessness are practically inconceivable. Here, Giddens has produced an insight that many sociological analyses of power and domination risk passing over, namely the fact that subordinates and those subject to power also have very substantial room for manoeuvre and that the rulers are dependent on the cooperation of the ruled should they wish to realize their goals. In this sense, the ruled too always have power; they can 'make a difference' through their action, at the very least pushing the ruler, who is to some extent dependent on them, in a particular direction. Thus, the ruler's potential to control people is never absolute, and Giddens rightly refers to a 'dialectic of control' or 'dialectic of domination', to capture the way in which 'the less powerful manage resources in such a way as to exert control over the more powerful in established power relationships' (ibid., p. 374).

This idea, which has incidentally always played a special role in literature and philosophy as well (one need only think of Diderot's late novel *Jacques the Fatalist and His Master* or the dialectic between servant and master described by Hegel in *Phenomenology of Spirit*), must certainly not be overstated, because the idea of the power of the ruled might perhaps tempt us all too easily into describing total institutions such as the prison and particularly the concentration camp in normatively problematic ways. On the other hand, we know from the analyses of Goffman and the symbolic interactionists that life in institutions, even in total institutions, is always 'negotiated' to some degree ('negotiated order' – again, see Lecture VI), and thus that two parties are always involved in the concrete organization of institutions and in the processes which occur within them; the ruled also have at least some room for manoeuvre at their disposal, however limited – they have 'power'.

It will come as no surprise that Giddens – very much in the tradition of conflict theory and in much the same way as Michael Mann – believes power to be based on more than just economics. Rather, Giddens uses a *multidimensional* concept of power, recognizing that positions of power may rest on various types of resource (he distinguishes between 'allocative' and 'authoritative' resources as ideal types), which may of course be economic, but also political, military or, we must bear in mind, knowledge-based. Giddens makes much of this last point, which surely owes a great deal to the work of the French theorist Michel Foucault (see Lecture XIV); rather than regarding knowledge and stocks of knowledge, ways of speaking, etc. as neutral or 'innocent', Giddens, like Foucault, sees them as possible means of structuring relations among people, and this may well mean structuring them in an *unequal* way.

So much for the outlines of Giddens' idea of 'power', which is still highly abstract. We emphasized earlier that Giddens' concept of power was defined as it was and equated with action in part because he attempted to develop a theory of order *from a consistently action theoretical perspective*. What exactly does this mean?

Giddens' way of tackling this problem takes some getting used to in certain respects, because he departs from the traditional style of theorizing with which we are familiar from the preceding lectures, but at the same time uses terms which you have met already but whose meaning has often been changed radically. This applies particularly to the conceptual duo of 'social integration' versus 'system integration' to which Habermas and Lockwood had already alluded, a conceptual toolkit of crucial importance to Giddens' theory of order. While Habermas and Lockwood, as different as their definitions may be in this regard, are at least in agreement that these two aspects must be grasped with the aid of different theoretical tools (issues of social integration with action theoretical tools, issues of system integration with functionalist ones), Giddens resists such theoretical dualism. In his opinion, there is no need to draw on functionalist analysis to develop an order theoretical framework. Rather, it is possible to construct a consistent action theoretical argument only if one makes proper use of insights into the connection between action and power.

Giddens had linked his concept of action, in contrast to other theorists of action, above all Habermas, very strongly to human corporeality, emphasizing in particular expressive behaviour, facial expressions and self-presentation in light of Goffman's insights. He thus attributes a special importance to immediate 'face-to-face' interaction, because this corporeality has a direct impact here. By 'social integration', Giddens understands the linkage between the acts of actors sharing the same space who are thus observing one another, that is, the linkage between acts in circumstances of *copresence*. In this thematic context, Giddens takes up to a large extent the order theoretical ideas of ethnomethodology and symbolic interactionism. He does not consider it necessary to refer to norms as did Parsons or the mutual modification of validity claims as did Habermas, in order to explain stable co-existence in circumstances of copresence. Order theoretical ideas of this kind seem to him either too superficial (as in the case of Parsons) or overly rationalistic (as in the case of Habermas). In contrast, he stresses that order is established at a deeper level, through the intelligibility of symbolic expression (both linguistic *and* physical) and through trust in the rationality of the everyday world (see again our remarks on the order theoretical arguments made by the ethnomethodologists in Lecture VII).

Things become interesting and truly innovative only when Giddens turns to the linkage of actions *beyond spatio-temporal distance* – actions carried out in situations in which the actors are *not* copresent. Here, what Giddens calls the problem of 'system integration' arises. He is no longer able to draw on conventional theories of order because the ethnomethodologists and interactionists, with their predominantly microsociological orientation, provided few convincing solutions, while Habermas, not to mention of course 'genuine' systems theorists, deployed the highly problematic functionalist toolkit, which Giddens rejects. How does he himself proceed?

Space and time play a key role in Giddens' distinction between 'social integration' and 'system integration'. But while the nature of the linkage is different because actors (must) act differently in circumstances of copresence than of absence, this does not compel us to take leave of action theory. Quite the reverse – and here, Giddens' reflections follow those of Michael Mann. One needs only to examine historically how people's or groups' capacity for action has changed over time, which technologies have developed to link people even across vast spatio-temporal distances, what capacities for power – and here the idea of the *production* or *accumulation* of power comes into play – have developed in different cultures in this regard. The concept of power, which is linked with action, is entirely sufficient to elucidate macrosociological realities; according to Giddens, we require no functionalist argument here.

Giddens develops his approach here in particularly graphic form in his *The Nation-State and Violence*, a book we mentioned earlier and which appeared a year after *The Constitution of Society*. In this work, whose main arguments are historical in nature, Giddens analyses the technical and technological prerequisites for early state formation in settings such as Mesopotamia, placing particular emphasis on the role of written records or writing, which made it possible to establish long-term domination in the first place. As he sees it, the invention of writing was a basic condition of the power-based integration of large numbers of people, because the storage of information was vital to the functioning of state administrations.

> Writing provides a means of coding information, which can be used to expand the range of administrative control exercised by a state apparatus over both objects and persons. As a mnemonic device, even the simplest form of the marking of signs makes possible the regular ordering of events and activities which could not be organized otherwise. Storage of information allows both for the standardizing of a certain range of happenings and, at the same time, allows them to be more effectively co-ordinated. A list is a formula that tallies objects or persons and can order them relative to one another. This is perhaps the most elementary sense in which writing, even in its simplest guise, enhances time-space distanciation, that is, makes possible the stretching of social relations across broader spans of time and space than can be accomplished in oral cultures.
>
> (*The Nation-State and Violence*, pp. 44–5)

The capacity to record information in written form facilitated a significant degree of 'surveillance' – a term which Giddens borrows from Foucault; state formation became conceivable for the first time. And the development of information storage and processing – in accordance with the insight that knowledge is power – was to play a crucial role throughout subsequent history. As Giddens shows with respect to the development of the early modern European state, printing, for example, facilitated a further major step in the production of power. The rulers in the emerging absolutist state were now as never before able to collect information, to control it and to construct centralized administrations in an entirely novel way in order to rule their subjects. In the age of nation-states – on the basis of a technology that was essentially already known – all this was merely further refined.

In this connection, one may of course wonder what the consequences of the spread of *computer technology* may be for power structures in contemporary states. Giddens himself does not systematically tackle this topic, but he would – in line with his thesis of the 'dialectic of domination' – surely reject the notion of a *one-sided* increase in domination. Despite the fact that the power of the centralized state certainly increased in the era of absolutism and in the age of the nation-states, the capacities of religious and political groups also grew (one need only think of the English dissenters or the intellectual circles of Enlightenment Europe with their critique of domination); these groups too made full use of the power of the printed word, and were thus able to produce counter-power. In much the same way, it is also possible to discern a contemporary 'dialectic' between the computer-aided power of state administrations and a counter-power held by social groups, based on the internet, which can never be fully controlled.

It is thus entirely possible – according to Giddens – to describe the linkage of actions carried out by large numbers of people across space and time on the basis of action theory. And one has no need of an actorless theory of order as provided by functionalism in order to do so. Indeed, such a functionalist theory of order is just what we do not need, as it is incapable of capturing the fluidity of social structures and the reality of the dialectic of domination and control, which is nothing more than an always precarious process of negotiation between various actors and groups of actors. This fact simply cannot be reconciled with the idea of solid structures and systems.

(C) These remarks on the long-range spatio-temporal concatenation of actions, the linkage of micro- and macro-structures with the aid of the concept of power, point to a special theory of order through which Giddens clearly sets himself apart from the ideas of Parsons, for example. For *macrosocial* order is not brought about through the pacification of conflicts of interest by means of norms and values. For Giddens, the problem of order arises at a more fundamental level. In this, his thinking resembles that of Garfinkel and Luhmann. However, the fact that Giddens, in his call for the temporal dimension of social processes to be taken into account, conceptually muddles the subjective experience of time and the objective temporality of processes (such as the variability of urban traffic flows at different times of the day) may be considered rather unfortunate. In any event, on this basis Giddens, very much like Michael Mann, pays particular attention to the technological mechanisms and resources, to the means of transport and communication, which make it possible to bind together large numbers of people in the first place. Norms, meanwhile, though not unimportant, are ultimately a secondary concern, because norms or values can be shared only *on the condition* that people are linked in extensive fashion (a linkage which is dependent on certain technologies). Values, ideologies, cultural patterns, etc. can be spread only on the basis of certain power capacities, in such a way that they affect not only a few people and groups but the majority of the population.

Logically enough, Giddens, like Mann, then bids farewell to the concept of society as central or fundamental to sociology, because one must first study history empirically to determine how stable networks formed between people on the basis of particular means of transport and communication, whether different networks overlapped, such that social structures developed featuring genuine, clear-cut spatial boundaries, etc. Like Mann, he warns against any assumption that premodern political structures were constituted in any way like the modern nation-state with its relatively homogeneous culture, policed boundaries, etc. Earlier empires and systems of domination looked quite different. There was no question of a relatively homogeneous culture if for no other reason than because no means of communication existed capable of spreading such a culture among large numbers of people, and there were also no clearly drawn boundaries: premodern empires tended to 'fray' at the edges. Power networks became increasingly weak on the periphery, far from the centre of the core polity. Even in ancient times, of course, there were political structures in which power was highly concentrated, the city-states being a prime example. But the transition from the absolutist state to the modern nation-state brought with it a further massive increase in the capacity for power, determined in part by the development of markets, industrial technology, the increasing administrative capacity of the state, that is, its ability to administer and monitor a large number of people, and above all by the interplay of all these factors:

> the modern state, as nation-state, becomes in many respects the pre-eminent form of power container, as a territorially bounded (although internally highly regionalized) administrative unity.
>
> (ibid., p. 13)

Reference to 'society' and its implicit conflation with the modern nation-state – so Giddens tells us – merely obscures the question of which specific features characterize this nation-state and set it apart from earlier 'forms of sociation'.

Here, though, Giddens wishes to take his leave not only of the concept of 'society'; he also wants to bid farewell, as indeed he must do, to the notion of a uniform and all-pervasive logic to which the processes within macro-structures are supposedly subject. With respect to modern (Western) nation-states, he considers, for example, the Marxian interpretation of modern Western 'societies' as 'capitalist societies' wrong simply because this characterization implies that social life features only one power resource on which all others depend – namely the economy. According to Giddens, however, it is empirically invalid to attempt to conceive of the functioning of these modern nation-states exclusively in terms of an economic logic and thus to reduce all other forms of power to this particular logic. Rather, Giddens takes the view that modernity and thus the nation-states were and are typified by a field of tension formed by various institutional complexes. In line with his distinction between several forms of power, which are based on specific resources and rules, he differentiates between the complexes of 'capitalism, industrialism and state system' (ibid., pp. 287ff.): the dynamic of *capitalism* was certainly an important point of departure in the rise of the modern age, but this dynamic was and is different from that of *technology*, which led to *industrial modernity*, as evident in the fact that industrialization was also possible in a *non*-capitalist context such as the Soviet Union and its sphere of influence. Again, the system of nation-states cannot be traced back either to industrialism or capitalism, but rather developed its own, dual dynamic. First, since the French Revolution at the latest, within the emerging European concert of nation-states (plural), a tremendous *military dynamic* arose which shaped the modern age at the most fundamental level. Giddens – again, in much the same way as Michael Mann – has developed a much stronger sense for the role of macrosocial violence than did Habermas or Luhmann, in whose theories this aspect plays as good as no role, an especially strange fact with respect to *German* theorists, in light of the enormous role played by state violence in the history of 'their society'. Second, the administrative apparatuses with their surveillance techniques, which, significantly, made possible the totalitarian forms of domination that typified the twentieth century, also developed their own dynamic, one which, once again, cannot be reduced either to industrial, capitalist or military processes.

Time after time, according to Giddens, individuals and groups have defended themselves against the danger that civil society might be overpowered by an omnipotent state, so that movements for democracy can be understood first and foremost as a consequence of the modern nation-state's administrative penetration of social relations. However, critics may question whether democracy can be understood solely in light of a dialectic of power and counter-power. When all is said and done – and the fact that Giddens has opted not to formulate a typology of action proves problematic here – ideas of equal rights, equality, the right to contribute to political decisions, fairness, etc. surely also have their cultural roots, and while processes of democratization are dependent on power structures, they cannot be adequately explained *by these alone*. It is evident here that Giddens' synthesis of power and culture is probably no more than half-successful, that his analytical focus – for all his action theoretical sophistication – is aimed too much at power as an aspect of action and not enough at its embedding in culture.

And yet, while Giddens draws heavily on Foucault in his use of the concept of 'surveillance' so important to his macrosociology, he is always at pains to reject Foucault's actorless conception of theory – and for this he deserves credit. Foucault's analyses, which we will be discussing in Lecture XIV, never identified the actors who use or advance the techniques of power; in other words, in the work of Foucault, power 'wanders' through history, but was not to be pinned down and classified, which is unacceptable to consistent action theorists such as Giddens. Further, in his analyses of power, Foucault always ran the risk of massively exaggerating the efficacy of power, because, at least until his late work, he had no real theoretical interest in actors and their actions. As Foucault sees it, the body was and is merely the object of techniques of power, an object profoundly moulded by techniques of power and discipline and which lacks any real subjectivity. Giddens, meanwhile, does not go this far; for him, actors always have the capacity to take action, and can thus – very much in line with the 'dialectic of domination' – always rebel, protest and struggle (see *Constitution*, p. 289). Giddens captures this contrast with Foucault by memorably declaring that Foucault's 'bodies' had no 'faces' – nothing in them looks back, showing the irreducible 'subjectivity' of these 'objects'.

The difference between Giddens and Luhmann is again apparent here. It may have occurred to you that Giddens' reference to the tensions between institutional complexes exhibits a certain similarity to Luhmann's radical thesis of the functional differentiation of modern societies, according to which the individual subsystems function exclusively in accordance with their own logic, no common code or common language exists and they can thus only be disturbed or irritated. The difference between the two theorists, however, is that Giddens considers such a *radical* separation between the institutional complexes or (sub)systems empirically implausible. Furthermore, and this is the crucial point, he makes the setting of boundaries between the complexes a matter for *the actors*: it is the actors who, however consciously or unconsciously, however perceptively or misguidedly, determine the internal logic of the institutional complexes and the boundaries between them.

This brings us to the end of this lecture, as well as to Giddens' ideas on social change. In our discussion of his theory of order, we mentioned that Giddens espouses a radically anti-functionalist approach. With respect to theories of change, functionalist thought was greatly inspired by evolutionary theory. There are, however, very different versions of evolutionary theory, quite apart from the fact that its further development occurred within a variety of disciplines. Parsons' evolutionary reflections (see Lecture IV), for instance, were guided by the idea of an alleged master process of 'differentiation', though, in line with his four-function scheme, he also identified other aspects of change such as 'adaptive upgrading', 'value generalization' and 'inclusion'. It can be fairly stated that subsequent sociological theories of evolution added little to this; one may in fact wonder whether Luhmann's evolutionary theses on social change constituted a step backwards from Parsons' insights, in that Luhmann's exclusive insistence on the topic of functional differentiation tended to airbrush out these other aspects of Parsonian theory. What is more, it remains very unclear in Luhmann's work who or what drives functional differentiation – other than the unique logic of intra-system communication, which he describes in strangely vague terms.

Because Giddens breaks radically with functionalism and is at most willing to countenance an empirical concept of system, asserting time and again that the acknowledged and unacknowledged, intended and unintended side-effects of actions disrupt the functionality of almost every system, he has little time for the idea of the 'evolution' of (social) systems driven by endogenous mechanisms. He is aware that actors are 'knowledgeable actors' who use various power resources to achieve their goals in specific and constantly changing ways. He is thus sceptical about the idea that history can be crammed into a linear (evolutionist) narrative. Precisely because of actors' resourcefulness and above all the side-effects of their actions, which can never be foreseen, history will always feature turning points and new beginnings, after which it may be possible to observe a continuous development – *for a time*. But because radical discontinuities may always occur, Giddens espouses a conception of history and change which he calls 'episodic'. According to him, episodes or epochs are all that can be delineated with a fair degree of clarity and coherence, but not the history of humanity as a whole in the sense of a unified narrative guided by evolutionary theory. It is impossible to identify specific 'master processes' (such as differentiation) or unambiguous examples of causality (such as the Marxist notion of class struggle) capable of adequately capturing this complex human history:

> there are no keys that will unlock the mysteries of human social development, reducing them to a unitary formula, or that will account for the major transitions between societal types in such a way either.
>
> (ibid., p. 243)

Social change is thus a far too convoluted process for us to describe, let alone explain it, through simple formulas. This also applies to the process of globalization, debated so intensely from the early 1990s in both the public sphere and the academy. Giddens, in keeping with his theoretical conception, understands globalization not primarily as an economic, but rather as a multidimensional process to be captured with the help of spatio-temporal categories:

> the concept of globalisation is best understood as expressing fundamental aspects of time-space distanciation. Globalisation concerns the intersection of presence and absence, the interlacing of social events and social relations 'at distance' with local contextualities. We should grasp the global spread of modernity in terms of an ongoing relation between distanciation and the chronic mutability of local circumstances and local engagements.
>
> (*Modernity and Self-Identity*, pp. 21–2)

It is not only global economic structures coming up against local contexts that change the world and how those affected perceive this world. Immigrants and refugees, long-haul tourism and the media also bring together contexts which used to be more or less 'reliably' separated – with incalculable consequences for personal identity. In light of this, Giddens elaborates on his diagnosis of the present era; because his ideas in this regard are palpably close to those of German sociologist Ulrich Beck, we shall discuss them in Lecture XVIII.

All in all, it is impossible to deny that Giddens' 'episodic' conception of history and change generates insights lacking in the often excessively linear evolutionary constructions, especially given that the role of macro-violence on a massive scale, which Mann and Giddens emphasize so often, undoubtedly provides further evidence of the *discontinuous* character of the historical process. At the same time, one may wonder whether Giddens' general critique of evolutionary theories is overdrawn in that people themselves constantly try to assure themselves about their history and try to see their life path as meaningful. They interpret 'the past in the light of a projected future for the purpose of interpreting and controlling the present' (Joas, 'A Sociological Transformation', p. 184); historical continuity is not a mere invention of sociologists or theorists, but is 'made' by subjects as well.

However much we may repudiate the search for a definitive formula capable of explaining history, there is no getting away from the need to integrate various pasts into a *single* history (see Lecture XVI on Ricoeur).

Our account of the attempts at theoretical synthesis made by Habermas, Luhmann and Giddens has familiarized you with the most influential writings in this field from the 1970s and 1980s. Later on, we shall be looking at other theoretical endeavours dating from this period as well as later developments. But first, in the following lecture, we get to grips with neo-Parsonianism. The authors to whom this label applies either lean heavily on the 'traditional' Parsonian theoretical framework, believing, despite all the criticisms made of Parsons, that his work represents in principle the 'correct' approach; or they specialize in macrosociological topics in a way that, while allowing systematic reflection on a theory of social change and perhaps even a theory of social order, makes work on the theory of action seem less pressing than it did in the writings of Parsons and later that of Habermas, Giddens and Luhmann. A contemporary theoretical synthesis, however, must surely keep pace with the insights generated by these three theorists.

XIII

The renewal of Parsonianism and modernization theory

In the preceding four lectures we outlined the most important attempts at synthesis made in the 1970s and 1980s; these aimed to fuse differing theoretical traditions and advance to a new grand theory à la Parsons. Do not let this lead you to false conclusions. Our claim that the centre of theoretical gravity shifted to Europe from around 1970 is not meant to imply that American sociology subsequently played no role at all theoretically. And our observation that Parsons was sharply criticized by neo-utilitarians, symbolic interactionists, ethnomethodologists and conflict theorists does not mean that the edifice of Parsonian thought lost all its appeal in the 1970s and 1980s. Rather, it became apparent that his highly comprehensive, multilayered, if sometimes inconsistent work offered a good deal of room for differing interpretations, enabling followers of Parsons to pursue their own paths, more or less independent of the thought of the 'master'. Above all, Parsons' *theory of social change* offered much scope for comprehensive revision. Parsons himself had in fact never stopped developing his ideas in this field (see Lecture IV). Yet because his evolutionary arguments became increasingly abstract, he could only go so far. The historical vagueness of such constructions generally held little appeal for those sociologists intent on serious empirical work.

This was the point of departure of so-called *modernization theory*, which can be understood only in light of Parsons' work but which was at variance with it in crucial respects. What is modernization theory? Simply put (on what follows, see Knöbl, *Spielräume der Modernisierung*, pp. 32f.), this was a theory of social change that attempted to grasp the developmental history of societies through comparative historical analysis. The assumptions were that

(a) modernization is a *global process* which began with the industrial revolution in Europe in the mid-eighteenth century (or perhaps even earlier), but which now increasingly affects all societies and is irreversible;
(b) historical development, that is, the process of modernization, *proceeds from so-called 'traditional' to 'modern' societies*, a sharp antithesis being assumed between modernity and tradition;
(c) in the traditional societies and countries of the Third World, personalistic attitudes, values and role structures dominate which – closely following Parsons' pattern variables (see Lecture III) – can be summed up

through terms such as *ascription, particularism* and *functional diffuseness* and which are to be interpreted as hindrances to economic and political development;
(d) in contrast, the modern societies of the European and North American cultural area are defined in terms of *achievement-related* and *universalist* values and *functionally specific* role patterns;
(e) the social changes leading to modernity will occur in relatively uniform and linear fashion in the various countries.

To put it even more simply: the goal of modernization theory was to provide a historical explanation for the rise of capitalist economics and democratic politics in Western Europe and North America while shedding light on the prerequisites for economic growth and democratization in *other* parts of the world. The whole system of ideas was designed to produce a macro-theory capable of competing with Marxism. Modernization theory countered the rigid Marxist concept of base–superstructure with the significantly more flexible theoretical toolkit of 'pattern variables'. These were inherently *multi*dimensional in nature, making it possible to capture the interplay between the great complexes of economy–politics–culture in a non-reductionist way. In contrast to the economism of the Marxian approach, no basic conceptual or theoretical assumptions were made regarding the causal primacy of economy, politics or culture.

In the 1950s and early 1960s, a theoretical construction of this kind was attractive for four reasons. First, for sociology more narrowly conceived, in contrast to Parsons' rather abstract writings, this approach was sufficiently concrete to provide a genuine basis for empirical work. Further, in the 1950s Parsons had yet to fully work out his ideas on social change; his theory of evolution was developed only in the following decade. The appeal of modernization theory lay, first of all, in the fact that it provided, for the first time, a universal and practicable theory of change, which could claim at least as much plausibility as Marxism. Second, by drawing on Parsons' pattern variables, modernization theorists could claim to be preserving the legacy of the classical figures of sociology. For as you will recall, Parsons produced his 'pattern variables' in order to provide a more nuanced understanding of the dichotomous concepts (*Gemeinschaft* versus *Gesellschaft*, 'mechanical' versus 'organic' solidarity, etc.) that cropped up so often in the work of the founding fathers of sociology, laying bare all their diversity and inherent contradictions. By drawing on Parsons' pattern variables, modernization theorists could claim, seemingly with justification, to have ensured the survival of the classical figures' undoubtedly still valid insights within the 'new' theory. What was overlooked here, though, was the fact that Parsons had ultimately formulated his pattern variables in order to *get beyond* those dichotomies, because he believed that while the classical figures were certainly on to something, social reality was far too complex to be grasped by means of such simple pairs of opposites. When modernization theorists stated that history could be described as a process through which 'traditional' societies became 'modern', with ascriptive, particularistic and functionally diffuse attitudes and role structures being replaced by achievement-related, universalistic and functionally specific ones, they ended up with the very dichotomies Parsons wished to avoid. But these differences from Parsons were generally papered over; modernization theory seemed too seductive, too elegant, to take seriously such nitpicking objections. In their own view, most modernization theorists stood firmly within the tradition of Parsons – a view which remained uncontested for so long in part because Parsons did relatively little to explicitly distance himself from modernization theory. Third, for the social sciences as a whole, and not just for sociology more narrowly understood, modernization theory was so interesting because it was conceived as an interdisciplinary approach. And its particular version of the 'pattern variables' did indeed appear both useful and inspiring to historians, political scientists, economists, psychologists and sociologists. Modernization theory thus entailed the promise of truly interdisciplinary social scientific research practice. Fourth, this theory also promised to be highly relevant to practice, the idea being that one could steer developmental processes in the non-Western world with the help of its insights.

The origins of modernization theory did in fact lie in a very specific 'practical' context; it was in a sense a response to attempts by the US government under President Truman to combat the influence of the Soviet Union in the countries of what was later called the 'Third World'. To this end, the American administration produced a major plan aimed at stabilizing these countries in 1949; they were to be supported economically to prevent them from coming under the influence of communism – in as much as they had not done so already. A kind of global Marshall Plan was called into being intended to help the poor non-European nations to advance economically with the aid of American money and know-how. Yet it rapidly became apparent that the work of development workers and experts in Latin America, Asia and Africa was not as straightforward as initially expected. Well-intended attempts to help often came to grief due to linguistic, and to an even greater extent cultural and social barriers, which must somehow be overcome without anyone quite knowing how. Social scientific experts were then drafted in; debates on the causes of developmental barriers started up, and certain argumentational patterns, drawing on the corpus of Parsonian theory, soon emerged with particular force. A dynamic notion of development based on the 'pattern variables' became the theoretical model thought most capable of describing, and explaining, processes of social change. This theoretical interpretation immediately triggered extensive interdisciplinary research which looked beyond the confines of the Western world at places in which systematic research had been almost inconceivable just a few years before. While Max Weber and Emile Durkheim had certainly tackled non-European topics, such as the economic ethics of the world religions or the world views of the native peoples of Australia and North America, they relied entirely on empirical research carried out by non-sociologists. With modernization theory, all this changed. The social sciences, sociology in particular, opened up both culturally and geographically, holding out the promise of relevance to practice: the analysis of obstacles to development in the 'poor' countries, performed using the tools of empirical social research, was to provide the key to overcoming them.

A number of important studies, among the magna opera of modernization theory and indeed of post-war sociology itself, were produced in the late 1950s and early 1960s: Robert Bellah's *Tokugawa Religion* from 1957, Daniel Lerner's *The Passing of Traditional Society* from 1958, Seymour Martin Lipset's (1922–2006) *Political Man* from 1959, Neil J. Smelser's *Social Change in the Industrial Revolution*, published in 1959, Walt Rostow's (1916–2003) *The Stages of Economic Growth* from 1960, David McClelland's (1917–98) *The Achieving Society* from 1961 and Gabriel Almond's (1911–2003) and Sidney Verba's (b. 1932) *The Civic Culture* from 1963 – works penned by sociologists and political scientists, economists and psychologists, whose arguments, though diverging in the details, were broadly in line with the five points identified above.

To give you a better idea of what our remarks so far, which have remained rather abstract, mean in reality, we shall briefly introduce you to the work of Daniel Lerner (1917–80), who both used the term 'modernization' itself in the sub-title of his book, greatly contributing to its popularization, and expounded a relatively simple, some would say simplistic, theoretical model.

According to Lerner, life in modern societies depends on a vast array of prerequisites. In order to be able to play any kind of active part in what goes on in a modern society, people require a high degree of psychological mobility (*The Passing of Traditional Society*, p. 202), a specific emotional state which Lerner calls 'empathy'. By this he means the capacity to think and act according to abstract criteria, in order to escape the narrow personal and familial horizons so typical of traditional societies. Modern societies function in line with certain principles, and because this is the case, the resignation to one's fate apparently so typical of traditional societies must be ruptured, just as the narrow, obstructive ties, generally to patriarchal family and kinship structures, must be overcome. For Lerner, 'empathy' is the only means of escaping the constraints of traditional society and understanding oneself as an *active member* of a modern society:

> Traditional society is nonparticipant – it deploys people by kinship into communities isolated from each other and from a center; without an urban–rural division of labor, it develops few needs requiring economic interdependence; lacking the bonds of interdependence, people's horizons are limited by locale and their decisions involve only other known people in known situations. Hence, there is no need for a transpersonal common

doctrine formulated in terms of shared secondary symbols – a national 'ideology' which enables persons unknown to each other to engage in political controversy or achieve 'consensus' by comparing their opinions.

(ibid., p. 50)

Lerner thus elaborated in great detail the mental or psychological characteristics of modern people or of those receptive to modernity. What he thought he had found in the Middle East in the 1950s were traditional societies that, while on the whole relatively static, showed the first stirrings of a modern dynamism. According to Lerner, such dynamic centres can be found predominantly in major urban conglomerations or nearby. Here, he asserts, we find the prerequisites for the development of (modern) psychological mobility. Lerner's rather simple thesis was that empathy-inducing knowledge and corresponding role models are nurtured only in places where mass media (newspapers, radio, etc.) are used to a sufficient degree, in other words within the sphere of influence of the major cities, with their media infrastructure. Lerner thought the ability to read and write was one of the, if not *the* key means of enhancing the psychological mobility of the general population. As the developmental process ran its course, particularly in cities, oral and direct forms of communication would increasingly be supplemented and to some extent replaced by modern mass media, making the proliferation of these media both an index of and a causal factor in the psychological change undergone by members of society as well as change affecting the entire society (ibid., p. 196).

While Lerner's theory of modernization was relatively simple in character and other authors were to argue in a more nuanced way, the idea that societies developed over time from 'traditional' into 'modern' was constitutive of the work of all theorists of modernization, not least because this figure of thought lent credence to progressive hopes of steering the development of non-European countries through the tight interplay of theory and practice.

But the paradigm of modernization theory, as outlined above with reference to the five key characteristics, was not to survive for terribly long. When all is said and done, its heyday lasted only around fifteen years. As early as the late 1960s, the criticisms directed at it became so severe that other macrosociological paradigms rose to prominence (see further below), ending the pre-eminence of modernization theory in describing and explaining large-scale processes of social change. There are various interpretations of why modernization theory so quickly became the target of criticism and was thus marginalized. Perhaps the most common goes back to Jeffrey Alexander ('Modern, Anti, Post, and Neo: How Social Theories Have Tried to Understand the "New World" of "Our Time"'), a student of Parsons whom we shall be taking a closer look at later on in this lecture. He claimed that modernization theory was, as it were, a victim of the *Zeitgeist*. It was in good working order and adaptable, but with the student rebellions of the late 1960s, a politicization of the social sciences had set in, as a result of which modernization theory lost all its appeal to the younger generation.

Modernization theory did in fact embody an unambiguous vision of 'modernity'; it presented the system of institutions and values as developed in various permutations in the Euro-American world as desirable. In line with this, the 'modernization' of the so-called Third World was seen as a process which would and should somehow bring it closer to this 'modern' institutional and value complex. But, as Alexander sees it, it was precisely this notion which the leftist student movement now set its sights on; to pursue this notion in the political climate spreading through the social science faculties of (American) universities no longer seemed opportune. The demonstrations and protests against the war in Vietnam and American imperialism, against the oppression of Blacks in America itself, etc., appeared to demonstrate that this American or Western system could by no means serve as a normative role model for the Third World. This, though, discredited the normative thrust of modernization theory: in the febrile atmosphere of the late 1960s and 1970s, it was interpreted by the predominantly left-wing intellectuals as an *ethnocentric* construct and thus mercilessly attacked as a theory whose goal was to force upon other nations the highly questionable and problematic Western system. Modernization theory was suspected of being imperialistic, which is why, according to Alexander, most young or fairly young social scientists turned to its major macrosociological competitor, Marxism, which became attractive as a critique of the foundations of Western societies. Modernization theory, Alexander concludes, fell victim to the left-wing *Zeitgeist*. In reality, though, he thought that its weaknesses were not so severe as to necessitate such renunciation. Modernization theory could therefore be profitably revived.

It is certainly possible to interpret the 'death' of modernization theory in the late 1960s in other ways – in connection with a different assessment of its capacity for renewal (see Knöbl, *Spielräume der Modernisierung* ['Modernization: The Room for Manoeuvre']). An alternative, rival interpretation suggests that modernization theory, rather than being 'killed off' from outside by the leftist *Zeitgeist*, disintegrated from within. Modernization theory was built upon rather unstable foundations; it had weak spots that could not be rectified. These were due in part to the fact that while it adopted certain conceptual tools from Parsonian theory, all in all it destroyed its complexity, developing a far too simplistic view of processes of social change not found in this form in the work of Parsons. From the outset, several facets of modernization theory proved problematic. While the opposition between 'traditional' and 'modern' societies seemed persuasive at first glance, it papered over the problem that modernization theory aspired to the status of a theory of social *change*, rather than one that merely describes differing social realities by means of a static typology. Who or what drives the shift from tradition to modernity? Which causal relationships are at play here?

Modernization theory proved incapable of coming up with any real answers to these questions. Reference to technological developments – such as Lerner's idea that the mass media break down the existing structures of traditional societies and trigger the spread of new, modern value patterns which then usher in economic dynamism – immediately raised the question of *how* and *by whom* these technological innovations were disseminated. These innovations are themselves dependent on economic preconditions (without economic growth, the spread and use of mass media will remain very limited), which quickly gave rise to the problem that this explanatory model was tautological. Lerner ultimately explained economic change as resulting from the influence of media, but these themselves can only have an impact on the basis of economic transformation. This was thus a circular explanation: the *explanans* (that which explains) was explained by reference to the *explanandum* (that which requires explanation) and vice versa.

Within the debate on modernization theory, this led to the insight that references to trends in technological development were insufficient if one wished to claim for this theory genuine explanatory potential. Attempts were thus made to produce clearer causal statements, to identify the *agents* of modernization – for instance, *social groups* – that advance the modernization of a society. Here too, though, difficulties arose, for it was often impossible to make clear-cut statements. Political elites, for example, were by no means always inclined to set off on the road towards *Western* modernity, often following the socialist model of society realized and propagated in Moscow or Beijing. While the middle classes, particularly engineers and other experts, seemed to be the grouping most likely to be interested in the Western model of society, there were generally so few of them in the countries of the Third World that they could not seriously be considered effective agents of modernization. Because scholars, probably quite correctly, did not think the rural masses likely to develop a society oriented towards the West either, it was very unclear within modernization theory who or which concrete groups might in fact drive this supposedly inescapable process. The causal question 'Who wants modernization and who is capable of making it happen?' thus remained unresolved, which did little to enhance the theory's impact or plausibility.

Finally, the core assumption of modernization theory soon began to appear dubious as well, namely the clear-cut distinction between traditional and modern structures. On closer inspection, it was by no means the case that 'traditional' features had vanished entirely from Western societies. From the vitality of religious traditions in the USA, seemingly the most modern Western society, and that country's constitutional patriotism, the evocation of a 200-year-old political and legal tradition, to the survival of monarchical structures in European countries such as Great Britain, it was possible to point to numerous phenomena which defied easy and unequivocal characterization as 'modern'. But if it is difficult to *clearly distinguish* the 'modern' from the 'traditional', modernization theory's *assumptions about change – from* the 'traditional *to* the modern' – automatically becomes problematic as well. Modernization theory had endowed Parsons' 'pattern variables' with historical dynamism and it would ultimately pay dearly for it. Parsons had developed his pattern variables in order to capture the often confusing *complexity* of societies in which, for example, functionally specific role patterns could certainly continue to exist alongside particularistic values. Most modernization theorists suppressed this insight by awarding one half of Parsons' pattern variables (see p. 69) to tradition (particularistic, functionally diffuse, ascriptive, etc.), and the other (universalistic, functionally specific, achievement-related, etc.) to modernity. Parsonian complexity was superseded by another dichotomous construction which was then, moreover, projected onto the historical process, resulting in the simplistic theory of change summed up in the phrase 'from tradition to modernity'.

Ultimately, as a consequence of these various difficulties facing modernization theory, its internal critique became increasingly vigorous towards the end of the 1960s and the theory fragmented and disintegrated from within. According to the rival interpretation to that of Alexander, it was not simply laid to rest by the alleged *Zeitgeist*; rather, the theorists dug a grave for their own theory. Modernization theory had proved too simplistic to be tenable.

This interpretation is supported by the fact that certain authors close to modernization theory exercised a special influence on the later development of sociological theory. This refers to those who did not merely simplify the Parsonian approach, but, quite to the contrary, tried to incorporate the complexity of Parsons' arguments. Some of Parsons' leading students tried to do just this. While it was not their aim to develop the kind of abstract universal theory constructed by Parsons, but rather to pursue theoretical *and* empirical interests at the same time, they did not evade Parsons' insights regarding the complex interleaving of various ('traditional' and 'modern') structures in almost all societies. This set some of them off along new theoretical paths that were to take them far from unadulterated Parsonianism and further yet from modernization theory.

The pre-eminent figure here is Edward A. Shils. While he published no monumental works of theory, he produced important studies and essays on a smaller scale that pointed the way for the international debate on theory both empirically and theoretically. Shils, a tremendously erudite scholar who worked at the University of Chicago as well as at elite British universities, where he influenced a large number of intellectual circles extending far beyond the discipline of sociology, has even been immortalized in literature, by none other than Saul Bellow, winner of the Nobel prize for literature; he appears in his novel *Ravelstein* under the name 'Rakhmiel Kogon' (see Bellow, *Ravelstein*, pp. 130ff.). But it is of course Shils' sociological work rather than his personal history that is of primary interest to us here. As you may recall, Shils co-authored certain books with Parsons in the early 1950s, including such crucial studies as *Toward a General Theory of Action* (1951) and *Working*

Papers in the Theory of Action (1953). Yet Shils was plainly more oriented towards the empirical than was Parsons, which was ultimately to lead him to new theoretical insights.

Shils became famous very early through a study in military sociology (see his essay, co-authored by Morris Janowitz [1919–88], 'Cohesion and Disintegration in the Wehrmacht in World War II', from 1948), which was also to inspire the small group research that flourished in the 1950s. What is more important in the present context, however, is the fact that he had already worked intensely on issues in the sociology of knowledge during this period, including the sociology of intellectuals, which enabled him to rectify some of the deficiencies of modernization theory. Shils was one of the authors who recognized that modernization theory required stable anchorage in action theory if it was serious about grasping the causes of modernization. His proposal was to take a closer look at the elites in the developing countries, particularly the intellectuals (see Shils, 'The Intellectuals in the Political Development of the New States'), because such groups featured major, if not crucial, potential for innovation. While this point of departure did not produce entirely clear results, because the study of intellectuals quickly showed that their behaviour could not be predicted as simply as one might have expected from a modernization theoretical perspective, Shils did much to develop and ultimately modify traditional modernization theory (on what follows, see Knöbl, *Spielräume der Modernisierung*, pp. 228ff.).

But Shils did not stop there. He attempted, by means of his own theoretical endeavours, to free himself from the fundamental difficulties which modernization theorists, but also Parsons himself, had got into. The key, implicit thesis informing his work was that *the conception of culture found in both modernization theory and Parsons was inadequate and that the roots of their difficulties lay precisely here*. Heavily influenced by Max Weber as well as certain authors affiliated with the earlier Chicago School of sociology (see Lecture VI), some of whom he had got to know personally, Shils' first step was to inquire into the relationship between culture and power. In this connection, he began to get to grips systematically with Weber's concept of charisma – with Durkheimian conceptual tools.

Following Durkheim (as well as Parsons; see Lecture IV), Shils' hypothesis was that certain ideas about the sacred exist in *every* society, including modern society. We can thus by no means assume that modernity entails and will continue to entail a comprehensive process of secularization inevitably resulting in the dissolution of all that is sacred, as Weber and the modernization theorists believed and continue to believe:

> All societies regard as sacred certain standards of judgment, certain rules of conduct and thought, and certain arrangements of action. They vary only in the intensity and self-consciousness of their acknowledgment,

the scope which they allow to the sacred, and the extent of participation in them.

(Shils, 'Tradition and Liberty: Antinomy and Interdependence', p. 156)

On this view, while the relationship with the sacred undoubtedly changes through the process of modernization, this change is better described in terms of sublimation than disappearance. To render this thesis more precise and plausible, Shils combines the Durkheimian concept of the sacred with the Weberian concept of charisma, equating the attribution of sacred qualities to certain things or individuals with that of charismatic qualities. Here, Shils backs up the thesis of the omnipresence of the charismatic and thus of the sacred in societies with the aid of anthropological reflections: he detects a universal 'need for order' which ultimately explains the attribution of charisma – in every society. Charisma is attributed to those with the power to establish and maintain order. Such people are viewed with a kind of sacred respect, which in turn enables their power to be used more efficiently to maintain order.

> The generator or author of order arouses the charismatic responsiveness. Whether it be God's law or natural law or scientific law or positive law or the society as a whole, or even a particular corporate body or institution like an army, whatever embodies, expresses, or symbolizes the essence of an ordered cosmos or any significant sector thereof awakens the disposition of awe and reverence, the charismatic disposition. Men need an order within which they can locate themselves, an order providing coherence, continuity, and justice.
>
> (Shils, 'Charisma, Order, and Status', pp. 125–6)

While Weber wished to apply the concept of charisma chiefly to individuals, Shils – as the above quotation shows – also relates it to political rulers, institutions, symbols and even specific classes. His aim here was to deprive Weber's concept of charisma of its generally disruptive and non-quotidian character, making charisma or the sacred normal, everyday 'phenomena', ones which *function to stabilize society* and which to some extent *maintain the routines within a society* for this very reason. His famous study of the coronation ceremony marking the ascent to the throne of Queen Elisabeth II in 1952 is a prime example here (see Shils and Young, 'The Meaning of the Coronation'). Shils thus interprets charisma not in terms of the dissolution, but of the stabilization of order.

With this basic idea, Shils is pursuing two goals. First, he wishes to explain more convincingly than structural functionalism the genesis and durability of ties to collective values. Parsons, and particularly modernization theorists, had done little to answer the question of how and why values become binding for the members of a society and can be lastingly accepted. Second, Shils wants to move away from classical modernization theory, which simply defined tradition as something that is absent from modern societies. As Shils saw it, it is impossible to separate the traditional and the modern in this way, and this is why he fused his hypotheses about the sacred and charisma with the concept of tradition. According to him, actions or phenomena are surrounded with the aura of tradition when the members of a society associate them with certain charismatic or sacred qualities:

> The unreflective reception of tradition is not an amoral, vegetative acceptance. There is an active, outgoing, positive tendency in the reception of tradition. The availability of a traditional rule or standard of judgement guides and stimulates a spontaneous moral tendency in man, a need to be in contact with the ultimately true and right, a sensitivity to the sacred, which reach out and seek the guidance and discipline of tradition.
>
> (Shils, 'Tradition and Liberty: Antinomy and Interdependence', p. 155)

Thus it is not the mere repetition of certain actions that explains the vitality of a tradition, but rather their ongoing embedding in a system of meanings centred on the sacred or charismatic. Because, so Shils asserts, such sacred meanings do not disappear even in modern societies, but are at most sublimated, it follows that traditions too do not simply cease to exist. Traditions, Shils tells us, are not mere ballast from the past. They live on. Even modern democratic societies depend on them – one need only think of national holidays, rituals such as inauguration ceremonies, oaths to the constitution, etc.

While traditions do not simply disappear in the modern world, they do of course depend on active acquisition and continuation. This is where Shils' *theory of elites* comes into play, in as much as he asserts that it is generally social elites that satisfy this universal need for order that explains the attribution of charismatic qualities. *Elites*, on Shils' view, are the concrete agents of the acquisition and continuation of tradition. Through their positions of power and authority, they guarantee the political, social and cultural order, which is why it is to them that charisma is ascribed and it is they who keep traditions alive: 'Great power announces itself by its power over order; it discovers order, creates order, maintains it, or destroys it. Power is indeed the central, order-related event' (Shils, 'Charisma, Order, and Status', p. 128). It is in this context that Shils introduces the conceptual pair of 'centre' and 'periphery', which he conceives from the point of view of cultural sociology, rather than economic geography or political economy like other authors. The associated thesis is that every society features an authoritative system of values and that it is thus possible to identify a central system of institutions supported by elites in every society. This 'centre' encompasses the prevailing order of symbols, values and beliefs within a society (Shils, 'Center and Periphery', p. 93), its influence extending to the 'periphery', that part of society beyond the centre. The charisma characteristic of elites is so powerful, their cultural achievements so impressive, that they cast their spell even over 'out-of-the-way' places.

Shils' theoretical move was a decisive step forward within Parsonianism. Though he did not manage to develop a consistent research programme on the basis of his reflections, he certainly paved the way for one. Because Shils worked with a novel conceptual apparatus including charisma and tradition, but also 'centre' and 'periphery', he was no longer compelled to understand 'culture', like the early Parsons, as a mere (action-free) context that 'floats' amorphously above the actors in no specific location (see Lecture III), or, like the late Parsons, as an equally actorless 'cybernetic system' (see Lecture IV). Rather, Shils, referring to *concrete actors* and the key importance of their cultural achievements, had opened up the opportunity to analyse culture in terms of *action theory* within a Parsonian framework (on Shils, see also Stephen Turner, 'The Significance of Shils'). It is no coincidence that it was a student of Shils who succeeded in developing his ideas further, gradually putting together a massive research programme extending far beyond Parsonianism, and even further beyond modernization theory, one that is hugely influential today.

This student was Shmuel N. Eisenstadt. Born in Poland in 1923, Eisenstadt arrived in Palestine, modern-day Israel, in 1935. In Jerusalem he became assistant to the famous sociologist and philosopher of religion Martin Buber (1878–1965), who, having emigrated from Germany, had occupied a chair in social philosophy and general sociology at the Hebrew University in Jerusalem since 1938. While still a young man, Eisenstadt sought contact with the leading sociologists of the day, in order to forge ties between Israeli sociology, which was fairly isolated, and the rest of the world. He met Edward Shils at the London School of Economics and Talcott Parsons at Harvard, who moulded him profoundly as well as involving him in the very lively debates on the development of structural functionalism and modernization theory. Ultimately, though, Eisenstadt followed his own path. He was undoubtedly influenced deeply by functionalism via his teachers Shils and Parsons. Yet in a lengthy process that was to last for decades and which is, it seems, not yet entirely complete even now, he freed himself from the original premises of functionalism and subjected it to a process of ongoing revision. The resulting theoretical construction can in fact scarcely be described as functionalist. To put it in somewhat drastic terms, Eisenstadt ultimately left functionalism's sphere of influence, having become increasingly aware of its weaknesses. The life-long influence of his early contact with the philosophy of Martin Buber with its emphasis on the creativity of human action was surely important here, as Eisenstadt himself attests in an autobiographical retrospective (see the introduction to Eisenstadt, *Power, Trust, and Meaning*).

But Eisenstadt is not just a theorist. His ongoing and rigorous revision of functionalism was always bound up with empirical analyses; he took up Max Weber's programme of comparative research on the world religions and their influence on processes of social change – surely the most impressive aspect of his work alongside his many theoretical achievements. We shall return to these empirical studies later, but first we would like to outline Eisenstadt's *theoretical* innovations, which incorporated a critique of Parsons and above all of conventional modernization theory; you will be familiar with some of his criticisms from the preceding lectures.

1. Eisenstadt embraced Shils' attempt to open up functionalism to action theory. Like Shils, he rejected Parsons' efforts to radicalize functionalism with a view to turning it into a systems theory, in which actors play practically no role or are no longer considered relevant as units of analysis because they merely fulfil the requirements of the system. According to Eisenstadt, it is vital that theoretical analysis include actors, and *collective* actors are thus of special interest to the study of macrosociological contexts. Urban dignitaries, religious leaders and their followers, bureaucracies, armies, etc. thus always played a major role in Eisenstadt's writings, and as with Shils, Eisenstadt is concerned to identify the *key* actors driving social change or, more specifically, processes of modernization. As Shils had done, Eisenstadt was to pay particular attention to *elites*.
2. The immediate consequence of ensuring the inclusion of actors is that, unlike Parsons, Eisenstadt no longer refers to processes of exchange between systems or subsystems. Rather, the processes of exchange are interpreted as actions and especially as *struggles* among bearers of power over (scarce) resources. To argue in this way, from a conflict theory perspective, is to bid farewell to a crucial component of functionalist thought, the presumption of equilibrium, as Eisenstadt underlined explicitly in subsequent reflections.
3. The point here is that if the analytical focus is already on actors, it is hard to see why only those actors 'internal to the system' should be taken into account. Eisenstadt is in fact receptive to the insight that one can study social processes adequately only if one pays heed to the effect of so-called exogenous influences and circumstances. Societies, after all, are not truly isolated entities, they are not fully autonomous and autarchic, but are always already in contact with other societies; they communicate, trade and fight wars with them, etc. But if this is the case, it becomes difficult to work with a model of society, like that of functionalism, which refers self-evidently to 'society' as the primary and ultimate point of reference in the analysis of systems. Suddenly, in view of the ever-increasing 'international' integration of 'societies', it also seems dubious that one can speak meaningfully of a social equilibrium describable primarily in terms of conditions and factors internal to the system. Eisenstadt was thus to make vigorous efforts to elaborate how societies are interconnected culturally, which again entails a significantly more dynamic conception of 'society' than was typical of traditional functionalism.

4. This inclusion of very different 'internal' and 'external' influences and actors also meant keeping a weather eye on the different consequences or results of processes of institutionalization and integration. While Parsonian functionalism never seriously discussed *how* certain values are institutionalized, and assumed the integration of societies and their stability rather than investigating them, for Eisenstadt this was simply not good enough. Because he placed such emphasis on the existence of (collective) actors in analysing social processes, he quickly came to appreciate that the institutionalization of values is a far from smooth and straightforward process. Values are amenable to interpretation – and actors fight for *their* interpretations, which is why there is always a struggle over the *correct* or *real* institutionalization of values. In line with this, societies are not integrated once and for all via a particular system of values; rather, it is always possible for existing forms of integration to be questioned, because opposing groups advance different interpretations of values and thus insist on a different approach to institutionalizing them.

A huge question mark is thus placed over the sociological theorem of differentiation – at least in the traditional sense. The concept of differentiation had been (re-)introduced within structural functionalism in order to outline the contours of social change. The assumption here was that there is a more or less inexorable, linear process of differentiation that underpins the shift from simple units to a multiplicity of ever more specialized units, which are in turn successfully integrated to form a complex unit, which increases the efficiency of the system as a whole (see Lecture IV). Eisenstadt completely rejects this conception of differentiation. For him, because the outcomes of processes of institutionalization and integration vary, we can in no way take it for granted that the institutionalization of values and the integration of societies will always succeed. There may be such a thing as a process of differentiation, but because such processes are driven by actors, the consequences and forms of differentiation – against the assumptions of functionalists and modernization theorists – cannot simply be deduced from theory. And there is certainly no guarantee that processes of differentiation will conclude successfully. In direct contrast to (Parsonian) functionalism and modernization theory, Eisenstadt produced a now famous typology of the consequences of differentiation, intended to furnish us with a more adequate understanding of social processes. He emphasizes that (a) institutional solutions may fail, (b) it is always possible to regress to a lower level of differentiation (de-differentiation), and thus that we cannot think of differentiation in terms of progress, (c) the possibility of partial differentiation cannot be excluded, that subdivisions of a society may become differentiated while others do not, almost inevitably resulting in 'non-simultaneous' social developments, and finally that (d) processes of differentiation may of course be successful, if institutions develop that are capable of integrating the new differentiated units (see Eisenstadt, 'Social Change, Differentiation, and Evolution', pp. 111ff.). But such successful differentiation is by no means the norm.

5. In light of this, we must drop the assumption, found in modernization theory and certain sociological theories of evolution, of unilinear development or steady progress. The historical process depends on specific conflictual circumstances in which actors find themselves, and successful differentiation cannot and should not simply be taken for granted: progress is anything but guaranteed. It is equally wrong to assume that the history of different societies will converge – on the Western model of society for example. According to Eisenstadt, we cannot simply assume that similar conflicts, with similar results, will arise everywhere, as do those who believe that the developing countries will sooner or later fall in line with Western-style modernization. Because there are conflicts between different groups as well as exogenous factors, one must reckon with contingencies, with unforeseeable processes which show time and again how absurd the assumption of linearity and convergence is.

6. One is thus bound to conclude that the modernity 'born' in Europe and then North America also arose from a specific and contingent set of circumstances, that a development was set in motion that was by no means necessary. This suggests that Westerners might be well advised to adopt a more modest view of their own past, destroying the self-certainty and sense of superiority vis-à-vis other cultures and civilizations and also making the dichotomy between tradition and modernity highly questionable. Because once one has acknowledged this contingency, one must seriously consider whether Western modernity itself was not the creation of a very specific tradition, the invention – this is ultimately Eisenstadt's interpretation – of a very specific cultural 'code' through which Western Europe and North America set themselves apart from other civilizations from the early modern period onwards, without having cause to assume that other regions will simply follow them. According to Eisenstadt, it was and is necessary to reckon with different traditions in the past, present and future, of which Western modernity is merely one – an insight directly opposed to *the* core assumption of modernization theory.

So much for Eisenstadt's theoretical innovations, which are bound to appear abstract unless one knows something about the objects of his work and his methods, especially given that Eisenstadt's thought, as we have pointed out, did not develop purely within a theoretical framework, but through grappling with empirical problems.

Although by no means unknown at this time in light of his already prodigious body of work, much of it published around the world, it was only in 1963 that Eisenstadt truly captured the attention of the international sociological community. This he did by producing an enormously ambitious book, *The Political Systems of Empires*, a comparative study of bureaucratic empires including ancient Egypt, the Inca empire, ancient China and Byzantium; he also tackled European absolutism. The striking thing about this work was not just the way in which it revised Parsonianism and modernization theory (his strong focus on political struggles between various actors, religious groups, rulers, bureaucracy, etc., which we referred to earlier, was in essence already evident here). What caused a stir was the vast scope of Eisenstadt's material, his comparative analysis of phenomena from very different times and regions and the fact that here an author associated with modernization theory was examining *the distant past*, something which rarely occurred within classical modernization theory. The vast majority of authors in that particular field tackled the 'recent' past, and at most European history since the Reformation, believing that their work was directly relevant to practice and thus that it was unnecessary to delve so far back into history. Eisenstadt took a very different approach. He too of course wished to produce findings of 'current' relevance. At the same time, however, he made it clear that for him history is more than an irksome prelude to present-focused sociology. His point of departure was that key events occurred *in the distant past* that set the future course of history. These must be understood in comparative context if one wishes to grasp the history of modernization, which began and proceeded so differently on different continents.

Probing times long past in this way was the only means of opening up new perspectives, as prefigured by Parsons with his theory of evolution (see Lecture IV), though Eisenstadt himself – and this is of signal importance – was not to follow Parsons down this particular theoretical path. For his goal was to produce a *non*-evolutionist theory of social change purged of the weaknesses of both classical modernization theories and sociological theories of evolution, a theory, in other words, whose starting point lies in action theory, one which takes conflicts between actors and contingent processes for granted. Eisenstadt took more than a decade, however, to design a theory that satisfied him. He was aided here by a debate that resurfaced in the mid-1970s in religious studies and the history of religion concerned with a fairly old idea, namely German philosopher Karl Jaspers' (1883–1969) thesis of the so-called *Achsenzeit* or 'Axial Age'.

In his 1949 study in the philosophy of history, *The Origin and Goal of History*, Jaspers had asked whether it is possible to conceive of history as a unity and delineate a structure underlying world history which might be considered valid regardless of one's particular standpoint. While the Christian Revelation was seen as the self-evident starting point and axis of world history even by Hegel, in the twenty-first century, in an age well aware of the dangers of ethnocentrism, this no longer seems possible: Jaspers correctly emphasized that 'an axis of world history, if such a thing exists, would have to be discovered ... as a fact capable of being accepted by all men, Christians included' (*Origin*,

p. 1). As improbable as it may seem to discover such a non-ethnocentric axis, Jaspers surprises by offering the reader just that. He was not the first to point to the empirical fact that the origins of *all* the major world religions, and ancient Greek philosophy too as it happens, lie in the period between 800 and 200 BC or can be traced back to this age, which he calls the Axial Age:

> The most extraordinary events are concentrated in this period. Confucius and Lao-tse were living in China, all the schools of Chinese philosophy came into being ... India produced the Upanishads and Buddha and, like China, ran the whole gamut of philosophical possibilities down to scepticism, to materialism, sophism and nihilism; in Iran Zarathustra taught a challenging view of the world as a struggle between good and evil; in Palestine the prophets made their appearance, from Elijah, by way of Isaiah and Jeremiah to Deutero-Isaiah; Greece witnessed the appearance of Homer, of the philosophers – Parmenides, Heraclitus and Plato – of the tragedians, Thucydides and Archimedes.
>
> (ibid., p. 2)

These parallel intellectual processes, which occurred largely independently of and thus did not influence one another, made themselves felt in the advanced civilizations of the eastern regions of the West, and in India and China. According to Jaspers, they superseded a mythical age, ushering in a period of systematic reflection on the basic conditions of human existence. Jaspers cannot and does not seek to explain why these events occurred in parallel. For him, it seems more important that these civilizations of the Axial Age might make sense of one another, because while their origins were different, *the intellectual issues confronting them were very similar* (ibid., p. 8).

Jaspers is vague about what exactly these issues involved – other than the beginnings of a more intensive consideration of what it means to be human. When religious historians and theologians again took up the idea of the Axial Age in the 1970s, however, something of a consensus emerged that the common thread running through all these religions and philosophies was best captured through the concept of *transcendence*. In other words, they were of the opinion that thinking in terms of transcendent categories is (or was) *the* characteristic feature of these Axial Age cultures. Precisely what, though, is meant by 'transcendence'?

The key point here is the fact that these religions and philosophies entailed a sharp quasi-spatial division between the worldly and the divine and that ideas were developed that asserted the existence of an *otherworldly, transcendent* realm. While the divine had been present *in* the world and formed *part* of the world in the mythical age, that is, while the divine and the worldly had never been truly separated and the spirits and gods could be directly influenced and manipulated, precisely because they were part of the world, or the realm of the gods at least functioned in much the same way as its earthly counterpart, with the new salvation religions and philosophies of the Axial Age a gulf opens up between the two. The main idea here is that the divine is what is real and true and entirely other, by comparison with which the earthly realm can only ever be deficient.

Thinking in this way involves more than merely making a distinction. An unprecedented *tension* arises between the 'mundane' (the worldly) and the transcendent, a tension with significant consequences. A kind of divine kingdom, for example, is no longer compatible with this idea. The ruler can no longer be godlike because the gods are in another place. What is more, there is an increasing trend towards compelling the ruler to justify his actions in light of divine imperatives. The ruler is of this world – and he must justify himself with reference to the real world of the beyond. A new form of critique (of the ruler) becomes possible, introducing an entirely new dynamic to the historical process in that one can always point out that the ruler is failing to live up to the divine commandments. At the same time, it also becomes possible to argue over the true nature of God or the correct interpretation of the divine commandments in a far more radical and dogged way, which was to lead, sooner or later, to conflicts as well as to the distinction between different ethnic and religious collectivities. Intellectuals – priests, prophets, etc. – now play a substantially more important role than they did before the Axial Age because, among other things, they have the difficult task of interpreting the gods' true, inaccessible intentions, which can no longer be grasped so easily through earthly categories. With the idea of transcendence, history opened up, that is, entirely new fields of conflict became conceivable. To put it more abstractly: the idea of transcendence entailed the idea of the fundamental need to reconstruct the mundane order. From now on, it becomes possible to conceive of changing the social order to bring it into line with divine principles; for the first time, it is possible to imagine deliberate revolutions. The ideas spawned in the Axial Age were so powerful that they triggered a new social dynamic.

Eisenstadt draws on these insights, his *Revolution and the Transformation of Societies: A Comparative Study of Civilizations*, which originally appeared in 1978, being the key text here. In a particular version of Jaspers' hypotheses, he perceives the starting point for a highly ambitious theoretical and research project intended to open up entirely new perspectives on the analysis of social change. Eisenstadt's thesis is that the tension between the mundane and the transcendent present in all these Axial Age religions was resolved in different ways in each case, with the result that the pace of change differed in the various Axial Age civilizations. To put it in a nutshell, Eisenstadt believes that he can produce a typology detailing the ways in which this tension was resolved. How are we to imagine this?

Eisenstadt's argument is as follows. In some civilizations, the tension was resolved by *secular* means, as for example in the case of Confucianism (and to some extent in classical Greece and ancient Rome) through the development of a metaphysics and ethics, which ultimately preserved and stabilized social relations:

> The thrust of the official Confucian civilizational orientations was that the resolution of this tension was attained through the cultivation of the social, political and cultural orders, as the major way of maintaining the cosmic harmony ... Accordingly, the Confucian orientation did stress the proper performance of worldly duties and activities within the existing social framework – the family, broader kin groups and Imperial service – as the ultimate measure of the resolution of the tension between the transcendental and the mundane order and of individual responsibility.
>
> (Eisenstadt, 'This Worldly Transcendentalism and the Structuring of the World', p. 171)

This secular resolution of the tension between the transcendent and the mundane understood salvation primarily as an *inner*-worldly affair. That is, people seek their religious salvation by cultivating the social order existing at a given time. In other words, the divine will is best served by getting on with one's allotted tasks *in the world* and slotting neatly into the social order, rather than withdrawing from this world by, for example, becoming a hermit.

But it was also possible to resolve this tension *religiously*; Eisenstadt distinguishes between the Buddhist and Hindu approaches, in which the transcendent realm was conceived in non-personal terms, and a monotheistic approach, in which a personified God is located outside of the universe (Eisenstadt, 'Cultural Traditions and Political Dynamics', pp. 163–4). The former variant understood salvation almost exclusively as *outside* of the world, that is, the actions of Buddhists and Hindus were geared so strongly towards an otherworldly order that for them *the transformation of the world could not be the goal of their efforts*. The monotheistic religions of Judaism, Christianity and Islam, meanwhile, oscillated between a purely other-worldly and purely this-worldly concept of salvation; *but if a this-worldly notion of salvation prevailed, the transformation of the world became an urgent priority.*

All of this sounds very complicated, as indeed it is. Let us pause briefly to summarize our discussion so far. Eisenstadt's core thesis was that the so-called Axial Age entailed the potential to massively accelerate the historical process – conditional upon the tension between the mundane and transcendent. However, the degree of 'acceleration' depended on the manner in which the tension was resolved. It thus makes sense that a purely other-worldly orientation, as in Buddhism and Hinduism, offered and continues to offer few stimuli for the reorganization of politics and society. Eisenstadt thus puts forward the further thesis that those civilizations which, as a result of their religious character, enabled believers to adopt a *this-worldly* orientation, particularly if these aimed at *changing* rather than cultivating society, have the greatest potential for extensive and rapid processes of change.

The notion of 'accelerated' or 'rapid' processes of change, one might object, is rather strange. What exactly does it mean? Can the pace of social change be straightforwardly measured? And what are the criteria? Eisenstadt, in fact, has none to speak of; he cannot, therefore, 'measure' anything in a natural scientific sense. However, he can at least back up his thesis of differing rates of change with supporting evidence. He calls our attention to a fact which only a scholar such as he, with a truly universal knowledge of history, would notice. He observes that 'revolutions', events characterized by rapid and sweeping social change, have by no means happened everywhere. 'Major revolutions' have in fact been possible only in Axial Age civilizations; or only in these have they been attempted or thought about.

'Major revolutions' (one would typically think of the American, French or Russian revolutions here) always had and have – so Eisenstadt believes – a rudimentary background in the history of ideas, one linked with the Axial Age notion of the fundamental need to reconstruct the world. In non-Axial Age civilizations – as the history of Japan was to show – the intellectual foundations were simply not present and influential actors thus lacked such major goals. Despite very rapid economic change in the nineteenth century, which seemed to offer every prospect of revolutionary uprisings or at least attempts at revolution, Japan has known no real revolutions, and has not even developed the requisite ideological models. Even the so-called Meiji Restoration or Meiji Revolution in the second half of the nineteenth century lacked the ideological and symbolic elements, the messianic and universalistic features, characteristic of the 'great revolutions' of North American and European modernity, but also generally found in all Axial Age civilizations (Eisenstadt, 'Cultural Premises and the Limits of Convergence in Modern Societies: An Examination of Some Aspects of Japanese Society', pp. 132 ff.).

Even if the ideological bases for revolutions were present in *all* Axial Age civilizations, this did not mean that revolutions took place in all of them. This, of course, always depended on specific constellations of actors as well (and this brings us again to the religious differences *between* Axial Age religions), on the specific way in which the tension between the mundane and the transcendent was resolved in each case. In relation to the latter, this meant that the nature of this resolution might 'suggest' the idea of the *total* overthrow of the existing order with particular force or tend to push it into the background. For Eisenstadt it is therefore no accident that it was in those civilizations moulded by monotheistic religions, in which *inner-worldly* action orientations were widespread, that the first 'great revolutions' occurred. An activism related to changing the world was a far more favourable condition for a revolutionary project than a stance of turning away from or preserving the world. Concretely, this means that there were important currents in Judaism, Christianity and Islam willing and able to come up with radical worldly goals.

The fact that, of the religions with an inner-worldly orientation, it was Christianity – rather than Islam, for example, whose roots also place it among the Axial Age religions – that proved a favourable environment for revolutions, was linked with the specific set of actors, that is, the particular *structural* conditions. Though Islam undoubtedly featured major messianic characteristics, still highly visible today, its specific political and geographical spread, that is, its extension beyond the Arabian peninsula, weakened the position of the cities and their citizenries. Key factors that had made the revolutionary dynamic in early modern Europe or North America possible in the first place were thus lacking. It was the Christian cultural complex that was not only to provide the ideas necessary to a particularly high degree of societal dynamism, but which was able to realize these on the basis of a certain set of structural circumstances. In early modern Europe, the pace of revolutionary change accelerated; after a number of intermediate steps, this was to give rise to the global domination of Western civilization that persists to this day.

So much for Eisenstadt's theoretical design. To repeat, his core thesis is that the various religions and the civilizations to which they gave rise feature a particular rate of change rooted, among other things, in the specific way in which transcendent tensions were resolved. Unlike Max Weber, Eisenstadt does not believe that magical or traditional elements in non-Western civilizations, that is, a low degree of rationalization of the religions found in them, explain the fact that they developed more slowly and ultimately lagged behind the West. He rejects this ethnocentric idea, emphasizing that the potential for rationality was and is present in all religions. It was merely used in different ways to resolve the tension between the transcendent and the mundane. Each civilization developed its own traditions in this regard, and in Europe and North America this produced a set of circumstances that gave rise to so-called (Western) 'modernity'.

Eisenstadt's notion of Western 'modernity' has little in common with that deployed by modernization theorists. The taproots of his modernity lie in the Judaeo-Christian tradition of the Axial Age, a tradition which, however, again underwent major change in the eighteenth century when a specific constellation of actors brought about revolutions; these created a new situation, rendered newly dynamic. Thus, according to Eisenstadt, Western modernity was not the somehow inevitable product of a historical principle. Rather, its origins were contingent, which also means that other civilizations may find it far from easy to follow our example as they develop. They have their own traditions, or better, their own modernities (plural). For Eisenstadt, the dichotomy of tradition and modernity no longer makes sense. All contemporary non-Western civilizations are modern. They have changed profoundly as a result of the European expansion beginning in the early modern era if not before. They have been crucially moulded by the collision with Europe. Other civilizations have processed and digested the impulses for change coming from the West, fusing them with their own traditions; they have developed *other* modernities in competition with the West, which is why Eisenstadt consistently refers to 'multiple modernities'.

All the points referred to above, which may sound like mere theoretical inference, Eisenstadt has backed up with 'weighty tomes'. His tremendous erudition has enabled him to 'digest' huge quantities of historical material and fathom historical processes in many regions of the world. His monumental *Japanese Civilization: A Comparative View* (1996) is probably the most impressive evidence of his working methods. Eisenstadt 'buried himself' in the literature on Japan in order to explain why this country, with no experience of an Axial Age, and which never adopted an Axial Age religion, nonetheless managed, during the nineteenth century at the latest, to catch up with the West economically and compete seriously with it; this it did despite its failure to spawn any revolutionary projects (as a result of its non-Axial Age origins), which in itself made it very different from the West.

Should you wish to acquire a more precise picture of Eisenstadt's working methods as well as the breadth of his historical-sociological interests, one of his shorter works, such as *Die Vielfalt der Moderne* ('The Diversity of Modernity'), will provide you with a good introduction. Here you will find Eisenstadt's analyses of the histories of Europe, the USA and Japan in condensed form. At the same time, this volume from 2000 provides an explanation, tailored to his Axial Age thesis, of the emergence of a wide variety of religious fundamentalisms in the present era (the messianic characteristics of the Axial Age civilizations being of key significance here), a phenomenon to which Eisenstadt has devoted much attention in recent times.

Eisenstadt's theoretical reflections, as we have seen, rest upon an admirable empirical knowledge of a huge variety of geographical and temporal contexts. In light of the breadth of his research it is fair to say that he is the only contemporary figure who could seriously claim the status of successor to Max Weber. Nonetheless, Eisenstadt's work has provoked a number of critical questions, of which we would briefly like to mention at least four.

1. In various publications produced from the 1960s onwards, Eisenstadt has pointed out that different – internal and external – actors and influences must be considered when analysing processes of social change. Yet one wonders whether Eisenstadt's embrace of the notion of the Axial Age has produced another basically endogenous perspective. Of course, Eisenstadt does not deny the existence of external influences. But because the civilizational dynamics are explained on the basis of specific *internal* intellectual or religious circumstances, external influences risk being downgraded. The next point is directly bound up with this.
2. In our account of Eisenstadt's work, we imperceptibly introduced the concept of civilization, which Eisenstadt himself uses. But this concept is

very difficult to define. Eisenstadt emphasizes cultural features. For him, civilizations are characterized by a very specific religious or philosophical problem. But we may question how coherent and homogeneous these civilizations really were and whether it is possible to distinguish between them so clearly. The criticism made by Anthony Giddens of notions of discrete 'societies' (see the previous lecture) can of course be applied to the concept of civilizations in much the same way. Furthermore, this means that if civilizations were not and are not entirely coherent, the notion of dynamics of change specific to civilizations is also ultimately problematic.

3. In examining the upheavals of the Axial Age, Eisenstadt inevitably concentrated on elites, because the historical sources for this period mostly fail to take account of the lives of the majority of the population. But Eisenstadt continues to argue from an elite theory perspective with reference to the modern age. Like his teacher Shils, he focuses on ideologies, that is, intellectual products formulated and bequeathed to history by elites. One might wonder whether the inclusion of the values and actions of broader social strata might lead to different conclusions about historical processes. One might argue, for example, against Eisenstadt, that revolutions often occurred for trivial reasons and were imbued with symbolic meanings *as the upheaval itself took place* or even *afterwards*, meanings which are all too easy to interpret retrospectively, and problematically, as an immanent, latent 'revolutionary project' that can be attributed to certain intellectuals.

4. Eisenstadt's focus on the Axial Age and its ideological upheavals runs the risk of downplaying the *structural* prerequisites for forms of social change in general and processes of modernization in particular. He certainly argues from a structural point of view when, time and again, he points explicitly to constellations of actors and elites. Yet on the other hand it is striking that phenomena such as colonialism and the associated brute force deployed against the peoples of Africa, South America, Australia and Asia play no real role in his analyses. It surely makes a difference whether 'modernization' took place under conditions of self-determination or external violence. Eisenstadt's work tells us little about how the problems of the Axial Age relate to *these* structural circumstances.

In our account of the renewal of Parsonianism and modernization theory we have so far restricted ourselves to the work of Edward A. Shils and Shmuel N. Eisenstadt. This is certainly justified given these authors' theoretical significance. But our approach should not inspire false conclusions. We wish to address two points perhaps most likely to lead to misunderstandings.

First, Parsons did of course have many other important students besides Shils and Eisenstadt. From the 1950s, an American sociology anchored in the Parsonian tradition was associated with the names of certain authors who continue to enjoy an excellent reputation to this day. We shall mention two representative figures here. Robert Bellah (b. 1927) was a close associate of Parsons and devoted much attention to processes of modernization in Japan as early as the 1950s. We have already cited his *Tokugawa Religion* from 1957, identifying it as a classical text in modernization theory. But at the same time, Bellah was significantly closer to Parsons' complex arguments than most other theorists of modernization, who worked with the relatively simple dichotomy between tradition and modernity.

Tokugawa Religion was first and foremost a groundbreaking historical investigation of certain patterns of values found in Japan which enabled this Asian country to start catching up with the West at a relatively early point, namely towards the end of the nineteenth century. Taking up a problem dating back to Weber, Bellah examined Japan, a country outside of the Euro-American cultural complex, for functional equivalents of the Protestant ethic, with its dynamic consequences. But his study was also important for another reason. It showed that the processes of industrialization that occurred in Japan had a very different character than in the USA for example. While economic values were paramount in US industrial society, this did not appear to apply in the case of Japanese modernization. In Japan, *politics* played a decisive role and economic values were subordinate to political ones. In concrete terms, this meant that the process of industrialization and modernization was implemented by political elites, and in a manner which must have seemed strange to Western observers, particularly Anglo-Saxons. Japanese modernity took off on the basis of close, particularistic ties binding all social elites to the imperial household. *Militaristic* values geared towards efficiency, which had been disseminated throughout society, particularly in the nineteenth century, also played a major role. This insight caused Bellah to question the clear division between the two halves of the 'pattern variables' taken for granted by almost all proponents of modernization theory. As this example shows, particularistic value orientations cannot be simply and smoothly ascribed to tradition. This also problematized the thesis of a unilinear process of modernization. According to Bellah, modernization does not simply lead to the unquestioned dominance of rational or secular values. This also means that religion, for example, does not simply disappear as modernization proceeds. Rather, and here Bellah argues in much the same way as Parsons and Shils, it is characterized by *new* forms and *new* settings. Bellah is thus not expounding a simple thesis of secularization as do many modernization theorists, but rather a theory of 'religious evolution'.

In the 1960s and 1970s, Bellah was to elaborate further this thesis of the enduring force of the religious in modern society, with the USA his primary 'object', in as much as he demonstrated how the political was consistently accompanied by religious motives – from the founding fathers in the eighteenth century to John F. Kennedy in the twentieth century. He deployed the concept of 'civil religion', borrowed from Rousseau, to gain greater purchase on this particular version of religion in a post-traditional world (see *Beyond Belief*). American identity – according to Bellah – still has deeply religious roots, and there is no sign that this is changing to any significant extent. In the 1980s and 1990s, Bellah contributed much to the empirical diagnosis of the contemporary era on the basis of these assumptions. We shall be taking a closer look at his contributions in Lecture XVIII.

Neil Smelser, the other Parsonian we would like to mention here, played an important role in the further development or opening up of Parsonianism. Having co-authored (with Parsons) *Economy and Society*, mentioned in Lecture IV, while still a student, Smelser subsequently prefigured certain developments in Parsonian theory or helped rid structural functionalism of certain deficiencies. In his 1959 *Social Change in the Industrial Revolution* (again, see Lecture IV), Smelser had done much to make the concept of differentiation a taken-for-granted part of modern sociology, a concept upon which Parsonian evolutionary theory was then to build and one which all functionalists right up to Luhmann were subsequently to make central to their work. Smelser never stopped grinding away at the concept of differentiation, but over the course of his career he revised his ideas, which originally were very simple. Today, he no longer assumes that differentiation is a unilinear process. Though he continues to assert that 'differentiation remains a commanding feature of a contemporary society' (Smelser, *Problematics of Sociology*, p. 54), he has shown emphatically in a number of studies that processes of differentiation entail psychological, political and social costs and may therefore be blocked (see his *Social Paralysis and Social Change*). Fundamentally, this means that he has adopted an Eisenstadtian position.

Smelser remedied the theoretical deficiencies of Parsonianism insofar as he was one of the first functionalists to grapple with the phenomenon of collective action, his particular focus being social movements. Parsons had no theory in this regard and apparently had no need of one, as he moved ever closer to an actorless systems theory emphasizing relations of exchange between subsystems. As Eisenstadt had done, Smelser more strongly emphasized the action theoretical aspects within structural functionalism and thus took an interest in collective actors, because they are clearly of special importance to explaining *macro*-processes. His *Theory of Collective Behavior* from 1962 was his attempt to interpret collective action neither on the premise that individual actors are entirely irrational nor on the premise that they are totally rational. Though the model developed by Smelser was anything but coherent (for a critique, see Joas, *The Creativity of Action*, pp. 204ff.), his work here did open up new research fields to functionalism.

Second, if we have laid particular emphasis on the work of Eisenstadt in this lecture on the renewal of Parsonianism, this does not mean that it had received a great deal of attention by the 1970s and early 1980s. At least in the 1970s, fate decreed that *all* those remotely close to Parsons generally had to operate on the margins of the sociological debates being carried on across the world. As mentioned earlier, this was largely due to the fact that, from the second half of the 1960s, Parsons' evolutionary reflections, along with those approaches that drew on Parsons but which were in fact quite new, such as that of Eisenstadt, were suspected of embodying a conservative ideology, however unfair this may have been. Parsons was straightforwardly identified with a rather simplistic modernization theory, in such a way that accusations of ethnocentrism continued to 'stick' to his students. As a result, from the 1960s on, most authors with macrosociological interests looked for other approaches, particularly ones as different as possible in every respect from a discredited modernization theory. For it was not only the internal construction of classical modernization theory that proved problematic, as evident in Eisenstadt's constant revision of this theory. Modernization theory had also patently failed at a practical level, the hopes placed in it coming to nothing. The vast majority of Third World countries failed to truly develop. In fact, the opposite seemed to apply. Many of these countries fell ever further behind the West, raising the question of whether the plight of the Third World could be traced back to *relations of exploitation* and thus to the West. What the West was doing to the countries of the Third World, according to the thesis being discussed as early as the 1960s, mainly by left-wing economists and sociologists specializing in South America, was not helping them to develop but ensuring their ongoing *under*development. These social scientists claimed that the societies of South America were being systematically plundered as a result of unfavourable terms of trade dictated by the West, aided and abetted by a rich but numerically tiny indigenous bourgeoisie that profited greatly from this set-up. A work by two Brazilian sociologists, Fernando H. Cardoso (b. 1931 and president of Brazil, 1995–2002) and Enzo Faletto (1935–2003), entitled *Dependencia y desarollo en América Latina* (*Dependency and Development in Latin America*) from 1969 became particularly famous in this connection. One of the key terms in the title, 'dependencia', was later used to designate a larger-scale theoretical programme, so-called dependencia or dependency theory. Here again, researchers worked with the conceptual duo of 'centre' and 'periphery', though unlike those in the work of Shils and Eisenstadt, these concepts were not understood in cultural terms with respect to a society or civilization, but were predominantly defined in *economic* terms and were *related to the entire world (economy)*. On this view, the centre – essentially meaning the Western countries – is exploiting the periphery, in other words the Third World.

In the 1970s, this approach was further radicalized as its exponents turned increasingly to the analytical tools of Marxism. This theoretical movement was associated above all with the name of the American Immanuel Wallerstein (b. 1930), originally a specialist in African history and politics. Deploying what he called 'world systems theory', Wallerstein pursued the hugely ambitious goal of writing a history of the world since the age of European expansion in the fifteenth century. With his starting point the notion that the world economy was and is centrally governed by certain world cities that control flows of money and trade (Seville and Amsterdam at the beginning of this period, London in the eighteenth and nineteenth centuries and finally New York City in the present era), Wallerstein described the system of nation-states as fundamentally dependent on economic structures. This furnished him with a theoretical skeleton key with which he could divide the world into 'centre', 'semi-periphery' and 'periphery'. He then went on to describe and explain macrosociological processes of change (see Wallerstein, *The Modern World-System*, 3 vols.; for a brief overview, see Wallerstein, *Historical Capitalism*).

While Wallerstein's model was clearly reductionist and many of his explanations were questionable, as he ultimately traced all historical phenomena back to processes of unequal economic exchange, world systems theory and similar approaches were certainly the most influential macrosociological paradigms in sociology worldwide in the 1970s and early 1980s. The empirical failure of modernization theory was all too obvious, while the Marxian highlighting of gross exploitation seemed to explain far more plausibly the failure of 'development'. Attempts to renew Parsonianism 'suffered' from this widespread view. The international macrosociological debate was unambiguously dominated by dependency theory or Wallersteinian world systems theory, in comparison with which Eisenstadt, for example, found himself in a very difficult position. Parsons and all (post-)Parsonians were on the defensive.

There are all kinds of reasons why Parsonianism nonetheless saw a turnaround from the mid-1980s at the latest. First, in light of the collapse of the Soviet Union and its satellite states, Marxism, at least that embodied by the communist regimes, was plunged into crisis in a way that could no longer be papered over. But even Western Marxism à la Wallerstein, and with it dependency theory, struggled to explain certain events, because, second, the so-called Asian tiger economies like South Korea and Taiwan were clearly developing in ways that clashed with their tenets. Third, as a result of all this, even modernization theory, which had previously been abandoned, underwent and is still undergoing something of a revival, because the Western system of values and institutions had proved superior after all – this at least was the implicit argument put forward in the 1990s by authors such as the American Edward A. Tiryakian, born in 1930, another important student of Parsons ('Modernisation: Exhumetur in Pace'), and the German Wolfgang Zapf (born in 1937; 'Die Modernisierungstheorie und unterschiedliche Pfade der gesellschaftlichen Entwicklung' ['Modernization Theory and Differing Paths of Societal Development']). Fourth and finally, Parsons himself was rediscovered by sociologists worldwide. At least some parts of his extensive and heterogeneous theoretical edifice were declared important and useful in unexpected quarters, by Jürgen Habermas for instance, as you may recall from Lecture X.

As a result of all this, the Parsonians suddenly returned to the centre of theoretical debates with renewed vigour. A new generation of sociologists, a good deal younger than Parsons, Shils, Eisenstadt, Bellah and Smelser, set about renewing Parsonianism from the roots up. In Germany, this theoretical movement was and is most strongly associated with the name of Richard Münch (b. 1945). Münch, currently professor of sociology at Bamberg, published a kind of rival product to Jürgen Habermas' *Theory of Communicative Action* in 1982 with his *Theory of Action: Towards a New Synthesis Going Beyond Parsons* and *Understanding Modernity: Towards a New Perspective Going Beyond Durkheim and Weber*. The key assertion in Münch's comparative analysis of these classical figures is that Talcott Parsons is the superior theorist because, by drawing on Kant, he developed a 'voluntaristic theory of action', a theory so comprehensive that it requires very little revision. Because Parsons took up Kantian ideas, so Münch thought, he was able to avoid all reductionisms, which crop up time and again in the works of Durkheim and Weber, but especially in that of contemporary theorists. Though the thesis that Parsons' work was Kantian at heart is disputed by some (in interpreting Parsons, authors such as Charles Camic (b. 1951) have placed substantially more emphasis on the economic ideas that moulded Parsons' early work, while Harald Wenzel (b. 1955) pointed to the influence of the American philosopher Alfred North Whitehead), Münch did much to reconstruct Parsonian thought. The nature of this reconstruction, however, can be understood only against the background of his critique of the work of Niklas Luhmann. According to Münch, Luhmann squandered Parsons' legacy and pushed functionalism in the wrong direction. Because Luhmann had radicalized functionalism unnecessarily, by asserting that differentiated subsystems are incapable of communicating and can do no more than disrupt one another, he had lost Parsons' original insight into the 'interpenetration' of subsystems. It is true, Münch tells us, that the subsystems have become largely differentiated in the modern era. But in Western modernity, the subsystems have *not* become *entirely* detached from one another: time and again, cultural patterns and values impact on the different systems. Western development in particular entailed the *mutual interpenetration of ethics and the world*. This, he claims, has changed little to this day. In contrast to Luhmann, but in agreement with Parsons, Münch thus insists that societies, including contemporary ones, feature *normative integration*. These emphatically normative components of Münch's theory also found clear expression in his subsequent studies, in which his definitions of modernity and comparative analysis of England and the USA or France and Germany came very close to cultural determinism (*Die Struktur der Moderne. Grundmuster und differentielle Gestaltung des institutionellen Aufbaus der modernen Gesellschaften* ['The Structure of Modernity: Basic Patterns and Differences in the Institutional Development of Modern Societies'] and *Die Kultur der Moderne* ['The Culture of Modernity'], 2 vols.). Münch has also produced numerous diagnoses of the present era in recent years.

Distancing himself more clearly from Parsons' work, the American Jeffrey C. Alexander (b. 1947) burst upon the scene in 1983 with the publication of a four-volume work entitled *Theoretical Logic in Sociology*. Here, he analysed the approaches of Marx, Durkheim and Weber; in much the same way as Münch, he praised Parsons' work as a superior theoretical synthesis. Alexander, however, made a good deal more than had Münch of the fact that Parsons quite often 'forgot' his own theoretical insights: his fundamentally multidimensional theoretical construct often became narrowed down because of a certain idealism (airbrushing out the material aspects of action for example); furthermore, he had often succumbed to the temptation of simply equating his theoretical models with reality, and his evolutionary analyses tended to present American society as the endpoint of history. Alexander was thus sharply critical of Parsons. But at the same time, he began to gather together the remaining functionalists and Parsonians, labelling the 'movement' that resulted 'neo-functionalism'. What lay behind this move? According to Alexander, while it was necessary to strengthen the action theoretical elements in Parsonian functionalism, this theory was basically in good working order. Indeed, even more surprisingly, in the 1970s at the latest a large number of sociologists reached maturity whose working methods are compatible with just such a renewed Parsonianism, modified in light of action theory. Functionalism – so Alexander tells us in 1985 – is by no means dead; in fact it lives on, even if the design of the theory is slightly different, making it appropriate to refer to '*neo*-functionalism'. These neo-functionalists, among whom Alexander, taking a rather liberal approach, includes a large number of quite different authors (Eisenstadt, Smelser and Bellah appear alongside Luhmann and even Habermas, see 'Introduction', 1985, p. 16), allegedly share at least five key theses: (1) Society is understood as a system or pattern amenable to analysis. (2) The focus of analysis lies more on action than structure. (3) The thesis of the integration of societies is a theoretical assumption rather than an empirical statement. (4) It is important to insist upon Parsons' distinction between personality, culture and society, as this is the only way of preventing reductionism and at the same time grasping the tense relationship between these three realms. (5) Differentiation is a crucial mode of social change (ibid., pp. 9–10; see also Alexander and Colomy, 'Toward Neo-Functionalism').

This last point seemed particularly important to the 'neo-functionalists', or at least to those who accepted that Alexander's label could be properly applied to them, which is why the literature sometimes refers to 'theorists of differentiation'. For differentiation theory, whose roots lay primarily in structural functionalism and modernization theory, was to be retained as the key tool for describing and explaining social change, which of course entailed a fairly radical departure from the original notions of differentiation. In light of new empirical findings, scholars in the field no longer took the positive effects of differentiation as their sole point of departure, but also discussed negative ones, blocked differentiation and de-differentiation, etc. (see Colomy, 'Recent Developments in the Functionalist Approach to Change'). Eisenstadt of course already saw things in this way in the 1960s. Yet, however positive this adoption of Eisenstadt's insights may have been, the neo-functionalists and (new) differentiation theorists were faced with an obvious question: what sense does it make to speak of 'differentiation theory' if one constantly refers to *exceptions* within this 'master process' of differentiation? If it is true that historical processes do not all lead to a particular goal, but rather contingent phenomena constantly crop up, etc., why must all of this be understood through the concept of differentiation in the first place? Differentiation theory thus makes a rather poor centrepiece of neo-functionalist theory because it rules out practically nothing (see Joas, *The Creativity of Action*, pp. 223ff.). Equally, one may ask what exactly the term 'functionalism' in the label 'neo-functionalism' is supposed to mean. This term too has become rather meaningless, because many of the authors described as 'neo-functionalist' say practically nothing about systems and functions. This is why functionalist 'traditionalists' among the 'neo-functionalists', such as Bernard Barber ('Neofunctionalism and the Theory of the Social System'), have called for greater attention to be paid to the concept of system, because this is the only sensible way to carry out functional analyses – but to no avail. For there is no consensus within the neo-functionalist 'movement' with regard to the concept of system. There are thus good reasons to doubt the coherence of 'neo-functionalism'.

This is not to say that the renewal of Parsonianism did not produce important insights or usher in significant developments. We would, however, suggest that no *coherent* theoretical framework, meaningfully summed up by a single label, has emerged from the legacy of Parsons' work. There is no 'neo-functionalism'; at most, there are individual authors who have rendered great services in renewing Parsonianism (Eisenstadt is surely the outstanding figure here), but in very different ways.

Today, Alexander seems to see things this way as well. He explicitly refrains from calling himself a 'neo-functionalist' any longer, as implied in the title of one of his more recent works, from 1998: *Neofunctionalism and After*. In fact, Alexander's importance lies not in the intriguing but problematic terms he has coined, but in the fact that he, along with other writers, has opened up the work of Parsons in a crucial respect. Chiefly from the 1990s on, he has immersed himself in the study of a diverse array of cultural analyses, in an effort to rectify a key deficiency of Parsonian theory. Parsons' account of 'culture' overstated its homogeneity, failing to bring out internal tensions. Further, his descriptions of specific cultures, rather than being based on empirical 'thick description' (an expression coined by Parsons' student, the cultural anthropologist Clifford Geertz, 1923–2006), are basically analytical constructs.

Alexander's project involves learning from cultural historians and anthropologists such as Clifford Geertz and Victor Turner (1920–83) and getting at processes of cultural change, particularly in terms of methodology. His aim is to show that cultural discourses are often structured in accordance with binary codes ('friend–enemy', 'pure–impure', etc.) and that their dynamics are anchored in this binarism (see 'Culture and Political Crisis: "Watergate" and Durkheimian sociology' or 'Citizen and Enemy as Symbolic Classification: On the Polarizing Discourse of Civil Society'; on Alexander's approach, see Wenzel, 'Einleitung: Neofunktionalismus und theoretisches Dilemma' ['Introduction: Neofunctionalism and Theoretical Dilemma']). Here, Alexander – with the same intention as Shils and Eisenstadt but in a somewhat different manner (see pp. 316ff.) – attempts to conceptualize 'culture' in a more nuanced way as the core feature of Parsonian theory. Parsons himself, strangely enough, largely failed to analyse culture. Unlike Shils, Alexander's concern is again more with the disruptive aspect of charisma or the sacred and the openness of the situations in which this disruption makes itself felt; unlike Eisenstadt, his focus is less on profound historical processes than on the recent past and the present, particularly the preconditions for a functioning civil society and the process of coming to terms with the Holocaust in the post-Second World War era. Alexander's writings provide strong evidence that drawing directly on Parsons' work can still be a fruitful endeavour and that his oeuvre will always attract scholars keen on interpreting and developing it further – whatever labels may be applied.

While we have taken account of the writings of the Israeli sociologist Shmuel Eisenstadt and his German colleague Richard Münch, this lecture was concerned mainly with American theoretical traditions. In the next three lectures, we enter a different national context, indeed, one might almost say a different world – that of France.

XIV

Structuralism and poststructuralism

Should you glance back over our lectures so far, you may come away with the impression that the development of modern sociological theory has been an overwhelmingly American, British and German affair, with other nations playing no more than a minor role. But the reality is quite different. The (geographical) focus of our account is due primarily to the fact that these national traditions of sociology were very much aware of and generally responded quickly to one another, allowing us to proceed more or less chronologically in the preceding thirteen lectures: 'First came Parsons, then his predominantly American critics, followed by attempts at synthesis in Europe by Habermas, Luhmann and Giddens, who in turn criticized each other, along with certain attempts to develop Parsons' legacy in modified form' – this has been the 'plot' of our story so far.

However, the simple elegance of this 'plot' cannot be sustained within the framework of our lectures – at least if one takes the *French* contribution to the development of modern sociological theory as seriously as it deserves. For until the late 1960s, the social sciences and humanities in France formed a continent apparently sufficient unto itself. This was bound up with the fact that there are vigorous and productive intellectual traditions in France that laid the foundations for a highly autonomous, not to say isolated national development. This was particularly apparent in the case of sociology. Here, the work of Emile Durkheim dominated to a degree unknown in other countries. Prior to the epoch-making rupture of the First World War, French sociology and the Durkheim school were practically identical, because by the time of his death in 1917, Durkheim had managed not only to mould the sociological debate, but to fill a large number of influential academic posts with his students. Durkheim was a tremendously successful builder of institutions, and it is almost solely down to him that sociology was able to gain a foothold so rapidly within the canon of university disciplines in France as a recognized subject. In his day, Max Weber by no means occupied a similarly unchallenged intellectual status within the social sciences in Germany, as is implied almost automatically nowadays when we refer to him as *the* classical German sociologist – quite apart from the fact that the institutionalization of sociology through the establishment of independent chairs occurred far later than in

France. In the USA, it is true, the subject was established at around the same time as in France, under the overall control of the department of sociology and anthropology at the University of Chicago. But there was no outstanding, utterly dominant figure at Chicago to match Durkheim's status within French sociology as a whole. The Chicago School was more of a network, while the Durkheim School entailed a clear hierarchy.

Until the First World War, then, Durkheim and the Durkheimians, though not without their rivals, were the undisputed point of reference (in both a positive and negative sense) of every sociological discussion in France, and the intellectual legacy of Durkheim and his successors remains alive to such an extent that even very contemporary theoretical debates within sociology cannot be understood without being located within the context of interpretations of Durkheim. We thus need to look briefly back over the development of French sociology in the twentieth century before we can address the theme of this lecture – French structuralism and poststructuralism. The roots of these theories also lie in an intellectual space deeply moulded by the work of Durkheim.

While Durkheim's ideas, which first made an impact in the late nineteenth century, have remained alive in France to the present day, with the demise of the 'master' the Durkheim School did of course become somewhat less important, a development reinforced by 'external' circumstances. For some of what Durkheim had achieved in establishing a school of sociological research rooted in his ideas was simply wiped out by the First World War, insofar as a fair number of his successful students fell on the field of battle. While the school survived after 1918 thanks to the efforts of one or two outstanding figures, most of Durkheim's remaining students were unable to inject fresh impetus, especially of the theoretical kind. Among these 'outstanding figures', Marcel Mauss (1872–1950) and Maurice Halbwachs (1877–1945) are particularly worthy of note; taught by Durkheim himself, they kept his legacy alive. Other key figures included Georges Bataille (1897–1962) and Roger Caillois (1913–78), who combined certain motifs found in Durkheim's sociology of religion with surrealism to create a theoretical mix of great interest, in a literary as well as sociological sense, at the short-lived Collège de Sociologie, founded in 1937; German intellectuals such as Walter Benjamin (1892–1940) and Hans Mayer (1907–2001) were in contact with these figures (see Mayer, *Ein Deutscher auf Widerruf. Erinnerungen* ['A German Until Further Notice: A Memoir'], vol. I, pp. 236ff.). All in all, though, it is fair to say that the Durkheim School, and along with it French sociology as a whole, suffered much the same fate in the 1920s as the Chicago School of sociology and sociology in Germany: innovative impulses gradually ran out of steam and these intellectual movements became generally more sterile.

One new and very remarkable development on the French intellectual scene, however, initially affecting philosophy more than sociology, was a new reception of 'German thought' beginning in the inter-war period. Hegel and Marx, along with Freud and phenomenological thinkers such as Husserl and Heidegger were re-read or read for the first time on a large scale – Russian émigré Alexandre Kojève (1902–68) being one of the key intermediaries here. Raymond Aron's assimilation of the work of Max Weber had particularly far-reaching consequences for sociology; after the war, Aron, mentioned in Lecture VIII, became one of France's leading journalists and a leading sociologist of war and of international relations. In the context of a fairly wide-ranging philosophical (and to some extent sociological) debate, very much moulded by German thought, a number of young intellectuals were growing to maturity; from the early 1940s on, while France was still under German occupation, they began to exercise a massive influence on French thought. Jean-Paul Sartre's *Being and Nothingness: An Essay on Phenomenological Ontology* from 1943 was the philosophical manifesto of a movement that truly came into its own following the end of the occupation and the Vichy regime under the label of 'existentialism' and which dominated intellectual debate in France in the late 1940s and 1950s. In circumstances of foreign rule and everyday collaboration with the Nazis, Sartre's early philosophical magnum opus was a despairing call for authenticity and responsibility, for a morality of the individual, especially that of the isolated intellectual in a repressive world. It was – as Sartre's biographer Annie Cohen-Solal (*Sartre*, p. 187) was to put it – the 'declaration of the absolute supremacy of subjectivity over the world' and thus 'a profoundly Cartesian work'.

After 1945, with this his basic stance, Sartre drove forward the philosophical debate, collaborating and sometimes clashing with other brilliant philosophers such as Maurice Merleau-Ponty. In parallel with this, Sartre's own literary works, as well as the novels produced by his wife Simone de Beauvoir (1908–86) and by Nobel Prize-winning novelist Albert Camus (1913–60), a long-time friend of Sartre until they fell out spectacularly over politics, awakened an attitude towards life that appealed to a broad public. Time after time, existentialism aroused massive interest among the reading public, in part because of the political controversies that so often surrounded it: for a time, Sartre expressed his support for the Communist Party of France. It was anything but clear how his theoretical subjectivism could be reconciled with membership of a Stalinist cadre party (see Kurzweil, *The Age of Structuralism*, pp. 2ff.).

This fusion of phenomenology, existentialism and left-wing radicalism dominated the intellectual life of France into the 1950s, but then began to lose influence, particularly – and this brings us to the real focus of the present lecture – in light of the emergence of a powerful counter-movement in the shape of 'structuralism'. It is hard to determine precisely why existentialism faded so rapidly as structuralism took off. Political reasons alone were certainly not the key factor here. While Sartre's confusing political involvements – such as his fluctuating membership of the Communist Party – may have disturbed many of his followers, the later structuralists were no different in this regard. Many of them were also heavily involved in left-wing politics or even doctrinaire agitators for the French Communist Party. Rather, we may have to attempt to explain this development from a philosophical point of view, as did Pierre Bourdieu and Jean-Claude Passeron ('Sociology and Philosophy in France since 1945: Death and Resurrection of a Philosophy without Subject'). On this view, as French philosophy and sociology developed over time, they oscillated constantly between an exaggerated subjectivism and excessive anti-subjectivism or objectivism, so that structuralism inevitably superseded the subjectivism characteristic of the golden age of Sartre. For structuralism (and here we offer simply an initial characterization, which we will flesh out later on) was a profound critique of the ideas found in the work of Sartre on the subject's capacity to choose, the individual's capacity for autonomous action or the always threatened but ever-present possibility of human self-realization. And it was all the easier to be critical because, for so long, Sartre did so little to open up philosophy to the individual disciplines within the humanities and social sciences. This applied especially to new and burgeoning subjects. He was, for example, as dismissive or hostile towards linguistics as he was towards Freudian psychoanalysis, as was only too apparent in *Being and Nothingness* (see esp. pp. 458ff. and 557ff.). This seemed unsatisfactory to those philosophers looking for new approaches and intellectual links, and it is thus no surprise that many of them actively sought to break with Sartre and his style of philosophizing (see Dosse, *History of Structuralism*, vol. I, p. 3). It was only in response to this that Sartre tried to do more to integrate the social sciences into his thought.

But let us take one step at a time. When we speak of 'structuralism', you will notice right away that it contains a term with which you are already familiar from its frequent appearance in the preceding lectures, that of 'structure'. And this constituent part of the word does in fact tell us something significant about the intentions of the theorists to whom this label applies:

> The structuralists are distinguished first and foremost by their ardent, powerfully held conviction that there is structure underlying all human behavior and mental functioning, and by their belief that this structure can be discovered through orderly analysis, that it has cohesiveness and meaning.
>
> (Gardner, *The Quest for Mind*, p. 10)

However, the characterization expressed in this quote does not seem particularly specific at first sight. Could not theorists such as Parsons, Luhmann, Habermas or Giddens, who have also worked with the concept of structure, also be labelled 'structuralists'? The answer is no, because structuralists have *a very specific understanding of structure*.

Parsons, together with most of the theorists we have dealt with so far, did *not* make the effort to clarify the concept of structure more precisely. When Parsons referred to 'structure', he generally meant no more than a kind of architectural plan, a model of parts, parts which fit together to form a greater whole. And the term has generally been used in sociology in similarly vague fashion since then. The term was and is something of a jack-of-all-trades, deployed to a diverse array of ends in every imaginable context, which is precisely why it is rarely defined in any detail. 'Urban structures', 'structures of the life-world', 'transportation structures', 'organizational structures', etc. – all terms in which the component 'structure' can scarcely mean the same thing.

Structuralists, on the other hand, have a more specific understanding of structures which emerged and developed in different (humanities) disciplines during the first half of the twentieth century as their exponents grappled with the special features of human language and human thought (see Caws, *Structuralism: The Art of the Intelligible*, pp. 11ff.). It was, however, *linguistics* that really, or at least most effectively, initiated the structuralist movement in the social sciences. The outstanding figure here was Ferdinand de Saussure (1857–1913), who sparked off something of a conceptual revolution within linguistics with his posthumously published lectures (see his 1916 *Cours de linguistique générale*, English title: *Course in General Linguistics*), which subsequently exercised a profound influence on the French structuralism of the 1950s and 1960s and thus the social sciences in France. What was so revolutionary about Saussure's ideas? Which changes did this Geneva-based linguist set in motion and why did his thought attract such a large cross-disciplinary following decades later? We must look first at Saussure's work if we are to understand the social scientific structuralism based upon it.

Research on human language was first carried out in a systematic and consistent way in the late eighteenth and early nineteenth centuries, with scholars taking an almost exclusively historical approach. Linguistics was often equated with historical philology, the primary aim being to place linguistic phenomena within the historical process, to investigate how words have changed over time, how, for instance, Latin words have adapted to the German language, how Middle High German and later New High German emerged from Old High German or how mother and daughter languages have developed out of one another. Influenced by (German) Romanticism, 'language families' or linguistic 'family trees' were the key concepts deployed by scholars, in order to portray the historical transformation of language(s), and present this as a process of organic change.

Saussure, and even more his later admirers and interpreters, broke radically with this historical philology and with the idea that the *historical* investigation of language is the primary object of linguistics. Rather, they concentrated – as researchers studying languages without written sources, such as those of native Americans, had already done – on the question of how a specific language is constructed internally and thus how it may be described in its *stable condition*. One, if not *the* crucial step in establishing this novel analytical focus was Saussure's distinction between the speech of individuals (*la parole*) and language as an abstract (social) system (*la langue*), the latter of which was to become the true object of his linguistics. Language

> is a fund accumulated by the members of the community through the practice of speech, a grammatical system existing potentially in every brain, or more exactly in the brains of a group of individuals; for the language is never complete in any single individual, but exists perfectly only in the collectivity.
>
> (*Course*, p. 13)

Which ideas underpinned this Saussurean distinction between *la parole* and *la langue*, which you may find rather implausible? Saussure's thinking ran roughly as follows. When I speak, that is, when I utter one or several sounds, this is a one-off occurrence. My repetition of the sound 'tree' never produces a totally identical physical pattern, as can easily be demonstrated by a sound meter. This applies even more strikingly when *different* people utter the word 'tree'. In light of the fact that a sound will always vary physically in this way, the question arises of how we know that these differing sound-waves refer to the same word, 'tree'? We know, according to Saussure, simply because we as hearers produce a kind of hypothesis through which we establish a connection between a particular physical sound and an *ideal* sound (the *signifier*); at the same time, we know that this ideal sound is associated with the idea of a trunk with branches and leaves or needles (here Saussure refers to the *signified*). Saussure calls the linkage of idea and sound, of signified and signifier, a 'sign' (ibid., pp. 65ff.). A sign is thus an immaterial entity consisting of a signifier and an (abstract) signified, the signifier referring to the idea of the tree and the signified, conversely, to the sound.

The relationship between signifier and signified clearly requires clarification. Here, Saussure dismisses the so-called representational model of language, *the notion of a quasi-natural relationship between signifier and signified*. According to Saussure, it is impossible to infer the meaning of a word from its sound. Conversely, there are no pre-existing ideas from which the sound of a word might 'naturally' arise. Rather, Saussure is of the opinion that the signifier is entirely independent of the signified (the term), or more generally that the signifier is randomly or arbitrarily assigned to the term. An example may serve to illustrate this. The three-syllable sound 'vehicle' has nothing to do with the abstract notion of an object that moves on wheels, as evident in the fact that the sound denoting the same concept is different in different languages, such as German (*Fahrzeug*). Which signifier is assigned to which signified does not of course depend on the individual speaker, but is a matter of convention. Languages have histories; at some point, a particular sign with a particular meaning 'took hold' – language, as Saussure never ceases to underscore, is social in nature.

> Of all social institutions, a language affords the least scope for [initiative]. It is part and parcel of the life of the whole community, and the community's natural inertia exercises a conservative influence upon it.
>
> (*Course*, p. 74)

The immateriality of the sign and the fact that language is a system of signs, which are based on conventions, justify Saussure's distinction between language (*la langue*) and the speech of individuals (*la parole*). Language very obviously exists independently of individual speakers; in fact, it assigns to speech its function in the first place. For it is only by dint of the fact that language is a stable, immaterial system of signs (Saussure was to state that language is form, not substance) that we can endow sounds, in all their different physical permutations, with a *fixed* meaning, that we can speak, no matter how often, and still be sure that we are producing the same meanings.

In light of all these preliminary considerations, particularly the assertion that the signifier is assigned arbitrarily to the signified, Saussure concludes that linguistic signs cannot be defined in their own terms *but only in association with other signs*. This applies to words as well as sounds. Within the word fields of a particular language, one which distinguishes for instance between 'believe', 'be of the opinion', 'know', 'assume', 'think', one word assigns meaning to another, for if a word did not exist, 'its content would be shared out among its competitors' (*Course*, p. 114). It is thus only because we have alternatives to the word 'believe' that this word is assigned a very specific meaning; 'believe' means something rather different from 'know' or 'think'.

An example from phonology makes this even clearer. The human being has an apparatus of articulation (vocal cords, tongue, lips, etc.), capable of producing an infinite variety of sounds. But each language in fact uses only a tiny proportion of all possible sounds. Some languages use nasal sounds, some use the unvoiced 's' more than the voiced; 'th' is unknown in German, as every German taking evening classes in English is painfully aware as he stumbles over this tricky sound. And the inhabitants of the 'Middle Kingdom' clearly struggle – this at least is the implication of many jokes about the Chinese – to pronounce the English 'r' correctly, because they are unfamiliar with the opposition between 'l' and 'r'. We can thus state that the structure of a language exhibits a certain logic, because only certain combinations of sounds are possible in certain languages, while others are not, because only certain distinctions are acknowledged, while others are not. Thus a language's phonological peculiarities cannot be revealed through examination of individual sounds, but only by analysing the *differences* and *combinatorics* characteristic of the individual phonemes (of the individual meaning-bearing sounds) (*Course*, p. 116).

On this view, the meanings of words and individual sounds are not produced by the sign as such, but rather by certain differences between the words within a particular word group or the oppositions between sounds – all specific to each language. We have to distinguish between words (and sounds) in order to be able to define them in the first place. Words or sounds take on meaning only when we delimit them, only by dint of their *difference* from other words or sounds. Thus, in order to understand language, we must think *relationally*, in terms of *relationships*, which would bring us neatly to the concept of *structure*, though Saussure himself, who preferred to speak of a *'system* of language', did not use the term in this way.

The thesis of the arbitrary nature of the relationship between the signifier and signified (and thus the arbitrary nature of the sign in general) and the proposition that language is a system of signs which can be made sense of only by analysing the relations between the signs, appeared to open up the possibility – and this explains to some extent the enthusiasm Saussure's ideas were to generate both within and outside of linguistics – of making linguistics (and later the social sciences) a strictly scientific affair. For on these premises, because there is no need to take account of the always problematic and contested issue of how subjects impart meaning, and one can focus solely on the relations between the signifiers which constitute meaning in the first place, it becomes possible to investigate language in highly objective and scientific fashion. The assumption here is that it is only by analysing objectively the combination of signifiers that we can outline the *structure* of the language, of which speakers or subjects are *unaware*, that we can demonstrate how meanings are constituted in the first place. In other words, Saussure's approach emphasized the primacy of an underlying system, which must be described objectively; while analysis of this system certainly leads us to meanings, they themselves are merely surface phenomena and thus only of secondary importance – a position which Sartre always vigorously resisted as he grappled with linguistics (again, see *Being and Nothingness*, e.g. p. 510).

Propelled by Saussure's insights, it seemed possible for linguistics to transform into a 'hard' discipline close to the natural sciences, though it took some time for scholars to reach this conclusion. For if Saussure's premises were correct, linguistics no longer had to be a historical science featuring all the interpretive problems with which historians and humanities scholars are always faced, but could produce seemingly objective, quasi-natural scientific knowledge. To put it in more general terms, it no longer seemed necessary for linguistics to take a hermeneutic approach. Hermeneutics (see Lecture IX, pp. 204ff.) is, as you know, based on the insight that we can get at the essence of symbolic orders only by means of interpretations. Because new interpretations are inevitable, however, these never lead to a final result that would bring the process of interpretation to an end. Structural linguists seemed able to avoid the hermeneutic 'problem' of the never-ending process of interpretation, believing that they could 'explain' linguistic systems objectively, and thus once and for all. It seemed possible to realize a scientific dream, according to which the structures of language could be penetrated down to the last detail, making it possible to grasp the genesis of meaning – *and without having to analyse the (linguistic) subject which in fact imparts meaning*. This seemed to pave the way for linguistics to rid itself of the subject (that endows the world with meaning), bringing us back once again to the interpretation outlined above, according to which French intellectual life oscillated constantly between a radical subjectivism and a radical anti-subjectivism (Dosse, *History of Structuralism*, vol. I, p. 59).

Saussure's (structural) methods were quick to attract followers; they were taken up by linguists in other countries – though with certain modifications – and generally roused broad interest in non-linguistic sign systems as well. For language is just *one* sign system among others, and why should other such systems (sign language, symbolic rites, polite forms of address, military signals) not be fathomed by means of a similar scientific toolkit? Ultimately, this was the view taken by Saussure himself, who envisaged a general theory of signs (which he called *sémiologie* or semiology, see *Course*, p. 15). It was thus only a matter of time until social scientists – fascinated by this way of thinking – also took up this idea, applying the structural method to non-linguistic sign systems, to ordered social relations.

One man in particular played a key role in France in this regard, a figure later described as the 'father of structuralism', the anthropologist and sociologist Claude Lévi-Strauss. He applied the conceptual model of structural linguistics to anthropology and sociology and developed a conception of 'structures' new to the social sciences in this particular form, a conception which may become clearer if you read the above quotation on p. 342 again more closely. The assertion here is that structuralists wished to get at the 'structure underlying all human behavior and *mental functioning*' (emphasis added). This was precisely Lévi-Strauss' hugely ambitious aim as he set about identifying the *unconscious structures of the human mind and of human culture*.

Claude Lévi-Strauss was born in 1908 in Brussels, Belgium, where he grew up in a family of Jewish-French intellectuals. He studied philosophy and law at the Sorbonne, but soon turned to anthropology and sociology, at which point he happened to be offered a position as professor of sociology at the University of São Paulo in Brazil. Lévi-Strauss took up this offer in 1934. When he had fulfilled his teaching commitments, he organized an expedition to central Brazil in 1938–9, during which he had the opportunity to carry out field research on the Nambikwara and Tupi-Kawahib. In 1939 he returned to France to do military service, but had to leave the country again in the spring of 1941 for political and 'racial' reasons following the Nazi victory. He went to New York, where he came into contact with leading American anthropologists such as Franz Boas (1858–1942) among others and became friends with an increasingly renowned Russian linguist, Roman Jakobson (1896–1982), who was the first to use the term 'structuralism', introducing him to a new field of knowledge, that of structural linguistics. Between 1945 and 1947, Lévi-Strauss worked as the cultural attaché at the French embassy in Washington before, drawing on his Brazilian fieldwork, he came to public attention towards the end of the 1940s with the publication of two anthropological books, one of them being *Les structures élémentaires de la parenté* (English title: *The Elementary Structures of Kinship*) from 1949, the founding text of structural anthropology. Further important publications – including a highly influential travelogue and literary masterpiece from 1955 on his experiences in Brazil entitled *Tristes Tropiques* – allowed him to rapidly ascend the scholarly career ladder; he was ultimately appointed to the chair in social anthropology at the famous Collège de France, the leading French institute of higher education, in 1959. A number of other important publications followed, of which a fair number were to have a significant impact on the neighbouring social sciences; Lévi-Strauss received various honours, including election to the Académie française in 1973, before becoming professor emeritus at the Collège de France in 1982.

If one reads the first major book by Lévi-Strauss, which was soon to become famous, *The Elementary Structures of Kinship*, one can understand even now the kind of earthquake it must have triggered in certain fields of the French social sciences. A fusion of philosophical reflection on the relationship between culture and nature, detailed ethnographic descriptions of highly complex kinship structures and elegant structuralist theory that claimed to penetrate this complexity, this text continues to exude a unique fascination, despite the knowledge that a number of the theses put forward by Lévi-Strauss have now been convincingly refuted by anthropologists.

The very title of the book is a provocation in certain respects; at the very least, it suggests that the author is not exactly lacking in self-confidence. For as you may have noticed, it recalls Durkheim's famous late work *The Elementary Forms of Religious Life*. But Lévi-Strauss is by no means posing as an orthodox Durkheimian here. On the contrary, he firmly rejects Durkheim's interpretation of the incest taboo, for example. However, Lévi-Strauss draws on a text produced by a famous student of Durkheim, Marcel Mauss, whom we have mentioned already, whose *Essai sur le don* (1923/24; English title: *The Gift: The Form and Reason for Exchange in Archaic Societies*) pointed to the overriding importance of gift exchange to the functioning of societies. According to Mauss, who happened to be Durkheim's nephew, the giving, receiving and reciprocal giving of gifts were the key mechanisms for establishing solidarity in archaic societies. For giving – whatever form this might take – is an opportunity to create reciprocity, because it results in expectations and obligations that create ties between people. How could Lévi-Strauss make use of Marcel Mauss' idea, given that he was concerned with the seemingly very different topic of kinship structures?

Lévi-Strauss presents a two-stage argument here. First, he claims that the difference between nature and culture is that there are no rules or norms in nature. It is only the establishment of rules and norms (conveyed through language) that makes cultural development possible in the first place; the human being becomes a cultural being only through norms and rules. '[The] absence of rules seems to provide the surest criterion for distinguishing a natural from a cultural process' (*The Elementary Structures of Kinship*, p. 8). Lévi-Strauss thus goes on to state that every human universal is an aspect of the natural world, while everything subject to a specific norm or rule is an aspect of culture. On this view, the role of culture is to replace chance occurrence with (orderly) organization and thus to secure the existence of the group as a group (ibid., p. 42). However, as Lévi-Strauss recognizes, this statement, in itself very clear and understandable, raises a problem as soon as one approaches a phenomenon that has long fascinated anthropologists, as well as Durkheim, namely the incest taboo. For this is without doubt a rule not observed with such strictness in the animal kingdom, but is, according to Lévi-Strauss, universal, that is, present in every culture:

> Here therefore is a phenomenon which has the distinctive characteristics both of nature and of its theoretical contradiction, culture. The prohibition of incest has the universality of bent and instinct, and the coercive character of law and institution. Where then does it come from, and what is its place and significance?
>
> (ibid., p. 10)

Here, Lévi-Strauss makes use of Marcel Mauss' ideas on exchange relations in archaic societies. For the incest taboo, the prohibition on marriage within a particular kinship group, ensures that people marry 'out'. A man or woman is thus passed on to another group. He or she must marry in to this group because the incest taboo forbids marriage within the group. The incest taboo thus necessitates 'exogamy' and guarantees that people are 'exchanged' *between groups*. Lévi-Strauss thus believes that kinship structures, which are based on the universal incest taboo, can be interpreted in much the same way as the gift or economic exchange. These structures always produce reciprocity and ties of solidarity, not least because people, particularly women, represent an economic good as a result of their capacity for labour: by forgoing the women in their group, men gain access to a more extensive 'marriage pool'. That is, they can expect an inflow of women and thus labour 'from outside' while concurrently creating relations of solidarity and reciprocity to other groups. Lévi-Strauss explains what this means in the case of certain particularly clear-cut kinship structures characterized by so-called 'generalized exchange':

> Generalized exchange establishes a system of operations conducted 'on credit'. A surrenders a daughter or a sister to B, who surrenders one to

C, who, in turn, will surrender one to A. This is its simplest formula. Consequently, generalized exchange always contains an element of trust (more especially when the cycle requires more intermediaries, and when secondary cycles are added to the principal cycle). There must be the confidence that the cycle will close again, and that after a period of time a woman will eventually be received in compensation for the woman initially surrendered.

(ibid., p. 265)

The incest taboo and the rule of exogamy thus exhibit clear functionality for groups. Because they establish ties between different groups, they also have a integrative effect. Lévi-Strauss also claims that marriage should literally be viewed as a form of exchange:

> Because marriage is exchange, because marriage is the archetype of exchange, the analysis of exchange can help in the understanding of the solidarity which unites the gift and the counter-gift, and one marriage with other marriages.

(ibid., p. 483)

Not only that, but the kinship system, like the system of gift exchange analysed by Marcel Mauss, is a *system of signs*, which may be studied in the same way as language – with fundamentally the same methods, namely those originally developed by structural linguistics. At the same time, Lévi-Strauss claims to be able to trace back the kinship structures, quite different in each society, to elementary principles, just as Saussure had tried to render transparent the complexity of human speech by laying bare the ideal structure of language (*la langue*). In fact, Lévi-Strauss even goes a step further. All these systems of signs – whether languages, kinship systems or systems of archaic gift exchange – ultimately *adhere to a specific logic inherent to the human mind*. If we could pin down this logic, then according to Lévi-Strauss this would provide us with the key to analysing symbolic representations of every kind. He was convinced

> that an internal logic directs the unconscious workings of the human mind, even in those of its creations which have long been considered the most arbitrary, and that the appropriate methods to be applied to it are those usually reserved for the study of the physical world.

(ibid., p. 220)

Lévi-Strauss had already made clear how he believes the human mind functions in *The Elementary Structures of Kinship*, albeit that this aspect was to find full expression only in his later work. The human mind is structured in 'binary' fashion, it 'works' with oppositions – an idea that Lévi-Strauss borrowed from his friend, the linguist Roman Jakobson. The latter expounded the thesis, a modified version of ideas found in the work of Saussure, that language is characterized not only by a clearly defined structure, but that this is a *binary* structure. It is possible to break language down into its component parts in as much as it is characterized by oppositions, between consonants and vowels, which are dull or sharp, hard or soft, etc. and which are opposed according to very specific rules in the various languages. Ultimately – Lévi-Strauss concludes – social sign systems such as the kinship and gift exchange systems also rest upon this opposition, as apparent, for example, in the distinction between 'inside' and 'outside' (in the case of endogamy or exogamy) or between giving and receiving (as with gift exchange and the reciprocity which rests upon it). Lévi-Strauss thus thought that while it may be going too far to state that

> 'human societies tend automatically and unconsciously to disintegrate, along rigid mathematical lines, into exactly symmetrical units' (James G. Frazer) ... perhaps it must be acknowledged that *duality, alternation, opposition* and *symmetry*, whether presented in definite forms or in imprecise forms, are not so much matters to be explained, as *basic and immediate data of mental and social reality which should be the starting-point of any attempt at explanation*.
> (ibid., p. 136; emphasis added)

Duality, as the basic structure of kinship relations, is certainly functional for groups, but it is observable in reality *not because* it is functional, but because it expresses the 'fundamental structures of the human mind' (ibid., p. 75). It is the structures of the mind that *unconsciously* steer human history along certain paths. Contingent, that is, unforeseeable events do of course occur over the course of human history, such as the migration of Indian tribes provoked by natural disasters, political upheavals, economic crises, etc.: 'However, ... the general result gives proof of *integrating forces which are independent of such conditions, and under the influence of which history has tended towards system*' (ibid., pp. 76–7; emphasis added).

Lévi-Strauss was to develop this form of analysis further over the course of time, attempting to apply the idea of the binary structure of all human cultural forms to other 'objects', not just the kinship system. Several volumes appearing since the mid-1960s under the title *Introduction to a Science of Mythology*, for example, are devoted to the structural analysis of myths, the subtitle of the first volume, *The Raw and the Cooked*, alluding to the thesis of the binarity of the human mind, specifically the idea that 'cooking' marks a key dividing line between nature and culture.

But it is not the conclusions presented in these very difficult books, themselves increasingly composed in line with aesthetic principles and structured like myths, which are of primary interest to us here. Rather, we wish to return to the theoretical background to Lévi-Strauss' ideas in order to cast light on why contemporaries found structuralist thought so fascinating.

Lévi-Strauss' influence on French intellectual life was certainly due in part to the 'romantic' motifs that crop up so often in his work. He always acknowledged his admiration for Jean-Jacques Rousseau and, particularly in his later writings, declared archaic or 'savage thought' (a notion reflected in the title of his book *The Savage Mind*) a kind of (superior) alternative to the scientific rationality of the West (on the romantic elements in the work of Lévi-Strauss, see Axel Honneth, 'A Structuralist Rousseau: On the Anthropology of Claude Lévi-Strauss'). This alone inevitably attracted the attention of those intellectuals who could not bear this Western civilization and its sometimes problematic consequences. The profoundly expressive images found in *Tristes Tropiques* for example – his literary travelogue mentioned earlier – allowed readers a glimpse of another, archaic world, soon to be lost for ever, one which served a good number of intellectuals as a kind of ersatz utopia during an era of decolonization when many of them were troubled by an increasingly bad conscience with respect to colonialism. But these romantic aspects of Lévi-Strauss' work were just one half of the picture. It also featured a seemingly contrasting and unmistakably *scientistic* aspect.

Lévi-Strauss emphasized on numerous occasions that his work was partly informed by or modelled on structural linguistics and the work of Marx. The study of language as promoted by Saussure, among others (see *Structural Anthropology*, vol. II, p. 9), and Marx's writings had helped him appreciate the importance of the *latent* structures which it is so vital to understand if one is to have any chance of explaining surface phenomena. With respect to the social sciences, 'latent' means that structuralists such as Lévi-Strauss sought to identify structures of which human beings *are not consciously aware*. As a direct result of this, it becomes possible to explain culture without recourse to subjects and their interpretations. It is in fact vital to do so. As Lévi-Strauss repeatedly underlines, the ideas expressed by members of the indigenous population with respect to how their society functions all too often contradict its actual organization (see for example *Structural Anthropology*, vol. I, p. 133). But this is no problem, for the discovery of unconscious structures is the very definition of anthropology, whose 'originality [is anchored in] the unconscious nature of collective phenomena' (ibid., p. 18). And it is this unearthing of unconscious elements by means of structural analysis that ensures the discipline's scientific status. Anthropology and sociology must thus take their lead from structural linguistics, the field within the social sciences and humanities that has come closest to approximating the natural sciences:

> of all the social and human sciences, linguistics alone can be put on an equal footing with the hard sciences. And this for three reasons: (a) it has a universal subject, the articulated language of which no human group is lacking; (b) its method is homogeneous (in other words, it remains the same, whatever the particular language to which it is applied, modern or archaic, 'primitive' or civilized); and (c) this method is based on some fundamental principles, the validity of which is unanimously recognized by specialists in spite of some minor divergences.
>
> (*Structural Anthropology*, vol. II, p. 299)

It was this (natural) scientific impulse, much more than its romantic motifs, which made Lévi-Strauss' structuralism attractive. He clearly had his finger on the pulse of French intellectual life when he used this theory to polemicize against 'unscientific' phenomenology and existentialism, both of which took individual experience as their point of departure and – labouring under the 'illusion of subjectivity' – believed this capable of explaining anything. Lévi-Strauss, meanwhile, believed that 'to reach reality one has first to reject experience, and then subsequently to re-integrate it into an objective synthesis devoid of any sentimentality' (*Tristes Tropiques*, p. 71). He thus criticizes Sartre's existentialism as a species of extreme Cartesianism which bases all its ideas on the individual ego. It is, he thought, imprisoned by a number of prejudices as a result (*The Savage Mind*, pp. 245ff.). Lévi-Strauss' critical characterization of the work of Sartre has a good deal to be said for it. But his solution to the problems of Sartrean philosophy is not to turn to theorists or theories of *inter*subjectivity, but rather – the pendulum swinging all the way back to the anti-subjectivism to which we referred earlier – to *deny all subjectivity in favour of the search for objective structures of mind*, structures whose effects pervade subjects without any help from them and which determine human society and its development. A way of thinking was born which held out the promise of a genuinely scientific approach, previously thought impossible, to the analysis of the most varied realms of social life. The idea of non-intentional systems of signs propagated in Lévi-Strauss' writings exuded the aura of strict objectivity and held out the prospect of placing the human sciences on a fully scientific basis. Many scholars thus gratefully embraced his ideas. If it was possible to understand kinship systems, economic systems and myths as systems of signs, why should it not be possible to apply the structural method to *all* social phenomena? Might not all the social sciences sign up to structural methods of analysis?

This was in fact attempted when the structuralist movement reached its peak in the mid-1960s. The structuralists succeeded – at least in terms of their public impact – in pushing non-structuralists further and further to the margins, to such an extent that figures such as Alain Touraine, admittedly a strong critic of structuralism, claimed that Paris in the 1960s had been 'occupied' by the structuralists. While this may appear to be overstating things, it is striking that structuralism seemed all-pervasive at the time. Psychoanalysis saw the rise of Jacques Lacan (1901–81) and his followers, who read Freudian theory in a particular, namely structuralist, way; in philosophy, sociology and political science, theorists such as Louis Althusser (1918–90) and Nicos Poulantzas (1936–79) set about reinterpreting the work of Marx, expunging all those elements they considered unscientific – and this applied especially to the former – by playing the later, allegedly scientific Marx with his critique of political economy and structuralist arguments off against the philosophizing and anthropologizing early Marx; Roland Barthes (1915–80) became the great, sensitive structuralist theorist of culture, analysing mass culture in France (*Mythologies* from 1957); and structuralist thought ultimately became an accepted feature even of history, in the shape of the (historicizing) philosopher Michel Foucault, who we shall be dealing with in a moment. These figures exercised a massive influence on the intellectual life of France. They dominated the French discursive context and eventually became intellectuals of international standing, at the point when – somewhat belatedly – structuralism 'spilled over' into other countries.

Nonetheless, the golden age of this 'original' or 'classical' structuralism did not last very long. Its star began to wane towards the end of the 1970s at the latest, which was linked in part with the personal tragedies suffered by these individuals. Poulantzas committed suicide by leaping from a window in 1979; Barthes was run over by a car and died in March 1980; Althusser strangled his wife in November 1980 and was admitted to a psychiatric institution; Lacan – afflicted by a disorder of the language centre – died in September 1981; and Foucault died of AIDS in 1984. The fact that these individuals suffered such tragic fates around the same time conveyed the impression that the structuralist era was definitely over (see Dosse, *History of Structuralism,* vol. I, pp. xx–xxi).

Looking back on these thinkers' intellectual legacy, one quickly notices – at least as far as the social sciences are concerned – the huge discrepancy between it and the initial euphoria that structuralism inspired. For the legacy of structuralism is not terribly impressive. Quite the reverse: Marxism lost ground in France from the time of the intensive debate on the crimes of the Gulag and has been critically weakened by the political caesura of 1989; in those cases where it is still intellectually alive, however, it has taken a form which has practically nothing to do with the ideas of Poulantzas and even less with those of Althusser; while Barthes' analyses of culture were frequently brilliant, they were too essayistic and playful to do justice to the more systematic requirements of cultural sociology; and the structuralist interpretation of psychoanalysis advanced by Lacan did no more than graze the outermost fields of the social sciences, particularly given that even within psychoanalysis, major doubts remained as to the seriousness of Lacan's project (critics mocked his often scarcely understandable writings with caustic references to 'Lacancan').

The situation is, however, quite different with respect to the legacy of Michel Foucault (1926–84), to whom we turn now in light of the tremendous importance of his work to many disciplines, including sociology. Foucault's appearance on the 'structuralist stage' was remarkable in that here was a philosopher with a strong *historical orientation* who adopted structuralist arguments. While Lévi-Strauss always underlined that structural anthropology certainly is or ought to be alert to historical processes, it was nonetheless clear that his real analytical interest lay in unchanging structures – and thus in society in a stable, as it were frozen state. He clearly favoured 'synchronic' analysis, that relating to the moment, over 'diachronic' or historical analysis – just as Saussure had distanced himself from historical philology, placing the synchronic point of view centre stage with his structural linguistics. When Foucault set about examining French or Western culture in a historically detailed way, this was new territory from a structuralist point of view.

Admittedly, it is a stretch to describe Foucault as a 'classical' structuralist à la Lévi-Strauss. Foucault undoubtedly adopted certain structuralist ideas. But he also used a good number of new theoretical elements, not found in this form in the work of the 'father of structuralism', leading a fair number of Foucault's interpreters to describe him as a *post*structuralist. But we need not (yet) be concerned with such conceptual pigeonholes. Nonetheless, one aspect is worth mentioning in this connection: Foucault did *not* share Lévi-Strauss' ambition to locate the basic, universal structures of the human mind. His work does not feature the scientist search for ultimate, foundational structures. This had partly to do with the fact that Foucault was heavily influenced by Nietzsche and those authors close to him, who were not prepared to see the history of the West as one of progress, and who had become hugely sceptical of the notion of a universal rationality valid in all circumstances. Foucault was fascinated by the 'dark' philosophers and writers of European modernity who, rather than celebrating the postulates of the Enlightenment with their optimism about progress, adopted an anti-Enlightenment position and strove at all times to question the supposed rationality of this Enlightenment. The fact that Foucault drew on this anti-Enlightenment tradition of thought in itself prevented him from signing up fully to Lévi-Strauss' scientific project.

Anyone wishing to take a closer look at the corpus of Foucauldian ideas is best advised to begin with his first major work, *Histoire de la folie à l'âge classique* from 1961 (English title: *Madness and Civilization: A History of Insanity in the Age of Reason*). This extremely detailed book, for which Foucault sifted through archives in numerous European countries, is an analysis of how the West deals with madness and of how people have thought about madness from the Renaissance to the early nineteenth century. Foucault's analyses were the source of a virtually irresistible fascination (to social scientists among others) because he suggested that our European civilization is characterized by a deep-seated dialectic of rationality and irrationality or madness, that madness is in fact only the flip-side of rationality, perhaps even the truth of rationality. At the very least, according to Foucault, the intense preoccupation with madness that recurs again and again throughout the history of the West suggests that we are dealing here with a truth from which reason has closed itself off.

> European man, since the beginning of the Middle Ages, has had a relation to something he calls, indiscriminately, Madness, Dementia, Insanity.

> Perhaps it is to this obscure presence that Western reason owes something of its depth ... In any case, the Reason–Madness nexus constitutes for Western culture one of the dimensions of its originality.
>
> (*Madness and Civilization*, p. xiii)

In his book, Foucault describes how, during the Renaissance, the madman was still integrated into society, or at least was not separated from it. During this era, madness was something one might encounter in everyday life. In what he calls the 'classical' age, however, the way in which people dealt with the madman began to change. The sixteenth century was distinguished by the invention of the hospital, in which the mad, along with the poor, the physically sick, criminals, etc. were locked up. We have here the beginnings of a comprehensive practice of internment, through which the madman (along with the other potential inmates) is separated out, that is, excluded from society. It is only towards the end of the eighteenth century that we see the separation of the mad from the rest of the interned, as the 'destitute' were separated from the 'irrational'. The madhouses and psychiatric institutions came into being in which the mad were for the first time handed over to the doctors and in which they – separated out from all others – became exclusively the object of medicine.

Foucault characterizes this historical process occurring since the Renaissance as an attempt to tame madness – but one which should by no means be conceived in terms of the Enlightenment notion of progress. For Foucault, the fact that the medical profession gained exclusive responsibility for dealing with madness in the nineteenth and twentieth centuries made madness a mere object. The truth of madness – which it was still possible to recognize at least during the Renaissance, when the madman was integrated into society – was lost to us; we became 'alienated' from madness (ibid., p. 277). Foucault is deeply suspicious of how reformers saw themselves, a self-image which is also the main point of reference for those who believe in scientific progress. The cordoning off of the infirm, criminals and the poor from the mad in the late eighteenth century, according to Foucault, was not anchored in humanistic motives, the desire to treat the mad in a more effectual and humane fashion; the sole motive was to protect the destitute from madness, chaining the mad all the more firmly to the practices of internment found in the madhouses and psychiatric institutions.

> It is important, perhaps decisive for the place madness was to occupy in modern culture, that *homo medicus* was not called into the world of confinement as an *arbiter*, to divide what was crime from what was madness, what was evil from what was illness, but rather as a *guardian*, to protect others from the vague danger that exuded through the walls of confinement.
>
> (ibid., p. 205; original emphasis)

Historically speaking, Foucault's reconstruction is in fact highly dubious. An alternative interpretation of his source material might be that the madman was tolerated so long as he was not considered a human being as you and I, but rather, as it were, a member of another species. Internment in an asylum might then be a first step towards the inclusion or integration of the mad.

At all events, Foucault subsequently continued his intellectual project, distinguished by a critical or sceptical view of the Enlightenment, with a number of historical studies, his history of criminal justice, the 1975 *Surveiller et punir. Naissance de la prison* (English title: *Discipline and Punish: The Birth of the Prison*) being particularly worthy of note. Foucault begins his book with an account, which will leave few readers unaffected, of the brutal public torture and execution of the patri- and regicide Damien in Paris in 1757. For Foucault, this beginning is of programmatic significance: he goes on to show how practices of punishment changed massively in subsequent decades. Increasingly, it was the conduct or the mind of convicts rather than the body that became the target of punishment. Physical penalties were applied less often, as was capital punishment, which was increasingly carried out away from public view. The focus of attention shifted instead to efforts to discipline the individual prisoner, to mould him in a particular way, to drill his body and mind. The symbol of this new conception of punishment was the birth of the modern prison. Dungeons and so on had of course existed since time immemorial. But what was new about the 'modern' prisons was that they were constructed architecturally and organizationally in such a way that prisoners could be monitored at all times or that the prisoners were made to feel constantly under surveillance. According to Foucault, this idea of surveillance and disciplining was expressed most clearly in the plans conceived by a man with whom you are already familiar from Lecture II. The utilitarian Jeremy Bentham was also one of the great penal reformers of his time. He propagated changes to techniques of punishment, drawing up plans for prisons in which the design of the cells, occupied by isolated prisoners, ensured that the guards could observe their doings from a central vantage point at all times. Through constant, uninterrupted surveillance, prisoners were to be disciplined and moulded in new ways, in order to bring them into line with the norms of society – an idea which persists to this day.

But – and this is, once again, typical of Foucault, as well as constituting the key message of the book – Bentham's 'panopticon', a prison in which the cells form a circle and the guard can see into all of them from his central vantage point (see *Discipline and Punish*, pp. 200ff.), along with the associated new forms of punishment, are not interpreted in terms of progress or humanization. There is in fact nothing outlandish about such an interpretation, particularly if one contrasts the new, in principle violence-free techniques of punishment with the scene of torture and execution described by Foucault at the beginning of the book. But Foucault makes a very different argument. For him, the transition from justice through torture to the prison merely represents a *restructuring of techniques of power*. While the aim is no longer to *destroy the body*, ever greater efforts are made to *exercise power over both mind and body as effectively as possible and to increase this power*. The rise of the prison is merely an element in the ensemble of entirely new techniques of power and disciplining which developed in the modern period. Following the army reforms in the early modern period, which entailed the first use of the systematic drilling of soldiers to ensure that they could load their rifles quickly and maintain their position or formation despite enemy fire, the bodies of the workers in the manufactories and factories were drilled in the same way. The birth of the prison was and is just one more strand in the web of power.

It is of crucial significance that Foucault's concept of power is not centralist, as we pointed out in the chapter on Anthony Giddens. Foucault does *not* imagine that there is an especially powerful being sitting somewhere, issuing orders and exercising power over the soldiers, workers or convicts. Power, according to Foucault, *is in fact locationless; it is decentralized, silent, inconspicuous, but all-pervasive*. Foucault's idea here captured perfectly the mood of many intellectuals following the failed rebellion of 1968. In a later publication, Foucault expressed the particular quality of his concept of power in his very dark and flowery language:

> Power's condition of possibility ... must not be sought in the primary existence of a central point, in a unique source of sovereignty from which secondary and descendent forms would emanate; it is the moving substrate of force relations which, by virtue of their inequality, constantly engender states of power, but the latter are always local and unstable. The omnipresence of power: not because it has the privilege of consolidating everything under its invincible unity, but because it is produced from one moment to the next, at every point, or rather in every relation from one point to another. Power is everywhere; not because it embraces everything, but because it comes from everywhere. ... power is not an institution, and not a structure; neither is it a certain strength we are endowed with; it is the name that one attributes to a complex strategical situation in a particular society.
>
> (Foucault, *History of Sexuality*, vol. I, p. 93)

This power is so pervasive and at the same time location-less in part because – and this brings us to another hallmark of Foucault's theory of power – it is directly bound up with 'discourses', specific forms of expression, including scientific forms. For Foucault, basing himself entirely on Nietzsche, this in turn means that science and the search for truth always produce power. Foucault puts forward this thesis, which may sound rather implausible, most clearly in the first volume of his *History of Sexuality*, which he began towards the end of his life. Foucault, who characteristically entitled this volume *La volonté de savoir* ('The Will to Knowledge'), takes issue here primarily with the Enlightenment and predominantly left-wing hypothesis of repression, according to which sexuality was suppressed and repressed in the 'dark' middle ages, plagued by inhibited Christian morality, and was liberated only by modern medicine, psychoanalysis, etc. Foucault takes a very different view of these processes. While it may be true that the social repression of sexuality by means of prohibition and censorship diminished in the early modern period, this does not mean that there was less regulation. Quite the opposite. Foucault identifies a huge increase in discourses about 'sex' in the eighteenth and nineteenth centuries; sex was probed biologically, medically, psychoanalytically, theologically, by moral philosophers, etc. Every form of sexuality was registered and described with the utmost precision. 'Sex' was subjected to scientific investigation down to the last detail, and the sciences also influenced how people saw themselves with respect to their sexual desires. According to Foucault, it is naive to think that this was about 'liberating' the human being or that this was at least an unintended effect of these discourses (*History of Sexuality*, vol. I, p. 130). Rather, *a new form of power* was produced, but we cannot ascribe responsibility for this to any central, controlling authority. Rather, these constantly expanding discourses led unintentionally to a disciplining and moulding of the human being, to an internalization of power practised by everyone without the need for anyone to tell them to do so. Science, as the search for truth, is a will to knowledge with incalculable power effects; Foucault's overall thesis is that it is impossible to separate truth from power. Again and again, therefore, Foucault's studies focused very consistently on the following questions: 'What are the rules of right that power implements to produce discourses of truth? Or: What type of power is it that is capable of producing discourses of power that have, in a society like ours, such powerful effects?' (Foucault, *Society Must be Defended*, p. 24).

The other and even more provocative thesis that Foucault derives from this is that these scientific discourses actually constituted the 'subject' in the first place. It was the unceasing penetration of the human being that gave rise to the concept of the subject in the first place. In other words, on this view, the subject is an effect of power or more precisely *an effect of specific techniques of power*, which have developed from the early modern period and particularly in the eighteenth and nineteenth centuries and which have subjected the human being to ever closer scrutiny. The human subject is thus not something that has always been there and will always be there. Rather, it was constituted historically by means of specific forms of power and, should the dominant forms of power change, may disappear again in exactly the same way. It is this idea that underpins the oft-cited passage on the 'end of man' or the 'death of the subject' in one of Foucault's major works from the mid-1960s, *Les mots et les choses*.

Une archéologie des sciences humaines (English title: *The Order of Things: An Archaeology of the Human Sciences*):

> One thing in any case is certain: man is neither the oldest nor the most constant problem that has been posed for human knowledge. Taking a relatively short chronological sample within a restricted geographical area – European culture since the sixteenth century – one can be certain that man is a recent invention within it. ... As the archaeology of our thought easily shows, man is an invention of recent date. And one perhaps nearing its end.
>
> (Foucault, *The Order of Things*, p. 387)

This thesis of the 'end of man' – and here Foucault's structuralist inheritance is clearly evident for the first time – was first and foremost a profound critique of (French) phenomenology, of Sartre, indeed of the philosophy of the subject in general (see Eribon, *Michel Foucault*, p. 156 or Dreyfus and Rabinow, *Michel Foucault: Beyond Structuralism and Hermeneutics*, pp. 44ff.). The subject cannot and must not be taken as the point of departure for philosophical analysis, because it is merely the product of the power relations pertaining during a particular historical phase. Structuralist anti-subjectivism is thus legitimized here by Foucault in a quite new way, namely historically.

Foucault's penchant for a synchronic approach to phenomena is another structuralist feature of his thought; astonishingly for a philosopher who worked so intensely with historical materials, it is virtually impossible to make out any real interest in the diachronic in his work. Foucault, as he himself hints in the foreword to the English edition of *The Order of Things* (p. xiii), was not really interested in issues of historical causality. He cannot, of course, entirely avoid such issues; but his primary interest lies in the *form* of discursive configurations *rather than their origins and development*. His analysis of the 'birth of the prison', for example, often includes brief references to possible links with nascent capitalism, but in principle it is left to the reader to contemplate the precise causal relationships involved. The omnipresence of power, the impossibility of pinning it down to a particular location, seems to evade questions of causality.

The motive underlying this conscious bracketing off of questions of causality becomes apparent if one takes a closer look at the concept of 'archaeology' appearing in the quotation above and in the subtitle of *The Order of Things*. With this concept, Foucault seems to be suggesting that his intention is to investigate when exactly the human being appeared historically as the object of knowledge. This also implies an anti-evolutionist approach. The 'archaeologist' of the human sciences certainly studies her historical sources to unearth and make visible the dark and hidden sides of our modern civilization, those preconditions for contemporary thought that were repressed in order that the radiant vision of the enlightened modern age, with its optimism about progress, could shine all the more brightly. But this exposure of repressed elements is not intended as therapy; this is not a cure designed to impart to the modern individual a better understanding of how he became what he is. Quite the reverse. Discourses – so Foucault tells us – alternate, in seemingly random and aimless fashion. They lie one on top of the other like the remains of past cultures in different layers of the earth, without any connection necessarily existing between them. In a universe in which power cannot be localized, little can be said about the genesis of discourses; and it certainly cannot be assumed that discourses can be converted into one another, that they build on one another, so that history can be regarded as 'development'. History in fact consists of the random playing out of power effects. It is a game in which there is no place either for the idea of progress or the search for any other kind of meaning. As well as archaeology, Foucault, following Nietzsche, also refers repeatedly to 'genealogy'. This term refers to a process of historical remembering concerned not with reinforcing value commitments, but with unmasking and destruction.

Foucault's concept of discourse, which, incidentally, differs fundamentally from that of Habermas (see Lecture X), is in fact basically synchronic in nature. The parallels with structural linguistics are obvious. In Foucault's early work, 'discourse' means no more than a system of statements, which are related to one another and which make up an ordered pattern. Over the course of his oeuvre, while Foucault continually 'embellishes' the term such that a 'discourse' may refer both to a wickerwork of statements as well as one made up of techniques of power in highly specific institutions (the law, health system, etc.), it is never entirely clear *how these 'discourses' change*. Just as Lévi-Strauss failed to ask where the structures of the mind come from, Foucault also systematically evaded the question of how we are to conceive of the genesis of discourses. Foucault elucidates the 'origin' of these discourses only insofar as he refers to a deep stratum, the so-called 'episteme', which is ascribed to every historical era but which he tells us no more about. Every age is characterized by this deep-seated epistemological schema, on the basis of which the discourses specific to the age take shape. Just as speaking is a function of language (Saussure) and kinship systems are a function of the basic structures of the human mind (Lévi-Strauss), according to Foucault, discourses and the associated power effects must be understood as a function of this deep stratum of the episteme which, while certainly typical of a given era, is not really amenable to *historical* study. Sartre, rebuked so often by structuralists and implicitly by Foucault as well, fittingly observed that

> Foucault does not tell us the thing that would be the most interesting, that is, how each thought is constructed on the basis of these conditions, or how mankind passes from one thought to another. To do so he would have to bring in praxis, and therefore history, which is precisely

what he refuses to do. Of course his perspective remains historical. He distinguishes between periods, a before and an after. But he replaces cinema with the magic lantern, motion with a succession of motionless moments.

(Quoted in Eribon, *Michel Foucault*, p. 163)

If one looks at the beginnings and the middle phase of Foucault's work, one cannot help but notice that his views became increasingly more radical over time. While it is true that he firmly rejected any kind of progressive optimism in his early work *Madness and Civilization*, at the same time he also played with the idea of acknowledging a fundamentally 'integral' truth – this was exactly what his account of the 'other' of reason was meant to express. Subsequently, however, his (Nietzschean) view of the universal nature of power increasingly dominated – truth itself becomes inseparably linked with power and is thus discredited. It has simply become impossible to escape the webs of power, and even the truth can no longer set us free.

It only remains to ask whether such a radical stance is plausible and theoretically productive (for a rather different critique, see the lecture on Anthony Giddens). There would appear to be good reason to doubt that it is, and the 'late' Foucault clearly came to the same conclusion – this at least is our contention. For even if one was to share many of Foucault's theoretical premises and accept many of his historical interpretations, one might wonder if it is really the case that we are trapped in a web of power. Is it fruitful, for example, to describe struggles for human rights as no more than discourses of power and declare all notions of 'liberation' a mere chimera? How can this theoretical stance possibly be reconciled with Foucault's political engagement? While it is true that he rejected the idea of a great struggle for liberation, he was very actively involved in many small-scale political and social battles (see Eribon's biography).

It is conceivable (see also Dosse, *History of Structuralism*, vol. II, pp. 336ff.) that Foucault asked himself these very questions, or at least similar ones, towards the end of his life. The multivolume work he planned to write on the history of sexuality, which he was unable to complete, has a distinctive feature. While the first volume of the *History of Sexuality* (1976) appeared at almost the same time as *Discipline and Punish* (1975), which we outlined earlier, and merely applies the universal conception of power found in the latter work to a new field (sexuality), the following two volumes, destined to be the last, are quite different in tone. Volumes II and III of his history of sexuality (*L'usage des plaisirs*, English title: *The Use of Pleasure*, and *Le souci de soi*, English title: *The Care of the Self*) appeared almost eight years after the first volume – a lengthy period, during which Foucault had obviously changed his views. He suddenly begins to refer to the 'subject', the 'self' – and in a way utterly at variance with his earlier, rather cynical perspective, though Foucault furnishes us with no autocritique in this regard. Rather, he describes how, in the period between the fourth century BC in Greece and the first few centuries AD in Rome, sexuality was constituted as a field of morality. Morals – so Foucault tells us – consist, on the one hand, of rules and codes and on the other of forms of subjectification, practices of the self, that is, ways of working on the self, such as asceticism (see *The Use of Pleasure*, pp. 30ff.). With tremendous empathy, he traces the constitution of the moral subject and delineates how sexuality was lived in Graeco-Roman antiquity in comparison to the later rigidity of Christianity. There is no sign here of any cynical, universalistic concept of power, as is clearly apparent in the brilliant title of the last volume, *The Care of the Self*, a volume in which Foucault not only distinguishes carefully between different forms of individualism (ibid., p. 42), but in which he also describes how the intensification of the care of the self in Stoic philosophy entailed a 'valorization of the other' (ibid., p. 149). In contrast to his earlier books, Foucault refers here to subjects, ones who, indeed, have discovered for themselves an authentic existence of sorts, subjects who cannot be described as the mere effects of techniques of power.

However one may assess this final, surprising shift in the development of Foucault's work, which inevitably raises significant doubts as to the plausibility and fruitfulness of the uncompromisingly universalistic view of power characteristic of the bulk of his writings, despite all the difficulties, Foucault's legacy has much to offer social theory. Through his novel version of the concept of power, Foucault has sensitized us to the fact that language too produces power effects, with which any social science sensitive to power must grapple. In this sense, Foucault's work is a continuation of the tendency to conceive of power relations with greater precision, a tendency which began with Talcott Parsons. The latter had extended the purely negative Weberian concept of power, based on the idea of a zero-sum game (see Lectures IV and XII), in such a way as to draw attention to the productive effects of power. What remained bracketed out in the case of Parsons, however, was the insight that while power may also be productive, this does not make it any less repressive. Foucault showed, for example, that the sciences have generated a massive increase in knowledge, but that their (positive) power effects have been associated with important mechanisms for disciplining and moulding subjects. Every discourse, including the scientific, always excludes someone or something while emphasizing something else. It is on this that its power is based. There is no need to take the dramatic step of turning this insight into a fundamental critique of science, featuring an equally fundamental relativism, as Foucault suggested and as many of his followers in fact did. An interpretation of his theses less intent on eliciting shock does not reduce his great importance to sociology. For an entire generation of social scientists, he opened up a new way of looking at the world. Feminist theorists in particular became alert to mechanisms of power as a result of his work, mechanisms which have nothing to do with brutal, outright violence, but which, because they are latent, may be no less effective (see Lecture XVII).

Foucault achieved another feat of sensitization. However much critics have assailed his totalizing interpretation of the modern age, his writings formed a necessary counter-balance to historical interpretations overly oriented towards progress and optimistic diagnoses of the present era, which had characterized sociology and especially modernization theory hitherto. Though his approach was controversial, Foucault, like no other before him, not even Adorno, drew our attention to the 'dark' sides of modernity, creating the space for an interpretation of this modernity that breaks with the confident faith in perpetual progress.

This brings us to the second topic of this lecture, so-called *post*structuralism or *neo*-structuralism. Although, once again, this phenomenon started life in France, neither of these terms is commonly used there; they are in fact a German, and even more an American invention. Nonetheless, it is quite possible to affix this label to French authors who, coming from the structuralist tradition, turned away from it and developed a new theoretical orientation. Foucault himself (see above) has been described as a poststructuralist by some interpreters, simply because he brought entirely new elements into play (his reference to Nietzsche and associated scepticism about Western rationality vis-à-vis Lévi-Strauss). Otherwise, Foucault paid very little attention to the concept of structure, which is why he has also been described as a 'structuralist without structures'. But Foucault's work always undoubtedly exhibited a great scholarly earnestness as he carried out his historical studies and examined various sources.

In the work of those we can, without classificatory headaches, call poststructuralists, this earnestness was and is not nearly so apparent. They are *post*structuralists because they have bid farewell both to the scientific concept of structure *and* the scientific ideals of a Lévi-Strauss. The scientific bathos is absent from their work, and an ironic relationship develops with the old dream of placing the human sciences on a firm scientific basis. Scepticism towards the scientistic project is the order of the day and 'serious scholarship' is increasingly replaced by a playful approach to texts.

In philosophy, this movement was to begin as early as the mid-1960s, though it really took off only in the late 1970s; it was strongly associated with the names of Jacques Derrida (1930–2004) and Jean-François Lyotard (1924–98). Why some scholars departed from the concept of structure used by Saussure or Lévi-Strauss is most clearly apparent in a critique put forward by the philosopher Derrida, which he formulated as early as the mid-1960s in *L'écriture et la différence*, his sights set on Lévi-Strauss (English title: *Writing and Difference*, see especially pp. 351–70). Derrida was more influenced by the phenomenology of Husserl and Heidegger, but attempted to beat structuralism at its own game. His point of departure was the following analysis. Reference to structures always confronts us with the question of the unity of these structures, for the coherence of every structure depends on reference to a core of meaning. In other words, only if a central idea exists is it possible to determine what is structure, that is, which elements are in fact part of the structure as opposed to surface phenomena. In the absence of any kind of idea that establishes order, reference to 'structure' is rather empty. What then is the centre of the structure? Who or what ensures its coherence? The classical structuralists such as Lévi-Strauss were clear about the fact that it is *not* the subject that gives the structure coherence. Who or what establishes this coherence remained unclear in their work. But *the fact that* such coherence exists, and must indeed exist, seemed to them beyond dispute. This is the starting point for Derrida's critique, as he points out how internally inconsistent this stance is. For if there really was such a thing as a centre of meaning, then – bearing in mind that, in line with the insights of linguistics, sense and meaning arise only through difference – such meaning would come into being only through the difference from other parts of the structure. But if this is the case, then this supposedly prominent meaning centre cannot really be so central, because it is an immediate component of the structure. Thus, according to Derrida, we are faced with a paradox. This is why he believes that the notion of a substance that establishes unity is a metaphysical one of which we need to rid ourselves. A further corollary is that, lacking a centre, the structure is anything but fixed or unchanging. Manfred Frank (b. 1945), interpreting Derrida's position, expressed this in the following well-chosen words:

> every meaning, every signification, and every view of the world is in flux, nothing can escape the play of differences, there is no interpretation of Being and the world that is valid in and of itself and for all times.
>
> (Frank, *What is Neostructuralism?*, p. 63)

But this destroys all the hopes formerly harboured by 'classical' structuralism of avoiding the constant uncertainty of (historical) explanation and interpretation by identifying a fixed, objective structure. Structures can be conceived only in *decentred* fashion; they too thus require interpretation, which is why – according to Derrida – there can be no once-and-for-all interpretation of texts (and social rules). As he puts it: 'The absence of the transcendental signified extends the domain and the play of signification infinitely' (*Writing*, p. 354). Thus, the reading of a text, the interpretation of an ordered social context, no longer entails the identification of a meaning, but rather a process of invention, of constantly creating anew, because there are no final interpretations. Derrida has since re-read a large number of philosophical texts, his comments at times revealing, at times arbitrary, and generally rhetorically overdrawn. It is ironic indeed that the objectivism of structuralism has led to such interpretive subjectivism.

Insights into the subjectivity of interpretation are also typical of *hermeneutic philosophy*. In contrast to the stance adopted by Derrida and his successors, however, it retained the assumption of a dialogue between interpreting subject and interpreted text. However, it is the theses put forward by Derrida that form the point of departure for poststructuralist philosophy, which is too multifaceted for us to provide a meaningful overview here (see the brilliant book by Manfred Frank, *What is Neostructuralism?*). As you may have deduced from our brief account, the poststructuralist debate within philosophy also generated challenges for the social sciences, particularly because the thesis of the existence of multiple selves – which are non-uniform in nature and constantly shift identity amid the play of signs – constituted a frontal assault on traditional social psychology and theories of socialization. For just as texts no longer admit of final, uniform interpretation, it is claimed that we can no longer attribute fixed identities to human beings and that they themselves can grasp their own existence only as a game of constantly shifting identities. Empirically, however, these assertions have little going for them (for a critique see Joas, 'The Autonomy of the Self: The Meadian Heritage and its Postmodern Challenge').

Of even greater importance to social theory as a whole was the work of the philosopher Jean-François Lyotard, in as much as he was more concerned to diagnose the present era than was Derrida. Lyotard's *The Postmodern Condition*, a 1979 text on the future of knowledge produced at the behest of the government of Québec, became particularly famous. Here, Lyotard makes some interesting observations about the political repercussions of new information and communication technologies and their consequences for a democratic society. But this was not the really interesting thing about this 'report'; ultimately, other authors had said much the same, authors who, moreover, were better informed sociologically and politically than Lyotard. The book's impact, the reason it became famous, lay in his thesis of the supposed 'end of metanarratives'. While modernity, according to Lyotard, was characterized by the fact that science functioned as the undisputed and unquestioned point of reference in every discussion, today – in the postmodern age – science is no more than *one linguistic game among others* and can lay claim to no more legitimacy than other discourses. 'Knowledge is not the same as science, especially in its contemporary form' (Lyotard, *The Postmodern Condition*, p. 18). On this view, there is no longer any clear-cut point of reference, no overarching discourse which, as the ultimate authority, encompasses and holds together all other discourses. In the postmodern age, science has to justify itself by referring to other non-scientific discourses, non-scientific 'narratives', a tendency which has allegedly become ever stronger since the emergence of the critique of reason, which first burst so dramatically upon the scene towards the end of the nineteenth century – Nietzsche being a key figure here (ibid., p. 39). However, the death or end of metanarratives, which place all individual stories within a large-scale, comprehensive interpretation of history, has not only affected the sciences, but also belief systems such as Marxism (it is worth noting here that Lyotard was himself a Marxist in the 1950s) and aesthetic theories which postulate a kind of progressive logic of artistic development, as expressed, for example, in the term 'avant-garde'. (The concept of postmodernity, whose roots lie in the most varied range of sources and in some cases stretch far back into history – see for example Welsch, *Unsere postmoderne Moderne* ['Our Postmodern Modernity'] – has taken off with particular vigour within architecture from the early 1970s, because observers considered further development of architectural styles impossible; all that remained was to combine earlier styles in ironic fashion. Genuine artistic progress seemed increasingly inconceivable to many architectural theorists and practitioners.)

What was provocative about Lyotard's theses concerning the inevitable plurality of language games was that he by no means described this 'death of the metanarrative' as a story of decline, but in terms of the opening up of new possibilities. In the postmodern age, according to Lyotard, people know about the end of metanarratives, but they feel no regret about it:

> Most people have lost the nostalgia for the lost narrative. It in no way follows that they are reduced to barbarity. What saves them from it is their knowledge that legitimation can only spring from their own linguistic practice and communicational interaction. Science 'smiling into its beard' at every other belief has taught them the harsh austerity of realism.
>
> (Lyotard, *The Postmodern Condition*, p. 41)

Politically, Lyotard's statement here was intended to affirm the existence of a huge variety of equally valid language games, forms of action, values and lifestyles within a society, a message which was positively embraced by the gay rights and women's movements and which, among other things, was a powerful stimulus for debates on multiculturalism in Western societies. *Sociologically and philosophically*, Lyotard's argument was an attack on both Parsons and Habermas, in as much as both of them – the former with reference to values, the latter with reference to a consensus to be achieved rationally – continued to adhere to traditional notions of uniformity. Lyotard's thesis of the inevitable plurality of all these 'language games' (a term coined by the philosopher Ludwig Wittgenstein, 1889–1951) may call to mind the debate described in the first lecture on Thomas Kuhn's concept of paradigms and his reference to their 'incommensurability'. Lyotard upped the ante considerably by describing all efforts to achieve uniformity and consensus as totalitarian or even as a species of terrorism. Even Habermas' discourse theory, which was meant to be free of domination, is ultimately repressive because it attempts to destroy the undeniable diversity of language games by means of a dubious metanarrative centred on the rational potential of language, which supposedly facilitates consensus (ibid., pp. 60ff.). Postmodernity – Lyotard concludes – is, however, profoundly plural, and indeed in every respect (for a critique of these theses, see Benhabib, 'Epistemologies of Postmodernism: A Rejoinder to Jean-François Lyotard').

Lyotard's original philosophical thesis of the inevitable plurality of language games and ways of life opened up a wide-ranging discussion on social theory and the diagnosis of the modern age. The sociological debate on so-called postmodernity saw the emergence of radical and not-so-radical, understandable, incomprehensible and quite implausible positions. It should be evident that the theses put forward by both Derrida and Lyotard entailed the risk of a deterioration of scientific standards. For if there can no longer be any fixed meanings and interpretations, and science is no more than one language game among many, we are but a short step away from the conflation of science and fiction, of high and popular culture, especially given that, under such premises, we can dispense with the methodical examination of empirical evidence. And a good number of authors did in fact succumb to the temptation to abandon scientific standards, the leading example perhaps being the sociologist Jean Baudrillard (1929–2007), whose daring theses made him a celebrity contributor to the culture pages of the international press. His 1976 book *L'échange symbolique et la mort* (English title: *Symbolic Exchange and Death*), for example, expounded the thesis of the end of production, according to which there is supposedly no longer any difference between labour and non-labour, production and consumption. Amid the play of signs, all clear distinctions have already become blurred; social and political categories have long failed to capture the phenomena for which they were created, so that the present is characterized by a simulation of reality and there is no longer any such thing as the real (one of his books, which appeared in German, was entitled 'The Agony of the Real', *Agonie des Realen*). But this did not stop him from producing eye-catching theses, whose origins clearly lie in some kind of Marxian cultural critique, which explains why a fair number of ex-Marxists converted to this way of thinking: 'The phase ... where "the process of capital itself ceases to be a process of production", is simultaneously the phase of the disappearance of the factory: society as a whole takes on the appearance of a factory' (*Symbolic Exchange and Death*, p. 18). It is hard to say which is the more astonishing, the simplicity and falseness of his proposition or the commanding way in which Baudrillard the sociologist ignores the highly nuanced findings of empirical social research. Baudrillard reached a creative 'peak' with his 1987 book *America*. In the run-up to the Gulf War of 1991, Baudrillard finally declared that the war would not take place; when it did, he saw no ground for self-criticism. His thesis that the war was played out solely in simulated form did in fact capture once again an important aspect of how this event was perceived; but he expressed this in such over-the-top fashion that while he was assured of the attention of the media, even erstwhile supporters began to turn away from him.

The debate on postmodernity thus strayed quite often into dangerous territory. Yet this was by no means always the case. The Marxian context produced a number of stimulating studies very much worth reading, as authors such as the geographer David Harvey (*The Condition of Postmodernity*), born in 1935, and the cultural theorist Frederic Jameson (*Postmodernism or, The Cultural Logic of Late Capitalism*), born in 1934, combined postmodern discourse with a Marxian cultural sociology. Beyond Marxian debates, the most systematic take on the debate on postmodernity was perhaps that of Zygmunt Bauman (see also Lecture XVIII), who opened up a new discussion of Lyotard's theses of the plurality of ways of living and language games against the background of debates on the Holocaust. Because, quite obviously, not all ways of living can be equally accepted (those of convinced Nazis for example, out to annihilate anyone 'different'), Bauman consciously steered the discussion back to a place in which it is possible to discuss very seriously an ethos of tolerance and develop a more plausible concept of difference. Within philosophy – though exercising a strong influence on some sociologists – the theses put forward by postmodern theorists were taken up by the neo-pragmatist Richard Rorty, whose dynamic contributions brought the topic of subjectivity into play, something which those participating in the poststructuralist debate on postmodernity had long and very consciously refrained from doing (see Lecture XIX).

Looking back on structuralism and poststructuralism, it is evident that they impacted on the social sciences first and foremost with respect to their *potential for diagnosing the present era*, particularly via the work of Foucault and Lyotard. The way in which these theories are constructed meant that they did not generate systematic statements on *social change*. And, logically enough, approaches which set out to decentre the subject and which postulate a radical anti-subjectivism have little to offer with respect to a *theory of action*. It is thus very hard to place structuralism and poststructuralism within the history of sociology. Our thesis that the development of sociological theory can be described in terms of the conceptual trio of 'social action–social order–social change' seems not to apply to them. It is perhaps for this very reason that both these theoretical approaches stood and still stand on the margins of the international theoretical debate in the social sciences rather than at its centre. For a time, however, they practically dominated the humanities more narrowly conceived, particularly literary studies. It is clearly vital to move beyond the constraints of the structuralist and poststructuralist approach in order to find points of contact within sociology. This is precisely what Pierre Bourdieu, whom we shall be tackling in the next lecture, did; despite the fact that his background lay in the French structuralist context, he again placed greater emphasis on action theory.

Finally, we would like to make some suggestions on further reading relevant to the present lecture. Should you wish to acquire a highly detailed and well-informed overview of the structuralist 'revolution' in France, François Dosse's two-volume *History of Structuralism* is indispensable. Manfred Frank's *What is Neostructuralism?* is an impressive series of lectures on post- or neo-structuralist thinkers from Lévi-Strauss through Foucault to Derrida. Your escort here, a brilliant philosopher, will guide you safely through the labyrinth of highly complex and often confusing poststructuralist debates. Should you wish to obtain a critical overview of the work of Michel Foucault, the most important of the authors examined here in terms of social theory, the relevant chapters in Axel Honneth's *Critique of Power* and *Michel Foucault: Beyond Structuralism and Hermeneutics* by Hubert Dreyfus and Paul Rabinow are the best places to look. Finally, the biographies by Didier Eribon (*Michel Foucault*) and James Miller (*The Passion of Michel Foucault*) provide a window on the life and circumstances of this extraordinary author.

XV

Between structuralism and theory of practice
The cultural sociology of Pierre Bourdieu

In this lecture we examine an author who moved towards a synthetic theoretical project at an early stage, in much the same way as Habermas, Luhmann or Giddens, and who thus became one of the most influential sociologists worldwide from the 1970s on. We are referring to Pierre Bourdieu, whose work was deeply moulded by the national intellectual milieu in which it developed, that of France in the late 1940s and 1950s, a milieu characterized by disputes between phenomenologists and structuralists. But it is not this national and cultural dimension that distinguishes Bourdieu's writings from those of the other 'grand theorists' treated in this lecture series. We have seen how much Habermas or Giddens, for example, owed to the academic or political context of their home countries. What set Bourdieu's approach apart from that of his German and British 'rivals' was a significantly stronger linkage of theoretical and empirical knowledge. Bourdieu was first and foremost an empiricist, who developed and constantly refined his theoretical concepts on the basis of his empirical work – with all the advantages and disadvantages that theoretical production of this kind entails. We shall have more to say about this later. Bourdieu is thus not to be understood primarily as a theorist, but as a cultural sociologist who systematically stimulated the theoretical debate through his empirical work.

Pierre Bourdieu was born in 1930 and is thus of the same generation as Habermas or Luhmann. The fact that Bourdieu came from a modest background and grew up in the depths of provincial France is extremely important to understanding his work. Bourdieu himself repeatedly emphasized his origins: 'I spent most of my youth in a tiny and remote village of Southwestern France ... And I could meet the demands of schooling only by renouncing many of my primary experiences and acquisitions, and not only a certain accent' (Bourdieu and Wacquant, *An Invitation to Reflexive Sociology*, p. 204). Despite these clearly unfavourable beginnings, Bourdieu was to succeed in gaining entry to the leading educational institutions in France, a fact of which many people became aware when he was elected to the famous Collège de France in 1982. This classic case of climbing the social and career ladder, the fact that Bourdieu had no privileged educational background to draw on, helped legitimize his pitiless take on the French education and university system and on intellectuals in general, a group he investigated in numerous studies over the course of his career. He thus made use of the classical sociological notion of the outsider, the 'marginal man', in order to lay claim to special, and above all especially critical insights into the functioning of 'normal' society.

> In France, to come from a distant province, to be born south of the Loire, endows you with a number of properties that are not without parallel in the colonial situation. It gives you a sort of objective and subjective externality and puts you in a particular relation to the central institutions of French society and therefore to the intellectual institution. There are subtle (and not so subtle) forms of social racism that cannot but make you perceptive.
>
> (ibid., p. 209)

However, Bourdieu's path to the production of a sociology of French cultural institutions and his path to sociology more generally was anything but straightforward or self-evident – a state of affairs with which we are familiar from the biographies of other major social theorists, such as Habermas and Luhmann, who also took some time to settle on a career in sociology. A highly gifted student, Bourdieu studied at the École Normale Superieure in Paris, where he took philosophy, the most prestigious subject in the French disciplinary canon. He initially seems to have wanted to concentrate on this subject, as he subsequently worked as a philosophy teacher in provincial France for a brief period, as is usual for those who go on to have an academic career in the humanities in France. But Bourdieu was increasingly disappointed by philosophy and developed an ever greater interest in anthropology, so that he ultimately became a self-taught empirically oriented anthropologist and later sociologist. This process of turning away from philosophy and towards anthropology or sociology was partly bound up with Lévi-Strauss' concurrent rise to prominence. With its claim to a strictly scientific approach, structuralist anthropology began to challenge philosophy's traditional pre-eminence within the disciplinary canon. Bourdieu was drawn towards this highly promising and up-and-coming subject. Structuralism's anti-philosophical tone held much appeal for him (see the preceding lecture) and often appeared in his own work, when he takes up arms against philosophy's purely theoretical rationality for example.

But Bourdieu's path to anthropology and sociology was also determined by external circumstances, insofar as he was stationed in Algeria during the second half of the 1950s while completing his military service. There, in the undoubtedly very difficult circumstances of the war of independence, he gathered data for his first book, a sociology of Algeria (*Sociologie de l'Algerie*, 1958) – in which he came to terms intellectually with his experiences in this French colony (see Derek Robbins, *The Work of*

Pierre Bourdieu, pp. 10ff.). In this setting, he also carried out field research among the Kabyle, a Berber people of northern Algeria, which led to the publication of a number of anthropological monographs and essays which, in collected and eventually expanded form, appeared as a book entitled *Outline of a Theory of Practice*. This work, published in French in 1972, and then expanded greatly for the English (and German) translation, became tremendously famous and influential because Bourdieu departed from the structuralism of Lévi-Strauss, in whose footsteps he had originally followed, and developed his own set of concepts, which held out the promise of a genuine theoretical synthesis.

At around the same time as these basically anthropological studies, Bourdieu began to utilize the theoretical insights they contained to subject *French* society to sociological analysis, particularly its cultural, educational and class system. With respect to the socially critical thrust of his writings, the work of Marx was in many ways his model and touchstone, and a large number of essays appeared in the 1960s which were later translated into English, for example *Photography – A Middle-brow Art*. In these studies, Bourdieu (and his co-authors) attempt to describe the perception of art and culture, which varies so greatly from one class to another, and to elucidate how class struggle involves contrasting ways of appropriating art and culture. Classes set themselves apart by means of a very different understanding of art and culture and thus reproduce, more or less unintentionally, the class structures of (French) society. Bourdieu elaborated this thesis in a particularly spectacular way in his perhaps most famous work of cultural sociology, *La distinction. Critique sociale du jugement* (1979; English title: *Distinction: A Social Critique of the Judgement of Taste*).

Bourdieu's subsequent publications merely complemented or completed a theoretical and research orientation set at an early stage. In terms of cultural sociology, two major studies have become particularly important: *Homo Academicus*, from 1984, an analysis of the French university system, particularly the crisis it faced towards the end of the 1960s, and *Les règles de l'art* (English title: *The Rules of Art*) from 1992, a historical and sociological study of the development of an autonomous art scene in France in the second half of the nineteenth century. Alongside these works, Bourdieu also published a steady flow of writings that fleshed out his theoretical ambitions, *Le sens pratique* (1980; English title: *The Logic of Practice*) and *Méditations pascaliennes* from 1997 (English title: *Pascalian Meditations*) being the key texts in this regard. But even in these basically theoretical studies, it is fair to say that he expands on the conceptual apparatus presented in *Outline of a Theory of Practice* only to a limited degree; above all, he defends it against criticisms. It is, however, almost impossible to discern any theoretical *development* here. Bourdieu's theory thus distinguishes itself from that of the other grand theorists dealt with so far. To deploy the language of the building trade once again, not only the foundation walls, but also the overall structure and even the roof were in place very quickly, while the later theoretical work related solely to the façade and décor. Since it was developed in the 1960s, his theory has thus remained basically the same.

It was solely Bourdieu's identity or role that seemed to change significantly over the course of time. While Bourdieu was always active politically on the left, this generally took a less spectacular form than in the case of other French intellectuals, occurring away from the light of day and basically unnoticed by most people. The fact that he pursued such activities away from the limelight was partly bound up with his frequently expressed critique of high-profile French intellectuals such as Jean-Paul Sartre, who frequently overshot the bounds of their specialisms and claimed a universal competence and public responsibility to which they were scarcely entitled. However, Bourdieu abandoned such restraint in the 1990s at the latest, until his death in 2002, when he increasingly emerged as a symbolic figure for critics of globalization, which almost automatically made him the kind of major intellectual he had never wished to be. His 1993 book *La misère du monde* (English title: *The Weight of the World: Social Suffering in Contemporary Society*) was conceived as a kind of empirical demonstration of the negative effects of globalization in different spheres of life and cultures. One has to give Bourdieu credit for having avoided a purely pamphleteering role to the very last. He was too strongly oriented towards empirical research, and his Durkheim-like ambition to strengthen the position of sociology within the disciplinary canon of France and to set it apart from other subjects, especially philosophy and social philosophy, was too strong for him to take on such a role. Bourdieu, so aware of power, had an ongoing interest in developing the kind of *empirical* sociological research which he favoured at an institutional level, as demonstrated in his role as editor of the journal *Actes de la recherche en sciences sociales*, which he founded in 1975 and which was accessible to a broad readership (on Bourdieu's intellectual biography, see the interview in *In Other Words: Essays Towards a Reflexive Sociology*, pp. 3–33).

Our account of Bourdieuvian theory will proceed as follows. First, we shall take a closer look at his early work, *Outline of a Theory of Practice*, which is of particular theoretical relevance as it features the basic elements of his arguments. Though we shall frequently draw on explanations and more precise formulations from subsequent works, our key aim is to lay bare why, and with the help of which ideas, Bourdieu tackled certain problems at a relatively early stage (1). Always bearing this early work in mind, and while presenting Bourdieu's key concepts, we shall then critically examine the model of action advocated by Bourdieu and the problems it entails (2). We then go on to present the overall architecture of Bourdieuvian theory and identify the nodal points within it (3), before presenting, as vividly and as briefly as possible, some characteristic aspects of Bourdieu's works of cultural sociology (4) and shedding light on the impact of his work (5).

1. We therefore begin with the early study of Kabyle society mentioned above, whose programmatic title requires explication: *Outline of a Theory of Practice*. Bourdieu – as intimated in our remarks on his intellectual biography – was caught up in the enthusiasm for Lévi-Straussian anthropology in the 1950s and began his anthropological research in Kabylia by focusing on key structuralist topics. Studies of kinship patterns, marriage behaviour and mythology were to provide insights into the logic of the processes occurring within this society, into the way in which it continually reproduces itself on the basis of certain rules. But Bourdieu's research had unexpected results. Above all, these did not confirm the structuralist premise of the constancy of rules (of marriage, exchange, communication), in line with which people supposedly always act. Rather, Bourdieu concluded that actors either play rules off against each other more or less as they see fit, so that one can scarcely refer to the *following* of rules, or follow them only in order to disguise concrete interests. This last is particularly apparent in the first chapter of the book, in which he scrutinizes the phenomenon of 'honour'. In Kabyle society, and in other places as well of course, honour plays a very important role; it seems impossible to link it with base economic interests because 'honourable behaviour' is directly opposed to action oriented towards profit. A man is honourable only if he is *not* greedy and *cannot* be bought. And in Kabyle society, the rituals by means of which one demonstrates that one's actions are honourable and that one is an honourable person are particularly pronounced. But Bourdieu shows that these rituals of honour often merely mask (profit-related) interests, that the actors see this link between honour and interests, or at least unconsciously produce it: people uphold rituals of honour *because* they enable them to promote their interests.

> The ritual of the ceremony of presenting the bridewealth is the occasion for a total confrontation between the two groups, in which the economic stakes are no more than an index and pretext. To demand a large payment for one's daughter, or to pay a large sum to marry off one's son, is in either case to assert one's prestige, and thereby to acquire prestige ... By a sort of inverted haggling, disguised under the appearance of ordinary bargaining, the two groups tacitly agree to step up the amount of the payment by successive bids, because they have a common interest in raising this indisputable index of the symbolic value of their products on the matrimonial exchange market. And no feat is more highly praised than the prowess of the bride's father who, after vigorous bargaining has been concluded, solemnly returns a large share of the sum received. The greater the proportion returned, the greater the

honour accruing from it, as if, in crowning the transaction with an act of generosity, the intention was to make an exchange of honour out of bargaining which could be so overtly keen only because the pursuit of maximum material profit was masked under the contests of honour and the pursuit of maximum symbolic profit.

(*Outline*, p. 56)

Rituals of honour thus conceal very tangible interests, which are overlooked if one merely describes the logic of the rules as do structuralist anthropologists. What is more, for precisely this reason, rules are by no means as rigid and have nothing like the determining effect on behaviour that orthodox structuralist authors assume. As Bourdieu observed, rules that do not tally with actors' interests are often broken, leading him to conclude that an element of 'unpredictability' is clearly inherent in human action with respect to rules and patterns, rituals and regulations (*Outline*, p. 9). This places a question mark over the entire structuralist terminology of rules and its underlying premises. Bourdieu puts forward the counter-argument that the following of rules is always associated with an element of conflict. If rules are not in fact ignored entirely, which certainly occurs at times, every rule-based act of exchange, every rule-based conversation, every rule-based marriage must *also* at least protect or enforce the interests of those involved or improve the social position of the parties to interaction. Rules are thus consciously instrumentalized by actors:

> Every exchange contains a more or less dissimulated challenge, and the logic of challenge and riposte is but the limit towards which *every act of communication* tends. Generous exchange tends towards overwhelming generosity; the greatest gift is at the same time the gift most likely to throw its recipient into dishonour by prohibiting any counter-gift. To reduce to the function of communication – albeit by the transfer of borrowed concepts – phenomena such as the dialectic of challenge and riposte and, more generally, the exchange of gifts, words, or women, is to ignore the structural ambivalence which predisposes them to fulfil a political function of domination in and through performance of the communication function.
>
> (ibid., p. 14; original emphasis)

Bourdieu accuses structuralism of having failed entirely to take account of how the action undertaken by social actors is related to interests in favour of a highly idealized description of rules and cultural patterns. People – according to Bourdieu – certainly manipulate rules and patterns; they are not merely the passive objects of social classification systems. Because actors pursue their interests, we must assume that there is always a difference between the 'official' and the 'regular' (ibid., p. 38) and between (theoretically) construed models and the *practice* of actors. It may be very helpful to identify social rules, but it is by no means sufficient if we wish to get at actors' *practice*:

> The logical relationships constructed by the anthropologist are opposed to 'practical' relationships – practical because continuously practised, kept up, and cultivated – in the same way as the geometrical space of a map, an imaginary representation of all theoretically possible roads and routes, is opposed to the network of beaten tracks, of paths made ever more practicable by constant use.
>
> (ibid., p. 37)

Ultimately, this is a profound criticism of structuralism (as the title *Outline of a Theory of Practice* indicates), particularly given that Bourdieu also resists applying the Saussurean paradigm of linguistic analysis, so inspiring for structuralists, to the social world (ibid., p. 24). In this way, he casts doubt on the theoretical and empirical fruitfulness of the structuralist anthropology and sociology of Lévi-Strauss.

> [The only way] the Saussurian construction ... could constitute the structural properties of the message was (simply by positing an indifferent sender and receiver) to neglect the functional properties the message derives from its *use* in a determinate situation and, more precisely, in a socially structured interaction. As soon as one moves from the structure of language to the functions it fulfils, that is, to the uses agents actually make of it, one sees that mere knowledge of the *code* gives only very imperfect mastery of the linguistic interactions really taking place.
>
> (ibid., p. 25; original emphasis)

Examining the actual practice characteristic of the 'objects of investigation' more closely, according to Bourdieu, reveals how inappropriate or insufficient structuralist analysis is. To put it in slightly more abstract terms, Bourdieu introduces elements of action theory into his originally structuralist theoretical framework, namely the idea of conduct at variance with the rules and related to interests. This was to change the structuralist paradigm markedly. As he was to state later in another publication, he objected in particular to the 'strange philosophy of action' inherent to structuralism, which 'made the agent disappear by reducing it to the role of supporter or bearer of the structure' (*The Rules of Art*, p. 179).

Yet Bourdieu does not break entirely with structuralism. He always remained attached to structuralist thinking, as evident in the fact that he termed his own approach 'genetic' or 'constructivist structuralism' (see for example *In Other Words: Essays Towards a Reflexive Sociology*, p. 123). The exact nature of this attachment, however, was to become clear only as his oeuvre developed. This is of course due to the predominantly empirical orientation of Bourdieu's work, which sometimes makes it appear unnecessary for him to locate and distinguish his own concepts with respect to other theoretical approaches. It is only in his next major theoretical work (*The Logic of Practice*, p. 4) that we find clear evidence of how structuralism 'influenced' him, when, for example, he praises it for the 'introduction into the social sciences of ... the relational mode of thought' and having broken with 'the substantialist mode of thought'. Bourdieu's thought leans heavily on structuralism (and on functionalism as well at times). Thus, for him, it is not the individual actor that is the key analytical lodestone; rather, it is the *relations* between actors or the relations between the positions within a system or – as Bourdieu was to say – within a 'field', that are crucial. 'Fields', to cite a definition provided by Bourdieu, are

> structured spaces of positions (or posts) whose properties depend on their position within these spaces and which can be analysed independently of the characteristics of their occupants (which are partly determined by them). There are general laws of fields: fields as different as the field of politics, the field of philosophy or the field of religion have invariant laws of functioning ... Whenever one studies a new field, whether it be the field of philology in the nineteenth century, contemporary fashion, or religion in the Middle Ages, one discovers specific properties that are peculiar to that field, at the same time as one pushes forward our knowledge of the universal mechanisms of fields.
>
> (*Sociology in Question*, p. 72)

According to Bourdieu, it is not useful to analyse the behaviour of individual actors in isolation, as many theorists of action do without further reflection, unless one also determines an actor's position within such a 'field', in which action becomes meaningful in the first place. 'Fields' offer options for action, but only *certain* options, which simply means that other options for action are excluded, that the actors are subject to constraints. The logic of action within the religious field is necessarily different from that in the artistic field, for example, because the constraints are different. These constraints and boundaries influence how prone actors – prophets and the faithful, artists and the viewing public – are to take action, which is why it is inevitably quite unproductive to restrict oneself to examining the biography of an actor, prophet, artist or author in order to explain religious or artistic phenomena (*Pascalian Meditations*, pp. 115ff.).

In light of this, Bourdieu consciously refrains from referring to 'subjects'; at most, he talks of actors. For him, actors are 'eminently active and acting' – a fact overlooked by structuralism. However, Bourdieu believes that Foucault's provocative structuralist notion of the 'looming end of man' or the 'death of the subject' is justified in as much as this was merely a way of stating the (structuralist) insight into the crucial significance of relations and relationships (within fields) and expressed the well-founded rejection of the idea, found in the work of Sartre and many other philosophers and sociologists, of a self-creating, autonomous subject (see the foreword to *Practical Reason*, pp. viii ff.). Time and again, Bourdieu was to defend this structuralist 'insight' with great vehemence; it was also the basis of his attacks on certain sociological or philosophical currents which, as he puts it, give sustenance to the 'biographical illusion'. Bourdieu mercilessly assails any notion that people create their own biography and that life is a whole, arising, as it were, from the subject's earliest endeavours and unfolding over the course of her life. He repeatedly points to the fact that the 'meaning and the social value of biographical events' are not constituted on the basis of the subject, but on the basis of actors' 'placements' and 'displacements' within a social space, which lends biographical events their meaning in the first place, the meaning which they ultimately take on for the actor (*The Rules of Art*, pp. 258ff.; see also *Practical Reason*, pp. 75ff.). Thus, rather than 'subjects', people are actors in a field by which they are profoundly moulded.

But we wish to avoid getting ahead of ourselves in our discussion of Bourdieu's work. Let us turn once again to his early book *Outline of a Theory of Practice*. Though this text is rather wordy in places, and Bourdieu was to provide a clearer explanation of his position only at a later stage, it undoubtedly set out his synthetic aspirations. For Bourdieu made it absolutely clear that all action theoretical perspectives are insufficient *in isolation*: neither symbolic interactionism nor phenomenological approaches within sociology such as ethnomethodology are capable of deciphering the really interesting sociological facts. For him, these approaches are too quick to adopt the actor's perspective; they take on his *naive* view of the givenness of the world, forgetting how crucial are *actors' positions in relation to one another* and to the field within which they move. To reinforce his 'objectivist' stance, Bourdieu borrows not only from structuralism, which seems to him overly idealistic in certain respects. He also draws on a 'concrete' materialist Marxism, when he points, for example, to the conditions of production on the basis of which marriage rituals take place and without which they cannot be understood:

> It is not sufficient to ridicule the more naïve forms of functionalism in order to have done with the question of the practical functions of practice. It is clear that a universal definition of the functions of marriage as an operation intended to ensure the biological reproduction of the group, in accordance with forms approved by the group, in no way explains Kabyle marriage ritual. But, contrary to appearances, scarcely more understanding is derived from a structural analysis which ignores the specific functions of ritual practices and fails to inquire into the *economic and social*

conditions of the production of the dispositions generating both these practices and also the collective definition of the practical functions in whose service they function.

(*Outline*, p. 115; emphasis added)

Critical of a theory of action which he describes as subjectivist, Bourdieu ultimately asserts the *pre-eminence of an objectivist form of analysis* in which the structures of a social field are determined *by the sociological observer* – structures that impose constraints on actors, of which they themselves are generally unaware. Loïc Wacquant, a sociologist closely associated with Bourdieu, has put this in the following way, drawing a comparison between the 'objectivism' of the Durkheimian method of analysis and that of Bourdieu:

> Application of Durkheim's first principle of the 'sociological method', the systematic rejection of preconceptions, must come before analysis of the practical apprehension of the world from the subjective standpoint. For the viewpoints of agents will vary systematically with the point they occupy in objective social space.
>
> (Bourdieu and Wacquant, *An Invitation to Reflexive Sociology*, p. 11)

At the same time, however, Bourdieu regards (objectivist) structuralism on its own as insufficient, as he does the equally objectivist functionalism, which ignores actors' perspectives. His sociological approach is intended to take full account of actors' power and capacity to act. But this means that Bourdieu wishes to sail, and indeed cannot avoid sailing – and he puts it explicitly in these terms – between the Scylla of 'phenomenology' or 'subjectivism' and the Charybdis of 'objectivism'. For him, all these forms of knowledge are deficient *in and of themselves*, which is why he wishes to develop a third mode of sociological understanding, his 'theory of practice', an approach which goes beyond 'objectivism' and takes what actors do seriously. This can succeed only if it is shown that there are '*dialectical* relations between the objective structures [of fields] … and the structured dispositions [of actors]' (*Outline*, p. 3; original emphasis; our insertions), that is, that action and structures determine one another through their interrelationship.

Attentive readers of the quote above may have noticed that what Bourdieu is trying to do here is familiar to us from the lecture on Anthony Giddens; Bourdieu also refers to 'structuring' or 'structuration'. Though this active conception never attained the systematic significance that it did in the work of Giddens (in part because Bourdieu was not a 'pure' social theorist and would probably have had no interest in developing the kind of social ontology present in the work of Giddens), it is nonetheless clear that Bourdieu is aiming to develop a stance which, in contrast to functionalists and structuralists, assumes that structures are 'made' and continuously reproduced by actors. But at the same time – in contrast to the ideas supposedly expounded by pure action theorists – he also emphasizes the profound and causal impact of these structures.

2. So far, we have defined Bourdieu's theoretical approach only vaguely; his cited statements generally represent declarations of intention which underline the need for a theoretical synthesis rather than provide one. When Bourdieu states that he wishes to proceed neither 'phenomenologically' nor 'objectivistically', this is a purely negative definition of his project. The question arises as to *how* he incorporates the action theoretical elements – the level of actors – into his approach, *how* he conceives, in concrete terms, the actions carried out by actors, who drive the process of structuration, which in turn structures their actions. Here, there is an evident need to scrutinize Bourdieu's relationship with utilitarianism and its theory of action, particularly in light of the fact that Bourdieu refers so often to actors' 'interests'. And a number of interpreters (see especially A. Honneth, 'The Fragmented World of Symbolic Forms') have in fact expounded the thesis that Bourdieu's approach represents an amalgamation of structuralism and utilitarianism, a hypothesis or interpretation of his work which, considering how he reacted to it, certainly infuriated Bourdieu like no other and which he rejected vehemently on numerous occasions. In fact, Bourdieu emerges as a harsh critic of utilitarianism and the rational choice approach in many of his writings – and it is very hard to reconcile key aspects of his work with the basic assumptions of utilitarian or neo-utilitarian arguments. Nevertheless, this does not render superfluous the issue of whether other, perhaps equally important aspects of his work are not redolent of utilitarianism. What then (again, see Lecture V) distinguishes Bourdieuvian actors from their utilitarian counterparts?

We have already hinted at Bourdieu's first criticism of utilitarian thought. Because it places the isolated actor centre stage, it ignores the relational method of analysis which, according to Bourdieu, is a prerequisite for attaining key insights into the functioning of the social world. This criticism is intended to apply not only to utilitarian theories, but in principle to all action theoretical approaches. His second criticism is more specific: Bourdieu assails utilitarian approaches for systematically failing to address the issue of the origin of utility calculations and interests. 'Because it must postulate *ex nihilo* the existence of a universal, pre-constituted interest, rational action theory is thoroughly oblivious to the social genesis of historically varying forms of interest' (Bourdieu and Wacquant, *An Invitation to Reflexive Sociology*, p. 125). In addition, in his anthropological studies, Bourdieu showed again and again that the rational-economic calculations typical of modern Western capitalism are not found in other societies in this form. Utilitarians, according to Bourdieu, thus turn a way of calculating actions that developed in modern capitalist societies into a human universal. More significant and more typical than this very well-known criticism is Bourdieu's third objection, that utilitarians confuse the logic of theory with the logic of practice:

> The actor, as [this theory] construes him or her, is nothing other than the imaginary projection of the knowing subject (*sujet connaissant*) into the acting subject (*sujet agissant*), a sort of monster with the head of the thinker thinking his practice in reflexive and logical fashion mounted on the body of a man of action engaged in action. ... Its 'imaginary anthropology' seeks to found action, whether 'economic' or not, on the intentional choice of an actor who is himself or herself economically and socially unconditioned.
>
> (ibid., p. 123)

Here, Bourdieu first of all addresses the fact that utilitarianism has a false notion of real action processes, which are for the most part not entirely rational and reflexive. The kind of rationality and reflexivity that utilitarianism takes for granted here is possible only under particular circumstances, in the sheltered world of science for example, but is quite rare under normal conditions of practice. Action is indeed concerned with realizing interests, but only rarely in the sense of the *conscious* pursuit of these interests. Here, Bourdieu is advocating a stance similar to that of Anthony Giddens, one close to American pragmatism (see its concept of 'habit'). According to Bourdieu, action generally adheres to a practical logic, which is often shaped by routine requirements and which thus has no need for the capacity for reflection demanded by rational choice theorists. Determined by socialization, earlier experiences, etc., certain action dispositions are stamped onto our bodies; for the most part, these can be retrieved without conscious awareness and predetermine what form action takes. Bourdieu captures this idea with the term 'habitus', originally found in the work of Husserl. A key term within his theory, he developed it at an early stage and was repeatedly to set himself apart from other theoretical schools with its help.

In *Outline*, he defines the habitus as a 'system of lasting, transposable dispositions which, integrating past experiences, functions at every moment as a *matrix of perceptions, appreciations, and actions* and makes possible the achievement of infinitely diversified tasks, thanks to analogical transfers of schemes permitting the solution of similarly shaped problems, and thanks to the unceasing corrections of the results obtained, dialectically produced by those results' (pp. 82–3; our emphasis). This sounds complicated, but is in fact easy to explain. Bourdieu assumes that, from childhood onwards, in the family, school and world of work, we are taught certain schemata of thinking, perceiving and acting, which generally enable us to respond smoothly to different situations, to solve practical tasks, etc. Our physical movements, our tastes, our most banal interpretations of the world are formed at an early stage and then crucially determine our options for action.

> Through the habitus, the structure which has produced it governs practice, not by the process of a mechanical determination, but through the mediation of the orientations and limits it assigns to the habitus's operations of invention. As an acquired system of generative schemes objectively adjusted to the particular conditions in which it is constituted, the habitus engenders all the thoughts, all the perceptions, and all the actions consistent with those conditions, and not others. ... Because the habitus is an endless capacity to engender products – thoughts, perceptions, expressions, actions – whose limits are set by the historically and socially situated conditions of its production, the conditioned and conditional freedom it secures is as remote from a creation of unpredictable novelty as it is from a simple mechanical reproduction of the initial conditionings.
>
> (ibid., p. 95)

As this quotation indicates, the concept of 'habitus' does not rule out a certain behavioural room for manoeuvre which enables conduct of a creative and innovative nature. On the other hand, however, we cannot step or break out of this habitual behaviour entirely, because the habitus is an aspect of our life story and identity. The attentive reader will discern how this links up with Bourdieu's investigations in cultural sociology and class theory. For it is clear that there is no one habitus in a society, but that *different* forms of perception, thinking and action are inculcated in different classes, through which these classes, and above all the differences between them, are constantly reproduced. But we are not yet concerned with this aspect. What is important here is that Bourdieu deploys the concept of habitus in the attempt to rid himself of the assumptions of utilitarianism and neo-utilitarianism, which are highly rationalistic and anchored in the philosophy of consciousness.

If, as we have seen, Bourdieu's explicit effort to set himself apart from utilitarianism is unambiguous and there are elements in his theoretical edifice which simply cannot be reconciled with utilitarian thought, why has he so often been accused of being 'close to utilitarianism' – and not only by malicious interpreters or cursory readers? The reason is that while Bourdieu has certainly criticized thinking in terms of economic utility, *the nature of his criticism is incapable of establishing clear distance between his approach and utilitarian ones.*

For as we saw in Lecture V, utilitarianism is also fairly differentiated internally insofar as the so-called neo-utilitarians have done away with some of the assumptions of traditional utilitarianism. Neo-utilitarians have, for example, rid themselves of the concept of utility, replacing it with the neutral term 'preferences', because only very few actions can be explained on the basis of purely (economic) calculations of utility. It is true that Bourdieu's critique of utilitarianism in its 'original' form goes further than this. The concept of habitus allows him to take leave, above all, of the model of the actor whose deeds are *consciously* rational. Yet at the same time, like *all* utilitarians, he continues to adhere to the notion that people (consciously or unconsciously) always pursue their interests – or preferences. According to Bourdieu, people are socialized into a 'field', where they learn how to behave appropriately; they understand the rules and internalize the 'strategies' indispensable to playing the game *successfully*. And the aim of these 'strategies' – a (utilitarian) concept used repeatedly by Bourdieu, although he is very aware of how problematic it is in view of his critique of utilitarianism (see Bourdieu and Wacquant, *An Invitation to Reflexive Sociology*, p. 128) – is to improve the player's position within a particular field or at least to uphold the status quo.

> It is not enough to say that the history of the field is the history of the struggle for a monopoly of the imposition of legitimate categories of perception and appreciation; it is in the very *struggle* that the history of the field is made; it is through struggles that it is temporalized.
>
> (*The Rules of Art*, p. 157; original emphasis)

The battle over the realization of actors' interests is thus a factor driving the historical change of fields. The strategies deployed in the field are not always concerned solely with attaining economic benefits – Bourdieu would roundly reject an economistic or primitive utilitarian perspective of this kind. The way he puts it is that the strategies are intended to procure those goods worth playing for within a particular field. This *may*, as in the field of the economy, be financial profit; in other fields, meanwhile, strategies are oriented towards enhancing one's reputation or honour (which cannot necessarily or immediately be converted into financial gain). But the priority will always be to realize those interests relevant within a particular field – in competition with others.

This line of argument no doubt entails a premise backed by typical utilitarian notions, with which we are already familiar within the context of conflict theory and to which Bourdieu explicitly refers: 'the social world is the site of continual struggles to define what the social world is' (Bourdieu and Wacquant, *An Invitation to Reflexive Sociology*, p. 70). The concept of 'struggle' crops up in his work as frequently as that of 'strategy'; in much the same way as in utilitarianism and conflict theory, there is quite often a hint of cynical pleasure in the observation of the hypocritical behaviour of the objects of inquiry, whose subjective motives are by no means to be believed:

> The most profitable strategies are usually those produced, without any calculation, and in the illusion of the most absolute 'sincerity', by a habitus objectively fitted to the objective structures. These strategies without strategic calculation procure an important secondary advantage for those who can scarcely be called their authors: the social approval accruing to apparent disinterestedness.
>
> (Bourdieu, *The Logic of Practice*, p. 292, fn. 10)

This close connection between utilitarian, conflict theoretical and Marxian arguments is even more clearly apparent in another key Bourdieuvian concept, that of 'capital', which complements or completes the concepts of 'field' and 'habitus'.

Bourdieu's concept of capital owes its existence to the following problem. Bourdieu must explain which goods the actors in the various fields struggle over, that is, what they are trying to achieve in deploying their various action strategies. He rejects the notion characteristic of (primitive) utilitarianism that social life is to be understood exclusively as a struggle over (economic) goods. For the same reason, he also criticizes Marxism, as it also focuses solely on the struggle over economic goods, while ignoring or neglecting other forms of dispute (see for example 'The Social Space and the Genesis of Groups', p. 723).

Bourdieu now takes the logical step already taken in much the same way before him by conflict theorists. *His concern is to bring out how social struggles are about more than just financial utility and economic capital.* But, peculiarly enough, the way in which he proceeds – once again, in much the same way as does conflict theory (see Lecture VIII) – does not entail a complete break with utilitarian or Marxian notions. For in order to determine more precisely what is at stake in social struggles, Bourdieu deploys the term 'capital', which originates in 'bourgeois' and Marxian economics, but he extends its meaning and distinguishes between *different forms* of capital. In *Outline of a Theory of Practice*, he criticizes Marxism for having utterly neglected what Bourdieu calls 'symbolic capital', a consequence of its preoccupation with economic capital. Bourdieu, using language highly redolent of utilitarianism, puts it as follows. Marx only recognized immediate economic interests and these were all he allowed in his theoretical edifice, relegating all other types of interest to the sphere of the 'irrationality of feeling or passion' (*Outline*, p. 177). But what one must do is apply economic calculations to *all* goods (utilitarians and conflict theorists would say: to all resources):

> contrary to naively idyllic representations of 'pre-capitalist' societies (or of the 'cultural' sphere of capitalist societies), practice never ceases to conform to economic calculation even when it

> gives every appearance of disinterestedness by departing from the logic of interested calculation (in the narrow sense) and playing for stakes that are non-material and not easily quantified.
>
> (ibid., p. 177)

According to Bourdieu, Marxism entirely disregards the fact that actions which at first sight seem irrational because they are not geared towards immediate financial gain may be a means of acquiring substantial benefits *of other kinds*, which Bourdieu calls 'symbolic profits' and which prompt him to refer to 'symbolic capital' as well as economic capital. Certain deeds – such as generous gifts, extravagant behaviour, etc. – enable people to accrue all kinds of distinction; such deeds are a symbol of one's own (outstanding) position, power, prestige, etc., allowing one to distinguish oneself from those of lower rank. This symbolic form of capital is of relevance to the class hierarchy in a society in as much as it can be converted into 'real' capital in certain circumstances. The great prestige enjoyed by an individual, the good reputation of a particular family, the ostentatiously displayed wealth of a great man often furnish people with opportunities to attain economic capital as well, in line with the motto: to everyone that has (symbolic) capital, (economic) capital shall be given. In this sense, there is nothing (economically) irrational about symbolic capital. Rather, the accumulation of symbolic capital is also a clever way of safeguarding one's prospects of obtaining economic capital. This symbolic form of capital is a kind of credit, on the basis of which economic opportunities constantly arise. In this sense, Bourdieu can state that symbolic capital represents a 'transformed and thereby *disguised* form of physical "economic" capital' (ibid., p. 183; original emphasis).

> It is thus by drawing up a *comprehensive balance-sheet* of symbolic profits, without forgetting the undifferentiatedness of the symbolic and material aspects of the patrimony, that it becomes possible to grasp the economic rationality of conduct which economism dismisses as absurd: the decision to buy a second pair of oxen after the harvest, on the grounds that they are needed for treading out the grain – which is a way of making it known the crop has been plentiful – only to have to sell them again for lack of fodder, before the autumn ploughing, when they would be technically necessary, seems economically aberrant only if one forgets all the material and symbolic profit accruing from this (albeit fictitious) addition to the family's symbolic capital in the late-summer period in which marriages are negotiated. The perfect rationality of this strategy of bluff lies in the fact that marriage is the occasion for an (in the widest sense) economic circulation which cannot be seen purely in terms of material goods.
>
> (ibid., p. 181; original emphasis)

But this great importance of symbolic capital is not, as this quotation referring to Kabyle society might lead us to presume, restricted to 'primitive' or pre-capitalist societies. It is true, as Bourdieu states, that pre-capitalist economies have a 'great need for symbolic violence' (ibid., p. 191) insofar as circumstances of unadulterated exploitation and great material inequalities were and are always papered over symbolically and thus concealed (or, conversely, realized in brutal fashion by means of physical violence). This, Bourdieu suggests, arguing in a very similar way to Marx, has changed in capitalism in that its practice of domination no longer depends on symbolic concealment, but can be legitimized in a very different way (through the ideology of fair exchange between goods, money and labour, for example). But this does not mean that symbolic capital plays no role in modern societies. Nothing could be further from the truth. It was to become Bourdieu's core project in the sociology of culture to analyse this 'symbolic capital' in modern societies, particularly modern French society, in a sober and sometimes cynical way. In his view, a convincing analysis of modern societies must go beyond economic forms of capital and pay heed to symbolic capital as well.

Subsequently, when he had more or less ceased to carry out anthropological studies and increasingly devoted himself to the analysis of French society, Bourdieu was to attempt to clarify more precisely this still relatively nebulous concept of 'symbolic capital'. In addition to economic capital, he introduced the distinction between 'cultural' and 'social' capital; sometimes he also refers to 'political capital', prompting observers and critics to refer to the 'inflationary' tendency affecting the concept of capital in his theory. There is no need for us to understand all these extensions and differentiations in detail. It is enough to point out that in his best-known writings Bourdieu distinguishes between economic, symbolic, cultural and social forms of capital. As the meaning of the term 'economic capital' ought to be fairly clear, we shall briefly clarify the other three types:

- Under the term 'cultural capital' he includes *both* works of art, books and musical instruments, in as much as this capital is present in the form of objects, *and* cultural capacities and cultural knowledge, in as much as these have been 'absorbed' by actors through earlier processes of socialization, *as well as* titles (such as doctor, along with those conferred by other degrees, etc.), because these demonstrate, as it were, the acquisition of cultural knowledge.
- 'Social capital', meanwhile, covers resources through which one demonstrates membership of or affiliation to a group, one's (distinguished) family background, one's attendance at a particular elite school or university; it refers to networks in the sense of social relationships upon which one may draw in order to realize certain goals, that which is colloquially known as the 'old boys' network' (see Bourdieu's essay 'The Forms of Capital').

- 'Symbolic capital' is something of a generic term emerging from the interplay of the economic, social and cultural types of capital: all three 'original' capital types lay the foundations for an individual's overall standing, good reputation, renown and prestige in society, thus determining his place in the hierarchy.

According to Bourdieu, these concepts of capital enable us to model a society's class structure. In his view, one ought to be aware that the forms of capital may sometimes be exchanged or translated into one another; their conversion is often possible. That is, in determining an individual's position within a society's class structure, it is vital to study both the *volume* of capital available to this individual as well as the *structure* of this capital (which shows which forms of capital this individual's total capital is composed of). To mention one example: professors would generally be located in the middling ranks of a modern society with respect to their economic capital, but at the same time they possess great cultural capital (they have a large number of titles, they not only own lots of books, but have even read many of them) and they often have a fairly large number of social relationships with a diverse range of circles, so that assessing their social position requires a multidimensional approach. To elucidate Bourdieu's mode of analysis, we have provided you with a model of class developed entirely on the basis of his theoretical framework, but in *simplified form*, as drawn up by Klaus Eder ('Klassentheorie als Gesellschaftstheorie' ['Class Theory as Social Theory'], p. 21, fn. 6), taking only the cultural and economic forms of capital into account, for the former West Germany (Figure 15.1). The vertical line is intended to indicate the *absolute* volume of available capital; the horizontal the *relative* proportion of both forms of capital.

According to this diagram, the volume of capital enjoyed by doctors and members of the independent professions is quite similar, though the composition of this capital is very different: while doctors possess a comparatively small amount of economic capital, their cultural capital is relatively great compared with private sector professionals. Farmers generally have neither particularly great economic nor cultural capital, while in the case of craftspeople one is struck again by the great discrepancy between relatively great cultural capital and relatively meagre economic capital, etc. Of course, we could argue endlessly over whether, for example, the cultural capital of craftspeople and professors in relation to one another is 'correct' here. And we would have to look closely at the methodological approach to determining capital that underpins this diagram. But this is of no concern to us here.

What we wish to get across is that subtle analyses of social structure of this kind provide a more convincing class theory, and above all one more in keeping with the times, than could orthodox Marxism. But that is not all.

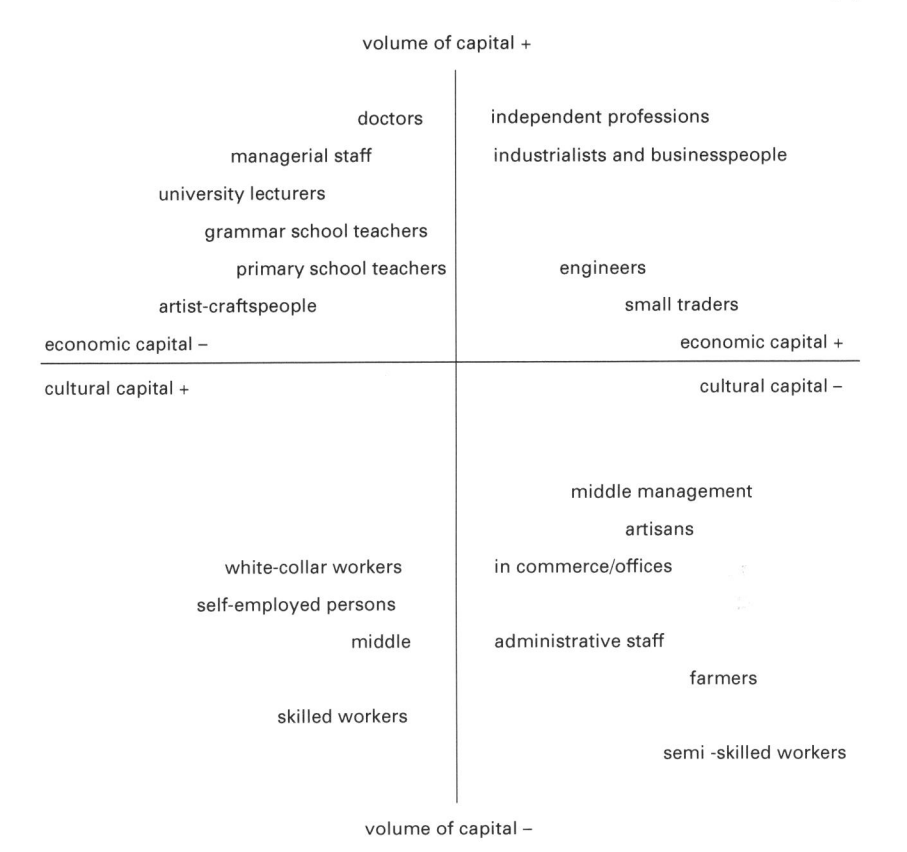

```
                    volume of capital +
                                    |
                    doctors         | independent professions
                managerial staff    | industrialists and businesspeople
            university lecturers    |
                grammar school teachers |
                primary school teachers | engineers
            artist-craftspeople     | small traders
economic capital –                  | economic capital +
                                    |
cultural capital +                  | cultural capital –
                                    |
                                    | middle management
                                    | artisans
            white-collar workers    | in commerce/offices
            self-employed persons   |
                    middle          | administrative staff
                                    | farmers
                    skilled workers |
                                    | semi-skilled workers
                                    |
                    volume of capital –
```

Figure 15.1

The introduction of differing concepts of capital remedies Marxism's obvious lack of a sociology of culture – and this is a key reason why Bourdieuvian theory seemed so appealing to ex-Marxists. The deployment of a sophisticated conception of capital allowed them a *degree* of distance from Marx, without requiring them to enter wholly new theoretical territory.

But at the same time – and this brings us back to our initial question concerning the traces of utilitarianism in Bourdieu's theoretical edifice – a concept of capital originating in the economy reinforces the utilitarian (and conflict theoretical) 'feel' of Bourdieuvian theory to which we referred earlier: the field of culture is described with fundamentally the same conceptual apparatus as that of the economy. For in both spheres, actors' interests play the decisive role; it is only the types of capital, and thus the forms of what is at stake, that differ. The main concern is always with profits and losses and the struggles and disputes over them. Bourdieu's model of action – coupled with his concept of habitus – always remains the same and takes fundamentally the same form with respect to the various fields.

> The theory of action that I propose (with the notion of habitus) amounts to saying that most human actions have as a basis something quite different from intention, that is, acquired dispositions which make it so that an action can and should be interpreted as *oriented toward one objective or another* without anyone being able to claim that that objective was a conscious design.
>
> (*Practical Reason*, pp. 97–8; emphasis added)

It thus comes as no surprise that Bourdieu formulates his ambitions with regard to the production of 'grand theory' in a language that does little to conceal its economistic or utilitarian taproots. The overriding and long-term goal of his work – as he was to express it – was to produce a 'general theory of the *economy* of practices' (*The Rules of Art*, p. 183; emphasis added), a theory capable of comprehensively interpreting the logic of the interest-based struggle over specific types of capital in very different fields.

As a result of these echoes of utilitarianism in his theory of action, 'supra-individual' or collective phenomena are also described solely under utilitarian premises: for Bourdieu, 'culture' is no more than a game in which different classes enforce their particular conceptions of aesthetics in an attempt to set themselves apart from other classes. Bourdieu sees the 'public sphere', the idea of the unconstrained and pluralistic exchange of political arguments prized so highly by Dewey and Habermas, primarily as something introduced for strategic reasons in the eighteenth and nineteenth centuries by a class of high-ranking bureaucrats, a means of asserting themselves against their competitors, such as the aristocracy (*Practical Reason*, pp. 23–4). As Bourdieu sees it, what is invariably at issue here – but by no means only here – is the acquisition of capital, though 'capital' can mean different things. In line with the rules that pertain within specific fields, actors pursue their interests as they relate *to these fields*, though, because they have become habituated to them, actors are not always aware of these interests. This is why, particularly in his later work, Bourdieu also uses the term *illusio* (from *ludus* = 'game') as an alternative to 'interests', to make it clear that these do not refer solely to (conscious) economic interests.

> I much prefer to use the term *illusio*, since I always speak of specific interests, of interests that are both presupposed and produced by the functioning of historically delimited fields. Paradoxically, the term interest has brought forth the knee-jerk accusation of economism. In fact, the notion as I use it is the means of a deliberate and provisional reductionism that allows me to import the materialist mode of questioning into the cultural sphere from which it was

expelled, historically, when the modern view of art was invented and the field of cultural production won its autonomy.

(*An Invitation to Reflexive Sociology*, pp. 115–16; original emphasis)

By deploying the term 'illusio', Bourdieu believes that he has distanced himself sufficiently and conclusively from utilitarianism. He also thinks he can do without a typology of action of the kind produced by Jürgen Habermas, with its distinction between purposive-rational and communicative action. Such a distinction, according to Bourdieu, would merely ignore the existence of different forms of non-material profit in disparate fields. For him, capital exists in various forms but action does not; actors do their best to accrue the different types of capital within the various fields. Habermas' typology of action is said to be merely an idealistic means of disguising this fact. Yet, despite all his criticisms of utilitarianism, Bourdieu overlooks the fact that this is exactly the position advocated by neo-utilitarians: they too make no mention of different types of action, referring only to actors' attempts to realize their various preferences. They too declare a typology of action absurd or useless, because action in itself is very easy to explain, as it always revolves around obtaining what one wants.

But it is not just Bourdieu's proximity to (neo-)utilitarianism, which was a recurrent feature of his work, that is remarkable here. Also of interest is the fact that Bourdieu's position appears not to be entirely consistent in itself. For even if we were to accept his 'theory of habitus', which does not assert that action is entirely determined, we would still be faced with the problem of explaining the actors' *room for manoeuvre* with respect to action, the flexibility of action *within the boundaries set by the habitus*. In concrete terms, within a field which demands a particular habitus, how are the various 'interests' realized by the actors? It should at least be conceivable that normative, affective, etc. forms of action play a role within the variable options for action opened up by the habitus. But a typology of action would be very helpful, if not essential, to shed light on this spectrum of action, because it is the only way of guarding against an overly narrow – perhaps, once again, utilitarian – conception of action. But Bourdieu does nothing to address this issue. He seems quite unaware of it, which suggests a lacuna in his theory. This is also apparent in the fact that, in his studies of art, for example, Bourdieu only illuminates writers' and painters' efforts to establish themselves and obtain distinction along with the constraints upon them, but remains strangely silent about their artistic creativity. This is not to say that this creativity can be described without reference to the logic of the various 'fields'. Bourdieu's critique of idealist notions of the artist's self-creation is quite justified. But if the habitus is not to be understood deterministically, the theorist must pay some attention at least to these *non-determined* aspects of action, that which we might call the 'creativity of action'.

3. We have now outlined Bourdieu's theoretical premises from a critical angle and presented his basic concepts of *field, habitus* and *capital* more or less in isolation from one another. Our concern now is to lay bare how these three concepts *connect* in Bourdieu's thinking and thus to present his theoretical construct in its entirety, as well as identifying the problematic features of its 'architecture'.

The concept of field or Bourdieu's references to fields (plural) form the logical starting point of Bourdieuvian theory. Social reality is composed of various fields, in which different rules apply, rules which actors have to follow if they wish to succeed in gaining profits – specific forms of capital – within this field. To repeat: the field of science obeys different rules than that of politics, education or sport. This is in a way reminiscent of theorems of differentiation, particularly Luhmann's systems theory. And in fact, Bourdieu is fairly close here to the idea advocated by Luhmann and his supporters that the social world has divided into various spheres, which can no longer be straightforwardly unified under conditions of modernity. And Bourdieu is faced with the same problems as confront this theory. He is unable to convincingly explain *how many fields there are* (Bourdieu seems to assume that there are a large number of fields, which he believes can be determined only by means of empirical historical investigation, though his references to this process of determination are not particularly helpful and his own research relates only to a few limited aspects of the social world; see *In Other Words*, p. 88) and *where exactly the boundaries between the fields lie*. Theorists of differentiation and Luhmann in particular have made detailed theoretical observations in this respect, though these too failed to satisfy entirely. Bourdieu on the other hand set about providing his notion of 'fields' with theoretical backup only very late in his career. His comments on the relevant problems are rather thin on the ground and are far from being as systematic as is the case in Luhmann's work. But one thing at least is clear: Bourdieu's 'field theory' can be distinguished from the assumptions characteristic of Luhmannian systems theory in at least two respects. First, in contrast to Luhmann, Bourdieu places struggle centre stage, that is, his fields are analysed in terms of conflict theory – a point which was never of any interest to Luhmann in his analyses of 'systems':

> If it is true that, in the literary or artistic field, for instance, one may treat the stances constitutive of a space of possibles as a system, they form a system of differences, of distinctive and antagonistic properties which do not develop out of their own internal motion (as the principle of self-referentiality implies) but via conflicts internal to the field of production. The field is the locus of relations of force – and not only of meaning – and of struggles aimed

at transforming it, and therefore of endless change. The coherence that may be observed in a given state of the field, its apparent orientation toward a common function ... are born of conflict and competition, not of some kind of immanent self-development of the structure.

(*An Invitation to Reflexive Sociology*, pp. 103–4)

Second, in contrast to Luhmann, Bourdieu does not assume that the fields are radically separate and that there is thus no prospect of establishing any kind of unity. It may be no coincidence that the Frenchman Bourdieu – citizen of a highly centralized country – attributed a kind of meta-function to the state. He understood the state as a 'meta-field' which is still capable of playing the role of 'arbiter' between the fields owing to its capacity to establish compelling norms (*Pascalian Meditations*, p. 127; see also *Practical Reason*, p. 33). With this thesis too, he set himself apart from radical theorists of differentiation and above all from Luhmann, but without, we underline, endorsing the idea that societies are integrated by norms, as is the case in the work of Parsons or Münch.

A special habitus is moulded by the rules which apply within the specific fields, and those who enter them inescapably (have to) adapt to this habitus. Scientists, politicians, sportspeople, etc. have a specific habitus detectable in how they talk, gesture, evaluate various issues, walk, etc. This does not mean that all politicians talk, gesture, evaluate, etc. in the same way, which would mean that their behaviour was fully determined. Bourdieu, as we have seen, defends himself against the accusation of determinism so often levelled against him (see for example Luc Ferry and Alain Renaut, 'French Marxism (Bourdieu)', pp. 153–84, in *French Philosophy of the Sixties*); he repeatedly emphasizes that actors adopt a particular habitus only with a certain, if high, degree of probability, and that this habitus also allows for the possibility of behavioural variation:

> Because the habitus is an infinite capacity for generating products – thoughts, perceptions, expressions and actions – whose limits are set by the historically and socially situated conditions of its production, the conditioned and conditional freedom it provides is as remote from creation of unpredictable novelty as it is from simple mechanical reproduction of the original conditioning.
>
> (*The Logic of Practice*, p. 55)

Despite all the variability, however, field-specific action as well as the fields as a whole are fairly stable. This is because, as a schema of perception, thinking and action (here Bourdieu adopts the insights of ethnomethodology), the habitus tends to be constantly confirmed or reproduced. Because the habitus has entered into people's bodies and become their identity, people (unconsciously) tend to uphold this identity. We wish to see our familiar world confirmed repeatedly and have no interest in destroying this trust in the meaningfulness of the everyday world. This means that through the 'systematic "choices" it makes among the places, events and people that might be frequented, the habitus tends to protect itself from crises and critical challenges' (ibid., p. 61). As a result, the types of habitus formed in the fields constantly reconfirm the fields in their original form, and the same process of structuration occurs on an ongoing basis.

> Because habitus ... is a product of a history, the instruments of construction of the social that it invests in practical knowledge of the world and in action are socially constructed, in other words structured by the world that they structure.
>
> (*Pascalian Meditations*, p. 148)

However, the habitus is not only the expression of 'differentiated' social fields, as one would say from a more systems theoretical perspective. Types of habitus are also the products of specific *class* realities, specific social milieus, which reproduce these realities and milieux:

> One of the functions of the notion of habitus is to account for the unity of style, which unites the practices and goods of a single agent or a class of agents ... The habitus is this generative and unifying principle which retranslates the intrinsic and relational characteristics of a position into a unitary lifestyle.
>
> (*Practical Reason*, p. 8)

Bourdieu's ongoing preoccupation with issues relating to the (French) education system was, among other things, intended to show that this class-based habitus is almost impossible to undo even by means of a seemingly meritocratic education system. In fact, in his view, the opposite applies. The education system continually reinforces these class-specific forms of behaviour, which is why it contributes to the ongoing reproduction of social inequality (see 'Reproduction') – a thesis with which we are familiar in much the same form from our discussion of conflict theorist Randall Collins in Lecture VIII.

Of course, this trope of the reproduction of social structures in near-identical form associated with the concept of habitus raises the question of how Bourdieu conceives of *social change* in the first place – especially given that he is cool towards the thesis that ideas or ideologies can do much to influence or change things. This becomes particularly clear in light of the classical sociological concept of the 'legitimacy of domination'. For Bourdieu, this figure of thought, which goes back to Max Weber, is problematic right from the outset because – through the concept of rational-legal domination for example – it suggests that there can be a somehow *conscious* discourse about the legitimacy of domination. But Bourdieu believes that domination functions quite differently. According to him, from childhood onwards people become accustomed to structures of domination as taken-for-granted features of the world. In institutions such as nurseries, schools and factories, the lower classes in particular have a self-evident acceptance of social inequality 'drummed into' them, which makes it almost impossible for them to turn these structures into an object of discourse (see *Practical Reason*, pp. 53–4). And domination is not maintained by means of ideologies or legitimizing discourses, of which many people could make neither head nor tail anyway, but by the constant practice of compliance with existing inequalities of power.

> If I have little by little come to shun the use of the word 'ideology', this is not only because of its polysemy and the resulting ambiguities. It is above all because, by evoking the order of ideas, and of action by ideas and on ideas, it inclines one to forget one of the most powerful mechanisms of the maintenance of the symbolic order, the *two-fold naturalization* which results from the inscription of the social in things and in bodies (as much those of the dominant as of the dominated – whether in terms of sex, ethnicity, social position or any other discriminating factor), with the resulting effects of symbolic violence. As is underlined by ordinary-language notions such as 'natural distinction' or 'gift', the work of legitimation of the established order is extraordinarily facilitated by the fact that it goes on almost automatically in the reality of the social world.
>
> (*Pascalian Meditations*, p. 181; original emphasis)

This stance, though, makes the potential of Bourdieuvian theory to contribute to a theory of change a yet more pressing issue, and it inspired some to accuse Bourdieu of (negative) hyperfunctionalism, because according to the logic of his theory, despite ongoing struggles within the fields, the (normatively problematic) unequal power structures are constantly reproduced and stabilized 'automatically', making it seem almost impossible to bring about a new situation. Bourdieu's ideas thus offer few stimuli for a theory of social change. *The Rules of Art* (p. 253), for example, states that processes of change in the fields of literature and painting are most likely to be triggered by those entering a field for the first time, in other words the *younger generation*. Bourdieu provided historical evidence of this by referring to Flaubert and Baudelaire, demonstrating how, as newcomers to the field of literature, they established and enforced their own new form of aesthetics, restructuring the field significantly. But to a genuine theory of social change this is of very little help. Bourdieu stated that in light of the forms of capital available within it, each field requires its own models of change. But because his studies focused on a few fields only, his work inevitably lacks general statements about social change.

4. The potential of Bourdieu's theory to cast light on the contemporary situation is most apparent in his critiques of globalization and writings in the sociology of culture, of which his 1979 book *Distinction* was to become particularly famous. Bourdieu had, however, formulated a conceptual and theoretical programme for this kind of study much earlier. This is perhaps expressed most impressively in the following passage:

> In fact, the least privileged groups and worst-off classes from an economic point of view appear in this game of circulation and distinction, *which is the real cultural game*, and which is objectively organized in line with the class structure, solely as a means of contrast, that is, as the element necessary to highlight the other, or as 'nature'. The game of symbolic distinctions is thus played out within that narrow space whose boundaries are dictated by economic constraints, and remains, in this respect, a game played by the privileged in privileged societies, who can afford to conceal the real differences, namely those of domination, beneath contrasting manners.
>
> ('Zur Soziologie symbolischer Formen' ['On the Sociology of Symbolic Forms'], pp. 72–3; emphasis added)

Culture, as Bourdieu claims in this quotation, is a game of distinction in which class differences are also expressed or visibly constituted for the first time. Analogously to his concept of cultural capital, which covers a great many things, including objects such as paintings and books, knowledge and skills and even titles, Bourdieu defines culture very broadly indeed; it also refers to aesthetic evaluations. In *Distinction*, he is primarily concerned to assert, provocatively, that even our seemingly most personal predilections – our opinions about how things taste, the aesthetic quality of a piece of music, the 'acceptability' of articles of clothing, etc. – are determined by a class habitus. His simple thesis is that 'taste' or aesthetic judgements classify the very individuals engaged in classification, because they reflect existing economic opportunities or economic constraints.

What is both provocative and fascinating here is not just how distraught we feel when Bourdieu takes such pleasure in casting doubt on our most sublime feelings and perceptions, tracing them back to seemingly banal or profane realities. Emile Durkheim's book *Suicide*, which interpreted what appears to be the freest of all free decisions – to take one's own life – as a *socially determined* phenomenon, was shocking in much the same way. Arguments of this kind contradict utterly our view of ourselves as self-determining beings, which is why they distress us so much. But Bourdieu's writings, especially *Distinction*, are provocative for another reason as well. Ultimately, he attempts to equate or at least associate aesthetics, the theory of the good and the true (in art), with banal quotidian tastes. Bourdieu wishes to show that what aesthetic theory acclaims as great music, great paintings and great literature is in reality nothing other than a form of perception derived from specific economic realities. According to Bourdieu, great art was and is always partly a product of class conflict; the ruling classes have managed to define *their* aesthetic perceptions as 'legitimate' art, concurrently veiling or airbrushing out entirely how this aesthetics is determined by class. The aim of his programme of 'anti-Kantian "aesthetics"' is thus to *expose* and *demystify*.

In this connection, he establishes the dichotomy between so-called 'luxury' and so-called 'necessity-driven' taste. The latter is typical of the lower strata and classes within a society. It is associated with immediate material problems of life, with the everyday experience of lack, with the sense of economic insecurity, etc. Under such circumstances it is supposedly impossible to devote a great deal of time and effort to refining one's behaviour. In line with this, the aesthetic perceptions and everyday behaviour of the lower strata are also very different from those of the ruling classes, as apparent even in their eating habits.

> In the face of the new ethic of sobriety for the sake of slimness, which is most recognized at the highest levels of the social hierarchy, peasants and especially industrial workers maintain an ethic of convivial indulgence. A bon vivant is not just someone who enjoys eating and drinking; he is someone capable of entering into the generous and familiar – that is, both simple and free – relationship that is encouraged and symbolized by eating and drinking together, in a conviviality which sweeps away restraints and reticence.
>
> (*Distinction*, p. 179)

But it is of course not only how people eat that distinguishes this necessity-driven taste; *what* is eaten is also fundamentally different from that typically consumed by the ruling classes. Bourdieu marshals a mass of statistical evidence and nuanced observational data to demonstrate how variable eating culture is, pointing out that the upper classes always tend, sometimes consciously, but more often unconsciously, to set themselves apart from the eating culture of the lower classes through the refinement of the mealtime experience, in order to develop 'distinction'. The extravagant tastes of the upper strata are always in part an attempt to demarcate themselves from others, to attain *distinction*, which ongoingly reproduces class differences and class boundaries. Intellectuals, businesspeople, journalists, etc. go to Chinese, Vietnamese and Burmese restaurants as a matter of course, something a worker, even if he could afford it, would never dream of doing because his notions of good food are very different. (All such observations, of course, represent snapshots of a particular historical period.) Anyone born into the upper classes is socialized into a particular taste in food and corresponding habitus, through which she almost automatically sets herself apart from individuals of other classes. It is not just their table manners but also their seemingly primal tastes that distinguish the 'aristocrats' from the 'plebeians'. This was true in the past, and according to Bourdieu it is true in the present as well.

A similar pattern is also apparent in the different ways in which members of different classes relate to art. Extravagant tastes and an aesthetics to match, because they are free of economic constraints, have no specific purpose and are seemingly disinterested, which is why members of the upper classes get a good deal more out of *abstract* art – Braque, Delaunay, Malevich or Duchamp – than the lower classes, who are unfamiliar with disinterested conditions and thus view art in close association with practical tasks of everyday life. They perceive a painting by Braque, for example, as incomprehensible or unappealing and are always more likely to hang a Spitzweg reproduction or one of Caspar David Friedrich's works in their sitting room than a Delaunay. 'Is that what they call art?' – this question is always on the tip of the worker's or petit bourgeois' tongue as he looks at a Malewitsch, while artistically inclined intellectuals may see a painting as particularly interesting and expressive precisely because it is rather inaccessible and – as Bourdieu would assume – one can thereby gain distinction, setting oneself apart from the philistines. Much the same applies to the realm of music. Insofar as workers listen to classical music in the first place, it tends to be Smetana's *The Moldau* rather than the unmelodic 'noise' of a Shostakovich.

Bourdieu never tires of tracking down similar patterns in the realms of sport, political opinion, film, clothing and leisure-time activities. For him, what is always evident here is that the ruling classes determine the legitimacy of a particular activity within the various cultural fields; it is they who, for instance, declare the latest forms of avant garde art to be *real* art on the basis of their need for distinction, while all that came before takes on an air of triviality, of the not truly artistic, especially if the lower classes begin to appropriate these now 'outdated' forms of art.

Taken together, Bourdieu's investigations cause him to expound the thesis that the habitus acquired within a particular class – as an ensemble of schemata of perception, cognition and action – defines a particular 'lifestyle' by means of which the classes set themselves apart from one another 'culturally'. The different types of lifestyle found within a society point to symbolic conflicts over the efforts made by members of different classes to achieve distinction. According to Bourdieu, this is precisely what we need to grasp, because this is the only way to adequately describe the class structure of a society and its dynamics, something which orthodox Marxism was incapable of doing as a consequence of its lack of, or blindness to, a theory of culture.

Bourdieu's account, rooted in cultural sociology, is of relevance to the diagnosis of the contemporary era in that his view of the perpetual reproduction of class-based inequality appears to leave little prospect that things will get better. To some extent at least, this is at variance with Bourdieu's role as a public critic of the French education system and of globalization, to which we alluded at the beginning of this lecture; one may ask how this engagement can be reconciled with his diagnosis of the apparently unalterable and stable nature of social structures. However, he himself believes that this 'contradiction' can be resolved by pointing to the fact that freedom is possible only if one knows and recognizes the laws governing how a society is structured. 'Sociology frees by freeing from the illusion of freedom' (Bourdieu, see Dosse, *History of Structuralism*, vol. II, p. 67). Constant references to people's supposed 'free will' may in fact form part of a discourse of power, if it ignores either the limits of one's own potential to take action or those applying to 'others'; conversely, the assertion that social relations are determined may be the point of departure for a discourse of liberation. And Bourdieu always claimed that his academic work was advancing just such a discourse of liberation. Especially during the final decade of his life, he tried to mobilize left-wing intellectuals to form a counter-power to what he saw as the ever advancing and threatening economization of every aspect of human life and the hegemony of laissez-faire liberalism. No one engaging in such activities can have an entirely pessimistic world view. Despite all his references to the constant reproduction of patterns of social inequality, his diagnosis of the modern era must entail an element of hope.

This brings us to the end of our account of Bourdieuvian theory. It only remains to briefly investigate its impact.

5. Bourdieu's writings have enjoyed a wide readership, and have exercised a magnetic effect well beyond the bounds of sociology, within which political sociology and the sociology of social inequality have benefited most from his ideas. In France, for example, Bourdieu gathered a large number of collaborators around him who went on to develop his research approach or applied it to new topics. Studies in historical sociology on specific strata and professional groups are the leading case in point, a representative example being Luc Boltanski's 1982 book *Les cadres. La formation d'un groupe sociale* (English title: *The Making of a Class: Cadres in French Society*).

In Germany, it is research on inequality that has most often drawn on Bourdieuvian theory, with a particular focus on the concept of lifestyle (for an overview, see the anthology edited by Klaus Eder, *Klassenlage, Lebensstil und kulturelle Praxis* ['Class Situation, Lifestyle and Cultural Praxis'] from 1989 and Hans-Peter Müller, *Sozialstruktur und Lebensstile* ['Social Structure and Lifestyles'] from 1992). But Bourdieu has been received in sometimes peculiar fashion, insofar as the concept of lifestyle in Germany (which is not, however, based solely on his ideas) has increasingly been separated out from the arguments of class theory. This has created the impression that people can more or less freely choose their lifestyle, inspiring the dubious assertion that it is thus almost impossible to discern 'real' classes in German society (see for example Gerhard Schulze, *Die Erlebnisgesellschaft. Kultursoziologie der Gegenwart* ['The Experiential Society. A Cultural Sociology of the Present'] from 1992). This is an argument quite alien to Bourdieu's way of thinking.

Turning to North America, a study published in 1992 by the French-Canadian Michèle Lamont (*Money, Morals, and Manners: The Culture of the French and the American Upper-Middle Class*) created quite a stir. This was a comparative study of social structure executed in the spirit of Bourdieu, but which went beyond him in as much as it took seriously the moral discourses of these classes, which Bourdieu tended to neglect, eschewing their immediate reduction to other factors. Lamont (b. 1957) brought out in impressive fashion how much the images and ideas of a morally good life and conduct differ among the upper-middle classes of American and French society and how well suited moral stances are to highlighting the boundaries between classes.

Bourdieu's influence on history was almost as great. Concepts such as 'capital', 'field' and 'habitus' clearly helped remedy certain theoretical shortcomings. A good example of this is a work which was certainly influenced by Bourdieuvian theory and which tackles a topic frequently subject to Bourdieu's attentions, one which we were unable to deal with in greater depth in this lecture. We are referring to the highly accessible book by Christophe Charle, *Naissance des 'intellectuels': 1880–1900* ('The Emergence of "Intellectuals": 1880–1900'), which brings out vividly how the image of intellectuals was constituted during this period of history and the various strategies pursued by these intellectuals to set themselves apart from their 'competitors' and free themselves from state and church.

The intellectual landscape of France, however, was and is by no means exclusively defined by structuralist, poststructuralist or 'genetic-structuralist' (Bourdieu) approaches. Sociologists and philosophers also became established there who saw themselves as nothing less than militant *anti*-structuralists; this was one of the key reasons they became so influential around the world. We turn to them and their writings in the next lecture.

XVI

French anti-structuralists

(Cornelius Castoriadis, Alain Touraine and Paul Ricoeur)

As discussed in Lecture XIV, structuralism dominated French intellectual life from the 1950s on. The decline in the significance of 'classical' structuralism, which set in towards the end of the 1970s, did little to change this. For at least some of the so-called post- or neo-structuralist authors who rose so rapidly to prominence remained very much indebted to the legacy of structuralism. This made it tremendously difficult for non-structuralist humanities scholars and social scientists to make their voices heard within France, particularly because such a stance was generally criticized or even denounced as 'subjectivism'. It is thus with some bitterness that the authors we are about to consider describe the period of structuralist hegemony. Cornelius Castoriadis, for instance, referred to a 'linguistic epidemic', which made clear thinking very difficult as a result of its 'simplistic pseudo-model of language' (Castoriadis, *Crossroads in the Labyrinth*, p. 120). The structuralists' 'hegemony' meant that certain non-structuralist French thinkers were for a long time more influential outside of France than inside it, because their writings did not face such huge (structuralist) barriers to reception in other countries. This has begun to change only recently. French intellectuals are now ready to acknowledge the significance of anti-structuralist thinkers (see also Lecture XX).

We begin our overview of the key French anti-structuralist social theorists and sociologists with an author who defies disciplinary categorization and was not even French, but who spearheaded the theoretical dispute with structuralism, and with Marxism, which was the main factor in his emergence as a central figure in the intellectual life of France, though his influence extended far beyond its borders. This was Cornelius Castoriadis.

1. Castoriadis was born in Constantinople in 1922, but grew up in Athens, at a time of great political instability, after his family was expelled from Turkey (on what follows, see Marcel van der Linden, 'Socialisme ou Barbarie' ['Socialism or Barbarism']). He joined the youth wing of the Greek Communist Party during the dictatorship of General Ioannis Metaxas, though he soon left when the communists elected to cooperate with the mainstream political parties in order to fight more effectively the Nazi occupation of Greece, which began in April 1941. In protest against

this alliance, Castoriadis joined a Trotskyite resistance group, which was of course also persecuted by the Germans, and later – following the end of German rule – by Stalin's communists themselves, when these temporarily gained power in 1944 and took drastic action against the Trotskyites, including many murders and executions.

Castoriadis, who had begun to study law, economics and philosophy while still in Athens, went to Paris to study philosophy in 1945 in the middle of the Greek civil war (1944–9), and was soon immersed in an intellectual atmosphere, described in Lecture XIV, characterized by passionate debates over Marxism and existentialism. In another political shift, he rapidly moved away from Trotskyism in this period, though not from the left-wing revolutionary project as such, leading him to found an independent political group in 1949 which published a now legendary journal, *Socialisme ou Barbarie*. The journal produced by this circle, which was to include later intellectual luminaries, some of whom we have met already, such as Claude Lefort, Jean-François Lyotard and Edgar Morin (b. 1921), was concerned primarily with the issue of how revolutionary groups could be organized without falling prey to the process of bureaucratization which appears to have occurred so often throughout history, a process with terrible consequences, as particularly apparent during and after the Russian Revolution.

While officially working as an economist, Castoriadis published numerous texts on Marxism, capitalism and the Soviet system of rule in this journal under various pseudonyms (as a foreigner, he was not allowed to engage in political activities); in the late 1950s his work was marked by an increasingly trenchant critique of Marx and from 1963 at the latest it was obvious that he had broken finally with the core ideas of historical materialism. Though this journal was discontinued by 1965, not least as a result of conflicts over the correct attitude towards Marxism, its major impact was to be felt only later. A fair number of the key actors in the student uprisings of May 1968 in Paris – such as Daniel Cohn-Bendit – were influenced by this journal's revolutionary approach (see van der Linden, 'Socialisme ou Barbarie', p. 1; see also Gilcher-Holtey, *'Die Phantasie an die Macht'. Mai 68 in Frankreich* ['"All Power to the Imagination": May 1968 in France'], pp. 47ff.).

Once *Socialisme ou Barbarie* had folded, Castoriadis began to train as a psychoanalyst. While he became a serious professional practitioner and his publications increasingly included psychoanalytic topics, this did not prevent him from continuing to pursue ambitions with regard to social theory. On the contrary, precisely because he drew on such a diverse range of disciplines, he was more successful than other authors in developing something new out of the shattered remains of Western Marxism, as his 1975 magnum opus *L'institution imaginaire de la société* (English title: *The Imaginary Institution of Society*) showed to such impressive effect. This was followed by numerous essay collections (*Crossroads in the Labyrinth*, which we have already mentioned, is one of those available in English), testimony to Castoriadis' inexhaustible productivity. When Castoriadis died in 1997, he left behind a large number of unpublished manuscripts, which have formed the basis for a series of posthumous publications; more are expected to appear in the future.

It is very hard to place Castoriadis' oeuvre within any of the theoretical approaches examined so far. It is simply too independent. It is easiest to characterize his theoretical stance negatively, by identifying those theories against which he polemicized most vehemently. To put it in a tripartite nutshell, Castoriadis was an anti-structuralist, anti-functionalist and anti-Marxist; his critique of each school of thought was highly original.

(a) It is of course not terribly surprising that Castoriadis grappled with structuralism in particularly intensive fashion; given its theoretical hegemony in France, this was unavoidable. Castoriadis was heavily influenced by the thought of Maurice Merleau-Ponty, a phenomenological theorist particularly interested in human corporeality and the intersubjectivity of the ego. To a significantly greater degree than Sartre and primarily in his later work, Merleau-Ponty tried to come to terms with structuralist ideas, particularly the phenomenon of language. He was a key influence on Castoriadis' critique of structuralism. Castoriadis accepts the key structuralist thesis of the arbitrary nature of the sign. But rather than stop there, he introduces elements into his theory of signs fundamentally at variance with core structuralist ideas.

Castoriadis believes that sign systems such as languages organize the world and thus refer to the world. Language is not, of course, a reproduction of the world. Neither does it represent the world as it is, as apparent in the fact that different languages produce differing perceptions of the world. Yet this does not mean that language is entirely disconnected from reality and thus arbitrary. Quoting Merleau-Ponty, Castoriadis asserts 'the being-thus of the world labours from within the apparently arbitrary nature of language' (Castoriadis, *Crossroads in the Labyrinth*, p. 125). Castoriadis thus wishes to depart from the *two*-dimensional concept of signs so typical of structuralism, from the idea that meanings can be deciphered solely in light of how signifiers are arranged in relation to one another, that signifieds are thus exclusively functions of the relations between signifiers. Instead, he wishes to advance to a *three*-dimensional concept of the sign which also takes the 'referents', that is, the world to which the signs refer, into account.

> The relativity of the thing as it appears in culture and language is indisputable, but no appeal can ever be made to it without

immediately invoking the obscure and unsayable irrelativity of things *sans phrase*. If language, and thought, exist, it is thanks to such innumerable and momentous facts as: there exist trees; there is an earth; there are stars; there are days – and nights. The trees grow in the earth. The stars come out at night. In this sense ... that which is speaks through language.

(ibid., p. 126; translation corrected)

Inclusion of the referent in his theory of signs inevitably entailed a turn away from structuralism. For, as Castoriadis sees it, this makes it clear that signs are not first and foremost objects in the world, but 'sign-objects', that is, they *refer to some aspect of reality*. But if signs do not simply mirror reality, this can only mean that they were 'created', invented, 'instituted'. 'The sign *qua* sign can exist only as an instituted figure, a form-norm, a creation of the social imaginary' (Castoriadis, *The Imaginary Institution of Society*, p. 252).

The arbitrary nature of the sign is thus testimony to the creativity of a society; it is an expression of this creativity that the society has settled on this sign rather than a different one to identify an object or state of affairs. Castoriadis thus placed the concept of subject, the concept of a collective subject, namely society, at the heart of his theory of signs.

If sign systems such as languages are an expression of societal creativity and languages also structure the world, this also explains why different societies and cultures organize different worlds with the aid of language. As Castoriadis states, every language, every culture, creatively generates certain core meanings around which speaking, thinking and acting are organized. And these core meanings become part of each cultural world, creating discrete realities.

> Whether it is a case of *mana, tabou, dike, chreon, sacer*, God; or of *polis, res publice, citizen, party*; or of *einai, reason, Geschichte*; or even of *chic, cute, gemütlich* – entities upon which everything rests and everything depends, but of which one can provide neither photograph nor logical definition – what binds them together, gives form to and organises the totality of a given culture ... as a referent that is both unreal and more than real.

(Castoriadis, *Crossroads*, pp. 130ff.)

With this thesis of the societal instituting of sign systems, Castoriadis 'reveals the meaning-originating accomplishments of the subject, behind structuralism's back, as it were' (Joas, *Pragmatism and Social Theory*, p. 161). But this should not be taken to mean that Castoriadis' notion of 'societal instituting' relates exclusively to processes of *collective* subjectivity. Far from it. He believes that language points above all to the creativity of the *individual*. As he sees things, language does not hem in the speaking subject. It does not place the subject at the mercy of a system of constraints, such that one would have to state, in typical structuralist fashion, that 'the subject is spoken'. Rather, 'language opens up an infinitive area of untrammelled mobility. But within this area, there must still be someone who moves, and we cannot think the being of language without thinking the being of the speaking subject' (Castoriadis, *Crossroads in the Labyrinth*, p. 133). New meanings appear and old, seemingly long-forgotten signifieds are brought back to life only because language is spoken by subjects and constantly changed by them. With his emphasis on the significance of the subject to the understanding of language, also found in the work of Merleau-Ponty, and indeed his emphasis on the role of individual and societal creativity, Castoriadis prepared to launch a profound attack on all those theories which rushed to downplay the historicity of human existence, ruining their chances of attaining an adequate understanding of social change and the special character of the social world. This brings us to his critique of functionalism.

(b) Castoriadis' first argument against functionalism is methodological and fairly conventional. As it is simply impossible, in contrast to functionalist thought in biology or medicine, to clearly identify *societal* needs, according to Castoriadis it is also impossible to determine the institutions that fulfil these needs.

> A society can exist only if a series of functions are constantly performed (production, child-bearing and education, administrating the collectivity, resolving disputes and so forth), but it is not reduced to this, nor are its ways of dealing with its problems dictated to it once and for all by its 'nature'. It invents and defines for itself new ways of responding to its needs as it comes up with new needs.
>
> (*Crossroads*, pp. 116ff.)

The last sentence in this quotation goes beyond the *traditional* critique of functionalism. Castoriadis highlights the fact that the world of institutions is always inseparably interwoven with the symbolic world. While it is true that institutions cannot be traced back to the symbolic realm itself, they exist only within it (ibid., p. 117). The achievement of institutions consists in

> relating symbols (signifiers) to signifieds (representations, orders, commands or inducements to do or not to do something, consequences for actions – significations in the loosest sense of the term) and in validating them as such, that is to say in making this relation more or less obligatory for the society or the group concerned.
>
> (ibid.)

For Castoriadis, it is this symbolic dimension of institutions which causes functionalism to come to grief; symbol systems adhere to no functionalist logic because while a symbol cannot do without a reference to reality, neither does its nature emerge of necessity out of this reference to reality (ibid., p. 118). Thus, since symbols correspond to no real processes, they cannot fulfil any functions in this regard. Rather, they are an expression of the creativity of a society that constantly creates new symbols, reinterprets old symbols, links symbols, etc. Ultimately, of course, this means that the symbolic realm *is not determined* and *neither are institutions*. But because functionalist thought assumes such determination, it denies the creativity of societies with respect to their institutions, entwined as they are with symbols. Instead of engaging in absurd attempts to trace institutions back to 'given' needs, Castoriadis asserts that the task of the social sciences is to investigate *how needs are defined culturally or socially and which institutions are created to satisfy these needs.*

All of this sounds quite unspectacular, but it has significant consequences, for a critique of certain premises found in Marxism, among other things. For if institutions are always interwoven with the symbolic and if at the same time all social relations are defined by institutions, this means that economic relations, the so-called 'base', are also instituted (ibid., pp. 124f.). But the immediate corollary of this is that there is nothing 'outside the society', nothing that would prescribe the social structures. The attempt, typical of Marxism, to label the economy a quasi-natural factor that moulds the social realm, is thus a dead end. For if the economy itself is a culturally variable product of social creativity, the typical Marxist references to the economy as determinant 'in the last instance' are absurd. Here we already find ourselves in the midst of Castoriadis' critique of Marxism.

(c) Castoriadis had already formulated the fundamentals of this critique in 1964/65 in the journal *Socialisme ou Barbarie*, but – in more complete form – it was published again in his magnum opus *The Imaginary Institution of Society*, in the first part of the book, under the heading 'Marxism and Revolutionary Theory'. Castoriadis adopts a peculiar approach here. He presents various readings of Marxism or historical materialism, demonstrating that all of these interpretations and explanations are ultimately theoretically untenable.

A first line of argument is present within the work of Marx and Engels, as well as many of their interpreters, which we might term a *technologically determinist version* of historical materialism. This asserts that one may 'explain the structure and the functioning of every society on the basis of the state of technique and the transition from one society to another by means of the evolution of this technique' (ibid., p. 66). This idea – so Castoriadis tells us – is underpinned by the premise that technology and technological development are autonomous phenomena, and thus, once again, by the idea of an extra-societal explanatory factor free of cultural meanings. But Castoriadis vigorously contests that technology has such an inherent tendency towards autonomous development and that technology can be understood as a kind of prime mover. His argument is as follows. Technological determinism assumes that nature 'is only there to be exploited by human beings' (ibid., p. 19). But this idea of nature is nothing other than an untenable generalization of our contemporary Western understanding of nature. Not all societies have developed this kind of instrumental relationship to their environment, just as science was not conceived solely as a means to exploit the environment in all societies.

> In Greek antiquity, the fact that the techniques applied to production remained certainly far behind the possibilities offered by the scientific development already attained cannot be separated from the social and cultural conditions of the Greek world, nor, most likely, from the attitude of the Greeks towards nature, labour and knowledge.
>
> (ibid., p. 19)

Whether technology is used to render nature disposable and whether this leads to uninterrupted technological, and possibly social, change thus depends on a society's attitude towards nature. According to Castoriadis, modern capitalism is a cultural product which is closely bound up with such a notion of dominating nature. Marx and Engels, and especially those advocates of Marxism arguing from a technologically determinist point of view, had wrongly generalized this idea, which first emerged with capitalism, applying it to all historical eras and thus reifying it as a social law. But, Castoriadis tells us, this is simply wrong historically. Technologies are also socially constituted. They are 'chosen'. They are dependent on the symbolic creativity of a society and are thus culturally variable with respect to their application.

But, secondly, the ideas of Marx or Engels also include *utilitarian motifs*, which are in turn often bound up with technological determinism. The assumption here is that the development of the forces of production is the engine of history and that there exists an 'invariable type of basic motivation for all individuals, broadly speaking, an economic motivation' (ibid., p. 25), which leads to the unceasing utilization and exploitation of people and nature. Here again, Castoriadis believes that anthropological and historical research on the various forms of human economic practice has long since refuted the assumption of such suprahistorical motivational constancy. Anyone seriously expounding such a utilitarian version of historical materialism would be extrapolating to the 'whole of history ... the movement and organization of present society' (ibid., p. 26).

A third way of reading Marxism consists in arguing that Marx's primary concern was to conceive of the *capitalist economy as a closed system* and to render this system comprehensible by means of his labour theory of value. Marx was convinced that he had deciphered the expression of value of goods, claiming that the relation of exchange between goods is determined in line with how much social labour is expended to produce these goods. But of course it turns out that this idea, which seems so persuasive in itself, is practicable only if one can compare labour with respect to its quantity and quality. Is this possible? And if so, how?

> In its actual reality, as 'concrete labour' (that of the weaver, the mason etc.), labour is heterogeneous; and the quantum of labour 'contained' in a yard of cloth produced on a machine is different from the quantum 'contained' in a yard of cloth woven on an old loom. So it *must* be a question, it can only be a question, of some other labour, a labour which in truth nobody has ever seen or done ... Simple, Abstract, Socially Necessary Labour.
>
> (Castoriadis, *Crossroads*, p. 263)

Marx thus hit on the idea of postulating the existence of 'simple abstract' or 'socially necessary' labour, allowing him to claim that there is a yardstick for comparing labour and thus a possibility of determining the relations of exchange between goods. Castoriadis, however, considers Marx's entire undertaking here quite absurd. For no one knows what, in concrete terms, 'socially necessary' labour means. The 'average' amount of working time necessary to produce a good cannot provide a yardstick either, because this would either assume that there is no technological change or 'that competition, constantly and effectively, actually brings actual labour time into line with average labour time' (ibid., p. 268). But this would be conceivable only on the utterly unrealistic assumption of perfect competition and thus ideal markets. What, then, is a fitting yardstick for defining socially necessary labour? Marx provides no clear answer. His attempt to define 'simple' or 'abstract' labour gets us nowhere, because according to Castoriadis, labour is quite obviously not a good like any other. The 'production' of labour occurs under conditions quite different from those applying to goods – and it is this that Marx overlooked or did not wish to acknowledge:

> But if the 'price' of airline pilots' labour power is higher than its 'value', it is absurd to suppose ... that street-sweepers will attempt to gain the necessary qualifications, and will be able to do so in

numbers sufficient to bring 'price' and 'value' back together again. Evidently, if capitalism were to reach the limits of development anticipated by Marx, the question would not be resolved but *suppressed*: *if* capitalism were *actually* to transform labour of every kind into unskilled labour within large-scale industry, there would no longer be anything but Simple Labor ... But this is not the case.

(*Crossroads*, p. 273; original emphasis)

But it is impossible to determine the value of labour because the worker's subsistence needs cannot be pinned down precisely (ibid., p. 320), and the capitalists lack sure and certain knowledge of the utility they might gain from buying the labour. Ultimately they can predict neither technological change nor how cooperative or refractory the workers will be (Castoriadis, *The Imaginary Institution of Society*, pp. 15f.). But if the value of labour cannot be determined with any certainty because establishing its price is a matter of negotiation, conflict and assessment, the other supposed 'laws of motion' of the capitalist economy formulated by Marx are not laws, but merely descriptions which may or may not apply in a specific historical situation.

Marx himself, so Castoriadis tells us, was certainly aware of the inconsistencies in his labour theory of value. His descriptions of the specific features of capitalism had always fluctuated between three irreconcilable interpretations: first, that it was capitalism itself that made people and the labour carried out by them entities of the same kind, second, that capitalism was only bringing to light that which was in any case always the same, but previously hidden, and third, that capitalism had in fact merely endowed dissimilar things with the *semblance* of sameness (*Crossroads*, p. 276). But all three interpretations cannot be correct simultaneously.

Castoriadis thus concludes his run through the various interpretive possibilities of Marxism or historical materialism with the assertion that none of them is seriously tenable and that Marx's theory as a whole must therefore be rejected. This uncompromising critique of Marx is significantly more radical theoretically than that of Habermas, but unlike the latter it does *not* lead Castoriadis to abandon the idea of the revolution or of a radical project of 'societal autonomy'. This has rather a lot to do with the specific features of Castoriadis' theory of action, which is built on very different foundations than that of Habermas. How are we to understand this?

Let us turn first to the different form taken by these two thinkers' critique of Marx. Habermas, as we saw in Lecture IX, accepted Marx's economic theory at least in terms of its applicability to liberal capitalism (in the eighteenth and nineteenth centuries). Only as a result of the intervention of the state, which became ever more comprehensive over the course of the twentieth century, and the increasing scientification of industrial production did the Marxian law of value lose its validity. This was *one* of the reasons why Habermas described the Marxian 'paradigm of production' as outmoded and wished to replace it with his theory of communicative action.

Castoriadis meanwhile declares Marx's economic theory fundamentally wrong; it even failed to capture the reality of economic relations in the nineteenth century. In his opinion, the 'paradigm of production' was always wrong, because, in much of his work at least, Marx adhered to a false or one-sided theory of action and thus automatically airbrushed out the creativity of individuals and societies. On the other hand, however, Castoriadis – and this is quite crucial and underlines how he differed from Habermas – continued to adhere to *certain* Marxian insights more strongly than the latter. Habermas, having broken with Marx, believed that he could advance to a plausible theory of action only if he developed one of his own by patiently critiquing existing sociological theories of action (such as utilitarianism or Parsons' normativist theory) and drawing on the theory of speech acts developed in the Anglo-American world. This approach resulted in the concept of 'praxis' or creative or productive activity, found in the work of Marx, being marginalized entirely, as it appeared neither in existing sociological theories of action nor in philosophies and theories of language.

This is just what Castoriadis wishes to avoid. He wishes to retain this concept of praxis, found mainly in Marx's early work, making it the core of his own theory. In order to do this, it seems to him necessary to trace this concept back historically – all the way to Aristotle, in whose work it plays a key role. Thus, while Habermas attempted to counter the reductions of a utilitarian or normativist concept of action by developing a theory of communicative action, Castoriadis does so through the concept of praxis. For him, as for Aristotle, praxis is also non-teleological action. It does not adhere to the means–ends schema or predetermined norms. Practical action means opening oneself up to the future and thus to uncertainty; it means creating something new, breaking out of a rational or normatively determined order.

> To do something, to do a book, to make a child, a revolution, or just doing as such, is projecting oneself into a future situation which is opened up on all sides to the unknown, which, therefore, one cannot possess beforehand in thought.
>
> (Castoriadis, *The Imaginary Institution of Society*, p. 87)

Castoriadis thus stands in the Aristotelian theoretical tradition, which played a rather subordinate role in twentieth-century philosophy though it had certain significant exponents (Michael Oakeshott, 1901–90; Alasdair

MacIntyre, b. 1929; and most famously Hannah Arendt), but which seems to have been undergoing a revival in recent times (see for example our remarks on Martha Nussbaum in the next lecture). This tradition modelled its theory of action predominantly on forms of *situational* action, such as educational or political action, in as much as the realms of education and politics are concerned neither with retrievable technical knowledge nor clearly prescribed norms of action and, moreover, not all the conditions of action are entirely transparent. Thus, in these realms, the actors must open themselves to the new and unknown as a matter of course.

More than any other exponent of this Aristotelian tradition, more even than Hannah Arendt, and more, of course, than Habermas, Castoriadis was to emphasize the productive and creative aspects of human action. One could sum up the comparison between Habermas and Castoriadis by stating that the former seeks to escape the straitjacket of the utilitarian or normativist model of action through the concept of 'communication', the latter through that of 'imagination', insofar as Castoriadis believes that it is this creative capacity that guides human action or human practice.

Castoriadis thus endows Aristotelianism with a powerful conception of creative imagination, as shown to impressive effect in his magnum opus *The Imaginary Institution of Society*. Here, Castoriadis describes the always creative nature of societies with tremendous argumentative force. Because institutions cannot be traced back to functionalities and the realm of the symbolic is simply not determined, new symbols are always being 'created', new meanings are always emerging, which lead to *new* institutions and thus drive social change in unpredictable directions. This idea of the rise of new symbols and thus new institutions is almost necessarily linked with a specific anthropological definition of the human being. For one must ask oneself *how* such new symbols can come into being in the first place. Castoriadis' answer is as follows:

> Man is an unconsciously philosophical animal, who has posed the questions of philosophy in actual fact long before philosophy existed as explicit reflection; and he is a poetic animal, who has provided answers to these questions in the imaginary.
>
> (ibid., p. 147)

The imaginary, the creative 'capacity of evoking images' (ibid., p. 127), is thus the result of how the human psyche functions. The 'imaginary' refers to something invented – 'whether this refers to a "sheer" invention ("a story entirely dreamed up"), or a slippage, a shift of meaning in which available symbols are invested with other significations than their "normal" or canonical significations' (ibid., p. 127). The imaginary must be expressed by means of the symbolic (language, culturally predetermined signs, etc.), which explains the special character of the symbolic. While it always refers to something real, it is also interwoven with imaginary elements. And for this very reason, because the imaginary makes use of the symbolic, and ongoingly alters it, plays with its meanings, etc., the symbolic is subject to a process of constant change. But this also means that because institutions are loaded with symbols, the social world never stands still. This insight leads Castoriadis to develop a fundamental critique of existing theoretical approaches within the social sciences (not just Marxism) and to produce surprising interpretations of numerous historical-social phenomena. He focused on five key topics.

(a) Castoriadis develops his insights, initially gleaned mainly from his critique of Marxism, into an *ontology of the indeterminate*, a non-deterministic theory of being. Because the symbolic rests upon the natural human capacity for imagination, because meanings are inseparably interwoven with this irreducible aspect of the imagination, meanings cannot be traced back to causal factors. The historical-social realm consists of chains of meaning which cannot be fully derived from chains of causality (ibid., p. 46). To put it differently, and perhaps more radically, this means that history and society feature a significant number of non-causal elements:

> The non-causal ... is not merely unpredictable but *creative* (on the level of individuals, groups, classes or entire societies). It appears not as a simple deviation in relation to an existing type but as the *positing* of a new type of behaviour, as the *institution* of a new social rule, as the *invention* of a new object or a new form – in short, as an emergence or a production which cannot be deduced on the basis of a previous situation, as a conclusion that goes beyond the premises or as the positing of new premises.
>
> (ibid., p. 44; original emphasis)

This statement is, of course, informed by Castoriadis' question as to whether it is possible to conceive of creative action in the first place if the world is a self-contained space determined by endless chains of causality. He disputes this and concludes that all social scientific theories based on such a causal scientific ontology of determination shut themselves off from these creative aspects of individual action and thus from societal creativity as well.

> History is impossible and inconceivable outside of the *productive* or *creative imagination*, outside of what we have called the *radical imaginary* as this is manifested indissolubly in both historical *doing* and in the constitution, before any explicit rationality, of a universe of *significations*. If [history] includes the dimension that idealist philosophers called freedom and which is more appropriately termed indeterminacy [then this lies in] *doing* [which] ...

posits and provides for itself something other than what simply is ... in it dwell significations that are neither the reflection of what is perceived, nor the mere extension and sublimation of animal tendencies, nor the strictly rational development of what is given.

(ibid., p.146; original emphasis)

These insights then prompt Castoriadis to produce a highly peculiar metaphor and come to some far-reaching conclusions: in his opinion, the historical-social world arises from a fluid, by no means fixed and ultimately indeterminable foundation. Borrowing from the language of volcanologists, Castoriadis refers to 'magma'. On this molten basis of countless ambiguous meanings, with its equally innumerable referential potential, societies are organized and instituted which establish *specific* meanings through language and actions, each society in its own way. Symbol systems develop, which may be called 'God', 'sin', 'taboo', 'money', 'nation' or 'capital'. They appear to be immutable, an indestructible bedrock, which is why social meanings and actions group around them over time. But, and Castoriadis underlines this again and again, because language and action open up the possibility of overcoming what is given, inventing new meanings or new forms of action and instituting them in turn (ibid., pp. 269f.), society never stands still. This also applies to those so invulnerable, rock-like symbol systems mentioned above. Thus, society must be understood as a kind of interplay between the instituted and the instituting; only in this way can we grasp its irrepressible creativity.

(b) Castoriadis also derives a clear normative stance from this insight, in which the idea of autonomy, for which no reason can be given, takes centre stage (ibid., p. 100). In negative terms, this means that societies are non-autonomous or alienated if they do 'not recognize in the imaginary of institutions something that is its own product' (ibid., p. 132). Such societies claim to be built on extra-social foundations such as 'God', 'nature', a timeless 'reason', etc., and attempt by means of these to establish institutions, meanings and symbols once and for all, thus evading their own capacity for organization and action. In other words, a heteronomous society rejects its own responsibility for instituting the new. However, Castoriadis rashly identifies religious faith, both at the individual and collective level, with heteronomy. In contrast to Touraine and especially Ricoeur (see below), this militant atheist fails to ask whether human autonomy may not be expressed with particular vigour through religion, thus setting itself apart from creative hubris.

Castoriadis is particularly interested in those historical eras in which social autonomy became a reality, or, to put it more cautiously, was at least a clearly recognizable possibility. According to him, this has not often been the case in human history: first in ancient Greece and then in Western modernity. He devoted several studies to the rise of Greek philosophy and the democracy he believed was closely bound up with it (see Castoriadis, 'The Greek Polis and the Creation of Democracy'; 'Aeschylean Anthropogony and Sophoclean Self-Creation of Anthropos'). In his view, in the fifth century BC, for the first time, a society, that of Greece, understood itself as sovereign and volunteered to regulate and organize its own affairs in autonomous fashion. A process of societal self-instituting occurred, that is, there was a break with the rules provided by the gods and a questioning of all existing authorities with the aim of consciously creating a society. To put it somewhat paradoxically, it was in ancient Greece that the *institutionalization of institutionalization*, the will to constantly question the old and the associated creation of the new, was conceived and to some extent realized for the first time, an idea fundamental to any democracy, as Castoriadis sees it.

Castoriadis' radical ideal of autonomy and democracy almost inevitably leads him to identify certain political forms as normatively superior, in marked contrast to the stance of Habermas for example (on what follows, see Arnason, *Praxis und Interpretation* ['Praxis and Interpretation'], pp. 236ff. and Kalyvas, 'The Politics of Autonomy and the Challenge of Deliberation: Castoriadis Contra Habermas'). Habermas never seriously investigated the genesis of norms and values, only ever the question of their *legitimation* within the political process. Logically enough, he expounds a theory of democracy according to which the key decisions ought to be taken within the political system, which is regulated in line with certain procedures, though monitored by a critical public sphere. On this view, politics guides processes of incremental, gradual change. Meanwhile, as a consequence of his enthusiasm for societal creativity, Castoriadis has a more radical understanding of politics. His sympathetic view of radical transformations and revolutionary ruptures, in which the self-activation of society finds particularly clear expression, is unmistakable. But here we are confronted with a remarkable state of affairs. Despite a critique of Marx significantly harsher than that of Habermas because it was developed from within the logic of Marx's thinking, Castoriadis, unlike Habermas, is *not* willing to abandon the revolutionary project. While he is unable to identify any specific agents of this revolutionary project, he is unwilling to relinquish either the idea of revolutionary action or the demand for *radical economic equality between human beings*, which he made to the very end regardless of the experience of such utopian projects so far. Castoriadis refuses to fall in line with what he saw as an ultimately liberal (Habermasian) theory of democracy free of utopian elements, because for him this would mean giving up the radical idea of autonomy. But the nature of any contemporary political programme that might arise from this remained astonishingly vague in his writings. The political upheavals of 1989 in Eastern Europe certainly confirmed that history is always punctuated by the emergence of something new, but by no means have they led to the development of institutions which Castoriadis would accept as an expression of an alternative modernity. The new developments characteristic of Europe's political institutions, on the other hand, have been equally free of any association with utopian yearnings.

(c) Though Castoriadis thus remains committed to the revolutionary project, he of course rejects the Marxian notion of the (socialist) revolution as the end of history – because human creative imagination means that history can in principle *never* be brought to a standstill. But for the same reason, he believes, non-Marxist prognoses of long-term developmental processes are also condemned to fail. This applies especially to such sociological constructs as the theory of rationalization drawing on Weber and the theory of modernization to some extent related to it (see Lecture XIII). Eisenstadt asserted that different civilizations reacted to the challenges of the West with their own cultural projects, making it improbable that these civilizations will converge in terms of their historical development, and Castoriadis was to make the same claim, though his justifications and explanations were different. Castoriadis does not fall back on the idea of the Axial Age or the thesis of the vitality of religious traditions in order to make the 'diversity of modernity' a plausible notion. For him, this diversity follows from the unpredictability of history as such and the fact that the historical-social realm includes non-causal elements, and that while the imaginary draws on existing symbols, it 'plays' with and changes them. It is societal creativity that inhibits linear developments over the very long term and which allows ruptures to occur, thus making a comprehensive developmental convergence improbable (see Castoriadis, 'Reflections on "Rationality" and "Development"').

But if all these ideas of a uniform 'rationalization' and 'modernization' were and are so implausible, why have they gained such currency and so many supporters? For Castoriadis, these ideas, which for the most part developed in the West, are imaginary meaning complexes, the expression of a heteronomy-inspired attempt to bring history to a standstill, to assert that it is more or less determined and cannot be changed through the human potential for creative action.

(d) According to Castoriadis, another heteronomous phenomenon, one unsurpassed in its terrible consequences, was totalitarianism (see 'Destinies of Totalitarianism'). In light of his own biography, Castoriadis was always trying to come to terms with the Soviet system of domination; he interpreted it as perhaps the most radical attempt ever to determine history, an attempt based on the imaginary idea of the total control of historical change. According to Castoriadis, the idea of a necessary developmental sequence, the emergence of capitalism followed by socialism, led almost inevitably to mass murder in order to repress counter-trends – from the paranoid eradication of all dissidents of left and right to the annihilation of 'unplanned' classes such as the kulaks. Though some of these interpretations were clearly overstated philosophically and Castoriadis' opinions on the Soviet Union (see his assertions regarding its military superiority over the West in the 1960s and 1970s) were not always correct, he did succeed in making a major impact on the social scientific and philosophical debate on totalitarianism burgeoning in France from the 1970s on (see David Bosshart, *Politische Intellektualität und totalitäre Erfahrung. Hauptströmungen der französischen Totalitarismuskritik* ['Political Intellectuality and Totalitarian Experience: Principal Currents in the French Critique of Totalitarianism']), a debate of which there was very little sign in Germany, to the detriment of its social sciences, and which leading German theorists such as Habermas and Luhmann neglected almost entirely.

(e) Castoriadis elaborated his thesis of the irreducibility of the imaginary most comprehensively and in the greatest detail not at the social but at the individual level, in his numerous contributions to psychoanalysis. We merely wish to indicate briefly here that he often saw his position as a counter-concept to the structuralist psychoanalysis of Jacques Lacan. What is remarkable about his stance, particularly against the background of Freudian psychoanalysis and sociological theories of socialization, is that he opposed an overly rationalistic conception of the process of becoming a subject and claimed that just as it is impossible for society to look at itself with complete clarity, this applies to the individual as well. The unconscious can neither be done away with nor can it be entirely elucidated. He was thus of the opinion that the Freudian challenge 'Where Id was, there Ego shall be' (*Wo Es war, soll Ich werden*), must be complemented by a second challenge: 'Where Ego is, Id must spring forth' (*Wo Ich bin, soll Es auftauchen*) (Castoriadis, *The Imaginary Institution of Society*, p. 104). This linking of these two demands also expresses his conception of moral autonomy. For in his view, this autonomy does not exist, as claimed for example within Kantian moral philosophy, if I can reflect upon moral issues only while disregarding my own inclinations, but only if I *perceive and acknowledge* my drives and desires *as my own*:

Desires, drives – whether it be Eros or Thanatos – this is me, too, and these have to be brought not only to consciousness but to expression and to existence. An autonomous subject is one that knows itself to be justified in concluding: this is indeed true, and: this is indeed my desire.

(ibid., p. 104)

The prerequisite for such a stance is Castoriadis' core thesis of the naturalness and irreducibility of the ego's achievements of imagination. For it is these achievements which make it possible to keep one's distance from both reality and one's own drives: 'I can learn to accept statements about reality as true even if they contradict my own wishes. Similarly, I can learn to acknowledge my drives as they are even if I do not want to follow them' (Joas, *Pragmatism and Social Theory*, p. 166). This is precisely what the last quote from Castoriadis says, as well as pointing out that reality and my drives are not directly accessible, but only via the achievements of my imagination.

Here again, Castoriadis points us to a topic that permeates his entire oeuvre – the creative potential of individuals and societies, which most schools of social theory, with the exception of pragmatism, have either ignored or given only marginal consideration.

2. It is fair to say that Alain Touraine, alongside Pierre Bourdieu perhaps the most prominent French sociologist of the final third of the twentieth century, has not pursued the same kind of comprehensive, multidisciplinary and philosophically ambitious project as Castoriadis. Compared to him, Touraine's preoccupations have been more modest; apart from anything else, he has been active solely within the field of sociology. But Touraine, some of whose work was directly influenced by Castoriadis and who has drawn on similar philosophical sources, has always managed to make impressive contributions to social theory over the course of various periods of his work.

The early work of this sociologist, born in 1925, seemed to have a clear empirical orientation. His first field of research was industrial sociology, and he rapidly became one of its most renowned French exponents. In fact, though, Touraine, who had studied under Parsons at Harvard, carried out this research from a clear theoretical angle, which quickly caused him to produce an uncompromising critique of Parsons. For as his workplace research showed, decisions in such settings were not made in the form of the mere application of norms and values as one would expect in light of Parsons' normativist paradigm. Rather, he demonstrated that the workers used existing values and cultural patterns as resources for the power struggles occurring within the firm. In contrast to Bourdieu, however, this observation did not cause him to adopt a quasi-utilitarian interpretation of culture. Rather, Touraine made it his task to solve a problem never satisfactorily dealt with in Parsons' work, that of the *origins* of cultural orientations.

In his first major purely theoretical study, *Sociologie de l'action* ['The Sociology of Action'] from 1965, he certainly criticizes Parsons *in part* from a conflict theory perspective, for placing far too much emphasis on the consensual aspects of social order. But unlike conflict theorists, Touraine is not prepared to disregard the role of values and norms entirely in analysing social processes. As he underlines, in human action instrumentally rational and value rational aspects are directly bound up with one another. This also applies to conflict-related action, for even in class struggles, the antagonists battle not only over purely material matters, but also normative claims. This last point was of course also a criticism of the economistic determinism of Marxian approaches and particularly of the political analyses favoured within the French Communist Party, which ignored the creative dimension of individual and collective action.

But it was precisely this creative dimension with which Touraine was concerned. One of the key influences here was Jean-Paul Sartre, whose philosophy of freedom was one of Touraine's points of departure in seeking to avoid the one-sidedness of Marxism, as well as the cultural determinism of Parsonian approaches. His sociology was to be one 'of *freedom*, one which is always in search of that movement through which the forms of social life are both constituted and fought against, organized and rejected' (*Sociologie de l'action*, p. 123; our translation – original emphasis). His recourse to basic Sartrean positions, however, was not unproblematic. Sartre's highly individualistic or even anarchistic philosophy made it difficult to conceive of sociality in the first place, and Touraine was compelled to try and produce something of a synthesis between Sartrean and Parsonian ideas. He had to emphasize the freedom and creativity of human action, without denying the existence of norms and values, as it is only through these that the stability of social relations is explicable in the first place.

The decisive, if not unproblematic step towards such a synthesis consisted in the fact that Touraine did *not* relate value-generating and creative action primarily to individuals. Rather, in order to avoid the anarchistic tendencies of Sartrean philosophy from the outset, he equated action with a concept of labour understood in terms of society as a whole: action as the labour 'of society'. With this collectivist concept of action, Touraine does not assume that 'society' should be regarded as a homogeneous whole or even as a coherent actor. He is simply pointing to the historically new fact that the development of modern societies has set free massive potential for the steering of social processes, which for the first time makes it possible for these societies to understand themselves as products and to recognize their own works and relations of production as something they themselves have created. For the first time in history, they can cease to accept norms and values as given. Instead, they can create and institutionalize these themselves through a conflictual process: 'Social action is the creation of a universe of cultural works by means of human labour; this creation can only be collective in nature' (ibid., p. 60; our translation).

This sentence expresses an idea which Touraine was to make the title of one of his major works of the 1970s, namely the idea of the self-production of society (*Production de la société* from 1973). The thesis which Touraine presented and fleshed out in various books from the late 1960s on (such as *La société post-industrielle* from 1969), is that in 'postindustrial' societies, in which knowledge and the sciences play an ever more important role, it is possible to discern an increasing capacity of these societies to have an effect on themselves. What is remarkable here is not so much that Touraine highlights the role of knowledge in social change and that of educational qualifications in the structure of an emerging form of society. A well-known American sociologist, Daniel Bell (b. 1919), did much the same thing in his 1973 book *The Coming of Post-Industrial Society*. Although he came later, he exercised a perhaps even greater influence than Touraine on the debate on how to interpret the contemporary era carried on in the 1970s. Of far greater significance is the fact that, alongside his diagnoses of the modern age, Touraine's intentions had at least as much to do with normative issues; the similarities to Castoriadis' stance are unmistakable here. For Touraine grounds sociologically that which Castoriadis described as the self-instituting of society and interpreted as a sign of its autonomy. The *possibility* of autonomy – as one might say in the language of Castoriadis – may indeed depend on certain cultural prerequisites; but it can be *realized* only if the necessary means are available, namely society's capacity to have an effect on itself generated by the sciences or, as Touraine was to call it, the 'historicity' of (postindustrial) society.

Touraine's hopes for social change enabled by knowledge and the sciences were not undergirded by a positivist faith in scientific-technological progress. Touraine is no exponent of social engineering, and he certainly did not believe that values, for example, can be demonstrated scientifically. Rather, he had his sights set – and his proximity to Castoriadis is apparent again here – on *breaking* with the contemporary capitalist form of society; he was inspired by the hope that new social and cultural models would be found that would supersede the old capitalist industrial society based solely on advances in production. His concern was thus to identify the key areas of conflict and contradictions of contemporary capitalist societies, which might provide starting points for collective actors whose priority is to create and bring to bear *new* social and cultural models.

Reference to collective actors of course immediately calls to mind the traditional labour movement. But Touraine had quickly abandoned all hopes in this regard. Neither experiences with the socialist or communist parties in France, nor with the ruling parties in the Soviet or Chinese sphere of influence could nourish the idea of a truly autonomous future society. Rather, it was the so-called 'new social movements' that took pride of place in his investigations. For the 1960s and 1970s were a time of major social awakening. With the students', women's and environmental movements, new collective actors appeared on the social and political stage which appeared to nourish Touraine's hopes. Were these not the movements that would move on from the goals of the old labour movement, propagating a new cultural model, one envisaging the democratic control of production and knowledge and thus the conscious steering of social change?

Touraine immediately set about studying these emerging social movements in a number of empirical studies. Through his analyses of the student, green and anti-nuclear movements, as well as research on regionalist movements in France, Solidarnosč in Poland and other social movements in Latin America, he became one of the leading authors in the sociology of social movements, publishing his magnum opus in this field, *The Voice and the Eye*, in 1978. These studies demonstrate how little one can conceive of 'institutionalization' as a peaceful, always successful process, as Parsons had alleged. In fact, social actors struggle over every definition of values and every institutional embodiment of values. Touraine's studies were, however, highly controversial, above all because of his methodology. This was not solely concerned with the observation from a distance of existing movements; rather, through the so-called method of 'sociological intervention', researchers intervened actively in events, with the goal of getting those 'under investigation' to reflect upon or even escalate extant conflicts. This of course entailed the risk that the researchers would impose external and theoretically defined conflicts on their 'objects of study'; this was the main criticism of this method.

Whatever their results and achievements, Touraine's studies in the field of social movements ultimately proved disappointing to him. In the 1960s, Touraine had set out to identify the key areas of conflict in postindustrial societies and thus the social movement which might embody a new cultural model of society, superseding, as it were, the old labour movement as an actor. But no such coherent movement had developed. Touraine had to concede, albeit very hesitantly, that it is impossible to identify one central conflict in postindustrial society. Rather, it is the fragmentation and splintering of the field of conflict that is apparent in such societies. The wide variety of 'new social movements' have not united to form *one* joint formation. This had partly to do with their problematic recruitment base. From the 1980s at the latest, the members of the independent and academic professions, which did in fact represent a substantial socio-structural recruitment reservoir for these new social movements in the 1970s and 1980s, proved significantly less homogeneous and 'reliable' than Touraine had originally hoped.

But Touraine proved a very quick study. Subsequently, he turned away from the sociology of social movements, and from the 1990s on increasingly focused on the historically grounded diagnosis of modernity. Here again though, the 'subject' so abhorred by structuralism and poststructuralism was to take centre stage – laying bare once again his anti-structuralist tendencies, informed by Sartre and Castoriadis. This is also interesting insofar as his theoretical differences with structuralism were also reflected in the political field of battle. At the same time as Pierre Bourdieu, so strongly influenced by structuralism (see the previous lecture), Touraine became one of the most important public intellectuals in France in the final two decades of the twentieth century, though his political positions generally differed greatly from those of Bourdieu, as became particularly apparent in the 1990s. For while Bourdieu was calling himself a critic of globalization during this period and on this basis supported the great strikes of 1995 in France, in which mainly public sector workers fought to retain their privileges, Touraine adopted Michel Crozier's (b. 1922) notion of the 'blocked society'. From the late 1980s on, Touraine – sometimes in agreement with the policies pursued by socialist leader Lionel Jospin, French prime minister between 1997 and 2001 – grew closer to certain liberal views, a rapprochement which Bourdieu (like Castoriadis) always firmly rejected. These differences were also evident in the foreign policy field, with Touraine, in contrast to Bourdieu, clearly coming out in support of NATO intervention in Kosovo in 1999.

But let us return to Touraine's historically grounded and, once again, anti-structuralist diagnoses of the contemporary world. With his *Critique of Modernity* (1992), he produced a book inspired by a number of works of intellectual history from the late 1980s on the nature of modernity, including *Sources of the Self* (1989), magnum opus of the Canadian philosopher and political scientist Charles Taylor, who attempted to identify the sources of modern identity and thus the bases of our modern-day capacity for moral judgement in a brilliant overview of Western thought. Touraine's project in this book is equally ambitious, but his concerns are quite different from those of Taylor. Touraine wishes to uncover the *points of friction* within modernity, the *politically controversial issues* and *conflicts* characteristic of this era and, above all, the social philosophies and societal models that accompany these disputes. In this connection he develops a thesis in which his theory of the subject clearly emerges.

As Touraine sees it, modernity has always been characterized by an *irresolvable tension between rationality and creativity, between rationalization* and *'subjectification'*. What he calls the 'classical' age of modernity, which reached its peak in the work of Rousseau and Kant, represented a new era in that it saw the thesis of the unity of humanity and the universe, formerly justified in religious terms, superseded by other ideas (*Critique of Modernity*, p. 19). Because the traditional religious answers no longer seemed possible in this classical modernity, they were replaced in philosophical contexts by arguments that worked with concepts such as 'reason' and 'society'. According to Touraine, the question of the unity of humanity and universe was thus answered either, as in the work of Kant, by reference to a trans-subjective reason or, as in the work of Rousseau, by reference to a rational and harmonious society. While some critics at the time questioned whether philosophical constructions of this kind truly do justice to the subjectivity of human beings and their potential for creative action, whether people are really so thoroughly embedded in societies and can be understood through the categories of reason, these constructions nonetheless seemed capable of laying claim to a fairly high degree of plausibility in the eighteenth century.

This plausibility did not endure however, in part because the surging tide of capitalist industrialization in the nineteenth century was making formerly fixed social structures increasingly shaky. The formerly perceived coherence finally collapsed, though theorists such as Marx and Durkheim refused to accept this and attempted to rescue it once again through various concepts such as 'totality', 'revolution' and 'organic solidarity' – their efforts desperate and in vain in the view of Touraine. They were in vain because of the all-too-apparent decomposition characteristic of modernity. For, first of all, collective phenomena or corporate actors arose which resisted old ideas of social rationality; Touraine refers to the nation and nationalism and big firms concerned solely with making a profit and their strategies. Second, changes seemed to be in the air at the individual level, as the previously assumed 'composed' rationality of the citizen was exposed to the unsettling, often anti-rational discourse of sexuality and to the advertising characteristic of mass consumption. The notion of unity between individual and social rationality so typical of 'classical modernity' thus collapsed, and as a result so did the idea of a clear correspondence between social progress and individual emancipation (ibid., p. 130). Parsons' sociology in the 1950s and 1960s is interpreted by Touraine as a final attempt, long since overtaken by history, to conceive of a harmonious, internally consistent modernity and to offer this as a normative ideal for the social sciences (see also Touraine's essay 'La théorie sociologique entre l'acteur et les structures').

Touraine's reconstruction of the intellectual foundations of modernity are intended to make clear that the subject has successfully resisted every 'attempt at integration' made since the beginning of the modern age or that it has proved impossible to place this subject within a timeless reason or a harmonious society – and that similar attempts in future are also bound to fail. But what does Touraine take this stubborn 'subject' to be? What does he mean by 'subjectification'? As he explains in subsequent books (*What is Democracy?* from 1994 and *Can We Live Together?* from 1997), the 'subject' can only be defined negatively. For according to him, the individual does not become a subject simply by being released from traditional ties within the context of modernization. In contrast to theorists of individualization (see Lecture XVIII), Touraine does not equate the concept of subject with that of a solitary and largely ego-centric individual. Rather, for Touraine – and here again he takes up certain Sartrean motifs – becoming a subject is first and foremost a *struggle*, a struggle over the possibility of autonomous action. Because, in the history of modernity, these struggles were rarely those of discrete individuals, but rather were carried on by people of like mind within the framework of various cultural movements, Touraine sometimes goes so far as to equate the concept of subject with that of the social movement (*Critique of Modernity*, p. 235). This does not, of course, mean that this subject is smoothly absorbed into these movements and collective identities. Quite the reverse: according to Touraine, subjectification occurs through resistance and struggles against tendencies towards desubjectification in totalitarian structures of domination, in social orders in which purely instrumental rationality appears to hold sway, *and* in suffocating communities.

Touraine thus not only sets himself apart from certain theorists of individualization, but also distances himself from the conception of the subject cultivated by symbolic interactionism and from the theories of communication and socialization expounded by those close to Habermas. In a way once again highly reminiscent of Sartre, Touraine insists that the subject features a non-social dimension, that we cannot treat it as something derivable from social relations, which, among other things, explains its capacity for resistance:

> Many give primordial importance to communications. I think, on the contrary, that the relationship with the self determines relations with others. This is a non-social principle which determines social relations. It means that, now that the long period in which we tried to explain the social solely in terms of the social is over, we can once more recognize that the social is based upon the non-social, and is defined only by the role it gives or refuses to give, to the non-social principle known as the Subject.
>
> (*Can We Live Together?*, p. 65)

Because Touraine assumes that individuals are radically different, he refuses to adhere to the Habermasian notion of an ideal communicative community, a notion which seems far too harmonious to him. The subject is, of course, endowed with reason – Touraine does not dispute this. But it is also 'freedom, liberation and rejection' (ibid., p. 58). All attempts to airbrush out these aspects of human action and the antagonism of human communication through a harmonious model of socialization and communication, fail to capture – so Touraine tells us – the special features of the subject. This is one of the key reasons why he attributes a decisive role in the formation of identity to the experience of sexuality (and not only infantile sexuality), an experience which resists complete verbalization and smooth comprehension with the tools of reason; and it is no coincidence that Touraine also points to transcendental experiences, because they evoke a subject that exhibits or may exhibit a fundamentally non-social, unsocialized and thus resistant attitude towards *social* impositions (ibid., pp. 85f.).

Touraine's reconstruction of modernity and his thesis that modernization is to be understood as a constant tension between rationalization and subjectification, lead him to generate insights of which at least four are worth mentioning in light of their differences from other theoretical approaches.

(a) In much the same way as Giddens and Eisenstadt, but in contrast to Habermas for example, Touraine does *not* attempt to distinguish modernity from other eras in normative terms, by attributing to Western modernity a more comprehensive rational potential than other eras or civilizations for example. For him, the disintegration of 'classical modernity' described above is still a process *within* this modernity, such that phenomena such as nationalism or totalitarianism, to which both he and Castoriadis pay such attention, are just as much a part of it as is democracy. Touraine thus refuses to view upsurges of nationalism, wars and the rise of dictatorships as insignificant mishaps within a historical process destined to result in a rationality that pervades society, a process that will cast off the last remnants of barbarism.

For similar reasons, he also refrains from attempts to define modernity *institutionally* with the aid of the concept of differentiation, in terms, for example, of the market economy, autonomous legal system, specialized state administrations and democratic institutions. His analysis thus remains open to *different paths to modernity*, which is imperative if one wishes to avoid singling out the Euro-American developmental path as the only possible one. Other parts of the world will probably not see the same coincidence of nation-state, market economy *and* democracy so fortuitously characteristic of present-day Europe and North America any time soon, though there should be no doubt about the fact that such regions are also modern. Touraine wishes to keep his mind open to this insight.

(b) Touraine has now abandoned the idea, which he cultivated for decades, of a society featuring *one* central conflict that supersedes the class conflicts of traditional industrial society and in which *one* massive new social movement emerges to establish a new model of society. Modern societies have clearly become far too fragmented for him to continue to expect one central conflict to emerge. In line with this, for him the hallmark of modernity is ambivalence rather than clear-cut conflicts, such that one can point only to the diverse range of struggles in which subjects are engaged on various fronts, against various opponents. This brings Touraine close to a position found in much the same form in the work of Zygmunt Bauman (see Lecture XVIII).

(c) Precisely because of his emphasis on subjects' struggles against all forms of desubjectification and his associated efforts to highlight the significance of transcendental experiences, Touraine, unlike theorists such as Habermas and Castoriadis for example, has a markedly more ambivalent relationship to processes of secularization. In any event, for Touraine secularization is not a fundamental hallmark or attribute of modernity (*Critique of Modernity*, p. 308). While he is clearly sceptical towards religious movements, always seeing embodied in them the risk that the subject will be overwhelmed, he also underlines that faith in God and religious forms of community are not in themselves at variance with modernization. This is a stance confirmed empirically in many parts of the world and one which acknowledges that secularization theory has failed on a grand scale when applied to the world as a whole, that it applies only to Western Europe (to some extent) and cannot account for the situation in North America.

(d) Finally, Touraine's reflections on democratic theory are also worthy of note, because here he battles on several social theoretical fronts. To turn to the first of these: Touraine, as a theorist of the 'new social movements', which so often articulate the desire for direct democracy, has developed a remarkable degree of scepticism towards such demands in his later work, and above all a dismissive attitude towards the revolutionary project – which makes his differences from Castoriadis particularly clear. His rejection of direct democracy is comprehensible only against the background of his theory of the subject. As he sees it, direct democracy always runs the risk of creating the illusion of the smooth integration of the individual into the community or society, because all political decisions are made directly and immediately by the people, that is, without the 'detrimental' interposition of representatives. This is suggestive of the idea of the people as a uniform body. According to Touraine, there is a lurking danger here that the subject may be subjugated to 'social imperatives', which is why such ideas tend towards totalitarianism. Democracy – so Touraine tells us – is certainly defined by the principles of equality and majority rule, but also by a guarantee of inalienable *civil rights* and a clear *limitation* of state power (*What is*

Democracy?, p. 96). In this respect, Touraine emerges as a rather conventional liberal, speaking in favour of representative democracy and a clear separation of civil society and politics (ibid., p. 37), that is, for political parties and the state to be free of direct political pressure and for individuals to be protected from the thoroughgoing politicization of their lives. In his opinion, the differentiated structures of Western liberal modernity therefore ought to be retained.

For this reason, he also rejects the revolutionary project advocated by Castoriadis. Touraine favours the stance of Claude Lefort (b. 1924), one of Castoriadis' 'old' comrades-in-arms in the circle around the journal *Socialisme ou Barbarie*, who became one of France's most innovative political philosophers. He set himself apart from Castoriadis politically at an early stage, speaking out against the rationalist idea of revolution because he considered it impossible for society to look at itself with any real clarity and thus thought it all too probable that the revolution would morph into totalitarianism (see Lefort, 'Interpreting Revolution within the French Revolution', 1988). According to Lefort, the idea of the revolution is based on the 'fantastic assertion that the postulates of thought, discourse and will coincide with self-being and with the being of society, history and humanity' (ibid., p. 106). Touraine concurs with his rejection of this fantastic notion because, as we have seen, he considers the tension between subject and society simply unavoidable and does not believe that it can be remedied by the revolutionary project.

As clearly as Touraine appears to adopt a liberal political position here, he is at the same time – and this is the second 'front' – anything but a naive liberal. He repeatedly calls for an active state whose task it is to strengthen groups' capacity for action such that this capacity may be brought to bear within social conflicts. His conception of the subject is not a privatist one; rather, it assumes that the identities of individuals and their interests crystallize only through social and political struggles.

But Touraine's theory of democracy also battles on a third 'front', as apparent in his differences from Jürgen Habermas' views on this subject. Touraine is just as sceptical as Habermas of the communitarian notion that there is a need for relatively stable collective ties if democracy is to function (see Lecture XVIII for more on communitarianism), because this downplays the radical differences between individuals and entails the risk of subjugating the subject. But Touraine also criticizes the idea, so fundamental for Habermas, that democracy can be conceived only as a universalist project. Touraine, in contrast, understands democracy as a way of life characterized by the inseparable presence of both universalist *and* particularist elements (ibid., pp. 14–15). For according to Touraine, if subjectification occurs especially within collective struggles, then we should view particularist movements with rather less suspicion than Habermas claims. This is evident in his assessment of nationalism. While Habermas, at once hopeful, expectant and self-confident, refers to the inevitable transition to postnational forms of sociation (Habermas, *The Postnational Constellation*; *The Inclusion of the Other: Studies in Political Theory*, p. xxxvi), Touraine finds it more difficult to denounce nationalisms and processes of ethnicization (Touraine, *Can We Live Together?*, pp. 202ff.). Touraine is certainly aware of the ambivalent nature of nationalism, and his condemnation of its dark sides is unequivocal, particularly given that nationalist movements have often subjugated the subject. Yet Touraine also knows that processes of ethnicization may be processes of political learning and that such processes also offer opportunities for political participation and thus the emergence of subjects. For him, therefore, these processes are not automatically associated with the rise of racism, for example, which is why he believes that democracy does not have to be defined, either empirically or normatively, as an exclusively universalist project.

Touraine's theoretical reorientation in the 1990s is certainly impressive. His theory of the subject, along with the analyses of the contemporary world which he builds upon it, are an important corrective to other approaches in social theory. A theoretical weakness, however, runs through Touraine's entire oeuvre. In his research on social movements he always showed more interest in fluid social processes than in established institutions. Yet these certainly exist. And even in the 1990s, which were such a productive and innovative time for him, he failed to remedy this relative lack of interest in institutions. Touraine does refer to subjectification and to the fact that subjects wrestle with the machinery of state, and with markets, resisting them and so on. But he does not really examine this 'machinery' or these markets more closely; often, he merely characterizes them by deploying the highly imprecise term 'anti-subject'. He is thus empirically neglectful, bracketing out analytically those elements which partly determine the processes of subjectification to which he has paid so much attention. What is more, he makes the theoretical mistake of hypostatizing the 'machinery' and institutions, in much the same way as did Jürgen Habermas with his concept of system. However, if one takes the thesis of the fluidity of social processes seriously, as Touraine always strove to do, one cannot restrict one's interests solely to social movements. Processes of change within seemingly stable institutions must also be taken into account. This is probably the greatest weakness of his analyses.

3. To close this lecture, we shall take a brief look at a French thinker who long lived in the shadows of French intellectual life, but who, despite being a

philosopher, is likely to play an increasingly important role in sociological theory or social theory because of his work on basic theoretical issues. We are referring to Paul Ricoeur (1913–2005). Rather like Maurice Merleau-Ponty, Ricoeur's earliest philosophical roots lay in the so-called 'Christian existentialism' of 1930s France. As a German prisoner of war, he then delved deeply into the philosophy of Husserl in particular. Towards the end of the 1950s at the latest, he was considered a rising star in the firmament of French philosophy. He was, however, rapidly marginalized by the up-and-coming structuralism in the mid-1960s. Ricoeur certainly dealt with structuralist *topics*, above all symbol systems and language. He also produced some of the most important critiques of structuralism, but structuralism was not to be his theoretical frame of reference, but rather a hermeneutics strongly inspired by phenomenology. A theoretical orientation of this kind was, however, considered hopelessly outdated in the 1960s. This intellectual marginalization, together with the student rebellions from 1968 on, which culminated in a violent attack on him by left-wing extremist students, caused Ricoeur to move abroad; he accepted a professorship at the Divinity School of the University of Chicago in 1970 as successor to the great Protestant theologian Paul Tillich, who died in 1965 (see Joas, 'God in France'; Dosse, *Paul Ricoeur. Les sens d'une vie*).

The breadth and scope of Ricoeur's oeuvre transcend the frame of these lectures on social theory. His writings range from an early phenomenology of the will through a symbolism of evil and a hermeneutics of the text to studies of Freud (see his well-known 1965 study *De l'interprétation. Essai sur Freud*; English title: *Freud and Philosophy: An Essay on Interpretation*) and a three-volume work *Temps et récit* from 1983 (English title: *Time and Narrative*). For our purposes, his most important contribution is his 1990 magnum opus *Soi-même comme un autre* (English title: *Oneself as Another*), in which Ricoeur attempts to clarify the concept of the self by means of a wide-ranging examination of both phenomenology and Anglophone analytical philosophy. On this basis, he ultimately proceeds to a profound discussion of ethics.

Through his hermeneutics of the self, he wishes to clarify a concept which appears very difficult or nebulous in itself. What do we mean when we speak of 'self' in everyday life? What exactly do philosophers, psychologists and sociologists mean when they refer to 'the self'? Does it mean that people always remain the same, that they do not change? Hardly, given that we are always learning, developing, etc. But what does it mean? A fair number of philosophical approaches, particularly analytical philosophy, while referring to 'identity' or 'self', seem to simply leave out of account the fact that 'the person of whom we are speaking and the agent on whom the action depends have a history, are their own history' (Ricoeur, *Oneself as Another*, p. 113). Ricoeur believes that the underlying problem can be solved only through painstaking terminological distinctions, if one takes apart, as it were, common or popular terms such as 'selfhood', 'ipséité' or 'Identität', in order to advance to more precise definitions. Ricoeur ultimately suggests that we distinguish between 'sameness' or 'idem identity' (*mêmeté*) and 'selfness' or 'ipse identity' (*ipséité*). The first terms refer merely to the identifiability of an individual over time, while 'selfness' or 'ipse identity' points to the self-established continuity of the individual despite the changes she has undergone. In other words, this means that if I state of an individual that she is the same, this does not imply an unchanging core of personality (ibid., p. 2). Rather, Ricoeur believes that 'selfness' is produced *narratively*, that we as individuals *tell* ourselves and others who we are and how we became what we are.

> The person, understood as a character in a story, is not an entity distinct from his or her 'experiences'. Quite the opposite: the person shares the condition of dynamic identity peculiar to the story recounted. The narrative constructs the identity of the character, what can be called his or her narrative identity, in constructing that of the story told. It is the identity of the story that makes the identity of the character.
>
> (ibid., pp. 147–8)

As the events in a person's life never end, the narrative too is never complete. Ricoeur refers to the 'narrative incompleteness' of life, and the 'entanglement of life histories', and finally to the 'dialectic of remembrance and anticipation' (ibid., p. 161). This argument, which he worked on with great earnestness, not only makes Ricoeur one of the key critics of all postmodern positions that virtually assert that identities can be freely chosen and that the (postmodern) self has fragmented entirely – positions which, as Ricoeur sees it, could be adopted only by ignoring the terminological distinctions put forward by him. He also reminds us that 'narrative' is an aspect of the formation of ipse identity and thus of life, a natural feature of human experience that inevitably has direct consequences for ethics: 'How, indeed, could a subject of action give an ethical character to his or her own life taken as a whole, if this life were not gathered together in some way, and how could this occur if not, precisely, in the form of a narrative?' (ibid., p. 158).

In the eighth and ninth essay in his book, Ricoeur presents an impressively dense and comprehensive analysis of contemporary ethical models, ultimately advancing to a position of his own, which admirably maintains the balance between a morality based on a universal justice à la Kant, Rawls and Habermas (see also Lectures XVII and XVIII) and an ethics of concrete morality anchored in the work of Aristotle and Hegel. Ricoeur is well aware of the weaknesses of universalist conceptions of justice, in as much as they all too easily fail to take account of people's concrete practices of living. But he by no means falls smoothly into line with the camp of 'theorists of Hegelian "Sittlichkeit"'. As he brilliantly puts it:

> If we did not pass through conflicts that shake a practice guided by the principles of morality, we would succumb to the seductions of a moral situation that would cast us, defenceless, into the realm of the arbitrary.
>
> (ibid., pp. 240–1)

Thus, according to Ricoeur, we have great need of Kantian universal rules in order to come to practically consistent conclusions; we cannot do without the ideas of Rawls and Habermas, even if they are inadequate on their own. But the choice is not between universalist morality and 'Sittlichkeit' or abstract arguments and convention – Ricoeur considers these false dichotomies. He prefers to speak of a 'dialectic between argumentation and conviction' (ibid., p. 287), a choice of terminology which emerges as entirely comprehensible when he discusses Habermasian discourse ethics. For according to Ricoeur, Habermas assumes a mere exchange of arguments that aims to 'extract ... the best argument' and eliminate the others, but like all universalist theorists of morality he overlooks the fact that it is *real-life issues* that are being discussed in the discursive situation. Arguments are not mere adversaries of conventions and traditions, but rather critical instances *within* convictions and real-life issues which can only be articulated narratively (ibid., p. 288). And these issues cannot be dismissed:

> What makes conviction an inescapable party here is the fact that it expresses the positions from which result the meanings, interpretations, and evaluations relating to the multiple goods that occupy the scale of praxis, from practices and their immanent goods, passing by way of life plans, life histories, and including the conceptions humans have, alone or together, of what a complete life would be.
>
> (ibid., p. 288)

Because it fails to recognize the close connection between arguments and real-life matters, Habermasian discourse theory is thus too ethically abstract. What interests us in the present context is, first, the fact that a similar distancing from Habermasian discourse ethics and thus from the theory of democracy that this implies occurs in the work of Ricoeur as is already familiar to us in the case of Touraine – a distancing, however, that was carried out with very different theoretical means than in Touraine's case. What is even more impressive is how consistently and precisely (his precision a result of his intensive engagement with analytical philosophy) Ricoeur moves towards a synthesis of Aristotelian and Kantian ethics, thus elegantly mastering a number of problems, some of which were viewed as insurmountable within the debate on liberalism and communitarianism, a debate very much rooted in American soil (see Lecture XVIII).

While Ricoeur's work seems far removed from traditional sociological concerns and he restricted his methodological investigations to the discipline of history, his ideas on interpretation, the connections between self-formation and narrative, and on ethics, open up a great many points of contact with general debates in social theory. Particularly against the background of the obvious decline in the importance of structuralist and post-structuralist thought in France (and beyond), it is little surprise that more and more social scientists are discovering how relevant Ricoeur's ideas are to them.

XVII

Feminist social theories

We refer in the title of this lecture to feminist social *theories*, the plural indicating that we are confronted with a fundamental problem in seeking to describe this field – namely the fact that there is no such thing as feminist social theory, but at best a variety of such theories. The theoretical landscape within feminism is so tremendously multifarious because feminist theorists, whose concrete goals and projects do not, of course, always tally, draw on very different theoretical building blocks to construct their arguments. You have encountered the vast majority of these theories in the previous lectures. While few feminists build directly on Parsonian ideas, a large number make use of conflict theoretical arguments, for example. And the strongest and most influential currents within the feminist debate at present can be traced back to ethnomethodological, poststructuralist and Habermasian positions. In addition, the strong influence of psychoanalysis is also unmistakable.

The question thus arises as to whether this heterogeneous theoretical field of feminism features any kind of common denominator, especially given that feminist debates are being carried on not just within sociology, but also in psychology, anthropology, history, philosophy and political theory; here, disciplinary boundaries play a rather minor role (see for example Will Kymlicka, *Contemporary Political Philosophy: An Introduction*, pp. 238ff.). This question is crucial, as it points to the risk that the feminist debate might become hopelessly fragmented. But there does in fact seem to be agreement that what feminist theories have in common is a shared normative or political goal which can be traced back to the historical origins of feminist theory building, which lie in the women's movement. The aim of all feminist approaches, so it is generally argued, is ultimately to *critique* relations of power and domination that discriminate against or repress women, and thus to *liberate* women from these relations. This is clearly apparent in a quote from the philosopher Alison M. Jaggar (b. 1942): 'In order to offer guides to action that will tend to subvert rather than reinforce women's present systematic subordination, feminist approaches to ethics must understand individual actions in the context of broader social practices, evaluating the symbolic and cumulative implications of any action as well as its immediately observable consequences' (Jaggar, *Feminist Ethics*, p. 98; see also Pauer-Studer, 'Moraltheorie und Geschlechterdifferenz' ['Moral Theory and Gender Difference'], pp. 35ff.). The same can certainly be said of social or political theory.

This normative political impetus characteristic of feminist theory (theories) thus offers grounds for demarcating the associated approaches from the discipline of gender studies, which has become so fashionable over the last two decades (see Regina Becker-Schmidt and Gudrun-Axeli Knapp, *Feministische Theorien* ['Feminist Theories'], p. 7). Feminist approaches, like gender studies, have a shared scholarly interest in how social and political relations between the sexes are and were organized. Gender studies can, however, be carried out in a 'neutral' way. A study of the ways in which masculinity is performed, for example, does not necessarily have to take a critical approach. For feminists, meanwhile, the task at hand is a different one. For them, the key concern is and will continue to be to *critique* existing social arrangements relating to gender.

However, we would underline straight away that the shared normative and political thrust of feminist theories cannot obscure the fact that this goal is pursued with very different conceptual and theoretical tools, threatening to cut this common thread. This is what makes every account of feminist social theory (theories) so difficult. This difficulty is even more pronounced in light of the topics considered in this lecture series. We asserted that *approaches to social theory* are always characterized by the central concern with issues of action, social order and social change and generally also by a desire to analyse the contemporary world. But of course not all feminist analyses satisfy these criteria for 'theory', just as we have not included sociological studies of class structure, state theory or the ethnic make-up of modern society in the core of modern social theory. Analyses of the disadvantaging of women and discrimination against them in (modern) societies are thus not, in our view, contributions to feminist *social theory* in themselves. This view compels us to neglect certain fields of feminist debate, just as we have largely ignored many fields and topics of research within mainstream sociology in order to focus on those contributions that can be meaningfully related to the other theoretical studies presented in this lecture series. It goes without saying that this selective approach does not allow us to undertake an exhaustive analysis of feminist writings.

We divide this lecture into three parts. First, in a brief historical survey, we will explain why, in our opinion, a genuinely feminist social theory is a relatively recent development (1). We then go on to ask which debates on the 'nature' of femininity defined the 1970s and 1980s (2) and why (this is the last and by far the longest part of the lecture) these approaches then made way for an intensive discussion of the relationship between 'sex' and 'gender', that is, the relationship between 'biological' and 'social' gender, and which theoretical positions play a role here (3).

1. As we have already suggested, the roots of feminist social theories lie in the women's movement. As an organized movement, this is now more than 200 years old, and within the context of women's struggle over equality,

theoretical concepts were of course constantly being formulated that were intended to play a supportive role in this struggle (on the German women's movement, see for example Ute Gerhard, *Unerhört. Die Geschichte der deutschen Frauenbewegung* ['Unheard Of: The History of the German Women's Movement']; on the women's movement in the USA, see Janet Zollinger Giele, *Two Paths to Women's Equality: Temperance, Suffrage, and the Origins of Modern Feminism*; a historically grounded comparison of different national feminisms is provided by Christine Bolt, *The Women's Movements in the United States and Britain from the 1790s to the 1920s*). Nonetheless, it is fair to say that *systematic* feminist theory building began in the 1960s *at the earliest*. This was, of course, mainly the result of the fact that the educational reforms of this period enabled an appreciable number of women to attend university for the first time. Interestingly enough, however, it was not the experience of attending university as such which was the key factor in the rapid development of a feminist consciousness and the resulting theoretical production, but the conduct of the male-dominated student movement in the late 1960s, which 'didn't care a damn about a silly woman's movement' (Firestone, *The Dialectic of Sex: The Case for Feminist Revolution*, p. 42). Many women activists discovered that their concern – achieving equality in every area of life – was simply ignored within a discursive landscape influenced primarily by Marxian arguments, because the unequal relationship between men and women was always interpreted merely as a 'secondary contradiction' of capitalism, whose significance supposedly could not be compared with that of the 'main contradiction' between wage labour and capital. For many male representatives of the student movement and the New Left, this line of argument served as a convenient excuse for conduct every bit as sexist as that of their opponents in the so-called 'bourgeois camp'. This caused many politically engaged women to begin to break away from or sever their ties with the New Left both organizationally and theoretically, as they came to realize that a new approach was necessary – not least in the field of social scientific research and theory building.

This process of striking out on their own took a number of forms. A whole string of women authors set about elaborating the *consequences* of gender relations in different spheres of society, for the most part through an empirical approach. They showed, for example, how unequally the labour market is structured, how and why domestic work, almost exclusively carried out by women, receives no social recognition and no remuneration, which welfare policies have tied and continue to tie women to the home and children and how they do so, which mechanisms obstruct the adequate political representation of women to this day, etc.

Theoretically ambitious feminists, however, quickly proceeded to analyse the *premises* of gender relations as well, asking whether and to what extent existing social scientific theories are capable of advancing our understanding of this subject. Feminists set about this in a huge variety of ways. By pointing to the biological differences between men and women, activist Shulamith Firestone (b. 1945) polemicized against the Marxist-oriented students' movement and its economic reductionism in her above-mentioned book *The Dialectic of Sex* from 1970. She described the conflict between the sexes as fundamental, more so than class struggle, explaining male chauvinism on this basis. In her 1975 book *Against Our Will: Men, Women and Rape*, the journalist Susan Brownmiller (b. 1935) highlighted men's ability and desire to engage in violence, especially sexual violence, claiming that '*all men* keep *all women* in a state of fear' (p. 15; original emphasis) as a result of this sexual violence, forcing women into a subordinate social position. Other women authors, meanwhile, tried to avoid such radical biologism. This seemed imperative to them primarily because such attempts at explanation are incapable of adequately elucidating the huge cultural differences in the always unequal relationship between the sexes, the 'endless variety and monotonous similarity' as anthropologist Gayle Rubin put it ('The Traffic in Women', p. 10). Once again, this opened up the possibility of drawing on the work of Marx, and even more that of Engels, in that the gender-specific division of labour in all its various forms was thought to explain the equally variable forms of gendered inequality. On this view, the relationship between the sexes is shaped equally by capitalism and the patriarchal family; (male) gainful employment and (female) domestic work are closely interwoven, endlessly reproducing the inequality between men and women, in other words, maintaining the power of men (see Walby, *Theorizing Patriarchy*). However, as Marxism lost importance in the 1980s, the influence of these approaches also waned, in the same way as the concept of patriarchy or male domination, used in a wide variety of theoretical approaches (not just Marxist feminism). This term, seen as a key feminist concept as late as the 1970s and early 1980s, was clearly considered too unspecific to generate nuanced empirical analyses, and was increasingly marginalized as a result (see Gudrun-Axeli Knapp, 'Macht und Geschlecht' ['Power and Gender'], p. 298). As Gayle Rubin precociously concluded:

> it is important – even in the face of a depressive history – to maintain a distinction between the human capacity and necessity to create a sexual world, and the empirically oppressive ways in which sexual worlds have been organized. Patriarchy subsumes both meanings into the same term.
> (Rubin, 'The Traffic in Women', p. 168)

In the wake of this conceptual reorientation within feminist social theory, a more vigorous microsociological orientation emerged from the 1970s and 1980s and a more determined theorizing of gender relations in general, enabling many feminists to link their work more strongly to 'traditional' social theory. It was no longer the 'great' historical causes of inequality between the sexes, which may never be truly clarified, that increasingly took centre stage in the feminist debate of the 1980s, but the question of what equality between the sexes actually means or could mean, what the advancement of women should entail if it is to reduce the discriminatory consequences of the differences between the sexes for women, which phenomena currently undergird the differences between men and women, and how these differences are reproduced day in and day out. In other words, while biologically inclined authors had always underlined the immutable difference between the sexes and supporters of the thesis of patriarchy had always emphasized the dominance of men, which they believe to have deep historical roots and to be almost impossible to bring to an end, more and more feminist thinkers began to ask how this difference between the sexes is continually produced and constructed in very concrete everyday ways. Issues were clearly being touched upon, at least on the margins, which are among the core problems of 'traditional' social theory. What is (male and female) action? What is a male or female subject? How and by what means is the gendered order reproduced? Our thesis is thus that feminist social theory (theories), at least in as much as it forms or aspires to form part of the canon of modern social theory, is of fairly recent origin, its roots stretching no further back than thirty years. We therefore begin our account in the 1970s and 1980s with those theoretical approaches that define the debate to this day.

2. During this period, the feminist debate oscillated constantly between two poles, two very different types of argument. A stance sometimes described in the literature as 'maximalist' tended to emphasize the differences between men and women. Of course, this was *not necessarily* backed up with reference to biological arguments, but instead and increasingly to gender-specific *processes of psychological development*. 'These scholars typically believe that differences are deeply rooted and result in different approaches to the world, in some cases creating a distinctive "culture" of women. Such differences, they think, benefit society and ought to be recognized and rewarded' (Epstein, *Deceptive Distinctions*, p. 25). The so-called 'minimalist position', meanwhile, underlined the great similarity between the sexes and the fact that existing differences between them are not immutable, but historically variable and thus socially constructed (ibid.).

In the 1970s and 1980s, the *new* perspectives on gender relations alluded to above were initially developed for the most part within various fields of psychology or within a sociology that worked largely with psychological arguments. It was the 'maximalist positions' that received the most attention. Two authors stand out in this regard, whose writings held much appeal for the neighbouring social sciences.

American sociologist Nancy Chodorow (b. 1944) tried to explain, from a psychoanalytic perspective, why women are continually affected by a psychological dynamic which underpins the maintenance of gender relations and thus their social subordination. Her thesis (see *The Reproduction of Mothering: Psychoanalysis and the Sociology of Gender* from 1978) is that girls' earliest relationships with their mothers play a decisive role. Chodorow's point of departure was the assumption that the development of gender identity in both sexes occurs at a fairly early stage, such that a kind of unchangeable core of personality exists by the age of five at the latest. If this thesis, widely expounded within psychoanalysis, is true and if it is also true that, at least in Western societies, it is nearly always mothers who are the main reference individual for children of both sexes, then according to Chodorow it is also clear that *the way in which gender identity is formed in the two sexes must be very different*:

> The earliest mode of individuation, the primary construction of the ego and its inner object-world, the earliest conflicts and the earliest unconscious definitions of self, the earliest threats to individuation, and the earliest anxieties which call up defenses, all differ for boys and girls because of differences in the character of the early mother–child relationship for each.
> (Chodorow, *The Reproduction of Mothering*, p. 167)

While girls develop their gender identity very much with reference to the mother, identifying with her and her actions, boys experience themselves as forming an *opposite pole* to the mother, classifying themselves as something different from the mother. As Chodorow explained, this means that male development is far more a matter of individuation, of the development of clear, indeed overly clear ego boundaries. Girls on the other hand, so Chodorow asserts, develop an individuality far more inclined towards 'empathy' with others, endowing them with the ability to respond to the needs and feelings of others. This also explains why men have more problems in their relationships with other people, while rigid forms of individuation are generally alien to women (ibid., pp. 167ff.).

Chodorow's analyses were aimed, first of all, at the deeply 'masculine' theoretical premises of psychoanalysis. Drawing on Freud, these raised the development of the *male* child to the status of norm, in light of which girls' development of an ego identity could only seem deficient (see especially chapter 9 of her book). Second, though, Chodorow also wished to explain why gender relations are continually reproduced in all their inequality. For Chodorow, girls' earliest relationships to their mothers and the way in which their gender identity develops always brings about a type of action which may be described as 'mothering' and which differs from the action performed by men in many ways in being strongly oriented towards relationships. These ideas also highlighted a specific normative stance. For Chodorow and her supporters neither believed that girls' identity formation and action are fundamentally deficient (ibid., p. 198), nor that the typical family relations that pertained in the America of the time, with their particularly strong emphasis on 'mothering', were the only possible, let alone ideal, form of parenting, particularly given that this 'mothering' reinforced the inequality of the sexes.

> Contemporary problems in mothering emerge from potential internal contradictions in the family and the social organization of gender – between women's mothering and heterosexual commitment, between women's mothering and individuation in daughters, between emotional connection and a sense of masculinity in sons. Changes generated from outside the family, particularly in the economy, have sharpened these contradictions.
>
> (ibid., p. 213)

A modified division of labour between men and women (with more women working outside the home and men carrying out more family duties) would, according to Chodorow, at least mitigate the ways in which gender identity currently develops, because mothers would no longer be children's sole reference individual. Under these circumstances, there would be a real chance of disrupting the ceaseless 'reproduction of mothering', with all its negative consequences for the autonomy of women.

Carol Gilligan, whose book *In a Different Voice* from 1982 was to exercise an even greater influence than that of Chodorow, took a similar normative tack. But the psychologist Gilligan (b. 1936 and also American) adopted a very different theoretical and psychological approach than the sociologist Chodorow with her *psychoanalytical* approach. Gilligan was the colleague of one of the most famous *developmental psychologists* of her time, Lawrence Kohlberg, who strongly influenced neighbouring disciplines with his ideas. Gilligan's findings, which amounted to a critique of Kohlberg, almost inevitably triggered an immediate response from moral philosophers and sociologists, given that Gilligan was questioning some of their key postulates.

Kohlberg, whose work influenced that of Jürgen Habermas (see Lecture X), among others, developed a theory concerning the moral development of children and adults, building on studies by Jean Piaget. His empirical investigations, he asserted, suggested that the development of a moral conscience is a multistage process. He distinguished between three different moral levels (pre-conventional, conventional and post-conventional), subdividing each level into two further sublevels (of no further interest to us here). On the *pre*-conventional level, the actor is claimed to obey certain moral rules only because, from an egocentric perspective, she wishes to avoid punishment. In this case, 'good' is anything that helps the actor to do this. Arguments and actions are *conventionally* moral if I, for example, see my moral obligations as consisting in meeting the expectations of my fellow human beings, because, for instance, I want them to see me as a 'good guy' and want them to like me or because I wish to contribute to the good of the whole of which I am part. We reach the *post*-conventional stage only when people act according to universal ethical principles, when their moral actions are based on a point of view formulated regardless of particular relationships and communities, a point of view anchored in rules that apply to and are acceptable to *everyone* (see Kohlberg, 'Moral Stages and Moralization', pp. 170ff.).

Kohlberg believed that moral development adheres to a very specific logic: over the course of their socialization, people successively pass through these three levels or six stages; an ascent occurs from pre-conventional through conventional to post-conventional morality, with their various substages. According to Kohlberg, not everyone reaches the highest moral level or highest moral stage; just a small number of adults will succeed in aligning their arguments and actions consistently with post-conventional, that is, universalist ethical or moral principles. The explosive thing about Kohlberg's studies, and this was Gilligan's discovery as well as her critique, was that women clearly almost never reach the *post*-conventional moral level, that unlike men they almost always remain on the level of conventional morality, the third and – more rarely – fourth substage of moral development:

> Prominent among those who ... appear to be deficient in moral development when measured by Kohlberg's scale are women, whose judgements seem to exemplify the third stage of his six-stage sequence. At this stage morality is conceived in interpersonal terms and goodness is equated with helping and pleasing others. This conception of goodness is considered by Kohlberg ... to be functional in the lives of mature women insofar as their lives take place in the home. Kohlberg [implies] that only if women enter the traditional arena of male activity will they recognize the inadequacy of this moral perspective and progress like men toward higher stages where relationships are subordinated to rules (stage four) and rules to universal principles of justice (stages five and six).
>
> Yet herein lies a paradox, for the very traits that traditionally have defined the 'goodness' of women, their care for and sensitivity to the needs of others, are those that mark them as deficient in moral development.
>
> (Gilligan, *In a Different Voice*, p. 18)

In light of this fact and in much the same way as Chodorow had done with respect to traditional psychoanalysis, Gilligan now concluded that the theoretical model of Kohlbergian developmental psychology was constructed on the basis of a profoundly male perspective and that it therefore failed to capture how women develop morally. Her thesis was that an unprejudiced study of women's moral development would produce a different result. According to her own empirical investigations, women deal with moral problems in a very different way than men, and their moral developmental path must therefore also be interpreted differently. On this view, while men tend to think and act according to abstract principles, women make judgements contextually and narratively, which Kohlberg always failed to take into account in designing his studies. Women's way of forming moral judgements underpins the development of a morality 'concerned with the activity of care'. While female notions of morality emphasize 'the understanding of responsibility and relationships', men tend towards an abstract morality of 'fairness', based on 'rights and rules' (ibid., p. 19).

Gilligan thus criticized her teacher Kohlberg for having produced a model of moral development which implicitly rests on a male conception of morality, on a morality of abstract rights or an ethics of justice. In light of this it was hardly surprising that women almost never reached the highest stages of the Kohlbergian developmental schema, that they generally emerged as incapable of or unwilling to act and argue according to abstract and universalist rules. Gilligan now countered Kohlberg's approach with a model intended to be more commensurate with how women develop, a multistage model of *care*, based on a context-sensitive and non-abstract 'ethic of care' (ibid., p. 74). This model – and this was the normative and political impetus of her arguments – also had implications for the form of social institutions, in that these must always satisfy the very different moral notions of women.

This sharp contrast between a male ethics of justice and a female ethics of care or sympathy sparked off a huge debate within and beyond the feminist movement. Some feminists sharply criticized Gilligan, accusing her, among other things, of propagating a morality of care that is merely a variant of slaves' morality in the Nietzschean sense. Some suggested that this way of seeing things was that of a liberal feminist with no understanding of power relations:

> Women are said to value care. Perhaps women value care because men have valued women according to the care they give. Women are said to think in relational terms. Perhaps women think in relational terms because women's social existence is defined in relation to men. The liberal idealism of these works is revealed in the ways they do not take social determination and the realities of power seriously.
>
> (MacKinnon, *Toward a Feminist Theory of the State*, pp. 51–2; on this debate, see Benhabib, *Situating the Self*, pp. 179f.)

Some of these harsh criticisms were unfair, as Gilligan had always emphasized that her morality of care did *not* imply the surrendering or denial of one's identity. A series of plausible objections was, however, raised against her studies and again, often by feminists. They assailed the inadequate empirical basis of her studies or her misinterpretation of this basis, asserting that the gender differences apparent in early childhood are by no means as significant as Gilligan assumed. For them, what Gilligan called a female morality of care was merely the historical expression of a specific morality of roles, which might change as a result of the increasing equality of women (Nunner-Winkler, 'Gibt es eine weibliche Moral?' ['Is There a Female Morality?']). In certain situations, men too certainly tend towards contextual and narrative reflections. Finally, Gilligan was criticized for ultimately leaving the *social* and *historical* fact of gender difference unexplained, that is, for merely positing it – in much the same way as Chodorow (Benhabib, *Situating the Self*, p. 178).

There is agreement, however, that despite all the elements deserving of criticism, the debate triggered by Gilligan opened up a huge discursive space and also impacted on debates within moral philosophy and sociology. For it rapidly became clear that universalist moral theories, corresponding to the *post*-conventional level of Kohlberg's developmental schema, are deficient in several key respects. The aim of such theories is to provide non-contextual rules for resolving moral issues in order to find solutions acceptable to everyone, rather than just to a specific group. The disadvantage of these theories is that it is almost impossible to use them to tackle problems such as those centred on the consequences of personal ties, the nature of friendship and sympathy and indeed the good life in general (see Pauer-Studer, 'Moraltheorie und Geschlechterdifferenz', p. 44). All universalist theories of this kind, anchored in the legacy of Kant, whether Habermasian discourse ethics or the moral philosophy of a John Rawls (see the next lecture), struggle with these theoretical blind spots, and this is why they attract criticism.

> Kant's error was to assume that I, as a pure rational agent reasoning for myself, could reach a conclusion that would be acceptable for all at all times and places. In Kantian moral theory, moral agents are like geometricians in different rooms who, reasoning alone for themselves, all arrive at the same solution to a problem.
>
> (Benhabib, *Situating the Self*, p. 163)

Habermasian discourse ethics, which asserts that validity claims to normative correctness must submit to intersubjective scrutiny in a context free of domination (see Lecture X), avoided such problems in that this ethics is from the outset constructed *dialogically*, and specifically does *not* assume a solitary subject. But even this discourse ethics is based on a very limited conception of morality and politics and a problematic distinction between norms and values, the right and the good, excluding many issues such as those mentioned above as not amenable to discussion or as non-moral or non-political. For the most pressing (moral) issues often emerge from that very personal, contextual sphere (ibid., p. 170), and they cannot be discussed through Habermasian discourse ethics as originally conceived, because they form part of the realm of values or of the good life and are therefore impossible to discuss from a universalist perspective. Even if one agrees with Habermas' distinction between the good and the right, between values and norms, this would nonetheless result in an unsatisfactory situation, for a moral theory which is in principle unable or unwilling to say anything about such urgent personal moral issues can only be considered deficient. And Gilligan's writings did in fact inspire moral theorists, and Habermas as well incidentally (see *Moral Consciousness and Communicative Action*, pp. 175ff.), to give more thought to the relationship between a morality of care and a morality of justice and to ask whether one depends on the other or whether – as Seyla Benhabib (b. 1950) thought – the origins of care and justice are both to be found within childhood development.

> In this ... respect, Habermas and Kohlberg have dismissed all too quickly a central insight of Gilligan and of other feminists: namely that we are children before we are adults, and that the nurture, care and responsibility of others is essential for us to develop into morally competent, self-sufficient individuals.
>
> (ibid., p. 188)

It is thus possible to interpret Gilligan's studies as something quite different than naive liberal feminism. Her research undoubtedly features an inherent critical potential, in as much as she brought to light the (male) subtext of certain moral theories. Here, Gilligan's theoretical (though not necessarily political) impulses overlap with those driving communitarian thinkers (see the next lecture). And they were and are entirely compatible with the efforts of feminist theorists who, drawing on Aristotelian philosophy, criticize the hyper-rationalist construction of most moral philosophies: flying in the face of everyday experience, these interpret emotions as merely irrational and thus ignore them. The brilliant philosopher Martha Nussbaum (b. 1947), who teaches at the University of Chicago, is one of the outstanding figures here. Nussbaum, the feminist, does not mean that we must enhance the status of emotions because women – as the cliché has it – are naturally (in other words biologically) more emotional than men. Nussbaum's position is a quite different one, namely that emotions are fundamentally influenced by the social context, that is, they are social constructions. Unsurprisingly, we must therefore conclude that in a society lacking in sexual equality, emotions are distributed unequally between the sexes, in that emotions are often reactions to situations of insecurity and dependency, to which women have always been more exposed than men for historical reasons. But – and this is one of Nussbaum's crucial philosophical and sociological theses – the claim that emotions are distributed unequally does *not* entail the assumption that women are more irrational. For even if women are supposedly more emotional than men in our modern Western society, it is also true that emotions are not merely empty, irrational phenomena, but are usually bound up with judgements about a specific subject. Rather than the ultimate in irrationality, emotions are thus ways of seeing the world (Nussbaum, 'Emotions and Women's Capabilities', pp. 366ff.). Nussbaum's conclusion, which is very much compatible with Gilligan's theses, is that moral philosophy and sociology do themselves no favours when they refuse to pay attention to certain everyday phenomena because, for no good reason, they jump to the conclusion that they are irrational. On this view, feminist theory has special potential, against the abstract or formal premises of a generally male-dominated philosophical and sociological debate, to bring new aspects into play which do greater justice to social reality (and not only that of women).

3. So much for the debates kicked off by Chodorow and Gilligan in the 1970s and early 1980s. As influential as their writings were, it is nonetheless fair to say that a number of other research traditions attained dominance, by the 1980s at the latest, which called the 'maximalist position' radically into question. Deploying a highly specific set of conceptual tools, these moved towards a more minimalist stance that emphasized the great similarity between the sexes. The distinction, common in the English-speaking world, between 'sex' and 'gender', took centre stage here, with 'sex' (anatomical and physiological differences between men and women and contrasting hormonal and genetic make-up) referring to that which is biologically determined and determinable and 'gender' referring to a socially and culturally acquired status.

Feminists and women's studies scholars drew attention to this distinction primarily to counter the typical male line of argument with respect to women's (inferior) 'nature' and insist that the distinctions between the sexes are a result of repression and discrimination with deep historical roots, rather than the result of a somehow natural or biological difference. Biology, on this view, does not determine a person's 'gendered nature'.

> Gender is a relational category. It is one that seeks to explain the construction of a certain kind of difference among human beings. Feminist theorists, whether psychoanalytical, postmodern, liberal or critical, are united around the assumption that the constitution of gender differences is a social and historical process, and that gender is not a natural fact.
>
> (ibid., p. 191)

From the 1980s on, the most lively theoretical debates within feminism were increasingly concerned to do away with 'essentialisms', such as the notion, still found in the work of Gilligan, of a 'universal essence called "femaleness"' (ibid., p. 192). The theoretical debate seemed to be shifting away from an emphasis on gender differences towards demonstrating the social and historical *construction* of such differences (Gildemeister and Wetterer, 'Wie Geschlechter gemacht werden' ['How to Make Genders'], p. 201). Initially, this means that scholars adhered to the distinction between 'sex' and 'gender' as this allowed them to describe the historical and cultural reasons why women's identity developed in the particular way it did. But over the course of time, it even seemed possible to radicalize the debate by abolishing the distinction between 'sex' and 'gender' completely, this time by adopting a radical new perspective. It could be argued that 'sex' versus 'gender', the 'biological' versus the 'social', involved a misleading distinction because even so-called 'biological sex' is not truly 'biological' or 'natural', but a construction. According to this surprising thesis, there is simply no natural biological sex. The debates that built on this thesis, however, did not lead to a coherent feminist theory, but once again to conflicting interpretations and normative-political conclusions.

(a) This debate got off to a brilliant and theoretically highly innovative start thanks to a book by two American sociologists, Suzanne J. Kessler (b. 1946) and Wendy McKenna (b. 1945). *Gender: An Ethnomethodological Approach*, from 1978, not only clarified that 'gender' is a 'social construction', which was certainly no revolutionary new insight at the time. Above all, it made it clear that almost no studies had been carried out on *how* people are classified as male or female. That is, according to Kessler and McKenna, even those who had emphasized the distinction between 'sex' and 'gender' never seriously analysed what exactly is going on when people ascribe a social gender to others, that is, on what basis 'gender attribution' takes place.

> Occasionally ... we do see people whose gender is not obvious ... It is then that we begin to consciously look for gender cues as to what they 'really' are. What do these cues consist of? In asking people how they tell men from women, their answer almost always includes 'genitals'. But, since in initial interactions genitals are rarely available for inspection, this clearly is not the evidence actually used.
>
> (Kessler and McKenna, *Gender*, p. viii)

In such non-obvious cases it is apparent that human interaction features a never-ending and highly complicated process, as a result of which a certain 'gender' is ascribed to those involved, on the basis of facts which do not necessarily have much to do with biological characteristics. According to these authors, something which seems self-evident and unproblematic is thus a social process based on multiple prerequisites. But it is not just the labelling of another person that is complex, 'living' or 'acting out' a specific gender identity is as well, as is particularly apparent in the phenomenon of transsexualism. For here, being a man or being a woman obviously does not depend on a given physical fact, but on the constant and laborious task of self-presentation as a man or woman carried out by the individual concerned, whose anatomical sex may have been surgically altered. 'Gender' is a 'practical accomplishment' (ibid., p. 163) or, as ethnomethodologists were later to put it, '*Doing gender* means creating differences between girls and boys and women and men, differences that are not natural, essential, or biological' (West and Zimmerman, 'Doing Gender', p. 137; emphasis added).

Those authors arguing in this way were able to draw on studies produced by the 'founders' of the ethnomethodological approach in the 1950s. Garfinkel's book *Studies in Ethnomethodology* (see Lecture VII) contains a long and highly interesting study ('Passing and the Managed Achievement of Sex Status in an "Intersexed" Person, Part 1', pp. 116–85) on the transsexual 'Agnes', an individual who was considered to be a boy until she was seventeen, a tendency reinforced by the fact that the biological attributes of sex were entirely 'normal'. Yet she felt herself to be a girl or woman, wished to live accordingly and had a sex-change operation as a result. Garfinkel described in detail the difficulties faced by this individual in living her new gender, how she had to learn to be a woman and how and why 'passing', the shift from one gender identity to another, is an ongoing task which demands ceaseless performance, because 'gender' is of tremendous importance in all matters of everyday life. According to Garfinkel, transsexuals such as Agnes constantly have to present themselves in such a way that no one discovers their 'original' gender. As Garfinkel and especially Kessler and McKenna explained, it is not the relatively rare phenomenon of transsexualism as such that is most interesting. Studies on the behaviour of transsexuals are of *general theoretical interest* as they provide insights into the way in which 'gender' is generally attributed and lived (or must be lived) by each woman and each man:

> It must be kept in mind, however, that we are studying transsexuals not because they create gender attributions in a particular unusual way, but because, on the contrary, they create gender in the most ordinary of ways, as we all do.
>
> (Kessler and McKenna, *Gender*, pp. 127–8)

So far, this may not seem particularly novel or provocative. It may appear that this ethnomethodological research approach merely subjected a well-known phenomenon to closer examination, bringing out in a more detailed way how 'gender' is socially constructed. In fact, though, the implications of the studies by Kessler and McKenna are significantly greater – as they made very clear. For if one assumes that 'gender' is constructed, the question also arises as to how social reality is constructed such that, at least in our society, two – and only two – genders always emerge: 'what kinds of rules do we apply to what kinds of displays, such that in every concrete instance we produce a sense that there are only men and women, and that this is an objective fact, not dependent on the particular instance?' (ibid., pp. 5–6). If it is also true that the ascription of 'gender' is a social process not directly dependent on biological sex, would it not be possible to imagine gender ascriptions that do *not* proceed dichotomously, that is, that do *not* distinguish between men and women or girls and boys? And indeed the authors point to anthropological studies which show that gender is not inevitably conceived in dichotomous terms. While biology is regarded as the basis of the attribution of gender in Western societies, that is, it is unquestioningly assumed that the origins of social gender lie in biological sex, that men have male genitals and women female ones and that this is necessarily so, this is certainly not the case in other cultures. Here, it has been observed that the ascription 'man' may be applied to a 'biological' woman, should she merely exhibit a particularly male role behaviour. In such cases, anatomical, physiological and similar facts played no role. It has also been observed that there are cultures in which people do not necessarily assume the existence of two genders, but of three or more.

> To say that gender identity is universal is probably true in the sense that all people know what category they belong to, but may be incorrect if we mean knowing whether they are male or female.
>
> (ibid., p. 37)

While this thesis is provocative enough in itself, Kessler and McKenna went on to expound another. They asked whether the biological determination by modern science of the human being as man or woman is not beset by far greater problems than is generally acknowledged – a near-heretical idea at the time. What if 'sex' as a 'biological' phenomenon is just as unclear and nebulous as 'gender'? There are in fact no entirely clear scientific criteria for determining sex. Neither an individual's anatomy nor hormonal 'constitution' nor genetic code offer unambiguous criteria of demarcation. Studies on hermaphroditism in babies and children established that for medical specialists, 'whether the infant with XY chromosomes and anomalous genitalia was categorized as a boy or a girl depended on the size of the penis. If the penis was very small, the child was categorized as a girl, and sex-change surgery was used to make an artificial vagina' (Lorber, *Paradoxes of Gender*, p. 38; for a similar take, see Hagemann-White, 'Wir werden nicht zweigeschlechtlich geboren …' ['There Are No Males or Females at Birth …'], p. 228). There was (and is) obviously no definitively distinguishing biological attribute, and time and again the rather subjective assessment of the size of the penis won out over seemingly objective criteria such as the genetic code. This observation cannot be much of a surprise for scholars drawing on ethnomethodology (see Lecture VII), which strongly influenced research in the sociology of science and whose investigations have repeatedly shown how greatly even laboratory work in the natural sciences is pervaded by everyday ideas. This is just what Kessler and McKenna point out, emphasizing that biological and medical research also rests on society's cultural preconceptions and thus always strives – (so far) unsuccessfully – to lend credence to the dubious thesis that there are two and only two genders (Kessler and McKenna, *Gender*, p. 77).

The arguments put forward by Kessler and McKenna thus tended to overturn the distinction between 'sex' and 'gender', fundamental for many feminists, through their radical or surprising thesis that even seemingly so clearly determinable 'biological sex' is not so clear-cut after all, but that once again social constructions are quite obviously at play. This is sometimes referred to as the 'null hypothesis' in the literature, which Carol Hagemann-White (b. 1942) defines as follows:

> The 'null hypothesis' still seems to me more open to the diversity of women's lives, more radical in its view of patriarchal oppression, namely, that there is no inevitable gender binarism prescribed by nature, only different cultural constructions of gender. After all, we know that the dedifferentiation and plasticity of human beings is extensive enough to trump any hormonal factors or elements that may be present in our physical constitution.
>
> (Hagemann-White, 'Wir werden nicht zweigeschlechtlich geboren …', p. 230)

Kessler and McKenna then linked this 'null hypothesis' with a clear normative-political programme. For in their view, the assumption that there are two dichotomous genders, so typical in our society, almost inevitably leads to the development of a gender-based *hierarchy*, a process in which women are immediately forced into a subordinate social position on the basis of long-standing power relations. If dichotomization is closely bound up with hierarchization and entails 'androcentric' consequences, then the task of feminist theory is to demonstrate that the dichotomy between the sexes is not given in nature. Only ridding ourselves of this dichotomy will provide us with the opportunity to establish relations of equality between individuals over the long term:

> Where there are dichotomies it is difficult to avoid evaluating one in relation to the other, a firm foundation for discrimination and oppression. Unless and until gender, in all of its manifestations *including the physical*, is seen as a social construction, action that will radically change our incorrigible propositions cannot occur. People must be confronted with the reality of other possibilities, as well as the possibility of other realities.
>
> (Kessler and McKenna, *Gender*, p. 164; original emphasis)

Primarily in the English-speaking world, a fundamental and wide-ranging debate on the relationship between 'sex' and 'gender' built on the work of Kessler and McKenna, a debate which quickly came to dominate because British and American anthropology had, as it were, already paved the way for it with studies on 'strange' (from a Western point of view) gender identities in other cultures. The debate took off less rapidly in other countries (see Becker-Schmidt and Knapp, *Feministische Theorien*, pp. 9ff.), in Germany at least only in the early 1990s, where an article by Regine Gildemeister (b. 1949) and Angelika Wetterer (b. 1949) played the key role. In 'Wie Geschlechter gemacht werden' (1992), they took up the debate previously carried on mainly in the English-speaking world. Very much like Kessler and McKenna, to whom they were in any case close because of their ethnomethodological orientation, they pointed out that the distinction between 'sex' and 'gender' is merely an apparent solution in that it merely shifts the biologism to another level. While such a distinction, they asserted, no longer assumes a *social* substance of 'femaleness', instead assuming the existence of a *biological* substance of this kind, this is problematic because no clear biological criteria exist capable of clearly determining sex. What is more, the assumed dichotomy between men and women also entails a latent biologism, because once again, biology is a rather poor guide to dichotomous constructions (Gildemeister and Wetterer, 'Wie Geschlechter gemacht werden', pp. 205ff.).

If this is the case, if the ideas of Kessler and McKenna are correct, then according to Gildemeister and Wetterer this has a number of consequences for sociological theory. For in this case, we can no longer continue to assume that there was once a *pre*social category 'woman' that somehow brought about a gender-specific differentiation at some point in history, which it then continually underpinned. The woman's supposedly physically weaker body, her vulnerability during pregnancy, etc. cannot then serve as the quasi-natural foundation of the gendered division of labour. For if nature and culture are both originary, one can just as well argue that women's childbearing capacity explains their (subordinate) status as that it was cultural and social processes which made this capacity a symbol of their subordinate social status. Anyone identifying women's (natural) capacity for childbearing as the cause of the gendered division of labour, however, is suppressing the fact that

> a hypothetical construction as complex as that of the 'supposition of the possibility of giving birth' is already the result of abstraction and of a classification which can be decoded only if we investigate the cultural meaning with which physical features are endowed in the course of the very process of social differentiation they supposedly explain.
>
> (ibid., p. 216)

While Gildemeister and Wetterer very much remained on the same argumentational tracks originally laid down by Kessler and McKenna, merely discussing the theoretical consequences of such an approach more carefully than their American counterparts, they do draw attention to a fairly unpleasant political consequence of their theoretical framework. It seems to them less and less clear what political goal a feminist approach adopting such a radical anti-essentialist stance might pursue – other than the rather vague hope of abolishing dichotomous distinctions, already articulated by Kessler and McKenna. For it is difficult to reconcile this with conscious attempts to improve the lot of women; at least, a substantial problem arises, because every policy aimed at the advancement of women must first determine who is a woman and who is not. But this, as Gildemeister and Wetterer conclude, merely reifies and redramatizes the old or traditional distinction between the sexes, which it was in fact the goal to get away from – a paradox from which 'there seems no prospect of escaping at the level of action theory' (ibid., p. 249).

It was in fact such political aporias that inspired the critique of this ethnomethodological approach within feminism. It was not only the vagueness of the political programme that attracted criticism. Some scholars also asked whether even these vague hopes were at all justified. For the thesis, found in the work of Kessler and McKenna as well as that of Gildemeister and Wetterer, that dichotomies almost automatically lead to hierarchization, is certainly open to doubt. Above all, one must ask: Does the reverse apply? Does doing away with dichotomies in favour of the notion of several possible genders really banish hierarchical thinking? Experiences with racism point towards a negative answer. Racists do not necessarily recognize just *two* skin colours, but in fact distinguish precisely between 'shades' of colour as they live out their prejudices. In this field at least, it is evident 'that increasing the number of categories offers us no protection from hierarchization, but rather increases the potential for differentiation and hierarchization' (Becker-Schmidt and Knapp, *Feministische Theorien*, p. 80). It is thus quite possible that similar mechanisms are at play in the field of gender relations and that the hoped-for equalizing effects of the abolition of a dichotomous conception of gender will not occur.

But this ethnomethodologically inspired feminism was also criticized for its internal theoretical weaknesses, which were already apparent in the work of the 'father' of ethnomethodology Harold Garfinkel, namely the failure to analyse institutional contexts. The near-exclusive concern with the basic prerequisites of all interaction – critics asserted – had generated an analysis in which institutions, as reasonably stable and orderly arrangements, played almost no role, pointing to meso- and particularly macrosociological shortcomings. This attracted criticism from feminists, who accused those authors deploying ethnomethodological arguments of having largely neglected the institutional contexts in which gender difference is produced (Heintz and Nadai, 'Geschlecht und Kontext' ['Gender and Context'], p. 77). For one would have to investigate empirically *when* and *under which concrete institutional circumstances* gender difference is dramatized or perhaps even de-dramatized. In which institutional contexts does a dichotomous notion of gender play a major role, and in which a fairly minor one? Empirically, one would have to assume that gender differences vary according to context, so that it is not just 'doing gender' that sociology ought to be concerned with. 'Undoing gender' must also be examined (see also Hirschauer, 'Die soziale Fortpflanzung der Zweigeschlechtlichkeit' ['The Social Reproduction of Gender Binarism']):

> For if gender affiliation really is an *achievement* ... then *undoing gender* is ... at least theoretically conceivable. *Undoing gender* as a performative achievement is just as complex as the production of gender, and, like it, by no means gender-neutral.
>
> (Heintz and Nadai, 'Geschlecht und Kontext', p. 82; original emphasis)

However, according to Heintz and Nadai, in order to meaningfully analyse this dialectic of 'doing' and 'undoing' gender, one would have to do some macrosociological groundwork. But in light of the current predominance of microsociological 'gender studies' and a similarly oriented feminist social theory, especially in Germany, there is little prospect of this (ibid., p. 79).

(b) This scepticism about the prospects of feminism embracing the macrosociological level to any great extent is not unjustified, given that there is another branch of feminist theory building, which is hugely influential internationally and which is intertwined with the *philosophical* debate on postmodernity moulded by poststructuralism. In this tradition of thought too, macrosociological analyses play only a subordinate role, in that it tends to consider the relationship between 'sex' and 'gender' at a basic theoretical level, though with the aid of some very different reference authors. Why the debate on so-called postmodernity was so attractive to some parts of the feminist movement may not be immediately apparent, but becomes comprehensible in light of the arguments described below, though these are often highly controversial among feminists.

From the outset, feminist theorists discussed whether the sometimes grotesquely distorted findings of science, which in many cases easily 'proved' women's physical, social, intellectual, etc. inferiority, were merely the expression of a flawed scientific *practice* or the result of an ultimately untenable idea of science (see Sandra Harding, 'Feminism, Science, and the Anti-Enlightenment Critiques'). In the first case, one could hope as a feminist that women's penetration of the core bastions of science would pull the plug on such flawed practice and provide more objective knowledge. But what if the second thesis is correct, if the project 'science' born in the European Enlightenment, which supposedly produces or at least aims to produce timeless truths, is itself questionable? The key stimuli for this second theory of science came from the debates on Kuhn's concept of paradigms (see Lecture I), in which radical critics such as Paul Feyerabend wished to bid farewell to scientific rationality as such, and from the analyses of Foucault (see Lecture XIV), according to which the simple fact that (scientific) truth is directly linked with power means that it cannot claim 'objective' status. These were precisely the arguments deployed by theorists of postmodernity such as Lyotard, who heralded the end of all metanarratives – including science. It is thus no surprise that some feminist social theorists enthusiastically took up postmodern arguments, as they appeared to provide the most comprehensible explanations for the existence of a misogynistic science.

Jane Flax postulated a necessary connection between postmodernity and feminism in a particularly vehement and radical way. She wishes to take leave of the entire project of European Enlightenment, because Kant's famous motto, the 'answer to the question: What is enlightenment?', namely 'Sapere aude! Dare to use your own reason', is suspected of resting on androcentric premises. This is not only because 'enlightenment philosophers such as Kant did not intend to include women within the population of those capable of attaining freedom from traditional forms of authority' (Flax, 'Postmodernism and Gender Relations in Feminist Theory', p. 42), but also because Kant's epistemological position rests on a specific male approach to constituting the subject and self-consciousness, which tends to exclude other forms of thought and rationality:

> In fact, feminists, like other postmodernists, have begun to suspect that all such transcendental claims reflect and reify the experience of a few persons – mostly white, Western males. These transhistoric claims seem plausible to us in part because they reflect important aspects of the experience of those who dominate our social world.
>
> (ibid., p. 43)

While Flax is aware of the dangers of relativism arising from an overly close connection between postmodernity and feminism (if truth or science is no more than a power game, how does feminist theory differ from other power games?), she nonetheless claims that feminist theory should be considered part of the anti-Enlightenment postmodern critique (ibid., p. 42). Because there is no transhistorical knowledge or truth, because knowledge is always contextual and the process of becoming a subject is relational rather than monological and discrete, feminist theory must also admit that it is incapable of producing once-and-for-all truths (ibid., p. 48). This is not easy to accept, but the route back to 'modernity' is impassable, because the core premises of the European Enlightenment, which laid the foundations of modernity, are simply too fraught with problems.

> The notion that reason is divorced from 'merely contingent' existence still predominates in contemporary Western thought and now appears to mask the embeddedness and dependence of the self upon social relations, as well as the partiality and historical specificity of this self's existence.
>
> (ibid., p. 43)

The question, of course, is whether such an interpretation of the Enlightenment in particular and the history of philosophy in general is not extremely one-sided, because it ignores a whole series of currents which aim to avoid, and succeed in avoiding, the very partiality that Flax laments. As is well known, not all modern philosophies have taken radical Cartesian doubt as their point of departure, not all modern social philosophies have anchored themselves in the discrete subject and not all modern epistemologies have claimed to produce timeless truths. This objection to Flax's ideas is certainly of signal importance, but this is not the place to examine it. For us, the crucial point is that the fundamentals of Flax's argument were widely shared. And no author has articulated them with greater impact than the American philosopher and professor of rhetoric Judith Butler.

Butler (b. 1956) achieved her international breakthrough in 1990 with the book *Gender Trouble*, the radical nature of its ideas making her something of a cult figure for feminists. Right from the start of the book, Butler left readers in no doubt as to her reference authors, namely the critics of reason Nietzsche and Foucault (*Gender Trouble*, p. x). This set the course for her argument, in that her concern, like that of Foucault in his early and middle works, is to 'deconstruct' the concept of the subject. Butler immediately makes this clear when she scrutinizes the subject of feminism, arguing that the category 'woman' simply does not exist, because gender identity is only ever formed in a culturally highly variable political context and is thus fluid (ibid., p. 1) – a stance which appeared so plausible in part because the differences between white middle-class women from the West and women from other classes, ethnic groups and parts of the world mean that they only rarely have the same interests and problems. On this view, the women's movement is now too differentiated, too international, for it to be meaningful to speak of 'women' as such.

In emphasizing the contextuality of gender identity, Butler initially differs only marginally from authors such as Kessler and McKenna with their ethnomethodological arguments. For she too asserts that 'sex', as a matter of 'biology', is not a prediscursive, anatomical given, but a 'gendered category' (ibid., p. 6) and that ultimately anatomical sex places no limits on gender identity (ibid., pp. 128f.). But she distanced herself from conventional ethnomethodological feminism with two key theses. First, she claims – though without a great deal of empirical evidence – that it is *hetero*sexual desire that first generates the fixation on two genders within societies: 'The heterosexualization of desire requires and institutes the production of discrete and asymmetrical oppositions between "feminine" and "masculine", where these are understood as expressive attributes of "male" and "female"' (ibid., p. 17). This does not appear particularly convincing, because in terms of desire homosexuals may also differentiate sharply between two genders. Ultimately, though, Butler is not primarily concerned to rehabilitate or privilege homosexual vis-à-vis heterosexual identity, but to do away with the concept and fact of a stable (personal) identity as such. This distinguishes her from ethnomethodological feminists in another respect as well. For she claims, second, that the concept of identity is misleading and that of the subject untenable, as are all philosophies which work with such a concept of the subject. According to Butler, there is simply no stable subject, because subjects do not 'exist' in themselves, but are constituted through language and language games, as she explains in more detail in a later work:

> My presumption is that speech is always in some ways out of our control. ... Untethering the speech act from the sovereign subject founds an alternative notion of agency and, ultimately, of responsibility, one that more fully acknowledges the way in which the subject is constituted in language, how what it creates is also what it derives from elsewhere. ... The one who acts (who is not the same as the sovereign subject) acts precisely to the extent that he or she is constituted as an actor and, hence, operating within a linguistic field of enabling constraints from the outset.
>
> (Butler, *Excitable Speech: A Politics of the Performative*, pp. 15–16)

There is, so Butler tells us, no subject to be found behind language. We are fundamentally spoken. With this idea, which she was later to retract to some extent (see Butler, *The Psychic Life of Power: Theories in Subjection*, especially pp. 1–31), Butler again radicalizes the ethnomethodological position. For while it demonstrated the *efforts* which transsexual individuals, for instance, must make in order to assert their gender identity over and over again, the extent to which 'gender identity' is a major 'accomplishment' and the centrality of the category 'gender' to everyday interaction, for Butler the issue of gender identity seems to morph into a relatively unstructured playing with identities, which are ultimately linguistic constructions (for a critique, see Schröter, *FeMale*, p. 42). The category 'woman', for example, is

> itself ... a term in process, a becoming, a constructing that cannot rightfully be said to originate or to end. As an ongoing discursive practice, it is open to intervention and resignification.
>
> (Butler, *Gender Trouble*, p. 33)

The political project of Butlerian feminism derives from this idea. While it is true that there is no prediscursive ego or subject, according to Butler this does not mean that there is no potential for action. Quite the opposite: precisely because the surplus of linguistic meanings prevents a once-and-for-all fixing of identities, it is always possible for new meanings to be generated and for linguistic signs to be interpreted in new ways. She understands identity as merely a kind of variable practice, as a 'signifying practice' (ibid., p. 144).

> Paradoxically, the reconceptualization of identity as an *effect*, that is, as *produced* or *generated*, opens up possibilities of 'agency' that are insidiously foreclosed by positions that take identity categories

as foundational and fixed. For an identity to be an effect means that it is neither fatally determined nor fully artificial and arbitrary.

(ibid., p. 147; original emphasis)

Though it is again very unclear *through whom or what* these signifying practices change (the concept of 'practice' surely implies a subject or at least action), Butler identifies the political goal of feminism in relatively straightforward fashion: the task of feminism must be to evade the dichotomous notion of gender firmly established in our society by means of parodic strategies, to 'confuse the binarism of gender'. It cannot be the task of feminism and its theorists to forge alliances because this would always run the risk of codifying a substance called 'woman' and thus the desirable diversity, fragility and fluidity of identities (ibid., pp. 14f.); neither should feminists aim to win over state authorities to their side, in order, for example, to achieve a ban on pornography. Butler's distrust of the state is far too great. For her, the only possible strategy appears to entail undermining the existing institution of gendered duality through the ironic treatment and parodying of linguistic and non-linguistic practices. With respect to the prohibition of pornography demanded by many feminists but which she rejects, she puts this as follows: 'In the place of state-sponsored censorship, a social and cultural struggle of language takes place in which agency is derived from injury, and injury countered through that very derivation' (*Excitable Speech*, p. 41). Just as racist discourse can be evaded through irony, it is possible to approach sexist remarks in much the same way, because meanings, including racist or sexist ones, cannot be pinned down once and for all. For Butler, the struggle of language is ultimately *the* key means of bringing the feminist project to a successful conclusion, that is, of abolishing gender duality entirely, such that – as Butler too hopes – there would no longer be any hierarchization. For without stable identities, enduring hierarchies too are practically inconceivable.

Butler's feminist project has enjoyed very wide appeal, not least because her theory presents 'readers with a fascinating world of social models of gender ... one which nurtures dreams of doing away with boundaries and feeds secret desires. Her texts give rise to exotic universes; they conjure up ideas of unfamiliar freedoms and make the constraints present in one's own life appear surmountable' (Schröter, *FeMale*, p. 10). Butler's stance has, however, attracted harsh criticisms as well, with the following three arguments playing a particularly prominent role. First, doubts were raised as to the adequacy of the basis on which Butler's project rests, namely her heavy borrowing from Michel Foucault, whose work profoundly influenced her overall argumentational style. At first sight, it does indeed seem very sensible for feminists to invoke Foucault, who probed into how power works as few others have done. However, because he claims that power transcends place, exists everywhere and thus nowhere, Foucault's understanding of power is too diffuse to allow the kind of concrete analyses of power relations that would be of value to the 'liberation struggle' being carried on by specific groups: 'his account makes room only for abstract individuals, not women, men, or workers' (Hartsock, 'Foucault on Power: A Theory for Women?', p. 169). This is, of course, partly linked with Foucault's conception of subjectivity: he famously declared that the subject (capable of taking action) is *dead* (see Lecture XIV). With certain theorists of feminism in mind, including Butler, critics have asked whether it is helpful to declare as the movement's 'patron saint' (Knapp, 'Macht und Geschlecht', p. 288) the very thinker whose universalist conception of power has blurred all distinctions between power, violence, legitimate rule and authority and who therefore refrained from subjecting existing social relations to a justifiable normative critique (Fraser, *Unruly Practices: Power, Discourse and Gender in Contemporary Social Theory*, pp. 27f.). Foucault, indeed, even questions subjects' capacity to take action, a fundamental precondition for any social movement, including, of course, the women's movement.

Seyla Benhabib has challenged the notion that radical Foucauldian or postmodern approaches can really be reconciled with the priorities of feminists, precisely because postmodern theorists evade the normative concerns of the women's movement. On this view, without the capacity to produce normative critiques and without recourse to a subject capable of taking action, the feminist theoretical project will destroy itself (Benhabib, *Situating the Self*, pp. 213ff.). Criticisms of Butler's Foucauldian, Nietzschean and postmodernist premises share the same concerns. Because, as an adherent of this theoretical tradition, Butler abandons the notion of an autonomous subject capable of taking action, she is ensnared in theoretical problems, which makes her own political project – centred on hopes of a linguistic struggle fought with parody and irony – seem highly questionable. For, as touched on briefly above, she fails to answer the question of *who* is capable of engaging in parody or irony, and it is impossible for her to answer it because she refuses to refer to subjects capable of taking action. In her recent writings Butler has tried to counter this objection by examining the concept of subject in more depth (see *The Psychic Life of Power: Theories in Subjection*): she at least refers to subjects here. But her theory of the subject, which she clearly derives exclusively from the late work of Foucault (see Lecture XIV), is so flimsy and formalistic in comparison with the extensive psychological and sociological literature on identity formation that important issues remain unclarified:

> What is it that enables the self to 'vary' the gender codes? To resist hegemonic discourses? What psychic, intellectual or other sources of creativity and resistance must we attribute to subjects for such variation to be possible?
>
> (Benhabib, *Situating the Self*, p. 218)

Second, also bound up with this point are criticisms of the diffuseness of Butler's political project. Critics assert that she is clearly concerned only to ceaselessly study discourses without ever considering how these are tied to objectified and institutional power relations (Knapp, 'Macht und Geschlecht', p. 305). On this view, Butler can straightforwardly place her hopes in the linguistic struggle, to be fought with the tools of irony and parody, precisely because she airbrushes out institutionalized power structures. But the question arises as to whether language is really everything. Martha Nussbaum, one of Butler's sharpest critics, has put this as follows:

> In Butler, resistance is always imagined as personal, more or less private, involving no unironic, organized public action for legal or institutional change.
>
> Isn't this like saying to a slave that the institution of slavery will never change, but you can find ways of mocking it and subverting it, finding your personal freedom within those acts of carefully limited defiance? Yet it is a fact that the institution of slavery can be changed, and was changed – but not by people who took a Butler-like view of the possibilities. It was changed because people did not rest content with parodic performance: they demanded, and to some extent they got, social upheaval. It is also a fact that the institutional structures that shape women's lives have changed.
>
> (Nussbaum, 'The Professor of Parody: The Hip Defeatism of Judith Butler', p. 43)

The critique is thus that Butler's entire theoretical construct is not only blind to the opportunities for political action open to the women's movement, but is incapable of explaining the past successes of feminism.

Third and finally (and this is closely bound up with the two criticisms mentioned above), Butler was also accused of linguistic idealism (see Becker-Schmidt and Knapp, *Feministische Theorien*, p. 89), insofar as her radical constructivism excludes the possibility that anything at all exists outside of language. Like ethnomethodologically inclined authors, Butler too asserts that 'sex' is a 'gendered category' and that there is thus no solid basis for a biological distinction between men and women. For her, this dichotomy is merely the product of heterosexual desire and is thus changeable in principle. Gender and gender identity are merely linguistic constructs and it is therefore always possible to evade them linguistically – through irony and parody.

However, taking a critical view not only of Butler but also of Kessler and McKenna, it is entirely possible to question whether this is really the case. Are *all* phenomena really linguistically or socially constructed and constructible? Hilge Landweer (b. 1956), for example, has rejected such radical constructivism, a view shared, incidentally, by Martha Nussbaum, though her arguments are different. Landweer asserts that every culture features the categorization of human gender. In this she is in agreement with ethnomethodological feminists as well as Butler. However (and here she begins to differ from these positions), she believes that the development of gender characteristics is closely linked with the *generative* binarism of human beings. She claims that the capacity to give birth is of fundamental importance to every culture and is the starting point for the definition of 'being a woman'. 'While it is true that this does not mean that gender is determined by nature, it does mean that there is an inescapable connection between generative dualism and how culturally variable concepts of gender are structured' (Landweer, 'Generativität und Geschlecht' ['Generativity and Gender'], p. 151). Landweer's thesis is thus that not everything is amenable to arbitrary construction, but that societies feature certain experiences, such as death and birth, which become 'hooks' for specific social constructions. These experiences cannot simply be avoided or annulled. Landweer thus considers Butler's assumption that 'gender difference is produced by discourse' just as naive and false as the essentialist notion that there 'are clearly identifiable natural differences in gender' (ibid., p. 156). According to Landweer, Butler wrongly draws a parallel between *linguistic* signs, which – as we know from Saussure – are random and arbitrary, and *physical* signs or features. But the signs of sex are not entirely arbitrary. There is such a thing as a physical and affective state of being, such as the ability to give birth, which cultural fantasies and linguistic expressions have to 'come to terms with':

> It is not the case that more or less genderless agents enter into a situation in which it is the particular play of signs that produces their positions on the basis of gender sameness or difference. ... Bodily affectivity may be performed, presented and demonstrated and is in this sense symbolic. It is of course possible to trace back the origins of emotions and their expression to social situations. But our involvement in the bodily-affective dimension is nevertheless a

phenomenon sui generis that enters into the 'production' of sociality as a pre-condition for processes of symbolization.

(ibid., p. 162)

According to this critique, Butler persistently ignores this insight. In light of the correct assumption that every reference to 'nature', 'substance' or 'body' is a linguistic event, that such terms are symbolic representations, she concludes that there is nothing outside of the system of language. But the notion of the linguistic or discursive construction of the world is meaningful only if one assumes that there is a reality beyond language (ibid., p. 164). This is an insight of great significance to feminist projects and theories, for theories in which the female body was and is always of eminent importance. Martha Nussbaum, arguing against Butler, puts this as follows:

> And yet it is much too simple to say that power is all that the body is. We might have had the bodies of birds or dinosaurs or lions, but we do not; and this reality shapes our choices. Culture can shape and reshape some aspects of our bodily existence, but it does not shape all the aspects of it. 'In the man burdened by hunger and thirst' as Sextus Empiricus observed long ago, 'it is impossible to produce by argument the conviction that he is not so burdened'. This is an important fact also for feminism, since women's nutritional needs (and their special needs when pregnant or lactating) are an important feminist topic. Even where sex difference is concerned, it is surely too simple to write it all off as culture.
>
> (Nussbaum, 'The Professor of Parody: The Hip Defeatism of Judith Butler', p. 42)

What is being questioned here is whether feminist theory does itself any favours when it goes down the kind of radical postmodernist and linguistic path trodden by Butler.

(c) This criticism is shared by the final school of feminist theory to be considered here, authors who are not prepared to simply abandon the legacy of the Enlightenment in postmodernist fashion, who recognize the macrostructural shortcomings of ethnomethodological and Butlerian writings and for whom the political naivety of these approaches is a thorn in the flesh. As Regina Becker-Schmidt (b. 1937) and Gudrun-Axeli Knapp (b. 1944) have shown (*Feministische Theorien*, pp. 146f.), as a result of the intense and fundamental theoretical discussion of the relationship between 'sex' and 'gender' within the international feminist debate, there have been practically no serious attempts to link philosophical and microsociological studies to meso- and macro-structural analyses, diminishing the explanatory potential of feminist theory. For both ethnomethodologically oriented feminism and Butler have been rightly criticized for failing to clarify in what way 'doing' or 'undoing gender' is dependent on superordinate institutional contexts and how language relates to these contexts. It is thus unsurprising that feminists try to adhere to 'more traditional' sociological theories, while reformulating them in accordance with the feminist project. The writings of Jürgen Habermas, for example, have attracted particular attention not only because they are felt to retain a concrete critical element which seems to be entirely lacking in the work of postmodern theorists and ethnomethodologists, but also because certain concepts found within Habermasian theory, such as that of the public sphere, seem well-suited to analysing political action within the context of society as a whole. Two theorists stand out in this regard, namely Seyla Benhabib, a philosopher and political scientist born in Istanbul in 1950 now teaching at Yale University, who we have frequently cited in this lecture, and Nancy Fraser (b. 1947), also mentioned earlier, to whom we shall now turn briefly to close this lecture.

Fraser, who is also a philosopher and political scientist and like Benhabib also teaches in the USA, has a very positive view of Habermas' theoretical project in many respects, because his theoretical framework, as developed in *The Theory of Communicative Action* for example (see Lecture X), allows for both a macrosociological research perspective and normatively substantial argument. Nonetheless, according to Fraser there is no getting away from certain weaknesses in Habermas' work, particularly from a feminist perspective. First of all, Habermas' rigid distinction between system and life-world, between socially and systemically integrated spheres of action, is implausible. We too drew your attention to the fundamental theoretical problems of his work in our second lecture on Habermas. Fraser's feminist angle of attack is, however, rather different in nature. Above all, she criticizes Habermas for restricting power and the analysis of power mainly to bureaucratic contexts, that is, to the political system. As a result, he is more or less closed, at a basic conceptual level, to the fact that families are also pervaded by (patriarchal) power and must carry out economic tasks, among other things. 'Habermas would do better to distinguish different kinds of power, for example, domestic-patriarchal power, on the one hand, and bureaucratic-patriarchal power, on the other – not to mention various other kinds and combinations in between' (Fraser, *Unruly Practices*, p. 121). Ultimately, as Fraser sees it, while Habermas reads it in a new way, he merely reproduces the old familiar division between the domestic or private sphere on the one hand, in which the raising of children is declared the domain of women, and the male domain of the (political) public sphere on the other. This prevents him from dealing with the fact that this division rests upon an unequal relationship between the sexes (ibid., p. 122).

Nonetheless, Fraser concedes that Habermasian theory has 'genuine critical potential' (ibid., p. 123). But this can be tapped fully only if we understand what she calls the 'social' differently from Habermas. This sphere of the social, so Fraser tells us, can no longer be equated with the 'traditional public sphere of political discourse defined by Jürgen Habermas' (ibid., p. 156). The 'social' is in fact the setting for the discourse on *all* problematic needs. This fundamentally open sphere of action crosscuts the family, economy and state; it is not identical with them. According to Fraser, even 'private' needs are subject to social debate. It is thus only logical that she, unlike Habermas, identifies at least two main types of institution, which discourses tend to depoliticize, namely the market *and* the family. For Fraser, Habermas' categorical framework was capable only of analysing the depoliticizing effect of the market, but not the fact that the traditional family also has such an effect in that it suppressed the needs of women. In this sense, Habermas also failed to see that the public sphere – which Fraser calls the 'social' – must in fact be defined in a rather broader or more comprehensive way. Habermas, she asserts, implicitly assumes that the meaning of the political, that which must be negotiated within the public sphere, is always already established (or was established in the past and then repressed by ideological mechanisms). He is then able to explain the new social movements – and thus the women's movement as well – only by pointing to the penetration of life-worlds by systemic imperatives. But for Fraser, this assumption of causality is simply wrong, at least in the case of feminism (ibid., p. 133). For the women's movement did not develop out of the defence of the life-world against systems, but because women demanded rights and made the formerly privatized relations pertaining within the patriarchal family a political issue. With respect to the question of women's rights, Habermas thus ignores the fact that not just legal equality between men and women, but also the issue of responsibility for raising children, payment or compensation for domestic labour, etc. are thoroughly political matters. According to Fraser, the 'social' is thus also a site of struggle over the meaning of the political, over *new* rights, not merely over *existing* political options or legal interpretations.

> Very briefly, I align myself with those who favor translating justified needs claims into social rights. Like many radical critics of existing social-welfare programs, I am committed to opposing the forms of paternalism that arise when needs claims are divorced from rights claims. And unlike some communitarian, socialist, and feminist

> critics, I do not believe that rights talk is inherently individualistic, bourgeois-liberal, and androcentric – rights talk takes on those properties only when societies establish the *wrong* rights.
>
> (ibid., p. 183; original emphasis)

Fraser's socialist feminism, which draws heavily on Habermasian theory, is clearly structured in a different way than that expounded by ethnomethodologically inspired authors or by Butler. It clearly expresses both her Enlightenment perspective and normative political programme, centred on demands for social rights for women and their struggle to achieve these rights. Fraser does not refer to the diffuse play of power and its omnipresence, or to irony and parody as the only options, but to concrete power structures which hamper the articulation of (women's) needs and which must be fought. This shows once again that feminist ideas can bear fruit only if feminists get to grips with the more general approaches characteristic of modern social theory.

XVIII

A crisis of modernity? New diagnoses

(Ulrich Beck, Zygmunt Bauman, Robert Bellah, and the debate between liberals and communitarians)

The discourse on modernity within the social sciences worldwide has reached a new level of intensity since the 1980s. This discourse was partly stimulated by the criticisms of postmodern theorists. In a certain sense, it was the diagnosis of 'postmodernity' which led scholars to reflect on 'modernity'. The assertion made by theorists of postmodernity that the conception of rationality characteristic of modernity is inevitably linked with aspects of power and can therefore by no means lay claim to universality was bound to inspire contestation. As we saw towards the end of Lecture X, authors such as Jürgen Habermas (*The Philosophical Discourse of Modernity*) refused to accept this assumption, sparking off a complex *philosophical* dispute over the foundations of modernity. But the discourse on modernity was not carried on solely with philosophical arguments. It also raised *genuine social scientific* questions, in as much as new problems arose in modern societies or there was a greater awareness of certain (old) problems than ever before. Sociology at least produced a number of spectacular diagnoses of the contemporary era, which were discussed not only within the discipline but which appealed to a broad public and demonstrated that, despite all the talk of disciplinary crisis, sociology can still contribute highly interesting analyses of contemporary societies. In this lecture we shall deal primarily with three authors who produced powerful diagnoses of the present era in the 1980s, whose effects continue to be felt to this day.

1. When Ulrich Beck (b. 1944) produced his *Risk Society: Towards a New Modernity* in 1986, few would have predicted how tremendously successful it was destined to be. At the time, Beck was an acclaimed professor of sociology at Bamberg, but was by no means well known beyond the boundaries of the discipline; at that point in time, he had published a number of studies on epistemology and occupational sociology which had been well received within the discipline but had failed to attract attention beyond it. In 1986, however, he managed to synthesize a wide variety of empirical findings on the developmental tendencies of modern industrial societies, collating them to produce an analysis of the contemporary era which then took on a particular plausibility in light of a historical event. The accident at the Chernobyl

nuclear power plant, which also occurred in 1986, with its thousands of victims and the radioactive contamination of huge areas, seemed to prove conclusively the thesis developed by Beck in this book, namely that we no longer live in a class society, but in a 'risk society'. Deploying a language which avoided the generally abstract sociological jargon typical of many of his colleagues and which did not conceal the author's dismay or his engagement with the issues, Beck attracted a massive readership.

The book's title and particularly its subtitle (*Towards a New Modernity*) already point to one of Beck's staple lines of argument, namely the claim that a historical rupture has occurred. His forceful thesis, toned down or relativized from time to time, is that previously existing structures are no longer present in the same form, that formerly fundamental social and political processes have lost their significance, making way for *new* dynamics. A rhetorical trope of this kind, which we have met already in the work of Jean-François Lyotard, for example, with his claim that 'metanarratives' have lost all legitimacy, must of course be convincingly backed up. Beck does this essentially by pointing to three novel trends characteristic of society as a whole, each of which he deals with in the three main sections of the book: (a) Contemporary society is a 'risk society' in which the conflicts and structures of traditional class society have lost significance in light of the massive risks produced by industry; (b) it is also a society in which earlier class-based social milieus have disappeared as a result of a massive surge of individualization; and it is (c) a society in which the relationship between politics and science which formerly applied is changing dramatically within the framework of so-called 'reflexive modernization'. We shall now examine these three observations on the contemporary world more closely.

(a) Let us turn first to the idea of the 'risk society', to that aspect of Beck's arguments which, as a result of Chernobyl, has perhaps attracted the greatest attention. Beck's forceful assertion here is that the class society of the nineteenth and early twentieth centuries, with its characteristic tendencies and trends, no longer exists, or at least no longer in such a way that accounts and analyses of the conflicts and processes so typical of class societies can still tell us much about contemporary societies. His diagnosis is that we are now living in a 'risk society' in which old (class) conflicts are being displaced by new conflicts in light of massive risks. The new risks, which are being produced in all industrial societies, do not affect only a specific class or stratum, but tend to affect *everybody*. It has become impossible to protect oneself against such risks and dangers at the *individual* level; the only effective way of countering them is by means of action across classes and even nations. For Chernobyl doused party functionaries as well as collective farmers with radiation; the exposure to radiation was not restricted to Ukraine, but was also detected more than a thousand kilometres away in Western and Northern Europe; chemical accidents are not only a threat to the workers in production plants, but also to those living within a fairly wide radius. Chemical substances do not distinguish between rich and poor, and no one can escape from polluted air for ever. Eventually, they will reach even the health resorts of the prosperous.

Thus, according to Beck, risks and industrial menaces crosscut the class structure; the degree of exposure to risks polarizes societies far less than the ownership of goods or means of production did in the past. Beck's thesis is thus that the existing social scientific tools for analysing class societies have now become obsolete.

> Reduced to a formula: *poverty is hierarchic, smog is democratic.* With the expansion of modernization risks – with the endangering of nature, health, nutrition, and so on – the social differences and limits are relativized. Very different consequences continue to be drawn from this. Objectively, however, risks display an equalizing effect within their scope and among those affected by them. It is precisely therein that their novel political power resides. In this sense risk societies are not ... class societies; their risk positions cannot be understood as class positions, or their conflicts as class conflicts.
>
> (Beck, *Risk Society*, p. 36; original emphasis)

What is this 'novel political power' to which major industrial risks supposedly give rise? To answer this question, Beck points to the special nature of such industrially produced risks. While it was fairly simple to gain an awareness of the problems characteristic of the early capitalist society of the eighteenth and nineteenth centuries at the time because the misery was visible, the poverty was perceptible and exploitation clearly apparent, this is certainly not so in the case of industrial risks. Contemporary menaces are not really tangible. We cannot feel atomic radiation. As consumers, we generally know nothing about the chemical contaminants in the food we consume and as laypeople we do not know what the side-effects of growing genetically modified plants may be. Beck draws attention to the fact that for the most part we only perceive contemporary menaces with the help of scientific knowledge. We cannot do so ourselves, which means that we either trust in the statements of scientists, come what may, or that we as laypeople have to educate ourselves about the science involved, if we wish to challenge the definitional monopoly of scientists, who have very much set the tone so far. For the only way of disputing the assertion that certain chemical substances are harmless, certain limits for pollution levels are sensible and a certain dose of radiation is safe 'as far as it is humanly possible to tell' is through one's own scientific expertise.

The scientific perception of risks is always based on highly complex interpretations of causality; processes of definition always play a major role in analyses of risk. This also means that the definitions produced by the tone-setting science are frequently disputed, as apparent in the simple fact that scientific appraisals often contradict one another. Such disputes among experts tend to leave the layperson at a loss. Beck sums up this observation with the striking claim that in the risk society, consciousness – knowledge – determines being (ibid., p. 53). For in contrast to class society, we are no longer directly affected by various dangers. Paradoxically, these dangers can be explained to us only by means of unfamiliar scientific knowledge. Beck suggests that this is beginning to give rise to an everyday consciousness which has never before existed in this form:

> For, in order to recognize risks at all and make them the reference point of one's own thought and action, it is necessary on principle that invisible causality relationships between objectively, temporally, and spatially very divergent conditions, as well as more or less speculative projections, be believed, that they be immunized against the objections that are always possible. But that means that the invisible – even more, that which is by nature beyond perception, that which is only connected or calculated theoretically – becomes the unproblematic element of personal thought, perception and experience. The 'experiential logic' of everyday thought is reversed, as it were. One no longer ascends merely from personal experience to general judgements, but rather general knowledge devoid of personal experience becomes the central determinant of personal experience.
>
> (ibid., p. 72)

According to Beck, those affected by risks or dangers are not competent to assess their status as affected, because they are dependent on natural scientific analyses. This subjects the natural sciences to a profound process of politicization. They no longer merely establish facts but determine the degree to which people are affected by a particular risk, by laying down maximum and minimum standards for example. According to Beck, this has explosive consequences. For given how great the risks we face in fact are, the public demands that scientists make absolutely no mistakes in determining acceptable pollution levels, yet constantly discovers that they have made such mistakes, which inevitably increases public distrust of the rationality of the natural sciences. It is becoming increasingly apparent that while the natural sciences imply control and prediction, this is exactly what they cannot provide because the side-effects which they produce cannot be controlled, while the chains of causality are too extensive and complex to make clear-cut statements. Who can really say whether a particular substance causes cancer, given that we come into contact with innumerable other substances in everyday life, about whose effects science as yet knows nothing, quite apart from the fact that it is unable to assess how they interact with other substances? But it is not just the aura of control and prediction that traditionally surrounded the natural sciences that is being profoundly undermined. Legal and moral concepts such as 'responsibility' are also proving problematic in the risk society because within the context of large-scale technical production systems based on the division of labour, which are closely entwined with the organs of the state, it has become almost impossible to identify *the* guilty party should a disaster occur.

Beck believes that this critique of the natural sciences, articulated above all by the green movement, is quite justified. In fact, the emerging problems point to a far more profound dilemma. For the applied sciences, particularly the natural sciences, were and are closely bound up with the idea of increasing productivity. Research is carried out first and foremost in order to make better products, facilitate more rational labour processes, etc. The natural sciences are thus incorporated into the logic of wealth distribution, and indeed in such a way that the risks and side-effects to which this distribution and production of wealth give rise are only ever paid attention in retrospect. According to Beck, the sciences suffer from 'economic short-sightedness', making them systematically blind to risks. It is thus wrong to refer to mere 'accidents' in the case of ecological disasters, for example; these are in fact systematically produced by the way in which scientifically guided production functions.

> As they are constituted – with their overspecialized division of labour, their concentration on methodology and theory, their externally determined abstinence from practice – the sciences are entirely *incapable* of reacting adequately to civilizational risks, since they are prominently involved in the origin and growth of those very risks. Instead – sometimes with the clear conscience of 'pure scientific method', sometimes with increasing pangs of guilt – the sciences become the *legitimating patrons* of a global industrial pollution and contamination of air, water, foodstuffs, etc., as well as the related generalized sickness and death of plants, animals and people.
>
> (ibid., p. 59; original emphasis)

Knowledge of these realities makes those living in the risk society both critical of science and believers in it. It is as yet impossible to say what the political consequences of this will be. Beck runs through several possible scenarios for the risk society. In light of the risks of modernization, which can scarcely be denied but are also impossible to clearly interpret, he refers to the possible rise of 'doctrinal struggles within civilization' (ibid., p. 40), as defenders and critics of contemporary industrial society and their science(s) come into conflict over the 'proper road for modernity'. We may enter an age which resembles 'in many respects ... the doctrinal struggles of the Middle Ages more than the class conflicts of the nineteenth and early twentieth centuries' (ibid.), especially given that the very fear of risks, which resist localization, seems to be playing an ever more important role. The pervasiveness of risks and the occurrence of major disasters may lead to an 'interventionist policy of the state of emergency' (ibid., p. 78), to a 'scientific and bureaucratic authoritarianism' (ibid., p. 79).

Yet Beck is no prophet of doom. His book also features optimistic elements, and these ultimately predominate. For he considers it possible that the increasing public awareness of risks may pave the way towards more positive forms of sociation. Beck refers to the fact that the pervasive nature of risks may bring down the barriers between overly specialized areas of responsibility, that science and politics, for example, may be de-differentiated or at least differentiated in a *different* way. This would open up the prospect of a new ecological morality no longer restricted to individual societies, but which, given the *global* nature of risks, could relate to the world as a whole. Beck thus evokes the 'utopia of a global society', which has only become possible with the demise of class society:

> Even if the consciousness and the forms of political organization for this are still lacking, one can say that risk society, through the dynamic of endangerment it sets in motion, undermines the borders of nation states as much as those of military alliances and economic blocs. While class societies are capable of being organized as national states, risk societies generate commonalities of danger which can ultimately be brought under control only within the framework of global society.
>
> (ibid., p. 47; translation corrected)

(b) In Beck's book, these remarks on the characteristic features of the risk society are immediately followed by another long section which analyses the contemporary world. Here, Beck sets out his 'thesis of individualization', which, however (and this is the first criticism), is not really linked closely with his remarks on the risk society, aside from the fact that processes of individualization, like major industrial risks, also dissolve the structures of class society and contribute to the 'demise of class and stratum'. In any case, Beck's theory of individualization is a variation on an old sociological theme, that of the (apparent) decline of traditional ties to community. His conclusion with regard to contemporary Western industrial societies is that a 'capitalism without classes' now exists 'with ... social inequality and all the related social and political problems' (ibid., p. 88), a capitalism in which crafting one's own individual biography is becoming a crucial task, one, moreover, that is proving too difficult for many. For

> ties to a social class recede mysteriously into the background. Status-based social milieus and lifestyles typical of a class culture lose their lustre. The tendency is towards the emergence of individualized forms and conditions of existence, which compel people – for the sake of their own material survival – to make themselves the centre of their own planning and conduct of life. ... In this sense, individualization means the variation and differentiation of lifestyles and forms of life, opposing the thinking behind the traditional categories of large-groups societies – which is to say, classes, estates, and social stratification.
>
> (ibid., p. 88)

This disintegration of formerly stable milieus and ways of life was caused, among other things, by the development of the welfare state, both in Germany and other Western societies, and the expansion of education which occurred in these countries from the 1960s on, which facilitated the collective advance of a broad range of social strata. Here, Beck refers to a collective 'elevator effect', which enabled the 'collective increase in incomes, education, mobility, rights, science, mass consumption', resulting in the 'individualization and diversification of life situations and lifestyles'.[1]

But this surge in individualization is evident not only in socio-economic terms. According to Beck, new forms of living together have also become apparent in the family and kin group, in as much as marriage is now understood as temporary togetherness. Individuals even cultivate relations with their relatives in a selective way – depending on how much they like them, for example. Marriage and kinship are no longer unchangeable institutions; they too have been infiltrated by individual freedom of choice. Roles are no longer predetermined, but constantly negotiated – which involves numerous conflicts, and consequences which are often detrimental to relationships.

---

[1] Due to differences between the English and German editions of *Risk Society*, some of these quotations are translations from the German original, *Risikogesellschaft* (see Bibliography).

> As modernization proceeds, the decisions and constraints on decision-making multiply in all fields of social action. With a bit of exaggeration, one could say: 'anything goes'. Who does the dishes and when, who changes the screaming baby's diaper, who takes care of the shopping and pushes the vacuum cleaner around the house is becoming just as unclear as who brings home the bacon, who decides whether to move, and why the nocturnal pleasures in bed must be enjoyed only with the daily companion duly appointed and wed by the registrar's office. Marriage can be subtracted from sexuality, and that in turn from parenthood; parenthood can be multiplied by divorce; and the whole thing can be divided by living together or apart, and raised to a higher power by the possibility of multiple residences and the ever-present potentiality of taking back decisions.
>
> (ibid., pp. 115–16; translation modified)

Of course, Beck does not take an exclusively positive view of this burgeoning individualization. He certainly appreciates that individuals have vastly more choices and freedoms than they used to. But the decline of milieus and stable ways of life also gives rise to uncertainties which individuals have to cope with. Poorly qualified women, who often slide into poverty following divorce, experience this in a particularly painful way.

(c) Finally, the third section of Beck's book is devoted to the relationship between politics and science in the 'risk society'. Here, he tackles in more depth issues which he had touched on already in the first section and elaborates on the concept of 'reflexive modernization'. Once again, Beck presents a brilliant if very one-sided critique of (natural) scientific rationality and research practice, by taking up and making more pointed arguments articulated by the environmental movement which was so strong in Germany in the 1980s. For Beck, however, this socially pervasive scepticism about, and criticism of, rationality does not indicate the end of modernity, as claimed by Lyotard for example. Rather, Beck believes that modernity has entered a new era in which the principles of modernity come to light more clearly than before. We are seeing the rise of a modernity which is no longer 'divided in half'. For while industrial society, with its naive faith in science, embodied 'simple modernity', the (justified) critique of science indicates the emergence of a new modernity, a 'reflexive modernity'. The critique of technology and science does 'not stand in contradiction of modernity, but rather is an expression of reflexive modernization beyond the outlines of industrial society' (ibid., p. 11). The side-effects and risks produced by industrial societies rebound on these societies when major disasters occur. But dealing with threats in the risk society, the very process of becoming aware of risks, has opened up the opportunity, for the first time, for this modernity to question and *reflect upon* its own foundations, with incalculable consequences for the political process. In a later book, Beck puts this as follows. The concept of 'reflexive modernization'

> connect(s) up with the traditions of self-reflection and self-criticism in modernity, but implies something more and different, namely ... the basic state of affairs that industrial modernization in the highly developed countries is changing the overall conditions and foundations for industrial modernization. Modernization – no longer conceived only in instrumentally rational and linear terms, but as refracted, as the rule of side-effects – is becoming the motor of social history.
>
> (Beck, *The Reinvention of Politics*, p. 3)

As mentioned earlier, Beck's synthesis of these three lines of argument resonated tremendously with many people. In Germany and beyond, *Risk Society* was read as a completely convincing description of the problems of Western industrial societies, prompting sociologists and social theorists to subject the concept of risk to thoroughgoing analysis, while Beck's thesis of individualization was for the most part enthusiastically received.

Beck's theory of individualization converged closely with that of Anthony Giddens, who had placed special emphasis on the transformation of intimate relationships in his books on modernity published in the 1990s. In *Modernity and Self-Identity* from 1991 and above all *The Transformation of Intimacy* from 1992, Giddens too asserted that a historical rupture had occurred in this regard (Giddens refers to 'high modernity' or, no doubt already influenced by Beck, to a 'second modernity'), pointing to the novel impact of expert knowledge on the form of two-person and family relationships. Here, he distinguished between three historical phases of the formation of intimacy. While in premodern times love was understood primarily as sexual passion, which people generally and self-evidently sought outside of marriage, this changed with the dawning of modernity. With the rise of the Romantic notion of love at the latest, when those in love married, they entered into a life-long, emotionally intense relationship, though the inequality of the sexes and thus a sharp distinction between gender roles were taken for granted. Only now, according to Giddens, in 'high modernity' and in an age of love as partnership, are gender roles and all family relationships de-traditionalized. Very much like Beck, Giddens also argues that contemporary relationships are being constantly negotiated. At the same time, individuals have become highly demanding with respect to the satisfaction of their emotional and sexual desires, causing them to search permanently for 'ultimate' fulfilment, though this can never be entirely achieved, a search in which people increasingly follow the guidance of experts. Seeking advice from therapists, from quasi-therapeutic books on child-rearing issues and sexual problems, has according to Giddens become as taken for granted as the reading of guides to the development of an impressive 'personality'.

No doubt in part because of this shared interest in issues of individualization, Giddens, director of the London School of Economics in the 1990s, invited Ulrich Beck to take up a post there. Giddens declared Beck's analysis of the modern world one of the most significant contributions of contemporary sociology. They began a fairly intense collaboration, examining new fields of interest. By the late 1980s, Giddens had turned to the problem of globalization, which he was keen to present as a cultural phenomenon rather than solely an economic one (see Lecture XII). Beck takes a similar approach in his 1997 book *What is Globalization?*, in which he weighs up the opportunities and risks which it entails, though he comes to no very clear conclusions in evaluating the phenomena typical of globalization. These arguments, with their prevailing mood of optimism, captured the Zeitgeist of the 1990s very well. Exaggerating only slightly, it is fair to say that the ideas expounded by Beck and Giddens helped define to a significant degree the debate on risks in modern societies, on individualization and the consequences of globalization as carried on in the culture sections of newspapers, though these ideas were subject to considerable criticism by sociologists. In any event, Ulrich Beck, now professor at the University of Munich and the LSE, has established and edits a book series published by Suhrkamp. Entitled *Edition Zweite Moderne*, this has introduced authors close to his ideas and those of Giddens to a wide readership.

In critically acknowledging Beck's writings, it is fair to say that his analyses of the risks involved in large-scale technical systems were tremendously fruitful (see also *Ecological Politics in an Age of Risk* from 1988), and that in the best tradition of the Enlightenment his work also helped a broad public appreciate the problems faced by modern industrial societies. Beck's approach must also be seen as a valuable, very much theoretically inspired critique of differentiation theory, or at least of those variants which pass off the way in which contemporary Western society is differentiated as more or less inevitable. Because Beck's arguments are genuinely anchored in action theory, his work is characterized neither by the cynical-fatalistic perspective of a Niklas Luhmann nor the views of doom-mongers and historical pessimists. In formulating his diagnosis of contemporary societies, Beck always makes use of an argumentational trope drawn from the legacy of Hegel and Marx, which states that it is always possible for crises to give rise to options for action and productive solutions. His thesis was and is that large-scale technical systems produce their own opponents, who keep alive the prospect of a better future. The concept linked with this hope is that of 'subpolitics', a politics 'from below' opposed to established styles and forms of politics, to a research practice blind to side-effects, and to the denial of citizens' right to decision by means of large-scale technical systems:

> Anyone who stares at politics from above and waits for results is overlooking the self-organization of politics, which – potentially at least – can set many or even all fields of society into motion 'subpolitically'.
>
> (Beck, *The Reinvention of Politics*, p. 99)

Because industrial modernization always produces unexpected side-effects, because side-effects such as risks and threats, individualization and globalization have become 'the motor of social history' within it (ibid., pp. 3, 22–3), there will always be criticism of this form of sociation and attempts to change course. For Beck, modernization is not a linear process. Rather, it can only be conceived as 'refracted' (ibid., p. 3). This is *not only* a criticism of the excessive faith in progress and unilinear view of history characteristic of a fair number of 'traditional' theorists of modernization and evolution. Beck is very much aware that the future is uncertain, that the side-effects produced by industrial society might prove uncontrollable and thus that society might conceivably move towards 'counter-modernities' of a normatively highly problematic nature. It is *also* a forceful critique of Niklas Luhmann's theory of differentiation, in that Beck assumes, quite rightly, that the concrete form which differentiation takes depends on (collective) actors. Beck is among the so-called 'constitution theorists' such as Giddens, Touraine and Eisenstadt, who 'set out to make social processes intelligible in terms of the actions of the members of a society without assuming there to be some underlying transhistorical developmental trend' (Joas, *The Creativity of Action*, p. 231). Beck makes it very clear that in 'reflexive' modernity, or the 'second' modernity differentiation itself has become a problem, that here the actors struggle to achieve the form of differentiation best suited to them. This includes a type of differentiation in which the subsystems are not – as Luhmann described it – entirely cut off from one another. One might say that his work raises the possibility of a 'democratization of the question of differentiation'. Thus, in his theory,

> the questions of functional differentiation are replaced by the questions of *functional coordination*, cross-linking, harmonization, synthesis, and so on. Once again, [the *and*] undermines the *either-or*, even in the realm of systems theory. *Differentiation itself is becoming a social problem*. The way systems of activity are delineated becomes problematic because of the consequences it produces. Why does one delimit science from economics, economics from politics or politics from science *in this way*, and why can they not be intermeshed and 'sectioned' *any other way* in regard

to tasks and responsibilities? How can subsystems be conceived of and organized as both functionally autonomous *and coordinated?*

(Beck, *The Reinvention of Politics*, p. 27; original emphasis)

Yet, much as one may admire the acuteness of Beck's insights and the persuasiveness of his analysis of the contemporary era, apparent once again in the quotation above, his arguments exhibit a number of weaknesses. At least four criticisms or questions arise.

(a) The rhetoric of historical rupture certainly exercises a certain fascination, but – and this applies to both Beck and Giddens – it tempts one to produce overly crude contrasts. One wonders, for example, whether the 'first modernity' was really manifest in highly stable social milieus and ways of life in the rigid way that Beck, seeking to bring out the contrast with the 'second modernity', describes. Conversely, one wonders whether all milieus have really disintegrated and individualization is as far advanced as Beck asserts. Are there not still major differences in how people in different strata and classes fashion their lives and will this not continue to be the case? If so, this would suggest that the structures of 'traditional' class society have not disappeared entirely after all. Ultimately, this strict division between eras leads to an old and highly problematic trope which also plagued 'conventional' modernization theory. The dichotomy between 'traditional' and 'modern' in this 'conventional' theory of modernization now crops up again in a new form, namely the dichotomy between 'modernity' and 'high modernity', 'first' and 'second' modernity, etc. Critics (see Alexander, 'Critical Reflections on "Reflexive Modernization"') thus suggest that, in light of its crude dichotomies, the theory of 'reflexive modernity' put forward by Beck and Giddens is not in fact a new theory but 'conventional' modernization theory in new garb.

(b) Beck's characterization of the (global) risk society and the new political dynamics occurring within it has been criticized in much the same way. Do risks really have such a levelling effect that class-specific problems no longer play any role? Or was this diagnosis of the modern world from 1986 not tailored too specifically to a very distinct situation in West Germany, at a time *before* reunification when the welfare state was still fairly stable, when it was still possible to believe that socio-economic problems and the resulting political processes would play an increasingly negligible role?

(c) Paradoxically, Beck's thesis of individualization seems so pithy because it deploys the concept of individualization as discussed within sociology in a rather indiscriminate way. The term 'individualization' features numerous shades of meaning. It may refer to the release of individuals from traditional forms of sociation as social structures change, the isolation and increasing loneliness of individuals or to people's increasing autonomy or increasing capacity for action. These are just three meanings among several contained within the concept of individualization, and none of them necessarily go hand in hand. It is no more inevitable that release from traditional forms of sociation generates isolation than that isolation automatically means an increase in individual autonomy (see for example Honneth, *Desintegration* ['Disintegration'], pp. 24ff.). But because Beck fails to clearly differentiate between these levels of meaning, his thesis of individualization has a 'shifting' character. His analysis of the modern world is certainly suggestive, but ultimately less clear than it appears at first sight because the reader is not quite sure what exactly is meant by 'individualization'.

(d) We have already alluded to the lack of any connection between Beck's diagnosis of the 'risk society' and his thesis of individualization. This is particularly apparent when Beck articulates his hopes of a better modernity by pointing to subpolitical forms of action and – much like Touraine in the late 1970s – declares the professions and experts the agents of subpolitics (see Beck, *The Reinvention of Politics*, p. 156). Here, the question arises of how collective action is possible in occupational fields whose members embody the very individualism described by Beck. We cannot, of course, exclude the possibility of such action, but Beck tells us nothing about how exactly individualization relates to forms of protest (with good prospects of success). Beck's analysis of the modern world thus proves more problematic and unclear than was and is generally recognized by the writers and readers of the culture sections of newspapers, in which his statements are often interpreted as empirically validated findings (for an attempt to take stock of the theoretical and empirical criticisms of Beck, see Richard Münch, 'Die "Zweite Moderne". Realität oder Fiktion?' ['The "Second Modernity": Fact or Fiction?']).

2. Turning now to Zygmunt Bauman, who caused quite a stir in the late 1980s and above all in the 1990s with his writings on the contemporary era, we would appear at first to find ourselves in familiar territory. For, especially in his most recent work, there are a fair number of arguments which recall certain aspects of the writings of Giddens and Beck dealt with above, such as the thesis of individualization; Bauman asserts, for example, that we must work on the assumption of a 'thoroughly individualized world' (see Bauman, *Postmodernity and Its Discontents*, p. 204). This proximity is not terribly surprising, given that Bauman's work was influenced by close contact with Giddens. But to describe Bauman's writings merely as another variant of the analysis of the contemporary era guided by the theory of individualization fails to capture their significance. For Bauman, the point of departure is a different one. Astonishingly, we have not yet encountered

it in this form over the course of these lectures. Bauman was one of the first social scientific authors to make the Holocaust the starting point for reflections on the nature of modernity and to develop his views on the contemporary era and on ethics *on this basis*.

Zygmunt Bauman was born in 1925, the son of Jewish-Polish parents. After the German invasion of Poland, he fled east to the Soviet Union, marching into Berlin in 1945 as a Soviet soldier. After the war, he had an academic career in Poland as a Marxist sociologist; he was removed from his teaching post in 1968 in the course of an anti-Semitic campaign by the Polish communists. He then went to Israel for a short time and taught in Tel Aviv, before finally ending up in Great Britain, at the University of Leeds, where he made a name for himself within British sociology as an expert on Marxism and hermeneutics. Only relatively late, from the mid-1980s, did he begin to publish writings on the contemporary world more narrowly conceived. *Modernity and the Holocaust* appeared in 1989, *the* book that underpinned his sudden rise to international prominence. He went on to publish a number of other writings, his arguments building partly on his study of the murder of the European Jews. Here, Bauman succeeded in raising (more) serious ethical issues within the debate on so-called postmodernity than had occurred hitherto.

Bauman's sensational interpretation of the Holocaust is that it was not a 'German crime' in the sense that it was solely the particular and unique social and political conditions in Germany that made industrial mass murder possible. Neither does he refer, as Daniel Goldhagen, for example, was to do a little later on (*Hitler's Willing Executioners: Ordinary Germans and the Holocaust*) to supposedly deeply rooted anti-Semitic German traits; unlike classical theorists of the Frankfurt School such as Theodor W. Adorno, he does not seek to explain National Socialism by citing the presence of a large number of authoritarian figures in Germany who made it possible for the Holocaust to happen: 'personal traits do not stop them from committing cruelty when the context of interaction in which they find themselves prompts them to be cruel' (Bauman, *Modernity and the Holocaust*, p. 154). Finally, he does not derive the Holocaust from the dynamics of capitalism, as many Marxists have tried and still try to do.

Bauman's thesis is more ambitious, and more explosive as a result. He claims that the Holocaust was closely linked with modern civilization. It was no accident within modernity, no foreign body, but was in fact profoundly entwined with modernity, and utterly inconceivable without it. 'The Holocaust is a by-product of the modern drive to a fully designed, fully controlled world, once the drive is getting out of control and running wild' (ibid., p. 93). It was thus not the anti-Semitism that has existed for centuries or even millennia that triggered the Holocaust. Bauman correctly points out that anti-Semitism does not and did not necessarily lead to violence, let alone the incomprehensible violence that occurred in the middle of the twentieth century.

> Alone, anti-Semitism offers no explanation of the Holocaust (more generally, we would argue, *resentment is not in itself a satisfactory explanation of any genocide*). If it is true that anti-Semitism was functional, and perhaps indispensable, for the conception and implementation of the Holocaust, it is equally true that the anti-Semitism of the designers and the managers of mass murder must have differed in some important respects from the anti-Jewish sentiments, if any, of the executors, collaborators and complaisant witnesses. It is also true that to make the Holocaust possible, anti-Semitism of whatever kind had to be fused with *certain factors of an entirely different character*.
>
> (ibid., p. 33; emphasis added)

Bauman believes he can identify these factors. In his view, the Holocaust was the result of bureaucratic procedures, and these in turn were the expression of a pursuit of non-ambiguity, clarity and order which has become ever more apparent within modernity, a pursuit which, as soon as the bureaucratic means were available, was realized in the most terrible way. Paradoxically, the murder of the European Jews as well as the millions killed in Stalin's camps were the ultimate consequence of the vision of a better, purer, more unambiguous society. As Bauman states, this mass murder was

> not the work of destruction, but creation. They were eliminated, so that an objectively better human world – more efficient, more moral, more beautiful – could be established. A Communist world. Or a racially pure, Aryan world. In both cases, a harmonious world, conflict-free, docile in the hands of their rulers, orderly, controlled.
>
> (ibid., p. 92)

The reason why the *Jews* in particular were targeted by modern 'rulers' and 'inspectors', was bound up with their position in European societies. Ostracized and never integrated, they were the very embodiment of opacity and undefinability – in societies striving for transparency and certainty, particularly since the dawning of the modern age (ibid., p. 56). Racism was an expression of this modern striving, in as much as it represented the scientized version of the attempt to define purity and impurity; it was underpinned by the idea of a perfect society, a radical idea conceivable in this way only *as a consequence of the European Enlightenment*. For it was the Enlightenment that first enthroned the unhindered objectifiability and plasticity of nature, thus creating the conditions in which it was possible to resolve the unease felt about 'impure' and indefinable people and groups in an active and systematic way, through the so-called 'final solution', that is, bureaucratically organized mass murder (ibid., pp. 68ff.). Here, Bauman adopts what historians call the 'functionalist' or 'structuralist' interpretation of Nazi rule and the Holocaust (though these terms have very little if anything to do with the functionalist and structuralist theories treated in these lectures), according to which the end results of Nazi policies are to be explained not on the basis of Hitler's or other leading Nazis' anti-Semitism, but in light of a specific momentum characteristic of the Nazi bureaucracy, which put policies into practice with great consistency, in fact with greater consistency than anyone had demanded.

> True, bureaucracy did not hatch the fear of racial contamination and the obsession with racial hygiene. For that it needed visionaries, as bureaucracy picks up where visionaries stop. But bureaucracy made the Holocaust. And it made it in its own image.
>
> (ibid., p. 105)

With this interpretation of the Holocaust, Bauman is advancing an interpretation of modernity which focuses laser-like on its dark side. He thus refuses to gloss over the nature of modernity and to save its 'integrity' by describing the Holocaust as a result of Germany's special path – and thus as a one-off accident. Bauman thus belongs among those thinkers who, like Foucault for example, do not believe in the overly harmonious self-image of modernity and wish to hold up a mirror to it as 'archaeologists' or 'genealogists'.

Many aspects of Bauman's analysis pick up the thread of writings in which the shock felt about the Holocaust found particularly clear social philosophical expression. The *Dialectic of Enlightenment* produced by the exiled exponents of the Frankfurt School, Max Horkheimer and Theodor W. Adorno, a book which is profoundly pessimistic about history, is a good example. In the lecture on Habermas, we dealt briefly with this work and its aporias. Echoes are also found in Hannah Arendt's analyses in *The Origins of Totalitarianism* from 1951, and particularly in her highly controversial book *Eichmann in Jerusalem: A Report on the Banality of Evil* from 1963, which also expounded the thesis of the bureaucratic character of national socialist mass murder. But given what we know today, Bauman and his 'forerunners' would have to answer a number of critical questions.

(a) Does the thesis of the bureaucratic character of the Holocaust not underestimate the emotional and spontaneous aspects of the mass murder of the European Jews, the pleasure taken in killing by many of the murderers involved and the underlying anti-Semitic motivation, which made possible the literal slaughter of countless numbers of people beyond bureaucratic directives? Not all Jews were murdered in a quasi-industrial and anonymous fashion in the gas chambers. The killing often occurred in contexts of face-to-face interaction between perpetrators and victims. Analyses such as those produced by Christopher Browning (*Ordinary Men: Reserve Police Battalion 101 and the Final Solution in Poland*), Wolfgang Sofsky (*The Order of Terror: The Concentration Camp*) and Daniel Goldhagen at the very least raise doubts about whether bureaucracy, and the modern pursuit of order and non-ambiguity which it embodies, ought to be viewed as the sole or even key factors in the Holocaust.

(b) We may also ask whether bureaucracy as such can possibly have been such a decisive factor. Was the crucial development not rather the way in which bureaucracy *became an autonomous force*, a process which had become possible within a particular political context, in other words, the unleashing of bureaucracy? This would at least relativize to a degree Bauman's uncompromising evaluation of modernity and of a profoundly modern institution.

(c) We may also ask whether Bauman's analysis, with its emphasis on the pursuit of order expressed within modernity, the attempt to eradicate the indeterminate, does not almost inevitably depict the historical process in an overly sweeping way. Theories about modernity as a whole must be conveyed in detail, with reference to the specific historical processes that led to the Holocaust. Would one not then have to give more weight to the decision-making processes of those in power, and – a particularly important question – pay more attention as well to the role of war in analysing the Holocaust, given that the so-called 'final solution' was adopted at the Wannsee Conference in Berlin in the context of total war? This would do nothing to change Bauman's gloomy vision of modernity. Quite the reverse: wars, far from a rare occurrence in modern times, would have to be paid greater heed as further 'dark' phenomena in an interpretation of modernity. But it might make it possible to explain the Holocaust more precisely than occurs in Bauman's book, which scarcely mentions war and its consequences as conditions of possibility for the Holocaust.

(d) Finally, we may wonder whether Bauman's overall vision of modernity, his near-exclusive focus on state power and bureaucracies, does not tempt us to push the 'positive' aspects of modernity into the background, such as modern forms of autonomy and democratic self-government. While Bauman does attempt to overcome the hopelessness of the *Dialectic of Enlightenment* by Horkheimer and Adorno, his analysis of the contemporary world is also overly gloomy in many respects; its 'darkness' sometimes echoes Foucault's perspective on modernity and seems similarly implausible at times (for a more detailed analysis, see Joas, *War and Modernity*, pp. 163ff.).

But Bauman, exhibiting tremendous productivity, did not stop at this diagnosis of modernity. In the 1990s, he seized the opportunity to link his reflections on modernity with what he called 'postmodern ethics', an ethics intended both to learn specific lessons from the Holocaust and the other dislocations of modernity and to take into account what he views as contemporary postmodern social relations.

In light of Bauman's reflections on the connection between Holocaust and modernity outlined above, it will come as little surprise that he is no longer able to believe in the idea of moral progress over the course of history, let alone that the structures and patterns of thought so typical of modernity could promote such moral progress (Bauman, *Postmodern Ethics*, p. 229). On the contrary: Bauman believes that the moral discourse of modernity itself has consistently produced insurmountable contradictions. For him, this discourse assumes that there are ethical prescriptions which are applicable to and which are bound to make sense to everyone, that it is possible to justify such moral rules in a consistent way and that there can be unambiguous resolutions of all morally contested predicaments. But according to Bauman, it is this very pursuit of non-ambiguity, purity and certainty which, in its most consistent and radical form, led to the Holocaust. Thus, if there is a lesson to be learned from history, it is that we have to put up with ambivalence and ambiguity. This applies in particular to the field of ethics and morality. We must therefore accept that a 'foolproof – universal and unshakably founded – ethical code will never be found' (ibid., p. 10). Furthermore, Bauman believes that moral phenomena are inherently non-rational and that morality is *not* to be found in organizations and institutions. Shaken deeply by the fact that, under fascism and communism, modern institutions such as the German and Soviet bureaucracy could eliminate all their members' moral scruples and legitimate mass murder without further ado, Bauman concludes that *it is impossible to locate morality within the social sphere*. Rather, morality is something deeply personal, something *pre*social – and we must recapture this insight *against* modernity, which would have social institutions or even society speak for the conscience of the individual, but which paved the way for the almost inconceivable crimes of the twentieth century because of this.

> To let morality out of the stiff armour of the artificially constructed ethical codes (or abandoning the ambition to keep it there), means to re-*personalize* it. Human passions used to be considered too errant and fickle, and the task to make human cohabitation secure too serious, to entrust the fate of human coexistence to moral capacities of human persons. What we come to understand is that that fate can be entrusted to little else; rather, that that fate may not be taken proper care of.
>
> (Bauman, *Postmodern Ethics*, p. 34)

Bauman's postmodern and person-oriented ethics leans on that of the moral philosopher Emmanuel Levinas (1906–95), born in Lithuania, and naturalized in France in the 1930s, for whom 'being for the other' was the basic mode of human subjectivity. This thinker, who elaborated his key motifs by grappling with Husserl and Heidegger, had for long been paid little attention, though Paul Ricoeur (see Lecture XVI) in particular made frequent mention of him. Only when those thinkers who initially adopted a highly relativistic stance turned to ethics, as in the case of Derrida, was Levinas' work paid more attention. As Bauman understands Levinas, who was deeply imbued with Talmudic scholarship, *ego* is responsible for *alter*; the experience of the other is always shaped by my moral obligation and responsibility with respect to this other – *regardless of whether this other will ever reciprocate my care*.

> In a moral relationship, I and the Other are not exchangeable, and thus cannot be 'added up' to form a plural 'we'. In a moral relationship, all the 'duties' and 'rules' that may be conceived are addressed solely to me, bind only me, constitute me and me alone as an 'I'. When addressed to me, responsibility is moral.
>
> (ibid., p. 50)

This responsibility of *ego* or the individual that characterizes Bauman's postmodern ethics does not lead to relativism, in contrast to the stance of more than a few postmodern authors, for whom, very much in line with Nietzsche, moral criteria are merely the expression of power interests. It is true, Bauman tells us, that it is impossible to justify a morality that applies to everyone. But this does not necessarily lead to a relativistic position, precisely because *ego* is constantly called upon to be there for the other, to take responsibility for him. His postmodern ethics – according to Bauman – does not, therefore, reflect an attitude summed up by the phrase 'nothing we can do about it' (ibid., p. 14).

But for Bauman, a postmodern ethics of this kind is not only justified in light of *past* (catastrophic) experiences with the societies and systems of thought that have characterized modernity, but also because the contemporary structures of the social rule out any notion of universality, overarching rationality and non-ambiguity in any case. The fluidity and transience of seemingly fixed social relations have become too obvious for that. Bauman states that fundamental social and cultural patterns have changed massively since 1945 or since the collapse of the Soviet empire at the latest. Like Giddens and Beck, he asserts that a fundamental historical rupture has occurred, and he attempts to lend plausibility to this idea in a rather similar way. He too refers to the decline of the nation and family as the social forms which formerly cushioned individual insecurity and thus guaranteed stability. Nothing, however, has replaced them, so that the individual is our only remaining point of reference. Privatized individuality is thus at the core of postmodernity – which has significant consequences for politics (see Bauman, *In Search of Politics*, pp. 38ff.). Bauman portrays these consequences in a markedly more negative way than Beck and Giddens. In his opinion, the advance of the market in the wake of 'neoliberal' policies and ideology has ultimately led to increasing insecurity; in light of the fundamental fragmentation of political relations, this is a threat both to civil society as well as the critical discourse of intellectuals. Thus, according to Bauman, rather than greater freedom as such, postmodernity merely instigated a shift from citizen to consumer (Bauman, *In Search of Politics*, p. 78).

Bluntly put, Bauman's thesis is that the typical figures of modernity were the soldier and the producer, both firmly integrated into state organizations and industrial firms distinguished by extreme harshness and stability. These figures, he claims, have declined in significance in contemporary conditions of postmodernity. They have been replaced by the 'tourist' as the typical embodiment of this postmodern framework, the epitome of the 'negation' of stable patterns: the tourist never truly belongs to the society in which he happens to be present, because he rapidly switches his place of residence, never really commits to anything and seeks short-term emotional gratification rather than stable relationships. For Bauman, the 'tourist' is the figure that represents, if you will, a kind of answer to the instability and insecurity of postmodern social structures and the irreversible ambivalence of postmodern culture.

> Human action has not become less frail and erratic; it is the world it tries to inscribe itself in and orient itself by that seems to have become more so. How can one live one's life as pilgrimage if the shrines and sanctuaries are moved around, profaned, made sacrosanct and then unholy again in a stretch of time much shorter than the journey to reach them would take? How can one invest in a lifelong achievement, if today's values are bound to be devalued and inflated tomorrow? How can one groom oneself for life's vocation, if skills laboriously acquired become liabilities the day after they become assets? When professions and jobs disappear without notice and yesterday's specialisms are today's blinkers?
>
> (Bauman, *Postmodernity and Its Discontents*, p. 88)

In light of the nature of postmodern social structures as he sees them, Bauman adopts, so to speak, a heroic yet sober attitude. As people affected by economic globalization, we must fight against these processes, but we can no longer do so with the conceptual tools of modernity. It has simply become impossible to produce universalist arguments that assume the existence of *one single* rationality, etc., because postmodernity is distinguished by irresolvable ambivalences. We must recognize that we live in a 'rainbow-like, polysemic and manifold culture, unashamedly ambiguous, reticent in passing judgements, perforce tolerant to others because, at long last, it becomes tolerant of itself, of its own ultimate contingency and the inexhaustibility of interpretive depths' (Bauman, *Modernity and Ambivalence*, p. 159). Here, Bauman emerges as a sharp critic of communitarian authors, whom he believes wish to do away with this need for tolerance in favour of the idea of a stable and value-laden community. Bauman opposes this idea. For him, in much the same way as Lyotard, neither a Habermasian consensus nor the communitarian idea of a values-based community is conceivable or even desirable. Instead, Bauman advocates the idea of a 'polycultural society' (*In Search of Politics*, p. 199), characterized by pluralism and tolerance.

Starting from these premises, we may question how, concretely, we are to imagine the battle against the effects of economic globalization, for example. For while Bauman always calls for solidarity between human beings and for the retention or expansion of a welfare state, as conceived in Great Britain at the end of the Second World War under the 'radical liberal' Beveridge (Bauman, *Postmodernity and Its Discontents* p. 205), he leaves his readers unclear about how this solidarity is to be brought about and where it is to come from, how the battle over certain institutions of the welfare state, as a *collective* and above all ongoing battle, can be fought (successfully) in the first place, if it is true, as Bauman states, that the thesis of individualization must be the ultimate point of departure of all political and normative analyses. But it is possible to question Bauman's postmodern ethics at an even more basic level. For it is surely hazardous, and contradicts utterly the insights gained by sociology in particular, to conceptualize moral feelings as *pre*social givens, as Bauman does in borrowing from Levinas. It may be true that a fair number of modern institutions have proved profoundly immoral. But this certainly does not mean that morality generally is 'learned' outside of all institutional contexts. It may well be that the Kohlbergian theory of moral development, for example, is overly cognitivist or rationalistic (see Lecture XVII). Conversely, however, criticisms of Kohlberg cannot seriously lead one to conclude that morality develops *beyond* social contexts. The debate between Kohlberg and Gilligan did *not* revolve around the issue of the social genesis of morality as such, but around the form of this social development and its consequences for the development of (gender-specific) morality – and for good reason. A theory of morality must of course be capable of showing how the shocking encounter with the 'Other' penetrates socially acquired morality; but this also represents a social rather than presocial experience (see Bernstein's argument with Levinas in *The New Constellation*, and Joas, *The Genesis of Values*, pp. 103ff.). Because Bauman does not really pay attention to these genuine sociological and social psychological issues, but simply anchors his arguments without further comment in Levinas' philosophical conception (though certain doubts crop up repeatedly in his work), one of the central foundations of his oeuvre as a whole remains theoretically undeveloped.

For a more serious attempt to deal with these empirical and theoretical-normative issues, touched upon but never really tackled by Bauman, we have to turn to an author whom we have met already in connection with the renewal of Parsonianism (Lecture XIII). We are referring to Robert Bellah, whose analysis of the contemporary era in the mid-1980s did much to stimulate the communitarian movement alluded to above.

3. To fully appreciate the sometimes heated debates on Bellah's book and on communitarianism, which first arose in the USA, we must first review at some length the special features of the social scientific landscape in the USA in the 1970s and 1980s. We have mentioned that the locus of theoretical work within the discipline of sociology shifted to Europe from around 1970. While theoretical approaches such as neo-utilitarianism and neo-Parsonianism always enjoyed a strong position in the USA in particular, the novel and above all synthetic approaches were chiefly developed in Europe, where the great scepticism towards overly theoretical foci was far less evident than within the highly professionalized world of American sociology. But in the early 1980s at the latest, parts of the American social sciences at least changed course perceptibly, not least under the influence of certain developments in (American) political science and philosophy. The USA had again become fertile ground for the ongoing development of social theory.

The developments to which we are referring are closely linked with the name of John Rawls (1921–2002), who initiated something of a revolution in both disciplines with his 1971 book *A Theory of Justice*, insofar as he managed to bring normative-political issues back to the centre of social theoretical debates. Rawls' book was so novel and inspired such enthusiasm, as well as such controversy, because since the Renaissance modern political thought had essentially moved between two extremes. To simplify somewhat, and disregarding controversies over interpretive details, we can state that the work of Niccolò Machiavelli (1469–1527) initiated a far-reaching polarization of political thought. As one of the first modern political thinkers, he attempted to eliminate ethical problems as central concerns of political philosophy. In his view, political theorizing should not concern itself with ethical issues, but solely with the actual conduct of political actors fighting for power or the strategies deployed in this power game. Machiavelli's writings thus formed the starting point for the division of ancient 'practical philosophy' into an exact science of political rationality on the one hand and a theory of morality on the other. A 'division of labour' was established between a theory of politics stripped of morality, which attended to the actual functioning of political institutions or systems without consideration of ethical issues, and a politically neutralized theory of morality or virtue, whose public relevance was no longer clearly apparent (see Otfried Höffe, *Strategien der Humanität* ['Strategies of Humanity'], pp. 11ff.). There has of course been no lack of attempts in the history of modern philosophy to bridge this chasm; opposing tendencies towards the renormativization of political thought have been far from unusual. Yet it is remarkable how strongly this 'division of labour' was retained and continued to imbue the structure of political-philosophical discourse until the 1960s. Particularly in the post-war era, normative political philosophy and empirical political science in the USA existed side by side but with almost no connections between them. Rawls' *A Theory of Justice* was the first major – and spectacular – attempt to re-establish the link between ethical issues and public decision-making processes in a period which saw little activity in this particular respect, and in such concrete fashion that the relevance of practical philosophy seemed immediately apparent. Rawls thus succeeded in linking the two currents of political-philosophical thought, formerly separated by a well-nigh unbridgeable chasm. His work thus triggered the spectacular return of normative issues to the centre of political theory.

The distinguishing feature of Rawls' work was his placing of the value of *justice* at the very centre of his theoretical reflections and his attempt to derive from it what a 'just' institutional and power structure of societies and a just distribution of goods might look like. Practical philosophy, Rawls was convinced, must begin with the *institutional structure of society as a whole*, because this has a decisive influence on the life chances of the society's members. A moral philosophical approach focused primarily on discrete individuals, he thought, would be largely ineffective given the complexity of modern societies. According to Rawls, there is very little prospect of tackling pressing moral issues of poverty, imbalances of power within society, etc. through an ethics focused solely on individual conduct. A theory of justice must therefore begin with basic social structures, which he expresses in the following way in one of the first sentences of the book: 'Justice is the first virtue of social institutions' (Rawls, *A Theory of Justice*, p. 3). But how do we know whether existing social institutions or societies are just? According to Rawls, this can be determined by asking a simple question, which goes something like this: 'Would rational human beings really establish existing institutions or societies if they had the chance to create new social structures from the bottom up?' If the answer is yes, the various institutions or societies are just. Of course, Rawls' question, as you will likely have noticed immediately, is very simple, too simple, because one can go on to ask what rationality is in the first place, who is to be considered a 'rational person', etc. This would seem to suggest that this Rawlsian question, which supposedly provides us with a precise criterion for assessing a society or its institutions, entails so many uncertainties and such opacity, that to resolve it in a way that satisfies everyone involved seems quite inconceivable.

Rawls was of course aware of the weaknesses of such a question, but did not believe that these rendered it meaningless. Rather, he thought that it was possible to remedy these through a kind of thought experiment, deployed in much the same way already in the history of philosophy – in the work of the social contract theorists of the European Enlightenment for example. Rawls' argument is as follows. When people attempt to assess rationally the justice of contemporary institutions or to discuss rationally a new and just society of the future, they inevitably have different desires, needs, values, life plans, political and religious beliefs, power resources, goods, etc. In view of all these differences, we cannot expect to reach a consensus. However, and this is Rawls' proposed thought experiment, such a consensus would be within reach and a rational decision acceptable to all, and therefore just, could be made, if the various people involved in the discussion *did not know their own needs, values, goals, resources, etc.* One would have to create a situation in which the parties to the debate were *not* in the picture about their own place in society, so that they would necessarily discuss the matter at hand in impartial fashion. Such a situation would look like this:

> First of all, no one knows his place in society, his class position or social status; nor does he know his fortune in the distribution of natural assets and abilities, his intelligence and strength, and the like. Nor, again, does anyone know his conception of the good, the particulars of his rational plan of life, or even the special features of his psychology such as his aversion to risk or liability to optimism or pessimism.
>
> (ibid., p. 137)

In this discussion a 'veil of ignorance' would hang over those involved and their individual place in society, to use Rawls' metaphor. And it is this veil that prevents people from agreeing, for example, to extreme differences in wealth or power in the basic social structure, because they would be faced with the possibility of being at the bottom of the social ladder. No one, for example, would vote for slavery, Rawls suggests, if she ran the risk of being a slave herself.

With this thought experiment, this idea of the 'veil of ignorance', Rawls believes that he now has a criterion at his disposal for assessing whether social structures or social decision-making processes are truly just. They are just if those affected by the structure of a society or by social policy decisions would have agreed to the establishment of these structures or to these decisions in such an artificial situation of ignorance.

All of this sounds rather abstract and one may suspect that it has no major political consequences. In fact, though, Rawls reaches conclusions on the basis of this idea of the 'veil of ignorance' which lead to fairly specific political demands. He claims that, under the veil of ignorance, the parties to the discussion would agree on two fundamental principles.

> First: each person is to have an equal right to the most extensive basic liberty compatible with a similar liberty for others.
>
> Second: social and economic inequalities are to be arranged so that they are both (a) reasonably expected to be to everyone's advantage, and (b) attached to positions and offices open to all.
>
> (ibid., p. 60)

The first principle states that in a state of ignorance people will incline towards a form of society in which basic rights such as freedom of expression, freedom of religion, the right to vote, legal security, the right to own property, etc. are guaranteed, because everyone wishes to enjoy these rights and is unwilling to risk losing them in a society that upholds none or only certain of them. Clause (b) of the second principle aims to establish a meritocratic society in which one's achievement rather than, for example, criteria of birth, determines one's position, in which aristocratic origins for instance are not a prerequisite for holding certain political offices. The first clause (a), which sounds harmless enough in itself and which has been discussed in the literature under the term 'difference principle', has in mind a kind of socio-political programme which is reminiscent in some ways of left-wing liberal thought (in the German sense), because this principle states that the organization of social inequality and accompanying distribution of goods can no longer occur 'naturally' in a future just society. For the expression 'to everyone's advantage' excludes, for example, that the wealth of a society as a whole increases at the expense of certain groups of people. For example, on this view, the argument that it is necessary to lower the wages of the lowest wage groups in order to maintain Germany's status as a good place to do business and to secure or augment the wealth of society as a whole, would presumably be deemed unjust. According to Rawls, who differs profoundly from Castoriadis' radical ideal of equality in this respect, social inequalities are often unavoidable; social inequalities will in fact often increase. But this is just only if the inequalities are also to the advantage of the least well-off. This is what the expression 'to everyone's advantage' means. To illustrate this through an example: it may well make sense to privilege the highest wage earners in a society by offering top management even more money in the hope that they add even more to the overall wealth of society through their efforts. But according to Rawls, this approach is feasible *in a just society* only if the lowest wage groups, the unemployed or welfare recipients will also gain appreciably from it, if this increase in society's wealth also benefits the underprivileged, through wage increases, increased unemployment benefit or more generous income support. Rawls' political philosophy thus leads to something of a dynamic conception of welfare; it may be read as a call for social policies oriented towards the well-being of the weakest in a society, but which also take into account the advantages of the division of labour, societal differentiation and thus social inequality, which must also be acknowledged.

As we have emphasized, Rawls' political philosophy attracted enormous interest. His idea of the 'veil of ignorance' prompted other thinkers to seek criteria for assessing just/unjust procedures in much the same way. While Habermas' idea of (domination-free) discourse (see Lecture X) exhibits significant differences from Rawls' figure of thought, it owes to it key insights, in as much as Habermas has always been oriented towards, and his work has always been informed by, the strengths and weaknesses of the Rawlsian programme.

While Rawls' argument was brilliant, there was no absence of criticism – one specific form of criticism in particular. From the early 1980s on, what attracted criticism was not so much the (socio-)political consequences of Rawls' programme as the highly individualistic premises of his line of argument as a whole. According to these critics, Rawls clung to an overly atomistic conception of human existence. This triggered an explosive controversy in social theory.

The controversy to which we are referring was initiated in spectacular fashion by the American political scientist Michael Sandel (b. 1953), who put together a brilliant critique of the idea that the just takes priority over the good, as assumed by Rawls, in his 1982 book *Liberalism and the Limits of Justice*. He thus laid the first milestone in the debate between so-called liberal and communitarian political philosophers that was now taking off.

Rawls began his political-philosophical reflections with the statement that 'justice is the *first* virtue of social institutions'. He was thus expounding the view that it cannot be the task of philosophy to label certain values, certain ways of life, certain social structures as good in themselves, as Aristotle for example did in a quite taken-for-granted way. For in a pluralistic society, such an endeavour would almost inevitably injure certain individuals' notions of the 'good life'. On this view, the task of contemporary philosophy can only be to determine *formal* criteria for bringing about *just* decisions. This is why Rawls insisted on the priority of the just over the good. All philosophy has to do is keep its eye on decisions, making sure they are fair and just; it is not for it to comment on which values and specific ways of life people ought to choose as they go about their lives.

It is this that Sandel criticizes. His thesis is that Rawls' individualist point of departure in conceptualizing the 'veil of ignorance' is implausible and quite incompatible with the notion of the 'difference principle'. It is not only Rawls that Sandel has in mind here, but he focuses on him because he considers him a particularly skilful exponent of a political-philosophical liberalism, which is problematic or internally incoherent because of its premises. He sums up the liberal premises with which he is unhappy as follows:

> society, being composed of a plurality of persons, each with his own aims, interests, and conceptions of the good, is best arranged when it is governed by principles that do not themselves presuppose any particular conception of the good; what justifies these regulative principles above all is not that they maximize the social welfare or otherwise promote the good, but rather that they conform to the concept of right, a moral category given prior to the good and independent of it.
>
> (Sandel, *Liberalism and the Limits of Justice*, p. 1)

Sandel wishes to tackle this basic 'liberal' conception of moral philosophy, which appeared in the work of Kant; he wants to challenge the Kantian and Rawlsian thesis of the primacy of that which is right and instead underline the limits of the principle of justice – which is why he called his book *Liberalism and the Limits of Justice*. Sandel draws attention to one consequence of Rawlsian philosophy in particular and the premise which it entails that the right has priority over the good. This states that principles of justice can be defined independently of conceptions of the good: 'This foundational priority allows the right to stand aloof from prevailing values and conceptions of the good' (ibid., p. 18). But, according to Sandel, this implies a definition of the human individual with major consequences. If we take Rawls (and other liberals) at their word, then this would mean that it is not the content of our goals, values, desires, etc. that play the decisive role in our identity, but merely our *capacity to choose* (rationally) certain goals, values and desires. Ultimately, though, this would mean that the self exists independent of its specific goals, desires, values, etc. Thus, what is assumed is 'a self which must be prior to the ends it chooses' (ibid., p. 19); the suggestion is of 'the unity of the self as something antecedently established, fashioned prior to the choices it makes in the course of its experience' (ibid., p. 21).

Thus, Sandel's criticism is that Rawls' theoretical construct as a whole presupposes a subject which is radically emptied, or which can be emptied, of all 'content', those specific desires, goals, values, etc. The liberal (Kantian or Rawlsian) concept of the person is that of an 'unencumbered self' and implies that individuals can distance themselves completely from their qualities, values and ties and choose them (rationally). This is the only way to uphold the priority of the right over the good. But can we seriously assume that people who feel deeply drawn towards certain values, distance themselves from these values in order to enter into a discourse on justice which may call these very values into question? Further, why should those who take part in the discussion comply with its findings? Rawls' individuals in his thought experiment are conceived so abstractly that it remains quite unclear whence they get the moral motivation to put the conclusions of the discussion seriously into practice. According to Sandel, the entire thought experiment is based on the unrealistic notion of an isolated and unencumbered self, which inevitably produces inconsistencies in Rawls' overall theoretical architecture.

This is clearly apparent in Sandel's analysis of Rawls' difference principle, when he examines his call for welfarist policies that take into account the most disadvantaged groups within a society. For this call for policies intended to integrate all groups within a society into a 'political community' automatically falls back on a language which acknowledges *intersubjective* goals and thus a particular idea of the good. This contradicts the highly individualistic premises of Rawls' thought experiment. 'In his discussion of the idea of social union, Rawls carries his intersubjective language from common assets to common ends and purposes, and in rhetoric that comes perilously close to the teleological, speaks of human beings realizing their common nature as well' (ibid., p. 81). Sandel's objection to Rawls here is much the same as Parsons' objection to the utilitarians, above all Hobbes (see Lecture II). Against the various attempts to solve the 'problem' of social order with utilitarian means, Parsons claimed that grasping the limits of these utilitarian premises themselves was the only real way of resolving anything. Sandel argues in much the same way with respect to Rawls, claiming that the normative demands entailed in his difference principle are comprehensible only if one abandons the highly individualistic premises of his 'veil of ignorance' situation.

Ultimately though this can only mean that these premises themselves are problematic, including the notion that the right takes priority over the good. Sandel thus calls for this relationship between the right and the good to be reversed – and this is the key issue in the dispute between so-called liberals and communitarians. The reasons for this are as follows. Anthropologically speaking, it is problematic to assume that people determine their goals and desires individually and more or less monologically, quite apart from the fact that such a notion, against our everyday intuition, conceives of the self as 'empty of substance': 'To imagine a person incapable of constitutive attachments ... is not to conceive an ideally free and rational agent, but to imagine a person wholly without character, without moral depth' (ibid., p. 179). Sandel counters this with the claim that people live in communities and formulate their goals, values and desires *in association with others*, that is, they are integrated into certain institutions and social structures. These (intact) social structures are necessary if the individual is to be able to understand himself in the first place. It is only when we are clear about what is 'good', what kind of way of life we want for ourselves, that we are in a position to discuss justice. Rawls' premises, meanwhile, abstain from the collective preconditions for individuality without which, according to Sandel, it is impossible for a subject to be constituted in the first place. And this is why – so Sandel tells us – Rawls' theoretical construct is beset with such tremendous difficulties.

But Sandel is not content to criticize the anthropological or basic conceptual framework of Rawlsian theory. His critique is also aimed at the assumption that the political stability of a given polity can be based exclusively on individual rights and otherwise has no basis in values. For Sandel, a merely 'procedural republic' has in reality no firm foundations; these lie in collective values which go beyond a mere orientation towards abstract or formal issues of justice. The American Sandel sees a severe crisis gripping American society and politics, a result of the fact that politics is now understood solely as a battle over rights, while the issue of what is good is neglected.

> In our public life, we are more entangled, but less attached, than ever before. It is as though the unencumbered self presupposed by the liberal ethic had begun to come true – less liberated than disempowered, entangled in a network of obligations and involvements unassociated with any act of will, and yet unmediated by those common identifications or expansive self-definitions that would make them tolerable. As the scale of social and political organization has become more comprehensive, the terms of our collective identity have become more fragmented, and the forms of political life have outrun the common purpose needed to sustain them.
>
> (Sandel, 'The Procedural Republic', p. 124)

American society is in crisis because of a dearth of common values which are the sole means of making a society truly stable. While Sandel himself has no specific common ethics to offer, he is convinced that Rawls' normative theory with its primacy of the just is quite incapable of resolving this crisis.

After some initial heated disputes, the debate between liberals and communitarians set in motion by Sandel, among others, led to a gradual rapprochement between the two positions. Authors such as the philosophers and political scientists Charles Taylor and Michael Walzer (b. 1935) in the communitarian camp were compelled to revise their stance, at least mildly, as were their liberal opponents, the champions of a procedural ethics such as Rawls or Jürgen Habermas, as we mentioned towards the end of Lecture X. The rapprochement revealed that the critique of certain forms of individualism is shared by both camps. Both distance themselves clearly from 'utilitarian' and 'expressivist' individualism, which has allegedly attained hegemonic status in American culture (and perhaps Western culture generally). The problems of such a utilitarian and expressivist individualism were analysed, not in a philosophical way, but in a comprehensive *sociological* study, by Robert Bellah and his colleagues, lending empirical substance to the rather abstract philosophical debates carried on hitherto.

Habits of the Heart: Individualism and Commitment in American Life by Robert N. Bellah, Richard Madsen, William M. Sullivan, Ann Swidler and Steven M. Tipton is one of the great analyses of the contemporary era produced in the 1980s. For the authors of this book, which first appeared in 1985, managed to produce a critique of an individualism gone astray, one backed up by solid research. Not only this, but the book also dealt with the crisis of modern societies diagnosed by Sandel, societies in which – on this view – the lack of a shared framework of values threatened to undermine social stability. As a student of Parsons in the 1960s, Bellah himself was already sensitized to such issues, having underlined in his studies on civil religion in America (see Lecture XIII) how the basic values of American society are anchored in religion. In this major study carried out in the 1980s, he continued his earlier work, though now on a substantially broader empirical basis and with respect to an issue significantly broader in scope.

The book's point of departure is a famous thesis put forward by Alexis de Tocqueville in his 1835 book *De la démocratie en Amérique* (English title: *Democracy in America*), namely that a dynamic relationship between private and public life is crucial to the survival of free institutions. On this view, democracy can be vigorous only if citizens are prepared to go beyond the immediate private context (family and kin) and to articulate their views as individuals in a public sphere, in circles of friends, associations, in political parties, etc. Withdrawal into the private sphere merely risks the development of an all-powerful and all-regulating state and thus, over the long term, the death of a free and democratic society.

Bellah and his collaborators adopted this thesis, using it as a foil for their diagnosis and critique of the contemporary world. They interviewed around 200 adults from the white American middle class, asking them about specific aspects of their private lives (their relationship to marriage, love and therapy) as well as their 'public' lives (their participation in clubs and associations or in local politics). In some ways, the findings confirmed Sandel's claims of crisis and in addition led to new insights with respect to the highly variable forms of modern individualism.

While Ulrich Beck, for example, made very little effort to distinguish between different types of individualism in his theory of individualism, Bellah and his colleagues saw this as their first priority task. In their interviews, as well as through historical surveys of significant figures in

American intellectual history, they identified a total of four types of individualism: a *biblical tradition* originating in the religiously inspired settlement era, a *republican tradition* dating back to the revolutionary period and oriented towards a Graeco-Roman conception of politics, and finally a tradition which must be subdivided into two currents, a *utilitarian* and *expressive* individualism.

Analysis of the interviews alone, however, produced a rather one-dimensional picture. While Tocqueville, who carried out his investigations in the 1830s, chiefly observed a religious and republican individualism and thought that it was these forms of individualism that explained the strength and vitality of the American polity and democracy, there is very little sign of them among the modern interviewees. The idea expounded, for example, by John Winthrop (1588–1649), the 'first Puritan' on American soil, that human freedom is a good which obliges him to respect God and His commandments, has lost influence in modern America. The same can be said of Thomas Jefferson's (1743–1826) idea of individuality. As co-author of the American Declaration of Independence, he regarded a purely formal freedom as inadequate. Drawing on the political traditions of the ancient world, he considered a polity worthy of respect only if the citizens truly have a say in decisions and play an active part in political life. Most of the interviewees lacked entirely the moral language of a Winthrop or Jefferson, and could neither understand let alone express the ideas to which they were referring. For contemporary individualism, so Bellah tells us, is either utilitarian, that is, largely concerned with short-term and generally materialistic utility calculations, or expressive, in other words, oriented towards satisfaction of emotional needs and the cultivation of oneself. According to Bellah, these two types of modern individualism can be attributed to two social types, which dominate modern American culture, as well as that of other countries: the manager and the therapist. These are said to embody the utilitarian and expressive individualism, respectively, that predominate at present.

According to Bellah, the remarkable thing about these undoubtedly radical individualisms is that, for the most part, people acting in this individualistic way simply lack the capacity to grasp how it might be possible to link their interests with those of others. They frequently suffer from a lack of social ties and relationships. Furthermore, they are unable even to define what they understand a 'good life' to be. The interviewees articulated (consciously or unconsciously) a sense of unease about their own unconnected lives, and often expressed opposition to the social hegemony of the managers and therapists. Yet they were unable to express this unease and opposition in a moral language which would have transcended this utilitarian and expressive individualism. According to Bellah, it is thus also important to 'find a moral language that will transcend ... radical individualism'

(Bellah, *Habits of the Heart*, p. 21). This is all the more pressing because quite obviously neither the professional advancement typical of utilitarian individualists nor the purely private cultivation of personal preferences characteristic of expressive individualists genuinely satisfies people, particularly given that in both cases they are faced with the problem of a social life lacking in depth and duration.

Bellah's thesis is that these difficulties can be resolved only if this radical individualism is replaced or at least supplemented by cultural orientations which formerly played a major role in American history, which have not disappeared entirely even now and which might facilitate identification with communities and living traditions. Only picking up the thread of the biblical and/or republican traditions which still exist in the USA – so Bellah tells us – can revitalize American democracy in the long term.

> If we are not entirely a mass of interchangeable fragments within an aggregate, if we are in part qualitatively distinct members of a whole, it is because there are still operating among us, with whatever difficulties, traditions that tell us about the nature of the world, about the nature of society, and about who we are as people. Primarily biblical and republican, these traditions are, as we have seen, important for many Americans and significant to some degree for almost all. Somehow families, churches, a variety of cultural associations, and, even if only in the interstices, schools and universities, do manage to communicate a form of life, a *paideia*, in the sense of growing up in a morally and intellectually intelligible world.
>
> (ibid., pp. 281–2; original emphasis)

This is the only way to prevent the (American) polity from disintegrating into a conglomeration of atomized individuals or becoming a collection of 'lifestyle enclaves', each of which consists only of those of like mind (communities centred on gay people, the white middle class, New Age enthusiasts, etc.) and which are therefore utterly incapable of communicating with *other* communities, let alone of taking joint political action. Just as Tocqueville observed, there is a need for a sensible balance between private *and* public life to ensure the vitality and stability of democracy.

Bellah's call for a community of substance rich in traditions should not be understood as a reactionary reversion to ways of life of the distant past. Quite the reverse: he longs for social movements which might guide a cultural shift towards a vigorous democratic culture, movements which would, for example, find inspiration in the ideals of the civil rights movement of the 1950s and 1960s, which was not, of course, centred on the pursuit of utilitarian interests or satisfying emotional needs, but rather the creation of a truly democratic political culture on the basis of which blacks and whites could struggle together over the best way to organize their political community.

The critique of the state of American society expressed by Bellah and his co-authors in *Habits of the Heart* and the associated diagnosis of the contemporary world were translated in another book into specific proposals on how to revitalize the American polity (Bellah et al., *The Good Society* from 1991). These range from calls to dismantle militaristic state structures (ibid., p. 78) to proposals for the democratization of the workplace (ibid., p. 101). It is important to underline these proposals because the rhetoric of community deployed by Bellah and the communitarians has often met with resistance in Germany, where it is categorized as conservative to reactionary – which is understandable to a degree given how the concept was misused by the Nazis (with their *Volksgemeinschaft* or national community). There is no doubt that there are conservative communitarians. But the concept of community has a quite different resonance in American intellectual history than in its German equivalent (Joas, 'Decline of Community? Comparative Observations on Germany and the United States') which is why some American progressives or left-wingers have adopted it, as evident in Bellah's concrete political demands.

It is due above all to the political instincts and organizational talents of one man that the 'Communitarian Network' emerged from these academic approaches as well as political developments from the early 1990s on. We are referring to Amitai Etzioni. Etzioni (b. 1929) is in a number of respects an interesting figure in the intellectual and political life of the USA (see his autobiography *My Brother's Keeper: A Memoir and a Message*). Born in Cologne as Werner Falk, the son of Jewish parents, he emigrated to Palestine with his family during the Nazi period, where he took part in the battles over the foundation of the State of Israel as a soldier. He studied sociology in Jerusalem under Martin Buber – whom we encountered in Lecture XIII as one of Shmuel Eisenstadt's key inspirations. Etzioni then continued his education in the USA, where he obtained his Ph.D. at Berkeley in 1958 with a study in the sociology of organizations. Having 'found a home' at Columbia University in New York City, he rapidly became one of the leading organizational sociologists in the USA. In 1968, he produced a highly ambitious work of social theory, whose significance was for a long time greatly underestimated. *The Active Society: A Theory of Societal and Political Processes* was a first attempt to produce a synthesis of sociological theory; it may in fact have appeared too soon, though it was no less significant for that. It was another fifteen years before anyone in Europe – authors such as Habermas, Luhmann and Giddens – undertook anything similar. In other words, Etzioni was the first to deviate from the Parsonian paradigm who also had a comprehensive, fully worked out theoretical *alternative* at hand (Joas, 'Macroscopic Action'). Etzioni's book successfully fused Parsonian elements, aspects of systems theory and cybernetics, conflict theory and insights from phenomenology and interactionism to analyse a crucial question: How can we conceive of collective action, and indeed of consensus, at the level of society as a whole? In answering this question, Etzioni manages to avoid numerous 'pitfalls' that have bedevilled a good number of theorists. Because he neither equates structure with the macro-level, nor action with the micro-level, he does not – like Habermas for example – hit on the problematic idea of dealing with macroscopic contexts solely with systems theoretical means. In much the same way as Giddens was to do, he deploys the concept of system (see Lecture XII) in an empirical-realistic rather than essentialist way. For him, systems exist if and only if it is possible to show feedback loops that underpin stable processes. At the basic conceptual level, Etzioni's work is thus informed by action theory. In detailed analyses, backed up with copious empirical data, on (scientific) knowledge, power and consensus, he attempts to render comprehensible how collective action and a process of mobilization affecting society as a whole can come about. In a way reminiscent of Alain Touraine's writings, he goes in search of an 'active society' in this book, asking how such a society could bring about macrosocial change. Though the book cannot, and does not wish to, deny its origins in the context of the turbulent 1960s (it is dedicated to Etzioni's students at Berkeley and Columbia) and certainly pursues normative aims, it must be underlined that Etzioni does not simply take a collective subject for granted (as in many schools of Marxism). Rather, he examines *empirically* under which specific circumstances collective actors and perhaps even macrosocial action can develop. He avoids truncating the answer to this question, as did Habermas by rushing to introduce the concept of system (see Lecture IX), and instead makes an effort to keep an open mind through a consistently action-theoretical approach.

Etzioni himself did not develop this promising theoretical approach any further – undoubtedly a peculiar aspect of his career. A certain disappointment about the meagre response to this work and the author's unceasing urge to make an impact at a practical political level will both have played their part here. For at the same time as carrying out his studies in the sociology of organization, Etzioni was also highly active in the field of peace and conflict research, before becoming increasingly engaged in politics in the 1970s; among other things, he was a close adviser to President and later winner of the Nobel Peace Prize Jimmy Carter. In the Reagan era, Etzioni focused on critiquing the paradigm of microeconomics and utilitarian theories as a whole, which exercised an increasing influence on the intellectual and political life of the USA. This led him to produce *The Moral Dimension*, mentioned in Lecture V, a book which undertook to update the critique of utilitarianism expounded by the classical figures of sociology and Talcott Parsons. In the 1990s, Etzioni then became the *spiritus rector* of the American communitarians and organizer of the 'Communitarian Network', intended to present and disseminate communitarian ideas in the public sphere and in the world of politics. Especially within the framework of this last activity, Etzioni placed the problem of the stability of modern societies, above all American society, at the centre of his reflections, concentrating on the question, already raised in the work of Sandel and Bellah, of how best to revitalize a society's 'communicative infrastructure'. In programmatic books such as *The Spirit of Community: The Reinvention of American Society* from 1993, he criticized contemporary American society for its lack of 'we-ness', its overemphasis on individual rights, and its concurrent devaluation of obligations to the community. For him, the priority is to establish a new relationship between individual and community, to strengthen the communicative infrastructures that facilitate the production of community or its revitalization. His proposals range from schools policy ideas such as strengthening the school class (ibid., pp. 107f.), through the establishment of 'National Service', a more or less obligatory year of service to be completed by young adults to the benefit of the community (ibid., pp. 113ff.), to tighter regulation of campaign financing.

Etzioni always rejects liberal claims that his ideas propagate an ultimately reactionary community life, a narrowly conceived form of commonality. For he does not want social ties for their own sake. Etzioni is only too well aware that communities may be repressive, which is why he argues 'that one attribute of a good society is that it is one in which strong communal bonds are balanced by similarly powerful protections of the self' (Etzioni, *The Monochrome Society*, p. 144). Communitarianism, as Etzioni understands it, is very far from any kind of naive or backward-looking idealization of community as such.

The debate on communitarianism is quite similar to that on 'civil society'. This debate was initiated largely by Eastern European dissidents in the 1970s, during the era of Soviet domination. With this normative concept, they pointed to a space beyond the state and beyond the reach of the state, but which was not solely private; it would be untouched by the control of the ruling communist parties, so that a genuinely democratic way of life might begin to develop. In the late 1970s and 1980s, this concept also played an increasingly important role in debates on social theory in the West, particularly because it could be easily linked with the Habermasian concept of the public sphere (see Lecture IX). 'Civil society' generally refers to a sphere of citizens' activity regulated neither by the state nor market (see for example Jean Cohen and Andrew Arato, *Civil Society and Political Theory*). In the early 1990s, the American political scientist Robert D. Putnam sparked off another debate with his thesis of the decline of 'social capital' in the USA, a debate that deploys this concept as well as other, related conceptual tools and which deals with a similar subject, namely the issue of where citizens' participation in the polity takes place and how intensive this participation is today (for an analysis of Germany in this regard, see Joas and Adloff, 'Transformations of German Civil Society: Milieu Change and Community of Spirit').

From Etzioni's perspective, all of these approaches are valuable but inadequate. His criticism is that 'civil society' can only ever be a subdivision or one aspect of the 'good society', as he understands it. For those who champion the idea of 'civil society', as well as Putnam, ultimately have practically nothing to say about whether certain forms of sociation are good or not. For them, all social groupings and ties appear to be of equal value, regardless of their form and goals. Participation in associations, clubs, political parties, social movements, etc. seems to be good in itself: 'one voluntary association is, in principle, as good as any other' (*The Monochrome Society*, p. 198). The communitarian Etzioni cannot and will not resign himself to a relativistic position of this kind. For in his opinion, the 'good society' is always centred on a core of clearly definable particular (not particularistic) values, which is why academics and all intellectuals cannot avoid statements about the varying degrees of normative desirability of different institutions and forms of participation.

Etzioni thus passes on to the exponents of the conception of civil society, so to speak, the criticism often made of communitarianism, namely that it is unable to distinguish between 'good' and 'bad' communities. But there is equally little reason why it should apply to them. Habermas' concept of the public sphere certainly has a strong normative dimension; the Eastern European dissidents had very precise ideas about which forms of civil society are democratic and which are not; and Putnam too has now modified his stance somewhat to take more account of the distinctions demanded by Etzioni.

But Etzioni is surely right to emphasize that strong values can and ought to be articulated within public debates. If there is no consensus about them, the society must have the chance to enter into what Etzioni calls a 'megalogue', a 'societywide dialogue, one that links many community dialogues into one often nationwide give-and-take' (ibid., p. 157). This is the only way to clarify existing normative differences. A 'good society' brought about by such a megalogue would, Etzioni contends, ultimately produce a significantly firmer stance towards social inequality than is possible with Rawlsian arguments. Etzioni does not consider Rawls' liberal attitude towards major social inequality acceptable. A good society, according to Etzioni, would reduce social inequalities rather more than demanded by the Rawlsian difference principle (ibid., p. 147). For we do not have to judge all forms of inequality to be good simply because the most disadvantaged nonetheless benefit from it. The attitude towards social inequality found in a particular society is based on strong evaluations which cannot simply be pushed aside – by the difference principle, for example.

Etzioni's programmatic political writings include a large number of conservative proposals, but also many left-wing or progressive ideas – as apparent in the critique of Rawls outlined above. As Etzioni himself states, the communitarian movement cannot be located clearly within the schema of left and right. There are significant similarities with the political writings of another major contemporary social theorist, namely Anthony Giddens, with his notion of a 'third way' for social democracy. The communitarians on the one hand and Giddens on the other exercised a major influence on the social democratic policy debate in Europe in the 1990s, their primary goal being to combat the etatist orientation, the fixation on the state, so typical of traditional social democratic parties and others. Their goal, and in this sense the communitarians and Giddens greatly resemble the prototypical liberal Rawls, was to help remoralize politics – not in a narrow-minded way, but by establishing a new link between normative reflections on what constitutes a desirable polity and empirical knowledge about its character and developmental tendencies. At present, political theory and social theory are thus coming into contact again with productive outcomes for both. Much the same can be said of the intellectual current that arose from the renaissance of ideas whose importance was quickly recognized in the history of the social sciences, particularly in the USA, but which was then subject to increasing marginalization: pragmatism and neo-pragmatism in its various permutations. It is to this current that we turn in the following lecture.

XIX

Neo-pragmatism

As our remarks on symbolic interactionism in Lecture VI laid bare, the founding generation of American sociology, such as George Herbert Mead and the members of the Chicago School of sociology, had close links with American pragmatist philosophy. It would in fact be fair to say that authors such as Mead played a crucial role in developing pragmatist ideas and harnessing them for the analysis of social processes and relations. There is thus no doubt that pragmatist philosophy strongly influenced the development of American sociology, at least until well into the 1930s.

But pragmatism's influence on sociology subsequently diminished markedly. One of the key factors in sociologists' increasing lack of interest in pragmatist thought was Parsons' contribution to the establishment of a sociological canon, a contribution which resulted, with some delay, from his *The Structure of Social Action*, first published in 1937. In Lectures II and III we alluded to the fact that those thinkers whom Parsons declared the key founding fathers of sociology (especially Weber and Durkheim) were exclusively European. American authors influenced by pragmatist thought he ignored entirely. Given the emerging dominance of Parsonian sociology in the late 1940s, it is unsurprising that the development of sociological theory occurred almost exclusively *without reference to pragmatist traditions*. Only in the 1960s did this begin to change to some extent, when symbolic interactionism positioned itself as a 'new' theoretical approach and as an alternative to Parsonianism. Yet symbolic interactionism was not really 'new'. As a student of George Herbert Mead, Herbert Blumer had tried to 'save' his teacher's insights during the Parsonian hegemony of the 1940s and 1950s – and he did in fact succeed in this, as became apparent in the upswing in symbolic interactionism in the 1960s (again, see Lecture VI). Thus, pragmatist thought certainly lived on in symbolic interactionism, though in a highly circumscribed fashion. For the key reference author for the symbolic interactionists was George Herbert Mead, while the other founding fathers of American pragmatism such as Charles Sanders Peirce, William James and John Dewey played a far less prominent role.

Alongside the symbolic interactionists, there were of course always individual figures within American sociology who felt indebted to pragmatism. Authors such as the conflict theorist C. Wright Mills (see Lecture VIII), for example, referred to pragmatist authors time and again in various connections (see his posthumously [1964] published dissertation *Sociology and*

Pragmatism: The Higher Learning in America). Particularly in his cultural criticism, he propagated ideas reminiscent of pragmatist reformist projects. Another significant figure was the great American sociologist of law and organizations Philip Selznick (b. 1919), who utilized the social psychological insights of Dewey in his famous study *TVA and the Grass Roots: A Study in the Sociology of Formal Organization* from 1949 to enhance the analysis of organizations. In a major late work from 1992 (*The Moral Commonwealth: Social Theory and the Promise of Community*) he referred copiously to pragmatist authors in his discussion of key issues in social theory.

It was a long time before pragmatism played any role in European post-war sociology. This changed only in the 1970s, when Jürgen Habermas, influenced by his friend, the philosopher Karl-Otto Apel (b. 1922), made extensive reference to Mead, Peirce and Dewey, in order both to attain a viable concept of intersubjectivity and to back up his discourse ethics. But despite the huge impact of Habermas' work, this seems to have encouraged others to look at pragmatism only to a moderate degree. It is fair to say that pragmatism played a rather minor role in the academic world of both the USA and Europe between 1945 and the late 1970s.

Subsequently, however, this began to change rapidly, and it was an American philosopher, namely Richard Rorty (1931–2007), who was chiefly 'responsible'. With his 1979 book *Philosophy and the Mirror of Nature*, he ushered in a spectacular pragmatist renaissance – though initially solely within philosophy. This renaissance had a great deal to do with the fact that Rorty declared John Dewey a philosopher of similar standing to figures such as Ludwig Wittgenstein and Martin Heidegger in a rather surprising way, describing these three thinkers as the three 'most important philosophers' of the twentieth century (*Philosophy and the Mirror of Nature*, p. 5). Dewey, who many in their ignorance had thought of as a rather boring philosopher of common sense, was soon regarded as an author of great relevance as a result of Rorty's book, a tendency reinforced by the fact that it seemed possible to connect his writings with the French poststructuralist thought becoming so fashionable at the time. What were Rorty's key ideas? Above all, how did he interpret the pragmatists and Dewey in particular? In this lecture, we shall first present the two most important philosophical representatives of neo-pragmatism (Rorty and Hilary Putnam) and the differences between them, before examining the attempts to develop a neo-pragmatist social theory by Richard Bernstein and one of the authors of the present work (Hans Joas).

Philosophy and the Mirror of Nature is a history of modern philosophical thought in which Rorty tries to understand the historical genesis of the idea of 'mental processes' before going on to criticize it and declare it null and void. Rorty's line of thought, which is quite a challenge to understand, goes something like this. Traditional modern philosophy since Descartes was largely a constant attempt to flee from history in that philosophy was tasked with producing *trans*historical – timeless – truths. And philosophers tried to get at the truth by clinging to the idea of consciousness as a mirror, the idea that alongside physical things there are *mental processes* or *conscious* processes that more or less adequately portray or 'mirror' physical things. The background to this was the assumption that people have privileged access to their own mental states, that they know these mental states better than anything else and that 'true' or 'objective' knowledge must therefore be directly linked with these inner mental processes. The assumption here is that correct knowledge or truth can be obtained if 'consciousness' succeeds in accurately representing objects or nature. Philosophers thus believed that 'consciousness' or the 'mental' must be declared the foundation of all philosophy, as this was the only way to generate certain and thus timeless knowledge.

Rorty tried to show that the notion of 'mental' as opposed to physical processes is unhelpful or even meaningless and that therefore the distinction between body and soul, substance and spirit is as well. The dualism that this entailed is untenable, because that which is called 'consciousness' in traditional philosophy can be described either in a more simple or different way. Rorty makes this clear in a critique of the German philosopher and mathematician Gottfried Wilhelm Leibniz (1646–1716), who expounded precisely such a dualistic position with his claim that it is ultimately impossible to see thoughts:

> why should we be troubled by Leibniz' point that if the brain were blown up to the size of a factory, so that we could stroll through it, we should not see thoughts? If we know enough neural correlations, we shall indeed see thoughts – in the sense that our vision will reveal to us what thoughts the possessor of the brain is having. If we do not, we shall not, but then if we stroll through *any* factory without having first learned about its parts and their relations to one another, we shall not see what is going on. Further, even if we could find no such neural correlations, even if cerebral localization of thoughts was a complete failure, why would we want to say that a person's thoughts or mental images were nonphysical simply because we cannot give an account of them in terms of his parts? To use an example from Hilary Putnam, one cannot give an account of why square pegs do not fit into round holes in terms of the elementary particles which constitute the peg and the hole, but nobody finds a perplexing ontological gap between macrostructure and microstructure.
>
> (*Philosophy and the Mirror of Nature*, p. 26)

According to Rorty, there is no compelling reason to accept the existence of mental and conscious processes and thus to perpetuate the Cartesian dualism between body and mind. It is sufficient to describe the discrete processes (thoughts) occurring in the brain as functional states of the overall complex that is the 'brain'. Thus, they can be understood, if at all, only if we comprehend the overall structure of the brain and how it works. But this does not require the idea of an 'immaterial consciousness', because functional states cannot be described as 'immaterial'. This is precisely what the last sentence of the above quotation is saying. The mere fact that we are unable to derive thoughts directly from the structures of the brain does not compel us to assume an ontological chasm between the two, just as there is no need to assume that such a chasm exists between physical micro- and macro-structures, solely because we cannot explain, in the language of elementary particles, why square pegs do not fit into round holes.

Rorty's radical stance is certainly not undisputed, and in his late writings his key source, the pragmatist philosopher Hilary Putnam, mentioned in the above quotation and dealt with later in this lecture, would certainly have questioned whether 'mental states' can truly be equated with 'functional' ones and whether one can do entirely without the idea of the mental (see for example Putnam, *Representation and Reality*, p. 1). Over time, Rorty himself also abandoned this radical physicalism. But this is not the key point here. For Rorty is primarily concerned to reconstruct historically the reasons why philosophers have clung so desperately to an undoubtedly problematic dualism. In his view, these reasons are closely associated with the name of Descartes, who set the project of philosophy off down the wrong track to some extent. According to Rorty, philosophy made a crucial mistake in seeking and identifying its foundations in an 'unquestionable' epistemology because of the idea that so-called 'consciousness' is a mirror of nature. Epistemologists such as Descartes and Locke as well as Kant were unable or unwilling to accept that knowledge cannot be conceived as timeless 'truth' at which one can get via some kind of consciousness, but that knowledge can be understood solely 'as a relation between a person and a proposition' (*Philosophy and the Mirror of Nature*, p. 141). But knowledge – according to Rorty – does not depend on internal intuition or a correct 'mental' representation of reality, but rather on the discursive practice carried on between two or more individuals arguing over statements and attempting to convince one another.

Rorty's stance may seem rather unspectacular at first sight. In fact, though, it has significant and controversial consequences. For Rorty thus evades the concept of truth which most people would take for granted. In his view, we can never hope to obtain (transhistorical) 'truth'. When we speak naively of 'true' and 'less true' statements, we are referring at best to 'differences in degree of ease in objecting to our beliefs' (ibid., p. 157; see also Rorty, *Truth and Progress*, pp. 1ff.). Thus, neither science nor philosophy is concerned with the production of (timeless) 'truth', but merely with justifying specific statements. The ways in which such justification occurs are a function of the practice of social discourse (*Philosophy and the Mirror of Nature*, p. 170) and thus context-dependent; they are spatio-temporally bounded rather than transhistorical, which is why there can be no definitively 'true knowledge', no ultimate foundation of knowledge.

> we understand knowledge when we understand the social justification of belief, and thus have no need to view it as accuracy of representation. Once conversation replaces confrontation, the notion of the mind as Mirror of Nature can be discarded. Then the notion of philosophy as the discipline which looks for privileged representations among those constituting the Mirror becomes unintelligible. ... If we see knowledge as a matter of conversation and of social practice, rather than as an attempt to mirror nature, we will not be likely to envisage a metapractice which will be the critique of all possible forms of social practice.
>
> (ibid., pp. 170–1)

Thus, though philosophy is concerned chiefly with the justification of statements, Rorty does *not* try to identify the *foundation* of philosophical argument, a 'metapraxis', as Habermas did through the idea of the potential rationality of language for example. Rather, Rorty places himself firmly within the tradition of 'anti-foundationalist thought', which (see his interpretation of Dewey, Heidegger and Wittgenstein) does not believe or no longer believes that there is any possibility of acquiring an unquestionable and transhistorical basis for (philosophical) argument. Thus, for Rorty all attempts to establish a (transhistorical) 'metapraxis' or 'metarationality' are a 'waste of time'. He thus sees himself as a 'contextualist' and is described as such by others (see Habermas, *Postmetaphysical Thinking: Philosophical Essays*, pp. 135ff. and *Truth and Justification*, pp. 116ff.). Rorty's arguments are contextualist because he asserts that justifications are valid only *within a particular language community* and are not accepted as rational beyond its boundaries. Rorty adheres to this position with great consistency. For as he sees things, philosophy itself is merely one community among many, featuring a specific language and specific explanatory conventions. Here, he bids farewell to the notion that philosophy is capable of laying claim to a somehow superior rationality. In his view, 'philosophy will have no more to offer than common sense (supplemented by biology, history, etc.) about knowledge and truth' (*Philosophy and the Mirror of Nature*, p. 176). Indeed he goes so far as to claim that 'understanding', 'knowledge' and 'truth', rather than foundational concepts, merely represent a compliment 'paid to the beliefs which we think so well justified that, for the moment, further justification is not needed' (Rorty, 'Solidarity or Objectivity?', p. 24).

If you recall Lecture I, which sought to answer the question 'What is theory?', you will probably have noticed that we already briefly touched on and discussed similar problems in connection with Thomas Kuhn's concept of paradigm. And Kuhn and the 'anarchist' philosopher of science Paul Feyerabend are in fact key reference authors for Rorty, in as much as they advocated, to some extent at least, the kind of contextualist conception of truth favoured by Rorty, with their reference to the 'incommensurability' of different (scientific) paradigms (see Rorty, *Philosophy and the Mirror of Nature*, pp. 330ff.). Rorty's uncoupling of language from reality, however, was going too far for Kuhn (see the quotation in an unpublished paper by Kuhn on Rorty in Thomas Haskell, *Objectivity is Not Neutrality*, p. 142).

But what does all of this have to do with pragmatism? Why is Rorty described as a neo-pragmatist or why does he apply the label of 'pragmatist' to himself? You may well be asking yourself such questions. Rorty's answer is as follows. Dewey, like his other two heroes, the late Wittgenstein and Heidegger, abandoned the notion of certain knowledge as a central goal of philosophy; they did not even attempt to provide philosophy with a transhistorical foundation. Wittgenstein, Heidegger and especially Dewey were not and had no desire to be 'systematic' philosophers. They were 'edifying' or 'pragmatic' thinkers:

> These peripheral, pragmatic philosophers are skeptical primarily *about systematic philosophy*, about the whole project of universal commensuration. In our time, Dewey, Wittgenstein, and Heidegger are the great edifying, peripheral, thinkers. All three make it as difficult as possible to take their thought as expressing views on traditional philosophical problems, or as making constructive proposals for philosophy as a cooperative and progressive discipline. They make fun of the classic picture of man, the picture which contains systematic philosophy, the search for universal commensuration in a final vocabulary.
>
> (*Philosophy and the Mirror of Nature*, pp. 367f.; original emphasis)

Now, perhaps with our remarks on American pragmatism in Lecture VI still in the back of your mind, you may well feel that, given that he lumps Dewey together with Heidegger and Wittgenstein, Rorty's understanding of pragmatism is rather unspecific, particularly in light of the fact that he says nothing at all about key aspects of pragmatist thought. Rorty simply ignores crucial topics and achievements of 'classical' pragmatism. It may be understandable that he was not particularly interested in the problem of the link between action and consciousness with which the 'classical' pragmatists were so preoccupied, as it is the very concept of consciousness that he wishes to leave behind. But it is surprising that Dewey's reflections on action and on the creativity of actors in problematic action situations play practically no role for Rorty; the same can be said of Mead's reflections on an anthropological theory of (symbolic) communication and on human beings' original sociality.

Rorty's descriptions and definitions of 'pragmatism' (which for him is merely the view that 'the idea of an accurate representation of the natural order of things' should not be taken seriously ['Is it Desirable to Love Truth?', p. 22]) are thus inevitably highly formal and rather unconvincing. It is probably down to Rorty's background in analytical philosophy (of language) that his main interest in American pragmatism relates almost exclusively to its potential for *epistemological critique* and less to the highly original analyses produced by Dewey and Mead on the *specific features of human experience and action*.

Rorty expresses his rather one-sided reaction to pragmatist ideas, particularly those of Dewey, in unequivocal terms:

> The culminating achievement of Dewey's philosophy was to treat evaluative terms such as 'true' and 'right' not as signifying a relation to some antecedently existing thing – such as God's Will, or Moral Law, or the Intrinsic Nature of Objective Reality – but as expressions of satisfaction at having found a solution to a problem: a problem which may some day seem obsolete, and a satisfaction which may someday seem misplaced.
>
> (Rorty, *Achieving Our Country: Leftist Thought in Twentieth-Century America*, p. 28)

He seems not even to be aware of Dewey's status as a theorist of action.

Rorty's theory of democracy is also very difficult to reconcile with the participatory ideals of a John Dewey or George Herbert Mead, a fact of which he is well aware (ibid., p. 96). Rorty emerges as a fairly conventional liberal, though his liberalism takes highly aesthetic rather than utilitarian forms. The point of departure for Rorty's reflections on democratic theory is his conviction, outlined above, that because no timeless truths exist in the realm of (political) values and norms, a sharp division between the public and private sphere is necessary. As Rorty states, it is very hard to reconcile the solidarity necessary to a (national) community with people's need to fashion their own existence (*Contingency, Irony and Solidarity*, p. xiv). But people must continue to have the opportunity to do so; individuals' specific needs must be protected – and this is the most pressing task for democratic institutions. But this they can do only if they are embedded in a liberal and ironic culture, distinguished by the fact that the people living in it refrain from enforcing 'truths', instead accepting the diversity of ways in which individuals design their lives. Rorty seems to demand little more than this from (liberal) democracy. In line with this, his definitions of the terms 'liberal' and 'liberal culture' also turn out to be strangely thin:

> I borrow my definition of 'liberal' from Judith Shklar, who says that liberals are the people who think that cruelty is the worst thing we do. I use 'ironist' to name the sort of person who faces up to the contingency of his or her own most central beliefs and desires – someone sufficiently historicist and nominalist to have abandoned the idea that those central beliefs and desires refer back to something beyond the reach of time and chance. Liberal ironists are people who include among these ungroundable desires their own hope that suffering will be diminished, that the humiliation of human beings by other human beings may cease.
>
> (*Contingency, Irony and Solidarity*, p. xv)

For Rorty, liberal culture is thus characterized not by specific values or indeed any kind of shared and binding ethos, as Parsons for example asserted; neither is it held together, as Habermas seems to assume, by philosophical convictions, but at most by a consensus that each citizen within this liberal culture ought to have the opportunity to fashion his life as he sees fit and that no one may treat others in a cruel or humiliating way (ibid., pp. 84–5). But he also emphasizes that the kind of liberal culture that he favours and a democratic polity based on it cannot truly be *justified* with respect to other forms of political organization; this liberal order is as contingent as any other political model, and there is no argument capable of marking out the liberal order as superior to any other. According to Rorty, arguments for or against a way of life are only ever persuasive *within* a language community. This sounds highly relativistic, but Rorty defends himself against this label. A position is relativistic only if it claims that every moral conception is as good as any other. But he does not advocate such a position. He is convinced that the liberal culture which he favours is far better than any rival order, *though this cannot be proven*.

> It is one thing to say, falsely, that there is nothing to choose between us and the Nazis. It is another thing to say, correctly, that there is no neutral, common ground to which an experienced Nazi philosopher and I can repair in order to argue out our differences.
> (Rorty, 'Trotsky and the Wild Orchids', p. 15)

Rorty's theory of democracy is thus not relativistic, but rather contextualist or, as Rorty himself says, 'ethnocentric'. Because Rorty does not believe in universalist justifications for norms and in any case views the persuasive power of philosophical arguments as negligible, he considers the belief in the possibility of lived solidarity being extended to all people and all cultures to be an illusion (*Contingency, Irony and Solidarity*, p. 191). According to him, the strength of feelings of solidarity depends on our interpretation of other people as 'similar' or 'dissimilar', an interpretation which has arisen from contingent historical circumstances and which cannot be enforced or reinforced by philosophical arguments. This does not mean that the extension of solidarity is not desirable. For Rorty, it is in fact a sign of moral progress – but *only from the perspective* (for which no further justification can be offered) *of a liberal culture*, which wishes to avoid cruelty as far as possible (see also his essay in *Truth and Progress*, pp. 167ff.).

As apparent from our remarks on Rorty's theory of democracy, his philosophical views can certainly be converted into political ideas. On the other hand, there is no getting away from the fact that his statements on this subject are anything but fully developed; in particular, they lack entirely any connection with issues in social theory. Rorty is certainly one of the best-known left-wing political commentators among American intellectuals, as he demonstrated once again in his impressive 1998 book *Achieving our Country: Leftist Thought in Twentieth-Century America*, mentioned earlier. But he neither discusses systematically what role the public sphere has to play in a liberal society nor reflects upon the fact that the notion of the necessary avoidance of 'cruelty' is highly elastic, because the term can be interpreted in very different ways. And Rorty shows no interest whatsoever in the problem, so crucial to social theory, of the sources or basis of interpersonal solidarity, something he too values, though the 'classical' pragmatists could tell him a thing or two about that (on these criticisms, see Richard Bernstein, *The New Constellation: The Ethical-Political Horizons of Modernity/Postmodernity*, pp. 264ff.; Thomas McCarthy, *Ideals and Illusions: On Deconstruction and Reconstruction in Contemporary Critical Theory*, pp. 25ff.; Hans Joas, *The Genesis of Values*, pp. 160ff.).

It is hardly surprising that Rorty's ideas on the (remaining) tasks of philosophy, his farewell to the concept of truth and his conception of liberal democracy inspired some vehement protest. And those who located themselves within the tradition of American pragmatism felt particularly provoked. Scholars in the field certainly recognized that Rorty had breathed new life into pragmatism and had inspired many more people to look into it through his writings, but most were highly sceptical as to whether the Rortyan conception of pragmatism had much to do with the projects pursued by the 'classical' pragmatists. The critique of Rorty's philosophical views was expressed with particular conciseness by Hilary Putnam, surely one of the best-known contemporary American philosophers and logicians, who has a certain amount in common with Rorty. For very much like Rorty, Putnam sees major similarities between authors such as Wittgenstein on the one hand and Dewey or Peirce on the other. And the work of both Rorty and Putnam is rooted in analytic philosophy; both authors began to move closer to pragmatist thought only gradually. In Putnam's case, however, and this underscores how he differs from Rorty, this occurs in a way which would surely fit more closely with the intentions of the 'classical' pragmatists.

Putnam (b. 1926) shares at least four 'classical' pragmatist premises. First, he consistently advocates an *anti-sceptical position*, adopting the Peircean anti-Cartesian argument mentioned in Lecture VI, namely that we cannot doubt everything at once and that the work of philosophy must be guided not by a method of doubt but only by genuine doubts and problems; second, Putnam shares the *fundamental fallibilist stance* of the 'classical' pragmatists, which states that our convictions might always turn out to be wrong and are not ultimate truths; third, he *disputes* the thesis that *it is possible to maintain a clear division between facts and values* and that we cannot discuss values by means of good arguments; fourth, he constantly emphasizes that *human thought is bound up with human practice*, with human attempts to get to grips with the natural and social environment (see Marie-Luise Raters and Marcus Willaschek, *Hilary Putnam und die Tradition des Pragmatismus* ['Hilary Putnam and the Tradition of Pragmatism'], p. 12).

By sticking consistently to all these pragmatist premises, Putnam was able to carve out a distinct position, particularly with respect to the work of Richard

Rorty. His proximity to *and* distance from Rorty are immediately apparent at the beginning of one of his most important works, namely *Reason, Truth and History* from 1981:

> The view which I shall defend holds ... that there is an extremely close connection between the notions of *truth* and *rationality*; that ... the only criterion for what is a fact is what it is *rational* to accept. (I mean this quite literally and across the board; thus if it can be rational to accept that a picture is beautiful, then it can be a *fact* that the picture is beautiful.) There can be *value facts* on this conception. But the relation between rational acceptability and truth is a relation between two distinct notions. A statement can be rationally acceptable *at a time* but not *true*.
>
> (Putnam, *Reason, Truth and History*, p. x; original emphasis)

Putnam thus shares with Rorty the idea that 'rationality' is not something transhistorical, but depends on arguments whose claims to plausibility make sense only in a specific context. Yet he does not draw the radical contextualist or relativist conclusions which Rorty seemingly feels compelled to do. For Putnam argues that not every rational justification is 'criterial', that is, relative to the criteria of rationality defined as such within a language game. Rather, Putnam believes (and the contrast with Rorty is clearly apparent here) that discussions on the nature of rationality always presuppose a concept of rational justification which transcends the specific contexts (a similar argument is also put forward, against Rorty, by Habermas; see *Truth and Justification*, pp. 144ff.). He makes this particularly clear in his analysis of Kuhn's 'incommensurability thesis', to which Rorty had frequently referred approvingly. Putnam asserts that this thesis contradicts itself – and that this is apparent in the internally inconsistent way in which its champions argue. It is namely impossible to claim that two paradigms are 'incommensurable' while at the same time attempting to describe and elaborate the differences between the two. For in doing so, one has abandoned the idea of 'incommensurability' and conceded that it is possible, to some extent at least, to translate the two paradigms one into the other.

> if Feyerabend (and Kuhn at his most incommensurable) were right, then members of other cultures, including seventeenth-century scientists, would be conceptualizable by us only as animals producing responses to stimuli (including noises that curiously resemble English or Italian). To tell us that Galileo had 'incommensurable' notions *and then to go on to describe them at length* is totally incoherent.
>
> (Putnam, *Reason, Truth and History*, pp. 115f.; original emphasis)

Ultimately, Putnam believes that both Feyerabend and Kuhn, as well as Rorty, have fallen foul of a false interpretation of the Wittgensteinian idea of language games: they interpret Wittgenstein as if he had conceived these language games – the rules of speech and argument that prevail within a specific culture – as self-contained mathematical calculations or computer programs. In this case, it would indeed be true that language games can in no way be translated into one another, because we would have to understand them as sign systems entirely closed off from one another (see Putnam, *Pragmatism: An Open Question*, pp. 33ff.). But neither Wittgenstein nor Dewey and the classical pragmatists understood language games in this way, which is why they did not come to the radical conclusions drawn by Kuhn or Rorty. Rorty at least, according to Putnam, cannot invoke Wittgenstein, let alone pragmatist traditions, to back up his stance here. These traditions never doubted the at least partial translatability of language games, which means that they would not view the idea of rational justification as solely context-dependent (see Putnam, *Renewing Philosophy*, p. 77 and *Pragmatism: An Open Question*).

The position outlined here with respect to the (at least partial) translatability of language games is bound up, among other things, with Putnam's conviction (and here once again he distinguishes himself clearly from Rorty) that *there undoubtedly are such things as objective values* (on what follows, see R. Bernstein, 'Putnams Stellung in der pragmatistischen Tradition' ['Putnam's Place in the Pragmatist Tradition'], pp. 41ff.). Putnam thus contradicts the notion that norms and ethical stances are purely subjective or culture- or paradigm-specific. Science, for example, is based on cognitive values such as coherence or simplicity, by means of which specific statements can be justified, through which, indeed, we gain access to the world in the first place. According to Putnam, this does not mean that we can always determine what exactly coherence or simplicity means in relation to a given case, but we can at least discuss the meaning of these values rationally. These values are thus 'objective', as objective as are other values in other (non-scientific) social spheres:

> A belief that there is such a thing as justice is not a belief in *ghosts*, nor is a 'sense of justice' a para-normal sense which enables us to perceive such ghosts. ... Ethics does not *conflict with* physics, as the term 'unscientific' suggests; it is simply that 'just' and 'good' and 'sense of justice' are concepts in a discourse which is not *reducible* to physical discourse. ... Talk of 'justice' ... can be *non*-scientific without being *un*-scientific.
> (Putnam, *Reason, Truth and History*, p. 145; original emphasis)

The clashes between Rorty and Putnam (again, see Putnam's critique of Rorty in *Renewing Philosophy*, pp. 67ff.) certainly made the wider scholarly community far more willing to look into pragmatism. Yet at the same time, the associated debates offered no real point of contact for social theory. While Putnam was markedly more rooted in the pragmatist tradition than Rorty, and while he gets a good deal more out of Dewey's understanding of democracy than does Rorty (Putnam, *Renewing*, pp. 180ff.), the debates which he stimulated were also carried on within the 'usual' *philosophical* frame of reference; social theoretical issues were touched upon all too rarely, and few scholars attempted to examine the theoretical approaches discussed in this lecture series. This is all the more surprising in that Putnam in particular always held to the pragmatist thesis that action and thinking are closely intertwined.

This abstinence with respect to social theory did not, however, apply to all thinkers with a debt to pragmatism, and least of all to Richard Bernstein, who was one of the few pragmatist philosophers to consistently take up sociological problems. From the outset, Bernstein (b. 1932 and, incidentally, a friend of Rorty's from their time as students together at the University of Chicago) was interested in American pragmatism, particularly the work of John Dewey, and made it the point of departure for his philosophical reflections. What sets Bernstein clearly apart from Rorty, but also from Putnam, is that his work is genuinely oriented towards social theory and, above all, his concern with the characteristics of *human action*. Thus, it was not primarily the 'classical' pragmatists' *epistemological* positions or their *critique of epistemology* that Bernstein took up, but rather their reflections on the *theory of action*. This interest was already apparent in one of his early books, namely *Praxis and Action: Contemporary Philosophies of Human Activity* from 1971. Here, Bernstein examines four different philosophical currents centrally concerned with human action or human practice, namely Marxism, the existentialism of Sartre (and of Kierkegaard, 1813–55), analytical philosophy, though its concept of action is highly formalistic, and American pragmatism with its champions Dewey and Peirce. Bernstein's strengths were already apparent in this early book. He not only provides an impressive demonstration of his capacity to mediate between different philosophical traditions and to 'translate' the various problems (his main task, as he sees it, being to make American philosophy familiar with intellectual developments in Europe). He also succeeds in identifying the subject of action as a basic problem of (contemporary) philosophy. In a highly nuanced way, he manages to 'praise' both the clarity of studies by analytical philosophers (of language) on the concept of action as well as Marx's 'radical anthropology' and his attempt to overcome the dichotomy between 'is' and 'ought' (*Praxis and Action*, p. 307), to pay tribute to Sartre's emphasis on the freedom of human action as well as Dewey's and Peirce's attempts to reconstruct 'practice ... informed by reason and intelligence' (ibid., p. 313).

Bernstein's insight into the centrality of the concept of action led him to comment critically on the philosophical and sociological debates kicking off in the 1970s from a Deweyan and Peircean perspective, as demonstrated to impressive effect in his next major book, *The Restructuring of Social and Political Theory* from 1976. Here, he grapples for example with the work of Alfred Schütz, the key source for phenomenological sociologists and ethnomethodologists (see Lecture VII) and with that of Jürgen Habermas, but on a rather broader basis than occurred in the work of Rorty or Putnam, who were chiefly interested in epistemology or its critique. As late as the 1990s,

Bernstein was still concerned with the topic of action. Largely because of his adherence to a pragmatic concept of action, Bernstein succeeds in mediating between Habermasian and postmodern positions, while also bringing to light, in a highly instructive way, the (hidden) ethical assumptions of postmodern thinkers (*The New Constellation*).

The debates between Rorty and Putnam thus provided pragmatism or neo-pragmatism with tremendous impetus, though *predominantly within philosophy*. Characteristically, it is generally only the epistemological aspect of pragmatism that is discussed, while the action theoretical potential of the writings of Dewey and Peirce, for example, tends to be neglected. Above all, only rarely are the *consequences* for social theory of the concept of action found in the work of the 'classical' pragmatists discussed in systematic fashion or is any attempt made to *build on* the pragmatist theory of action.

In this sense, it is indeed possible to speak of a 'missing pragmatic revival in *American social science*' (Alan Wolfe), for the new, almost fashionable topicality of pragmatism has thus far scarcely affected the social sciences more narrowly conceived. And this applies not only to the USA, but also to Europe. There are, however, exceptions. The German sociologist Hans Joas (b. 1948), one of the authors of the present work, has gone to particular lengths to further develop the sociological and social theoretical aspects of pragmatism. Taking 'classical' pragmatist premises as his point of departure, he has worked towards a fundamental reorientation of action theory. In what follows, the work of one of the two authors responsible for the present synopsis is therefore presented in the third person. This is undoubtedly a delicate matter, but we believe that it chimes best with this book's status as textbook.

Joas, currently head of the Max Weber Centre for Advanced Cultural and Social Studies at the University of Erfurt and professor of sociology at the University of Chicago, positioned himself firmly in the tradition of American pragmatism from the very beginning of his career. His dissertation *G. H. Mead: A Contemporary Re-examination of His Thought* from 1980 was the first comprehensive reconstruction of Mead's entire oeuvre produced in Europe as well as an attempt to confront Meadian social theory with central trends in continental philosophy and sociology. Mead was presented to readers as a thinker who, in light of his penetrating analyses of the connection between action and consciousness, had managed to resolve numerous action theoretical problems, at which European social theorists had long slaved away, always in vain, and who also succeeded in producing the first truly viable concept of *inter*subjectivity through his anthropological theory of communication.

But the goal of this early book went far beyond the mere reconstruction of a past thinker. Joas was initially concerned with the fact that neither symbolic interactionism, which built on Mead's legacy in highly fragmentary fashion, nor Marxism or critical theory with their unmistakably deficient understanding of action, intersubjectivity and democracy, seemed theoretically adequate.

Consistent with this, Joas began to tread his own path. Among other things, this increasingly meant taking up and putting to use the full sweep of 'classical' pragmatism. He drew increasingly on the writings of Dewey and later those of William James as well. As Joas self-critically concedes in a later preface to *G. H. Mead*, he became fully aware of the significance of Dewey only after completing his dissertation:

> If one's interest is directed mainly toward a theory of intersubjectivity, Mead certainly is the more important author. But if the 'practical' moment in my formula 'practical intersubjectivity' is to be taken seriously, then Dewey's much better and much more comprehensively elaborated pragmatism is essential.
>
> (*Pragmatism and Social Theory*, p. 243)

In any event, his thorough reading of Dewey helped him produce a critique of traditional models of action theory and formulate his own theory of action in the early 1990s, when *The Creativity of Action* was published.

The Creativity of Action interleaves arguments of a systematic nature with those concerning the history of theory. The first part of the book is dedicated to showing that in formulating their theory of action or drawing up typologies of action, the classical figures of sociology had tremendous difficulty coping with the phenomenon of human creativity. Joas demonstrates this with reference to the writings of Durkheim, Tönnies, Simmel and not least Max Weber. Weber develops a seemingly exhaustive typology of action that distinguishes between instrumentally rational, value rational, traditional and affectual action, while also referring time and again to historical or social phenomena that clearly evade such a typology in his evidence-based writings. The concept of charisma, for example, so Joas tells us, plays an outstanding role in Weber's oeuvre as a whole, particularly his sociology of domination, but it is far from clear which type of action 'charisma' comes under in the first place. Charismatic modes of action clearly

> do not fit in with Weber's typology of action ... Naturally, any typology which, like Weber's, contains a more or less clandestine residual category is able to classify all phenomena, although the quality of the classification then leaves much to be desired. What is decisive, however, is that the principle underlying this typology does not do justice to that dimension of action which is revealed in exemplary fashion in charismatic action, namely the creative dimension.
>
> (Joas, *The Creativity of Action*, p. 47)

On the one hand, then, it is characteristic of Weber's work that charismatic phenomena play an outstanding role within it. For it is these that change the historical process and generate something new under the sun. The creative dimension is clearly evident in these phenomena. Yet it is this dimension that Weber's theory of action leaves out of account.

But as Joas sees things, Weber is not an isolated case. For the classical figures as a whole failed to smoothly integrate 'their thoughts on a theory of creativity into the rest of their work' (ibid., p. 69). That is, these figures were constantly confronted with phenomena that laid bare this problem of creativity without, however, managing to place it firmly and consistently within a theoretical framework.

The fact that this problem of creativity occupies such a marginal position within sociology is all the more astonishing in that this topic played a significant role within modern intellectual history as a whole. As Joas tries to show in the second part of the book, 'metaphors' of creativity such as the Marxian concept of production and that of revolution were the key focus of intellectual discussion in the mid-nineteenth century, as was the concept of 'life' within the *Lebensphilosophie* of the late nineteenth century and the concept of (creative) 'intelligence' in the pragmatist thought of the early twentieth century. None of these phenomena, which resist easy conceptualization, could be captured through a theory of action geared towards the model of normative or rational action; they compelled theorists to produce 'esoteric' reflections and to formulate theories of creativity, though they never managed to couple these with a plausible and above all sociologically applicable theory of human action.

This is just what Joas seeks to do in the third part of the book, which sketches the fundamentals of such a theory. As apparent in the book's title, his aim is not to alert us to a particular type of action, which we might call 'creative action' in contrast, for instance, to other (routinized) forms of action. Rather, he tries to show that there is an inherent creative aspect to *all* action. This is why he refers to the 'creativity *of* action'. Joas puts it like this:

> My intention is therefore to provide not a mere extension to, but instead a fundamental restructuring of the principles underlying mainstream action theory. It is not that common typologies of action are simply incomplete; rather, I am calling into question the very principle on which these typologies are based. Any typology of action can be said to be complete, formally speaking, if it overtly or covertly deploys a residual category into which all those phenomena fall which it cannot explicitly grasp conceptually. It by no means follows, however, that such a typology actually has the power to reveal phenomena.

(ibid., p. 145)

By this 'fundamental restructuring of the principles underlying mainstream action theory', Joas means that almost all theories of action, in economics, philosophy, psychology and indeed sociology, took so-called 'rational action' as their point of departure. If we limit ourselves to sociology, this can easily be demonstrated in the work of such different authors as Weber, Parsons and even Habermas. For Weber's theory of action is clearly constructed in such a way that value rational, traditional and affectual action exhibit rational deficiencies in comparison with instrumentally rational action. In *The Structure of Social Action*, Parsons supplements the model of rational action merely with that of normative action. He remains attached to a teleological model of action in that he interprets instrumentally rational or normative goals of action as given, and thus interprets the carrying out of action merely as the realization of preformulated goals (see Lecture II). And even Habermas constructs his model of action in such a way that – in line with the various ways in which action relates to the world – instrumentally rational or strategic action serves as the starting point from which to advance to concepts of action that exhibit more ways of relating to the world and in which a greater potential for rationality develops (see Lecture X). As different as these three authors' action theories may be, all are united by their point of departure: 'rational action'. According to Joas, this is problematic for at least two reasons. First, these models of action never ultimately succeed in capturing the problem of creativity. Their point of departure in 'rational action' always automatically produces a 'non-rational counterpart' (ibid., p. 146) and thus the problem, which we have met already, of residual categories which cannot really be placed within the typology of action. Second, the even more basic problem is that this rational action is simply posited as given or self-evident, while no questions are raised as to which fundamental assumptions underpin this idea itself.

In order to avoid misunderstandings, we would underline that Joas does not wish to call into question the fact that rational models of action may be and often are empirically useful. He merely wishes to contest the tendency to deploy such models of action without systematically discussing their foundations. This may appear to be an overly thorough and even unnecessary approach. In fact, though, it is a vital first step if one is to produce a fundamental critique of traditional action theories in the way Joas intends, as well as a version of the problem of creativity beyond the reach of these theories of action. In other words, this is the only way to advance to a quite different 'understanding of (instrumental) rationality and normativity' (ibid., p. 148).

As Joas states, all theories of action which work with the model of rational action assume 'firstly that the actor is capable of purposive action, secondly that he has control over his own body, and thirdly that he is autonomous vis-à-vis his fellow human beings and his environment' (ibid., p. 147). Yet all three presuppositions are anything but self-evident. Our first task must therefore be to examine them systematically, asking which theories are available to us that can shed light on these as yet unquestioned premises.

1. If we focus on the first assumption that as a rule actors try to realize their intentions according to the means–ends schema, we soon find ourselves confronted with a number of highly persuasive philosophical and

sociological critiques. These cast doubt on the notion that the means–ends schema is obviously the best way to interpret human action. As we have seen (Lecture XI), in his early writings Niklas Luhmann vehemently rejected the model of bureaucracy and organization advocated by Max Weber and Robert Michels, that is, the idea that we can understand organizations as functioning in line with priority objectives. But Luhmann was certainly not the only sociologist who had good reason to question the usefulness of the means–ends schema. Theorists of action also expressed major doubts about its inevitability: one need only think of Jürgen Habermas and his model of communicative action, which he characterized as non-teleological, insofar as discourse has no aim as such, but must be understood as open in terms of its outcome (see Lecture X). A look through the sociological literature alone thus demonstrates that we do not necessarily have to interpret social phenomena and social action in a teleological way.

Joas also embraces this insight, but draws very different and in part more radical conclusions than Luhmann and Habermas. While Luhmann soon abandoned action theory, set about developing a functional-structural theory and – later on – a highly abstract (autopoietic) systems theory (as a result, among other things, of his critique of classical organization theory), and while Habermas merely understands communicative action as non-teleological but otherwise fails to analyse strategic, instrumentally rational or norm-oriented action any further, Joas adopts a different strategy. In contrast to Luhmann, he remains a theorist of action, but unlike Habermas, he questions whether even instrumentally rational and norm-oriented action can be interpreted far more adequately under premises which do not describe all action as teleological from the outset. Here, his authoritative source is John Dewey, who did more than anyone else to undermine the belief in the smooth applicability of the means–ends schema when analysing human action (and thus even influenced Luhmann).

According to Joas, what Dewey teaches us is that goals of action are more than merely the anticipations of future states. In fact, they also organize action very immediately in all its contemporaneity. A reciprocal relationship thus exists between the goals and means of action.

> the goals of action are usually relatively undefined, and only become more specific as a consequence of the decision to use particular means. Reciprocity of goals and means therefore signifies the interaction of the choice of means and the definition of goals. The dimension of means in relation to the dimension of goals is in no way neutral. Only when we recognize that certain means are available to us do we discover goals which had not occurred to us before.
>
> (ibid., p. 154)

On this view, the pragmatists and especially Dewey had convincingly brought out the general fluidity or changeability of goals *as action is being carried out*, goals which cannot as a rule be interpreted as set, and thus rigid, from the outset. The intelligent pursuit of goals is distinguished by a creative weighing up of options for action and available means. And this applies both to instrumentally rational and *moral action*. This is hugely significant because it has immediate consequences for a theory of morality. This is also crystal clear in Dewey's ethical stance, in as much as he distances himself in no uncertain terms from rigid theories of morality that understand moral action as mere adherence to 'pre-existing' ultimate values or norms:

> Every sacralization of an end as a value per se conceals from the actor the further consequences of his definition of goals and choice of means, as though in some miraculous way these would not occur or could be ignored.
>
> (ibid., p. 155)

Thus, by drawing on Dewey, along with other philosophical traditions, Joas is able to show that an empirically substantial analysis of action must necessarily go beyond the means–ends schema, that 'neither routine action nor action permeated with meaning, neither creative nor existentially reflected action can be accounted for using this model' (ibid., p. 156). But if this is the case, the question immediately arises as to why the action-theoretical fixation on the means–ends schema observable throughout the history of the social sciences took hold in the first place and above all why it has held its ground for so long without inspiring much in the way of opposition.

According to Joas, the answer emerges when we realize that theories of action are generally built atop the Cartesian dualism of body and mind, world and ego. Only under this premise was it plausible to conceive of objectives as rational, planned goals separate from action, to imagine that these goals are *first* set by means of a mental process, before (physical) action is *subsequently* carried out. This also implied a further dichotomy, namely that of perception and thinking on the one hand and action on the other. If, however, one accepts the pragmatist critique of Cartesianism (again, see Lecture VI), one sees a very different relationship between action and perception or thinking as well as the possibility of dropping the teleological model of action geared towards the means–ends schema.

> The alternative to a teleological interpretation of action, with its inherited dependence on Cartesian dualisms, is to conceive of perception and cognition not as preceding action but rather as a phase of action by which action is directed and redirected in its situational contexts. According to this alternative view, goal-setting does not take place by an act of the intellect *prior to* the actual action, but is instead the result of a reflection on aspirations

> and tendencies that are prereflective and have *already always* been operative. In this act of reflection, we thematize aspirations which are normally at work without our being actively aware of them. But where exactly are these aspirations located? They are located in our bodies. It is the body's capabilities, habits and ways of relating to the environment which form the background to all conscious goal-setting, in other words, to our intentionality. Intentionality itself, then, consists in a self-reflective control which we exercise over our current behaviour.
>
> (ibid., p. 158; original emphasis)

Thus, pragmatism suggests that critical examination of the concept of ends will lead us to take seriously both the corporeality of action in general and the creativity of specific acts. Crucial here is the emphasis on the situation, the 'situational context'; the 'concept of "situation" is a suitable replacement for the means–end schema as the primary basic category of a theory of action' (ibid., p. 160). For it is the *specific situation in which action occurs*, in which processes of perception and cognition occur, in which plans and goals are formulated in the first place; these are then constantly modified or even reformulated when new situational interpretations crop up: 'Our reflective response to the challenge presented to us by the situation decides which action is taken' (ibid., p. 161). These situational challenges thus require new and creative solutions rather than the unwavering pursuit of goals and plans formulated at a particular point in time. Motives and plans are products of reflection within *action situations*, not (antecedent) causes of action.

A pragmatically informed critique of the means–ends schema thus provides, via the concept of the situation, an insight into the creativity of all action. And it also produces an emphasis on the corporeality of action – an aspect which Anthony Giddens has dealt with in much the same way (though within a rather different context at times), but which other theories of action have tended to neglect entirely. For people do not reflect on situational challenges in a highly rational or abstract-intellectual way. Rather, we do so because our 'corporeal-practical way of relating to the world', the everyday flow of action, our basically unconscious habits, routines and accustomed perceptual modes can no longer be maintained, and the situation demands creative solutions.

> If we adopt the understanding of intentionality that I am putting forward here ... goal-setting becomes the result of a situation in which the actor finds himself prevented from continuing his pre-reflectively driven forms of action. In this situation, he is forced to adopt a reflective stance on his pre-reflective aspirations.
>
> (ibid., p. 162)

Again, it should be clear that such a conception of intentionality is bound to have consequences for a theory of morality, among other things. For not only the pursuit of instrumentally rational goals, but also norm- or value-related action can be grasped more adequately from the perspective of a non-teleological logic. For once again, it is only in concrete action situations that we find out 'what satisfies our aspirations and what accords with our values. Both the concretization of values and the satisfaction of needs depend on exercising powers of creativity' (ibid., p. 163).

2. In analysing the second unquestioned assumption found in most theories of action, that actors are in control of their bodies, Joas points out that we must first clarify through which developmental stages people attain effective control of their bodies and how they are then able to relax this control again, at least temporarily. We can assume neither that people are capable of doing as they like with their bodies as if these were mere objects, nor that this control over the body is always exercised in the same way. After all, when we laugh or cry, we lose such control to some extent, without this being regarded as pathological. The assumption that actors control their bodies is thus by no means a straightforward one.

Drawing on analyses produced by philosophical anthropology and the writings of Maurice Merleau-Ponty and George Herbert Mead, Joas now shows that the capacity for action exists in the first place only on the basis of a 'body schema' or 'body image' constituted in childhood. The 'actor's awareness of the morphological structure of his own body, its parts and its posture, its movements and its limits' (ibid., p. 175) enables him to actively affect his world. Here, though, 'awareness' does not mean a clearly articulated reference to one's own body. For it is the preconscious or prereflective achievements of the body upon which we necessarily rely in order to be able to act – again, this is a thesis with which we are already familiar from our discussion of Giddens' approach and one which evades the dualism of body and mind.

The most impressive account of the *significance* of the body schema is that of Maurice Merleau-Ponty, who refers to phantom limbs. An individual whose arm has been amputated both feels his (missing) arm and constantly focuses on it, yet at the same time he must ignore it again and again. Merleau-Ponty interprets this 'feeling' of the arm neither as a 'physical' phenomenon, for the sensory receptors no longer exist, nor as a purely 'psychological' one, as it is certainly not the case that the amputee merely wishes to suppress the fact of the amputation. Rather, Merleau-Ponty opts out of this body–mind dualism and argues that:

> The phantom arm is not a representation of the arm, but the ambivalent presence of an arm ... To have a phantom arm is to remain open to all the actions of which the arm alone is capable;

it is to retain the practical field which one enjoyed before mutilation ... The patient therefore realizes his disability in so far as he is ignorant of it, and is ignorant of it precisely to the extent that he knows of it.

(Merleau-Ponty, *Phenomenology of Perception*, pp. 81–2)

Thus, because action is also a corporeal phenomenon, we are oriented towards certain aspects of the world. The world is available to us prereflexively. The body schema is both the result of each individual's biography, in which this practical relation to the world has always played a role, and at the same time a process that is never finally complete. For the consciousness of one's body necessarily changes through ageing processes, pregnancy, illnesses or amputations, for example. The actor must therefore constantly preconsciously construct and reconstruct this body schema. The body is *prereflexively* and habitually oriented towards certain changing practical relationships to the world. This means that action theory cannot simply assume that we consciously control our bodies.

While Merleau-Ponty illustrated the significance of the body schema very nicely, his explanations of how it develops, how we are to conceive of the genesis of the body schema in terms of socialization theory, were highly fragmentary. Merleau-Ponty merely implies that the experience of the body is always partly bound up with the experience of the other's body, and thus that the foundations of our (bodily) experience cannot be conceived on the basis of the isolated individual, but only intersubjectively. Yet American pragmatism, especially the work of Mead, features detailed studies of this very subject. Long before Merleau-Ponty, Mead made 'prelinguistic infant communication a part of the explanation of the constitution of the body schema' (Joas, *The Creativity of Action*, p. 181) and provided a plausible account of how the child's relationship to objects is based on the model of role-taking and the capacity to identify with an individual. This way of dealing with things is retained when the child grows up. For Mead,

> the cooperation of the hand and eye first forms 'things', that is, permanent objects, if we impute a substantive inner quality to the object, which then exerts the pressure which we experience as resistance in our relation to the object. This 'inner quality' is to be understood not as something that is located within the object, somewhere beneath its surface, but rather has an active, resisting quality, whose effective core is located in the object. In our practical handling of the object we assume that it has an 'inner quality', that is, that it innately, independently of us, is able to offer resistance.
>
> (ibid., p. 182)

It is possible for this notion of an interior of objects that offers us resistance to arise because the small child is always involved in social interactions and, even if she as yet has no awareness of the boundaries between herself and the world, she already responds to the parents' or other reference persons' gestures. At an early stage in the child's development, there is already communication through gestures, which presupposes identification with the parties to interaction – the parents. And this role-taking provides the child with a model of how to deal with physical objects, in that things too are assumed to have an interior that offers resistance. Having an effect on objects is thus understood in much the same way as having an effect on those with whom one interacts, which occurs by means of gestures, together with the reactions which these trigger, which in turn have an effect on the child.

But while this clarifies the origins of the specific features of action vis-à-vis physical objects, it is not enough to explain the genesis of the body schema itself. According to Mead, this arises only when we attain, through further processes of communication, a form of self-identification which acknowledges the otherness of inanimate objects, their non-sociality. Only then does it become possible for the child to distinguish between the body and other physical objects or between his own body and consciousness (ibid., pp. 182f.). And only then is the child able to gain control over his own body, a fact always merely taken for granted in conventional theories of action.

If it is true that the body is not merely a given for the actor, but is accessible only through a body schema constituted intersubjectively, then the actor's relationship to his body is profoundly shaped by the structures of the social relations in which he grew up.

3. This brings us directly to the third assumption found in most theories of action, namely that the human being is autonomous vis-à-vis other people and the environment. Here, Joas draws on his dissertation and its interpretation of the work of George Herbert Mead, in that Mead did more than anyone else to counter this assumption and to emphasize the *primary sociality* of the actor. Briefly, Mead's anthropological theory of communication enabled him to clarify how a coherent self develops only through communicative relationships. For Mead, individuality is not biologically predetermined. It is a 'result that depends on many preconditions' (ibid., p. 188) – another fact to which most theories of action fail to pay sufficient attention. But what is at issue here is not only the genesis of individuality, but also the always fragile conditions for its maintenance.

This reconstruction of the premises of the rational model of action has significant consequences. It should be clear by now that any account of action processes that fails to pay heed to the corporeality of the actor and his primary sociality risks ignoring key aspects of interactions.

Above all, though, the critique of the means–ends schema assumed by many theories of action and the emphasis on the creative aspects of all action must be accompanied by a significant analytical reorientation of key fields of sociological research. A theory of action informed by pragmatist ideas that takes the creativity of action seriously must – so Joas asserts – have *consequences for macrosociology* as well. Joas discusses this in the fourth section of the book, taking a close look at two fields in particular. He tries to show that in as much as research on social movements takes its lead from the rational model of action, it overlooks crucial features of collective action. For, because of their basic conceptual apparatus, both theorists of resource mobilization (see Lecture VIII), whose understanding of the origins of social movements is anchored in conflict theory or utilitarianism, and researchers such as Neil Smelser (see Lecture XIII), who interpret them in terms of the accomplishment or realization of specific predetermined normative goals, ignore the fact that such movements – as symbolic interactionists, among others, tried to show (see Lecture VI) – feature the emergence of *new* values and goals of action which are generated only *in situations* of mass action. The insight that action is not determined by utility calculations and values arrived at through contemplation thus applies to collective action as well; new definitions of the situation emerge as interacting actors carry out action, definitions which demand a creative interplay of means and ends and which thus make possible the genesis of *new* values.

A neo-pragmatist perspective requires similar revisions of 'traditional' macrosociological theories of social change. If we take seriously Joas' model of action, it is impossible to understand history as the automatic outcome of processes of rationalization and differentiation, as Weberians and above all theorists of differentiation in the tradition of Parsons have always assumed. Rather, it rapidly becomes apparent that actors find themselves confronted with new situations that force them to come up with *creative solutions* – a process which simply cannot be captured by a functionalist logic. Here, Joas' position is very close to that of Castoriadis (see Lecture XVI) who, on the basis of different theoretical premises, also placed special emphasis on the topic of creativity, prompting him to sharply criticize functionalism (of the kind whose arguments are anchored in theories of differentiation). Joas is also sympathetic towards the critique of functionalism put forward by Giddens and Beck. According to Joas, it may well be meaningful to speak of 'differentiation', but we must bear in mind that it is the actors who drive this differentiation, rather than any inherent system logic. Thus, setting himself clearly apart from functionalist theorists, Joas refers to the 'democratization of the differentiation question' in order to underline that, *contra* Luhmann, it is actors rather than theorists who determine the concrete form of differentiation processes and their inevitability.

One of Hans Joas' students, Jens Beckert (b. 1967 and currently director of the Max Planck Institute for the Study of Societies in Cologne), has shown with reference to this pragmatist model of action that economic sociology has a particularly pressing need for the idea of creative action. For, first of all, the analyst of market processes is constantly faced with uncertain decision-making situations in which the actors must come up with creative solutions for want of any solid basis on which to make their decisions. Second, innovation, so crucial to production and market processes, depends almost inevitably on a model of action that places great emphasis on actors' creativity (see Jens Beckert, *Beyond the Market: The Social Foundations of Economic Efficiency* and Joas and Beckert, 'Action Theory').

Joas has pursued further some of the topics insufficiently developed in *The Creativity of Action* in subsequent publications, elaborating more precisely the associated ideas. This applies particularly to the above-mentioned field of macrosociology, with Joas' chief and consistent concern being to grapple with theories of differentiation and modernization. Since the mid-1980s, in much the same way as Anthony Giddens, Joas has paid particular attention to the phenomenon of war and violence in the modern age. Tackling this subject seemed so worthwhile precisely because modern sociology has generally 'avoided' this issue, which has often given rise to a highly problematic progressive optimism (see Joas, *War and Modernity*, especially pp. 29–42). The sociological analysis of wars, their causes, development over time and consequences can do much to relativize the ideas of progress so common in sociology and particularly modernization theory. Studying wars is also useful because they are a prime example of the impact of contingency, of the non-necessary, upon history. Wars are thus not only phases that tend to be neglected because they represent a 'dark' element within a process of 'development' that is often depicted very positively. They are also nodal points of history, because the experience of war and the consequences of wars open up *unpredictable* possibilities for actors. This sets in motion a vast number of *new* processes, which brings out the absurdity of the popular notion that history is linear. To put it in terms of action theory, the actors respond to the 'situation' of war by creatively generating new plans. The concept of 'creativity', it should be underlined, entails no normative evaluation. The creative projects that have arisen during and after wars have by no stretch of the imagination all been morally 'good', as is clearly evident in the now common references to the 'birth of fascism from the spirit of the First World War'.

Thus, by subjecting wars to close scrutiny, Joas is able to relativize macrosociological theories of change. His increasing focus on religions (Joas, *Do We Need Religion? On the Experience of Self-Transcendence*) has a similar function, for the analysis of religious phenomena can also furnish us with insights into macrosociological processes of change. Modernization theorists' simplistic assumption that secularization is a necessary component of modernization has become increasingly implausible.

Alongside this focus on specific fields of social scientific research, Joas has further developed and systematized his genuinely theoretical arguments. His 1997 book *The Genesis of Values* is the key example here. As he did in 1992, Joas again links arguments concerned with the history of theory and of a systematic nature to answer a seemingly straightforward question: How do value commitments arise?

> My intention is ... to look out for those action contexts and types of experience in which the subjective feeling that something is a value has its origin.
>
> (Joas, *The Genesis of Values*, p. 10)

The point of departure here is the observation that modern social theorists from Parsons to Habermas have constantly referred to values, but mostly without making a serious attempt to clarify the *genesis* of values and, above all, to analyse *how people come to feel attached to certain values*. Joas' key thesis with respect to the history of theoretical development is that this topic did in fact attract the interest of acclaimed authors during a specific period of Euro-American intellectual history. Joas tells us that thinkers such as Friedrich Nietzsche, William James, Emile Durkheim, Georg Simmel, Max Scheler and John Dewey attempted to investigate this very problem between the late nineteenth century and the 1930s, with varying motives and very different conceptual tools – and results. On this view, the debate subsequently petered out for various reasons before one of the leading figures in the communitarian debate, Canadian philosopher Charles Taylor, picked up this thread again in systematic fashion in the 1980s (ibid., p. 124). As fraught with problems as these thinkers' expositions always were, Joas' assertion is that if we subject their work to systematic scrutiny, and, above all, if we contrast their arguments and deploy the strengths of some to remedy the weaknesses of others, we shall see that the origin of values lies 'in experiences of self-formation and self-transcendence' (ibid., p. 1).

Let us turn to the first part of this thesis. Values and value commitments first develop in childhood and adolescence, when the individual self takes shape; when, for example, personal identity is formed through the dialogical or, if you will, harmonious process of separating from, and discontinuation of, parental care. But we must always keep in mind that both individual and collective identities may certainly be constituted in response to the experience of power and exclusion as well; a wide range of values may result. Turning once again to a macrosociological phenomenon discussed above, the experience of violent conflict may lead to a (militaristic or fascist) glorification of violence or to a profound attachment to pacifist values. But the origins of values and value commitments also lie – and this is the second part of Joas' thesis – in the experience of self-transcendence in extraordinary situations, such as religious rituals or moments of collective ecstasy, through the 'confrontation with death; shame and guilt, remorse and humility; the opening of the self in conversation and in the experience of nature', etc. (ibid., p. 164), as elaborated by a number of the authors discussed by Joas, insights we could surely build upon by producing a detailed phenomenology of the experience of values.

This theoretical answer to the question of the genesis of values is the point of departure for an empirical research programme. It is crucial to distinguish between various aspects of the concept of 'genesis' if this idea is to bear fruit in historical sociology.

> Firstly, it can involve the original historical promulgation of a value; secondly, the defence of this value by a small, but growing, group of disciples; thirdly, the genesis of a new commitment in individuals (through conversion, for example) to values which are by no means historically new; fourthly and finally, a resuscitation of values which have lost their drive or sunk into oblivion.
>
> (ibid., p. 165)

It is vital to keep in mind at all times that *contingent circumstances* play a decisive role in the genesis of values; values follow no developmental logic, and the process of attachment to specific values is not a more or less inevitable one. Rather, values are 'born', adopted and disseminated in concrete action situations. Joas' current investigations centre on the historical and sociological study of the origins of human rights and the ideal of universal human dignity, and on analysing the twentieth century with an eye on contingency. The key focus of interest is moral universalism in its various concrete historical forms.

The highly charged question which arises, from both a social scientific and philosophical point of view, is how to reconcile the contingent way in which values develop with claims of a universalist morality. In attempting to solve this problem, Joas approaches the position of Paul Ricoeur which, as we stated in Lecture XVI, anticipates the productive integration of communitarian and liberal approaches. However, Joas' own attempt to mediate between these positions is based on arguments other than those deployed by Ricoeur; once again, his line of argument owes much to pragmatist premises.

As we have mentioned on a number of occasions, pragmatist ethics was consistently developed with the actor's perspective in mind. For Dewey and Mead, this meant that it was the solving of concrete action problems that stood centre stage, rather than the abstract justification of norms. This leads ultimately to a critique of 'traditional' theories of morality. Mead, for example, assails Kant because 'the categorical imperative as such could only serve to subject actions to a universalization test, but not to discover which actions were adequate in the first place' (ibid., p. 170). The object of Mead's criticism was the assumption found in Kantian ethics that specific guides to action could only be anchored in rules with which everyone must comply. For Mead, though, this is not the case at all, because the actor is faced with a concrete situation and is thus compelled to decide how to act 'under contingent conditions'. For him, it is therefore 'not the justification which is uppermost, but the specification of the good or the right in an action situation' (ibid., p. 171).

Because pragmatists consistently argue from an action theory perspective, the concept of 'situation' plays a crucial role for them with respect to moral theory as well – and this informs Joas' neo-pragmatist attempt to mediate between liberals and communitarians. According to Joas, we cannot do without the Kantian categorical imperative, or another universalizing rule, when we examine moral alternatives. In this sense, of course, the right always has a place within moral discourse, as Mead also conceded; as is well known, he did not reject the notion of the categorical imperative. On the other hand, however, decisions themselves cannot be derived from a universalizing rule, but must be made under conditions of situational contingency. This means that we can state neither that the right takes priority over the good (the liberal position), nor that the good has precedence over the right (as communitarians would assert). All people can do is reflect on each and try to strike a balance between them:

> If ... one assumes a theory of action which anchors intentionality in the situation-specific reflection on our pre-reflective conations, then it becomes clear that the right can only ever be an examining authority ... In these situations we can only ever achieve a reflective equilibrium between our orientations. Certainly, the extent to which we subject our orientations to this test may vary. For this reason, there is in the point of view of the right a perpetual, unflagging potential to modify the good, in order to enable it to pass the universalization test. But it does not follow from the universality of the right that, in action situations, we should give precedence to the right over all other considerations as a matter of course – nor that we should not do this.
>
> (ibid., p. 173)

This means that there exists a highly charged interrelationship between universal norms and particular values. At all events, it is impossible to derive specific values from universal norms. At the same time, with respect to political theory, this means that we cannot claim that there is no place for particular values in a constitutional state characterized by universal norms, as Habermas for instance long assumed. Rather, we must work on the assumption that the particular value systems of Western democracies certainly feature rules

> which can be viewed as translations of universal moral rules into particular political institutions. These ... inevitably remain particular, and, each time they are imported into another culture, must always be examined in order to assess whether their particularity is a particularism. The notion, however, that in order to overcome particularism, particularity itself must disappear, overlooks the necessarily contingent character of values.
>
> (ibid., p. 175)

Here, then, Joas, in contrast to Habermas (see Lecture X), is asserting that it is neither empirically plausible nor argumentatively imperative to conceive of the integration of societies solely in terms of universalist legal norms. Rather, and this lays bare his proximity to communitarianism, it is entirely possible (and empirically credible) to think about the cohesion of societies in terms of specific, and thus particular, values, without necessarily coming into conflict with the universal norms highlighted by liberals. A stance such as this, which serves as intermediary between liberals and communitarians, also implies a critique of Habermasian discourse ethics, in as much as this excludes questions about values by arguing that they cannot be universalized, which creates tremendous difficulties. Joas has much sympathy for the intentions underlying Habermasian discourse ethics. But he believes that this ethics can be deployed productively only if the problem of values, to which Habermas fails to pay attention, is adequately dealt with. A reformed discourse ethics would at least have to take account of the following aspects of values, whose empirical relevance is clearly evident in Joas' view:

> The discourse tests that to which people feel themselves evaluatively drawn. Without value commitment, they cannot feel motivated to participate in the discourse and keep to its rules; and they feel themselves bound to the result of the discourse only when this arises from their value commitment, or when the experience of participation itself produces value commitment.
>
> (ibid., p. 182)

What is required, alongside a theory of rational discourse, is thus a corresponding logic of communication about values (for a preliminary outline, see Joas, 'Values versus Norms: A Pragmatist Account of Moral Objectivity'). Joas' proximity to Ricoeur, so clearly apparent here, again underlines forcefully our assertion in Lecture I that the development of social theory cannot be understood as a random series of disparate theories. Rather, it is apparent that common problems exist which at times lead to convergence. Learning processes among liberals and communitarians have brought about a rapprochement between once sharply divided positions; and a similar modification of, for example, the content of Habermasian discourse ethics, has proved possible both within a German–American neo-pragmatist framework and a French anti-structuralist and hermeneutic one. It is wrong to imagine that the internationalization of developments in social theory that has occurred since the Parsonian hegemony came to an end has automatically led to an inexorable process of fragmentation. This will also become apparent in the next and final lecture, in which we turn our attention to the current state of social theory.

XX

How things stand

Looking back over Lectures IX–XIX, there can be no doubt that the classical approaches and those schools that evaded integration into the edifice of Parsonian theory were joined by new and promising syntheses in the field of social theory in the 1970s and 1980s. But these were merely additions to the stock of existing approaches. They did not succeed, as their exponents undoubtedly intended, in dominating the field of social theory institutionally rather than merely synthesizing it intellectually. Thus, despite the widespread desire to produce syntheses, it is by no means easy to sum up the current state of social theory. Furthermore, the recent past has seen far-reaching historical changes of a global nature, such as the collapse of the Soviet empire, which it will take some time for social theorists to digest. In this concluding lecture, we therefore wish to avoid creating the impression that there is a straightforward solution to every problem. Rather, we offer you a tableau of the contemporary situation, an overview of the most recent creative trends, intended to help orient you within this confusing field and with respect to your own studies. You should of course keep in mind at all times that these new trends are all in one way or another further developments of the work of the theorists or theoretical schools dealt with in the preceding lectures. The current situation thus comprises both the most recent studies as well as the potential of all the theories we have examined so far. This final lecture serves to complement and bring up to date what has gone before; this is not the crowning moment at which all the strands are neatly brought together. But this introduction to open questions and contemporary developments may encourage you to bring to bear your own perspectives in the field of social theory and thus to carry this discourse on into the future, a discourse whose post-war history we have presented here.

1. Let us begin by scrutinizing how contemporary scholars have elaborated on the particularly ambitious and widely acknowledged theoretical syntheses by Habermas, Luhmann, Giddens and Touraine. Giddens' theory of structuration has certainly seen the least degree of further development. Giddens himself has not attempted to extend his action theoretical programme, and none of his students has seriously, and above all systematically, attempted to do so. This stagnation may be due to the nature of Giddens' theory building. In contrast to Habermas and Luhmann, his synthesis was from the

outset based only to a minor degree on a deep philosophical grasp of his field of work. He tended instead to draw on empirical observations from heterogeneous fields in order to elaborate his basic ideas. This was certainly an advantage in terms of how his work was received, but it did not pave the way for further systematic work. We can thus dip into his work as a source of stimulation, but it failed to spawn its own school.

Things are rather different with respect to Luhmannian theory. Unlike Giddens, a number of Luhmann's students followed firmly in the footsteps of the 'master' and managed to exercise a significant influence within sociology, especially in Germany. Admittedly, Luhmann's project raised the question of whether it was even possible to 'elaborate' on his theory in a literal sense, given the profoundly radical and consistent way in which Luhmann carried out his theoretical work. 'Had Luhmann himself not already said everything?' There is no denying that the Luhmann school features a certain epigonality. There are, however, exceptions, Luhmann's student Rudolf Stichweh (b. 1951), his successor as chair of sociology at the University of Bielefeld and now professor in Lucerne (Switzerland), being the prime example here. He has distinguished himself within the systems theory debate through a strong historical orientation and by focusing consistently on the sociology of science and the professions on the one hand and the sociology of so-called 'world society' on the other.

Through a number of historical studies, Stichweh has not only provided an account of the early phase of differentiation of the European academic system (*Der frühmoderne Staat und die europäische Universität. Zur Interaktion von Politik und Erziehungssystem im Prozeß ihrer Ausdifferenzierung (16.–18. Jahrhundert)* ['The Early Modern State and the European University. The Interaction between Politics and the Education System in the Course of their Differentiation (16th–18th Century)']), but, by elaborating more precisely on differentiation theory, has revealed the peculiarity and complexity of the differentiation of academic disciplines, which it is impossible to capture convincingly with the conceptual tools of segmentary or functional differentiation. Stichweh thus renders systems theory open to a more empirically adequate account of modernity than was (and continues to be) possible with the original Luhmannian approach, with its generally overstated thesis of the absolute primacy of functional differentiation in the modern age.

> On the one hand, disciplinary differentiation differs from functional differentiation in that rather than, for example, assigning complementary subproblems of the system to specific subsystems for processing, it operates via the internalization of the differentiation of environmental sectors. On the other hand, disciplinary

differentiation differs from segmentary differentiation in that the units which it places side by side are not fundamentally identical, but are defined by their non-identity with other units.

(Stichweh, *Wissenschaft, Universität, Professionen. Soziologische Analysen* ['Science, University, Professions. Sociological Analyses'] p. 22)

Since the mid-1990s, Stichweh has also striven to update Luhmann's ideas on 'global society' in an attempt to bolster systems theory's standing as a source of convincing interpretations within the heated debate on so-called globalization. Luhmann had referred to 'global society' as early as the mid-1970s, a step he justified primarily in terms of communication theory. The claim here is that contemporary global communicational connectivity, brought about by novel means of communication and transportation, has rendered the notion of national societies meaningless both empirically and theoretically. We can only meaningfully speak of *one* 'global society'. There are two interesting things about Stichweh's elaboration of Luhmann's ideas. First, he goes further than Luhmann in attempting to explain why the similar-sounding notion of 'world system', anchored in Wallersteinian Marxism, and theories of 'globalization' found in other theoretical contexts (see Beck or Giddens) are wrong. According to Stichweh, the economically based centre–periphery distinction so central for Wallerstein rests on an 'old European' conceptual model that fails to capture the fact of functional differentiation characteristic of modernity (Stichweh, *Die Weltgesellschaft* ['Global Society'], pp. 15 and 199). On this view, the distinction between world cities and rural regions, between core and peripheral states, etc. is of diminishing empirical relevance as functional differentiation proceeds apace. For related reasons, the concept of globalization is also inadequate 'because it focuses primarily on the genetic factor of the expansion or delocalization of phenomena formerly limited to a particular location. It fails, however, to do so from the perspective of a system arising concurrently at a higher systemic level, which uses mechanisms of globalization to develop its own structure' (ibid., p. 14). It thus fails to probe the systemic nature of the world as such.

Second, Stichweh's arguments with regard to 'global society' are worthy of note because, in contrast to Luhmann, he pays serious attention to normative structures. Luhmann himself always showed an almost cynical lack of interest in such issues. Regardless of whether the notion of 'global society' is really as fruitful as its champions imagine, and of whether the shift away from the nation-state that tends to go along with it proves a rash move, what is interesting from the point of view of social theory is the extent to which Stichweh also leans on Parsons, asserting that states within the 'global society' are faced with obligations thrown up by modernity. Concretely, they have normative obligations to take welfarist measures (ibid., p. 58). His work is thus marked by a cautious distancing from Luhmann's strong anti-normativism, which no longer seems tenable in this form, particularly with respect to empirical analyses.

This distancing from Luhmann is even more apparent in the work of another leading systems theorist, namely Helmut Willke, also professor of sociology at the University of Bielefeld. At first sight, Willke (b. 1954) appears to share Luhmann's key theoretical assumptions, when he claims 'that the centrifugal dynamic of functional differentiation drives a metamorphosis of the principle underlying how society is ordered, a pervasive shift towards the heterarchic, polycentric and decentralized organization of autonomous subsystems of society' (Willke, *Ironie des Staates. Grundlinien einer Staatstheorie polyzentrischer Gesellschaft* ['The Irony of the State. Key Features of a Theory of the State for the Polycentric Society'], p. 7). Like Luhmann, he rejects the idea that politics should be seen as a supreme, central authority that steers society, one that dominates or directs the other subsystems. But Willke neither endorses Luhmann's notion of 'global society' (see *Supervision des Staates* ['The Supervision of the State'], pp. 9f.), nor does he share the radicalism shown by Luhmann, who seemed to have nothing but scorn for the idea that politics can usefully steer anything. This places him among the ranks of those political scientists and sociologists who felt increasingly disappointed by the thrust of Luhmannian theory from the 1980s on. If Luhmann's theoretical programme still seemed hugely attractive in the 1970s, because the notion of the inherent logic of subsystems appeared to shed light on contemporary phenomena such as the inability of Western societies to reform themselves, Luhmann's ever more extreme pessimism regarding the impact of government policies, which was merely logically derived rather than empirically proven, was bound to meet with resistance eventually, particularly in the field of political sociology. Authors such as Fritz Scharpf and Renate Mayntz at the Max Planck Institute for the Study of Societies in Cologne increasingly moved away from the Luhmannian theoretical programme with which they had worked for a time, attempting, in contrast to Luhmann, to grasp the interplay of collective actors, in order to describe political processes and above all to explain why politically guided reform projects have been successful in some societies yet not in others (on the differences between Luhmann and Scharpf, see their 1989 clash in *Politische Vierteljahresschrift*).

Willke too has ultimately taken the same step. In a surprising move, he has drawn, among other things, on Amitai Etzioni's great work *The Active Society*, discussed in Lecture XVIII. Willke makes a spirited attempt to probe the potential for a plausible theory of political control which, in contrast to Luhmann's approach, integrates action theory to the extent that Willke's arguments make much of differing constellations of corporative actors (*Systemtheorie III: Steuerungstheorie* ['Systems Theory III: The Theory of Political Control'], pp. 21ff.). Willke understands democratic politics as a key type of societal control alongside that provided by the market and by hierarchies. For him, democratic control is now conceivable only in terms of 'distanced engagement', that is, in terms of contextual control. Politics (that is, democratic politics) can no longer hope to command or issue instructions to the other subsystems. Willke agrees with Luhmann here. But (and this underpins its potential to exercise an influence) it can take on a supervisory role; it can encourage the other functional systems to reflect upon themselves:

> The reason why, given the equality in principle of all functional systems within a functionally differentiated modern democracy, it should be politics that takes on the role of supervisory authority, is not to be found in any kind of primacy of politics, however residual, but in the specific function of politics itself: its responsibility for the production and safeguarding of the collective goods indispensable to the society. This functional explanation implies two elementary principles of political supervision. First, only those decisions that touch on the 'essentials' of the production and safeguarding of collective goods are subject to political supervision. Second, political supervision does not replace decisions made by its own decisions – which would amount to an infringement of the autonomy enjoyed by the functional systems. Rather, in the event that the shortcomings of a questionable decision have been discursively established, supervision is restricted to 'referring back', that is, to pointing the functional system towards a revision of its options, towards a reconsideration of its policy options.
>
> (*Ironie des Staates*, p. 335)

The extent to which this opening of Luhmannian theory to action theory will set a precedent, and the extent to which this step can be reconciled with the Luhmannian notion of 'autopoietic' (sub-)systems in the first place (see also the critical observations by Schimank, *Theorien gesellschaftlicher Differenzierung* ['Theories of Social Differentiation'], pp. 196ff.), will only become apparent through future discussions of a more comprehensive and perhaps more fundamental nature. But what already seems clear is that if they fail to embrace action theory, the empirical relevance of arguments anchored in systems theory is likely to diminish markedly, while systems theory as a whole will sink into sterility.

From the late 1980s, a similar cautious distancing from the 'head of the school' as occurred in the 'Luhmann camp' has also marked anti-structuralist sociology around Alain Touraine. Touraine 'attracted' a large number of talented collaborators and students, at least some of whom have gone their own ways. Notably, these collaborators, with François Dubet

(b. 1946) and Michel Wieviorka (b. 1946) being the leading examples, have done empirical research in a much wider area. While Touraine focused mainly on social movements in his empirical studies, which formed the basis for his reflections on the contemporary era, his students began to subject a broader range of topics to *empirical* examination in an attempt to render Touraine's theoretical ideas more plausible. Dubet's research foci lie not only in the field of social movements, but also in urban sociology, the sociology of youth, immigration, occupations and education (see for example Dubet, *La galère. Jeunes en survie* from 1987; Dubet and Didier Lapeyronnie, *Les quartiers d'exil* ['Districts of Exile'] from 1992; Dubet, *Le déclin de l'institution* ['The Decline of the Institution'] from 2002), while Michel Wieviorka has become well-known, among other things, as a result of his analyses of terrorism and racism (see Wieviorka, *Sociétés et terrorisme*, 1988, English title: *The Making of Terrorism*; Wieviorka et al., *La France raciste* ['Racist France'], 1992; *La violence* ['Violence'], 2004; *The Lure of Anti-Semitism*, 2007).

This expansion of empirical research was no accident. It was the expression of an increasing distance from theoretical notions cultivated by Touraine, at least in the middle developmental phase of his work. While he clung stubbornly, into the 1980s, to the idea that a new, major social movement was set to emerge that would take the place of the earlier labour movement and never entirely abandoned this notion even in the 1990s, Dubet and Wieviorka have broken more radically with such ideas. In their view, social structures have become too heterogeneous and unstable to justify such thematic focus on *one emerging* social movement. They therefore quite consciously opt to study a whole spectrum of what used to be called 'social problems', though they have given up any hopes that these problems might somehow mobilize large groups of people.

It was Dubet who went furthest in producing explicit theoretical observations on these topics (see *Sociologie de l'expérience* ['The Sociology of Experience'] from 1994). In much the same way as his teacher Touraine, he criticizes the ideas typical of so-called 'classical sociology', which suggest that individuals are seamlessly integrated into stable 'societies' through the internalization of norms, though his critique is even harsher. According to Dubet, we can no longer assume such a degree of unity between individual and institution, between individual and society. Rather, the institutional structures of societies have begun to crumble and are in the process of disintegration; as a result, actors are compelled to adhere to very diverse and often incompatible logics of action. Ultimately, this means that the (Tourainian) idea of a central social conflict can no longer reflect reality (*Sociologie de l'expérience*, p. 15), for even such an idea, influenced by conflict theory, is based on the (false) assumption of a *unity* against which specific actors might struggle. Dubet thus underlines more decisively than did Touraine in his late work (again, see Lecture XVI) that the idea of a 'historical subject' must be abandoned and that the differences between social movements (plural!), with their differing forms of mobilization and differing projects, must be regarded as normal (ibid., pp. 214ff. and 258).

As Dubet tries to show through his own empirical studies, a split has occurred between system/institution/society on the one hand and actors on the other, a split which we cannot get to grips with using the conceptual tools of 'classical sociology'. The 'classical' autonomous individual (in a Weberian or Durkheimian sense) no longer exists, while concepts such as 'alienation', 'crisis' or 'contradiction', whose origins lie in the Marxist context, no longer provide any real purchase on reality (ibid., p. 58). As Dubet makes clear, the experience of 'alienation', for example, can be articulated only in a stable institutional context, from which one feels excluded or alienated. But this no longer applies, because subjects are now concerned solely with the constant (sometimes despairing) search for identity, an identity whose stability can no longer be guaranteed by any institution (ibid., p. 18).

On this view, then, systems and institutions have lost their previous, or perhaps merely assumed, hyperstability, their power to integrate individuals. Dubet's exaggerated, though not entirely implausible observation, no doubt aimed at structuralisms and systems theories of all kinds, is that sociology has responded sensibly to this: most of the theories of action that have attracted attention since the 1990s (ibid., p. 79) feature a justified scepticism towards all hyperstable constructions of structure and system. Dubet wishes to endorse this development, and indeed to take it further. He suggests replacing the term 'action' with that of 'social experience', as the latter is free of the problematic assumptions of rationality characteristic of the concept of action:

> Experience is a cognitive activity, a way of constructing what is real, of 'verifying' it, of *experimenting* with it. Experience constructs those phenomena beyond the categories of reason and rationality.
>
> (ibid., p. 93; original emphasis)

However, Dubet develops this interesting concept of 'experience', so significant to American pragmatism (see Dewey, *Experience and Nature*), no further in terms of theory. His concept of experience thus remains no more than a label intended to raise the profile of a diagnosis of the contemporary era that places great emphasis on the dissolution of stable institutional forms. Without serious efforts to flesh out the concepts of action and experience, however, this diagnosis will never be entirely persuasive. In light of this, it will be intriguing to observe the theoretical path trodden by members of the 'Touraine camp' in future.

The clearest reorientations initiated by students and colleagues have probably occurred with respect to Jürgen Habermas. Axel Honneth (b. 1949), professor of philosophy at the University of Frankfurt and Habermas' successor as chair, is the leading example here. Honneth, Habermas' assistant in the 1980s, moved towards a social theory which may be described as 'conflict theoretical' in a very broad sense at an early stage; he attempted to strengthen certain motifs found in Habermas' early work that fell increasingly out of sight as his oeuvre developed. This was already evident in Honneth's 1986 dissertation on critical theory, Foucault and Habermas (Honneth, *The Critique of Power: Reflective Stages in a Critical Social Theory*). Honneth criticized Habermas' distinction between system and life-world and the theory of evolution that underpins it (see Lecture X), because it conceals the fact that the institutional structure of society was and is the result of battles and processes of negotiation between groups in every field. According to Honneth, Habermas' specific approach with respect to evolutionary theory causes him to describe the historical relationship between systems and life-world as a quasi-automatic (learning) process and thus ruins its chances of achieving 'an understanding of the social order as an institutionally mediated communicative relation between *culturally integrated groups* that, so long as the exercise of power is asymmetrically distributed, takes place through the medium of *social struggle*' (Honneth, *Critique of Power*, p. 303; emphasis added).

Honneth went on to develop this conflict theory in his 1992 postdoctoral thesis (*The Struggle for Recognition: The Moral Grammar of Social Conflicts*), in which, as the title indicates, the concept of 'recognition' played a crucial strategic role in theoretical terms. While Honneth endorses Habermas' ideas in many respects, he wishes to understand his 'communication paradigm ... not in terms of a theory of language but of recognition' (*Disrespect: The Normative Foundations of Critical Theory*, p. 74). What does this mean, and above all, what is the thrust of Honneth's arguments?

What is clear is that the term 'recognition', found in the early Hegel, which is intended to capture the moral development of humanity as a sequence of different social struggles, best expresses Honneth's 'conflict theoretical' intentions. As Honneth sees things, there are several advantages associated with this perspective. The historical process can thus be interpreted, first of all, as a social struggle between various social groups or classes over a particular institutional structure, one which will continue as long as groups or classes feel that they have not received sufficient recognition. Elsewhere, Honneth expresses this as follows:

> Hegel, anticipating a materialist objection to cognitivist theories of development, traces the moral learning process characteristic of the human species back to the negative experiences of a practical

struggle carried on by subjects over the legal and social recognition of their identity. A critical social theory can still benefit from a concept of 'social struggle' transformed in this way because it opens up the theoretical possibility of interpreting the historical process as a directed sequence of moral conflicts and disputes.

(Honneth, 'Moralische Entwicklung und sozialer Kampf. Sozialphilosophische Lehren aus dem Frühwerk Hegels' ['Moral Development and Social Struggle: Social Philosophical Teachings from the Early Hegel'])

But the concept of recognition not only enables us to retain the theory of conflict found in Marx, which gradually dropped out of sight in Habermas' theory. At the same time, as the conclusion of the above quotation suggests, the concept of recognition also allows us to escape from Marxian economism, in as much as Marx reduced the struggle between social classes as far as possible to the idea of a merely *economic conflict of interest*. 'Recognition' is far broader in scope. The feeling that such recognition is not forthcoming is not only the result of economic disadvantages, but also of cultural contempt, linguistic discrimination, etc. This last point not only makes it possible to move beyond Marxist theories, but also to produce a well-founded critique of universalist moral theories such as that of Rawls, in that Honneth can rightly point to the fact that feelings of disrespect do not result solely from the experience of the unfair distribution of goods in society. Furthermore, the concept of recognition offers an easy way into a wide range of current debates in which the topic of collective rights is considered – such as feminist discussions of women's rights and debates centred on multiculturalism that tackle the political representation of ethnic and linguistic groups. Finally, the concept of recognition tones down the rationalistic character of Habermas' diagnosis of the contemporary world, which always understands social pathologies solely as system-induced limitations on a comprehensive everyday communicative rationality. According to Honneth, there are certainly other social pathologies, such as the dissolution of social 'binding power', and these can be better captured through a theory of communication informed by the theory of recognition than through Habermas' theoretical toolkit (*Disrespect*, p. 73).

If it is true, as Honneth claims is demonstrated by various historical studies and by research informed by socialization theory, that both the action undertaken by groups and classes and individual moral conduct are guided by intuitive notions of justice; if it is true, therefore, that notions of justice play a role in both cases, notions bound up with 'respect for one's own dignity, honour or integrity', then any social theory anchored in theories of communication must proceed differently than Habermas suggested. For it is clear then that 'the *normative presupposition* of all communicative action is to be seen in the acquisition of social recognition' (ibid., p. 71; emphasis added). Honneth thus criticizes Habermas for failing to discuss this prerequisite, for having left out the moral foundation of all communication, making his diagnosis of the contemporary world very one-sided and implausible in certain respects.

This position, however, as Honneth is well aware, demands considerably more explanation. He needs to deal with at least two problems. First, he is compelled to elaborate different forms of recognition and disrespect. This he did to a certain extent in the book *The Struggle for Recognition*, where he set out the specific understandings of the concept of recognition and disrespect as found in the work of Hegel and Mead. But he needs to go well beyond the mere exegesis of these two thinkers and at the very least elaborate what recognition and disrespect might mean in the first place, through a kind of *formal anthropology*. Honneth himself refers to the 'difficult problem', 'of replacing Habermas' universal pragmatics with an anthropological conception that can explain the normative presuppositions of social interaction' (ibid., p. 72). Honneth has made a start on this in recent essays, particularly those in which he defends his programme against critics (ibid., pp. 129–43; his most detailed exposition so far is found in Nancy Fraser and Axel Honneth, *Redistribution or Recognition?*). But we may wonder whether this is not to expect too much of the concept of recognition, far beyond its original task. A conflict-oriented conception of intersubjectivity may not necessarily answer all the questions that arise when one attempts to ground the social sciences in terms of action theory.

But it seems absolutely crucial for Honneth to produce a convincing anthropologically grounded phenomenology of recognition and disrespect because – and this is the second problem – this is the only means of developing a research programme centred on what he calls the 'pathologies' or 'paradoxes of capitalist modernization' (see Honneth, 'Zur Zukunft des Instituts für Sozialforschung' ['On the Future of the Institute for Social Research'], pp. 62f.) that is truly capable of competing with other diagnoses of the contemporary world, including that of Habermas. In principle, Honneth must determine exactly when and where genuine cases of disrespect occur in modern societies. The work of the Institute for Social Research in Frankfurt, which still exists and has always been associated with critical theory, and whose current director is none other than Axel Honneth, will reveal the extent to which this can succeed. In any event, it is clear that the thrust of Honneth's theoretical work represents a clearer shift away from the 'head of the school' than in the other cases discussed here. Rather than a sign of the poor quality of Habermas' original theory, this is evidence of its openness, which appears to allow other authors to develop it further in a huge variety of ways.

2. In point one we referred to French sociology and social theory only with respect to the contemporary elaboration of Touraine's theory, to how his students have developed his ideas. We could do the same for Bourdieu's work, pointing to such interesting students as Loïc Wacquant (b. 1960). But this seems like a misguided approach to us as it would overlook more significant changes in French social theory since the 1990s.

These changes have seen a younger generation move sharply away from structuralism and poststructuralism and turn towards French (Ricoeur), German and Anglo-Saxon theories of action. Historian of science François Dosse has called this process the 'humanization of the social sciences'. The younger generation 'finally seems to have found the words and mental equipment to pursue its quest for meaning without teleology, to express its sensitiveness to historicity without historicism, and its taste for acting without activism' (Dosse, *The Empire of Meaning: The Humanization of the Social Sciences*, p. xx). This shift is generating a wealth of important studies at present, and our survey would be inadequate without a fairly detailed account of recent French social theory.

The terms used by Dosse seem overly abstract at first sight, but they become clearer if we look at who or what this younger generation is turning against. The clearest stance in this regard is probably that adopted by Luc Boltanski (b. 1940; a student of Bourdieu as it happens) and Eve Chiapello (b. 1965). These authors emphasize that the French sociology of the 1960s and 1970s – and they are referring here both to genuine structuralism and Bourdieu – was caught up in a strangely contradictory argumentational structure. On the one hand, social reality was said to be governed by unchanging laws. On the other hand, the very social scientists who made such claims lent their support to left-wing movements which aimed to intervene actively in the course of events, to change things. But there was another evident contradiction. On the one hand, these scholars laid claim to a scientific rigour that inevitably unmasked individuals' moral values and ideals as ideologies. Yet on the other hand, as scientists, these writers themselves also had critical ideals; their attempt to get at the truth would otherwise be meaningless.

> This tension is particularly evident in Pierre Bourdieu's sociology of domination. Its goal is to reveal 'mechanisms' with the help of which domination is practised everywhere and at all times, a domination that is presented as an iron law and which also claims to advance the liberation of individuals as a liberation from external power and interference. But if, in the final analysis, all relationships can be reduced to conflicts of interest and power relations, if a law immanent to the social order is at work here, what is the point in exposing these relationships with an indignant critical tone,

rather than coolly identifying them in the style of an entomologist studying the society of ants?

(Boltanski and Chiapello, 'Die Rolle der Kritik in der Dynamik des Kapitalismus und der normative Wandel' ['The Role of Criticism in the Dynamic of Capitalism and Normative Change'], p. 460)

This anti-structuralist line of argument, which is also anti-Bourdieu, is elucidated by those 'abstract' terms brought into play by Dosse to characterize the theoretical projects pursued by the younger generation. For those such as Boltanski and Chiapello, who criticize the structuralists and Bourdieu, avoid arguing in 'teleological' fashion, that is, assuming that history has a final destination, and eschew 'historicism', in other words the assumption that social processes unfold in an inevitable way, in line with a set pattern. Aware of historical contingencies, such a critic will tend to proceed with careful consideration, rather than play the prophetic 'activist' with the (false) consciousness of one who believes history is on his side. We have just encountered a term, 'contingency', which clarifies why ethnomethodology and symbolic interactionism, for example, which had been ignored almost entirely for decades by French intellectuals, are being embraced so willingly by this younger generation. For among other things, it is the insights furnished by the so-called interpretive paradigm (see Lectures VI and VII) which show that actors reach decisions in very specific *situations* and under *contingent* circumstances. The interactionist or ethnomethodological thesis was that action cannot simply be predicted or derived and that actors do not simply act in conformity with norms or rules, but constantly *negotiate* and *modify* these norms and rules in a highly complex *process of interpretation*. This was clearly an effective way of expressing with greater theoretical precision what had previously been no more than a sense of unease with the structuralist system of thought.

Such a new action-theoretical perspective triggers a reassessment of the role of values and norms. While structuralist sociology tended not to take these seriously, merely interpreting them as an ideological mask or as the expression of a false consciousness, this younger generation appears to be drawing near once again to a classical issue of social theory, namely 'the issue of social order and how it is "presented" ... without reducing it *a priori* to the mere interplay of forces which the actors are unable to influence' (ibid.). This also implies that one take seriously the values and norms of actors, the nature of their criticisms and justifications, without rushing to denounce them as ideologies. Boltanski and Chiapello sum this up by stating memorably that sociology, which is supposedly so critical (in other words, structuralist-determinist) will ultimately have to be replaced by a *sociology of criticism* (ibid.).

Boltanski in particular pursued such a project in a number of publications written with various co-authors, perhaps the most impressive being *On Justification: Economies of Worth* (1991), a collaboration with the economist Laurent Thévenot. As the authors state at the very beginning of their study, they have set themselves the task of producing a typology of the various justificatory logics deployed by actors in discourse and demonstrating empirically how consensus is justified and produced, while aiming to avoid the conventional dichotomy between consensus and conflict (*On Justification*, p. 25). They first survey the history of political philosophy, identifying six 'regimes of justification' frequently deployed in different situations to legitimize or criticize certain decisions in a general way. In highly original language, the authors refer to six *cités* or 'cities'. In the history of political philosophy, a particular type of city formed the background to individuals' ambitions to achieve greatness (*grandeur*) and in line with this individuals had to invoke different arguments within public discourse. The *civitas Dei* of St Augustine (354–430), for example, demanded a different discourse, the invocation of different justifications, than Adam Smith's city of merchants. Concretely, Boltanski and Thévenot distinguish between the *cité inspirée* (in which greatness is an attribute of that which is holy, that is, justificatory strategies refer to the sacredness of given circumstances or the holiness of an individual), the *cité domestique* (greatness is an attribute of the first born, the oldest, etc.), the *cité de l'opinion* (in which greatness depends on the opinions of numerous others), the *cité civique* (greatness is an attribute of the political representative, who represents the collectivity), the *cité marchande* (greatness is a quality of those who know how to make the most of market opportunities) and the *cité industrielle* (in which greatness is calculated according to the efficiency of given measures) (ibid., pp. 83ff.).

Equipped with the results of this discourse analysis, which may strike you as strange, Boltanski and Thévenot now set about studying processes of decision-making and discussion in businesses. This project, especially as pursued by Boltanski, leads to at least three significant theoretical insights. First, it is evident that all six forms of justification are deployed within the sphere of the economy, though of course to varying degrees, that the economy too features more than one dominant strategy of legitimation. This also means that the various decision-making situations are ambiguous, as they always involve a process of negotiation between different actors, who, moreover, bring very different arguments into play (see Wagner, 'Die Soziologie der Genese sozialer Institutionen' ['The Sociology of the Genesis of Social Institutions'], p. 472). An approach genuinely anchored in action theory, as found within the interpretive paradigm, is thus particularly appropriate to the study of economic decision-making processes. This project is, however, intended to go considerably further than this: Boltanski is always concerned to establish how these processes are linked with the macro-level – and this is the second theoretically important point. In recent collaborations with Eve Chiapello he has shown how a new 'spirit' of capitalism, a new *cité*, a *cité par projets*, has formed historically since the 1980s, how concepts such as creativity, flexibility and innovation have superseded the capitalist discourse of efficiency that marked the mid-twentieth century (Boltanski and Chiapello, 'Die Rolle der Kritik', pp. 463ff.; see also Boltanski and Chiapello, *Le nouvel esprit du capitalisme* from 1999, English title: *The New Spirit of Capitalism*). In order to bring this out, the authors were compelled to develop a typology of the various historical stages of capitalism, that is, to engage in the kind of macro-analysis at which the advocates of the interpretive paradigm have tended to baulk. Boltanski and Chiapello underline that their notion of the 'spirit' of capitalism does not imply an idealistic approach involving the mere study of discourses without paying attention to 'real' economic structures. Rather, they claim that justificatory discourses have an effect on this 'real reality', that these legitimize certain forms of capital accumulation in the first place, thus making it possible 'to mobilize those forces which hinder accumulation. If we take seriously the justificatory strategies we have outlined, not all profits are legitimate, not all personal enrichment is just and not all accumulation – no matter how important and rapid – is permissible' (Boltanski and Chiapello, 'Die Rolle der Kritik', p. 463). This last is in part a sideswipe at both Marxist and neo-classical positions within economics, insofar as these continue to make reference to capitalism as a homogeneous phenomenon, and at its norm-free 'logic' or at market participants' calculation of utility to the exclusion of all else.

Third and finally, Boltanski's project is also an explicit attempt to contribute to a sociology of social change: it investigates how new regimes of justification, new *cités*, are brought into being in the first place, how they are enforced and what role elites play in this.

> The transformation of regimes of justification generally seems bound up with the emergence of groups which try to get round those obstacles standing in the way of the long-term continuance of their advantages or the extension of these advantages. They attempt to find new routes to success and recognition, which allow them to forego the selection criteria legitimate at a particular point in time.
>
> (ibid., p. 472)

Though Boltanski and Chiapello make no explicit mention of this, their 'dynamic model of normative change' offers many points of contact with the kind of theory of culture expounded by those close to Shmuel N. Eisenstadt; at the same time, it implicitly criticizes theories of differentiation that take no account of actors.

Within French sociology, those studies carried out by scholars close to Boltanski certainly stand out. But a large number of other authors made their voices heard in the 1980s and 1990s whose concerns with respect to theoretical strategy closely resemble those of Boltanski, but who are active in sometimes very different fields of inquiry. We cannot go into all the important works here, but we want to mention at least a few noted authors to give you a feel for the scope of the contemporary French discursive context. The sociologist Louis Quéré (b. 1947) was originally a member of the circle around Alain Touraine and carried out research on social movements, but has increasingly devoted himself to the ethnomethodological research programme. The historian and philosopher Marcel Gauchet (b. 1946 and founder of the journal *Le Débat* together with the historian Pierre Nora) was one of the authors deeply involved in the philosophical debate on totalitarianism and democracy that took off among those close to Claude Lefort and Cornelius Castoriadis, particularly in the 1970s. In the 1980s, he then took up the problem of the continuity and discontinuity of history through the example of religious experience, asking what role religion has played after it was ousted from the official state system of institutions in the eighteenth century and what has replaced it – a problem which touches not only on aspects of democratic theory but also on issues of individual identity (see Gauchet, *The Disenchantment of the World*, originally published in French in 1985). Finally, the sociologist Alain Caillé (b. 1944), a student of Claude Lefort, is also a very interesting author in that he became the central figure of a small group which set itself the task of combating the influence of utilitarianism in the social sciences. To this end, it founded a journal in the 1980s entitled *La Revue du MAUSS – Mouvement Anti-Utilitariste dans les Sciences Sociales*. Though the journal never had a very large circulation, it was important as it became a publishing forum for many of those French authors identified by Dosse as the 'new generation' of anti-structuralists. It is, of course, no accident that the journal's title recalls that great, classical figure of French sociology, Marcel Mauss, nephew of Durkheim and author of the famous essay *The Gift* (see also Lecture XIV). In a number of studies, Caillé revisited the topic dealt with in this essay. He tried to show that the gift is not only a distinguishing feature of primitive societies, but that the principle of reciprocity inherent to it also determines the behaviour of actors in modernity in key ways (Jacques Godbout and Alain Caillé, *The World of the Gift*). Marcel Hénaff (b. 1943) has gone furthest in developing these impulses (*Le prix de la verité: Le don, l'argent, la philosophie* ['The Price of Truth: The Gift, Money and Philosophy']).

However, it is sociologist of science Bruno Latour who has probably become best known internationally. Latour (b. 1947) is a member of a fairly large international research network that has set itself the task of producing an anthropology of the sciences. Going beyond these studies, which may be said to lie within the sociology of science, he came to a number of conclusions interesting both in terms of social theory and in a political and philosophical sense. In *Nous n'avons jamais été modernes* from 1991 (English title: *We Have Never Been Modern*), Latour demonstrates how the fact that scientists construct their objects has produced an immutable fusion of nature and society, which we must take into account:

> The ozone hole is too social and too narrated to be truly natural; the strategy of industrial firms and heads of state is too full of chemical reactions to be reduced to power and interest; the discourse of the ecosphere is too real and too social to boil down to meaning effects.
>
> (Latour, *We Have Never Been Modern*, p. 6)

Science has thus created a whole range of hybrids, 'quasi-objects' which are neither merely natural things nor people or subjects. If we take this seriously, political questions immediately arise. How do we deal with these quasi-objects that have become part of society? How do we represent them? Latour's response is to call for a 'Parliament of Things' (ibid., pp. 142ff.), a kind of self-reflexive democracy in which the people's representatives are aware that they are often referring to quasi-objects, to social-natural things, and in which they are aware that they must represent these very things. Rather than the mere representation of interests, such a democracy would involve a ceaseless process of reflection on this unavoidable fusion of society and nature in parliament and the public realm, a fusion we need to face up to and whose consequences we must live with.

While Latour's political vision is not terribly specific, he persuasively argues, on the basis of his studies in the sociology of science, that modernity – which was and is closely bound up with science – has always been distinguished by two groups of practices. On the one hand, scientists' achievements of construction constantly created hybrid beings, while on the other, people tried desperately to deny this hybridity and to refer to *one* nature and *one* society – each clearly separate from the other (ibid., p. 10). Latour demonstrated that this ambivalence has characterized modern scientific and social history from the outset. The title of his book, *We Have Never Been Modern*, is also derived from this insight. On this view, modernity has never been one-dimensional; the ambivalence described by Latour has always pertained. Theorists of both classical modernity and postmodernity are thus wrong, as they all work with a one-dimensional (positive or negative) notion of modernity.

> We have never plunged into a homogenous and planetary flow arriving either from the future or from the depths of time. Modernization has never occurred. There is no tide, long in rising,

that would be flowing again today. There has never been such a tide. We can go on to other things – that is, return to the multiple entities that have always passed in a different way.

(ibid., p. 76)

According to Latour, we should now acknowledge this ambivalence and accept the fact that the fusion of nature and society in the shape of hybrid objects is unavoidable. This would not only enable us to leave behind us the unedifying debates between moderns and postmoderns. We would also gain a new and more adequate view of the problems facing our world.

This brings us to the end of our brief survey of the most recent developments in the French intellectual landscape, which seemed so important to us primarily because the emerging, large-scale process of opening to the action theoretical approaches discussed in this lecture holds considerable promise for the future. For only by combating structuralism and the related approaches to social theory can the potential inherent in French traditions of thought truly be tapped – to the benefit of the international 'scientific community'.

3. Since the 1980s, an interdisciplinary movement has increasingly made its presence felt which lends much plausibility to our assertion in Lecture I that there are undoubtedly 'corridors' between the theoretical paradigms and thus that the notion of incommensurability is wide of the mark. We are referring to the so-called 'new institutionalism'. As the term itself suggests, there were institutionalist theorists and theoretical approaches at an earlier point in time. Prime examples are American sociologists and economists such as Thorstein Veblen (1857–1929), John Commons (1862–1945) and Wesley Mitchell (1874–1948), who criticized the classical assumptions of economics and emphasized that individuals are integrated into institutions in a way that clashes with the classical economists' assumption that they are interested solely in maximizing their utility (in the market). Such 'old' institutionalist approaches were not, however, found only in the USA. In Germany, the so-called Younger Historical School of Political Economy, which is associated with the name of Gustav Schmoller (1838–1917), pursued similar objectives, and in fact kicked off a mode of thought which was to influence the American economists mentioned above. The founding fathers of sociology can also be described as 'institutionalists', Durkheim as well as Weber; both were very aware that cultural patterns and institutions have a decisive influence on the motivations underlying individuals' actions. Finally, Talcott Parsons must also be mentioned in this connection. If you recall Lectures II and III, Parsons, borrowing from Durkheim, placed great emphasis on the non-economic prerequisites for economic action, drawing attention in particular to the importance of institutionalized values. In this sense, Parsons too was an 'institutionalist'.

But why was there a need, as there manifestly was, for a movement that placed renewed emphasis on institutionalist ideas? The answer is fairly simple – and it too underlines the value of beginning our lecture series with Talcott Parsons. Many of Parsons' insights were lost to the world in the 1960s and 1970s, as were the insights of the classical figures of the social sciences (on what follows, see Paul J. DiMaggio and Walter W. Powell, 'Introduction' and W. Richard Scott, *Institutions and Organizations*, pp. 2ff.). In political science, for example, so-called behaviouralism took hold with the advance of certain empirical research methods, an approach that regarded institutions as merely marginal and worked on the assumption that they are no more than the sum of the actions taken by discrete individuals, possessing no further significance. The theory and sociology of organizations, meanwhile, often adhered to a utilitarian conceptual model that was incapable of grasping certain empirical phenomena such as organizations' need for legitimacy. And in economics it became ever clearer that microeconomic assumptions about the cognitive capacities of actors are empirically false because there are limits to the absorption of information, and that trust plays a key role in the market – without it, it would be impossible to guarantee that contracts are complied with in a cost-effective way. We cannot grasp these phenomena solely by referring to utility-maximizing actors and taking as our basis a utilitarian model of action. It has thus become ever more apparent that institutions must be brought back into social scientific analysis.

A turn towards the analysis and theorizing of institutions thus began from the 1980s in various fields of research, though the approaches taken by the disciplines were very different. While the Nobel prize winner Douglass North (b. 1920) tackled the problem of institutions with the help of a utilitarian perspective within economics, focusing particularly on the issue of which institutional structures are responsible for the ongoing existence of inefficient market mechanisms (North, *Institutions, Institutional Change and Economic Performance*, 1990), the utilitarian model of action had already been subjected to closer scrutiny in the other social sciences. Economic, organizational, political and historical sociology placed considerably more emphasis on the normative constraints on actors in institutions, their world views and how these guide their action, their cognitive schemata, their practices of acting and thinking as learned at work, etc., as well as the dimension of (political) power. Only by including these phenomena could it plausibly be explained why, for example, markets do not 'obey' the laws of the microeconomic paradigm and why organizations and political processes cannot be analysed meaningfully with the model of the rational actor (see Paul DiMaggio, 'The New Institutionalisms: Avenues of Collaboration' and Peter A. Hall and Rosemary C. R. Taylor, 'Political Science and the Three New Institutionalisms').

The debate on the so-called 'new institutionalism' is still in a state of flux at present, and there is no doubt that it has provided and continues to provide empirical research with significant impetus. Yet it is very unlikely to become established as a theoretical movement in its own right, as the parties to the debate are coming from such different starting points. Rational choice assumptions are being modified and the Parsonian model of institutions is being extended by insights from conflict theory, ethnomethodology and cognitive psychology. This is happening, however, within the individual disciplines in very different ways, and even within one and the same discipline institutionalist theorists often argue very much in line with the various theoretical schools which we have introduced to you in the preceding lectures. We cannot, therefore, dismiss out of hand the suspicion that this 'new institutionalism' is not a truly coherent theoretical movement, but rather a label applied to what are in fact very disparate research projects, which have only one thing in common, namely their concern with institutions (this is also unintentionally apparent in the anthology edited by Andrea Maurer and Michael Schmid, *Neuer Institutionalismus. Zur soziologischen Erklärung von Organisation, Moral und Vertrauen* ['New Institutionalism: The Sociological Explanation of Organizations, Morality and Trust']).

Nevertheless, the field of institutionalist thought has generated one sociological grand theory that is currently attracting a great deal of attention around the world and is in competition with globalization theories. The 'world polity' approach is closely associated with the name of the American sociologist John W. Meyer. Long a lecturer at Stanford, since the 1970s Meyer has consistently advanced a corresponding theoretical programme based on empirical research on the worldwide spread and consolidation of uniform institutional patterns.

The preoccupations of the 'world polity' approach can be clarified most simply with the help of the ideas advanced by Meyer and his colleagues with respect to problems of political science (see Thomas and Meyer, 'The Expansion of the State'). If, for instance, we look at the recent history of the international system of states, then – according to Meyer – we are immediately struck by the similarity of form characteristic of the different states: more or less all of them have uniform bureaucratic structures; at the ministerial level, the fields of politics are divided up in line with the same model almost everywhere; political processes are expedited with similar means – and all this regardless of the very different national cultural contexts and conflicts.

This of course poses a theoretical problem. Meyer's thesis is that this surprisingly large degree of structural similarity between states cannot be plausibly explained with the aid of functionalist or power theoretical arguments. For given the very different national contexts, it cannot be due to functional requirements if bureaucratic structures of the same kind are developed everywhere; and it makes equally little sense to assume that actors with an awareness of power (classes, political parties, trade unions, etc.), which inevitably have very different interests in the specific national contexts, would wish to establish the same state structures everywhere. Hence, Meyer's conclusion is that the form taken by states and the specific design of the state system cannot be explained 'from the bottom up' (in light of the interests of individual or collective actors for example), but only 'from the top down': the specific features of the state and of the state system must be derived, as it were, from the presence of far-reaching principles, from a 'world culture' or 'world polity' in other words, which brings us to the term characteristic of this macro-level approach. Only if we postulate the existence of such a world culture, according to Meyer, is it possible to grasp why states have been established and continue to be established in accordance with very similar ('isomorphic') structural characteristics.

What may appear to be no more than the outcome of fairly abstract theoretical deduction has, however, been substantiated by Meyer and his colleagues from the 1970s on in a number of empirical analyses, chiefly in the sociology of education and organizations. Meyer has shown, for example, that universities with at least superficially similar courses, comparable degrees, etc. have spread everywhere. In much the same way, it was possible to show that very similar passages can be found in the constitutions of almost all states founded after 1945, referring, for example, to human rights and democratic procedures, though clearly these passages are not necessarily a genuine expression of the particular national cultures. In Meyer's view, this indicates that a world culture has now become institutionalized that exercises a significant structuring influence on the processes and types of process occurring across the world. In other words, it is the world culture that frequently determines which policies and structures organizations and states must adopt – which educational goals are to be pursued, which requirements a university system must fulfil, etc.

How, though, are we to describe this world culture? According to Meyer, it consists of several, originally Christian-Protestant values, with some of the key dimensions here being the emphasis on the intrinsic value of the individual, the acceptance of rationally grounded authority and faith in a progress achieved through rational means. In Meyer's view, these values or principles shape profoundly the actions of individual and collective actors within world society, and these actors in turn refer to these in a taken-for-granted way when, for example, they wish to justify their actions. To violate them openly is unacceptable and is sanctioned. They are the premises of all action, which almost no one seriously questions any longer; in other words, they have been institutionalized throughout the world culture.

Meyer does not claim that this world culture as described by him – as we might suspect – inevitably leads to peace and harmony in the world. In his opinion, there will continue to be conflicts, not least because attempts to establish certain structures derived from this world culture in various regional contexts have provoked and continue to provoke violent resistance (one need only think of the idea of a unified, rationally structured state, and of how attempts to enforce it have often inspired the development of ethnic minorities and caused them to protest). But even if severe conflicts occur, the protagonists almost always make reference to the rational principles of the world culture. As Meyer states, if they wish their demands to be heard within the world at large, even fundamentalist or ethnic movements refer to such rational principles or specific rights anchored in the world culture (Meyer *et al.*, 'World Society and the Nation State').

The institutionalist 'world polity' approach (sometimes also known as the 'world society' approach), which, incidentally, overlaps with some of the ideas emanating from the Luhmannian theoretical camp, which also uses the concept of the world society (see p. 530 in this chapter), is surely one of the most interesting contemporary macrosociological theoretical programmes with clear empirical aspirations. However, there is some doubt as to the explanatory potential of this approach. In his studies in the sociology of organization, Meyer himself has always stressed the potential for actual organizational processes to be 'de-coupled' from culturally required standards of rationality ('Institutionalized Organizations'). This, as Meyer states explicitly, must also be taken into account when examining 'isomorphisms' (or processes of structural adaptation) determined by the world culture: the structures and processes may indeed be very similar or may be growing very similar on the surface, but is this also true of structures and processes beneath the surface? The sociology programmes and the name of a particular degree at a Third World university may sound very similar to those of the University of Chicago. But on the whole this will tell us very little about the state of the particular institution or about the standards students are expected to achieve. We cannot rule out the possibility that Meyer's world culture approach, with its emphasis on world cultural isomorphisms, simply fails to get to grips with far more important social processes (for a critique, see Wolfgang Knöbl, *Die Kontingenz der Moderne. Wege in Europa, Asien und Amerika* ['The Contingency of Modernity: Pathways in Europe, Asia and America'], pp. 30–45).

4. As we near the end of our lecture series, we would like to alert you to three problem areas with which many social scientists are currently concerned both conceptually and theoretically and which thus form the foci of current debate. The relevance of these problems to the diagnosis of the contemporary age is beyond doubt. But our remarks here should not divert your

attention away from the fact that the various theoretical currents outlined in the preceding lectures have also generated important recent studies.

(a) Bruno Latour's thesis of a modernity which in fact never happened already points to one of these issues hotly debated at present, namely the issue of the cultural composition of Western modernity. How coherent was and is this modernity? What internal cultural tensions does it entail? The scholars who have focused on this topic were motivated by the one-dimensional notion of modernity deployed by theorists of modernization and theorists of postmodernity, from which they wished to set themselves apart. It is thus no surprise that the currently most innovative interpretations of modernity and its history are so-called 'non-identitarian interpretations' (Johann P. Arnason, 'Totalitarismus und Modernisierung'), ones, that is, in which the ruptures and contradictions of this era find clear expression. On this view, Western modernity was not and is not a coherent complex, which explains, among other things, its turbulent history.

We are already familiar with such non-identitarian interpretations from our lecture on the French anti-structuralists. In his reconstruction of Western modernity, Alain Touraine drew attention to what he saw as the immutable opposition between subjectification on the one hand and de-subjectification through systems on the other, further developing an idea found in much the same form in the work of Cornelius Castoriadis. The latter referred to the idea of autonomy first formulated in ancient Greece, which came into its own again with the European Enlightenment but which was always under threat from heteronomy. Castoriadis draws a sharp contrast between democracy on the one hand and a capitalism that promotes heteronomy or a totalitarian state apparatus on the other, enabling him to enter the highly interesting and productive debate on the concept of totalitarianism.

But the origins of perhaps the most comprehensive and persuasive reconstruction of the cultural tensions characteristic of modernity lie in a different context. This reconstruction was produced by the communitarian philosopher and political scientist Charles Taylor (b. 1931), mentioned above. His impressive *Sources of the Self: The Making of the Modern Identity* from 1989 is a major attempt to identify the sources or traditions that nourish or potentially nourish our modern identity at present. This he does by taking us on a tour through Western intellectual history. Taylor identifies three traditions that arose in different historical eras: a high regard for introspection ('inwardness') that stretches back to Augustine and Descartes, a positive attitude towards everyday life and work ('affirmation of ordinary life'), for which we largely, but not exclusively, have the Reformation to thank, and finally a receptiveness to a Romantic interpretation of nature and a high regard for the creative and expressive ('the voice of nature'). These different elements of tradition certainly allow us to develop a rich and multifaceted identity if we achieve a balanced relationship between them. Yet at the same time, they are also the cause of numerous tensions which appear not only within individuals but also Western culture as a whole. Taylor refers to three main tensions or conflicts within modernity. First, demands are made for universal justice, freedom and equality, which everyone is happy to support in principle and which have been achieved to a considerable extent, particularly in Western democracies. Yet at the same time, there is great uncertainty about what constitutes a good life, about strong evaluations and highest goods beyond those principles with which we can all agree (Taylor, *Sources*, p. 495). Second, there is clearly an immutable conflict between the instrumentalism required in everyday life and the world of work and the Romantic protest against this one-sided and sometimes deadening form of rationality. Third and finally, it has proved impossible to achieve a consensus on the question of whether our moral standards can always be reconciled with our efforts, and our desire, to achieve a rich and varied identity and what takes priority in specific cases as we seek to realize this identity (ibid., pp. 498f.).

Taylor has done much to render this understanding of these extensive tensions within modernity, which he initially discusses in rather abstract terms, useful to concrete political analysis. In a number of essays he has tried to show the extent to which they are at least partly reflected in the political conflicts and circumstances of modern Western societies (see for example his essay 'Legitimation Crisis?' in the volume *Philosophy and the Human Sciences*, pp. 248ff.).

Cosmopolis: The Hidden Agenda of Modernity by Stephen Toulmin, a historian and philosopher of science born in London in 1922, appeared in 1990, not long after Taylor's *Sources of the Self*. His book takes up Richard Rorty's ideas on the status of Wittgenstein, Heidegger and Dewey within modern philosophy. Toulmin's central concern can be summed up as follows. If these great twentieth-century philosophers are right and knowledge really does lack any firm foundation, if, that is, as the title of a famous book by John Dewey puts it, the 'quest for certainty' is in vain, we are bound to ask when and under what circumstances this quest began. It is not enough then, like Rorty, merely to couch one's arguments in terms of the history of philosophy and point to the internal construction of the Cartesian system of thought. Rather, our task must be to examine in greater detail the (philosophical) transition from the Middle Ages to the modern era which began with Descartes – by connecting the history of ideas with social history (Toulmin, *Cosmopolis*, p. 12).

In this connection, Toulmin underlines that modernity draws on at least two traditions which arose in two different historical eras. While the Renaissance produced the literary and humanistic inheritance of modernity, with Erasmus of Rotterdam (1467–1536), Michel de Montaigne (1533–92) and William Shakespeare (1564–1616) its perhaps most impressive representatives, Descartes (1596–1650) seemed to belong to an entirely new era. He was a representative of the scientific and systematic-philosophical thinking which Toulmin sees as constitutive of the second tradition of modernity. Toulmin's question is how, in a fairly short period of time, such a radical cognitive change as this shift away from the Renaissance could occur. Here, he presents us with a surprising political interpretation. According to him, the Cartesian project, Descartes' search for a firm basis for knowledge, for certainty in other words, was due neither to the logic of philosophical development nor did it merely arise from the author's individual biography. Rather, it is possible to show that Descartes' search for certainty began in a situation of great political upheaval and uncertainties. The era of the Thirty Years War and the political turmoil in France, during which political groupings fought each other with weapons, religious doctrines and ideologies, inspired a state of mind among the philosophically interested which Toulmin describes as follows:

> If Europeans were to avoid falling into a skeptical morass, they had, it seemed, to find *something* to be 'certain' about. The longer fighting continued, the less plausible it was that Protestants would admit the 'certainty' of Catholic doctrines, let alone that devout Catholics would concede the 'certainty' of Protestant heresies. The only other place to look for 'certain foundations of belief' lay in the epistemological proofs that Montaigne had ruled out.
>
> (ibid., pp. 55–6; original emphasis)

Descartes thus rejects the humanist scepticism of Montaigne, his doubts as to whether it is in any way meaningful to seek secure knowledge, because for Descartes, at a time of civil war and political murder, the philosophical search for certainty seems the only plausible way out. As Toulmin sees things, Descartes' philosophical project, and Newton's natural scientific one, were not primarily the result of logical or practical considerations. Rather, their roots lie in a politico-religious context; it is thus no accident that the Newtonian world view, for instance, was promoted and accepted most rapidly in the centralized nation-states (ibid., p. 119).

Such an interpretation is significant for two reasons. First, it clarifies how modernity has always been characterized by a fair degree of cultural tension, between the scientific search for certainty on the one hand and humanistic-literary endeavours on the other. But what is more interesting, and this is the second reason, is that Toulmin's account suddenly casts a dark shadow on European intellectual history, never seen before in this form. For according to him, far from an untroubled departure for new shores, the birth of Cartesian thought and the scientific world view was a fraught process dependent on a number of factors. Within Descartes as an individual, this tradition of thought is in fact closely bound up with the experience of violence, war and civil war, which have played a hugely important role in European history as a whole. It is thus apparent that key institutions (one need only think of the nation-state) would never have emerged over the course of European modernity without war. Not only this, but the same applies to significant intellectual currents seemingly far removed from politics.

Finally, the German social scientist Peter Wagner (b. 1956), currently teaching in Trento (Italy), is another prominent contributor to the debate on the cultural tensions within modernity. His postdoctoral thesis at the Free University of Berlin, *A Sociology of Modernity: Liberty and Discipline* from 1994, provides a historical sociology of modern institutions. Within modernity, Wagner distinguishes between various eras: a liberal modernity of the nineteenth century, an organized modernity from the early twentieth century and a long-term crisis of this organized modernity evident from around 1960, which has allegedly led to the dissolution of formerly established institutional practices and to a plurality of new ones. In a way that recalls Castoriadis and Touraine, but also Foucault, Wagner shows how the idea of freedom so characteristic of modernity has been constantly thwarted by the disciplinary practices that are also its distinguishing features. The strength of his book undoubtedly lies in the fact that he attempts to interpret this conflictual constellation of modernity not only in terms of intellectual or philosophical history, but also through the prism of institutional theory. What was always lacking in the work of Touraine, for example, namely an in-depth engagement with institutions, is tackled head on by Wagner, who investigates the transformation of political and market-related processes as well as those affecting academia. This enables him to produce a *sociologically* more substantial picture of the ruptures and conflicts of modernity than the French anti-structuralists have so far managed to do. Yet we may still wonder whether, with his thesis of the interplay of freedom and discipline, he has not succumbed to a dichotomous way of thinking in much the same way as the French authors, a way of thinking which is constantly in danger of underestimating the complexity of modernity and the diversity of its traditions. But in any event, his claim that modernity is and will continue to be characterized by immutable tensions and problems, for which there will be no general solutions, is of key importance: 'There is no end to disputes over justification, once different orders of justification are at play' (Wagner, *Theorizing Modernity: Inescapability and Attainability in Social Theory*, p. 10). Wagner, however, goes beyond the mere philosophical confirmation of an immutable pluralism of values (ibid., pp. 19f.), in that he tries to show through historical-sociological evidence how *different actors* in modernity have responded to these irresolvable tensions *at different times*; his current research thus aims (and a certain closeness to Toulmin and direct link with Joas are apparent here) to *historicize* the quest for certainty described by Dewey (and Rorty) exclusively in terms of the history of ideas.

You will have noticed that very different interpretations are possible within the framework of the discourse on the cultural tensions within modernity. We wanted to bring home to you that there is no *one* true and final interpretation either in sociology or history. Rather, we are faced with more or less comprehensible reconstructions, whose plausibility is partly context-related, because, for example, in interpreting history different aspects are interesting and important to different authors and to different historical generations. Yet this is not bound to lead to absolute relativism. If you take a closer look at the (historical) interpretations of modernity that we have outlined, you will undoubtedly notice that they do not really contradict one another in any fundamental way, but are in fact complementary. The very same 'conflict of interpretations' is also to be found in the 'multiple modernities' discourse of such importance at present, a discourse which cannot be considered in isolation from the debate on the internal cultural tensions within Western modernity.

(b) You have already encountered the 'multiple modernities' discourse in Lecture XIII, where we presented Shmuel N. Eisenstadt as the key reference author in this regard. Our aim here is to introduce you to other important contributors to this debate and to identify some of the problems with which the debaters are currently grappling (for an initial overview, see the issue of the American journal *Daedalus*, Winter 2000, entitled 'Multiple Modernities').

The origins of the debate on the 'diversity of modernity' certainly lie in the reception of Max Weber. Eisenstadt himself was heavily influenced by Weber and tried at an early stage to outline a programme of comparative research as ambitious as that carried out by Weber, to some extent at least, in his studies in the sociology of the world religions.

However, with the possible exception of the group around Parsons and his students, to which Eisenstadt also belonged, Weber's programme of study in this respect was not very well known internationally, and in the 1960s and 1970s was mainly discussed in Germany. There, it was above all Weber's theory of rationalization that caught scholars' attention and also aroused their interest in the overall context of his comparative analyses in the sociology of religion. We pointed out in Lecture X that Habermas made use of Weber's ideas on rationalization to formulate an interpretation of the genesis of modernity informed by evolutionary theory and to lend credence to his diagnosis of the contemporary age, centred on the threat posed to the life-world by systems. Yet it would have been almost impossible for him to draw on Weber's theory of rationalization, had not another German sociologist already subjected it to systematic study before him. We are referring to Wolfgang Schluchter (b. 1938), who interpreted Weber's work primarily through the prism of his writings in the sociology of religion and the highly complex theory of rationalization to be found there and who has done more than anyone else to introduce Weber's work into theoretical debates, centred on understanding contemporary society, as a competitive alternative (Schluchter, *The Rise of Western Rationalism: Max Weber's Developmental History*).

Internationally, however, interpretations of modernity based on rationalization theory have won relatively little recognition, despite the great influence of Jürgen Habermas. The suspicion that this Weberian theory of rationalization was a legacy of German idealism, imbued with the notion that mind develops in line with its own inherent logic, was clearly too great. Indeed, many doubted whether it was appropriate to interpret Weber in terms of his theory of rationalization in the first place: British sociologists such as Anthony Giddens and Michael Mann seemed to have rather more time for Weber as a *conflict* theorist than as a supposed theorist of rationalization. In this sense, it would be wrong to state that the debate on rationalization theory, largely native to Germany, did much to help pave the way for the 'multiple modernities' discourse. Moreover, it was possible to view Weberian or Habermasian/Schluchterian rationalization theory merely as a more sophisticated version of modernization theory, while the overall thrust of the 'multiple modernities' discourse clearly runs counter to modernization theory.

But Schluchter did not stop at the reconstruction of Weber's work through the prism of rationalization theory; he attempted to consider Weber's theory of religion, his studies of ancient Judaism, of Confucianism and Taoism, Hinduism and Buddhism, Islam and ancient and Western Christianity in light of the modern-day knowledge of the social sciences and humanities. In a series of international conferences, in which Eisenstadt, among others, generally participated and which generated a number of high-calibre anthologies (see the books edited by Schluchter in the bibliography), it became clear that highly disparate models of society had developed in different regions of the world and that as a result the process of modernization has also inevitably taken a wide variety of forms. In this sense, Schluchter was certainly one of the initiators of the debate on 'multiple modernities'; but he has so far done more to lay the ground for this debate than to shape it.

Some of the most important contributions to the discourse on the diversity of modernity have come from an author whose roots lie in a tradition quite different from that of Eisenstadt and Schluchter: Johann Arnason. Born in Iceland in 1940, he studied in Prague in the 1960s; following the Soviet invasion of Czechoslovakia in 1968, which brought brutally to an end the experimental 'socialism with a human face', he moved to Germany, where he was part of the circle around Jürgen Habermas. Until recently he was professor of sociology at La Trobe University in Melbourne and editor of one of the most interesting international social theory journals, *Thesis Eleven*.

Arnason began his academic career as a straightforward social philosopher, his energetic pursuit of an empirically grounded analysis of modernity taking off only in the late 1980s. Here, always mediating between Habermasian theory and the French anti-structuralists such as Touraine and Castoriadis, he applied the insights he had already won into social theory to empirical research in a surprising way. Among other things, he produced an important book on the Soviet model of society (*The Future That Failed: Origins and Destinies of the Soviet Model* from 1993) while increasingly focusing on analysing the history and society of Japan and East Asia from the 1990s on (see *Social Theory and Japanese Experience: The Dual Civilization* from 1997; *The Peripheral Centre: Essays on Japanese History and Civilization* from 2002). Here, drawing on Castoriadis' ideas on creativity, one of his central claims was that the political history of these regions cannot be understood as an endogenous development. Rather, 'developments' in the Soviet Union and in Japan must be interpreted as creative counter-projects to Western modernity; the Soviet model of society is best interpreted as an attempt to catch up with and overtake Western societies with different, namely totalitarian means, one that failed in the most terrible way.

Arnason adopts Eisenstadt's theory of civilization in certain respects, as he too is convinced that it is vital to examine entire civilizations and their inherent cultural tensions if one wishes to understand the dynamics of the societies within those civilizations. But he modifies this approach in one crucial respect. One of his criticisms is that Eisenstadt understood the idea of the Axial Age too much as a cultural programme within a civilization that runs relatively independently of other events, in autonomous fashion. Arnason on the other hand proposes a theory of civilization in 'processual garb', which takes account of *contact* between civilizations as a key variable; it thus takes on a decidedly trans-civilizational and transnational tenor. This is broadly in line with the aims underlying Wallerstein's world system theory, which it proved impossible to fully realize as a consequence of his economism. Arnason's approach provides a significantly more dynamic view of processes of change. Rather than falsely attributing an archaic logic to Japanese development, for example, as Eisenstadt had done, Arnason's analysis privileges the strategy of adoption *and* processing of foreign cultural patterns so successfully pursued during many eras of Japanese history (see also Knöbl, *Spielräume der Modernisierung*, pp. 330ff.).

Recently, Arnason has also begun to investigate something which Eisenstadt never managed to address directly, namely the adequacy of the concept of civilization. Eisenstadt had assumed that there simply *are* civilizations, determined by religious developments, and that these are *the* key units of reference for sociological analysis. We criticized Eisenstadt for this in Lecture XIII. Our argument was that the concept of civilization is not much clearer than the 'traditional' sociological concept of 'society'. Though it has become fashionable nowadays to refer to the end of the nation-state and a question mark has increasingly and rightly been placed over the concept of society linked with it, we should not merely replace it with other unclear or nebulous concepts. Arnason tackles this criticism and in his most recent book (*Civilizations in Dispute: Historical Questions and Theoretical Traditions* from 2003) he tries, first of all, to take stock of the various concepts of civilization used in the social sciences before going on to tease out their strengths and weaknesses. Whatever one thinks of the results of Arnason's analyses, it should be clear that civilization theory can maintain its current appeal within the debate on 'multiple modernities' only through such theoretical endeavours and conceptual clarifications.

Alongside the question of the adequacy of the concept of civilization, the debate on 'multiple modernities' is also moulded by another controversy, namely the assessment of cultural and structural factors in research on processes of social change. The concept of civilization generally presupposes a heavy emphasis on cultural factors, particularly when, as in the case of Eisenstadt and his Axial Age thesis, it is introduced in terms of the sociology of religion. But one may wonder whether such a perspective truncates or distorts certain things. Despite all the economistic arguments that it entails, is not Wallersteinian world system theory, for example, justified in as much as it discusses the obstacles to economic development – and thus both structural and exogenous factors – for countries lying outside of North America and Western or Central Europe? The Swedish sociologist Göran Therborn (b. 1941), now professor at the University of Cambridge, has expressed this problem in a very particular way. He has tried to show that it is entirely possible to refer to several paths to or through modernity in the style of Eisenstadt, without adopting the *endogenous* perspective characteristic of his theory of civilization, with its near-exclusive emphasis on *cultural* factors, and without sharing Wallerstein's economism. Therborn refers to four such paths of modernization: European modernization, the modernization of the New World (North and South America, Australia, New Zealand), the modernization of, for example, Japan, induced by *exogenous* factors but implemented in autonomous fashion, and the violent modernization that took place in the so-called 'colonial areas', that is, the rest of the world, where modernity came literally 'from the barrel of a gun' with all the consequent cultural traumas (Therborn, *European Modernity and Beyond: The Trajectory of European Societies, 1945–2000*, p. 5; see also Therborn, 'The Right to Vote and the Four World Routes to/through Modernity', 1992). Whatever one thinks of Therborn's proposal, it seems clear that an approach such as this, which takes seriously colonial history and all its extreme violence, opens our eyes to other, no less important aspects of modernity than Eisenstadt's approach, which is culturalist and informed by the theory of civilization, and which works primarily with endogenous factors. In future, we can therefore expect key arguments within the debate on the 'diversity of modernity' to revolve around the assessment of structural and cultural, endogenous and exogenous factors. In a series of penetrating essays, another Swedish sociologist and political scientist, Björn Wittrock (b. 1945), has tried to break new ground here by means of a cultural theory informed by discourse theory and the sociology of knowledge, his arguments embedded in a perspective of global history.

(c) Therborn's reference to the 'barrel of a gun' and the violent 'modernization' of many parts of the world underlines that both an adequate theory of social change and a plausible diagnosis of the contemporary world must take account of macrosocial violence. Our brief mention of Toulmin's *Cosmopolis* showed that even key cultural achievements of modernity are understandable only if we include the history of violence in Europe (and America) in our analyses. At a time of international instability, when war almost seems to have become a 'normal' political option once again, it is absolutely crucial that social theory dedicate itself to this issue. This has not yet happened on a sufficient scale. Attempts have of course been made, by Giddens, Joas and Toulmin for example, to pay heed to this dark side of modernity. On the whole, though, social theory and sociology lack the sensory apparatus required to tackle the topic of war and peace in analyses of the contemporary era. This is generally left to the neighbouring discipline of political science, which, however, often seems rather uninterested in this subject, with the exception of the specialized field of international relations. What scholars forget is that several of the founding fathers of sociology consistently discussed this topic in their various studies. Only within British social theory (we have mentioned, for example, the work of Michael Mann, whose theoretical toolkit is centred on four power networks and ascribes a good deal of importance to military power – see Lecture XII) has the attempt even been made to produce the kind of systematic conceptual apparatus vital to formulating a theory of social change sensitive to violence. On the whole, though, in light of the growing significance of armed conflicts since the end of the Cold War, this seems insufficient for a social theory that aspires to cast light on the contemporary era (see Michael Mann, *The Incoherent Empire*).

But it is also of great importance to study the subject of war and the other dark sides of modernity in depth because social theory's crucial task will be to clarify which criterion it applies to history and where it gets its normative criteria from. For if it is *not* certain, as modernization theorists assume, that the normative achievements of modernity will prevail (Joas, *War and Modernity*, pp. 53f.), if it is *not* the case that liberty, the rule of law and democracy, for example, will be established without resistance or that these values are secure for ever more even in the West, then the question of whether we can speak of social progress in the first place arises with renewed vigour. To what extent is it appropriate to refer to processes of moral learning with respect to entire societies? Are we not compelled, as postmodern authors tend to do, simply to declare such questions meaningless or, like Anthony Giddens, to adopt a radically discontinuous view of history? Or could there be another route out of this predicament, because subjects interpret their own history, organizing the present against the background of their concept of history and thus always maintaining at least a degree of continuity to the past, their hopes and experiences, their achievements and their suffering? If we can no longer work on the assumption that history is moving towards a specific goal which embodies all that is good, if we no longer believe that moral progress is part and parcel of history, then social theory must inevitably acquire its normative stance *without* recourse to evolutionist and teleological presuppositions.

In any case, it will not be enough for social theory merely to describe events in the past and present. Normative questions will always 'intrude', demanding an answer. Though we cannot simply borrow the answers provided by Parsons and the classical figures of sociology, the questions with which they were concerned remain constitutive for the social sciences. Thus, mediating between normativity and history is and will remain central to how social theory understands itself, and to its role within modernity.

BIBLIOGRAPHY

Abbott, Andrew (1988), *The System of Professions: An Essay on the Division of Expert Labor*. Chicago: University of Chicago Press.

Adler, Patricia, Peter Adler and Andrea Fontana (1987), 'Everyday Life in Sociology', *Annual Review of Sociology* 13: 217–35.

Adorno, Theodor W. (1976 [1969]), *The Positivist Dispute in German Sociology* [*Der Positivismusstreit in der deutschen Soziologie*]. London: Heinemann.

Adorno, Theodor W. and Max Horkheimer (1979 [1944]), *Dialectic of Enlightenment* [*Dialektik der Aufklärung. Philosophische Fragmente*]. London: Verso.

Adorno, Theodor W., Else Frenkel Brunswick, Daniel Jacob Levinson and Robert Nevitt Sanford (1950), *The Authoritarian Personality*. New York: Harper.

Alexander, Jeffrey C. (1982), *Theoretical Logic in Sociology*. Volume I: *Positivism, Presuppositions, and Current Controversies*. Berkeley and Los Angeles: University of California Press.

(1982), *Theoretical Logic in Sociology*. Volume II: *The Antinomies of Classical Thought: Marx and Durkheim*. Berkeley and Los Angeles: University of California Press.

(1983), *Theoretical Logic in Sociology*. Volume III: *The Classical Attempt at Theoretical Synthesis: Max Weber*. Berkeley and Los Angeles: University of California Press.

(1983), *Theoretical Logic in Sociology*. Volume IV: *The Modern Reconstruction of Classical Thought: Talcott Parsons*. Berkeley and Los Angeles: University of California Press.

(1985), 'Introduction', in Jeffrey C. Alexander (ed.), *Neofunctionalism*. London: Sage, pp. 7–18.

(1987), *Twenty Lectures: Sociological Theory since World War II*. London: Hutchinson.

(1988), 'Culture and Political Crisis: "Watergate" and Durkheimian Sociology', in Jeffrey C. Alexander, *Durkheimian Sociology: Cultural Studies*. Cambridge: Cambridge University Press, pp. 187–244.

(1994), 'Modern, Anti, Post, and Neo: How Social Theories Have Tried to Understand the "New World" of "Our Time"', *Zeitschrift für Soziologie* 23, 3: 165–97.

(1996), 'Critical Reflections on "Reflexive Modernization"', *Theory, Culture & Society* 13, 4: 133–8.

(1998), 'Citizen and Enemy as Symbolic Classification: On the Polarizing Discourse of Civil Society', in Jeffrey C. Alexander (ed.), *Real Civil Societies: Dilemmas of Institutionalization*. London: Sage, pp. 96–114.

(1998), *Neofunctionalism and After*. Malden, MA and Oxford: Basil Blackwell.
Alexander, Jeffrey C. and Paul Colomy (1985), 'Toward Neo-Functionalism', *Sociological Theory* 3, 2: 11–23.
Almond, Gabriel and Sidney Verba (1989 [1963]), *The Civic Culture: Political Attitudes and Democracy in Five Nations*. Newbury Park, London and New Delhi: Sage.
Arendt, Hannah (1958), *The Human Condition*. Chicago: University of Chicago Press.
(1958 [1951]), *The Origins of Totalitarianism*. New York: Meridian Books.
(1964 [1963]), *Eichmann in Jerusalem: A Report on the Banality of Evil*. New York: Viking Press.
(1970), *On Violence*. London: Allen Lane.
Arnason, Johann P. (1988), *Praxis und Interpretation. Sozialphilosophische Studien*. Frankfurt am Main: Suhrkamp.
(1993), *The Future that Failed: Origins and Destinies of the Soviet Model*. London and New York: Routledge.
(1996), 'Totalitarismus und Modernisierung', in Lars Clausen (ed.), *Gesellschaften im Umbruch*. Frankfurt am Main: Campus, pp. 154–63
(1997), *Social Theory and Japanese Experience: The Dual Civilization*. London and New York: Kegan Paul.
(2002), *The Peripheral Centre: Essays on Japanese History and Civilization*. Melbourne: Transpacific Press.
(2003), *Civilizations in Dispute: Historical Questions and Theoretical Traditions*. Leiden: Brill.
Barber, Bernard (1992), 'Neofunctionalism and the Theory of the Social System', in Paul Colomy (ed.), *The Dynamics of Social Systems*. London: Sage, pp. 36–55.
Barthes, Roland (1972 [1957]), *Mythologies* [*Mythologies*]. London: Jonathan Cape.
Baudrillard, Jean (1978), *Agonie des Realen*. Berlin: Merve.
(1988 [1986]), *America* [*Amérique*]. London: Verso.
(1993 [1976]), *Symbolic Exchange and Death* [*L'échange symbolique et la mort*]. London: Sage.
Bauman, Zygmunt (1989), *Modernity and the Holocaust*. Cambridge: Polity Press.
(1991), *Modernity and Ambivalence*. Oxford: Polity Press.
(1993), *Postmodern Ethics*. Oxford: Blackwell.
(1997), *Postmodernity and its Discontents*. Cambridge: Polity Press.
(1999), *In Search of Politics*. Cambridge: Polity Press.
Beck, Ulrich (1986), *Risikogesellschaft. Auf dem Weg in eine andere Moderne*. Frankfurt am Main: Suhrkamp.
(1992 [1986]), *Risk Society: Towards a New Modernity* [*Risikogesellschaft. Auf dem Weg in eine andere Moderne*]. London: Sage.
(1995 [1988]), *Ecological Politics in an Age of Risk* [*Gegengifte. Die organisierte Unverantwortlichkeit*]. Cambridge: Polity Press.

(1997 [1993]), *The Reinvention of Politics* [*Die Erfindung des Politischen*]. Cambridge: Polity Press.

(2000 [1997]), *What is Globalization?* [*Was ist Globalisierung?*]. Cambridge: Polity Press.

Becker, Gary S. (1981), *A Treatise on the Family*. Cambridge, MA and London: Harvard University Press.

Becker, Howard S. (1963), *Outsiders: Studies in the Sociology of Deviance*. New York: Free Press.

Becker-Schmidt, Regina and Gudrun-Axeli Knapp (2001), *Feministische Theorien zur Einführung*. Hamburg: Junius.

Beckert, Jens (2002 [1997]), *Beyond the Market: The Social Foundations of Economic Efficiency* [*Grenzen des Marktes. Die sozialen Grundlagen wirtschaftlicher Effizienz*]. Princeton and Oxford: Princeton University Press.

Bell, Daniel (1973), *The Coming of Post-Industrial Society: A Venture in Social Forecasting*. New York: Basic Books.

Bellah, Robert (1985 [1957]), *Tokugawa Religion: The Cultural Roots of Modern Japan*. New York and London: Anchor Books.

(1991 [1970]), *Beyond Belief: Essays on Religion in a Post-Traditional World*. Berkeley, Los Angeles and London: University of California Press.

Bellah, Robert, Richard Madsen, William M. Sullivan, Ann Swidler and Steven M. Tipton (1985), *Habits of the Heart: Individualism and Commitment in American Life*. Berkeley and London: University of California Press.

(1991), *The Good Society*. New York: Knopf.

Bellow, Saul (2000), *Ravelstein*. London: Viking.

Bendix, Reinhard (1963 [1952]), 'Social Stratification and Political Power', in Reinhard Bendix and Seymour Martin Lipset (eds.), *Class, Status and Power: A Reader in Social Stratification*. Glencoe: Free Press, pp. 596–609.

(1966 [1960]), *Max Weber: An Intellectual Portrait*. London: Methuen.

(1974 [1956]), *Work and Authority in Industry: Ideologies of Management in the Course of Industrialization*. Berkeley, Los Angeles and London: University of California Press.

(1986), *From Berlin to Berkeley: German Jewish Identities*. New Brunswick, NJ: Transaction Books.

Benhabib, Seyla (1984), 'Epistemologies of Postmodernism: A Rejoinder to Jean-François Lyotard', *New German Critique* 33: 103–26.

(1992), *Situating the Self: Gender, Community and Postmodernism in Contemporary Ethics*. Cambridge: Polity Press.

Berger, Peter L. and Thomas Luckmann (1971 [1966]), *The Social Construction of Reality*. Harmondsworth: Penguin.

Bergson, Henri (1912 [1889]), *Time and Free Will: An Essay on the Immediate Data of Consciousness* [*Essai sur les données immédiates de la conscience*]. London: George Allen.

Bernstein, Richard (1971), *Praxis and Action: Contemporary Philosophies of Human Activity*. Philadelphia: University of Pennsylvania Press.

(1976), *The Restructuring of Social and Political Theory*. Oxford: Blackwell.

(1992), *The New Constellation: The Ethical-Political Horizons of Modernity/Postmodernity*. Cambridge, MA: MIT Press.

(2002), 'Putnams Stellung in der pragmatistischen Tradition', in Marie-Luise Raters and Marcus Willaschek (eds.), *Hilary Putnam und die Tradition des Pragmatismus*. Frankfurt am Main: Suhrkamp, pp. 33–48.

Bittner, Egon (1967), 'Police Discretion in Emergency Apprehension of Mentally Ill Persons', *Social Problems* 14, 3: 278–92.

Blau, Peter M. (1964), *Exchange and Power in Social Life*. New York, London and Sidney: John Wiley & Sons.

Blumer, Herbert (1969), 'The Methodological Position of Symbolic Interactionism', in Herbert Blumer, *Symbolic Interactionism: Perspective and Method*. Englewood Cliffs, NJ: Prentice-Hall, pp. 1–60.

(1969), *Symbolic Interactionism: Perspective and Method*. Englewood Cliffs, NJ: Prentice-Hall.

(1975), 'Comment on Turner, "Parsons as a Symbolic Interactionist"', *Sociological Inquiry* 45, 1: 59–62.

(1981), 'George Herbert Mead', in B. Rhea (ed.), *The Future of the Sociological Classics*. London: Allen & Unwin, pp. 136–69.

(1990), *Industrialization as an Agent of Social Change: A Critical Analysis*. New York: Aldine de Gruyter.

Bolt, Christine (1993), *The Women's Movements in the United States and Britain from the 1790s to the 1920s*. Amherst: University of Massachusetts Press.

Boltanski, Luc (1987 [1982]), *The Making of a Class: Cadres in French Society* [*Les cadres. La formation d'un groupe social*]. Cambridge: Cambridge University Press.

Boltanski, Luc and Eve Chiapello (2001), 'Die Rolle der Kritik in der Dynamik des Kapitalismus und der normative Wandel', *Berliner Journal für Soziologie* 11, 4: 459–77.

(2005 [1999]), *The New Spirit of Capitalism* [*Le nouvel esprit du capitalisme*]. London: Verso.

Boltanski, Luc and Laurent Thévenot (2006 [1991]), *On Justification: Economies of Worth* [*De la justification. Les économies de la grandeur*]. Princeton and Oxford: Princeton University Press.

Bosshart, David (1992), *Politische Intellektualität und totalitäre Erfahrung. Hauptströmungen der französischen Totalitarismuskritik*. Berlin: Duncker & Humblot.

Boudon, Raymond (1982), *The Unintended Consequences of Social Action*. New York: St. Martin's Press.

Bourdieu, Pierre (1970), *Zur Soziologie der symbolischen Formen*. Frankfurt am Main: Suhrkamp.

(1977 [1972]), *Outline of a Theory of Practice* [*Esquisse d'une théorie de la pratique, précédé de trois études d'ethnologie kabyle*]. Cambridge: Cambridge University Press.

(1982), *Leçon sur la leçon*. Paris: Les Editions de Minuit (reprinted as the closing chapter of *In Other Words*; see below).

(1984 [1979]), *Distinction: A Social Critique of the Judgement of Taste* [*La distinction. Critique sociale du jugement*]. Cambridge, MA: Harvard University Press.

(1985), 'The Social Space and the Genesis of Groups', *Theory and Society* 14, 6: 723–44.

(1986 [1983]), 'The Forms of Capital', in John Richardson (ed.), *Handbook of Theory and Research for the Sociology of Education*. New York: Greenwood Press, pp. 241–58.

(1988 [1984], *Homo academicus* [*Homo academicus*]. Cambridge: Polity Press.

(1990 [1980]), *The Logic of Practice* [*Le sens pratique*]. Cambridge: Polity Press.

(1990 [1987]), *In Other Words: Essays Towards a Reflexive Sociology* [*Choses dites*]. Cambridge: Polity Press.

(1993 [1980]), *Sociology in Question* [*Questions de sociologie*]. London: Sage.

(1996 [1992]), *The Rules of Art* [*Les règles de l'art. Genèse et structure du champ littéraire*]. Cambridge: Polity Press.

(1998 [1994]), *Practical Reason: On the Theory of Action* [*Raisons pratiques. Sur la théorie de l'action*]. Cambridge: Polity Press.

(1999 [1993]), *The Weight of the World: Social Suffering in Contemporary Society* [*La misère du monde*]. Cambridge: Polity Press.

(2000 [1997]), *Pascalian Meditations* [*Méditations pascaliennes*]. Cambridge: Polity Press.

Bourdieu, Pierre and Jean-Claude Passeron (1971), *Die Illusion der Chancengleichheit. Untersuchungen zur Soziologie des Bildungswesens am Beispiel Frankreichs*. Stuttgart: Ernst Klett Verlag.

(1981), 'Soziologie und Philosophie in Frankreich seit 1945: Tod und Wiederauferstehung einer Philosophie ohne Subjekt', in Wolf Lepenies (ed.), *Geschichte der Soziologie. Studien zur kognitiven, sozialen und historischen Identität einer Disziplin*. Volume III. Frankfurt am Main: Suhrkamp, pp. 496–551.

Bourdieu, Pierre and Loïc J. D. Wacquant (1992), *Invitation to Reflexive Sociology* [*Réponses pour une anthropologie réflexive*]. Cambridge: Polity Press.

Browning, Christopher R. (1992), *Ordinary Men: Reserve Police Battalion 101 and the Final Solution in Poland*. New York: Aaron Asher Books.

Brownmiller, Susan (1975), *Against Our Will: Men, Women and Rape*. London: Secker & Warburg.

Butler, Judith (1990), *Gender Trouble*. New York and London: Routledge.

(1997), *Excitable Speech: A Politics of the Performative*. New York and London: Routledge.

(1997), *The Psychic Life of Power: Theories in Subjection*. Stanford, CA: Stanford University Press.

Camic, Charles (1979), 'The Utilitarians Revisited', *American Journal of Sociology* 85, 3: 516–50.

(1989), '*Structure* after 50 Years: The Anatomy of a Charter', *American Journal of Sociology* 95, 1: 38–107.

(1991), 'Introduction: Talcott Parsons before *The Structure of Social Action*', in Charles Camic (ed.), *Talcott Parsons: The Early Essays*. Chicago: University of Chicago Press, pp. ix–lxix.

Cardoso, Fernando H. and Enzo Faletto (1979 [1969]), *Dependency and Development in Latin America* [*Dependencia y desarrollo en América Latina. Ensayo de interpretación sociológica*]. Berkeley and London: University of California Press.

Castoriadis, Cornelius (1983), 'Destinies of Totalitarianism', *Salmagundi* 60: 107–22.

(1984 [1978]), *Crossroads in the Labyrinth* [*Les carrefours du labyrinthe*]. Brighton: Harvester.

(1984/85), 'Reflections on "Rationality" and "Development"', *Thesis Eleven* 10/11: 18–35.

(1987 [1975]), *The Imaginary Institution of Society* [*L'institution imaginaire de la société*]. Cambridge: Polity Press.

(1997), 'The Greek Polis and the Creation of Democracy', in David Curtis (ed.), *The Castoriadis Reader*. Oxford: Blackwell, pp. 267–89.

(2001), 'Aeschylean Anthropogony and Sophoclean Self-Creation of Anthropos', in Johann P. Arnason and Peter Murphy (eds.), *Agon, Logos, Polis: The Greek Achievement and its Aftermath*. Stuttgart: Franz Steiner, pp. 138–54.

Caws, Peter (1988), *Structuralism: The Art of the Intelligible*. Atlantic Highlands, NJ: Humanities Press.

Chalmers, A. F. (1986), *What is this Thing Called Science?* Second Edition. Milton Keynes and Philadelphia: Open University Press.

Charle, Christophe (1997), *Vordenker der Moderne. Die Intellektuellen im 19. Jahrhundert*. Frankfurt am Main: Fischer.

Chazel, François (1994), 'Away from Structuralism and the Return of the Actor: Paradigmatic and Theoretical Orientations in Contemporary French Sociology', in Piotr Sztompka (ed.), *Agency and Structure: Reorienting Social Theory*. Yverdon, Switzerland and Langhorn, PA: Gordon and Breach, pp. 143–63.

Chodorow, Nancy (1978), *The Reproduction of Mothering: Psychoanalysis and the Sociology of Gender*. Berkeley and London: University of California Press.

Cicourel, Aaron V. (1964), *Method and Measurement in Sociology*. New York: Free Press.

(1981), 'Basic and Normative Rules in the Negotiation of Status and Role', in David Sudnow (ed.), *Studies in Social Interaction*. New York: Free Press, pp. 229–58.

Cohen, Jean and Andrew Arato (1992), *Civil Society and Political Theory.* Cambridge, MA: MIT Press.
Cohen-Solal, Annie (1987 [1985]), *Sartre: A Life* [*Sartre. 1905–1980*]. New York: Pantheon Books.
Coleman, James (1982), *The Asymmetric Society.* Syracuse, NY: Syracuse University Press.
  (1990), *Foundations of Social Theory.* Cambridge, MA: Harvard University Press.
Collins, Randall (1971), 'Functional and Conflict Theories of Educational Stratification', *American Sociological Review* 36, 6: 1002–19.
  (1975), *Conflict Sociology: Toward an Explanatory Science.* New York, San Francisco and London: Academic Press.
  (1979), *The Credential Society: An Historical Sociology of Education and Stratification.* New York: Academic Press.
  (1985), *Three Sociological Traditions.* New York: Oxford University Press.
  (1986), *Weberian Sociological Theory.* Cambridge: Cambridge University Press.
  (1998), *The Sociology of Philosophies: A Global Theory of Intellectual Change.* Cambridge, MA and London: Harvard University Press.
  (2008), *Violence: A Micro-Sociological Theory.* Princeton: Princeton University Press.
Collins, Randall, Janet Saltzman Chafetz, Lesser Rae Blumberg, Scott Coltrane, Jonathan H. Turner (1993), 'Toward an Integrated Theory of Gender Stratification', *Sociological Perspectives* 36, 3: 185–216.
Colomy, Paul B. (1986), 'Recent Developments in the Functionalist Approach to Change', *Sociological Focus* 19, 2: 139–58.
Colomy, Paul B. and David J. Brown (1995), 'Elaboration, Revision, Polemic, and Progress in the Second Chicago School', in Gary Alan Fine (ed.), *A Second Chicago School? The Development of a Postwar American Sociology.* Chicago and London: University of Chicago Press, pp. 17–81.
Coser, Lewis A. (1956), *The Functions of Social Conflict.* London: Routledge.
  (1967), *Continuities in the Study of Social Conflict.* New York and London: Free Press.
Dahrendorf, Ralf (1958), 'Out of Utopia: Toward a Reorientation of Sociological Analysis', *American Journal of Sociology* 64, 2: 115–27.
  (1972 [1957]), *Class and Class Conflict in Industrial Society* [*Soziale Klassen und Klassenkonflikt in der industriellen Gesellschaft*]. London: Routledge.
  (1972), *Konflikt und Freiheit. Auf dem Weg zur Dienstklassengesellschaft.* Munich: Piper.
  (1986 [1955]), 'Struktur und Funktion. Talcott Parsons und die Entwicklung der soziologischen Theorie', in Ralf Dahrendorf, *Pfade aus Utopia. Zur Theorie und Methode der Soziologie.* Munich and Zurich: Piper, pp. 213–42.
  (1988), *The Modern Social Conflict: An Essay on the Politics of Liberty.* London: Weidenfeld & Nicolson.
  (2002), *Über Grenzen. Lebenserinnerungen.* Munich: C. H. Beck.

Denzin, Norman K. (1977), 'Notes on the Criminogenic Hypothesis: A Case Study of the American Liquor Industry', *American Sociological Review* 42, 6: 905-20.
  (1984), *On Understanding Emotion*. San Francisco, Washington and London: Jossey-Bass Publishers.
  (1991), *Images of Postmodern Society: Social Theory and Contemporary Cinema*. London, Newbury Park and New Delhi: Sage.
Derrida, Jacques (1978 [1967]), *Writing and Difference* [*L'écriture et la différence*]. London: Routledge.
Dewey, John (1925), *Experience and Nature*. London: George Allen & Unwin.
  (1930 [1929]), *The Quest for Certainty*. London: George Allen & Unwin.
DiMaggio, Paul J. (1998), 'The New Institutionalisms: Avenues of Collaboration', *Journal of Institutional and Theoretical Economics* 154: 696-705.
DiMaggio, Paul J. and Walter W. Powell (1991), 'Introduction', in Walter W. Powell and Paul J. DiMaggio (eds.), *The New Institutionalism in Organizational Analysis*. Chicago and London: University of Chicago Press, pp. 1-38.
Dosse, François (1997 [1991f.]), *History of Structuralism*. 2 vols. [*Histoire du structuralisme*]. Minneapolis and London: University of Minnesota Press.
  (1998 [1997]), *The Empire of Meaning: The Humanization of the Social Sciences* [*L'empire du sens. L'humanisation de sciences humaines*]. Minneapolis: University of Minnesota Press.
  (2000), *Paul Ricoeur. Les sens d'une vie*. Paris: La Découverte.
Douglas, Jack D. (1967), *The Social Meanings of Suicide*. Princeton: Princeton University Press.
Dreyfus, Hubert L. and Paul Rabinow (1982), *Michel Foucault: Beyond Structuralism and Hermeneutics*. Chicago: University of Chicago Press.
Dubet, François (1987), *La galère. Jeunes en survie*. Paris: Fayard.
  (1994), *Sociologie de l'expérience*. Paris: Éditions du Seuil.
  (2002), *Le déclin de l'institution*. Paris: Éditions du Seuil.
Dubet, François and Didier Lapeyronnie (1992), *Les quartiers d'exil*. Paris: Éditions du Seuil.
Durkheim, Emile (1982 [1895]), *The Rules of Sociological Method*. London: Macmillan.
Eder, Klaus (1989), 'Klassentheorie als Gesellschaftstheorie. Bourdieus dreifache kulturtheoretische Brechung der traditionellen Klassentheorie', in Klaus Eder (ed.), *Klassenlage, Lebensstil und kulturelle Praxis. Theoretische und empirische Beiträge zur Auseinandersetzung mit Pierre Bourdieus Klassentheorie*. Frankfurt am Main: Suhrkamp, pp. 15-43.
Eder, Klaus (ed.) (1989), *Klassenlage, Lebensstil und kulturelle Praxis. Theoretische und empirische Beiträge zur Auseinandersetzung mit Pierre Bourdieus Klassentheorie*. Frankfurt am Main: Suhrkamp.
Eisenstadt, Shmuel N. (1963), *The Political Systems of Empires*. New York: Free Press.
  (1973), *Tradition, Change and Modernity*. New York: Wiley-Interscience.

(1978), *Revolution and the Transformation of Societies: A Comparative Study of Civilizations*. New York: Free Press.

(1981), 'Cultural Traditions and Political Dynamics: The Origins and Modes of Ideological Politics' (Hobhouse Memorial Lecture), *British Journal of Sociology* 32, 2: 155–81.

(1985), 'This Worldly Transcendentalism and the Structuring of the World: Weber's "Religion of China" and the Format of Chinese History and Civilization', *Journal of Developing Societies* 1, 2: 168–86.

(1989), 'Cultural Premises and the Limits of Convergence in Modern Societies: An Examination of Some Aspects of Japanese Society', *Diogenes* 37: 125–47.

(1992), 'Frameworks of the Great Revolutions: Culture, Social Structure, History and Human Agency', *International Social Science Journal* 133: 385–401.

(1995), 'Introduction', in Shmuel N. Eisenstadt, *Power, Trust and Meaning: Essays in Sociological Theory and Analysis*. Chicago: University of Chicago Press, pp. 1–40.

(1995), 'Social Change, Differentiation, and Evolution', in Shmuel N. Eisenstadt, *Power, Trust and Meaning: Essays in Sociological Theory and Analysis*. Chicago: University of Chicago Press, pp. 106–22.

(1996), *Japanese Civilization: A Comparative View*. Chicago and London: University of Chicago Press.

(2000), *Die Vielfalt der Moderne*. Weilerswist: Velbrück.

Elias, Norbert (1982 [1937]), *The Civilizing Process*. 2 vols. Oxford: Blackwell.

Elster, Jon (1979), 'Imperfect Rationality: Ulysses and the Sirens', in Jon Elster, *Ulysses and the Sirens: Studies in Rationality and Irrationality*. Cambridge: Cambridge University Press, pp. 36–111.

(1983), *Sour Grapes: Studies in the Subversion of Rationality*. Cambridge: Cambridge University Press.

(1999), *Alchemies of the Mind: Rationality and the Emotions*. Cambridge: Cambridge University Press.

Emerson, Richard M. (1962), 'Power-Dependence Relations', *American Journal of Sociology* 27, 1: 31–41.

Epstein, Cynthia Fuchs (1988), *Deceptive Distinctions: Sex, Gender, and the Social Order*. New Haven and London: Yale University Press.

Eribon, Didier (1991 [1989]), *Michel Foucault [Michel Foucault (1926–1984)]*. Cambridge, MA: Harvard University Press.

Erikson, Kai (1966), *Wayward Puritans: A Study in the Sociology of Deviance*. New York: John Wiley & Sons.

Esser, Hartmut (1993), *Soziologie. Allgemeine Grundlagen*. Frankfurt am Main and New York: Campus.

(1999–2000), *Soziologie. Spezielle Grundlagen*. 6 vols. Frankfurt am Main and New York: Campus.

Etzioni, Amitai (1968), *The Active Society: A Theory of Societal and Political Processes*. New York: Free Press.
— (1988), *The Moral Dimension: Towards a New Economics*. New York: Free Press.
— (1993), *The Spirit of Community: The Reinvention of American Society*. New York: Crown.
— (2001), *The Monochrome Society*. Princeton and Oxford: Princeton University Press.
— (2003), *My Brother's Keeper: A Memoir and a Message*. Lanham, MD: Rowman & Littlefield.
Ferry, Luc and Alain Renaut (1990 [1985]), 'French Marxism (Bourdieu)' in Luc Ferry and Alain Renaut, *French Philosophy of the Sixties: An Essay on Anti-Humanism* [*La pensée 68. Essai sur l'antihumanisme contemporain*]. Amherst and London: University of Massachusetts Press, pp. 153–84.
Feyerabend, Paul (1982), *Science in a Free Society*. London: Verso.
Firestone, Shulamith (1971), *The Dialectic of Sex: The Case for Feminist Revolution*. London: Jonathan Cape.
Flax, Jane (1990), 'Postmodernism and Gender Relations in Feminist Theory', in Linda J. Nicholson (ed.), *Feminism/Postmodernism*. New York and London: Routledge, pp. 39–62.
Foucault, Michel (1977 [1975]), *Discipline and Punish: The Birth of the Prison* [*Surveiller et punir. Naissance de la prison*]. London: Allen Lane.
— (1979 [1976]), *The History of Sexuality.* Volume I: *The Will to Knowledge* [*Histoire de la sexualité. La volonté de savoir*]. London: Allen Lane.
— (1986 [1984]), *The History of Sexuality.* Volume III: *The Care of the Self* [*Histoire de la sexualité. Le souci de soi*]. London: Pantheon.
— (1987 [1984]), *The History of Sexuality.* Volume II: *The Use of Pleasure* [*Histoire de la sexualité. L'usage des plaisirs*]. London: Penguin.
— (1988 [1961]), *Madness and Civilization: A History of Insanity in the Age of Reason* [*Histoire de la folie*]. New York: Vintage.
— (2001 [1966]), *The Order of Things: An Archaeology of the Human Sciences* [*Les mots et les choses*]. London: Routledge.
— (2002 [1996]), *Society Must be Defended: Lectures at the Collège de France, 1975–1976* [*Il faut défendre la société*]. New York: Picador.
Frank, Manfred (1989 [1984]), *What is Neostructuralism?* [*Was ist Neostrukturalismus?*]. Minneapolis: University of Minnesota Press.
Fraser, Nancy (1989), *Unruly Practices: Power, Discourse and Gender in Contemporary Social Theory*. Minneapolis: University of Minnesota Press.
Fraser, Nancy and Axel Honneth (2003), *Redistribution or Recognition? A Political-Philosophical Exchange*. London: Verso.
Fraser, Nancy and Linda J. Nicholson (1990), 'Social Criticism without Philosophy: An Encounter between Feminism and Postmodernism', in Linda J. Nicholson (ed.), *Feminism/Postmodernism*. New York and London: Routledge, pp. 19–38.
Freidson, Eliot (1970), *Profession of Medicine: A Study of the Sociology of Applied Knowledge*. New York: Dodd, Mead & Co.

Friedman, Debra and Michael Hechter (1988), 'The Contribution of Rational Choice Theory to Macrosociological Research', *Sociological Theory* 6, 2: 201–18.
Fühmann, Franz (1978), 'Drei nackte Männer', in Franz Fühmann, *Bagatelle, rundum positiv. Erzählungen*. Frankfurt am Main: Suhrkamp, pp. 7–22.
Gardner, Howard (1976), *The Quest for Mind: Piaget, Lévi-Strauss and the Structuralist Movement*. London: Quartet Books.
Garfinkel, Harold (1959), 'Aspects of the Problem of Common-Sense Knowledge of Social Structres', in *Transactions of the Fourth World Congress of Sociology*. Volume IV: *The Sociology of Knowledge*, pp. 51–66.
—— (1963), 'A Conception of, and Experiments with, "Trust" as a Condition of Stable Concerted Actions', in O. J. Harvey (ed.), *Motivation and Social Interaction*. New York: Ronald Press, pp. 187–238.
—— (1967), *Studies in Ethnomethodology*. Englewood Cliffs, NJ: Prentice-Hall.
—— (1991), 'Respecification: Evidence for Locally Produced, Naturally Accountable Phenomena of Order, Logic, Reason, Meaning, Method, etc. in and as of the Essential Haecceity of Immortal Ordinary Society, (I) – an Announcement of Studies', in Graham Button (ed.), *Ethnomethodology and the Human Sciences*. Cambridge: Cambridge University Press, pp. 10–19.
Garfinkel, Harold and Harvey Sacks (1970), 'On Formal Structures of Practical Actions', in Edward Tiryakian and John MacKinney (eds.), *Theoretical Sociology: Perspectives and Developments*. New York: Appleton-Century-Crofts, pp. 337–66.
Gauchet, Marcel (1997 [1985]), *The Disenchantment of the World: A Political History of Religion* [*Le désenchantement du monde*]. Princeton: Princeton University Press.
Gehlen, Arnold (1956), *Urmensch und Spätkultur*. Bonn: Athenäum.
—— (1968 [1940]), 'Mensch und Institutionen', in Arnold Gehlen, *Anthropologische Forschung. Zur Selbstbegegnung und Selbstentdeckung des Menschen*. Reinbek: Rowohlt, pp. 69–77.
—— (1988 [1940]), *Man: His Nature and Place in the World* [*Der Mensch. Seine Natur und Stellung in der Welt*]. New York: Columbia University Press.
Gerhard, Ute (1992), *Unerhört. Die Geschichte der deutschen Frauenbewegung*. Reinbek: Rowohlt.
Gerhardt, Uta (ed.) (1993), *Talcott Parsons on National Socialism*. New York: Aldine de Gruyter.
Giddens, Anthony (1971), *Capitalism and Modern Social Theory*. Cambridge and New York: Cambridge University Press.
—— (1973), *The Class Structure of the Advanced Societies*. London: Hutchinson.
—— (1976), 'Classical Social Theory and the Origins of Modern Sociology', *American Journal of Sociology* 81, 4: 703–29.
—— (1976), *New Rules of Sociological Method*. London: Hutchinson.
—— (1979), *Central Problems in Social Theory: Action, Structure and Contradiction in Social Analysis*. Basingstoke: Macmillan Press.

(1981), *A Contemporary Critique of Historical Materialism*. Volume I: *Power, Property and the State*. Basingstoke: Macmillan Press.
(1982), 'Commentary on the Debate', *Theory and Society* 11, 4: 527–39.
(1984), *The Constitution of Society: Outline of the Theory of Structuration*. Cambridge: Polity Press.
(1985), *The Nation-State and Violence. Volume Two of A Contemporary Critique of Historical Materialism*. Cambridge: Polity Press.
(1987), 'Structuralism, Post-structuralism and the Production of Culture', in Anthony Giddens, *Social Theory and Modern Sociology*. Cambridge: Polity Press, pp. 73–108.
(1989), *Sociology*. Cambridge: Polity Press.
(1990), *The Consequences of Modernity*. Stanford, CA: Stanford University Press.
(1991), *Modernity and Self-Identity: Self and Society in the Late Modern Age*. Cambridge: Polity Press.
(1992), *Transformation of Intimacy*. Cambridge: Polity Press.
(1994), *Beyond Left and Right: The Future of Radical Politics*. Cambridge: Polity Press.
(1998), *The Third Way: The Renewal of Social Democracy*. Malden, MA and Cambridge: Polity Press.
Giele, Janet Zollinger (1995), *Two Paths to Women's Equality: Temperance, Suffrage, and the Origins of Modern Feminism*. New York: Twayne Publishers.
Gilcher-Holtey, Ingrid (1995), *Die 'Phantasie an die Macht'. Mai 68 in Frankreich*. Frankfurt am Main: Suhrkamp.
Gildemeister, Regine and Angelika Wetterer (1992), 'Wie Geschlechter gemacht werden. Die soziale Konstruktion der Zweigeschlechtlichkeit und ihre Reifizierung in der Frauenforschung', in Gudrun-Axeli Knapp and Angelika Wetterer (eds.), *Traditionen Brüche. Entwicklungen feministischer Theorie*. Freiburg: Kore, pp. 201–54.
Gilligan, Carol (1982), *In a Different Voice: Psychological Theory and Women's Development*. Cambridge, MA and London: Harvard University Press.
Glaser, Barney G. and Anselm L. Strauss (1966 [1965]), *Awareness of Dying*. London: Weidenfeld & Nicolson.
(1967), *The Discovery of Grounded Theory: Strategies for Qualitative Research*. New York: Aldine de Gruyter.
Godbout, Jacques and Alain Caillé (1998 [1992]), *The World of the Gift [L'esprit de don]*. Montreal and London: McGill-Queen's University Press.
Goffman, Erving (1956), *The Presentation of Self in Everyday Life*. Edinburgh: Edinburgh University Press.
(1961), *Asylums: Essays on the Social Situation of Mental Patients and Other Inmates*. Garden City, NY: Doubleday & Co.
(1963), *Stigma: Notes on the Management of Spoiled Identity*. Englewood Cliffs, NJ: Prentice-Hall.
(1972 [1971]), *Interaction Ritual: Essays on Face-to-Face Behaviour*. Harmondsworth: Penguin.

(1975 [1974]), *Frame Analysis: An Essay on the Organization of Experience.* Harmondsworth: Penguin.
Goldhagen, Daniel J. (1996), *Hitler's Willing Executioners: Ordinary Germans and the Holocaust.* London: Little, Brown.
Goldstone, Jack A. (1994), 'Is Revolution Individually Rational? Groups and Individuals in Revolutionary Collective Action', *Rationality and Society* 6, 1: 139-66.
Gottschall, Karin (1997), 'Sozialkonstruktivistische Perspektiven für die Analyse von sozialer Ungleichheit und Geschlecht', in Stefan Hradil (ed.), *Differenz und Integration. Die Zukunft moderner Gesellschaften. Verhandlungen des 28. Kongresses der Deutschen Gesellschaft für Soziologie in Dresden 1996.* Frankfurt am Main and New York: Campus, pp. 479-96.
Habermas, Jürgen (1963), 'Literaturbericht zur philosophischen Diskussion um Marx und den Marxismus', in Jürgen Habermas, *Theorie und Praxis. Sozialphilosophische Studien.* Frankfurt am Main: Suhrkamp, pp. 387-463.
(1969), *Technik und Wissenschaft als 'Ideologie'.* Frankfurt am Main: Suhrkamp.
[(1971), *Toward a Rational Society: Student Protest, Science and Politics.* London: Heinemann].
(1973 [1963]), 'Between Philosophy and Science: Marxism as Critique' ['Zwischen Philosophie und Wissenschaft. Marxismus als Kritik'], in Jürgen Habermas, *Theory and Practice.* Cambridge: Polity Press in association with Basil Blackwell, pp. 195-252.
(1973 [1967]), 'Labour and Interaction: Remarks on Hegel's "Jena Philosophy of Mind"' ['Arbeit und Interaktion. Bemerkungen zu Hegels "Jenenser Philosophie des Geistes"'], in Jürgen Habermas, *Theory and Practice.* Cambridge: Polity Press in association with Basil Blackwell, pp. 142-69.
(1976 [1973]), *Legitimation Crisis* [*Legitimationsprobleme im Spätkapitalismus*]. London: Heinemann.
(1978 [1968]), *Knowledge and Human Interests* [*Erkenntnis und Interesse*]. London: Heinemann.
(1983 [1971]), *Philosophical-Political Profiles* [*Philosophisch-Politische Profile*]. Cambridge, MA: MIT Press.
(1984-7 [1981]), *The Theory of Communicative Action* [*Theorie des kommunikativen Handelns*]. London: Heinemann.
(1987 [1981]), 'The Paradigm Shift in Mead and Durkheim: From Purposive Activity to Communicative Action', in Jürgen Habermas, *The Theory of Communicative Action*, Volume II [*Theorie des kommunikativen Handelns*]. Cambridge: Polity Press, pp. 1-92.
(1989 [1962]), *The Structural Transformation of the Public Sphere: An Inquiry into a Category of Bourgeois Society* [*Strukturwandel der Öffentlichkeit. Untersuchungen zu einer Kategorie der bürgerlichen Gesellschaft*]. Cambridge, MA: MIT Press.
(1990 [1983]), *Moral Consciousness and Communicative Action* [*Moralbewußtsein und kommunikatives Handeln*]. Cambridge, MA: MIT Press.

(1991 [1976]), 'Toward a Reconstruction of Historical Materialism' ['Zur Rekonstruktion des Historischen Materialismus'], in Jürgen Habermas, *Communication and the Evolution of Society*. Cambridge: Polity Press, pp. 130–77.

(1992), *Postmetaphysical Thinking: Philosophical Essays*. Cambridge: Polity Press.

(1996 [1992]), *Between Facts and Norms: Contributions to a Discourse Theory of Law and Democracy* [*Faktizität und Geltung. Beiträge zur Diskurstheorie des Rechts und des demokratischen Rechtsstaats*]. Cambridge: Polity Press.

(1998 [1996]), *The Inclusion of the Other: Studies in Political Theory* [*Die Einbeziehung des Anderen. Studien zur politischen Theorie*]. Cambridge, MA: MIT Press.

(2003), *Truth and Justification*. Cambridge, MA: MIT Press.

Habermas, Jürgen and Niklas Luhmann (1971), *Theorie der Gesellschaft oder Sozialtechnologie – Was leistet die Systemforschung?* Frankfurt am Main: Suhrkamp.

Haferkamp, Heinrich and Wolfgang Knöbl (2001), 'Die Logistik der Macht. Michael Manns Historische Soziologie als Gesellschaftstheorie', in Michael Mann (ed.), *Geschichte der Macht. Die Entstehung von Klassen und Nationalstaaten*. Band 3, Teil II. Frankfurt am Main and New York: Campus, pp. 303–49.

Hagemann-White, Carol (1988), 'Wir werden nicht zweigeschlechtlich geboren...', in Carol Hagemann-White and Maria S. Rerrich (eds.), *FrauenMännerBilder. Männer und Männlichkeit in der feministischen Diskussion*. Bielefeld: AJZ Verlag, pp. 224–35.

Hall, John A. (1985), *Powers and Liberties: The Causes and Consequences of the Rise of the West*. Oxford: Basil Blackwell.

(1994), *Coercion and Consent: Studies in the Modern State*. Cambridge: Polity Press.

Hall, Peter A. and Rosemary C. R. Taylor (1996), 'Political Science and the Three New Institutionalisms', *Political Studies* 44, 5: 936–57.

Hall, Peter M. (1972), 'A Symbolic Interactionist Analysis of Politics', *Sociological Inquiry* 42, 3/4: 35–75.

(1987), 'Presidential Address: Interactionism and the Study of Social Organization', *The Sociological Quarterly* 28, 1: 1–22.

Hall, Peter M. and Dee Ann Spencer-Hall (1982), 'The Social Conditions of the Negotiated Order', *Urban Life* 11, 3: 328–49.

Harding, Sandra (1990), 'Feminism, Science, and the Anti-Enlightenment Critiques', in Linda J. Nicholson (ed.), *Feminism/Postmodernism*. New York and London: Routledge, pp. 83–106.

Hartsock, Nancy (1990), 'Foucault on Power: A Theory for Women?', in Linda J. Nicholson (ed.), *Feminism/Postmodernism*. New York and London: Routledge, pp. 157–75.

Harvey, David (1989), *The Condition of Postmodernity: An Enquiry into the Origins of Cultural Change*. Oxford: Basil Blackwell.

Haskell, Thomas (1998), *Objectivity is Not Neutrality: Explanatory Schemes in History*. Baltimore: Johns Hopkins University Press.
Hechter, Michael (1987), *Principles of Group Solidarity*. Berkeley, Los Angeles and London: University of California Press.
Heilbron, Johan (1995), *The Rise of Social Theory*. Minneapolis: University of Minnesota Press.
Heintz, Bettina and Eva Nadai (1998), 'Geschlecht und Kontext. De-Institutionalisierungsprozesse und geschlechtliche Differenzierung', *Zeitschrift für Soziologie* 27, 2: 75-93.
Hénaff, Marcel (2002), *Le prix de la vérité: Le don, l'argent, la philosophie*. Paris: Éditions du Seuil.
Heritage, John (1984), *Garfinkel and Ethnomethodology*. Cambridge and New York: Polity Press.
Hettlage, Robert and Karl Lenz (eds.) (1991), *Erving Goffman – ein soziologischer Klassiker der zweiten Generation*. Stuttgart: UTB.
Hirschauer, Stefan (1994), 'Die soziale Fortpflanzung der Zweigeschlechtlichkeit', *Kölner Zeitschrift für Soziologie und Sozialpsychologie* 46, 4: 668-92.
Hirschman, Albert (1977), *The Passions and the Interests: Political Arguments for Capitalism Before its Triumph*. Princeton and Guildford: Princeton University Press.
Hobbes, Thomas (1914 [1651]), *Leviathan*. London: J. M. Dent & Sons.
Hochschild, Arlie (1979), 'Emotion Work, Feeling Rules, and Social Structure', *American Journal of Sociology* 85, 3: 551-75.
—— (1983), *The Managed Heart*. Berkeley and London: University of California Press.
Höffe, Otfried (1985), *Strategien der Humanität. Zur Ethik öffentlicher Entscheidungsprozesse*. Frankfurt am Main: Suhrkamp.
Homans, George C. (1950), *The Human Group*. New York: Harcourt, Brace & World.
—— (1958), 'Social Behavior as Exchange', *American Journal of Sociology* 63, 6: 597-606.
—— (1961), *Social Behavior: Its Elementary Forms*. London: Routledge.
—— (1964), 'Bringing Men Back In', *American Sociological Review* 29, 5: 809-18.
Honneth, Axel (1989), 'Moralische Entwicklung und sozialer Kampf. Sozialphilosophische Lehren aus dem Frühwerk Hegels', in Axel Honneth, Thomas McCarthy, Claus Offe and Albrecht Wellmer (eds.), *Zwischenbetrachtungen im Prozeß der Aufklärung. Jürgen Habermas zum 60. Geburtstag*. Frankfurt am Main: Suhrkamp, pp. 549-73.
—— (1990), 'A Structuralist Rousseau: On the Anthropology of Claude Lévi-Strauss', *Philosophy and Social Criticism* 16, 2: 143-58.
—— (1991 [1986]), *The Critique of Power: Reflective Stages in a Critical Social Theory* [*Kritik der Macht. Reflexionsstufen einer kritischen Gesellschaftstheorie*]. Cambridge, MA and London: MIT Press.
—— (1994), *Desintegration. Bruchstücke einer soziologischen Zeitdiagnose*. Frankfurt am Main: Fischer.

(1995 [1990]), 'The Fragmented World of Symbolic Forms: Reflections on Pierre Bourdieu's Sociology of Culture', in Axel Honneth and Charles W. Wright (eds.), *The Fragmented World of the Social: Essays in Social and Political Philosophy* [*Die zerrissene Welt des Sozialen. Sozialphilosophische Aufsätze*]. Albany: State University of New York Press, pp. 184–201.

(1995 [1992]), *The Struggle for Recognition: The Moral Grammar of Social Conflicts* [*Kampf um Anerkennung. Zur moralischen Grammatik sozialer Konflikte*]. Cambridge: Polity Press.

(2000), *Das Andere der Gerechtigkeit. Aufsätze zur praktischen Philosophie*. Frankfurt am Main: Suhrkamp.

(2001), 'Die Zukunft des Instituts für Sozialforschung', *Mitteilungen des Instituts für Sozialforschung* 12: 54–63.

(2007) *Disrespect: The Normative Foundations of Critical Theory*. Cambridge: Polity Press.

Honneth, Axel and Hans Joas (1988 [1980]), *Social Action and Human Nature* [*Soziales Handeln und menschliche Natur. Anthropologische Grundlagen der Sozialwissenschaften*]. Cambridge: Cambridge University Press.

(2002), *Kommunikatives Handeln. Beiträge zu Jürgen Habermas' 'Theorie des kommunikativen Handelns'*. Erweiterte und aktualisierte Ausgabe. Frankfurt am Main: Suhrkamp.

Horster, Detlef (1997), *Niklas Luhmann*. Munich: Beck.

Hughes, Everett C. (1994), 'Professions', in Everett C. Hughes, *On Work, Race, and the Sociological Imagination*, ed. and intro. Lewis A. Coser. Chicago and London: University of Chicago Press, pp. 37–49.

Husserl, Edmund (1970 [1936]), *The Crisis of European Sciences and Transcendental Phenomenology* [*Die Krisis der europäischen Wissenschaften und die transzendentale Phänomenologie*]. Evanston: Northwestern University Press.

Irrgang, Bernhard (1993), *Lehrbuch der evolutionären Erkenntnistheorie*. Munich and Basel: Ernst Reinhardt.

Jaggar, Alison M. (1993), 'Feministische Ethik. Ein Forschungsprogramm für die Zukunft', in H. Nagl-Docekal and H. Pauer-Studer (eds.), *Jenseits der Geschlechtermoral. Beiträge zur feministischen Ethik*. Frankfurt am Main: Fischer, pp. 195–218.

James, William (1978 [1907]), *Pragmatism: A New Name for Some Old Ways of Thinking*. Cambridge, MA and London: Harvard University Press.

Jameson, Fredric (1991), *Postmodernism, or, The Cultural Logic of Late Capitalism*. London and New York: Verso.

Jaspers, Karl (1953 [1949]), *The Origin and Goal of History* [*Vom Ursprung und Ziel der Geschichte*]. London: Routledge.

Joas, Hans (1993 [1986]), 'The Unhappy Marriage of Hermeneutics and Functionalism: Jürgen Habermas' Theory of Communicative Action', in Hans Joas, *Pragmatism and Social Theory* [*Pragmatismus und Gesellschaftstheorie*]. Chicago and London: University of Chicago Press, pp. 125–53.

(1993 [1992]), 'Pragmatism in American Sociology', in Hans Joas, *Pragmatism and Social Theory* [*Pragmatismus und Gesellschaftstheorie*]. Chicago and London: University of Chicago Press, pp. 14-54.

(1993 [1992]), 'A Sociological Transformation of the Philosophy of Praxis: Anthony Giddens's Theory of Structuration', in Hans Joas, *Pragmatism and Social Theory* [*Pragmatismus und Gesellschaftstheorie*]. Chicago and London: University of Chicago Press, pp. 172-87.

(1996 [1992]), *The Creativity of Action* [*Die Kreativität des Handelns*]. Oxford: Polity Press.

(1997 [1980]), *G. H. Mead: A Contemporary Re-examination of His Thought* [*Praktische Intersubjektivität. Die Entwicklung des Werkes von G. H. Mead*]. Cambridge, MA: MIT Press.

(1998), 'The Autonomy of the Self: The Meadian Heritage and its Postmodern Challenge', *European Journal of Social Theory* 1: 7-18.

(1998/99), 'Macroscopic Action – On Amitai Etzioni's Contribution to Social Theory', *The Responsive Community* 9: 23-31.

(2000 [1997]), *The Genesis of Values* [*Die Entstehung der Werte*]. Chicago: University of Chicago Press.

(2001), 'The Gift of Life: Parsons' Late Sociology of Religion', *Journal of Classical Sociology* 1, 1: 127-41.

(2002), 'Values versus Norms: A Pragmatist Account of Moral Objectivity', *The Hedgehog Review* 3, 1: 42-56.

(2002 [2000]), *War and Modernity* [*Kriege und Werte. Studien zur Gewaltgeschichte des 20. Jahrhunderts*]. Oxford: Polity Press.

(2003), 'Gott in Frankreich. Paul Ricoeur als Denker der Vermittlung', *Merkur* 57: 242-6.

(2003), 'Max Weber und die Entstehung der Menschenrechte. Eine Studie über kulturelle Innovation', in Gert Albert, Agathe Bienfait, Steffen Siegmund and Claus Wendt (eds.), *Das Weber-Paradigma. Studien zur Weiterentwicklung von Max Webers Forschungsprogramm*. Tübingen: Mohr Siebeck, pp. 252-70.

(2007 [2004]), *Do We Need Religion? On the Experience of Self-Transcendence* [*Braucht der Mensch Religion? Über Erfahrungen der Selbsttranszendenz*]. Boulder: Paradigm Publishers.

Joas, Hans and Frank Adloff (2002), 'Milieuwandel und Gemeinsinn', in Herfried Münkler and Harald Bluhm (eds.), *Gemeinwohl und Gemeinsinn*. Volume IV: *Zwischen Normativität und Faktizität*. Berlin: Akademie Verlag, pp. 153-85.

Joas, Hans and Jens Beckert (2001), 'Action Theory', in Jonathan H. Turner (ed.), *Handbook of Sociological Theory*. New York: Kluwer Academic, pp. 269-85.

Kalyvas, Andreas (2001), 'The Politics of Autonomy and the Challenge of Deliberation: Castoriadis Contra Habermas', *Thesis Eleven* 64: 1-19.

Kessler, Suzanne J. and Wendy McKenna (1978), *Gender: An Ethnomethodological Approach*. Chicago and London: University of Chicago Press.

Kippenberg, Hans G. and Brigitte Luchesi (eds.) (1978), *Magie. Die Sozialwissenschaftliche Kontroverse über das Verstehen fremden Denkens*. Frankfurt am Main: Suhrkamp.

Kitsuse, John I. (1962), 'Societal Reaction to Deviant Behavior: Problems of Theory and Method', *Social Problems* 9, 3: 247–56.

Knapp, Gudrun-Axeli (1992), 'Macht und Geschlecht. Neuere Entwicklungen in der feministischen Macht- und Herrschaftsdiskussion', in Gudrun-Axeli Knapp and Angelika Wetterer (eds.), *Traditionen Brüche. Entwicklungen feministischer Theorie*. Freiburg: Kore, pp. 287–325.

—— (1997), 'Differenz und Dekonstruktion. Anmerkungen zum "Paradigmenwechsel" in der Frauenforschung', in Gudrun-Axeli Knapp, *Differenz und Integration. Die Zukunft moderner Gesellschaften. Verhandlungen des 28. Kongresses der Deutschen Gesellschaft für Soziologie in Dresden 1996*. Frankfurt am Main and New York: Campus, pp. 497–513.

Kneer, Georg and Armin Nassehi, *Niklas Luhmanns Theorie sozialer Systeme*. Munich: Wilhelm Fink.

Knöbl, Wolfgang (2001), *Spielräume der Modernisierung. Das Ende der Eindeutigkeit*. Weilerswist: Velbrück.

—— (2007), *Die Kontingenz der Moderne. Wege in Europa, Asien und Amerika*. Frankfurt am Main and New York: Campus.

Knorr-Cetina, Karin (1981), *The Manufacture of Knowledge: An Essay on the Constructivist and Contextual Nature of Science*. Oxford: Pergamon.

Kohlberg, Lawrence (1996), 'Moral Stages and Moralization', in Lawrence Kohlberg, *The Psychology of Moral Development*. San Francisco and London: Harper & Row, pp. 170–206.

Kuhn, Thomas S. (1962), *The Structure of Scientific Revolutions*. Chicago and London: University of Chicago Press.

Kurzweil, Edith (1980), *The Age of Structuralism: Lévi-Strauss to Foucault*. New York: Columbia University Press.

Kymlicka, Will (1990), *Contemporary Political Philosophy: An Introduction*. Oxford: Clarendon Press.

Lamont, Michèle (1992), *Money, Morals, and Manners: The Culture of the French and the American Upper-Middle Class*. Chicago and London: University of Chicago Press.

Landweer, Hilge (1994), 'Generativität und Geschlecht. Ein blinder Fleck in der sex/gender-Debatte', in Theresa Wobbe and Gesa Lindemann (eds.), *Denkachsen. Zur theoretischen und institutionellen Rede vom Geschlecht*. Frankfurt am Main: Suhrkamp, pp. 147–76.

Larson, Magali Sarfatti (1977), *The Rise of Professionalism: A Sociological Analysis*. Berkeley, Los Angeles and London: University of California Press.

Latour, Bruno (1993 [1991]), *We Have Never Been Modern* [*Nous n'avons jamais été modernes. Essai d'anthropologie symétrique*]. New York and London: Harvester Wheatsheaf.
Leach, Edmund (1989), *Claude Lévi-Strauss*. Chicago: University of Chicago Press.
Lefort, Claude (1988), 'Interpreting Revolution within the French Revolution', in Claude Lefort, *Democracy and Political Theory*. Oxford: Polity Press, pp. 89-114.
Lemert, Edwin M. (1975), 'Das Konzept der sekundären Abweichung', in Friedrich W. Stallberg (ed.), *Abweichung und Kriminalität. Konzeptionen, Kritik, Analysen*. Hamburg: Hoffmann und Campe, pp. 33-46.
Lenski, Gerhard (1966), *Power and Privilege: A Theory of Social Stratification*. New York: McGraw-Hill.
Lerner, Daniel (1965 [1958]), *The Passing of Traditional Society: Modernizing the Middle East*. New York: Free Press.
Lévi-Strauss, Claude (1966 [1962]), *The Savage Mind* [*La pensée sauvage*]. London: Weidenfeld & Nicolson.
— (1968 [1958]), *Structural Anthropology* [*Anthropologie structurale*]. London: Allen Lane.
— (1973 [1955]), *Tristes Tropiques* [*Tristes Tropiques*]. London: Jonathan Cape.
— (1977 [1949]), *The Elementary Structures of Kinship* [*Les structures élémentaires de la parenté*]. Boston: Beacon Press.
Lidz, Victor (2000), 'Talcott Parsons', in George Ritzer (ed.), *Blackwell Companion to Major Social Theorists*. Oxford: Basil Blackwell, pp. 388-431.
Lipset, Seymour Martin (1988 [1959]), *Political Man: The Social Bases of Politics*. Baltimore: Johns Hopkins University Press.
Lockwood, David (1956), 'Some Remarks on *The Social System*', *British Journal of Sociology* 7: 134-46.
— (1964), 'Social Integration and System Integration', in George Zollschan and Walter Hirsch (eds.), *Explorations in Social Change*. London: Routledge, pp. 244-57.
— (1992), *Solidarity and Schism: 'The Problem of Disorder' in Durkheimian and Marxist Sociology*. Oxford: Clarendon Press.
Lorber, Judith (1994), *Paradoxes of Gender*. New Haven and London: Yale University Press.
Luhmann, Niklas (1964), *Funktionen und Folgen formaler Organisation*. Berlin: Duncker & Humblot.
— (1970), 'Funktionale Methode und Systemtheorie', in Niklas Luhmann, *Soziologische Aufklärung 1. Aufsätze zur Theorie sozialer Systeme*. Opladen: Westdeutscher Verlag, pp. 31-53.
— (1970), 'Funktionen und Kausalität', in Niklas Luhmann, *Soziologische Aufklärung 1. Aufsätze zur Theorie sozialer Systeme*. Opladen: Westdeutscher Verlag, pp. 9-30.

(1970), 'Soziologie als Theorie sozialer Systeme', in Niklas Luhmann, *Soziologische Aufklärung 1. Aufsätze zur Theorie sozialer Systeme.* Opladen: Westdeutscher Verlag, pp. 113–36.

(1970), 'Soziologische Aufklärung', in Niklas Luhmann, *Soziologische Aufklärung 1. Aufsätze zur Theorie sozialer Systeme.* Opladen: Westdeutscher Verlag, pp. 66–91.

(1972 [1968]), *Zweckbegriff und Systemrationalität. Über die Funktion von Zwecken in sozialen Systemen.* Frankfurt am Main: Suhrkamp.

(1979 [1968]), *Trust and Power* [originally published in German as two separate volumes, *Vertrauen and Macht*]. Chichester: Wiley.

(1980), *Gesellschaftsstruktur und Semantik. Studien zur Wissenssoziologie der modernen Gesellschaft.* 4 vols. Frankfurt am Main: Suhrkamp.

(1983 [1969]), *Legitimation durch Verfahren.* Frankfurt am Main: Suhrkamp.

(1986 [1982]), *Love as Passion: The Codification of Intimacy* [*Liebe als Passion. Zur Codierung von Intimität*]. Cambridge: Polity Press.

(1989 [1986]), *Ecological Communication* [*Ökologische Kommunikation. Kann die moderne Gesellschaft sich auf ökologische Gefährdungen einstellen?*]. Cambridge: Polity Press.

(1989), 'Politische Steuerung. Ein Diskussionsbeitrag', *Politische Vierteljahresschrift* 31, 1: 4–9.

(1990 [1981]), *Political Theory in the Welfare State* [*Politische Theorie im Wohlfahrtsstaat*]. Berlin: de Gruyter.

(1995 [1984]), *Social Systems* [*Soziale Systeme. Grundriß einer allgemeinen Theorie*]. Stanford, CA: Stanford University Press.

(1997), 'Biographie im Interview', in Detlef Horster, *Niklas Luhmann.* Munich: Beck, pp. 25–45.

(1997), *Die Gesellschaft der Gesellschaft.* 2 vols. Frankfurt am Main: Suhrkamp.

(2000), *Die Politik der Gesellschaft.* ed. André Kieserling. Frankfurt am Main: Suhrkamp.

Lukács, Georg (1971 [1923]), *History and Class Consciousness: Studies in Marxist Dialectics* [*Geschichte und Klassenbewußtsein*]. London: Merlin Press.

Lynch, Michael, Eric Livingston and Harold Garfinkel (1983), 'Temporal Order in Laboratory Work', in Karin Knorr-Cetina and Michael Muller (eds.), *Science Observed: Perspectives on the Social Study of Science.* Beverly Hills and London: Sage, pp. 205–38.

Lyotard, Jean-François (1984 [1979]), *The Postmodern Condition: A Report on Knowledge* [*La condition postmoderne*]. Manchester: Manchester University Press.

MacKinnon, Catharine A. (1989), *Toward a Feminist Theory of the State.* Cambridge, MA and London: Harvard University Press.

Maines, David R. (1977), 'Social Organization and Social Structure in Symbolic Interactionist Thought', *Annual Review of Sociology* 3: 235–59.

(1982), 'In Search of Mesostructure: Studies in the Negotiated Order', *Urban Life* 11, 3: 267–79.

(2001), *The Faultline of Consciousness: A View of Interactionism in Sociology*. New York: Aldine de Gruyter.
Mann, Michael (1986), *The Sources of Social Power*. Cambridge: Cambridge University Press.
Marwell, Gerald and Ruth E. Ames (1981), 'Economists Free Ride, Does Anyone Else? Experiments on the Provision of Public Goods, IV', *Journal of Public Economics* 15: 295–310.
Marx, Karl (1970 [1919]), *A Contribution to the Critique of Political Economy*. London: Lawrence & Wishart.
Marx, Werner (1987), *Die Phänomenologie Edmund Husserls. Eine Einführung*. Munich: Fink.
Maurer, Andrea and Michael Schmid (eds.) (2002), *Neuer Institutionalismus. Zur soziologischen Erklärung von Organisation, Moral und Vertrauen*. Frankfurt am Main and New York: Campus.
Mauss, Marcel (1990 [1923/24]), *The Gift: The Form and Reason for Exchange in Archaic Societies [Essai sur le don]*. London: Routledge.
Mayer, Hans (1982), *Ein Deutscher auf Widerruf. Erinnerungen*. Volume I. Frankfurt am Main: Suhrkamp.
McCarthy, John and Mayer Zald (1977), 'Resource Mobilization and Social Movements: A Partial Theory', *American Journal of Sociology* 82, 6: 1212–41.
McCarthy, Thomas (1978), *The Critical Theory of Jürgen Habermas*. London: Hutchinson.
(1991), *Ideals and Illusions: On Reconstruction and Deconstruction in Contemporary Critical Theory*. Cambridge, MA and London: MIT Press.
McClelland, David (1961), *The Achieving Society*. New York and London: Free Press.
Mehan, Hugh and Houston Wood (1976), 'Five Features of Reality', in Jodi O'Brien (ed.), *The Production of Reality*. Thousand Oaks and London: Pine Forge Press, pp. 365–80.
Meltzer, Bernard N., John W. Petras and Larry T. Reynolds (1975), *Symbolic Interactionism: Genesis, Varieties and Criticism*. London and Boston: Routledge & Kegan Paul.
Merleau-Ponty, Maurice (1962 [1945]), *Phenomenology of Perception [Phénoménologie de la perception]*. London: Routledge.
Merton, Robert K. (1957), 'Continuities in the Theory of Reference Groups and Social Structure', in Robert K. Merton, *Social Theory and Social Structure*. Revised and enlarged edition. Glencoe, IL and New York: Free Press, pp. 281–386.
Meyer, John W. (1977), 'Institutionalized Organizations: Formal Structure as Myth and Ceremony', *American Journal of Sociology* 83, 2: 340–63.
Meyer, John W., John Boli, George M. Thomas and Francisco O. Ramirez (1997), 'World Society and the Nation-State', *American Journal of Sociology* 103, 1: 144–81.

Mill, John Stuart (1992 [1863]), 'Utilitarianism', in John Stuart Mill, *On Liberty and Utilitarianism*. New York: Alfred A. Knopf, pp. 113–72.
Miller, James (1993), *The Passion of Michel Foucault*. New York: Simon & Schuster.
Mills, C. Wright (1956), *The Power Elite*. New York: Oxford University Press.
— (1959), *The Sociological Imagination*. New York: Oxford University Press.
— (1964), *Sociology and Pragmatism: The Higher Learning in America*. New York: Paine-Whitman Publishers.
Müller, Hans-Peter (1992), *Sozialstruktur und Lebensstile. Der neuere theoretische Diskurs über soziale Ungleichheit*. Frankfurt am Main: Suhrkamp.
Mullins, Nicolas C. and Carolyn J. Mullins (1973), 'Symbolic Interactionism: The Loyal Opposition', in Nicolas C. Mullins, *Theories and Theory Groups in Contemporary American Sociology*. New York: Harper & Row, pp. 75–104.
Münch, Richard (1984), *Die Struktur der Moderne. Grundmuster und differentielle Gestaltung des institutionellen Aufbaus der modernen Gesellschaften*. Frankfurt am Main: Suhrkamp.
— (1986), *Die Kultur der Moderne*. 2 vols. Frankfurt am Main: Suhrkamp.
— (1987 [1982]), *Theory of Action: Towards a New Synthesis Going Beyond Parsons* [translation of part of *Theorie des Handelns. Zur Rekonstruktion der Beiträge von Talcott Parsons, Emile Durkheim und Max Weber*]. London: Routledge.
— (1988 [1982]), *Understanding Modernity: Toward a New Perspective Going beyond Durkheim and Weber* [translation of part of *Theorie des Handelns. Zur Rekonstruktion der Beiträge von Talcott Parsons, Emile Durkheim und Max Weber*]. London: Routledge.
— (2002), 'Die Zweite Moderne: Realität oder Fiktion? Kritische Fragen an die "Theorie reflexiver Modernisierung"', *Kölner Zeitschrift für Soziologie und Sozialpsychologie* 54, 3: 417–43.
Nagl, Ludwig (1992), *Charles Sanders Peirce*. Frankfurt am Main and New York: Campus.
Nagl-Docekal, Herta (2000), *Feministische Philosophie. Ergebnisse, Probleme, Perspektiven*. Frankfurt am Main: Fischer.
Nipperdey, Thomas (1996 [1983]), *Germany from Napoleon to Bismarck 1800–1866* [*Deutsche Geschichte. 1800–1866. Bürgerwelt und starker Staat*]. Dublin: Gill & Macmillan.
North, Douglass C. (1990), *Institutions, Institutional Change and Economic Performance*. Cambridge: Cambridge University Press.
Nunner-Winkler, Gertrud (1991), 'Gibt es eine weibliche Moral?', in Gertrud Nunner-Winkler (ed.), *Weibliche Moral. Die Kontroverse um eine geschlechtsspezifische Ethik*. Frankfurt am Main and New York: Campus, pp. 147–61.
Nussbaum, Martha C. (1995), 'Emotions and Women's Capabilities', in Martha C. Nussbaum and Jonathan Glover (eds.), *Women, Culture and Development*. Oxford: Oxford University Press, pp. 360–95.

(1999), 'The Professor of Parody: The Hip Defeatism of Judith Butler', *New Republic*, 22 February: 37–45.

Offe, Claus and Helmut Wiesenthal (1980), 'Two Logics of Collective Action: Theoretical Notes on Social Class and Organizational Form', *Political Power and Social Theory* 1: 67–115.

Oliver, Pamela E. and Gerald Marwell (1988), 'The Paradox of Group Size in Collective Action: A Theory of the Critical Mass. II', *American Sociological Review* 53, 1: 1–8.

—— (2001), 'Whatever Happened to Critical Mass Theory? A Retrospective and Assessment', *Sociological Theory* 19, 3: 292–311.

Olson, Mancur Jr. (1965), *The Logic of Collective Action*. Cambridge, MA: Harvard University Press.

Opp, Karl-Dieter (1994), 'Der "Rational Choice"-Ansatz und die Soziologie sozialer Bewegungen', *Forschungsjournal NSB* 2: 11–26.

—— (1994), 'Repression and Revolutionary Action', *Rationality and Society* 6, 1: 101–38.

Parsons, Talcott (1939), 'Actor, Situation and Normative Patterns: An Essay in the Theory of Social Action' (unpublished manuscript).

—— (1964 [1951]), *The Social System*. New York and London: Free Press.

—— (1964), 'Democracy and Social Structure in Pre-Nazi Germany', in Talcott Parsons, *Essays in Sociological Theory*. New York: Free Press, pp. 104–23.

—— (1964), 'The Motivation of Economic Activities', in Talcott Parsons, *Essays in Sociological Theory*. New York: Free Press, pp. 50–68.

—— (1964), 'The Professions and Social Structure', in Talcott Parsons, *Essays in Sociological Theory*. New York: Free Press, pp. 34–49.

—— (1966), *Societies: Evolutionary and Comparative Perspectives*. Englewood Cliffs, NJ: Prentice-Hall.

—— (1967), 'Full Citizenship for the Negro American?', in Talcott Parsons, *Sociological Theory and Modern Sociology*. New York: Free Press, pp. 422–65.

—— (1967), 'On the Concept of Political Power', in Talcott Parsons, *Sociological Theory and Modern Society*. New York: Free Press, pp. 297–354.

—— (1968 [1937]), *The Structure of Social Action: A Study in Social Theory with Special Reference to a Group of Recent European Writers*. 2 vols. New York and London: Free Press.

—— (1969), 'On the Concept of Influence', in Talcott Parsons, *Politics and Social Structure*. New York and London: Free Press, pp. 405–38.

—— (1969), 'On the Concept of Value-Commitments', in Talcott Parsons, *Politics and Social Structure*. New York and London: Free Press, pp. 439–72.

—— (1971), *The System of Modern Societies*. Englewood Cliffs, NJ: Prentice-Hall.

—— (1974), 'Comment on Turner, "Parsons as a Symbolic Interactionist"', *Sociological Inquiry* 45, 1: 62–5.

—— (1978), *Action Theory and the Human Condition*. New York and London: Free Press.

Parsons, Talcott and Edward A. Shils (1951), *Toward a General Theory of Action*. Cambridge, MA: Harvard University Press.

Parsons, Talcott and Neil Smelser (1956), *Economy and Society: A Study in the Integration of Economic and Social Theory*. London: Routledge.

Parsons, Talcott, Robert F. Bales and Edward A. Shils (1953), *Working Papers in the Theory of Action*. New York and London: Free Press.

Pauer-Studer, Herlinde (1993), 'Moraltheorie und Geschlechterdifferenz. Feministische Ethik im Kontext aktueller Fragestellungen', in H. Nagl-Docekal and H. Pauer-Studer (eds.), *Jenseits der Geschlechtermoral. Beiträge zur feministischen Ethik*. Frankfurt am Main: Fischer, pp. 33–68.

Peirce, Charles S. (1934), 'The Fixation of Belief', in Charles Hartshorne and Paul Weiss (eds.), *Collected Papers of Charles Sanders Peirce*. Volume V: *Pragmatism and Pragmaticism*. Cambridge, MA: Harvard University Press, pp. 358–87.

(1934), 'Some Consequences of Four Incapacities', in Charles Hartshorne and Paul Weiss (eds.), *Collected Papers of Charles Sanders Peirce*. Volume V: *Pragmatism and Pragmaticism*. Cambridge, MA: Harvard University Press, pp. 156–89.

Plummer, Ken (1991), 'Introduction: The Foundations of Interactionist Sociologies', in Ken Plummer (ed.), *Symbolic Interactionism*. Volume I: *Foundations and History*. Aldershot and Brookfield: Edward Elgar Publishing, pp. x–xx.

Pope, Whitney, Jere Cohen and Lawrence E. Hazelrigg (1975), 'On the Divergence of Weber and Durkheim: A Critique of Parsons' Convergence Thesis', *American Sociological Review* 40, 4: 417–27.

Popper, Karl Raimund (1989), *Logik der Forschung*. Ninth edition. Tübingen: Mohr.

(1992 [1934]), *The Logic of Scientific Discovery* [*Logik der Forschung*]. London: Routledge.

Psathas, George (1976), 'Die Untersuchung von Alltagsstrukturen und das ethnomethodologische Paradigma', in Richard Grathoff and Walter Sprondel (eds.), *Alfred Schütz und die Idee des Alltags in den Sozialwissenschaften*. Stuttgart: Enke, pp. 178–95.

Putnam, Hilary (1981), *Reason, Truth and History*. Cambridge: Cambridge University Press.

(1988), *Representation and Reality*. Cambridge, MA and London: MIT Press.

(1992), *Renewing Philosophy*. Cambridge, MA and London: Harvard University Press.

(1995), *Pragmatism: An Open Question*. Oxford: Blackwell.

Raters, Marie-Luise and Marcus Willaschek (2002), 'Hilary Putnam und die Tradition des Pragmatismus', in Marie-Luise Raters and Marcus Willaschek (eds.), *Hilary Putnam und die Tradition des Pragmatismus*. Frankfurt am Main: Suhrkamp, pp. 9–29.

Rawls, John (1972 [1971]), *A Theory of Justice*. Oxford: Clarendon Press.

Rex, John (1970 [1961]), *Key Problems of Sociological Theory*. London: Routledge.
Reynolds, Larry T. and Nancy J. Herman-Kinney (eds.) (2003), *Handbook of Symbolic Interactionism*. Walnut Creek, CA: Alta Mira Press.
Ricoeur, Paul (1970 [1965]), *Freud and Philosophy: An Essay on Interpretation* [*De l'interpretation. Essai sur Freud*]. New Haven and London: Yale University Press.
— (1984f. [1983f.]), *Time and Narrative*. 3 vols. [*Temps et récit*]. Chicago: University of Chicago Press.
— (1992 [1990]), *Oneself as Another* [*Soi-même comme un autre*]. Chicago and London: University of Chicago Press.
Rock, Paul (1991), 'Symbolic Interaction and Labelling Theory', in Ken Plummer (ed.), *Symbolic Interactionism*. Volume I: *Foundations and History*. Aldershot and Brookfield: Edward Elgar Publishing, pp. 227-43.
Rödel, Ulrich (ed.) (1990), *Autonome Gesellschaft und libertäre Demokratie*. Frankfurt am Main: Suhrkamp.
Rorty, Richard (1980), *Philosophy and the Mirror of Nature*. Oxford: Basil Blackwell.
— (1989), *Contingency, Irony, and Solidarity*. Cambridge: Cambridge University Press.
— (1991), 'Solidarity or Objectivity?', in Richard Rorty, *Objectivity, Relativism and Truth*. Cambridge: Cambridge University Press.
— (1998), *Achieving Our Country: Leftist Thought in Twentieth-Century America*. Cambridge, MA and London: Harvard University Press.
— (1998), *Truth and Progress*. Cambridge: Cambridge University Press.
— (1999), 'Trotsky and the Wild Orchids', in Richard Rorty, *Philosophy and Social Hope*. London: Penguin, pp. 3-20.
— (2000), 'Is it Desirable to Love Truth?', in Richard Rorty, *Truth, Politics and 'Postmodernism'*. Assen: Van Gorcum, pp. 1-22.
Rostow, Walt W. (1971 [1960]), *The Stages of Economic Growth: A Non-Communist Manifesto*. Cambridge: Cambridge University Press.
Rubin, Gayle (1975), 'The Traffic in Women: Notes on the "Political Economy" of Sex', in Rayna R. Reiter (ed.), *Toward an Anthropology of Women*. New York and London: Monthly Review Press, pp. 157-210.
Ryan, Alan (1991), 'When It's Rational to be Irrational', *The New York Review of Books*, 10 October: 19-22.
Sacks, Harvey (1972), 'Notes on Police Assessment of Moral Character', in David Sudnow (ed.), *Studies in Social Interaction*. Glencoe: Free Press, pp. 280-93.
Sandel, Michael J. (1982), *Liberalism and the Limits of Justice*. Cambridge: Cambridge University Press.
— (1993), 'The Procedural Republic and the Unencumbered Self', in Colin Farrelly (ed.), *Contemporary Political Theory: A Reader*. London: Sage, pp. 113-25.
Sartre, Jean-Paul (2003 [1943]), *Being and Nothingness: An Essay on Phenomenological Ontology* [*L'être et le néant. Essai d'ontologie phénoménologique*]. London: Routledge.

Saussure, Ferdinand de (1983 [1915]), *Course in General Linguistics* [*Cours de linguistique générale*]. London: Duckworth.
Scharpf, Fritz W. (1989), 'Politische Steuerung und Politische Institutionen', *Politische Vierteljahresschrift* 31, 1: 10–21.
— (2000), *Interaktionsformen. Akteurzentrierter Institutionalismus in der Politikforschung*. Opladen: Leske & Budrich.
Schegloff, Emanuel A. (2001), 'Accounts of Conduct in Interaction: Interruption, Overlap, and Turn-Taking', in Jonathan H. Turner (ed.), *Handbook of Sociological Theory*. New York: Kluwer Academic, pp. 287–321.
Schelling, Thomas C. (1960), *The Strategy of Conflict*. Cambridge, MA: Harvard University Press.
— (1978), *Micromotives and Macrobehavior*. New York and London: W. W. Norton & Co.
Schelsky, Helmut (1977 [1975]), *Die Arbeit tun die anderen. Klassenkampf und Priesterherrschaft der Intellektuellen*. Munich: dtv.
— (1984 [1957]), *Die skeptische Generation. Eine Soziologie der deutschen Jugend*. Frankfurt am Main, Berlin and Vienna: Ullstein.
Schimank, Uwe (1996), *Theorien gesellschaftlicher Differenzierung*. Opladen: Leske & Budrich.
Schiwy, Günther (1978), *Der französische Strukturalismus*. Reinbek: Rowohlt.
Schluchter, Wolfgang (1981 [1979]), *The Rise of Western Rationalism: Max Weber's Developmental History* [*Die Entwicklung des okzidentalen Rationalismus. Eine Analyse von Max Webers Gesellschaftsgeschichte*]. Berkeley and London: University of California Press.
— (1998), *Die Entstehung des modernen Rationalismus. Eine Analyse von Max Webers Entwicklungsgeschichte des Okzidents*. Frankfurt am Main: Suhrkamp.
Schluchter, Wolfgang (ed.) (1981), *Max Webers Studie über das antike Judentum. Interpretation und Kritik*. Frankfurt am Main: Suhrkamp.
— (1983), *Max Webers Studie über Konfuzianismus und Taoismus. Interpretation und Kritik*. Frankfurt am Main: Suhrkamp.
— (1984), *Max Webers Studie über Hinduismus und Buddhismus. Interpretation und Kritik*. Frankfurt am Main: Suhrkamp.
— (1985), *Max Webers Sicht des antiken Christentums. Interpretation und Kritik*. Frankfurt am Main: Suhrkamp.
— (1988), *Max Webers Sicht des okzidentalen Christentums. Interpretation und Kritik*. Frankfurt am Main: Suhrkamp.
— (1999 [1987]), *Max Weber and Islam. Interpretations and Critiques* [*Max Webers Sicht des Islams. Interpretation und Kritik*]. New Brunswick, NJ: Transaction.
Schröter, Susanne (2002), *FeMale. Über Grenzverläufe zwischen den Geschlechtern*. Frankfurt am Main: Fischer.
Schulze, Gerhard (1992), *Die Erlebnisgesellschaft. Kultursoziologie der Gegenwart*. Frankfurt am Main and New York: Campus.

Schütz, Alfred (1972 [1932]), *The Phenomenology of the Social World* [*Der sinnhafte Aufbau der sozialen Welt. Eine Einleitung in die verstehende Soziologie*]. London: Heinemann.
Schütz, Alfred and Thomas Luckmann (1974/1989 [1979/1984]), *The Structures of the Life-World*. 2 vols. London: Heinemann.
Schwingel, Markus (2000), *Pierre Bourdieu zur Einführung*. Hamburg: Junius.
Scott, Richard W. (1995), *Institutions and Organizations*. Thousand Oaks, London and New Delhi: Sage.
Sebeok, Thomas A. and Jean Umiker-Sebeok (1980), *'You Know My Method': A Juxtaposition of Charles S. Peirce and Sherlock Holmes*. Bloomington: Gaslight Publications.
Selznick, Philip (1966 [1949]), *TVA and the Grass Roots: A Study in the Sociology of Formal Organization*. 'With a new preface by the author'. New York: Harper.
(1992), *The Moral Commonwealth: Social Theory and the Promise of Community*. Berkeley, Los Angeles and London: University of California Press.
Shibutani, Tamotsu (1988), 'Herbert Blumer's Contribution to Twentieth-Century Sociology', *Symbolic Interaction* 11, 1: 23-31.
Shils, Edward A. (1958), 'Tradition and Liberty: Antinomy and Interdependence', *Ethics* 68, 3: 153-65.
(1966), 'The Intellectuals in the Political Development of the New States', in Jason L. Finkle and Richard W. Gable (eds.), *Political Development and Social Change*. New York, London and Sydney: John Wiley & Sons, pp. 338-65.
(1982), 'Center and Periphery', in Edward A. Shils, *The Constitution of Society*. 'With a new introduction by the author'. Chicago and London: University of Chicago Press, pp. 93-109.
(1982), 'Charisma, Order, and Status', in Edward A. Shils, *The Constitution of Society*. 'With a new introduction by the author'. Chicago and London: University of Chicago Press, pp. 119-42.
Shils, Edward A. and Morris Janowitz (1948), 'Cohesion and Disintegration in the Wehrmacht in World War II', *The Public Opinion Quarterly* 12, 2: 280-315.
Shils, Edward A. and Michael Young (1953), 'The Meaning of the Coronation', *Sociological Review* 1, 2: 63-81.
Simmel, Georg (1964 [1908]), *Conflict* [a translation of chapters from *Soziologie. Untersuchungen über die Formen der Vergesellschaftung*]. New York: Free Press.
Simon, Herbert A. (1959), 'Theories of Decision-Making in Economics and Behavioral Science', *American Economic Review* 49, 3: 253-83.
Smelser, Neil J. (1960 [1958]), *Social Change in the Industrial Revolution: An Application to the Lancashire Cotton Industry 1770-1840*. London: Routledge & Kegan Paul.
(1962), *Theory of Collective Behavior*. New York and London: Free Press.
(1991), *Social Paralysis and Social Change*. Berkeley: University of California Press.

(1997), *Problematics of Sociology: The Georg Simmel Lectures, 1995*. Berkeley, Los Angeles and London: University of California Press.
Snow, David A. and Phillip W. Davis (1995), 'The Chicago Approach to Collective Behavior', in Gary Alan Fine (ed.), *A Second Chicago School? The Development of a Postwar American Sociology*. Chicago and London: University of Chicago Press, pp. 188-220.
Sofsky, Wolfgang (1997 [1993]), *The Order of Terror: The Concentration Camp* [*Die Ordnung des Terrors. Das Konzentrationslager*]. Princeton and Chichester: Princeton University Press.
Srubar, Ilja (1988), *Kosmion. Die Genese der pragmatischen Lebenswelttheorie von Alfred Schütz und ihr anthropologischer Hintergrund*. Frankfurt am Main: Suhrkamp.
Stichweh, Rudolf (1991), *Der frühmoderne Staat und die europäische Universität. Zur Interaktion von Politik und Erziehungssystem im Prozeß ihrer Ausdifferenzierung (16.-18. Jahrhundert)*. Frankfurt am Main: Suhrkamp.
(1994), *Wissenschaft, Universität, Professionen. Soziologische Analysen*. Frankfurt am Main: Suhrkamp.
(2000), *Die Weltgesellschaft. Soziologische Analysen*. Frankfurt am Main: Suhrkamp.
Strauss, Anselm (1977 [1959]), *Mirrors and Masks: The Search for Identity*. London: Martin Robertson.
(1978), *Negotiations: Varieties, Contexts, Processes, and Social Order*. San Francisco, Washington and London: Jossey-Bass Publications.
(1982), 'Interorganizational Negotiation', *Urban Life* 11, 3: 349-67.
(1993), *Continual Permutations of Action*. New York: Aldine de Gruyter.
Stryker, Sheldon (1987), 'The Vitalization of Symbolic Interactionism', *Social Psychology Quarterly* 50, 1: 83-94.
Taylor, Charles (1975), *Hegel*. Cambridge: Cambridge University Press.
(1985), 'Legitimation Crisis?' in Charles Taylor, *Philosophy and the Human Sciences: Philosophical Papers 2*. Cambridge: Cambridge University Press, pp. 248-88.
(1985), *Philosophy and the Human Sciences: Philosophical Papers 2*. Cambridge: Cambridge University Press.
(1989), *Sources of the Self: The Making of the Modern Identity*. Cambridge, MA: Harvard University Press.
Therborn, Göran (1992), 'The Right to Vote and the Four World Routes to/through Modernity', in Rolf Torstendahl (ed.), *State Theory and State History*. London, Newbury Park and New Delhi: Sage, pp. 62-92.
(1995), *European Modernity and Beyond: The Trajectory of European Societies, 1945-2000*. London: Sage.
Thomas, George M. and John W. Meyer (1984), 'The Expansion of the State', *Annual Review of Sociology* 10: 461-82.
Thompson, Edward P. (1963), *The Making of the English Working Class*. London: Victor Gollancz.

Tilly, Charles (2003), *The Politics of Collective Violence*. Cambridge: Cambridge University Press.
Tiryakian, Edward A. (1991), 'Modernization: Exhumetur in Pace (Rethinking Macrosociology in the 1990s)', *International Sociology* 6, 2: 165-80.
Tocqueville, Alexis de (2003 [1835/1840]) *Democracy in America* [*De la démocratie en Amérique*]. London: Penguin.
Toulmin, Stephen (1990), *Cosmopolis: The Hidden Agenda of Modernity*. New York: Free Press.
Touraine, Alain (1965), *Sociologie de l'action*. Paris: Éditions du Seuil.
(1974 [1969]), *The Post-Industrial Society* [*La société post-industrielle*]. London: Wildwood House.
(1977), *The Self-Production of Society*. Chicago and London: University of Chicago Press.
(1981 [1978]), *The Voice and the Eye* [*La voix et le regard*]. Cambridge: Cambridge University Press.
(1992), 'La théorie sociologique entre l'acteur et les structures', *Schweizerische Zeitschrift für Soziologie/Revue suisse de sociologie* 18, 3: 533-5.
(1995 [1992]), *Critique of Modernity* [*Critique de la modernité*]. Oxford: Blackwell.
(1997 [1994]), *What is Democracy?* [*Qu'est-ce que la démocratie?*]. Boulder: Westview Press.
(2000 [1997]), *Can We Live Together? Equality and Difference* [*Pourrons-nous vivre ensemble? Égaux et différents*]. Oxford: Polity Press.
Tugendhat, Ernst (1982 [1976]), *Traditional and Analytical Philosophy: Lectures on the Philosophy of Language* [*Vorlesungen zur Einführung in die sprachanalytische Philosophie*]. Cambridge: Cambridge University Press.
Turner, Jonathan H. (1974), 'Parsons as a Symbolic Interactionist: A Comparison of Action and Interaction Theory', *Sociological Inquiry* 44, 4: 283-94.
(1998), *The Structure of Sociological Theory*. Sixth edition. Belmont: Wadsworth Publishing Company.
Turner, Ralph (1962), 'Role-Taking: Process versus Conformity', in A. Rose (ed.), *Human Behavior and Social Processes: An Interactionist Approach*. London: Routledge & Kegan Paul, pp. 20-40.
(1970), *Family Interaction*. New York and London: John Wiley & Sons.
Turner, Ralph and Lewis M. Killian (1972), *Collective Behavior*. Second edition. Englewood Cliffs, NJ: Prentice Hall.
Turner, Stephen (1999), 'The Significance of Shils', *Sociological Theory* 17, 2: 125-45.
(2003), 'The Maturity of Social Theory', in Charles Camic and Hans Joas (eds.), *The Dialogical Turn*. Lanham, MD: Rowman & Littlefield, pp. 141-70.
Van der Linden, Marcel (1997), 'Socialisme ou Barbarie: A French Revolutionary Group (1949-65)', *Left History* 5, 1: 7-37.
Wagner, Helmut R. (1983), *Alfred Schütz: An Intellectual Biography*. Chicago and London: University of Chicago Press.

Wagner, Peter (1993), 'Die Soziologie der Genese sozialer Institutionen – Theoretische Perspektiven der "neuen Sozialwissenschaften" in Frankreich', *Zeitschrift für Soziologie* 22, 6: 464–76.

— (1994 [1995]), *A Sociology of Modernity: Liberty and Discipline* [*Soziologie der Moderne. Freiheit und Disziplin*]. London: Routledge.

— (2001), *Theorizing Modernity: Inescapability and Attainability in Social Theory*. London, Thousand Oaks and New Delhi: Sage.

Walby, Sylvia (1990), *Theorizing Patriarchy*. Oxford: Basil Blackwell.

Wallerstein, Immanuel (1974f.), *The Modern World-System*. 3 vols. New York: Academic Press.

— (1983), *Historical Capitalism*. London: Verso.

Warner, Stephen R. (1978), 'Toward a Redefinition of Action Theory: Paying the Cognitive Element Its Due', *American Journal of Sociology* 83, 6: 1317–67.

Weber, Max (1975 [1908]), 'Marginal Utility Theory and the So-called Law of Psychophysics' ['Die Grenznutzlehre und das "psychophysische Grundgesetz"'], *Social Science Quarterly* 56: 21–36.

— (1979), *Economy and Society: An Outline of Interpretive Sociology* [*Wirtschaft und Gesellschaft. Grundriß der verstehenden Soziologie*]. Berkeley and London: University of California Press.

Weingarten, Elmar and Fritz Sack (1976), 'Ethnomethodologie. Die methodische Konstruktion der Realität', in Elmar Weingarten, Fritz Sack and Jim Schenkein (eds.), *Ethnomethodologie. Beiträge zu einer Soziologie des Alltagshandelns*. Frankfurt am Main: Suhrkamp, pp. 7–26.

Welsch, Wolfgang (2002), *Unsere postmoderne Moderne*. Berlin: Akademie Verlag.

Wenzel, Harald (1990), *Die Ordnung des Handelns. Talcott Parsons' Theorie des allgemeinen Handlungssystems*. Frankfurt am Main: Suhrkamp.

— (1993), 'Einleitung: Neofunktionalismus und theoretisches Dilemma', in Jeffrey C. Alexander, *Soziale Differenzierung und kultureller Wandel*, ed. Harald Wenzel. Frankfurt am Main and New York: Campus, pp. 7–30.

— (2001), *Die Abenteuer der Kommunikation. Echtzeitmassenmedien und der Handlungsraum der Hochmoderne*. Weilerswist: Velbrück.

West, Candace and Don H. Zimmerman (1987), 'Doing Gender', *Gender & Society* 1, 2: 125–51.

Wieder, D. Lawrence and Don H. Zimmermann (1976), 'Regeln im Erklärungsprozeß. Wissenschaftliche und ethnowissenschaftliche Soziologie', in Elmar Weingarten, Fritz Sack and Jim Schenkein (eds.), *Ethnomethodologie. Beiträge zu einer Soziologie des Alltagshandelns*. Frankfurt am Main: Suhrkamp, pp. 105–29.

Wiesenthal, Helmut (1987), 'Rational Choice. Ein Überblick über Grundlinien, Theoriefelder und neuere Themenakquisition eines sozialwissenschaftlichen Paradigmas', *Zeitschrift für Soziologie* 16, 6: 434–49.

Wieviorka, Michel (1993 [1988]), *The Making of Terrorism* [*Sociétés et terrorisme*]. Chicago and London: University of Chicago Press.

(2004), *La violence*. Paris: Ballard.

(2007), *The Lure of Anti-Semitism: Hatred of Jews in Present-Day France*. Leiden: Brill.

Wieviorka, Michel (ed.) (1992), *La France raciste*. Paris: Éditions du Seuil.

Wiggershaus, Rolf (1994 [1988]), *The Frankfurt School: Its History, Theories and Political Significance* [*Die Frankfurter Schule. Geschichte – Theoretische Entwicklung – Politische Bedeutung*]. Cambridge: Polity Press.

Willke, Helmut (1987), *Systemtheorie. Eine Einführung in die Grundprobleme*. Stuttgart and New York: Gustav Fischer Verlag.

(1992), *Ironie des Staates. Grundlinien einer Staatstheorie polyzentrischer Gesellschaft*. Frankfurt am Main: Suhrkamp.

(1995), *Systemtheorie III: Steuerungstheorie. Grundzüge einer Theorie der Steuerung komplexer Sozialsysteme*. Stuttgart and Jena: Gustav Fischer Verlag.

(1997), *Supervision des Staates*. Frankfurt am Main: Suhrkamp.

Wilson, R. Jackson (1968), *In Quest of Community: Social Philosophy in the United States, 1860–1920*. New York, London, Sidney and Toronto: John Wiley & Sons.

Wolfe, Alan (1998), 'The Missing Pragmatist Revival in American Social Science', in Morris Dickstein (ed.), *The Revival of Pragmatism*. Durham, NC: Duke University Press, pp. 199–206

Zald, Mayer N. and John D. McCarthy (1987), *Social Movements in an Organizational Society: Collected Essays*. New Brunswick, NJ and Oxford: Transaction Books.

(2002), 'The Resource Mobilization Research Program: Progress, Challenge, and Transformation', in Joseph Berger and Morris Zelditch, Jr. (eds.), *New Directions in Contemporary Sociological Theory*. Lanham, MD: Rowman & Littlefield.

Zapf, Wolfgang (1996), 'Die Modernisierungstheorie und unterschiedliche Pfade der gesellschaftlichen Entwicklung', *Leviathan* 24, 1: 63–77.

AUTHOR INDEX

Abbott, Andrew 146
Abendroth, Wolfgang 201
Adler, Patricia 149
Adler, Peter 149
Adloff, Frank 498
Adorno, Theodor W. 201, 207–8, 213–14, 228, 236, 244, 364, 476, 478–9
Alchian, Armen R. 95
Alexander, Jeffrey C. viii, 9–10, 17–18, 45, 92, 289, 312–13, 315, 336–8, 474
Allen, William R. 95
Almond, Gabriel 311
Althusser, Louis 353–4
Ames, Ruth E. 121
Anderson, Perry 284
Apel, Karl-Otto 501
Arato, Andrew 497
Arendt, Hannah 216, 297, 411, 478
Aristotle 212, 410, 429, 488
Arnason, Johann P. 414, 550, 556–7
Aron, Raymond 186, 341

Bales, Robert 75–6
Barber, Bernard 337
Barthes, Roland 353–4
Bataille, Georges 340
Baudelaire, Charles 395
Baudrillard, Jean 368
Bauman, Zygmunt 369, 425, 463, 475–84
Beauvoir, Simone de 341
Beck, Ulrich 280, 307, 463–75, 481–2, 492, 522, 531
Becker, Gary S. 94, 120
Becker, Howard S. 142–3
Becker-Schmidt, Regina 433, 448, 450, 457, 459
Beckert, Jens 523
Bell, Daniel 419
Bellah, Robert 311, 331–2, 335–6, 463, 484, 492–5, 497
Bellow, Saul 315

Bendix, Reinhard 178–81, 184–5, 189, 196
Benhabib, Seyla 368, 440–3, 456–7, 460
Benjamin, Walter 340
Bentham, Jeremy 26–7, 50, 94, 97, 120, 357
Berger, Peter L. 172
Bergson, Henri 291
Bernstein, Richard 16, 483, 501, 508, 510–12
Beveridge, William 483
Bismarck, Otto von 206
Bittner, Egon 171
Blair, Tony 290
Blau, Peter M. 106–7
Blumer, Herbert 130–41, 143–4, 146–7, 152, 185, 500
Boas, Franz 347
Bolt, Christine 434
Boltanski, Luc 399, 539–43
Bosshart, David 416
Boudon, Raymond 108, 113, 116, 118
Bourdieu, Pierre ix, 149, 190, 237, 342, 369, 371–400, 417, 421, 539–40
Braque, Georges 398
Brecht, Bertolt 261
Brown, David J. 137
Browning, Christopher R. 479
Brownmiller, Susan 435
Buber, Martin 319, 495
Butler, Judith 453–9, 462

Caillé, Alain 543
Caillois, Roger 340
Camic, Charles 21, 43, 49, 335
Camus, Albert 341
Cardoso, Fernando H. 333
Carter, Jimmy 496
Castaneda, Carlos 168
Castoriadis, Cornelius 401–17, 419, 421, 424–6, 487, 522, 543, 550, 553, 556

AUTHOR INDEX

Caws, Peter 343
Chafetz, Janet Saltzman 193
Chalmers, A. F. 15
Charle, Christophe 400
Chiapello, Eve 539–40, 542
Chodorow, Nancy 437–9, 441, 443
Cicourel, Aaron V. 153–4, 156, 167, 171
Cohen, Jean 497
Cohen, Jere 50, 497
Cohen-Solal, Annie 341
Cohn-Bendit, Daniel 402
Coleman, James S. 119–20
Collins, Randall 142, 187, 189–90, 192–4, 196, 394
Colomy, Paul B. 137, 336–7
Commons, John 545
Cooley, Charles Horton 20, 44–5, 124
Coser, Lewis A. 176–8, 180–1, 185, 189, 194, 196
Crozier, Michel 421

Dahrendorf, Ralf 183–6, 189, 193–4, 196–7, 200, 202–3, 281–2
Darwin, Charles 7, 86
Davis, Phillip W. 145
Delaunay, Robert 398
Denzin, Norman K. 137, 140, 147, 148
Derrida, Jacques 364–6, 368, 370, 481
Descartes, René 125–7, 159, 501, 503, 550–3
Dewey, John 44, 125, 127, 266, 390, 500–1, 504–6, 508, 510–13, 516–17, 524–5, 535, 551, 554
Diderot, Denis 298
DiMaggio, Paul J. 546
Dosse, François 170, 342, 347, 354, 362, 370, 399, 428, 539–40, 543
Douglas, Jack D. 171
Dreyfus, Hubert L. 360, 370
Dubet, François 534–5
Duchamp, Marcel 398
Durkheim, Emile x, 1–2, 13, 20, 23, 25, 36, 41–2, 46, 50, 72, 91, 142, 167, 171, 176, 180, 186, 228, 236, 287, 310, 316–17, 335–6, 339–40, 348–9, 374, 380, 396, 422, 500, 513, 524, 535, 543, 545

Eder, Klaus 388, 399
Eisenstadt, Shmuel N. 319–23, 325–30, 332–8, 415, 424, 473, 495, 542, 554–8
Elias, Norbert 284
Elster, Jon 118–19
Emerson, Richard M. 107
Engels, Friedrich 12–13, 54, 186, 406–7, 435
Epstein, Cynthia Fuchs 436
Erasmus of Rotterdam 552
Eribon, Didier 360, 362, 370
Erikson, Kai 143
Esser, Hartmut 8, 18, 120
Etzioni, Amitai 95, 102, 121, 495–9, 532

Faletto, Enzo 333
Ferry, Luc 393
Feuerbach, Ludwig 256
Feyerabend, Paul 16, 229, 451, 504, 509
Firestone, Shulamith 434–5
Flaubert, Gustave 395
Flax, Jane 451–3
Foucault, Michel 299, 301, 304–5, 354–64, 369–70, 378, 451, 453, 455–6, 478–9, 536, 553
Frank, Manfred viii, 365–6, 370
Fraser, Nancy 456, 460–2, 538
Freidson, Eliot 146
Freud, Sigmund 55, 60, 62, 341–2, 353, 416, 428, 437
Friedman, Debra 96
Friedrich, Caspar David 398
Fühmann, Franz 106

Galilei, Galileo 159, 509
Gardner, Howard 342
Garfinkel, Harold 150–6, 158, 160–4, 166–7, 170, 172, 185, 295, 302, 445, 450
Gauchet, Marcel 543
Geertz, Clifford 337–8
Gehlen, Arnold 256–8, 265, 266
Gerhard, Ute 434
Gerhardt, Uta 55
Giddens, Anthony ix, 51–2, 57, 149, 170, 237, 280–1, 283–4, 287–307, 330, 339, 342, 358, 362, 371, 380, 382,

424, 471–5, 481–2, 495–6, 499, 518–9, 522–3, 529–31, 555, 559
Giele, Janet Zollinger 434
Gilcher-Holthey, Ingrid 402
Gildemeister, Regine 444, 448–9
Gilligan, Carol 438–44, 483
Glaser, Barney G. 140, 146
Godbout, Jacques 543
Goffman, Erving 141–42, 196, 231, 236, 294, 298–9
Goldhagen, Daniel J. 476, 479
Goldstone, Jack A. 115
Gramsci, Antonio 212

Habermas, Jürgen ix, 22, 83–4, 130, 159, 198–204, 206–52, 260, 264, 269–70, 281–3, 287, 289, 292, 294, 296, 299–300, 304, 307, 334–6, 339, 342, 361, 367, 371–2, 390–1, 409–11, 414, 416, 423–7, 429–30, 432, 438, 441–2, 460–2, 463, 478, 483, 488, 491, 495–8, 501, 504, 507, 509, 511–2, 515–16, 524, 526–9, 536–8, 555–6
Haferkamp, Heinrich 285
Hagemann-White, Carol 447
Halbwachs, Maurice 340
Hall, John A. 286–7
Hall, Peter A. 546
Hall, Peter M. 148–9
Harding, Sandra 451
Hartsock, Nancy 456
Harvey, David 369
Haskell, Thomas 505
Hazelrigg, Lawrence E. 50
Hechter, Michael 96, 114
Hegel, Georg Wilhelm Friedrich 46, 216, 222–6, 243, 298, 323, 341, 429, 472, 536–8
Heidegger, Martin 158, 291, 341, 364, 481, 501, 504–5, 551
Heilbron, Johan 46
Heintz, Bettina 450
Hénaff, Marcel 543
Herder, Johann Gottfried 47–50, 135, 256
Heritage, John 151, 155, 166
Hintze, Otto 181
Hirschauer, Stefan 450

Hirschman, Albert 30
Hitler, Adolf 25, 55, 159, 207, 478
Hobbes, Thomas 27–32, 98, 108, 156, 490
Hobsbawm, Eric 284
Hochschild, Arlie 140
Höffe, Otfried 485
Hoffmann, E. T. A. 261
Homans, George C. 98–107, 120
Honneth, Axel 248, 256, 352, 370, 381, 475, 536–8
Horkheimer, Max 200–1, 207–8, 228, 236, 244, 478–9
Horster, Detlef 280
Hughes, Everett C. 141, 145–6
Husserl, Edmund 156–61, 166, 259, 291, 341, 364, 382, 428, 481

Irrgang, Bernhard 272

Jaggar, Alison M. 432
Jakobson, Roman 348, 350
James, William 125, 260–1, 291, 500, 513, 524
Jameson, Frederic 369
Janowitz, Morris 316
Jaspers, Karl 323–5
Jefferson, Thomas 493
Jevons, William Stanley 27
Joas, Hans viii, ix, 43, 48, 50, 53, 91, 125, 127, 236–7, 240, 248, 256, 266, 280, 290, 307, 332, 337, 366, 404, 417, 428, 473, 479, 483, 495, 498, 501, 508, 512–17, 519–27, 554, 559
Jospin, Lionel 421

Kalyvas, Andreas 414
Kant, Immanuel 31, 175, 211, 335, 422, 429–30, 441, 451–2, 489, 503, 525–6
Keller, Gottfried 106
Kennedy, John F. 219, 331
Kessler, Suzanne J. 444–9, 453, 458
Kierkegaard, Søren 511
Kippenberg, Hans G. 169
Kitsuse, John I. 143
Knapp, Gudrun-Axeli 433, 435, 448, 450, 456–7, 459
Kneer, Georg 272, 280

AUTHOR INDEX

Knöbl, Wolfgang viii, 86, 285, 308, 313, 316, 549, 557
Knorr Cetina, Karin 172
Kohlberg, Lawrence 223, 438–42, 483
Kojève, Alexandre 341
Kuhn, Thomas S. 11–17, 229, 367, 451, 504–5, 509–10
Kurzweil, Edith 341
Kymlicka, Will 432

Lacan, Jacques 353–4, 416
Lamont, Michèle 400
Landweer, Hilge 458
Lapeyronnie, Didier 534
Larson, Magali Sarfatti 191
Latour, Bruno 543–5, 550
Lavoisier, Antoine Laurent de 11
Lefort, Claude 402, 426, 543
Leibniz, Gottfried Wilhelm 502
Lemert, Edwin M. 143
Lenski, Gerhard 186–7
Lerner, Daniel 311–2, 314
Levinas, Emmanuel 481, 483–4
Lévi-Strauss, Claude 347–55, 361, 364–5, 370, 372–3, 375, 377
Lidz, Victor 91
Lipset, Seymour Martin 311
Livingston, Eric 172
Locke, John 30–1, 98, 503
Lockwood, David 181–5, 189, 196, 200, 281–4, 287, 299
Lorber, Judith 447
Luchesi, Brigitte 169
Luckmann, Thomas 160–1, 172, 239
Luhmann, Niklas ix, 22, 83–4, 201, 226, 242, 249–81, 287, 289, 296, 302, 304–5, 307, 332, 335–6, 339, 342, 371–2, 392–3, 416, 472–3, 495, 516, 522, 529–33
Lukács, Georg 225
Luther, Martin 38, 102, 206
Lynch, Michael 172
Lyotard, Jean-François 364, 366–9, 402, 451, 464, 470, 483

Machiavelli, Niccolò 484
MacIntyre, Alasdair 411
MacKinnon, Catharine A. 440
Madsen, Richard 492

Maines, David R. 138, 149
Malevich, Kazimir 398
Malinowski, Bronislaw 21, 56
Mann, Michael ix, 284–7, 299–300, 302–4, 307, 555, 559
Mannheim, Karl 172
Marshall, Alfred 23, 39, 40–2, 45, 48, 86, 180, 228, 236
Marshall, Thomas H. 284
Marwell, Gerald 114, 121
Marx, Karl 3, 12–13, 20–1, 46, 54, 56–9, 78, 108, 114, 172, 178–81, 184–6, 194, 197, 202–4, 211–12, 216–17, 219–25, 237, 243–4, 256, 283, 288, 303, 309, 334, 336, 341, 352–3, 369, 373, 385, 387, 389, 402, 406–10, 414–15, 422, 434–5, 472, 511, 514, 537
Maturana, Humberto R. 272–4
Maurer, Andrea 547
Mauss, Marcel 340, 348–50, 543
Mayer, Hans 340
Mayntz, Renate 532
McAdam, Doug 115
McCarthy, John D. 115, 192
McCarthy, Thomas 248, 251, 508
McClelland, David 311
McKenna, Wendy 444–9, 453, 458
Mead, George Herbert x, 1, 20, 44–5, 52, 124–5, 127–31, 134, 140, 147, 152, 163, 216, 228, 236, 500–1, 505–6, 512–13, 519–21, 525–6, 538
Mehan, Hugh 162, 168
Meltzer, Bernard N. 142, 148
Merleau-Ponty, Maurice 158, 341, 403, 405, 519–20
Merton, Robert K. 52, 66, 93, 176, 295
Metaxas, Ioannis 401
Meyer, John W. 547–9
Michels, Robert 112, 263, 265–6, 516
Mill, John Stuart 26–7
Miller, James 370
Mills, C. Wright 92–3, 181, 500
Mitchell, Wesley 545
Montaigne, Michel de 552
Morin, Edgar 402
Mosca, Gaetano 186
Müller, Hans-Peter 107, 399
Mullins, Carolyn J. 139

Mullins, Nicolas C. 139
Münch, Richard 92, 335–6, 338, 393, 475

Nadai, Eva 450
Napoleon Bonaparte 286
Nassehi, Armin 272, 280
Newton, Isaac 552
Nietzsche, Friedrich 246, 355, 358, 361–2, 364, 366, 440, 453, 481, 524
Nipperdey, Thomas 286
Nora, Pierre 543
North, Douglass C. 546
Nunner-Winkler, Gertrud 441
Nussbaum, Martha C. 411, 442–3, 457–9

Oakeshott, Michael 410
Oberschall, Anthony 115
Offe, Claus 112
Oliver, Pamela E. 114
Olson, Mancur Jr. 108, 110–17, 185
Opp, Karl-Dieter 113

Pareto, Vilfredo 23, 40–2, 45, 48, 51–2, 86, 180, 186, 228, 236
Park, Robert 44, 124, 147
Parsons, Talcott viii, xi, 19–28, 30–94, 98–100, 102–3, 105, 108, 122–5, 131–5, 137–9, 141, 145–6, 150–6, 161, 166–7, 170, 173–83, 185, 187–93, 195, 197–9, 206, 218, 221, 226–8, 235–6, 238, 240–2, 247–54, 258–60, 265, 268–71, 273, 277, 281, 283, 286–8, 290–2, 295–7, 300, 302, 305, 307–10, 312–13, 315–17, 319–21, 323, 330–9, 342–3, 363, 367, 393, 410, 417–18, 420, 422, 432, 490, 492, 495, 497, 500, 506, 514–15, 522, 524, 529, 531, 545–7, 554, 560
Passeron, Jean-Claude 342
Pauer-Studer, Herlinde 432, 441
Peirce, Charles S. 4–5, 9, 125–6, 157, 500–1, 508, 511–12
Petras, John W. 142, 148
Piaget, Jean 223, 438
Plessner, Helmuth 256
Plummer, Ken 130

Pope, Whitney 50
Popper, Karl Raimund 5–12, 15, 17, 213–15
Poulantzas, Nicos 353–4
Powell, Walter W. 546
Proust, Marcel 291
Psathas, George 166
Putnam, Hilary 501–3, 508–12
Putnam, Robert D. 497–8

Quéré, Louis 543

Rabinow, Paul 360, 370
Raters, Marie-Luise 508
Rawls, John 429–30, 441, 484–91, 498–9, 537
Reagan, Ronald 220, 496
Renaut, Alain 393
Rex, John 181–5, 189, 193, 196, 281–2, 284
Reynolds, Larry T. 142, 148
Ricardo, David 27
Ricoeur, Paul 307, 401, 413, 428–31, 481, 525, 527, 539
Robbins, Derek 372
Rock, Paul 143
Roosevelt, Franklin D. 22
Rorty, Richard 369, 501–12, 551, 554
Rostow, Walt W. 311
Rothacker, Erich 200, 204
Rousseau, Jean-Jacques 186, 331, 352, 422
Rubin, Gayle 435
Ryan, Alan 120

Sack, Fritz 161
Sacks, Harvey 161, 170–1
Sandel, Michael J. 488–92, 497
Sartre, Jean-Paul 158, 186, 341–2, 346, 353, 360–1, 374, 379, 403, 418, 421, 423, 511
Saussure, Ferdinand de 343–7, 350, 352, 355, 361, 364, 377, 458
Scharpf, Fritz W. 117, 532
Schegloff, Emanuel A. 170
Scheler, Max 172, 256, 524
Schelling, Friedrich Wilhelm Joseph 200
Schelling, Thomas C. 117–18

Schelsky, Helmut 250, 262, 279
Schimank, Uwe 533
Schluchter, Wolfgang 555–6
Schmid, Michael 547
Schmidt, Helmut 219
Schmoller, Gustav 545
Schröter, Susanne 454–5
Schulze, Gerhard 400
Schütz, Alfred 159–63, 172, 239, 511
Scott, Richard W. 546
Searle, John 230
Selznick, Philip 501
Shakespeare, William 552
Shibutani, Tamotsu 144
Shils, Edward A. 76, 315–20, 330–1, 333, 335, 338
Shklar, Judith 506
Shostakovich, Dmitri 398
Simmel, Georg 2, 20, 45, 52, 107, 130, 177–8, 185, 193–4, 206, 513, 524
Simon, Herbert A. 121
Skinner, B. F. 101, 103
Smelser, Neil J. 78–9, 85, 311, 332, 335–6, 522
Smetana, Bedrich 398
Smith, Adam 20, 30–1, 49, 94, 98, 116–17, 541
Snow, David A. 145
Sofsky, Wolfgang 479
Sombart, Werner 21
Sorokin, Pitirim 21
Spencer, Herbert 44, 48, 85–6, 88–9
Spitzweg, Carl 398
Srubar, Ilja 160
Stalin, Joseph 203, 402, 477
Stichweh, Rudolf 530–1
Strauss, Anselm 135, 137, 140, 146–9
Sullivan, William M. 492
Swidler, Ann 492

Taylor, Charles 47–8, 421, 491, 524, 550–1
Taylor, Rosemary C. R. 546
Thatcher, Margaret 220
Therborn, Göran 558
Thévenot, Laurent 541
Thomas, George M. 547

Thomas, William Isaac 20, 44–5, 124, 147
Thompson, Edward P. 284, 288–9
Tieck, Ludwig 261
Tillich, Paul 428
Tilly, Charles 192
Tipton, Steven M. 492
Tiryakian, Edward A. 334
Titmuss, Richard M. 284
Tocqueville, Alexis de 46, 178, 180, 492–4
Tönnies, Ferdinand 20, 72, 513
Toulmin, Stephen 551–4, 558–9
Touraine, Alaine ix, 53, 280, 353, 401, 413, 417–27, 430, 473, 475, 496, 529, 533–5, 539, 543, 550, 553, 556
Truman, Harry S. 310
Tugendhat, Ernst viii
Turner, Jonathan H. 131, 196–7
Turner, Ralph H. 139, 152–3
Turner, Stephen xi, 319
Turner, Victor 338

van der Linden, Marcel 401–2
Varela, Francisco J. 272–4
Veblen, Thorstein 545
Verba, Sidney 311

Wacquant, Loïc 371, 380–1, 384, 539
Wagner, Helmut R. 160
Wagner, Peter 541, 553–4
Walby, Sylvia 435
Wallerstein, Immanuel 333–4, 531, 557–8
Walzer, Michael 491
Warner, Stephen R. 51
Weber, Max x, 1–2, 13, 20–1, 23, 25, 42, 50, 69–71, 78, 81, 91, 97, 159, 176, 178, 180–2, 185–6, 194, 206, 208, 228, 236, 244–5, 263–6, 287–8, 297, 310, 316–17, 319, 328–9, 331, 335–6, 339, 341, 363, 394, 415, 500, 512–16, 535, 545, 554–5
Weingarten, Elmar 161
Weizsäcker, Carl Friedrich von 201
Welsch, Wolfgang 367
Wenzel, Harald 83, 335, 338
West, Candace 445

Wetterer, Angelika 444, 448–9
Whitehead, Alfred North 335
Wieder, D. Lawrence 168
Wiesenthal, Helmut 98, 106, 112
Wieviorka, Michel 534
Wiggershaus, Rolf 201
Willaschek, Marcus 508
Willke, Helmut 280, 532–3
Wilson, R. Jackson 44
Winthrop, John 493
Wittgenstein, Ludwig 367, 501, 504–5, 508–10, 551
Wittrock, Björn 558
Wolfe, Alan 512
Wood, Houston 162, 168

Young, Michael 317

Zald, Mayer N. 115, 192
Zapf, Wolfgang 334
Zimmerman, Don 168, 445
Zola, Emile 34

SUBJECT INDEX

action
  affective 69, 70, 72, 391
  collective 108–14, 117, 118, 144,
    145, 148, 179, 197, 226, 227,
    245–6, 320, 321, 332, 418,
    419–20, 473, 475, 496, 522,
    532, 548
  communicative 215, 216, 219, 233–7,
    240, 246, 391, 410, 516, 537–8
  coordinating/coordination of 33–4,
    39, 62, 65, 155, 209, 234, 238,
    239–40
  expressive 47–50, 135, 244, 256
  flow of 290–1
  instrumentally rational
    (instrumental rationality)
    42, 69, 70, 190, 193, 195, 209,
    212, 215–18, 221, 230, 234,
    235, 237, 238, 240, 263, 265,
    268, 282, 418, 423, 471, 513,
    515–17, 519
  situation(s) of 28, 32, 33, 34, 38, 51,
    60, 102, 116, 123, 124, 126–8,
    151, 155, 233, 234–5, 239, 505,
    518–19, 525, 526
  social 1, 18, 19, 64, 66, 144, 147, 154,
    369, 419, 470
  strategic 195, 218, 233, 234, 235, 237,
    238, 240, 515, 516
  traditional 69, 70, 513, 515
  utility-oriented 27, 28, 30, 31, 40,
    45, 50–95, 97–8, 107, 108, 114,
    119, 120, 195
  value rational 69, 70, 513
  voluntaristic theory of 23, 34–5,
    38, 40, 42, 45–6, 50, 53, 55,
    180, 335
'action frame of reference' 38–9, 47,
  48, 50–1, 52, 53–4, 55, 60, 62,
  68, 84, 132, 135, 146, 151, 236,
  290, 291, 295
actors
  constellation of 327, 328, 330

corporative 119, 532
AGIL scheme 76, 83–5, 87, 277
autonomy 292, 293, 379, 409, 413,
  416–17, 419, 475, 521, 550
autopoietic systems/autopoietic turn
  249, 272, 273–4, 277, 516, 533
Axial Age (Achsenzeit) 323–30, 415,
  556, 557

body 129, 293–4, 305, 357, 459, 515,
  518, 519–21
  body schema/body image 519–21
  corporeality 163, 237, 293, 294,
    299–300, 403, 518, 521
  dualism of body and mind/soul 294,
    502, 519
breaching experiment 161–3, 167, 168,
  170
bureaucracy 89, 92, 194, 244, 260,
  263–4, 265–7, 323, 402, 460, 468,
  477–80, 516, 547–8

capital
  cultural 387–8
  economic 385–8
  forms of (Bourdieu) 385–92, 400
  social 387
  symbolic 385–8
capitalism/capitalist 12, 21, 29–30,
  54, 56–8, 97, 108, 179, 190, 204,
  209, 213, 217–20, 225, 239, 241,
  245, 288, 303–4, 309, 360, 381–2,
  385–7, 402, 407–9, 416, 419, 422,
  434, 435, 465, 469, 476, 538, 542,
  550
Cartesianism *see* body, dualism of
  body and mind/soul
change, social (theory of) 18–19, 66,
  85, 87–90, 118, 138–9, 147, 170,
  174–5, 178–9, 180, 184–5, 192,
  196–7, 202, 223, 224–5, 282, 296,
  305–7, 308–9, 310, 312, 313–15,
  320, 321, 323, 326–30, 334, 336–8,

599

369, 394–5, 405, 407, 411, 419–20, 433, 496, 522, 523, 542, 557, 558–9
charisma 316–19, 338, 513
Chicago School of sociology 124, 129–30, 139, 144, 147–8, 316, 340, 500
communication *see* action, communicative
communication (systems theory) 259, 268, 275–6, 278, 306, 531
communitarianism x, 248, 426, 430, 442, 461, 483, 484, 488, 490, 491, 495–9, 524–8, 550
complexity (reduction of) 258–9, 267, 269, 276
conflict theory/sociology 146, 173, 174–98, 199, 202, 203, 221, 281–7, 299, 308, 320, 384–5, 389, 392, 418, 432, 496, 522, 534, 536, 547, 555
consciousness
  collective 41–2
  moral 223, 438
  philosophy of 125, 126, 127, 383
  self- 125–7, 128, 134, 157–8, 259, 275, 291, 502–3, 505, 512, 520, 521
contingency/contingent 138, 171, 179, 250, 260–2, 322, 351, 483, 506–7, 523, 525–6, 527, 540
contract (theory of) 37, 42, 98, 108, 486
convergence thesis 23–6, 39, 43, 48–9, 50, 180
creativity 138, 153, 212, 237, 266, 319, 383, 392, 404–5, 406, 407, 410, 411, 415, 417, 418, 421–2, 505, 513–15, 517–19, 522–3, 542, 551, 556
critical theory/Frankfurt School 207–9, 213, 215, 228, 236, 245, 289, 476, 478, 512, 536, 538

democracy 55, 88, 89, 90, 92, 112, 178, 206–7, 209, 242, 245, 268, 280, 304, 309, 366, 414, 420, 424–7, 430, 479, 492–4, 497–9, 506–8, 510, 512, 527, 533, 543, 544, 548, 550, 551, 559

theory of 414–15, 425, 426, 506, 507, 543
democratization 197, 304, 309, 473, 495, 522
dependency theory 333–4
diagnosis of the times/of the contemporary era 18, 217–20, 241–5, 274, 276, 286, 288, 290, 307, 332, 336, 364, 366, 368, 369, 399, 419, 421, 463–99, 535, 537–8, 549, 555, 558
differentiation (theory of) 87–90, 142, 179, 241–3, 245, 265, 268, 276, 278, 279–80, 305, 321–2, 332, 336–7, 392–3, 424, 448, 449, 469, 472, 473, 488, 522–3, 530–1, 542
  de-differentiation 321, 337, 468
  functional 77, 78, 268–70, 273–4, 278–9, 305–6, 530–2
discipline 284, 305, 357–9, 363, 553
discourse 16, 232, 338, 358–62, 363, 366, 457, 458, 461, 488, 490, 510, 519–21, 527, 541–2
  discourse theory/ethics 367, 430, 441–2, 501, 527, 558
distinction 190, 386, 391, 395, 396–8
domination 37, 106, 113, 180, 181, 184, 187–8, 192, 195, 196, 197, 209, 215, 241, 246, 263, 298, 301–2, 303, 304, 305, 328, 367, 376, 387, 394–6, 416, 423, 432, 435, 441, 513, 539

ethnomethodology 51, 123, 124, 150, 174, 185, 191, 206, 217, 221, 237, 259, 266, 289, 290, 291, 295, 300, 308, 379, 393, 432, 445–50, 453–4, 457–8, 459–60, 462, 511, 540, 543, 547
evolution (theory of) 46, 86–8, 89, 175, 179, 197, 223–5, 227, 240, 241–3, 273, 286, 305–8, 309, 322, 323, 332, 333, 336, 473, 536, 555
evolutionary universals 89, 92
evolutionism/evolutionist 40, 44, 48, 85–6, 86–7, 224, 323, 360, 559
exchange theory 98, 106
  gift exchange 348–51, 376
existentialism 158, 341, 353, 402, 511
  Christian 428

falsification/falsificationism 7–13, 15, 17, 58, 97, 105, 212
feminism 173, 193, 363, 432–62, 537
field (Bourdieu) 378–80, 384, 385, 389–94, 395, 398, 400
functionalism 56–9, 67, 74–5, 77, 79, 84, 85, 89, 92, 98–103, 119, 124, 133, 137–9, 145, 147, 151, 176–7, 178, 180, 183, 185, 186, 189–90, 193, 218, 226–7, 228, 240–1, 242, 249, 250, 251, 252–6, 258, 273, 274, 276, 281–3, 287, 295–7, 299–300, 302, 305–6, 319–21, 332, 335–7, 378, 379–80, 403, 405–6, 522, 547
'equivalence functionalism'/ functional equivalence (Luhmann) 254–6, 261, 268
neo-functionalism 22, 336–8
structural functionalism 66, 144, 175, 176, 180, 182, 183, 184, 187, 251, 252, 317, 319, 332, 336

game theory 116–18, 234, 297
gender 192, 433, 435–8, 441, 443–9, 449–51, 453–60, 483
identity 437, 438, 445, 446, 448, 453, 454–8
relations xi, 192, 434, 435, 436–7, 450
roles 193, 471
globalization 3, 13, 54, 286, 306, 374, 399, 472–3, 482, 483, 531, 547
opponents/critics of 54, 374, 396, 421

habitus 382–5, 390, 391–4, 396, 398, 400
hermeneutics 204–7, 214, 227, 346, 366, 428, 528
heteronomy 413, 415, 550
historical sociology 197, 283–5, 525, 546

identity/identity formation (see also gender: identity)128–9, 140, 141, 147, 231, 247, 248, 289, 307, 366, 383, 393, 421, 424, 428–9, 437–8, 441, 444, 453, 454–5, 457, 489, 524, 535, 537, 543, 550–1
collective 247, 491
imaginary, the 404, 411–12, 413, 415, 416
individualism/individualistic/ individualist (theoretically) xi, 27, 44, 95, 115, 418, 488, 490
anti-individualistic 100
individualism (as diagnosis of the times) 90–1, 363, 492–4
individualization 3, 423, 464, 468–72, 474, 483
inequality, social 29, 106, 186–9, 190, 192, 394–5, 399, 435–6, 437–8, 469, 471, 487–8, 498
'instituting' (Castoriadis) 404, 413–14, 419
institutionalism, new 545–7
institutionalization 62, 65, 67, 72, 100, 182, 279, 321, 414, 419, 420, 545, 548
institutions 63, 65, 78, 82, 88, 89, 92, 99–100, 106, 136, 137, 142, 148, 177, 189–90, 210–1, 226, 257–8, 264, 280, 283, 298–9, 313, 317, 318, 321, 334, 361, 395, 405–6, 411–15, 424, 427, 440, 450, 461, 480, 483, 484, 485–6, 490, 498, 534–6, 545–9, 553
'total' 141–2, 298
integration 75, 84–5, 88, 138, 176, 183, 184, 223, 247, 253, 268–9, 284, 285–6, 297, 301, 321, 335, 336, 350, 393, 425, 490, 527, 534, 535, 536, 545
social vs. systemic 238–40, 281, 282–3, 299–300, 460
internalization 42, 44, 62, 65, 67, 134, 139, 153–6, 359, 384, 534

intersubjectivity 128, 130, 133, 137, 215, 221, 224, 231, 294, 403, 441, 490, 501, 512–13, 520, 521, 538

labelling theory/approach 143, 191
labour 57, 80, 138, 204, 213, 215–17, 219–20, 224, 237, 349, 368, 387, 408–9, 418–19, 434, 461
   division of 64, 88, 179, 193, 194, 435, 438, 449, 467, 488
   movement 284, 420, 534
   sociology of occupations and work 145
language 128, 130, 155, 164, 166, 171, 209–11, 212, 213, 220, 229–30, 235, 236, 240, 243, 246, 260, 294, 343–7, 350–1, 352, 361, 363, 377, 403–5, 411, 413, 428, 454–5, 457–60, 504–5, 507
   games 367, 369, 454, 509–10
law/legal (system) 89, 151, 171, 194–5, 205, 244, 247–8, 268–70, 273, 277, 424, 461, 467, 487, 527
   sociology of law/legal sociology 262, 270, 501
liberalism 31, 218, 288, 399, 409, 415, 421, 426, 440, 442, 443, 482, 488–90, 491, 497, 498, 499, 506–8, 525, 526–8, 553
life-world (Lebenswelt) 159–62, 217–18, 219, 239–41, 243, 244, 259, 296
   colonization of the 243, 244
   vs. system 237–9, 240–3, 244, 245–7, 460, 461, 536, 555

Marxism 12–13, 57, 102, 108, 109, 178, 180, 181, 185–6, 187–8, 193, 200–4, 206–7, 209, 211, 215, 216–18, 221, 224, 225–6, 227, 261, 281, 284, 285, 286, 288, 306, 309, 313, 333–4, 354, 367, 368, 379, 385–6, 388–9, 398, 401–3, 406–8, 409, 412, 418, 435, 475–6, 496, 511, 512, 531, 535, 537, 542

means–ends schema/scheme 42, 50, 234, 237, 410, 515–18, 522
medium/media (symbolically generalized) 79–83, 85, 241–2, 244, 273, 297
modernization 92, 308–11, 313–17, 320, 322, 323, 330–1, 415, 423, 424, 425, 465, 468, 470, 473, 524, 544, 556, 558
   'reflexive modernization' 464, 470–1
   theory ix–x, 73, 87, 90, 308–11, 312–18, 319–20, 321–3, 328, 330–4, 336, 364, 415, 473, 474, 523–4, 550, 555, 559
money 79–83, 241–2, 243–4, 247, 277, 334, 387, 413

nation-state xi, 12–13, 109, 276, 285–6, 301–4, 334, 424, 468, 531, 552–3, 557
normativist functionalism 55, 59, 66, 84, 123, 283
normativity (in scientific statements) x, 2, 3, 97–8, 120, 204, 214, 260, 413, 432–3, 456, 483–5, 490, 491, 497–9, 532, 559–60
norms 35–40, 42, 45, 46, 48, 50–1, 53, 59, 61–2, 65, 66, 67, 69, 73, 78, 99–100, 103, 106, 108, 114, 119–20, 123–5, 132, 134–5, 141, 145, 151–6, 161, 166, 167–8, 180, 181–3, 187, 195, 221, 231–2, 234–6, 238, 248, 253, 260, 261, 270, 281, 291, 300, 302, 349, 357, 393, 410, 414, 417–19, 442, 506, 507, 510, 514–17, 525, 526–7, 534, 540

organization(s) 103, 108, 110–4, 119, 136–7, 142, 148–9, 179, 226, 254, 258, 260, 263–7, 299, 480, 516, 546–9
organizational sociology 106, 148, 250–1, 262–3, 264–6, 270, 495, 496, 501, 516, 546, 548–9

paradigm/paradigm shift 14–17, 170, 228, 367, 451, 504, 509–10, 545
phenomenology 124, 156–61, 174, 218, 239, 259–60, 290, 291, 341, 353, 360, 364, 371, 379, 380, 403, 428, 496, 511
positivism 6–8, 15, 23, 28, 33–5, 38, 41–3, 46, 154, 180, 419
  dispute over 201, 213–14
postmodernity/postmodern 147, 229, 246, 366–8, 369, 429, 443, 451–2, 456, 459–60, 463, 476, 480–3, 512, 544–5, 550, 559
power/power relations/power structures 29, 31–2, 41, 79–83, 106–7, 113, 143, 144, 145, 148, 174, 181–3, 184, 186, 188–9, 191–2, 194, 195, 197, 209, 213, 229, 241–2, 243, 244, 247, 270, 281–2, 283–7, 289, 292, 297–305, 306, 316–17, 318, 358–63, 374, 380, 395, 432, 435, 440, 447, 451–2, 456–7, 459, 460, 462, 463, 484–6, 496, 524, 536, 539, 546, 547–8
  networks of 285–6, 287, 303, 559
practical philosophy 484–5
pragmatism x, 44–5, 53, 124–30, 141, 146, 147, 149, 152, 156, 174, 214, 233, 237, 248, 259, 260, 265, 266, 290–1, 293–4, 382, 417, 499, 500–26, 535
  neo-pragmatism 48, 52, 135, 232, 237, 369, 499, 500–28
praxis (concept of) 212–13, 215–17, 237, 410
preferences 95–6, 115, 135, 141, 154, 384, 391
professions (sociology of) 54–5, 73, 139, 145–6, 148, 190–1, 388, 399, 475, 530
public sphere 112, 210–1, 260, 390, 414, 460–1, 491, 492, 494, 497–8, 506, 507, 544
  public/collective goods 109–12, 116, 533

rational choice 8, 10, 17–18, 98, 107, 111–17, 119–21, 123, 195, 199, 221, 229, 240, 295, 381, 382, 547
rationalization 97, 190, 208, 209, 220, 236, 328, 415, 421, 424, 522, 555
recognition 136, 146, 434, 536–8, 542
religion/religious 50, 85, 88, 90–1, 175, 248, 261, 273, 277, 301, 311, 314, 319–20, 323–30, 331–2, 378, 413, 415, 422, 425, 486, 487, 492, 493, 523, 525, 543, 552, 557
  sociology of 175, 180, 236, 340, 554–5, 557
resource mobilization approach 115, 144, 191, 195, 522
'the right' vs. 'the good' 442, 489–90, 526
risk society 463–8, 470, 474
roles (social, status)/role theory (see also gender, roles) 64–7, 71, 74, 87, 100, 129, 134, 139, 152–3, 155, 176, 269, 308–10, 315, 469
role-taking 129, 153, 520–1
routine(s)/habits 71, 145, 221, 257–8, 292–4, 382, 517, 518

secularization 90–1, 248, 316, 331, 425, 524
signs 344–7, 350–1, 353, 366, 368, 403–4, 411, 454–5, 458, 510
social movements (see also labour: movement) 113–15, 144–5, 174, 178–9, 191–2, 194, 195, 220, 244, 245–6, 276, 278–80, 332, 420–1, 423, 425, 427, 456, 461, 467, 470, 494, 498, 522, 534–5, 549
social order (theory of) 18–19, 30–8, 39, 50, 55–6, 58–60, 63–5, 66, 71, 78–9, 84, 87, 89, 92, 94, 98, 108, 125, 155–6, 167, 170, 174–5, 183, 186, 188, 212, 227–8, 237–41, 247, 253, 260–1, 281, 287–8, 295–7, 299–302, 305, 307, 317–18, 325–6, 365, 369, 418, 433, 479, 490, 536, 540

order, factual 35–6, 182, 238
order, negotiated 148–9, 264, 266, 298
order, normative 35–6, 181–2, 238
solidarity 82, 138, 247, 348, 349–50, 483, 506, 507–8
mechanical vs. organic 72, 309, 422
structuralism x, 289, 339–70, 371, 372–3, 375, 376–81, 400, 401, 403–5, 416, 421, 428, 431, 478, 535, 539, 540, 545
anti-structural thinking 400, 401–31, 528, 533, 540, 543, 550, 553, 556
poststructuralism 229, 246, 339–70, 400, 421, 431, 432, 451, 501, 539
structuration 288–9, 295, 296, 380–1, 394, 529
structure 342–3, 345–53, 354–5, 361, 364–5, 380–1, 383
subjectivity 231, 305, 341, 353, 366, 369, 404, 422, 456, 481
desubjectification 423, 425
macro-, large-scale, species-, superordinate-, collective, great subjects 204, 222, 224–6, 227, 243, 496
subjectification 363, 421, 423–4, 426–7
symbol/symbolic/symbolization 61–2, 64, 81, 128, 130, 145, 155, 300, 317, 318, 346, 347, 350, 395, 396, 398, 405–6, 407, 411–13, 415, 428, 458–9, 505
symbolic capital *see* capital, symbolic
symbolic interactionism 45, 51, 52, 116, 123–49, 150, 151, 152, 153, 156, 163, 173, 174, 185, 191, 206, 214, 221, 230, 236, 237, 264, 266, 289, 290, 291, 293, 298, 300, 308, 379, 423, 500, 512, 522, 540
symbolically mediated interaction 130, 228, 236

systems (concept of) 59–67, 71, 74–85, 103, 136–7, 217, 221, 226–7, 239, 240–7, 252–5, 258, 264–5, 268–9, 271–8, 283, 289, 295–7, 305, 306, 320, 335, 337, 427, 496, 530–3, 535
action system/system of action 37, 41, 60–3, 74, 83, 84–5, 221, 238, 274
cultural system 61–4, 71, 74, 81, 82, 83–4, 88
personality system 61–4, 71, 74, 84
social system 59, 61–6, 71, 74, 75, 78, 84, 85, 176, 177–8, 182, 253–4, 258–9, 264, 268, 273, 274–5, 276, 282–3, 296
subsystems 77–85, 88, 217–18, 219–20, 220–1, 242, 243, 253–4, 259, 270, 273–4, 275–7, 282–3, 305, 320, 332, 335, 473–4, 530, 532–3
system of signs *see* signs
system vs. life-world *see* life-world vs. system
world system theory 333–4, 531, 557

totalitarianism/totalitarian 200, 207, 226, 227, 304, 367, 415–16, 423, 424, 425–6, 478, 543, 550, 556
tradition/traditional (*see also* action: traditional) 72, 257, 308, 311–12, 314–15, 318–19, 322, 328–9, 331, 415, 423, 461, 469, 471, 474–5, 493–4, 550–1, 552, 553
vs. modernity 73, 87, 90, 257, 308, 310, 312, 313–15, 318, 322, 331, 474
truth 6, 7, 230, 232, 261–2, 268–70, 275, 355–6, 358, 359, 362, 451–2, 502, 503–4, 506, 508–9

utilitarianism/utilitarian 23–4, 26–8, 32–5, 37–41, 42–3, 44, 46, 47, 49–50, 53, 55, 60, 94–8, 101–2, 105, 107, 139, 141, 156, 174, 180, 229–30, 234, 283, 288, 357, 381–5, 389–91, 407–8, 410,

411, 417, 490, 494, 496, 506, 522, 543, 546
neo-utilitarianism 94–122, 123, 124, 132, 133, 134, 135, 136, 152, 154–5, 173, 174, 185, 191–2, 195, 229, 240, 261, 308, 381, 383–4, 391, 484
'utilitarian individualism' *see* individualism (as diagnosis of the times)

validity claims 230–3, 234, 243, 294, 300, 441
value commitment 38, 76, 77, 79–80, 82–3, 188, 248, 361, 524–7
value generalization 88–9, 305
values 35, 37–40, 42, 44, 46, 50–1, 53–4, 59, 61–2, 64–6, 67, 71, 76, 78, 84–5, 90, 91, 100, 102, 107, 108, 123, 132, 134, 137–8, 151, 152–4, 156, 176, 180, 183, 187–8, 194–5, 236, 247–8, 253, 260, 261, 266–70, 282, 283, 284, 291, 302, 308–9, 314, 315, 318, 321, 330, 331, 334, 335, 417–20, 442, 482–3, 486, 488–92, 498, 506, 508–9, 510, 517, 519, 522, 524–5, 526–7, 539, 540, 545, 548, 554
genesis of 53, 317, 414, 522, 524–5
verification 6–9

war 32, 118, 187, 286, 289, 368, 479, 523, 552–3, 558–9
of all against all 29, 156
world society 548–9

Printed in Great Britain
by Amazon